Music Listening Today

SIXTH EDITION

Music Listening Today

Charles Hoffer
University of Florida

Darrell Bailey
Indiana University Purdue University Indianapolis

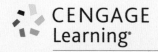
CENGAGE
Learning

Australia • Brazil • Mexico • Singapore • United Kingdom • United States

CENGAGE Learning®

Music Listening Today, Sixth Edition
Charles Hoffer, Darrell Bailey

Product Director: Monica Eckman

Product Manager: Sharon Poore

Content Developer: Sue Gleason Wade

Associate Content Developer: Erika Hayden

Senior Product Assistant: Rachael Bailey

Media Developers: Chad Kirchner/Liz Newell

Marketing Manager: Jillian Borden

Senior Content Project Manager: Lianne Ames

Art Director: Linda May

Manufacturing Planner: Julio Esperas

IP Analyst: Jessica Elias

IP Project Manager: Farah Fard

Production Service: Cenveo Publisher Services

Compositor: Cenveo Publisher Services

Text Designer: Curio Press

Cover Image: © Todd Rosenberg; all rights reserved

Library of Congress Control Number: 2014943333

ISBN: 978-1-285-85812-8

Cengage Learning
20 Channel Center Street
Boston MA 02210
USA

Cengage Learning is a leading provider of customized learning solutions with office locations around the globe, including Singapore, the United Kingdom, Australia, Mexico, Brazil, and Japan. Locate your local office at **www.cengage.com/global.**

Cengage Learning products are represented in Canada by Nelson Education, Ltd.

To learn more about Cengage Learning Solutions, visit **www.cengage.com.**

Purchase any of our products at your local college store or at our preferred online store **www.cengagebrain.com.**

Printed in the United States of America

Print Number: 01   Print Year: 2014

To Mimi

About the Cover

The Chicago Symphony Orchestra (CSO) annually performs more than 150 concerts, including a free concert for the community each year. Pictured is the conductor, Riccardo Muti, Zell Music Director, Chicago Symphony Orchestra, leading the Orchestra in September 2010 in a free concert in Chicago's Millennium Park that was attended by more than 25,000 people. The CSO also offers many community and education programs, some of which are free, throughout the year. Learn more about Muti at RiccardoMutiMusic.com, and read stories about the CSO and the other ensembles and artists presented at the CSO's Symphony Center, at CSOSoundsandStories.org. Thanks to Riccardo Muti, the CSO, and photographer Todd Rosenberg for their courtesy in providing this photo. Photo copyright: Todd Rosenberg; all rights reserved.

Brief Contents

Contents

Preface

How can the authors make the new edition of *Music Listening Today* even more useful in providing information and promoting listening skill for students who are not music majors? In essence, by writing it for the twenty-first-century student who is daily connected to technology and its uses.

THE BOOK

Let's start with the book itself.

- Chapter 1's introduction to music listening has been heavily revised to describe more effectively how music contributes to the quality of people's lives.
- A choral work has been added in Chapter 6, specifically Biebl's "Ave Maria" for male chorus.
- The music of the Classical period now includes Mozart's Piano Concerto No. 21.
- The section on Romantic music features Mendelssohn's Violin Concerto.
- The first two chapters in Part 6 (Chapters 29 and 30) have been reversed, to place the introduction to twentieth-century music first in that part.
- In Chapter 34, New Sounds and New Techniques, special attention is paid to the coverage of twentieth- and twenty-first-century music through the inclusion of a "telematic" opera in which audiences at various locations around the world can interact with the performers through mobile devices.
- Chapters 38, Popular Music since 1950, and 39, Music for Stage and Film, have been thoroughly updated, to incorporate recent artists and film composers.
- Chapter 41, Folk Music of Europe and the Americas, now includes coverage of native Alaskan music.
- Chapter 43, Music of Asia, now branches out to include the native music of Australia.

But that's not all that makes the new edition an important aid in advancing the teaching and learning in music appreciation courses. The changes that truly make the new edition more exciting and effective involve a new ancillary program named MindTap. It has the potential to dramatically alter the nature of music appreciation courses. This includes the option of accessing the entire course within the reach of a mobile device.

FOR STUDENTS

The appearance of this icon 🔵 MindTap on the pages of the book indicates that something special in terms of a relevant video or self-study quiz is available in MindTap for both students and instructors. These MindTap items include the following:

1. The recordings of the music studied in the book available in streaming audio, in MindTap. This allows the works to appear exactly where they are discussed in the book. No longer will there be a concern about locating an example. Furthermore, the music is now available for download onto smartphones, tablets, and other computing devices.

2. Links to more than 140 carefully selected YouTube videos that add a visual element to the content being studied. For example, students will be able to watch videos such as the original choreographed version of Stravinsky's *The Rite of Spring*; listen to composers such as John Williams, John Adams, and Ellen Zwilich talk about their music; and view a snake charmer in India at work.

   These videos are almost as good as–perhaps in some ways better than–being there. Close-ups of performers, their instruments, and even the conductor are now possible. For popular music and the movies, this literally brings students onto the stage and into the studio, as seen in interviews with directors and composers.

   In addition, students will find popular and world music examples to expand their horizons in learning about music.

3. An Active Listening Guide for every work studied in the book. These guides (see Figure P.1) provide a real-time visualization of the music moving in perfect synchronization as it is played and describing what is happening in the music. Translations are also presented for all vocal works in a foreign language. The cursor can be dragged to any place in the work to listen to and compare specific points in the music as many times as one may wish.

   When using an Active Listening Guide, it is impossible for a student to become lost when listening to a work, no matter how long or complex it is.

FIGURE P.1
ACTIVE LISTENING GUIDE SCREEN

4. Interactive demonstrations of the main "Elements of Music."

5. Listening Practice Activity quizzes consisting of listening questions for each work presented in the book, as well as informational and listening Chapter Quizzes at the end of each chapter. These quizzes are available for student review and practice. However, they can also be graded, if the instructor wishes.

6. Six brief "Hear It Now" and four "Connecting the Dots" lectures illustrating points that are difficult to describe in words.

7. A video performance of Britten's *Young Person's Guide to the Orchestra*.

8. A glossary of musical terms in addition to the presence of more frequently used terms embedded directly in the Active Listening Guides.

FOR INSTRUCTORS

These features are available for instructors:
MindTap provides a logical sequence for the teaching/learning process:

1. Each chapter begins with an activity in the form of a video excerpt that engages students with questions for them to consider.

2. Objectives for the chapter are spelled out.

3. Information and examples are then presented related to the objectives.

4. Learning is evaluated through information and listening questions.

At the Instructor's Companion Site:

1. Examinations may be created for any grouping of chapters and in any allocation between information and listening questions as specified by an instructor. From a bank of about 550 information questions and 200 listening questions computers can randomly bring up the number and type of questions the instructor wants. Instructors can add or modify existing questions, and have examinations automatically graded.

2. Updated and improved PowerPoint lectures for each chapter can be individually customized by the instructor.

3. An instructors' manual contains many suggestions for making classes more interesting and effective.

ACKNOWLEDGMENTS

We wish to thank the following professors for their reviews and suggestions offered for the sixth edition:

W. Scott Ball, Southern Adventist University

Jim Bates, Otterbein University

James Bergman, Pierce College and Santa Monica College

Valerie Calhoun, Gordon State College

Alfred Cochran, Kansas State University

Joel Denson, Gaston College

Juel Iwaasa, Wenatchee Valley College

Mildred Lanier, Jefferson State Community College

Lucinda Lear, Hawkeye Community College

Ryan Mackey, Central Christian College of Kansas

Sylvia Mann, California State University, Dominguez Hills

Maria Williams, University of Alaska Anchorage

Thanks also to the many persons in editorial, production, and marketing who contributed to this sixth edition: Sharon Adams Poore, Sue Gleason Wade, Elizabeth Newell, Rachael Bailey, Brian Giordano, Chad Kirchner, Jillian Borden, and Lianne Ames. The authors also want to recognize Doug Short, whose pioneering work contributed the evolution of today's Active Listening Guides.

Charles especially wants to thank his wife, Mimi, for her loving patience during the many hours he spent making revisions for this edition. As an experienced instructor of music appreciation courses, she was able to offer many valuable suggestions and was very helpful in reading the manuscript and offering encouragement. Darrell would also like to thank his wife, Herminia, for her support and encouragement. An expert in global teaching and learning in the art and museum communities, she enhanced both the PowerPoints and other instructor resources.

—Charles Hoffer and Darrell Bailey

About the Authors

Charles Hoffer is currently professor of music at the University of Florida in Gainesville. Born and raised in East Lansing, Michigan, he earned his undergraduate degree in music education from Michigan State University. He received his master's degree in music literature from the Eastman School of Music, and his Ph.D. in music and higher education from Michigan State.

In addition to teaching in school districts for several years, he taught at the State University of New York's College for Teachers at Buffalo, for eighteen years at Indiana University in Bloomington, and for more than twenty-five years at the University of Florida. He has taught music appreciation courses at all three of these universities. Decades ago his textbooks in music appreciation were the first to introduce Listening Guides, which are now standard fare in almost all music appreciation textbooks. His *Music Listening Today* was the first to offer ancillary Active Listening Guides, which provided a comprehensive visualization of the music in perfect synchronization with the recording.

Dr. Hoffer is passionate about teaching music appreciation to college students who are not music majors. He believes the course represents the best and often the only chance for students to develop their listening skills and acquire musical knowledge at a level well beyond their normally limited music education in middle and high school.

Darrell Bailey is currently professor of music at Indiana University Purdue University Indianapolis in the Purdue University department of music and arts technology. Born and raised in Bluefield, Virginia, he studied piano from six years of age and organ in high school. He earned two undergraduate degrees in organ performance and music, and a master's degree in music teaching from the Oberlin College Conservatory of Music. His Ed.D. degree in computer-based music education was received from the University of Illinois.

In addition to teaching in public and private schools, he taught at Oberlin Conservatory and at the Indiana University School of Music in Bloomington. Later, he was the founding director of the music program of the IU School of Music in Indianapolis. Subsequently, he founded the new media program at Indianapolis and was the founding executive associate dean of the first School of Informatics in the United States. He has taught courses in music appreciation, computer-based music technology, media arts and sciences (new media), vocal pedagogy, keyboard improvisation, and choral methods, and has conducted large university-level choral ensembles. He was the designer and developer of the original Active Listening Guides for *Music Listening Today*, beginning with the first edition in 1999.

Dr. Bailey has traveled to over twenty-five countries and presented at national and international conferences. His insight into global music teaching and learning, using social networking tools, provides students with rich contemporary lecture and online experiences. He is an advocate of the live music performance experience as a major component in building a lifelong engagement with music for students who are not music majors.

PART 1

The Nature *of* Music

1

Music Listening *and* You

START...

experiencing this chapter's topics with an online video activity that your instructor may assign.

READ...

the complete chapter text in a rich interactive eBook!

Learning Objectives

1 Recognize how much music contributes to the quality of life.
2 Differentiate concert music from other, everyday types of music.
3 Recall eight ways to listen to music more effectively.
4 Apply your new information about listening to two different pieces of music.

It must be hard for animals out in the wild. For their entire lives they struggle to find enough to eat, avoid predators, and keep from freezing in cold weather. On the other hand, their wants are simple. They don't care whether the walls of a cave are plain or ugly, they eat almost any food as long as it's of the right type, and they have no preferences in music or entertainment. They largely get through life. They exist.

It's different with humans. We need to stay warm and dry in bad weather, and avoid physical predators. But we really want more out of life. We care what the walls of our rooms look like, we can sometimes be downright fussy about what we eat, and we have definite preferences in music. We want to do more than exist. If music and other arts and entertainment didn't exist, we wouldn't physically die. Instead, our lives would be much more drab. This fact can be expressed in a simple formula:

$$\text{Existence} \neq \text{Just living}$$

FIGURE 1.1

MUSIC HAS BEEN WITH US SINCE THE DAWN OF CIVILIZATION. THE ANCIENT EGYPTIANS EVEN SENT THEIR DEAD TO THE AFTERLIFE TO THE ACCOMPANIMENT OF MUSIC PAINTED ON THEIR TOMB WALLS. FROM THE TOMB OF NENKHEFETKA, SAQQARAH, OLD KINGDOM, C. 2400 B.C.E.

Egyptian/The Bridgeman Art Library/Getty Images

The importance of music to people is demonstrated by the fact that it has been around since the dawn of civilization in every part of the world (Figure 1.1) from the remote Aboriginal areas of Australia to the streets of Chicago and Moscow. In fact, its importance is present in so many ways that it's easy to overlook them. Just about every film and television show contains some music. Music is included in public events such as the pregame activities at ball games, the grand openings of malls, and the swearing-in ceremonies of public officials. People are exposed to music in supermarkets, airports, and worship services. Except for the time we're in our room or apartment, we can hardly avoid music!

BIMODAL LISTENING

The fact that music is everywhere has created special challenges for both students and instructors in music appreciation courses. The problem is that we grow up hearing so much music in so many situations that we learn not to pay attention to it. We would be mentally exhausted if we tried.

Often, music's role is simply to contribute to a nonmusical purpose. Its acoustical qualities become secondary. We may recognize bits and pieces of some music, such as the first 15 seconds of a theme for a particular television show or a song. But no one attributes much musical importance to it. We don't, for example, download the theme music of the top-rated television shows or a collection of the fight songs for universities in the Big Ten Conference.

Instead, we treat music in these situations as "sonic wallpaper." We have, therefore, for most of our lives, learned not to pay careful attention to music. Then we enroll in college and take this course, in which we are urged to listen very carefully to music. That's difficult to do after years of not paying much attention to it!

It will really help your ability to listen and appreciate concert music if you can develop two different outlooks and sets of expectations about music. You need to become a *bimodal listener*. First, there is the usual casual approach in which you don't pay a lot of attention to it (Figure 1.2). For most of the music you encounter, just being aware of it is adequate. It's music that a person just sort of absorbs.

FIGURE 1.2

MOST MUSIC THAT YOU ENCOUNTER IS MUSIC THAT YOU JUST ABSORB WHILE DOING SOMETHING ELSE.

Second, there is the careful, conscious effort to perceive the qualities that exist in concert music. In the case of concert music, which is most of the music covered in this course, consider it music for very careful listening and thought. This type requires mental effort and focused attention. It calls on you to know the difference between hearing music and listening to it.

ORDINARY MUSIC AND EXTRAORDINARY MUSIC

There is a type of music that exists primarily for its psychological and artistic qualities. It was created to be listened to very carefully. It is referred to as "concert music" or "art music," but many people also call it "classical music." (In this course the term *Classical music* refers to a specific type of concert music that is first presented in Chapter 15.) It is usually composed for performance in situations where people do nothing but listen to it. It is music with exceptional qualities that people find psychologically rewarding. It could be thought of as "music for careful listening." The word *art* describes such objects that are created with outstanding skill and devotion. Often, the word *fine* is coupled with *arts* to distinguish between objects that can be made by most people and those that demand exceptional skill, effort, and talent—such as concert music.

It's true. Concert music is heard far less often and in far fewer places than the various types of popular music we encounter every day. Virtually no performer or composer of concert music makes the millions of dollars that some popular musicians do from the sales of their recordings and concert tickets, and they are given nowhere near the public attention by the media and general public. Few people play it on their radios or listening equipment, or encounter it at parties or other social occasions. So why is concert music the main (although not the exclusive) fare in music appreciation courses? And why is it considered culturally so important?

It comes down to the difference between things that are ordinary and things that are extraordinary. Most of what we encounter in life is ordinary—the clothes we wear to class, the food we eat, the work we do, the pictures we see in advertisements and magazines, and the music we hear. Usually we don't give a lot of thought to ordinary things, because they are—ordinary. They aren't bad or worthless; they're just easily forgotten or overlooked. If someone asks you what you had for dinner two days ago, you would probably need to think a bit to remember, if indeed you could recall it at all. But suppose you had a dinner at an especially good restaurant and were served something truly delicious; then that experience would be easy to remember. That's why almost all everyday music is "here today, gone tomorrow," but much concert music is "here today, here tomorrow."

Fortunately, we don't need to eat extraordinary food at every meal (although that *is* an attractive thought). Nor do we need to listen only to music of extraordinary quality. But there are times when such experiences are truly enjoyable and psychologically meaningful. And as a part of a college education, it is proper and right that you gain at least a basic level of listening skill and knowledge so that you can understand and value musical works of extraordinary quality. It would be unfortunate to acquire a college degree and be culturally illiterate about music and the arts.

"I Know What I Like"

Everyone likes to listen to at least one kind of music. Usually, it's the type of music they are familiar with—and usually it's the only kind they listen to. The saying "I know what I like" is true. But so is the phrase "I like what I know." It isn't surprising that people feel most comfortable and competent with the music they know. The problem with stopping at this comfort level, however, is that it usually confines you to only a tiny bit of the rich world of music.

Suppose you had the chance to advise a person from a foreign country about what to see on a tour of the United States. You might suggest seeing the part of the country where you live, and that would be fine. But is that all a visitor should experience of the United States? What about its other great cities and natural wonders? The analogy with music seems clear. There is a vast and varied world of music out there. Why confine yourself to just one small portion of it and miss out on other kinds of music that could enrich your life?

Music and Expectations

The matter of time seems to have become more important to people in the twenty-first century. Today we are used to fast food and quick instant messaging. When working at a computer, for example, we expect it to bring up the right screen in a few seconds, or else we become impatient and wonder what's wrong.

A hundred years ago people seemed to be much less busy. They cooked meals over stoves, sent handwritten letters via "snail mail," and accepted the fact that crossing the Atlantic Ocean took more than a week. They also attended and enjoyed performances of music that lasted for an hour or more.

What's different today? People's expectations of time. Maybe it's like this. If you lived a 45-minute commute from your college, probably the first few times you made the trip it seemed long and slow. After the commute became familiar, you would become much less aware of the time and effort it requires. Why? Because your attention and expectations will have changed. Knowing this, we should not expect lots of short, lively pieces of music when we listen to concert music. Instead, we should relax and enjoy the fascinating and satisfying sonic qualities that concert music offers.

LISTENING TO CONCERT MUSIC

Because most works of concert music are more substantial in terms of what happens in them, they often require some guidance to be understood and appreciated (Figure 1.3). They also require a degree of skill in hearing what is happening with the sounds. Both information and listening skill need to be present. The good news is that the efforts at gaining knowledge and listening skill are well worthwhile in terms of your enjoyment of

FIGURE 1.3
Most works of concert music are substantial and require guidance in order to be understood and appreciated.

music that is better than ordinary. For these reasons a music appreciation course essentially has two basic goals:

1. Acquire useful information about music and musical works.
2. Develop the ability to hear most of the features contained in them.

Just knowing that a musical work was composed by a particular person and contains certain techniques of composition is of limited usefulness. On the other hand, listening to a musical work but not understanding its features can be an unpleasant waste of time. Think about this analogy: You could get around campus by hopping along on one leg. But it's far more successful and enjoyable if you walk using both legs. It's much the same in dealing with most of the music you will study in this course. It's a good idea to remember this simple equation:

Useful information + Careful listening = Enjoyable and meaningful listening to concert music

Here are several suggestions to help you in listening to music more effectively:

1. Take advantage of the ancillary aids for improving listening available with this book, especially the Active Listening Guides, which are available online. They are very useful for following vocal works in foreign languages and recognizing patterns of themes and similar aspects of music.
2. Make use of the Listening Guides in the pages of the book which provide a timetable for each work and outline its features. This can help you understand what happens in it. The timings for the various features in a work are accurate only for the Sony recordings that accompany this book. Different recordings of a work will probably have similar times, but will not be exactly the same and will not match what you see in the Listening Guides.
3. Utilize the special listening program that is associated with this book. For example, many chapters include online demonstrations of the elements of music and aspects of music that are difficult to describe in words.
4. Spread out the times when you listen to the music for this course. Cramming doesn't work well in developing skill in listening to music. Instead, listen to the same musical work several times over a couple of days. In fact, this is probably the best suggestion for developing skill in listening, especially if you listen carefully.
5. Avoid thinking up visual images. Concentrate on the musical sounds, not on any images that might come to mind. They can be distractions when listening.
6. Notice the feelings that the music encourages. Usually they are much more complex than just "happy" or "sad."
7. Realize that the Listening Guides and Active Listening Guides are only aids in learning to listen to music more fully. Eventually you will need to listen to music without any visual aids, because that's the way you will encounter it when you attend a performance or listen to a recording.
8. Know that remembering is essential for understanding concert music. At any particular moment, only a millisecond of a piece of music can be heard. What was sounded before that millisecond exists only in a person's memory. What will be heard in future moments can only be a guess based on what was heard previously.

Hearing music is not like seeing artwork. An entire painting or piece of sculpture can be viewed in a few seconds. If memory were made an essential part of looking at a painting, it might go something like this: An unfamiliar picture is covered except for one thin, vertical opening. You can see the picture only through that opening as it moves across the painting from one side to the other. Your comprehension of the picture results from (1) your memory of what you've seen, (2) the tiny portion you can see through the opening, and (3) your guess about what you will see as the opening moves along.

Would this be a difficult way to view a picture? Definitely! But that's the way music is perceived, and that is why memory is so important in listening to music. To pursue the analogy further, the more times you see the opening move across the picture, the better you will recall its images and the more accurate your comprehension of the whole picture. That is why listening to a musical work several times is so important and useful.

TWO MUSICAL WORKS FOR CAREFUL LISTENING

Talking and reading about music are useful up to a point, but the true enjoyment comes when you get to apply what you have learned to a piece of music. Two quite different works are presented here. One was written to be performed by a symphony orchestra and is in a lively style. The other is an especially beautiful song written for a choir.

"Hoe-Down" from *Rodeo*

"Hoe-Down" from *Rodeo* (see Listening Guide) by the American composer Aaron Copland is in the style of square dance music, so it probably will sound somewhat familiar to you. It is one part of a longer work that Copland composed for the ballet *Rodeo*. Today it is heard often, including in TV commercials, apart from the ballet itself. As you can tell from looking at its Listening Guide, it has three sections arranged in an *ABA* pattern.

AARON COPLAND
"Hoe-Down" from *Rodeo* (1942)

LISTENING GUIDE

Form: Three-part (*ABA*)

Download 1

3 minutes 30 seconds

0:00   Orchestra begins with rather loud and fast music.

0:40   First section (A) begins with strings and other instruments playing this theme.

0:48   Violins continue with "square dance" music as brasses and lower strings sound chords off the beat.

1:20   First theme repeated.

1:39   Trumpet plays theme for the second section (B).

2:11   Violins and other instruments take up square-dance theme.

2:50   After the music slows down, the first theme is played again.

3:10   First theme is played again before "Hoe-Down" closes with three quick chords.

(continued)

LISTEN TO... this selection streaming.

 WATCH... an Active Listening Guide of this selection.

 WATCH... a performance of this ballet online.

 DO... an online Listening Practice Activity related to this selection, which your instructor may assign for a grade.

In "Hoe-Down" Copland took a simple folk song and created an artistic piece of music, something more than ordinary square dance music. Did you notice the use he made of a short pattern of notes? They appear several times at the beginning of the work and also at the beginning of the first theme. Did you also notice places where the music slows down and becomes quieter, only for the more vigorous music to start up again? It is features like these that make it more interesting to listen to than just ordinary square dance music

Aaron Copland

De Agostini Picture Library/Getty Images

Aaron Copland (1900–1990) was born in Brooklyn, New York, the son of Russian-Jewish immigrants. His family had little money, so he took his first music lessons from an older sister. He also studied books and scores at the New York Public Library. After graduating from high school, he studied piano and harmony in New York.

In 1921 Copland went to the American School of Music at Fontainebleau in France. The teacher there was a remarkable woman named Nadia Boulanger. Copland became the first of a long list of young American composers to study with her.

Copland became interested in jazz in the late 1920s, and several of his compositions contain elements of jazz. In the early 1930s, his music tended to be more abstract. He began to be concerned, however, about the gap between concert audiences and contemporary compositions. Copland wrote, "It made no sense to ignore them and to continue writing as if they did not exist. I felt that it was worth the effort to see if I couldn't say what I had to say in the simplest possible terms."

His efforts at greater simplicity were successful, and he was able to retain the interest and respect of trained musicians while at the same time pleasing the general concert-going public. Many of his best-known works are excellent examples of music with an American quality. In addition to his music, he lectured at many universities and wrote several very readable books about music.

Best-Known Works

Orchestra
- *A Lincoln Portrait*
- *El salón Mexico*

Ballet
- *Billy the Kid*
- *Rodeo*
- *Appalachian Spring*

Film scores
- *Of Mice and Men*
- *The Red Pony*
- *Our Town*

Rutter's "Open Thou Mine Eyes"

The choral tradition of English church music is marked by a very polished, refined quality with pitches perfectly in tune. One reason for its beautiful quality is the use of boys with unchanged voices on the soprano and alto parts. When boys are between the ages of about ten and thirteen, their voices have a special brilliance and clarity that disappears once their voices change. The use of boys' voices is developed in England in choir schools in which the students study music extensively as well as their other academic subjects. Several recordings for this book have boys singing the treble parts, including the works by Josquin, Palestrina, and Handel's "Hallelujah Chorus."

John Rutter

JMEnternational/Redferns/Getty Images

John Rutter (b. 1945) was born in London and attended the Highgate School. He went on to study music at Clare College, Cambridge University. While there, he published his first compositions and conducted for recordings. Although he has written a wide range of music, he is known mainly for his choral works, including four *Carols for Choirs* anthologies with Sir David Willcocks.

From 1975 to 1979, he was director of music at Clare College. He gave up that position to devote more time to composing and to form the Cambridge Singers, a professional chamber choir that primarily makes recordings. He has conducted

or lectured at many universities and concert halls throughout the English-speaking world. He has been honored by Westminster Choir College in the United States and by the Archbishop of Canterbury in England.

Best-Known Works

Choral
- *Gloria*
- *Requiem*
- *Magnificat*
- *Psalmfest*
- *Mass for Children*

John Rutter is one of many excellent composers whose works are largely associated with the English/Anglican choral tradition. Over the years he has written or arranged a number of religious choral works. "Open Thou Mine Eyes" (see Listening Guide) is based on a poem by Lancelot Andrewes (1555–1626) and was commissioned by the Texas Choral Directors Association in 1980. It is a beautiful, simple work, one that many choirs are able to sing well and one that listeners can easily enjoy.

JOHN RUTTER
"Open Thou Mine Eyes" (1980)

Genre: Church anthem

Form: *A A B A A*

Download 2

2 minutes 35 seconds

0:00   Sopranos sing opening verse.

Open thou mine eyes...

0:28   Altos enter, and sopranos divide into two parts; repeat first verse.

LISTENING GUIDE

(continued)

0:57 Tenors and basses sing contrasting section.

O Lord God…

1:17 Upper and lower voices combine as A melody returns.

Vouchsafe to me…

1:55 Opening words and melody sung again by sopranos as other voice parts hum accompaniment.

2:21 Music closes quietly with moving notes in alto and tenor parts.

 LISTEN TO… this selection streaming.

WATCH… an Active Listening Guide of this selection.

WATCH… a performance of this selection online.

DO… an online Listening Practice Activity related to this selection, which your instructor may assign for a grade.

These musical examples of Copland and Rutter have provided a preview of the variety and richness of concert music. The hope is that they have whetted your appetite for the wealth of music created for careful listening.

MAIN POINTS OF CHAPTER 1

1. Music contributes much to the quality of life.
2. Music exists for many different purposes, each of which encourages a particular type of music.
3. People tend to enjoy the type of music they know and that meets their expectations. It is usually the only kind they listen to.
4. Concert/art music is an extraordinary type of music created for the mental and emotional satisfactions it provides. Most people need some guidance in order to perceive its qualities.
5. Learning to listen to music perceptively is an essential part of a music appreciation course.
6. It is important to connect information about a musical work with what is heard in that work.

 PRACTICE…
your understanding of this chapter's concepts by working once more with the chapter's Active Listening Guides online.

 DO…
online quizzes that your instructor may assign for a grade.

Rhythm

Learning Objectives

1 Give examples of beat as the regular pulse of much Western music.
2 Explain the significance of the 2:1 ratio in the notation of rhythm.
3 Provide examples of how syncopation works.
4 Define the basic symbols involved in the notation of rhythm.
5 List the sequence of terms for tempo, from slowest to most rapid.
6 Apply what you have learned about rhythm to two very different pieces of music.

START...
experiencing this chapter's topics with an online video activity that your instructor may assign.

Music is a "time" art. Paintings and pieces of sculpture occupy space, but the "canvas" of music is time. Because all music occupies time, all of it has rhythm, even when it's not a toe-tapping rhythm that makes it easy to mark the time. The term for the orderly flow of music through time is **rhythm**. It is a comprehensive word that includes beat, meter, and tempo.

READ...
the complete chapter text in a rich interactive eBook!

BEAT: MUSIC'S PULSE

The **beat** is the regular pulse found in most music. It is what people tap as they listen, and it is most easily heard in marches and dance music when it is marked by the sound of the drum. Although the beat can be sensed most of the time in a musical work, it is not always sounded clearly. For example, a drum doesn't need to tap the beat throughout a piece of music, although it often does in dance music and marches.

Furthermore, not all music has a beat, although most of the music we hear in the United States today does. It is central to most of the music of the Western world. In fact, our sense of meter depends on the presence of beats.

Usually, beats are heard and felt in a steady, even succession. If they are erratic, the effect is something like listening to a person who says a few words very rapidly, and then some more words very slowly, and then some words moderately fast, and so on. It is tiring and irritating to listen to someone talk with such changes of speed. The speed with which beats occur in music can change within a piece of music, but usually the changes are gradual and occur by design of the composer and performer.

WATCH...
an online demo that will help you sense the beat.

METER: THE PATTERNS OF BEATS

The human mind has a tendency to seek out patterns in what is heard and seen. It is easier to remember a telephone number such as 555-1212 than 555-2719 because 1212 has a pattern.

When people hear groups of beats, even though the beats may be exactly as strong as one another, their minds tend to group them into twos, threes, or fours; only occasionally are groups larger than four. Instead of beat-beat-beat-beat-beat-beat and so on, the mind tends to perceive **beat**-beat **beat**-beat **beat**-beat or **beat**-beat-beat **beat**-beat-beat. The grouping of the beats (not the notes) into patterns is called **meter**.

Meter is very evident in group cheers and rap music. Here is an example of a cheer (the 1 represents the more strongly stressed beat or the **downbeat**):

1   2   **1**   2   **1**   2   **1** 2

<u>Two</u> bits, <u>**four**</u> bits, <u>**six**</u> bits, a **<u>dol</u>**lar,

1   2   **1** 2   **1**   2   **1** 2

<u>**All**</u> for <u>**Den**</u>ver, **<u>stand</u>** up and <u>**hol**</u>ler!

Here is an example of meter in a poem, "The Raven," by Edgar Allan Poe:

| U | U | U | U

<u>**Once**</u>   up<u>**on**</u>   a   <u>**mid**</u>night <u>**drear**</u>y,

| U | U | U | U

<u>**As**</u>   I   <u>**pon**</u>dered <u>**weak**</u> and <u>**wear**</u>y,

The familiar song "Jingle Bells" has an easily felt two-beat meter. The beats are marked with short vertical lines.

In contrast, the song "America" ("My Country 'Tis of Thee") has an easily felt three-beat meter.

Beats normally follow a metrical pattern. If they don't, the music has not been arranged correctly. For example, the punctuation of the following sentence tends to obscure its meaning: *Every piece of. Music can be enjoyed, for its sounds. And rhythm.*

Syncopation

Sometimes the emphasis, called **accent**, is deliberately placed off the beat. **Syncopation** happens either by adding the emphasis where it is not expected or by removing it from where it is expected. Here is an example of syncopation from the song "Dixie":

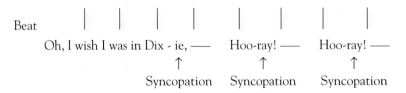

In the example, the *ie* of *Dixie* and the *ray* of *Hooray* occur halfway through beats instead of on the beat. The syncopation could be removed from the melody and the accent would fall normally, but the song would lose much of its character.

THE NOTATION OF RHYTHM

Music existed long before a system for writing it down was devised. In fact, even today most folk music and jazz are rarely written down. In other words, the sounds used in music and the notation of those sounds are two quite different matters. Hearing the rhythm and other elements of music is clearly the more important and valuable of the two. Knowing about the notation of rhythm, however, usually helps in learning and understanding music better.

Although the applications of the system of notating rhythm can be quite complex, the basic system is rather simple: It consists of various combinations of note heads, stems, and flags.

Stem

Flag

Note head

As the combinations progress from an empty oval to a solid head with a stem and flag(s), each note is sounded one-half the length of time that the previous note sounds.

A whole note ○ usually receives four beats.

A half note ♩ usually receives two beats.

A quarter note ♩ usually receives one beat.

An eighth note ♪ usually receives half a beat.

A sixteenth note ♪ usually receives a quarter of a beat.

And the opposite is also true: As the notes change from solid heads, stems, and flags toward empty ovals, the length of the note played doubles. Therefore, all other things being equal, a passage of music that contains notes with many filled-in heads and flags is going to move quickly.

Horizontal beams are often used in place of flags when two or more notes occur in the same beat.

The notation of silences, called **rests**, uses different symbols:

A whole rest ▬ hangs down from the fourth line of the staff.

A half rest ▬ is placed on top of the third line of the staff.

A quarter rest ⸕ has a distinctive shape.

An eighth rest ⸜ resembles a fancy number 7.

A sixteenth rest ⸝ looks like an eighth rest but with one more flag.

As can be seen from looking at the different note lengths, the system for notating rhythm is built on a 2:1 ratio, with note lengths being either one-half or double the length of the other. The 2:1 ratio is even carried over into the use of the dots that are sometimes placed to the right of a note. The dot to the right of a note tells a performer to increase the length of the note by one-half. So a note that is two beats long becomes three beats when a dot is added. Dotted notes are used extensively when the beat is divided into threes instead of twos.

The note with a solid head and a stem ♩ (a quarter note) is most frequently used to represent the beat, although any note can serve that purpose. For example, the following three lines of notes sound exactly alike when performed, even though they look different from one another.

The reason they sound the same is the different numbers at the beginning of each line. This vertical combination is the **meter signature** or **time signature**. This is one of two ways the meter of a piece of music is indicated in notation.

Usually, these pairs of numbers are placed at the beginning of a work or section. In some contemporary works, however, the meter changes every few measures, so meter signatures are sometimes found within the work.

The top number of a meter signature usually indicates the number of beats in the measure, and the bottom number usually indicates the type of note that should receive one beat. In the first example above, the eighth note (♪) receives the beat; in the middle example, it is the quarter note (♩); and in the last example, it is the half note (𝅗𝅥). The notation of silences using rests follows the same ratios.

The other way in which music notation indicates the pattern of beats is by vertical lines that enclose the beats in the pattern. These units of rhythm are called **measures**. The vertical lines are called *bar lines*, possibly because they resemble bars on a window.

Music students learn that the first beat of a measure is normally performed somewhat more strongly than the other beats in the measure.

TEMPO: THE SPEED OF BEATS

 WATCH...
an online demo that will let you experiment with different tempos.

Another important aspect of rhythm is **tempo**, which is the speed of the beats. The tempo of a piece of music can be indicated in two ways. One is by a metronome marking such as ♩ = 84. A metronome is a clocklike device (either windup or electronic) that indicates the beat with audible ticks and/or a flashing light. Metronomes can be set to provide exactly the desired number of beats per minute. With a few exceptions, most tempos in music range between one and three beats per second.

The other way of indicating tempo is through the use of words, which are usually in Italian. These verbal descriptors are general, such as *very fast, moderate,* and *slow.* Because the terms are general, the tempo of a work marked *Allegro* will differ somewhat from one performer or conductor to the next. The words indicating tempo not only provide guidance for performers, they also appear in concert programs and liner notes to identify the large, independent sections, or movements, of instrumental works.

The following are the more common terms for tempo.

Largo	Very slow, broad
Adagio	Slow, leisurely
Grave	Very slow, heavy
Andante	"Walking," moderate
Moderato	Moderate
Allegro	Moderately fast, moving briskly
Allegro molto	Much allegro, very brisk
Vivace	Lively

| *Presto* | Very fast |
| *Prestissimo* | As fast as possible |

Other words are often attached to the indications of tempo. These usually describe the style of the music, not the tempo. Examples of additional words include *con fuoco* (with fire or force), *sostenuto* (sustained), and *con brio* (brusque). Sometimes modifiers such as *meno* (less) and *piu* (more) are added. Two Italian terms affecting tempo that have close parallels in English are *ritardando* (retard, or slow down) and *accelerando* (accelerate, or speed up).

Notes and beats are not the same thing. Although a tempo may be slow, many notes can be played during the beat, giving the impression of much motion. On the other hand, the tempo may be fast, but if the duration of the notes is long, the sense of movement is reduced. Of course, all things being equal, more notes are heard when the tempo is fast than when it is slow.

RHYTHM IN BIZET'S *FARANDOLE*

In the world of concert music, it's customary to pronounce names and terms in the language of the particular country. For that reason the last name of the French composer Georges Bizet is pronounced "bee-ZAY." He composed twenty-seven pieces of music to go with the play *L'Arlésienne* (*The Woman of Arles*) by Alphonse Daudet. Later, his friend Ernest Guiraud arranged the music into two suites. *Farandole* (see Listening Guide) is from Suite No. 2.

Georges Bizet

Bizet (1838–1875) first learned music from his parents and was admitted to the Paris Conservatory at about the age of ten. By age seventeen he had composed Symphony in C, which was not performed until 1935. He was awarded the Prix de Rome and began composing music mostly for the theater and opera. For a variety of reasons, much of his music was not well received, and he earned his living arranging music and giving piano lessons.

After serving in the national guard in the Franco-Prussian War in 1870, Bizet was commissioned to write incidental music for Daudet's play *L'Arlésienne* (*The Woman of Arles*). The play was not successful, but fortunately Bizet's music survived.

Most of Bizet's fame is the result of his opera *Carmen*. Its plot is built around the gradual decline of Don José, a simple, honest soldier, caused by his infatuation with Carmen, a Spanish gypsy girl who worked in a cigarette factory. The music is filled with one colorful and beautiful song after another. At first it was not well received and was condemned for its "obscene" text. Apparently, the patrons of the Opéra Comique, which was something of a family theater in those days, did not enjoy watching Don José's life being ruined by the amoral Carmen. Today *Carmen* is perhaps the best-known and best-loved opera in the world.

Bizet had poured enormous effort into *Carmen* and was worn out by months of rehearsal and tension. His sensitive nature was simply unable to tolerate its initial cool reception. He died three months after its premiere.

Best-Known Works

Orchestra
- Symphony in C
- *L'Arlésienne*, Suites 1 and 2

Opera
- *Carmen*

For the main melody, Bizet chose an old song called "Marche de Turenne" from the Provence region of France. The tune is still sung at Christmastime in English under the title "The March of the Kings." Some marches have been written for processions or coronations, and they are slower. Marches at football games are usually played at a much faster tempo than military marches. This march is moderately fast.

GEORGES BIZET
Farandole from *L'Arlésienne*, Suite No. 2 (1872)

LISTENING GUIDE

March tempo, 4-beat meter

Download 3

3 minutes 7 seconds

0:00   Orchestra plays first theme at a march tempo in strong four-beat meter. The first three notes of the theme occur on the beat.

0:33   Tempo becomes faster as second theme enters. The first beat of each measure is emphasized. Music grows in intensity.

0:55   Orchestra repeats second theme.

1:17   Strings play second theme. Tempo remains fast.

1:27   Strings play first theme at a fast tempo.

1:39   Woodwinds play second theme.

1:44   Tempo remains fast, and four-beat meter returns as strings play opening theme.

1:56   Woodwinds take up second theme.

2:18   Orchestra combines both first and second themes. Marchlike rhythm of the music continues.

2:52   *Farandole* concludes in a flurry of sound.

LISTEN TO... this selection streaming online.

WATCH... an Active Listening Guide of this selection online.

WATCH... a performance of this selection online.

DO... an online Listening Practice Activity related to this selection, which your instructor may assign for a grade.

Bizet's *Farandole* has both a marchlike and a dancelike theme. Notice that the march and the dance have different meters, as you can see from meter signatures of the music notation in the musical examples. As you listen, try counting the march 1-2-3 1-2-3 instead of 1-2 1-2. You will quickly sense that the music is in two- or four-beat meter, because the three-beat pattern just doesn't seem to fit.

POLYRHYTHM

African music has a well-deserved reputation for its exciting rhythms. "Mitamba Yalagala Kumchuzi" (see Listening Guide) is a good example. It comes from the Zaramo tribe of the coastal region near Dar es Salaam in Tanzania in East Africa.

What makes the rhythm of this music exciting is the appearance of several rhythms at the same time, what is referred to as **polyrhythm**. When you hear "Mitamba Yalagala Kumchuzi" for the first time, it may seem like one of the drummers is lost and coming in at the wrong time. Not so. Instead, he is playing a different pattern. As the music progresses, other performers join in with their own particular patterns. Although you might

FIGURE 2.1
AFRICAN DRUM ENSEMBLE

AFRICAN MUSIC
"Mitamba Yalagala Kumchuzi"

Polyrhythm

Download 4

1 minute 33 seconds

0:00 One drummer begins playing two sounds, high and low. Other drummers soon enter. Several different rhythmic patterns are heard at the same time. Rattles enter.

0:43 A singer begins and is answered by other singers. The rhythmic patterns continue in drums and rattles.

1:00 Lead singer exchanges portions of the music with other singers in a call-and-response pattern.

(continued)

LISTEN TO... this selection streaming online.

 WATCH... an Active Listening Guide of this selection online.

 WATCH... a related video online.

DO... an online Listening Practice Activity related to this selection, which your instructor may assign for a grade.

expect rhythmic confusion because of the different patterns occurring at the same time, the effect is exhilarating.

Rhythm is not the only interesting feature of "Mitamba Yalagala Kumchuzi." The recording was made with five goblet drums, four cylindrical drums, and tines rattles. Each type of drum (Figure 2.1) has its own distinctive quality of sound, and these different qualities add to the music. The **call-and-response** pattern between the vocal soloist and the group is also characteristic of African music.

MAIN POINTS OF CHAPTER 2

 PRACTICE...
your understanding of this chapter's concepts by working once more with the chapter's Active Listening Guides online.

 DO...
online quizzes that your instructor may assign for a grade.

1. Rhythm is the flow of music through time.
2. The beat is the steady pulse found in almost all music in Western civilization.
3. *Meter* refers to the pattern with which certain beats are emphasized.
4. The notation of rhythm is based on a 2:1 ratio of notes and rests.
5. Tempo is the speed of the beats, not the notes.
6. Syncopation exists when the emphasis occurs where it is not expected or is omitted where it is expected.
7. Polyrhythms are created when two or more rhythmic patterns occur at the same time.

Melody *and* Harmony

START...
experiencing this chapter's topics with an online video activity that your instructor may assign.

READ...

the complete chapter text in a rich interactive eBook!

It is obvious that most music contains sounds that are higher or lower than others. These differences in high and low sound are a very important element of music.

PITCH: THE HIGH AND LOW OF SOUNDS

In many cultures pitch is described in terms of large/small or masculine/feminine. As used in Western music, the word **pitch** refers to the highness or lowness of a sound. It is the result of the number of vibrations made by the sound-making instrument—the human vocal cords, the reed of the clarinet, the string of the violin, and so on. The greater the number of vibrations, the higher the sound. For example, a sound-producing medium vibrating 440 times per second produces the standard pitch for the note A above middle C. Orchestras tune to this pitch; wind bands tune to B-flat, which is 456 vibrations per second.

Pitches by themselves are not music. To be useful in music, pitches must meet one of these three conditions:

- Be a part of a series of pitches that forms a logical unit of music—melody
- Be a part of two or more logical series of pitches sounded in contrast with each other—counterpoint
- Be a part of several pitches sounded at the same time—harmony

WATCH...
an online demo that will let you play different pitches.

MELODY: PITCHES IN A COHESIVE SERIES

The first of these conditions—a series of pitches that forms a cohesive entity—is referred to as **melody**. The important words here are *cohesive* and *entity*. The pitches must seem to belong together and be a unit—an entity. Not just any sequence of pitches will do. What causes some melodies to be memorable and emotionally moving and others to seem forgettable and senseless? No one really knows, although from time to time scholars attempt to provide general melodic guidelines. For example, a series made up of the same pitch sounded again and again has little chance of being a melody that anyone will want to sing or listen to; it lacks musical interest and variety. On the other hand, a melody in which the pitches seem to have little relationship to each other won't work either; it lacks a sense of unity. A good melody achieves a balance between unity and variety.

Melodies are what people generally remember in music. The melody is what they whistle, sing, and focus their attention on when listening to music. You can probably recall the opening melody of Bizet's *Farandole*. Some melodies over the centuries have acquired names of their own. In many Protestant churches, the Doxology is sung to a melody named "Old Hundredth." The names of the melodies of hymns are sometimes given in the hymnals just under the title.

Many melodies are known by their words, such as "Take Me Out to the Ball Game" and "Anchors Away!" Some melodies have two or more different sets of words. What we know in the United States as "My Country 'Tis of Thee" ("America") is the national anthem of England, where its first words are "God save our glorious queen."

Two other terms are sometimes used as synonyms for **melody**. The word *tune* is a less formal term, the implication being that a tune is less serious and complex than a melody or theme. A **theme** identifies an instrumental melody that plays an important role in a musical work. A theme is of interest both for its musical qualities and for what the composer does with it during the course of the piece. In some cases, quite average themes have become the basis for great musical works. A prime example of this is the famous four-note theme in Beethoven's Symphony No. 5, which is presented in Chapter 21.

Pitches in Music Notation

The representation of pitch in music notation is partly graphic. The horizontal lines and the spaces between them provide a visual image of the distance from one pitch to another. Both lines and spaces are used to represent pitches. The five lines and their spaces make up the staff. The higher a note is placed on the staff, the higher it sounds.

Middle C

The clef (French for "key" and meaning the key to the staff) sets the general level of pitch for the five lines. For example, in the treble clef, which is indicated by the symbol 𝄞, the inside curl goes around the line for G above middle C. In the bass clef indicated by 𝄢, the two dots straddle the line for F below middle C. The relationship between the two clefs can be seen when they are combined, as shown here.

Treble clef

Middle

Bass clef

Only the first seven letters of the alphabet are used in music. The notes can be modified by a sharp (♯), raising the pitch one half-step, or a flat (♭), lowering the pitch one half-step. Knowing the names of notes is *not* essential to appreciating music.

Much as words are read on the page, notes placed one after another in a row are to be performed sequentially. Notes that are aligned vertically on the page are sounded at the same time as a cluster or group, called a chord. Chords, too, are read from left to right across the page.

Therefore, notation gives you a visual representation of what the music sounds like. It can help you sense and remember what you hear.

Features of Melodies

We can better understand melodies by considering their various dimensions and features.

LENGTH Some melodies are short and concise; others stretch out over many measures. The themes in "Hoe-Down" are clear and to the point, but in contrast, the melody for Rodrigo's *Concierto de Aranjuez*, discussed in Chapter 4, is more flowing.

RANGE Some melodies stay within a narrow range of pitches. Others spread out over a wide pitch distance.

STEPS AND LEAPS Some melodies, such as the beginning of "Row, Row, Row Your Boat," move by small steps from one note to the next. Other melodies leap to a note a distance away. As we all know from the occasional strain of singing "The Star-Spangled Banner," it opens with several leaps that carry it over a considerable range: The word *leap* may seem to be an exaggeration for any note that is not adjacent, but it is the appropriate term.

CONTOUR Each melody has its own outline, or contour, just as each city has its own skyline. In fact, melody is often referred to as the "line" or "melodic line." Figure 3.1 shows the contour for the first several measures of "The Star-Spangled Banner." Figure 3.2 shows the contour of "America":

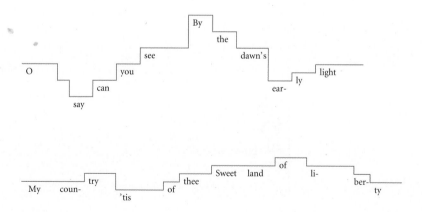

FIGURE 3.1
CONTOUR OF "THE STAR-SPANGLED BANNER"

FIGURE 3.2
CONTOUR OF "AMERICA"

DECORATIVE NOTES In some melodies each note seems solid and unadorned. The Shaker hymn melody is a prime example of a straightforward, undecorated melody. "Simple Gifts" (see Listening Guide) is an American Shaker song from around 1840. Notice that the melody moves in a steplike progression complemented by infrequent leaps.

LISTENING GUIDE

ARRANGED BY AARON COPLAND
"Simple Gifts" (1950)

Download 5

1 minute 40 seconds

0:00 Short introduction played by strings; then the singer begins.

'Tis the gift to be sim - ple, 'tis the gift to be free

> 'Tis the gift to be simple, 'tis the gift to be free,
> 'Tis the gift to come down where you ought to be.

The melody for the next two lines is very similar to that of the first two.

> And when we find ourselves in the place just right,
> 'Twill be in the valley of love and delight.

0:32 Contrasting section begins.

When true sim - pli - ci - ty is gained

> When true simplicity is gained.
> To bow and to bend we shan't be ashamed.

0:41 The melody of the second two lines returns, but with new words and a few small changes.

> To turn, turn will be our delight,
> 'Til by turning, turning we come round right.

0:58 Music and words of the opening four lines are repeated exactly.

1:25 Strings play a short concluding section.

1:34 "Simple Gifts" ends with a cadence.

LISTEN TO... this selection streaming online.

WATCH... an Active Listening Guide of this selection online.

WATCH... a video that provides insight into the Shaker lifestyle and beliefs online.

DO... an online Listening Practice Activity related to this selection, which your instructor may assign for a grade.

FIGURE 3.3
A Shaker Kitchen   Notice
that everything is hung neatly
in place from pegs in the upper
molding.

The Shakers were a religious sect that earned its name from the members' "shaking" when they felt the spirit of God. They lived a simple, celibate life and developed a number of communities in New England and Kentucky. They are known today for the simple, elegant furniture they designed (Figure 3.3).

What Affects the Impression of a Melody?

Just about everything affects the impression a listener gains of melody.

Accompanying Music The accompanying music is like a stage setting in that it contributes to the overall effect of a play. Copland's arrangement of the American Shaker song "Simple Gifts" demonstrates the skillful creation of accompanying music to enhance the melody. He makes the setting clear and simple, which is in keeping with the simple character of the song and its text.

Tone Qualities and Instruments A melody played on a flute gives listeners one impression, whereas the same melody played on a guitar gives another. Some melodies seem more suited for certain instruments than for others; a very decorative melody sounds fine on a violin or flute but would sound cumbersome played by a trombone. Copland used the melody for "Simple Gifts" in his ballet *Appalachian Spring*, which is presented in Chapter 36. In that music the melody is altered to suit the attributes of the different instruments that play it.

Rhythm The rhythmic properties of a melody can make a big difference. Imagine singing "Jingle Bells" very slowly. This merry winter song would sound like a funeral dirge. In other cases, average melodies are sometimes successful because of their distinctive rhythmic qualities.

Phrases You can't exactly see phrases in music as you can in written text, which is punctuated with commas and periods. **Phrases** are there in the logical groupings of notes, which vary in length as much as phrases in language do. For example, in the song "America" the words and notes for "My country 'tis of thee" form a short phrase that is coupled to the next short phrase, "sweet land of liberty," leading to the phrase "of thee I sing" to form a logical musical entity.

Style of Performance If you sing a melody such as "America" in short, detached notes instead of in a flowing, singing style, it will seem to be a different song, one you almost certainly will not like as much.

QUALITY OF PERFORMANCE The same piece played by two performers, one who is exceptionally able and another who is mediocre, can leave listeners with very different impressions of the music. Outstanding performers can make what are considered average pieces sound fresh and vital, and less able performers can make exceptional works sound pedestrian.

COUNTERPOINT: MELODIES SOUNDED TOGETHER

Melodies can be combined in one of two ways. One is as a *round* (Figure 3.4). Perhaps you have known about rounds since you were in elementary school. In a round, exactly the same music is sung, but each line starts at a specified time interval. For example, one group of singers sings, "Are you sleeping? Are you sleeping?" and then the second group follows, singing the same melody and words while the first group continues on with "Brother John, Brother John." The process continues with additional groups joining in until the round is sung a given number of times and the last group concludes singing alone.

FIGURE 3.4
ROUND

When one group or instrumental part periodically follows another exactly, it is called **imitation**. When the imitation continues for an entire song or section of music, it is called *strict imitation*, as in a round. The term *round* implies a short song. A **canon** is a somewhat longer and more complex piece than a round in strict imitation. The word *canon* means "by the rule." (When spelled with one *n*, the word has nothing to do with the artillery weapon.)

The second way to combine melodies is to design two different and distinctive lines of music to be performed at the same time. The term for this is **counterpoint** (Figure 3.5), a term that came from medieval times, when notes were called "points." A composer may add a line of counterpoint to an existing melody, or he or she may compose two fresh lines. Usually, the two lines have somewhat different characters; that is part of the reason why counterpoint is interesting to listen to. One line of melody is likely to be more solid and have longer note values than the other.

FIGURE 3.5
COUNTERPOINT

HARMONY: PITCHES SOUNDED TOGETHER

If melody is the horizontal line in music with its sounds occurring one after another, **harmony** is the vertical aspect with sounds occurring at the same time. To illustrate this concept, let's return to "The Star-Spangled Banner." Here are the first seven notes in its melody:

Aligned vertically, these same notes form the B-flat major chord, which is the tonic (home) chord in the key of B-flat.

The preceding sentence contains a number of points about harmony that need to be explained.

KEY OR TONAL CENTER Both melodies and harmonies usually have a **tonal center** and are in a **key**. The music tends to move away from and then back to this center. The musical example of "The Star-Spangled Banner" is in B-flat. Like most music we know, the national anthem of the United States ends and centers around its tonal center. If it were to end on any note other than B-flat, it would sound incomplete—as if someone had made a mistake.

MODULATION Can the tonal center or key change during a musical work? To use the musical term for changing key, can the music *modulate*? Definitely! Not only *can* it change key, but in works longer than a song, it usually *does*. **Modulations** help make the music sound fresher. If the music goes on too long in the same key, it can become boring. Most of the music you hear modulates every so often, but usually people aren't aware that the key has changed.

SCALES A **scale** is a series of pitches that goes upward or downward according to a prescribed pattern. Most scales contain seven different pitches, but a five-note scale is often found in Asian music and some folk music. Few melodies contain a complete scale one note after another, but generally scales are the underlying "skeleton" of melodies and harmonies. The scale for "The Star-Spangled Banner" is B-flat C D E-flat F G A B-flat. Although an alteration or two can occur in a song (and there is one in "The Star-Spangled Banner"), most of the notes come from that scale.

CHORDS A **chord** is three or more pitches sounded together. Usually, the notes of chords follow an every-other, checkerboard pattern. For example, the chord for the tonal center in B-flat is B-flat D F, which are the first, third, and fifth notes in that scale. This chord is called the **tonic chord** and is indicated with the Roman numeral I. A chord can be built on each step of a scale, but the I, IV (subdominant), and V (dominant) chords are used more often than the other chords.

All this should make the earlier reference to notes forming the tonic chord on B-flat clearer now.

OCTAVES You may have noticed that the B-flat scale mentioned earlier began and ended on B-flat. The second B-flat is an **interval** (the distance between two pitches) of an octave higher than the lower B-flat. An **octave** is eight notes higher or lower than another note with the same name. Each octave has double (if it is higher) or half (if it is lower) the number of vibrations of the other. When sounded, octaves blend very well with one another.

The note A above middle C vibrates 440 times per second. With each octave higher, the A vibrates at 880, 1,760, and 3,250. With each descent, the A vibrates at 220, 110, 55, and 27 1/2, which is—the lowest note on the piano. The limits of human hearing range from about 20 to 20,000 vibrations per second.

MAJOR/MINOR Two patterns of scales, **major** and **minor**, are traditional in the music of Western civilization. The main difference between the scales is in the third step, which is one half-step lower in the minor scale. The chords based on these scales are also affected by this difference. To listeners, major and minor sound different from one another, but one is by no means better or more pleasing than the other. *Farandole* by Bizet, discussed in the Listening Guide in Chapter 2, has a marchlike theme in minor and a dancelike theme in major. This offers you a chance to listen to its particular qualities.

 WATCH...
an online demo to listen to examples of major and minor chords, and also to hear the same song in major and in minor.

CONSONANCE/DISSONANCE **Consonance** implies agreement and equilibrium. **Dissonance** implies the opposite—tension and disequilibrium. If you push your hand down on a keyboard, depressing all the keys under your hand, you will get a very dissonant sound. If you press down every other white key, a rather consonant chord will be sounded. There are no clear standards, however, as to what is consonant or dissonant. These two terms are subjective and relative. Therefore, it is more accurate to think in terms of degrees of consonance or dissonance.

HARMONIC PROGRESSIONS AND CADENCES Because music moves through time, so do chords. They have a logic and a sequence, just as notes do in a melody. If you start on C on a keyboard, play the white keys up to B, and then stop without playing the C an octave above where you started, you will be left with an incomplete feeling—somewhat like someone saying to you, "I have a great idea! Why don't we... [silence]."

A progression of chords can give listeners the feeling of either conclusion or incompleteness. Certain patterns of two chords have become traditional for "punctuating" music. These patterns are called **cadences**. Usually, they appear at the ends of phrases, and they give a sense that the music is going to come to either a musical comma or a period. The word *cadence* is also used to describe the pattern played by the drum in a marching band, but this usage is, of course, quite different from the chord patterns discussed here.

TEXTURE AND THE WAYS PITCHES ARE USED

In music, the word **texture** refers to the basic approaches in the use of pitches. It does *not* refer to the smoothness or roughness of a melody. The three terms describing texture are *monophonic*, *homophonic*, and *polyphonic*. Bizet's *Farandole* (see Listening Guide) contains portions in each of these three textures.

The word for a melody alone, with no other accompanying sounds, is **monophonic** (Figure 3.6).

The term for a melody with accompaniment is **homophonic** (Figure 3.7).

The presence of two or more lines with melodic character creates a **polyphonic** texture (Figure 3.8).

FIGURE 3.6
MONOPHONIC TEXTURE

FIGURE 3.7
HOMOPHONIC TEXTURE

Chords

FIGURE 3.8
POLYPHONIC TEXTURE

GEORGES BIZET
Farandole from *L'Arlésienne*, Suite No. 2 (1872)

Download 3

3 minutes 7 seconds

0:00 Orchestra plays marchlike opening theme (A) in a minor key with simple accompaniment.

0:16 Strings play A theme in imitation. The texture is polyphonic.

0:33 High woodwinds play a faster, lighter theme (B) in a major key with accompaniment. Music slowly grows in intensity.

1:16 Strings play B theme in major with a homophonic texture.

1:27 Strings play A theme at a lively tempo. Music returns to minor, and the texture is monophonic.

1:38 Woodwinds play B theme as texture becomes homophonic.

1:44 Strings play A theme in minor. The texture is monophonic but changes to homophonic when lower strings add accompaniment.

1:55 Woodwinds take up B theme in major as texture remains homophonic.

2:18 Orchestra plays both A and B themes at a loud dynamic level. The texture is polyphonic, and music remains in a major key.

3:04 Music concludes with several short chords.

 LISTEN TO... this selection streaming online.

 WATCH... an Active Listening Guide of this selection online.

DO... an online Listening Practice Activity related to this selection, which your instructor may

assign for a grade.

Homophonic and polyphonic textures are relative, and they are sometimes used at different places in the same work. Composers often include musically interesting patterns in an accompanying part, but these parts lack enough melodic character to be considered another line of music. Occasionally, works that are basically polyphonic include portions containing mostly chords, and vice versa.

MAIN POINTS OF CHAPTER 3

1. Sound is created by molecules vibrating and colliding with one another in the air. The more rapid the vibrations, the higher the pitch of the sound.

2. The first seven letters of the alphabet are used to designate pitches. These letter names are repeated for each octave. Each note in an octave is either half (making it lower) or twice (making it higher) the number of vibrations of the note with the same name in the adjacent octave.

3. Pitch levels are depicted in notation on a graphlike staff. Higher notes use the treble clef (𝄞) and lower notes use the bass clef (𝄢), with a half-step higher indicated by a sharp (♯) and a half-step lower indicated by a flat (♭).

4. A melody is a series of consecutive pitches that form a logical entity. Most melodies can be divided into shorter groups of notes called phrases. A listener's impression of a melody is very much affected by other factors in the music such as the accompanying music and instruments or voices performing it.

5. Harmony is the simultaneous sounding of pitches, usually in chords containing three or more notes. Chords vary from sounding pleasing (consonant) to tense (dissonant). Most chords are built in an every-other note pattern such as C-E-G.

6. The music in almost all songs and instrumental works centers around one particular note. Changes of this center (key), called modulations, occur rather often.

7. Scales are the tonal framework around which music is created. Three types of scales predominate in the music of Western civilization: major, minor, and the five-note pentatonic scale. Music using the major scale tends to have a brighter quality than music in minor. Music using the pentatonic scale often has a folklike or Asian quality.

8. Texture in music refers to the basic arrangement of the lines of melody and harmony. Homophonic texture with its melody-plus-accompaniment character is most familiar to us today. Polyphonic texture has two or more different melodic lines occurring at the same time. Monophonic texture consists of only one line of music performed alone.

9. Two types of polyphony or counterpoint exist in music. One occurs when a melodic line is imitated in follow-the-leader fashion several beats later, which happens in a round or canon. The other exists when two different lines with melodic character occur at the same time.

 PRACTICE...
your understanding of this chapter's concepts by working once more with the chapter's Active Listening Guides online.

 DO...
online quizzes that your instructor may assign for a grade.

Dynamics, Timbre, *and* Organization

START...
experiencing this chapter's topics with an online video activity that your instructor may assign.

Learning Objectives

1. Describe the nature and role of dynamics in music.
2. Differentiate the basis of timbres among instruments and voices.
3. Define the essential element of organization in music.
4. Describe the features of different forms in music.
5. Analyze the different elements of music in *Concierto de Aranjuez*.

Loudness and tone quality have much impact on how music sounds. Whatever the relative importance of the four basic elements of music (pitch, rhythm, dynamics, and timbre), they amount to little unless they are combined in an organized way.

READ...
the complete chapter text in a rich interactive eBook!

DYNAMICS: THE LOUD AND SOFT OF MUSIC

Every sound has some degree of loudness, or else it could not be heard. The amount of loudness can range from barely audible to earsplitting, although concert music rarely reaches that level of loudness. The term for the levels of loudness in music is **dynamics**. Sometimes the word *volume* is used for dynamics, but technically speaking it is not the correct term.

Loudness can be measured precisely in terms of *decibels*. A food processor reaches a level of 85 decibels, and a New York subway train produces about 100 decibels, which requires shouting over its noise to carry on a conversation. At 120 decibels, rock concerts reach levels louder than those of a jackhammer or a chainsaw. The difference between 100 and 120 decibels may not seem all that much until you consider that the decibel scale is logarithmic; that is, 110 decibels is ten times louder than 100, and 120 decibels is 100 times louder than a subway train. Listening to loud music or sounds for several hours causes a temporary partial hearing loss. Doing so often over a period of years can cause a noticeable permanent hearing loss (Figure 4.1).

Dynamic levels in music are indicated only in a general way through the use of terms or symbols representing those terms. Table 4.1 lists the commonly used Italian terms and symbols for dynamics.

TABLE 4.1
TERMS AND SYMBOLS FOR DYNAMICS

Term	Symbol	Meaning	Pronunciation
fortissimo	*ff*	very loud	for-TIS-si-moh
forte	*f*	loud	FOR-tay
mezzo forte	*mf*	moderately loud	MET-zo FOR-tay
mezzo piano	*mp*	moderately soft	MET-zo pee-AH-noh
piano	*p*	soft	pee-AH-noh
pianissimo	*pp*	very soft	pee-ah-NIS-si-moh

FIGURE 4.1

Pat Benatar (performing here in 2012 with her husband, Neil Giraldo) is the national spokesperson for "It's Hip to H.E.A.R.," a national initiative whose aim is to educate baby boomers about the importance of hearing health. Benatar says that she knows "firsthand the risks of hearing loss and how it affects your quality of life. Many of my friends have suffered permanent hearing damage, and my husband Neil and I both take proactive steps to protect our hearing health. Unfortunately, many of my peers are in denial."

Larry Marano/Getty Images

WATCH...

an online demo that will help you hear the effect of changes of loud and soft in music.

An increase in dynamic level is indicated by the word **crescendo** (cre-SHEN-doe), abbreviated **cresc.**, and shown by the sign ⟨. The opposite of crescendo is **decrescendo** (DAY-cre-shen-doe), which is abbreviated **decresc**, and indicated by the sign ⟩.

Not all changes in dynamics are gradual. Some notes are marked to be accented (>) or suddenly emphasized **sforzando**, abbreviated as **sfz**. Some changes in dynamic level are to be made suddenly and are indicated by the Italian word **subito**, meaning suddenly loud or soft.

TIMBRE: COLOR IN MUSIC

The fourth basic element of sound is tone quality, its color, which is known as **timbre** (TAM-ber). Timbre in music is as important as color is in a picture.

Every musical instrument and every voice has its own particular tone quality or timbre. If a trombone, clarinet, violin, guitar, flute, and the human voice sound middle C, as all of them can, each will produce it with a different quality. Furthermore, if two or more of them produce the same pitch at the same time, yet another timbre will result.

Why do people and instruments have their own characteristic tone quality? The reason is a bit complicated but worth examining. Almost all musical sounds have pitch (A, D-sharp, G, and so on). But in addition to their fundamental pitch, they also produce small bits and pieces of other pitches, called *partials*, that make up the overtone series for that particular pitch. It's somewhat like getting fries and a soft drink when you order a combination at a fast food place, except in the case of overtones or partials you get many more than a couple of items. The number and the strength of these various partials are what create the timbre of a sound; they make a clarinet sound like a clarinet and a guitar sound like a guitar.

A pitch can be divided in half either by touching the string at half its length or by dividing the air column in half on a wind instrument by opening a key or changing lip tension. Such a division produces a pitch one octave higher than the fundamental. Divide the string or air column into thirds, and a pitch one octave and five notes higher is heard. Divide it into four parts, and a pitch two octaves higher is sounded. The pattern of pitches produced by dividing a string or other sound-producing mechanism into equal parts is called the **overtone series** or the **harmonic series**.

The pattern of the overtone series is exactly the same for every pitch on every instrument. Here are the first seven overtones for the note C:

Because the timbre of a sound is determined by the number and strength of the partials, the tone quality of instruments can be reproduced on a tone synthesizer. High-quality synthesizers can come surprisingly close to imitating the authentic timbre of an instrument. They cannot produce foolproof imitations, however, because the sounds they produce are *too* consistent, *too* perfect. Because of the subtleties of sound produced by some instruments, technicians make actual recordings (called *samples*) of an instrument's sounds and enter them into a computer for use in electronically produced music.

The timbre of a pitch played on an instrument or sung by a human being is not the same from beginning to end. The beginning of a sound may have a distinct hard quality that quickly blends into its basic timbre, which often changes slightly as it's being sustained. In fact, many singers, especially in popular music, make wide changes in timbre as they sing a pitch. These changes usually make the music more interesting and expressive.

Composers and arrangers are very conscious of the different timbres of instruments and voices. They learn in courses in orchestration and arranging, for example, that the low notes of the flute are mellow, whereas its high notes are more shrill. They also know that adding French horns to a melody played by cellos will give strength and richness to the sound. The possibilities for combinations of timbres are limitless.

ORGANIZATION: ORGANIZED SOUNDS = MUSIC

Seeing one dot alone has little meaning, but three dots arranged like those in Figure 4.2 outline a triangle and have more meaning than just three dots. Everyone who has taken a psychology course knows this basic principle of Gestalt-cognitive psychology: The whole is greater than the sum of its parts. This principle certainly applies to music. Composers work with a virtually infinite universe of possible combinations of rhythm, pitch, dynamic level, and timbre. But music, which is often defined as *organized sounds occurring in a specified span of time*, is more than just its accumulated total of notes and rhythms and timbres. Something more—and better—is created when they are combined and organized by a skillful composer or improviser. The whole truly becomes greater than the sum of its parts.

Consider again the song "Simple Gifts." It reveals a strong sense of organization. It has a three-part symmetrical pattern, and its phrases have a logical forward motion followed by points of repose. Its chords fit the notes of the melody, and their simple arrangement by Copland adds to the idea the song is expressing. The rhythms used in "Simple Gifts" also fit the words and are organized into patterns. And, best of all, the musical elements are combined into a musically satisfying entity.

The definition of music as organized sound has two implications. One is that any organized group of sounds occurring in a span of time meets the criteria for music. You may or may not enjoy hearing a particular group of sounds, but as long as they are organized, they fulfill the definition of music.

FIGURE 4.2
THE WHOLE IS GREATER THAN THE SUM OF ITS PARTS.

The other implication is that listeners will understand music much better if they can consider how sounds are organized. Why? Because the organization of sounds is the very stuff of music. Ignoring what is taking place in a musical work is a little like watching a football game with no understanding of the action while you sit around waiting for the final score.

Listening to music carefully and thoughtfully requires listening for what happens in the music, which in turn means listening for how the elements are manipulated by the composer and performer.

Form: Planning in Music

Over the centuries a number of general plans for organizing music have evolved. These general plans are called **forms**. They are the result of the trial-and-error efforts of hundreds of composers over hundreds of years. Forms were given names long after they were developed and used often. Musicians discovered, for example, that a three-part pattern with the first and third parts almost the same provides a satisfying logic in a musical work. Someone tried it, and other composers and listeners liked it.

Composing a form is not, however, like filling out a job application in which certain specific information must be supplied. Instead, forms in music are constructed around one or more of three broad, general considerations: repetition, variation, and contrast.

REPETITION Because music exists in time, the repetition of ideas in music is probably much more important than in the other fine arts. "Simple Gifts," for example, has a three-part form, with the middle part concluding with music similar to the last two lines of the first part. The first melody, the *a* section of the song, begins, "'Tis a gift to be simple …"; the contrasting melody, the *b* section, follows, "When true simplicity is gained …"; and then the *a* section is repeated, "'Tis a gift to be simple.…"

Letters of the alphabet are used to designate the parts of a work. When the parts are short, the letters are in lowercase. Therefore, the form of "Simple Gifts" is *a b a*, or what is termed *ternary form*. The prime (′) sign is used to indicate that the material is slightly different from its identifying letter. When longer sections of music are repeated, uppercase letters are used.

VARIATION A second broad approach to form is through varying the musical material—to repeat the same basic material but with changes.

CONTRAST A third broad approach is by contrast. In "Simple Gifts" the *b* portion of the song has a different melody and words. The contrasting sections in longer works may have a different melody as well as different tempos, keys, dynamic levels, and instruments. Even when a work does not repeat material, it usually contains contrasting sections unless it is quite short.

Because there are many different musical forms, they cannot successfully be discussed in just one chapter. Forms will be presented and discussed at the appropriate places throughout the book.

Genre and Movements

Form in music is largely the result of the pattern in which themes are heard. The word **genre** refers to a quite different aspect of music. It refers to the type of music— symphony, jazz, chamber music, oratorio, and so on. Think of the word as a synonym for "type of music." By the way, it is a French word that is pronounced with a soft *g*.

Many instrumental works are divided into large, independent sections called **movements**. In a sense, they are standalone pieces that have been grouped together by the composer to constitute a larger work. Usually, the movements in a multimovement work have a contrasting character in terms of tempo and other musical qualities. Some of the time they are also loosely related by key. These individual movements often follow their own particular form.

RODRIGO'S *CONCIERTO DE ARANJUEZ*

An important genre in concerto music is the concerto. The essential element of a **concerto** is the contrast between a soloist or small group and the remainder of the orchestra. In the case of Rodrigo's *Concierto de Aranjuez* (see Listening Guide), the solo instrument is a guitar. Many concertos also provide a chance for the soloist to show off his or her technical skill, which Rodrigo's *Concierto* certainly does.

Joaquín Rodrigo

Archive of the Victoria and Joaquín Rodrigo Foundation

Joaquín Rodrigo (1901–1999) was born in Sagunto, Spain. At the age of three he became blind as a result of diphtheria. His music studies began at an early age, and they later took him to France, where he studied with the composer Paul Dukas. After his marriage in 1933 to the Turkish pianist Victoria Kamhi, Rodrigo returned to Spain, but civil war broke out there in 1936 and lasted for three years. During that time he lived in Paris and Germany. He later returned to Spain, and in 1940 his *Concierto de Aranjuez* received a highly successful premiere.

This work was written at a time of tragic events in his native country and in his personal life. Their first child had died in childbirth, and there were concerns that Victoria also would not survive. It has become one of the best-loved pieces of classical music and a cornerstone in the repertoire for the guitar.

Rodrigo wrote of his desire to evoke the world of late eighteenth-century Aranjuez in this concerto—and the courts of Charles IV and Ferdinand VII, the lovely buildings and the gardens and fountains of the royal Aranjuez palace situated on the Tagus river. This is the Spain of the early Goya, of majas and toreros, and of "Spanish rhythms returned from America" (in Rodrigo's own words).

Rodrigo occupied an outstanding position in twentieth-century Spanish musical life, and his 170 compositions include concertos, choral and orchestral works, some 60 songs, pieces for piano and guitar, and music for the ballet and theater. He is recognized worldwide as a great ambassador of Spanish music. His musical language, drawn from both Classical and nationalist sources, underpinned a melodic gift of remarkable eloquence.

In 1996 he received Spain's highest distinction, the Prince of Asturias Prize, with a citation noting that his name joined those of Falla, Granados, and Albeniz among the classics of Spanish music, and underlining his definitive achievement of having given dignity and universality to the Spanish guitar as a concert instrument.

Best-Known Works

Guitar and orchestra
· *Concierto de Aranjuez*
· *Fantasia para un gentilhombre*

Joaquín Rodrigo
Concierto de Aranjuez, Second Movement (1939)

Genre: Concerto

Download 6

10 minutes

0:00   The guitar begins softly strumming four chords.

0:06   English horn plays the main theme. It begins with a short, three-note motive followed by a melody with a tender, mournful quality.

0:40   Guitar repeats the theme with decorative notes.

1:13   English horn plays the theme five notes higher.

1:48   Guitar repeats the theme in a more decorated version.

2:25   Cellos play a contrasting figure, followed by violins and English horn.

2:48   Guitar and woodwinds exchange portions of the theme.

4:00   Guitar plays a version of the theme on its low strings. The music grows more stern.

4:58   Oboe plays a fragment of the theme, answered each time by the guitar.

5:33   Flutes and woodwinds play rapidly repeated notes.

5:56   Guitar softly begins a cadenza. The theme is embedded in the repeated notes.

6:35   Three-note motive is played four times, each time one octave lower.

7:08   Basic pattern of four notes ascending, then four notes descending, begins. Music slowly becomes more intense and passionate.

7:50 Cadenza climaxes as the orchestra enters with a loud, short chord, followed by guitar's rapidly repeated chords.

7:59 Orchestra plays the main theme passionately, but then ends quietly with the flute, oboe, and guitar.

9:02 Guitar returns, quietly playing a portion of the theme, with two lines that seem to answer each other.

9:41 Movement seems to fade into space as it closes with the guitar and violins playing high, ethereal notes.

LISTEN TO... this selection streaming online.

WATCH... an Active Listening Guide of this selection online.

WATCH... a performance of this selection online.

DO... an online Listening Practice Activity related to this selection, which your instructor may assign for a grade.

Only the second of the *Concierto*'s three movements is presented in the body of the book. Usually, second movements are melodious and have a slow tempo, and Rodrigo follows that tradition. The first and third movements are online. Musical works can be examined in terms of how their melodies, rhythms, and timbres are organized. The second movement of *Concierto de Aranjuez* seems especially well suited for such analysis.

MELODY The basic outline of the melody—its "musical skeleton"—consists of a long note, and then the melody moves up two notes before returning to the original long note. Next, the melody ascends for four notes and then works its way down note by note to four notes below where it began. Up to this point, all the melodic movement has been to adjacent notes.

But there is much more than its melodic skeleton. Rodrigo also adds many quick-moving, decorative notes. These notes are especially noticeable when the guitar takes its turn playing the melody. Then three quick, accented notes begin the melody (♪♪♩), something often found in Spanish music. This short melodic figure is heard frequently throughout the music and contributes to the unity of the movement. Such brief figures are called **motives** when they act as a unifying element in a musical work. By the way, the word *motive* has nothing to do with the reasons why the composer wrote the music!

TIMBRE Much of the second movement of the *Concierto* has a tender, melancholy quality, due in large part to the tone qualities of the English horn and the guitar.

HARMONY The quiet, uncomplicated accompaniment adds to the tenderness of the music while allowing the melody to be clearly heard.

RHYTHM The rhythm is slow and steady with four beats to the measure. Because this movement features the melody, its rhythm is not as noticeable as it is in many works, including the other movements of *Concierto de Aranjuez*.

FORM AND ORGANIZATION The movement opens with the melody played by the English horn; then the guitar enters playing a more elaborate version of the melody. The melody returns two more times between contrasting sections and a long cadenza for the guitar. But that's not all. Rodrigo has the music build ever so gradually to a rather lengthy section for the guitar alone. This section also begins quietly but then slowly increases to a truly passionate level of intensity as the orchestra again takes up the theme with its three-note motive. The music just seems to float away as the movement ends.

The section for guitar alone is called the **cadenza**. Cadenzas allow the soloist to play paraphrases of the themes in a free-sounding and often technically stunning style. Cadenzas are almost always featured in one or more movements of solo concertos.

Everything about the second movement of *Concierto de Aranjuez* works. All the elements are organized into a musically satisfying entity. The entire second movement really is greater than the sum of its parts.

MAIN POINTS OF CHAPTER 4

1. The term for the degree of loudness in music is *dynamics*. Dynamics are indicated in a general way by the terms *forte* for loud (abbreviated *f*) and *piano* for soft (abbreviated *p*). These basic terms are often modified; for example, fortissimo (abbreviated *ff*) for very loud.

2. Gradual changes in dynamic level are indicated by the abbreviation cresc. for crescendo (get louder) or decresc. for decrescendo (get softer). The symbol for crescendo is ⎯◁⎯, and the opposite is used for decrescendo ⎯▷⎯.

3. Timbre refers to the tone quality of an instrument or voice. It is determined by the number and strength of the partials sounding in the overtone series. That series is the pattern of pitches that results when a string or column of air is divided in half or at other fractional points.

4. Music is organized sounds occurring in a specific span of time. Often, portions of music are organized according to forms or patterns of music. These forms make use of three general aspects of music:

   - Repetition: —Generally repeating the same musical ideas.
   - Variation: —The same basic musical ideas are repeated but varied.
   - Contrast: —Entirely different musical ideas are presented.

5. Letters in italics are used to designate forms. The larger sections of a work are indicated by capital letters, whereas short sections of a work are indicated in lowercase letters.

6. A concerto features contrast between a small group and a larger group or a soloist and a larger group. Concertos often contain a section called a *cadenza*, where the soloist plays alone a free-sounding, often technically impressive, section based loosely on one or more of the themes of the music.

PRACTICE...

your understanding of this chapter's concepts by working once more with the chapter's Active Listening Guide online.

DO...

online quizzes that your instructor may assign for a grade.

Orchestral Instruments

Learning Objectives

1 Recognize, from listening, the general timbre and range of the four families of instruments in a symphony orchestra.

2 Describe the basic means by which the various instruments in an orchestra produce sound and play pitches.

3 Explain the difference between the percussion instruments that play pitches and those that don't.

START...
experiencing this chapter's topics with an online video activity that your instructor may assign.

Sounds are produced when something causes the molecules in the air to rapidly collide and bounce off one another, something like balls on a pool table. What a musical instrument does is control and shape the vibrations in a particular way. In doing this, instruments provide the element of tone color or timbre (pronounced TAM-ber) in music.

Most musical instruments can be examined for their capabilities in doing four actions:

1. Producing their characteristic sound
2. Modifying their basic timbre
3. Playing different pitches
4. Starting and stopping their sounds

READ...
the complete chapter text in a rich interactive eBook!

The instruments that make up the symphony orchestra (Figure 5.1) can be grouped into families according to the way they produce sound.

STRING INSTRUMENTS

The difference among the four main string instruments in the orchestra is mostly one of size. The *violin* (Figure 5.2) is the smallest and has the highest pitch. It is held under the chin when played. There is no difference between the instruments used for the first and second violin sections. Only the music written for them differs.

The *viola* (vee-OH-lah) is somewhat larger than the violin but is still played under the chin. Its general range is five notes lower than that of the violin.

The *cello* (CHEL-low, officially known as the *violoncello*) rests on the floor when played and is supported between the player's knees (Figure 5.3). It is one octave lower than the viola.

The *double bass* (pronounced BASE) has several other names: *bass viol, contrabass,* and *string bass* (Figure 5.4). Players of the instrument stand or can sit on a high stool when playing. With its sloping shoulders, the shape of its body is slightly different from that of the other string instruments, and its strings are tuned four notes apart, not five like the other string instruments.

The *harp* is quite different. It's a large instrument that sits on the floor with many strings that are strummed or plucked. Its strings are modified to play different pitches through the use of a pedal mechanism.

The strings are the backbone of the symphonic orchestra, with their number equaling that of all the rest of the instruments put together. By far the largest number are

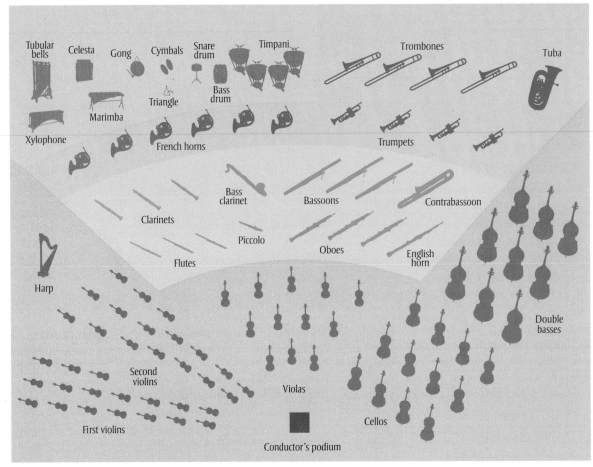

FIGURE 5.1

THE INSTRUMENTS OF THE SYMPHONY ORCHESTRA ARE GROUPED INTO FOUR FAMILIES ACCORDING TO THE WAY THEY PRODUCE SOUND: STRINGS, WOODWINDS, BRASSES, AND PERCUSSION. THIS ILLUSTRATION SHOWS A TYPICAL SEATING PLAN, ALTHOUGH EXACT NUMBER AND PLACEMENT OF THE INSTRUMENTS CAN VARY.

FIGURE 5.2

THE VIOLIN THE HORSEHAIR BOW DRAWN ACROSS THE STRINGS SETS THEM VIBRATING. THE VIBRATIONS ARE CONDUCTED THROUGH THE BRIDGE AND AMPLIFIED BY THE INSTRUMENT'S LARGELY HOLLOW BODY. THE POSITION OF THE PLAYER'S FINGERS PRESSING DOWN ON THE STRINGS ON THE FINGERBOARD DETERMINES THE PITCHES THAT ARE PLAYED.

Randy Batista Photography

AFP/Getty Images

FIGURE 5.4
THE DOUBLE BASS THE FINGERBOARD IS GLUED TO THE NECK OF THE INSTRUMENT BUT DOES NOT TOUCH THE HOLLOW BODY.

Randy Batista Photography

FIGURE 5.3
THE CELLO NOTICE THE RAPID ROCKING OF THE LEFT HAND TO CREATE THE SMALL VARIATIONS IN PITCH KNOWN AS *VIBRATO*.

violins (about twenty-four to thirty), with at least twelve violas, twelve cellos, and eight basses.

Sound Production

String instruments produce sounds by vibrating strings. This is done in two ways: by drawing a bow across the string and by plucking the string with the finger.

The bow was originally slightly arched like the bow used in archery. But over the years, its curve was reduced and then curved slightly inward toward the hair, which allowed for more flexibility in the types of bowing. The hair on a bow is from the tail of a horse. If you look at it through a microscope, you will see hundreds of tiny depressions in it. The uneven surfaces of the hair catch on the string, causing it to vibrate. Usually, players of string instruments apply rosin to the bow hair to help it catch the string better.

A string vibrating by itself doesn't produce much of a sound. The vibrations need to be amplified, which is the purpose of the body of the string instrument. The strings are held off the body by a wooden bridge. The vibrations of the strings are conducted through the bridge to the largely hollow body of the instrument.

Modifying the Basic Timbre

The timbre of string instruments can be affected in several ways. One is to rock the left hand back and forth in small, rapid motions. This creates a **vibrato** (vih-BRAH-toe), which adds warmth to the tone quality by causing small alterations of pitch. All advanced string players use vibrato when playing.

Another way of affecting the timbre of a string instrument is to place a **mute** over the bridge. This small wood or plastic device softens the sound and makes it more mellow.

The timbre of string instruments is also affected by the way the bow is drawn across the string. More pressure on the bow makes the tone more harsh. Several different styles of bowing are used, each of which affects the tone and expressive qualities of the sounds.

Regulating Pitch

Different pitches are achieved on a string instrument (1) by the particular string being played; (2) by the length of string allowed to vibrate, which is regulated by the player; and (3) occasionally by the way the string is fingered. All orchestral string instruments (except the harp and some double basses) have four strings. The strings each have a different thickness, are made of different materials, and are tuned five notes apart (except for double basses) by tightening or loosening the pegs at the end of the instrument.

As can be seen in the photos, the neck extends from the instrument, and a fingerboard is attached to the neck. The player depresses a string firmly against the fingerboard to shorten the string and thereby makes the pitch higher. The player's fingers must be placed at exactly the right spot; otherwise, the sounds are out of tune.

String instruments can also play *harmonics*, which are the notes in the overtone series above the basic pitch. The player can touch the string lightly at various points to create a *natural harmonic* or use a combination of depressed first finger and lightly touching with the little finger to produce an *artificial harmonic*. Both types of harmonics have a high, ethereal sound.

It is possible to sound two or three notes at the same time on string instruments. These combinations of notes are called *double stops* or *triple stops*.

Starting and Stopping Sound

The motion of the bow across the string usually determines how long a sound is produced. String players learn several different styles of bowing. Some styles have abrupt, clear-cut beginnings and endings of the sounds, but others are very smooth with less distinct beginnings and endings. Sounds that are made by plucking with the first finger of the right hand, called **pizzicato**, are short and cannot be sustained. Occasionally, the left hand will pluck an open string in flashy solo works.

WOODWIND INSTRUMENTS

The *flute* (Figure 5.5) used to have a wooden body, but since about 1900 silver-nickel bodies have been universally favored because of their more brilliant sound. The flute generally plays notes higher than those of the reed instruments. It has a smaller cousin, the *piccolo*, which sounds one octave higher than the flute.

The *oboe* is made of grenadilla wood, which comes from the island of Madagascar. It has to be carefully treated to prevent cracking. The instrument has a distinctive plaintive quality. The *English horn* is neither English nor a horn. It is basically a large oboe with a bulb-shaped bell. It sounds five notes lower than the oboe.

The *clarinet* (Figure 5.6) has a wide range, but its timbre differs quite a bit from its low notes (very mellow) to its high notes (quite shrill). Clarinets are made from the same wood as oboes. They come in several sizes, including the bass clarinet, which looks like a wooden saxophone.

The *bassoon* (Figure 5.6) has a distinctive appearance, which, with its reddish brown or black finish, looks somewhat like a long bedpost. Like the clarinet, it has a wide range, but it is more than an octave lower in pitch. The *contrabassoon* sounds another octave lower than the bassoon, going almost to the lowest note on the piano.

FIGURE 5.5
THE FLUTE TO GENERATE VARIOUS PITCHES, WOODWIND INSTRUMENT PLAYERS USE COMPLEX KEY MECHANISMS TO OPEN AND CLOSE HOLES THAT REGULATE THE LENGTH OF A COLUMN OF VIBRATING AIR.

Saxophones have a metal body and a distinctive J shape, except for the soprano saxophone, which has a straight body like that of a clarinet. Saxophones use a single reed clamped on a mouthpiece and come in a variety of sizes.

A symphony orchestra has two flutes and a piccolo, two oboes and an English horn, two clarinets and a bass clarinet, and two bassoons and a contrabassoon. Saxophones are not regular members of the symphony orchestra.

Sound Production

With the exception of the flute, the woodwinds produce sound through vibrating reeds (Figure 5.7). The reeds are cut from cane that looks like bamboo. In the case of the clarinet, a single reed is clamped on a mouthpiece. The oboe and bassoon play double reeds, with two reeds wired together facing each other.

The flute produces sound by the "stopped pipe" principle. It is possible to blow across the top of a bottle or jug and produce a sound. The sound is created by the collision of the air going down into the bottle meeting the air coming back out.

FIGURE 5.6
CLARINETS AND BASSOONS

Modifying Basic Timbre

All the woodwinds except the clarinet can be played with a vibrato, especially the flute. Only in jazz is a vibrato used on the clarinet.

Advanced oboists and bassoonists make their own reeds, which is something of an art. The cutting and shaping of the double reed has a noticeable effect on the timbre of the instrument.

No mutes are used on woodwind instruments.

Regulating Pitch

All woodwind instruments regulate pitch by shortening or lengthening the column of air inside the instrument. This is done by *key* mechanisms that open or close holes. Some of the fingerings are quite complicated, however. The closer an open hole is toward the end of the instrument in the player's mouth, the higher the pitch will be—usually.

The qualification is included in the preceding sentence because all the woodwinds can move into a new and higher level of pitch by either overblowing at the octave (as on the flute) or opening a key that causes the instrument to overblow (as on the oboe, clarinet, and bassoon).

Starting and Stopping Sounds

Sounds are usually started when air is allowed to go through the instrument as the player's tongue is pulled off the reed, or away from the upper teeth in the case of the flute. Flute players can also use an action called *double tonguing* to articulate notes very quickly. Flutists can also achieve an effect called *flutter tonguing*.

FIGURE 5.7
DOUBLE REEDS AN OBOE REED
(TOP) AND A BASSOON REED.

BRASS INSTRUMENTS

The *trumpet* is the highest-pitched brass instrument. It has three piston valves that change the length of tubing. The *cornet* is similar to a trumpet except that its tubing is more like a cone; the trumpet's tubing is more cylindrical. The configuration of the tubing affects the timbre of the instruments, with the trumpet having a more brilliant quality and the cornet a more mellow timbre.

The *French horn* (Figure 5.8) contains more than sixteen feet of tubing that is coiled so that it can be handled more conveniently. It has three or four rotary valves, which

FIGURE 5.8

FRENCH HORN MOST HIGH-QUALITY FRENCH HORNS ARE ACTUALLY DOUBLE HORNS, WHICH MAKES IT EASIER TO PLAY THE RIGHT NOTES. A VALVE REGULATED BY THE THUMB CONTROLS WHICH PART OF THE HORN IS USED.

are operated by the player's left hand. Rotary valves turn to open up different lengths of tubing instead of moving up and down as piston valves do. Most of the time, a player inserts his or her right hand into the bell of the instrument to modify the timbre.

The most unusual feature of the French horn isn't visible. All the other brass instruments use the overtone series starting one octave above the fundamental pitch. The French horn uses the overtone series starting two octaves above the fundamental pitch. This means that the notes with the same fingering are closer together and that much precision is needed to produce the desired pitches. The French horn has a rather wide range, however.

The *trombone* is the only orchestral instrument today that uses a slide to regulate the length of its tubing. It sounds one octave lower than the trumpet. The *bass trombone* is somewhat larger than the more common tenor trombone, and it can play several notes lower.

The *tuba* is the largest and lowest in pitch of the brass instruments. Its role is similar to that of the double bass in the string section in playing the important bass line. The tuba seldom gets to play solos. Like the double bass, however, when played well it has a pleasing quality.

A symphony orchestra usually has three trumpets, four French horns, two trombones and a bass trombone, and one tuba.

Sound Production

All brass instruments produce sound by the membranes of the player's lips vibrating into a cup-shaped mouthpiece (Figure 5.9) which can vibrate a thousand or more times each second. The buzzing sound is then amplified through a metal tube with a flared bell at the end. For ease of handling, the metal tubing on brass instruments is curled once or twice.

Modifying Sound

All brass instruments occasionally use mutes that are placed in the bell of the instrument to alter the timbres. The mutes come in a variety of shapes and materials, including one resembling a rubber sink plunger and another called a "wah-wah mute." A vibrato can be used when playing brass instruments, especially in solo passages.

Trumpet   French horn   Trombone   Tuba

FIGURE 5.9

BRASS MOUTHPIECES

Regulating Pitch

The pitches on brass instruments are controlled in two ways. One is by subtle changes in the lips, which produce the different pitches of the overtone series. This phenomenon is best explained by considering the bugle. A bugle has no mechanism for changing pitch. All its different pitches are the result of changes in the tension of the bugler's lips. Only the sounds of the overtone series can be produced, however. These are the ones heard in bugle calls. All brass instruments can play the "bugle" pitches.

In addition, all brass instruments in an orchestra have either a valve or a slide mechanism (Figure 5.10) that allows the player to change the length of tubing. That means that a new overtone series is made available when the length of the tubing is changed. The various combinations of valves and slide positions therefore make it possible for the player of a brass instrument to sound any pitch within the range of the instrument.

Starting and Stopping Sounds

Brass instrument players start and stop sounds with their tongues, with the sound beginning as the tongue is pulled back from behind their upper teeth, opening the air stream. They can tongue very rapidly by *double* or *triple tonguing*.

PERCUSSION INSTRUMENTS

Percussion instruments can be divided into those that play pitches and those that don't. The *glockenspiel* (Figure 5.11), *xylophone*, *marimba*, and *vibraphone* are all percussion instruments that have metal or wooden bars arranged like the piano keyboard. They are played with mallets, or sticks with padded ends. The glockenspiel has metal bars that produce high tinkling sounds. The xylophone has wooden bars and produces dry, brittle sounds. The marimba is like a xylophone except for hollow tubes hanging below each bar that allow the sound to resonate after the bar has been struck. The vibraphone also has tubes, but in addition has an electrically driven device that adds vibrato to the sounds.

Timpani (Figure 5.12) are two or more kettledrums of different sizes tuned to different pitches. Five are used in symphony orchestras today, and three are a minimum for works composed after 1800. The player positions the timpani around him or her in a semicircular arrangement. The mallets used in playing the timpani have round, padded heads. Professional players have several pairs of mallets of differing firmness to fit the needs of the music.

The *celesta* looks like a small piano, but it is more like a glockenspiel that is operated from a keyboard. *Chimes* sound different pitches. The player strikes the top of the metal tube with a wooden hammer.

The *snare drum* (Figure 5.13) is the most prominent percussion instrument that does not sound a definite pitch. It is constructed around two hollow rings that are five or more inches apart. The rings have calfskin or plastic stretched over them. The bottom surface has several strands of wire, called *snares*, that rattle against it. The snares give the drum its characteristic crisp sound. The snare drum is played with a pair of wooden sticks.

The *bass drum* is the largest percussion instrument, sometimes having a diameter of four feet or more. It is placed on its side and hit with a single beater with a round, padded head.

The *cymbals* (Figure 5.14) are large metal disks that are struck against each other with glancing blows. A single cymbal can also be suspended and struck with a stick or a wire brush.

FIGURE 5.10

TROMBONE BRASS-INSTRUMENT PLAYERS CAN VARY PITCH BY SUBTLE CHANGES IN THEIR LIPS AND BY MECHANICAL ADJUSTMENT OF THE LENGTH OF THE TUBING THROUGH WHICH VIBRATING AIR PASSES.

FIGURE 5.11
XYLOPHONE

FIGURE 5.12
TIMPANI

FIGURE 5.13
SNARE DRUM

FIGURE 5.14
CYMBALS

FIGURE 5.15
TRIANGLE

The *triangle* (Figure 5.15) is made of metal and is shaped like a triangle. It is struck with a metal beater while suspended. The *tambourine* has a single calfskin head stretched over a wooden or metal hoop. The rim hoop contains small metal disks that rattle when moved. The player shakes the tambourine or hits it against the heel of the other hand to produce sounds.

Percussion players get to play a number of unusual instruments. For instance, they play something called a *whip*, which is actually two flat pieces of wood that are slapped together. Occasionally, they even get to sound whistles and car horns.

Fortunately for the orchestra's budget, percussionists play more than one instrument, but not at the same time. Orchestras have four regular percussion players and hire extras when needed.

Sound Production

Percussion instruments make sounds when struck or shaken. None of them can sustain sound, something that all string (except the harp), woodwind, and brass instruments can do. Some percussion instruments are hit together, others are struck with a stick or a beater, and a few are operated from a keyboard.

Modifying Sound

Sticks and beaters are made from different materials and in different sizes, and each has an effect on the sound produced. Occasionally wire brushes are used, and sometimes beaters with round, padded heads are required. Drumsticks come in a variety of sizes. The manner in which percussion instruments are struck or rattled varies and thus can alter the sound produced.

Regulating Pitch

Many percussion instruments do not sound definite pitches. But there are a number of percussion instruments that do. One group has wooden or metal bars arranged in the manner of a piano keyboard. The large kettledrums (timpani) regulate pitch with a foot pedal mechanism or handles at the edge of the drumhead that change the tension in the drumhead.

Starting and Stopping Sounds

Because percussion instruments cannot sustain sounds, there is little problem with stopping sounds. An exception involves the ring of cymbals, chimes, and the timpani. Sometimes percussion players must dampen the sound of these instruments immediately after playing them to keep them from ringing too long and intruding on the music that follows.

LISTENING FOR INSTRUMENTS

Being able to identify the timbres of various instruments as you listen helps you understand and enjoy music more. You can learn to do this better by noticing the sounds of instruments as they are pointed out in the Listening Guides and Active Listening Guides, and in *The Young Person's Guide to the Orchestra*.

Benjamin Britten

Benjamin Britten (1913–1976) was born in the seacoast town of Lowestoft, England, the son of a dental surgeon father and a musical mother. He began putting patterns on paper before he was five, and by the time he was six or seven, the notes became associated with what he had in mind. By the age of fourteen, he had composed a number of works for piano and voice. He was given a scholarship to the Royal College of Music, and by the age of twenty-one was earning his living largely as a composer.

He immigrated to the United States in 1939 but returned to England in 1942. He toured America again several times, usually giving performances with his life-long companion, tenor Peter Pears.

Britten wrote for every medium and for varied levels of musical difficulty.

He once said of composing: "It is the easiest thing in the world to write a piece virtually or wholly impossible to perform—but—that is not what I prefer to do. I prefer to study the conditions of the performance and shape my music to them."

Best-Known Works

Opera
- *Peter Grimes*
- *Albert Herring*
- *Billy Budd*

Orchestra and voice
- *War Requiem*
- *Serenade for Tenor, Horn, and Strings*

Choral
- *A Ceremony of Carols*

It is the most sophisticated work created to demonstrate orchestral instruments. First, it presents the instruments first by families, and then a variation for each instrument, which is followed by a short fugue. The instruments play the melody of the fugue in the same order in which they played their variation on the theme. The work closes with the opening theme in long notes and the fugue melody sounding simultaneously.

BENJAMIN BRITTEN
The Young Person's Guide to the Orchestra

LISTENING GUIDE

Variations and Fugue on a Theme by Purcell, Op. 34

Theme, variations, and fugue

Download 7

17 minutes 23 seconds

Theme

0:00   Orchestra plays the theme at a loud dynamic level in a minor key.

(continued)

0:42	Woodwinds play the theme in a major key.
1:11	Brasses play the theme.
1:42	Strings play the theme.
2:07	Percussion, especially the timpani, play the theme.
2:26	Entire orchestra plays the theme.

Variations

3:00	Variation 1. Flute and piccolo play high, fast notes.
3:28	Variation 2. Oboes sound a plaintive, melancholy melody.
4:33	Variation 3. Clarinets play rapidly moving notes.
5:15	Variation 4. Bassoons play a humorous melody.
6:11	Variation 5. Violins play a dancelike variation with rhythmic accompaniment.
6:56	Variation 6. Violas play a slow melody with a wide range.
7:46	Variation 7. Cellos play a rich, flowing variation.
8:43	Variation 8. Double basses play a variation with three-note patterns that ascend one pitch level each phrase and then descend one pitch level each phrase.
9:42	Variation 9. Harp plays the theme in an upside-down version.
10:32	Variation 10. French horns play variation built around chords.
11:15	Variation 11. Trumpets feature marchlike figures.
11:49	Variation 12. Trombones and tuba play a heavy, majestic variation.
12:51	Variation 13. Percussion instruments play a variation that starts with the timpani, followed by the bass drum and cymbals, tambourine, triangle, snare drum, Chinese wood blocks, xylophone, castanets, gong, and the whip.

Fugue

14:45	Piccolo presents the main melody of the fugue.

The main theme is played by the instruments in this order:

14:51	Flute
14:58	Oboes
15:04	Clarinets
15:13	Bassoons
15:23	First violins
15:27	Second violins
15:29	Violas
15:37	Cellos
15:42	Double basses
15:53	Harp
16:04	French horns
16:08	Trumpets
16:17	Trombones and tuba

16:24 Percussion

16:32 Both themes are combined: Brasses play the slower opening theme while upper strings and woodwinds continue with the fugue.

17:00 Percussion enters loudly.

17:19 The work ends with a long, full-sounding chord.

LISTEN TO... this selection streaming online.

WATCH... an Active Listening Guide of this selection online.

WATCH... a video online that will help you review what you have learned about orchestral instruments.

DO... an online Listening Practice Activity related to this selection, which your instructor may assign

for a grade.

For nearly 200 years, the symphony orchestra has been the most important ensemble in instrumental concert music. The instruments that it comprises have a special place in listening to symphonic music. They provide the palette of musical sounds for both composers and listeners.

MAIN POINTS OF CHAPTER 5

1. The instruments in a symphony orchestra are traditionally divided into four groups: strings, woodwinds, brasses, and percussion. Each of these families of instruments differs in how sounds are produced, basic timbres are modified, different pitches are created, and sounds are started and stopped.

2. Violins, violas, cellos, and double basses produce sound when a bow is drawn across their strings or a string is plucked (pizzicato). Harps can only be plucked. String players rapidly rock their left hand back and forth (vibrato) to add warmth to the sound.

3. Pitches on string instruments are determined by where a player places a finger on one of the strings. It is also possible to play on more than one string at a time. Several different styles of bowing can be used.

4. Flutes, clarinets, oboes, and bassoons constitute the woodwind family. All were originally made of wood, but because of their more brilliant sound, metal flutes replaced their wooden predecessors. Oboes and bassoons produce sound through the use of two cane reeds wired together, whereas clarinets use a single cane reed on a mouthpiece. Flutes employ a stopped-pipe principle, in which air entering a pipe collides with air moving out to produce sound.

5. A vibrato can be used on all woodwinds except the clarinet, which uses it only in jazz style. Different pitches are produced by opening and closing holes and/or depressing and releasing keys. Sounds on woodwind instruments are started and stopped by the action of the player's tongue.

PRACTICE...

your understanding of this chapter's concepts by working once more with the chapter's Active Listening Guide online.

DO...

online quizzes that your instructor may assign for a grade.

6. Members of the brass family include trumpets, French horns, trombones, and tubas. All are made of metal. Sounds are produced on them by a buzzing action of the player's lip membranes against a mouthpiece. All produce the pitches of the overtone series. By changing the length of the tubing, by opening and closing valves, or by moving the slide on the trombone, all pitches within the range of the instrument are available.

7. Percussion instruments all produce sound by being shaken or struck, usually by sticks or beaters. Some percussion instruments produce definite pitches. This group includes xylophones, chimes, and timpani. Others sound no definite pitch and include snare and bass drums, cymbals, and castanets.

Other Musical Instruments

Learning Objectives

1 Describe how the human voice functions for singing.
2 Differentiate the instruments used in a wind band from those in a symphony orchestra.
3 Distinguish how the keyboard instruments—piano, harpsichord, and pipe organ—create sounds.
4 List a variety of other popular and electronic instruments.
5 Prepare to attend a concert as part of your music appreciation course.

START...
experiencing this chapter's topics with an online video exercise that your instructor may assign.

The instruments of the symphony orchestra are often discussed together because they make up a rather standardized musical organization. But these instruments represent only one segment of the instruments used to make music throughout the world. This chapter examines the other important types of instruments.

READ...
the complete chapter text in a rich interactive eBook!

THE VOICE

It may seem odd to talk about the **voice** as an instrument, although singers often refer to a person's voice as his or her "instrument." But it can be examined using the same categories that were used for orchestral instruments. The reason we don't usually think of the voice as an instrument is that we are born with it. We learn to use it for talking and to some extent for informal singing without any special instruction, something that is usually needed to play most instruments competently.

Sound Production

The voice produces sound through the vibration of the vocal cords in the larynx, or what is commonly called the voice box. Air and enough tension in the cords are required before these cords can produce sound.

Having enough air for breathing and enough for singing for an audience without the aid of amplification are two quite different matters. Because singing involves sustaining vowel sounds, good singing requires much control over the air. The muscular floor below the lungs, called the diaphragm, must provide a sufficient amount of breath support. The lungs are not muscles, hence the importance of the diaphragm. The vocal cords must also be tightened; otherwise, no sound can be sustained.

Modifying Basic Timbre

The timbre of vocal sounds is determined by the shape of the oral and nasal cavities inside the head, as well as the cheeks and tongue formation. Each vowel has its particular formation, which is altered by the placement of the throat and tongue and the shape of the mouth and lips. An infinite number of shadings of timbre are possible.

Regulating Pitch

The pitch of a vocal sound is determined by the amount of tension in the vocal cords in relation to their length and thickness. The shorter the cords and the tighter they are stretched, the higher the pitch.

The difference between men's and women's voices is caused largely by the length of the cords. The vocal cords of an adult male are normally about twice the length of a woman's, and they are also thicker. A larger larynx is required for a man's cords, which explains the more prominent Adam's apple.

Starting and Stopping Sounds

Vocal sounds are controlled by the action of the diaphragm in pushing air through the larynx. Sounds can also be choked off in the throat, but that doesn't sound very attractive, so it is usually avoided in singing.

Types of Voices

Voices in choral singing are traditionally divided into four classifications. The higher, lighter women's voice is called **soprano**. The darker, lower women's voice is called **alto**. In the case of men, the higher voice is called **tenor**, and the lower, deeper voice is called **bass** (pronounced "base"). Solo voices are classified using these four basic terms, which are often abbreviated in choral music as *SATB*. Additional modifiers such as *mezzo*, *dramatic*, and *lyric* are sometimes used in classifying voices. Most of the terms for classifying solo voices are not as well standardized as the four main classifications.

The voice is an instrument in one other way. Training is normally required to achieve the maximum power, beauty, range, and expression. It is, of course, possible to sing simple songs without any formal training. For almost all persons, however, lessons are needed to sing more difficult pieces or to have much power without the aid of a microphone.

What Is Singing?

The styles of singing vary tremendously around the world and in the present-day United States. Some singing is smooth and has an intimate quality, whereas other singing is raucous and sounds almost like shouting. Some styles sustain pitches for long periods of time, while in other styles the syllables in words are hardly sustained or hardly have pitch. In fact, singers in popular music try to cultivate an individual style and timbre. These differences are in addition to range and type of voice. The style of singing that is typical of one type of music can be very out of place in another style. It's the same with clothes. College students don't go to class wearing a swimsuit or a tuxedo. Yet both items of apparel are appropriate in other situations.

THE CHORAL EXPERIENCE The singing styles of choral groups also vary widely. Here are two examples from myriad possibilities around the world.

The first work is "Ave Maria" by Franz Biebl (see Listening Guide). It offers listeners not only beautiful sounds but also, at several points, a tapestry of vocal lines that are woven together to create a rich tonal fabric. It was composed for unaccompanied male voices, although it has also been arranged for choral groups consisting of men and women. Part of its appeal is not only the musical work itself, but also the performance on the recording by the male chorus Chanticleer. The singers' voices join together to produce a velvety sound that is perfectly in tune. In fact, "Ave Maria" owes much of its success to Chanticleer, who made it a hit in America and Europe in the early 1970s.

FRANZ BIEBL
"Ave Maria" (1964)

Download 8

7 minutes 25 seconds

0:00	(Chant) *Angelus Domini nuntiavit Mariae, Et concepit de Spiritu sancto.*	The angel of the Lord announced to Mary, and she conceived by the Holy Spirit.
0:19	(Choral) *Ave Maria, gratia plena. Dominus tecum, Benedicta tu in mulieribus, et benedictus fructus ventris, Jesus.*	Hail Mary, full of grace. The Lord is with thee. Blessed art thou among women, and blessed is the fruit of Thy womb, Jesus.
1:49	(Chant) *Maria dixit: Ecce ancilla Domini fiat mihi secundum verbum tuum.*	Mary said: Behold the handmaiden of the Lord, let it be done to me according to Thy word.
2:09	(Repeat: "Ave Maria" choral section)	
3:39	(Chant) *Et verbum carro factum et habitavit in nobis*	And the word was made flesh and dwelt among us.
3:53	(Repeat: "Ave Maria" choral section)	
5:32	(Choral) *Sancta Maria, mater Dei ora pro nobis peccatoribus nunc et in hora mortis nostrae*	Holy Mary, Mother of God pray for us sinners now and at the hour of our death.
6:48	*Amen*	Amen

 LISTEN TO... this selection streaming online.

 WATCH... an Active Listening Guide of this selection online.

 WATCH... a performance of this selection online.

 DO... an online Listening Practice Activity related to this selection, which your instructor may assign for a grade.

Franz Biebl

Franz Biebl (1906–2001) was not a giant among twentieth-century composers. He joins a rather long list of composers who are known largely because of their one exceptional composition that became a favorite of concert audiences. For Biebl, that work was his "Ave Maria." He was born in Germany, worked in the 1930s as a church musician, and directed choirs at the distinguished Mozarteum in Salzburg, Austria. He was drafted into the German army in World War II and was captured. He then spent nearly three years in a prisoner-of-war camp near Battle Creek,

(continued)

Michigan. So it's possible that he heard barbershop singing at some point during those years.

The remaining years of his life were spent as a church musician in Fürstenfeldbruck, Germany. "Ave Maria" might never have become famous were it not for the director of the Cornell University Glee Club, Thomas Sokol, to whom Biebl gave a number of his compositions in 1970.

The work quickly become well known to concert audiences, especially after its performances by men's vocal ensemble Chanticleer, shown performing in the photo that accompanies this biography.

Best-Known Works

Choral
• "Ave Maria"

Biebl's use of harmony is impressive. He divides the voice parts so that at points in "Ave Maria" there are five different pitches. In addition, in a couple of places he has changes of harmony that sound much like what is heard in American barbershop quartet singing.

Our second example of singing is a religious song, "Hohonolofatsa" (see Listening Guide), sung by the Soweto Gospel Choir (Figure 6.1) from the Union of South Africa. Notice the vocal and stylistic differences between the English and African songs. Because good singing depends very much on the particular type of music, no singing style is inherently better than another; the styles are just different. Both are very enjoyable to listen to.

The Soweto choir is a testament to humankind's ability to develop wonderful music from miserable conditions. The word *Soweto* comes from the official name (South Western Township) for the large townships just outside of Johannesburg, the largest city in the Union of South Africa. Strict racial segregation known as apartheid was instituted by the ruling white National Party in 1948, which forced thousands of nonwhites to live in grinding poverty and denied them citizenship and its benefits. Segregation affected virtually every area of life, especially governmental services. Apartheid finally ended in 1993.

The Soweto Gospel Choir was founded in late 2002, and in its short history the group has enjoyed one success after another. Its fifty-two members have sung in Europe and Asia and several times in the United States, including a performance for former President Bill Clinton. One of the choir's albums reached No. 1 on *Billboard*'s World Music Chart. At times it has toured as two twenty-six-voice choral groups. Many of their songs are accompanied by a four-piece band and percussion. The singing plus the colorful costumes and dancing make for a performance that audiences around the world applaud enthusiastically.

FIGURE 6.1
SOWETO GOSPEL CHOIR

SHAUN CURRY/Stringer/AFP/Getty Images

SOWETO GOSPEL CHOIR
"Hohonolofatsa"

Download 9

3 minutes 15 seconds

**Translation from Zulu: Bless everything in the name of our Lord.
By his name everything is blessed.**

0:00   Choir opens with progression of four chords.

0:11   Basses sing a repeated pattern on word "Hoho."

0:26   Tenors join in singing with repeated contrasting figure.

0:42   Chords return as basses continue repeated figure.

1:06   Sopranos enter singing "nolofatsa."

1:38   Frequent exchanges among the parts on "nolofatsa."

2:09   Quick exchanges of phrases among the four parts continue.

2:39   Clapping accompaniment introduced.

3:08   Tempo slows, leading to final chords.

 LISTEN TO... this selection streaming online.

 WATCH... an Active Listening Guide of this selection online.

 WATCH... a performance of this selection online.

 DO... an online Listening Practice Activity related to this selection, which your instructor may

assign for a grade.

WIND BAND INSTRUMENTS

Wind bands (Figure 6.2) vary in size from thirty to more than a hundred players. The wide range in the size of a wind, or *concert*, band indicates that its instrumentation is not as well standardized as that of the symphony orchestra. The larger groups usually produce a more massive sound, and the smaller groups achieve greater clarity. The larger bands also use more players on many of the parts.

As the name indicates, wind bands are composed almost entirely of brasses and woodwinds plus percussion. Some bands include one double bass but no other string instruments.

Wind bands also include a number of instruments not usually found in a symphony orchestra. Additional brass instruments include cornets and euphoniums or baritone horns, which sound one octave lower than a trumpet. Because tubas are difficult to carry while marching, an instrument with the same range and similar timbre was developed in the band of John Philip Sousa. The appropriately named sousaphone is coiled over the player's shoulder and has a large flared bell that faces straight forward.

© Richard Thornton/Shutterstock.com

FIGURE 6.2
SCHOOL BANDS, INCLUDING MARCHING BANDS, ARE COMMON IN THE UNITED STATES, IN SOME PROVINCES OF CANADA, AND MORE RECENTLY, IN SOME SCHOOLS IN JAPAN AND AUSTRALIA.

Wind bands also include saxophones of different sizes: alto, tenor, and baritone. Many times alto and bass clarinets are used in wind bands, and sometimes the low-pitched contrabass clarinet as well.

The wind band is largely an American institution. Bands are seldom found in schools and colleges in the rest of the world. Most bands in other countries are associated with the military. Even in the United States, the most musically recognized professional bands are the armed services bands in Washington, DC.

TRADITIONAL KEYBOARD INSTRUMENTS

Harpsichord

The *harpsichord* (Figure 6.3) looks something like a grand piano but it operates quite differently. Often it has two keyboards, called *manuals*, plus knobs that affect the couplings of strings to the keys. Sometimes the pattern of black and white keys is exactly the opposite of what it is on the piano.

The sound of the harpsichord is more delicate and lighter than that of the piano. Probably for this reason, it fell out of favor with composers after about 1750 because they preferred the more powerful sounds of the piano. However, it enjoyed a revival of interest in the twentieth century.

Piano

The *piano* (Figure 6.4) is a historically younger instrument than the harpsichord, being first constructed in Italy around 1709. Behind or underneath the strings, depending on the type of piano, is the *soundboard*, which amplifies the vibrations of the strings. Throughout its history, the piano has had a differing number of keys. Today that number is standardized at eighty-eight, although keyboards on almost all electronic pianos usually have fewer keys.

There are two types of pianos, the upright and the grand. The *grand* piano is long and flat, ranging from five and one-half to nine feet in length. With its longer strings and larger soundboard, the sound of the grand piano is superior to that of the upright piano. Concert music is therefore always performed publicly on a grand piano. The *upright* piano is the type usually seen in homes because of its lower cost and smaller size.

 WATCH...
a short video online that demonstrates how the plucking action on a harpsichord works.

 WATCH...
an online video that demonstrates the parts and key mechanism of the upright piano.

FIGURE 6.3
THE HARPSICHORD CAN BE HEARD IN THIS TEXT'S MUSIC COLLECTION, IN BRANDENBURG CONCERTO NO. 5 BY J. S. BACH.

FIGURE 6.4
THE PIANO IS REPRESENTED IN THE TEXT'S MUSIC COLLECTION WITH WORKS BY CHOPIN, LISZT, RACHMANINOFF, AND DEBUSSY.

Grand pianos usually have three pedals. One pedal holds the dampers off the strings so that they can ring freely. Another pedal holds the dampers off only certain strings, usually those in the lower half of the keyboard. The third pedal moves the entire mechanism so that the hammers do not strike all the strings for each pitch and thus creates a softer sound. On an upright piano, this pedal moves the hammers closer to the strings, which makes it easier to play the sounds more softly.

Pipe Organ

Although it has a keyboard—usually two or more—the *pipe organ* (Figure 6.5) is a quite different instrument from the harpsichord and piano. Instead of strings, the pipe organ has pipes—hundreds and hundreds of them—into which air is pumped. A piano has a set of strings that produces a uniform timbre. The pipe organ has many sets, or *ranks*, of pipes, each with a large complement of pitches and each with a different timbre. In fact, a large pipe organ can have as many as seventy ranks of pipes; medium-sized organs have forty or so. A rank of pipes is activated when a knob is pulled, and combinations of knobs can be set up in advance to be activated with the hand or foot. The number of combinations of timbres in a high-quality organ is enormous.

A pipe organ has several keyboards or manuals; generally, these keyboards have sixty-one keys. The different manuals make it easier for the organist to change back and forth between ranks of pipes.

A special feature of a pipe organ is the *pedalboard*, which is played with the feet. The pedalboard looks like a series of blond and black wooden slats that have been arranged in the pattern of the keyboard. It sounds many of the low pitches on the organ. Good organists can execute remarkably difficult passages with their feet on the pedalboard. The feet also control pedals for changing dynamic level that look like accelerators on an automobile.

The high cost of professional-quality grand pianos and pipe organs has encouraged the adoption of electronic versions of both instruments. Although electronic organs can

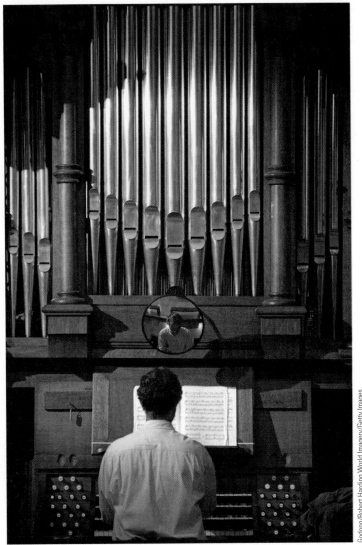

Godong/Robert Harding World Imagery/Getty Images

FIGURE 6.5

THE PIPE ORGAN HAS BEEN CALLED "THE KING OF INSTRUMENTS." IT CAN BE HEARD IN THIS TEXT'S MUSIC COLLECTION IN J. S. BACH'S TOCCATA AND FUGUE IN D MINOR.

sound quite good, they are also very expensive. For that reason cheaper and therefore less authentic organs are usually heard.

Sound Production

Keyboard instruments produce sounds in one of three ways: (1) In the case of the piano, a hammer of firmly packed felt strikes a string. (2) In the case of the harpsichord, a plectrum or quill plucks a string. (3) In the case of a pipe organ, air is released into a pipe.

Modifying Basic Timbre

It is not possible to make obvious changes in the timbre of the piano or harpsichord. Subtle differences are possible on the piano by the using the pedals and the manner in which the keys are depressed. The pipe organ contains many timbres, which are activated by pulling various knobs or pushing buttons.

Regulating Pitch

The particular pitches sounded on a piano or harpsichord depend on the keys that are depressed. Unless coupled by some mechanical means, which is possible on larger harpsichords, only the pitch of the depressed key is sounded. The pitch of the strings on the harpsichord and piano depends on how tightly they are stretched. The tension, and therefore the pitch, of a string is regulated by the person tuning the instrument. The tuner twists the tuning pins with a wrench until the correct pitch is achieved.

Keyboard instruments also differ from those found in bands and orchestras in that they can easily sound more than one pitch at a time. Therefore, a keyboard instrument can play both a melody and its accompanying part simultaneously. For this reason, keyboard instruments are basically solo instruments; only occasionally are they played in ensembles consisting of only keyboard instruments.

Starting and Stopping Sounds

Sounds on keyboard instruments start when a key is depressed. On the piano and harpsichord, the sounds soon fade or decay; they cannot be sustained, as they can on a pipe organ. Normally, they end as soon as the damper returns to the string. This action can be delayed by holding down the key, or, more commonly, holding down a pedal that keeps all the dampers from returning to the strings. Through the skillful use of the pedal, pianists can affect the listeners' impressions of the music.

Changing Dynamic Level

The harpsichord does not allow the player to alter the dynamic level by the amount of finger pressure; in other words, hitting a key harder does not make it sound louder. The only way to change the dynamic level on a harpsichord is to couple the two keyboards so that the sound is doubled an octave higher on the second keyboard.

It's different for the piano. It can be played very softly or very loudly, depending on how forcefully the keys are pressed. Interestingly, the piano's name comes from its capability for making dynamic changes. It was originally named *pianoforte*, which in Italian means "soft loud."

The person playing the pipe organ can increase or decrease the number of pipes sounding and can also raise or lower a foot pedal to change dynamic level.

POPULAR INSTRUMENTS

Guitar

Versions of the *guitar* have existed for hundreds of years in different parts of the world, but it probably originated in the Near East. Actually, the acoustic (nonelectric) guitar of today is not all that different from its ancestors. Some of the older versions had four strings instead of the six used today, and guitars have been constructed in many different sizes. It's easy to strum a few chords in G major on the guitar. It is not at all easy to play complicated music on it, however. Rodrigo's *Concierto de Aranjuez*, for example, is a very difficult piece to play correctly.

All guitars produce sounds from the strumming or plucking of the strings by the player. The vibrations of the strings are then resonated by the hollow body of the instrument. The neck of the instrument, where the players place their fingers, has metal strips running across it. These strips, called *frets*, help players find the right place on the fingerboard.

The guitar has two relatives. One is the *banjo*, which has a plastic or parchment head stretched over a hoop and no back. The head gives the banjo a brilliant sound. The other is the *ukulele*, a small four-string guitar.

Accordion

The *accordion* is basically a small organ that the player holds between his or her arms. Air is pushed through the instrument by the in-and-out motion of the player pumping air through the bellows. The sounds are produced by small metal reeds, one for each pitch. The short keyboard is used for playing the notes of the melody, and the chords are sounded by pushing the buttons. One button sounds an entire chord. Expensive accordions can produce several somewhat different timbres.

ELECTRONIC INSTRUMENTS

Electronic instruments are divided into two groups. One group consists of instruments that electronically alter and amplify the sounds of the player. The *electric guitar* (Figure 6.6) is the most prominent of this type of electronic instrument. Unlike the traditional acoustic guitar, the body of the electric guitar is not hollow, even though it is shaped somewhat like a guitar. Instead, it holds the strings and various control knobs, as well as a lever for adding vibrato to the tones. Players still place their fingers on the fingerboard as with the conventional guitar, but there the similarity ends.

The sounds of drums are often altered in popular music by electronic means. As with the electric guitar, electronic drums can produce wider differences in dynamic levels and alter the timbre to some degree.

The other group of electronic equipment is used in creating music. This group includes synthesizers (Figure 6.7), computers, and tape and disc players. The sky's the limit with such equipment today. Any type of sound and rhythm can be produced. And performances of the music are always flawless! There are no performers in the traditional sense who can affect the musical results—a fact that has both good and bad points.

Paula Tripodi/Getty Images

FIGURE 6.6
BLUES ARTIST B. B. KING PLAYS AN ELECTRIC GUITAR HE CALLS LUCILLE.

ICP-UK / Alamy

FIGURE 6.7
TODAY'S DIGITAL SYNTHESIZERS ARE COMPACT, SOPHISTICATED SYSTEMS THAT CAN PRODUCE REALISTIC SOUNDS.

In the 1950s, electronic music was largely confined to the manipulation of magnetic tape. Composers could alter the speed of the tape, splice in other sounds, record different music on two tracks for performance together, and so on.

A generation later, technology had moved from analog to digital processing and production. In *analog* music, sounds are recorded in a continuous, uninterrupted form. Dynamic levels, for example, are changed by increasing or decreasing the power.

In *digital* recording, discrete, noncontinuous bits of information, usually in the form of numbers, are produced, sorted, or analyzed. How is this possible? Computers can process these bits of data at an incredible rate of speed. It is the same principle used in motion picture film. The reel of film contains thousands of individual pictures. When they are projected at the rate of twenty-four per second (*much* slower than a computer!), the eye perceives the individual pictures to be a continuous flow.

The complaint about electronically produced music is that it has a certain manufactured quality about it. To overcome this problem, synthesizers can now store recorded samples of the actual complex sounds of instruments and then have them available anytime the composer wants them. The use of recorded samples is, appropriately, called *sampling*. For example, the sound of a snare drum is complex, with its abrupt beginning and ring in the drum after a tap. Technology can come close to imitating it but does not really capture all the nuances of the tap on a drum or the sounds of other instruments. The inclusion of traditional instrumental sounds on the hard drive helps make the electronic music sound more musical.

WATCH…
a series of videos online, on some creative uses of unusual musical instruments.

CONCERT ATTENDANCE TIPS

Students in music appreciation courses usually attend concerts as a part of the course work. Here are a few tips about attending concerts.

Types of Concerts

Recitals are usually for two to five performers in a medium-sized room or hall. They usually last about one hour or so.

Song recitals involve one singer with piano accompaniment in a medium-sized room or hall. Songs are quite often in a foreign language.

Large ensemble concerts are for large groups such as bands, orchestras, and choral groups. Because many performers are involved, they are held in large concert halls or auditoriums. They are usually longer than recitals.

Operas are dramas in which all the words are sung. In addition, they include scenery, costumes, and actions, and the singers are accompanied by an orchestra. Many operas are in foreign languages, but simultaneous translations are sometimes run on a screen above the stage or a low screen where footlights are placed. Many operas last for two or more hours. They are performed in concert halls or opera houses.

Popular music concerts can be held most any place, ranging from small auditoriums to stadiums and other outdoor venues. Almost all the music at these concerts is miked, and the performances are very casual, often with some audience participation.

Audience Conduct

The main purpose of attending a classical music concert is to listen carefully and attentively to the music being performed. Therefore, there should be no distractions such as

- talking or whispering
- shuffling programs or other objects
- eating or drinking
- looking at or using a portable device

Applause at instrumental concerts is appropriate at the end of every work, but only after the final movement of a multimovement work. Applause is expected after sizable solos or duets in operas and musicals and after solos at concerts of popular music. Sometimes at the conclusion of an outstanding concert, the audience will give the performers a standing ovation. If you aren't sure about what to do, wait to see what the rest of audience does before starting to applaud or stand.

Often a performing group will perform an extra piece or two in response to the applause of the audience. Such pieces, called *encores*, are short and attractive. They are announced verbally by the performer.

Performance Customs

Soloists often memorize their music so that they are not distracted with turning pages and will have a more direct rapport with the audience. Accompanists in recitals do not memorize their music and may have someone turn pages for them. Performers in stage productions must, of course, memorize their music as well as their movements on stage. Because of the number and character of the parts in chamber and orchestral music, such music is rarely memorized. Conductors sometimes conduct without the music in front of them. This does not mean they have memorized every part. Rather, they know the work in a general way, which is adequate for conducting it in a performance.

Orchestra and band concerts tend to follow certain customs. Because the conductor is the leader of the ensemble, he or she is treated with special respect. The conductor is the last to enter the stage and the first to leave when a lengthy work is completed. The audience applauds when the conductor enters. After a work is completed, the conductor often recognizes the efforts of the musicians by shaking hands with the first-chair violinist, in the case of a symphony orchestra. This player sits at the front of the violin section and is referred to as the concertmaster or concertmistress.

Soloists are special guests, so they are treated with even more deference than the conductor. They precede the conductor on and off the stage and receive applause on their own.

The concertmaster follows another tradition by being the last player to enter before the conductor. He or she points to the various sections of the orchestra, and they play a long tone to tune their instruments to the standard pitch of A440. The random sounds made by the musicians prior to that time are just their informal warming up.

Professional orchestras and bands have no systematic procedure for coming on stage. Some choral groups, however, enter row by row.

Orchestral players wear black suits or dresses. Singers in choral groups wear robes or black suits and dresses, except when performing "lighter," more popular music.

The Printed Program

People attending a recital or concert are usually given a program listing the music that will be performed. Rarely are the musical works announced from the stage, except in the case of popular music. The program sometimes contains many advertisements, which give people who arrive early something to read and provide income for the performing group.

On one side of the page, usually the left, the program lists the titles of the compositions. On the opposite side it lists the names of the composers or arrangers. Titles in foreign languages are often not translated. Each movement of a multimovement instrumental work is usually listed by its tempo (traditionally in Italian) and is indented and placed below the title.

Programs for song recitals list each song by title and composer. Opera programs look more like a program booklet for a play, listing acts and scenes, as well as a synopsis of the story. Programs sometimes contain notes and narrative material interspersed among the ads. These remarks may be helpful, but sometimes they are written in a complex style using language that nonmusicians find difficult to understand.

Dress Up for Concerts?

The idea of people attending concerts wearing fancy clothes has long since passed. Usually it is enough to wear nice, clean clothes. Shorts, tank tops, flip flops, and such should be avoided. Dress for evening concerts is usually more formal than for an event that takes place during the daytime. Dress for popular music concerts can be very informal.

Preparation for a Concert

In one sense, you don't need to prepare for a concert. All you need do is attend, listen attentively, and enjoy it. But you will find it more satisfying if you know what works will be performed. Then you can check in your textbook to see if the work might be described in it, or at least the composer of the work discussed. A little knowledge beforehand will help you better understand what you will hear. It will also help you in writing a report of the concert, in case that should be needed.

Don't let concerns about inadequate musical knowledge prevent you from attending and enjoying concerts or recitals. The enjoyment is not the same as going to a sports event or a theme park. It's different. Attending a concert is more subtle, more thoughtful, more lasting, more refined. Going to a performance can be an enriching experience in your life, and it can provide you with something that can't be achieved in any other way.

MAIN POINTS OF CHAPTER 6

1. The human voice is an important "instrument" in music. It produces sound as air causes the vocal cords in the larynx to vibrate.

2. The pitch of vocal sounds is regulated by the length and tension of the vocal cords. Women have shorter vocal cords; therefore, they produce a higher pitch than men. Women in choral groups usually sing the soprano (higher) part or the alto (lower) part. Men in choral groups usually sing the tenor (higher) part or the bass (lower) part.

3. Styles of singing vary enormously in America and around the world according to the type and style of the music.

4. Wind bands usually contain no string instruments. Instead, they often include saxophones, baritone horns, cornets, and a different type of tuba called a sousaphone.

5. Harpsichords, pianos, and pipe organs are instruments that control their pitches from a keyboard. Harpsichords create sounds when strings are plucked by a mechanism, whereas pianos produce sounds when hard felt hammers strike strings. Pipe organs create sound when air is blown through pipes and can produce a wide array of timbres.

6. Electric guitars are shaped like other guitars, but they are actually electronic instruments. Many versions of electronic keyboards also have achieved wide popularity.

7. Electronic music is created by synthesizers working in conjunction with computers. Early versions of electronic music were created by manipulating tape. Today electronic music is created using digital recording technology.

 PRACTICE...
your understanding of this chapter's concepts by working once more with the chapter's Active Listening Guides online.

 DO...
online quizzes that your instructor may assign for a grade.

PART 2

Early, Medieval, *and* Renaissance Music

1000 BC	AD 1	500
Historical Events		
● Early Hellenic civilization (1100 BC)	Roman Empire (c. 500 BC–AD 476)	Charlemagne (AD 747–814)
● Greek city-states (800 BC–AD 476)	● Birth of Jesus (AD 1)	Feudalism (9th–14th centuri...
Golden Age of Athens (5th cent. BC)	Separation of Eastern ● and Western Empires (AD 476)	● Rome falls (AD 476)
Visual Arts		
	● Parthenon built in Athens (top right) (447–432 BC)	
	Myron, *Discus Thrower* (c. 450 BC)	
	Colosseum built in Rome (AD 70–80)	
Literature and Theater		
○ Homer, *Iliad and Odyssey* (c. 750 BC)		
Dionysia n festivals (c. 200 BC)		
Sophocles, *Oedipus Rex* (c. 429 BC)		
Cicero (106–43 BC), Virgil (70–19 BC), Plutarch (AD 46–120)		
Philosophy and Science		
Socrates (469–399 BC), Plato (c. 427–347 BC)		Boethius (c. 480–525)
Aristotle (384–322 BC)		
Music		
Pythagoras discovers acoustical ratios (555 BC)	Pope Gregory codifies liturgy and chant (c. 600) ●	
Plato advocates music for all citizens (c. 360 BC)		

Heritage Images/Hulton Archive/Getty Images

| 00 | 1450 | 1500 | 1550 | 1600 |

usades (1096–1270)

Papal schism (1378–1417)

Copernicus (1473–1543)

Council of Trent (1545–1563)

niversities founded
088)

"Black Death" ●
(mid-1300s)

Exploration of New World (early 15th cent.–early 17th cent.)

Spanish Armada defeated
(1588)

● Magna Carta signed (1215)

Gutenberg invents movable type (1439)

● Luther initiates Reformation (1517)

Great cathedrals
constructed

Ghiberti (1378–1455)

Dürer etchings
(1496–1514)

● Leonardo, *Mona Lisa*
(1503–1506)

St. Peter's built in Rome
(1506–1626)

● Giotto, *Madonna . . .*
(c. 1305–1310)

● Van Eyck, *Arnolfini
Marriage* (1434)

Michelangelo, *David*
(near right) (1501–1504) ●

Donatello (c. 1386–1466)

● Botticelli, *Adoration
of the Magi* (1475)

Brueghel, *Landscape with
Fall of Icarus* (c. 1555) ●

Titian, *St. John, the Baptist* (c. 1540) ●

Dante, *The Divine Comedy* (1308–1321)

Rabelais (1494?–1553)

Ariosto, *Orlando Furioso* (1591)

Marlowe, *Essays* (1586–1593)

Boccaccio, *Decameron* (c. 1350–1353)

Spenser (1552–1599)

Chaucer, *The Canterbury Tales* (1387–1400)

Shakespeare, *Romeo and Juliet* (1595)

lard (1079–1142)

● Erasmus, *In Praise of Folly* (1511)

Thomas Aquinas, *Summa Theologica*
(1225–1274)

● Machiavelli, *The Prince* (1513)

More, *Utopia* ●

● Luther, *Ninety-five Theses* (1517)

● Hildegard, *Ordo virtutum* (left) (c. 1130)

● Bass voice part introduced
Josquin, *Pange lingua Mass* (1515)

Organum develops (c. 1000)

● First music book published (1501)

Motets begin at Notre Dame (c. 1250)

Palestrina, "Sicut cervus" ●
(c. 1577)

Weelkes, "As Vesta . . ." ●
(1590)

Early Western Music

START...
experiencing this chapter's topics with an online video activity that your instructor may assign.

READ...
the complete chapter text in a rich interactive eBook!

Learning Objectives

1 Describe the nature of music in ancient Greek and Roman times.
2 Place music in the context in which it existed in the Middle Ages.
3 List the features of Gregorian chant.
4 Describe the characteristics of a morality play.

There has always been music. Every civilization throughout recorded history and every tribe, even in the remotest parts of the world, had and still has some form of music. We know this because pictures from the various times and places show people singing or playing instruments, and writers have described music and music making. Often, musical traditions have been passed from one generation to another for as long as anyone can determine.

But there is a problem: No one really knows what this music sounded like until the advent of the phonograph and sound recording, which wasn't available until about a hundred or so years ago. Music notation didn't develop to anywhere near its present state until the fifteenth century, and it was used mostly for concert and church music, which is part of the reason they receive the greater share of attention in music history courses. It's difficult to devote much attention to a particular kind of music when no one is sure how it sounded.

ANCIENT GREEK AND ROMAN TIMES

"Western civilization" is a broad concept consisting of the culture that developed in ancient Greece and then spread throughout Europe and eventually to North and South America. It includes political and religious beliefs, laws, customs, and arts. Traditionally, the contrasts with the Eastern civilizations of the Middle East and Asia were considerable, although they are rapidly being diminished today.

From about 800 BC to the fall of the Roman Empire in AD 476, Western civilization was dominated by various city-states around the Mediterranean Sea. The first were the cities of Greece, especially Athens. Then came the Roman Empire, which dominated most of the known world from the Middle East to England. Although both Greece and Rome were replaced, they left their imprint in architecture, literature, and ways of thinking. In fact, about fifteen hundred years in the future these civilizations would be considered by educated persons as a high point to be admired and copied.

Greek civilization reached its acme in Athens in the fifth century BC. It produced astounding accomplishments for its time. Its architecture (Figure 7.1) can be seen in countless buildings even today. Great works of sculpture were created. Philosophy flourished with Socrates, Plato, and Aristotle, who also is often credited with starting scientific thinking. Great poets such as Homer and dramatists such as Sophocles were active in the Western world. The ancient Athenians were far ahead of their contemporaries in their type of government, which had the citizens meet and vote in civic matters. In fact, the word *democracy* comes from the Greek word *demos*, meaning "people." Greek religious beliefs revolved around a pantheon of gods and goddesses.

FIGURE 7.1
The Parthenon The Greeks built this celebrated temple for the goddess Athena in the fifth century BC. It defines the classical style still seen in architecture today.

© 123455543/Shutterstock.com

The Greeks, especially those living in Athens during the Golden Age of Pericles, valued music very much. The philosopher Plato (c. 427–347 BC) considered music an essential part of the education of all citizens. One reason for his advocacy of music was his belief that music influenced moral character. The idea that music could influence behavior largely disappeared with ancient Greek civilization, but remnants of it in various guises are still with us today. About 555 BC, Pythagoras found that the vibrations of certain intervals—the distances from one pitch to another—can be represented in mathematical ratios. As was characteristic of the Greeks at that time, he ascribed philosophical qualities to those ratios, calling those with simple ratios such as 2:1 and 3:2 "perfect." Pythagoras is also well known for his contributions to geometry and the theorem named after him.

The ancient Greeks also developed several musical instruments. One of these was the harplike lyre, which is often seen as a musical emblem today.

Music was found in many Greek dramas, too. The chorus did not sing. Instead, it chanted in a singsong style. Poets such as Homer sang their epic tales in singsong fashion, perhaps accompanied by a simple harplike instrument.

The Roman Republic followed, and the Romans simply took over much of what the earlier Greeks had done. They even adopted and expanded on their religious beliefs but renamed the gods. Zeus, king of the gods, became Jupiter; and Athena, goddess of the arts, became Minerva.

The Romans were militarily strong. They managed an empire that stretched for a thousand or more miles around the Mediterranean Sea. Holding such a huge empire together was quite an accomplishment when there was no communication faster than a man on a horse. But the character and quality of the Roman Empire deteriorated over the centuries, and it collapsed more than it fell to the invading Vandals and Visigoths from the north.

The Romans had music, too. Probably most of it was taken over from the Greeks. The Romans emphasized military music more than the Greeks did.

THE MIDDLE AGES

With the fall of the Roman Empire in AD 476, Western civilization slipped into what some historians call the "Dark Ages." For more than five hundred years following the fall of Rome, life in the Middle Ages centered around the manor and the monasteries.

Scala/Art Resource, NY

FIGURE 7.2

MUSIC AND THE ARTS DURING THE MIDDLE AGES WERE DEVOTED TO THE WORSHIP OF GOD. BOOKS WERE HAND LETTERED AND DECORATED BY MONKS, AS SHOWN IN THIS CAPITAL *C* FOR *CANTATE DOMINO* ("SING TO THE LORD").

A system of feudalism bound peasants to the land and to the lord of the manor. People did not place a great emphasis on life, because they thought that either Jesus would come again and bring a new era or they would soon have a better life after they died. It is hard for us living in America today to understand the hold that otherworldly concerns had on many people during that time, but the impact of this attitude was profound. Life was different and hard for most people in the Middle Ages. In short, it was grim.

Monasteries dotted the countryside throughout Europe and England. These monasteries preserved the writings and culture of the ancient world (Figure 7.2). But there was little interest in the civilizations of the Greeks and Romans, which were considered pagan and to be avoided.

MUSIC IN THE MIDDLE AGES

Christianity had no standard musical practices for its first three centuries. It adopted some aspects of Judaism, including daily prayer hours and the reciting of psalms between the leader and congregation. The fact that the early Church included singing in its worship is recorded in Matthew 26:30, Mark 14:26, and other, nonbiblical writings. As the Church expanded throughout Asia Minor into Europe, it adopted other musical practices.

Slowly, the Church at Rome became predominant, and the bishop of Rome became the pope. In an effort to bring order to worship practices, about the sixth century Pope Gregory I directed that the Church's worship and music be codified. Although Gregory I was not a musician himself, the music that resulted is known as Gregorian chant. The Church now had a **liturgy**—a body of rites prescribed for worship. The most important and frequent service is the **Mass**.

The Mass and Its Music

The Mass is central in the Roman Catholic Church. It is a ceremony that reaffirms in a symbolic way the connection between the believers and Jesus Christ through the reenactment of the Last Supper. The Eucharist, or Holy Communion, is the sharing of bread and wine and the miracle of that event.

The term *Mass* comes from the Latin phrase that ends the service: "Ite missa est." The Mass may be spoken or sung, but in the United States today it is largely spoken. It contains several parts. Some portions vary according to the particular day in the Church year. These parts are called the **Proper**, because they are proper for a certain day in the Church calendar. Some parts are repeated in each Mass; these are called the **Ordinary**, because they are ordinarily included.

The sections of the Ordinary are:

Kyrie This is a short prayer using Greek words instead of the usual Latin. The text means, "Lord, have mercy on us; Christ, have mercy on us."

Gloria This section offers praise to God in Latin with the words, "Glory to God on high."

Credo This rather long statement of belief in Latin ("We believe in one God, …") is recited or sung in a reciting style.

Sanctus This follows the consecration of the elements when the priest raises the bread and wine for everyone to see. The Sanctus begins with the words, "Holy, holy, holy."

Agnus Dei This section is based on the Latin words that mean "Lamb of God, who takes away the sins of the world, have mercy on us and grant us peace."

Because the Ordinary appears in all Masses, it has been selected by many composers over the centuries as the text for musical works. Ludwig van Beethoven, Wolfgang Amadeus Mozart, and Franz Joseph Haydn—and Igor Stravinsky in the twentieth century—have composed "concert" Masses not intended for use in worship services. Josquin and Palestrina and other composers of the sixteenth century composed shorter Masses for worship purposes.

A **Requiem** is a Mass for the dead. It omits the Gloria and Credo but adds a section called **Dies irae** ("Day of wrath"), referring to the day of final judgment.

Until Vatican Council II (1964–1967), the Roman Catholic Church specified the content and words for every service, which are in Latin. Since then, more freedom has been permitted, however, and vernacular (non-Latin) languages are now used. Unfortunately, most chants and music for Masses lose their impact when translated so, much of the inspiring traditional music is no longer heard today.

Gregorian Chant

Gregorian chant is very different from the music you usually hear today. Its features include:

- Nonmetrical rhythm: Although there are groups of notes, you will have no inclination to tap your foot as you listen to it.
- Monophonic texture: There is no harmony.
- Smooth contour: Its notes generally move by step to the next note.
- *Modal* scales: The melodies generally do not follow the familiar major or minor scale patterns.
- A reverent and restrained mood: No attempt is made to reach out and grab the listener's emotions.
- The texts are in Church Latin, not English or other languages.
- Certain texts are sung at Mass only by priests.

Gregorian chant is not concert music. Its goal is to contribute to worship. This it does for persons who understand its attributes.

The music example discussed is the "Dies irae" from the funeral or Requiem Mass (see Listening Guide). It is probably the best-known line of chant, especially its first several notes, because many composers in the nineteenth century used it to represent death or evil. Its opening phrase is shown in two versions. One is the traditional four-line staff and square notes of the Roman Catholic Church in medieval times. The other shows the pitches of the chant on a five-line staff similar to the way music notation looks today.

Gregorian musical notation of the Middle Ages

The same phrase in modern music notation

In 1994 a recording of chant by the monks at the monastery of Santo Domingo de Silos in Spain became the fastest-selling classical CD in history. It sold more than two million copies and reached number five on the US pop charts. The monks used the royalties to help the needy in Third World countries and for badly needed repairs to the twelfth-century monastery.

ANONYMOUS
"Dies irae" opening (c. 600)

Genre: Gregorian chant

Form: *a a b b*

Download 10

1 minute 2 seconds

0:00	*Dies irae, dies illa*	Day of wrath, that day
	Solvet saeclum in favilla,	the world will dissolve into ashes,
	Teste David sum Sibylla.	as witness David and the Sibyl.
0:14	*Quantus tremor est futurus,*	What trembling there will be
	Quando Judex est venturus,	when the Judge shall come;
	Cuncta stricte discussurus!	all shall thoroughly be shattered!
0:28	*Tuba mirum spargens son*	The wondrous trumpet, spreading its sound
	Per sepulchra regionem,	to the tombs of all regions,
	Coget omnesante thronum.	will gather all before the throne.
0:45	*Mors stupebit et natura,*	Death will be stupefied, also nature,
	Cum resurget creatura	when all creation arises again
	Judicanti responsura.	to answer to the Judge.
1:02	Recording fades as "Dies irae" continues.	

 LISTEN TO... this selection streaming online.

 WATCH... an Active Listening Guide of this selection online.

 DO... an online Listening Practice Activity related to this selection, which your instructor may

assign for a grade.

Hildegard's *Ordo virtutum*

Most of the creators of Gregorian chant are anonymous. Humility was a virtue in the Middle Ages, especially among the religious men and women. One known composer of the/this chant was a remarkable woman named Hildegard of Bingen.

Hildegard's *Ordo virtutum* (*Play of the Virtues*) is a morality play, probably written for the dedication of a convent church (see Listening Guide). In the play, a soul gives in to the temptations of the devil. The soul is saved through the intervention of the sixteen virtues. The Virtues are Knowledge of God, Humility, Discipline, Compassion, Mercy, Victory, Discretion, Patience, Charity, Obedience, Faith, Hope, Chastity, Innocence, World Rejection, and Heavenly Love. The work contains about eighty chantlike melodies. All the parts were sung by nuns, except the role of the devil, which was played by a priest. He does not get to sing. Instead, he talks.

Little except the vocal music has survived from most of these medieval plays. Performances today require some creativity in terms of the instruments and staging used.

HILDEGARD OF BINGEN
Ordo virtutum, excerpt from Scene 4 (c. 1150)

LISTENING GUIDE

Genre: Morality play

Download 11

3 minutes 50 seconds

Devil:

0:00 *Que es, aut unde venis?*
Tu amplexata es me, et ego foras eduxi te.
Sed nunc inreversione tua confundis me—
ego autem pugna mea deician te!

Who are you, where do you come from?
You were in my embrace, I led you out.
Yet now you are going back, defying me—
But I shall fight you and defeat you!

Penitent Soul:

0:22 *Ego omnes vias meas malas esse cognovi,*
et ideo fugi a te.
Modo autem, o illusor, pugno contra te.
Ine tu, o regina Humilitas, tua medicamine
adiuva me!

I realize that all my ways were wicked,
so I fled from you.
But now, you fraud, I'll fight you face to face.
Come, Queen Humility, with your medicine
give me aid!

Humility (to Victory):

1:30 *O Victoria, que istum in celo superasti,*
curre cum militibus tuis et omnes ligate,
Diabolum hunc!

O Victory, you who once bested this in the heavens.
run now, with all your military manner,
and all of you, tie up this fiend!

Victory (to the Virtues):

2:00 *O fortissimi et gloriosissimi milites,*
venite, et adiuvate me istum fallacem vincere.

Most brave and glorious warriors,
come, and help me to eliminate this false one.

The Virtues:

2:32 *O dulcissima bellatrix, in torrente fonte*
qui absorbuit lupum rapacem—
o gloriosa coronata, nos libenter
militamus tecum contra illusorem hunc.

O sweetest warrior, in the scorching torrent
that swallowed up the rapacious wolf—
o glorious crowned one, how freely
we will fight at your side against the faker.

Humility (to the Virtues):

3:11 *Ligate ergo istum, o Virtutes preclare!*

Tie him up then, you shining virtues!

The Virtues:

3:28 *O regina nostra, tibi parebimus,*
et precepta tua in omnibus adimplebimus.

O our queen, we obey you,
and we will follow your orders completely.

LISTEN TO... this selection streaming online.

WATCH... an Active Listening Guide of this selection online.

WATCH... a performance of this selection online.

DO... an online Listening Practice Activity related to this selection, which your instructor may assign for a grade.

Hildegard of Bingen

Heritage Images/Hulton Archive/Getty Images

Hildegard of Bingen (1098–1179) was the tenth child of a noble German family. At the age of eight, she was given to a group of nuns to be raised in a Benedictine monastery. Giving a son or a daughter to the Church was a common practice at that time.

She was a multitalented woman and a powerful abbess. She wrote seventy poems and nine books. More than seventy of her musical compositions have been preserved—hers is one of the largest bodies of work of any medieval composer. Her interests ranged from religious visions to natural sciences to theology. She was especially interested in the healing properties of plants. She also developed an alternative alphabet that she used in her writings.

In addition to *Ordo virtutum*, Hildegard composed a large number of liturgical songs. The music itself retains some of the character of Gregorian chant, but its melodies are more soaring and move outside the vocal range normally used for chants. In addition, she was careful to maintain a close relationship between the character of the music and the text, which was rare at that time. Because music notation had not yet been developed, the rhythm in her music is left to the performers.

MAIN POINTS OF CHAPTER 7

PRACTICE...
your understanding of this chapter's concepts by working once more with the chapter's Active Listening Guides online.

DO...
online quizzes that your instructor may assign for a grade.

1. Western civilization and its music developed over 2,500 years ago in the city-states around the Mediterranean, especially Athens.

2. The only music preserved in written form from ancient times is Gregorian chant. It was the basis for the Mass in the Christian Church.

3. Certain Gregorian chants are designated for particular days in the Church calendar, and these chants are called the Proper of the Mass. The Ordinary of the Mass is sung or said at nearly all Masses.

4. The Requiem is the funeral Mass. It includes the "Dies irae" chant, which means "Day of Wrath," referring to the final judgment.

5. The music of Gregorian chant is monophonic, sung unaccompanied in Latin by monks and priests, and has no metrical rhythm. It is intended for worship, not for concert performances.

6. A number of morality plays with music were created to educate listeners about the Christian faith. The music for these plays is similar to Gregorian chant in character.

Medieval Music

START...

experiencing this chapter's topics with an online video activity that your instructor may assign.

Learning Objectives

1 List the major intellectual and artistic accomplishments of the medieval period.
2 Describe the nature of organum and rhythmic modes.
3 List the characteristics of medieval motets.
4 Describe the nature of secular music during medieval times.

READ...

the complete chapter text in a rich interactive eBook!

Change came very slowly in the Middle Ages. The Holy Roman Empire ruled over much of central Europe, but Europe was actually a loose confederation of many small states. People lived mostly in small rural communities, often called manors. Communication and travel were difficult and slow, accomplished on foot or on horseback. So what was true in one place could be unheard of fifty miles away.

MEDIEVAL TIMES

Although very gradual, changes did take place in society and in music. There were several catalysts toward a more enlightened outlook: increased contacts with the Byzantine civilization to the east, better economic conditions and trade, and the influence of education in the monasteries.

The period from about 1100 to 1450 has come to be known as the medieval, or sometimes the Gothic, period. The use of the word *Gothic* to designate a particular artistic or musical style has little to do with its use in describing a mystery or horror story. Instead, these centuries were marked by continued progress away from the other-worldly outlook that was so strong during the preceding hundreds of years. The major intellectual movement of the time was Scholasticism, a highly organized and systematic philosophy culminating in the *Summa Theologica* (*Summary of Theology*) by Thomas Aquinas (1225–1274).

Another feature of the medieval period was chivalry, which glorified women and idealized kindness and refined manners. It may have existed more as an ideal than it did in reality. There was an emphasis on the community—the guild, the Church, or the feudal manor; individualism was not encouraged. Many works of art and music were created by artists who did not attach their names to their creations and whose identities are not known.

The medieval period saw the founding of universities. It was also the time when many of the great cathedrals were built. Literary accomplishments were achieved in this period with the poems of the troubadours, the romantic legends of a Celtic chieftain named Arthur, and *The Divine Comedy* by Dante Alighieri.

Giotto's *Madonna and Child* (Figure 8.1) has a planned, posed look. This work from the fourteenth century was originally part of a polyptych, or series, of paintings. Several points are worth noting about this painting.

First, it was part of a *polyptych*. This word contains the same stem word as *polyphony*, a feature of medieval and Renaissance music. Second, it has a flat, two-dimensional look; only a little shading was used to outline the figures. Third, the outline of the *Madonna and Child* is in a three-quarter position and creates an elegant Gothic shape broken

FIGURE 8.1

MADONNA AND CHILD BY
GIOTTO DI BONDONE. THIS
EARLY RENAISSANCE PAINTING
STILL CONTAINS ELEMENTS OF THE
GOTHIC STYLE IN ITS SHAPE AND
TWO-DIMENSIONAL LOOK, BUT
IT ALSO FORETELLS INTELLECTUAL
QUALITIES FOUND IN THE MUSIC
OF JOSQUIN AND PALESTRINA.

only by the almost geometric figure. Fourth, the hands and faces are not very lifelike. Madonna's hand looks as though it could be attached to a mannequin. Fifth, the painting is not very realistic. The Child has a mature face and body for an infant; he is also far too big to be held with one arm. Sixth, the gold background shows the influence of Byzantine or eastern European art. But whatever its limitations, it is nevertheless a compelling work of art.

POLYPHONY

Gregorian chant was monophonic, with only a single line of melody. How did music move beyond that to polyphony? Probably at first the Church musicians simply added a second line of music that moved in strict parallel motion with the original line, somewhat as the two front wheels on a car move exactly parallel to each other. Scholars suspect that initially such parallel lines, called **organum**, were sung without actually being written down. Some of the monks and priests probably tried singing the same line of chant at different pitch levels. Examples of organum began to appear in notation about AD 1000, and at first the added line matched the original chant note for note. But organum in strict parallel motion is not polyphony.

Gradually, the second part of organum began to show more independence, which marks the beginning of polyphony. Sometimes it would move for a note or two in the opposite direction. Over the years, the second line became even more independent by having several notes to the one note in the original line.

As the idea of polyphony developed, the notes of original Gregorian chant were made longer, sometimes to the point of sounding almost like a steady, continuous sound. The long-note values of the chant became so extended that the chant melody was hardly recognizable, which did not seem to bother the creators of this music. Perhaps they justified this practice because they knew that the music was still based on chant. And the second part, with its several moving notes, certainly did give the music a richer and more interesting quality than that of the original monophonic chant. Shortly before AD 1200, organum became even more interesting when musicians added two lines above the original line of chant. Eventually, a few works included four different lines to be sung simultaneously.

This more complex organum was developed at the Cathedral of Notre Dame in Paris by two composers whose names are known: Léonin (active from about 1150 to 1201) and his successor, Pérotin (c. 1160–1236).

Pérotin's "Alleluia, Diffusa est gratia"

Many pieces of music were created to express adoration for the Virgin Mary. In this work (see Listening Guide), the chant is presented in the usual monophonic texture of Gregorian chant.

The complete work is longer than can be presented here. The "Alleluia" section comes back twice in the complete work. The word "Alleluia" is sung with several notes for each syllable, which was probably intended to give the sense of spiritual joy. It consists of four phrases. The first, having the most notes, is repeated the first time it's heard. The second phrase reaches the highest pitch level. The third phrase continues the chant with the words "in aeternum". The fourth is calmer and has a narrower range.

The music opens with quite long notes before the upper parts begin singing several notes on each syllable of the word "Diffusa" and the words that follow. The lowest line, called the *cantus firmus*, sounds the notes of the chant in long-note values. It became the structure around which the notes of the moving parts are constructed.

By the thirteenth century, another feature had been added to organum: somewhat regular rhythmic patterns. Composers grouped notes into six long-and-short note patterns that are roughly equivalent to the metrical patterns used in analyzing metrical patterns in poetry. For example, ♩♪ is trochaic meter, whereas ♪♩ is iambic meter, and so on. These patterns (called **rhythmic modes**) helped to keep the polyphonic lines of music together, as well as added variety to the music. Notice that the "Alleluia" part of Pérotin's music is sung without a metrical pattern, whereas the word "Diffusa" begins a section with a somewhat steady rhythmic patterns. Music notation during the Gothic period did not contain bar lines. The patterns were indicated by brackets called *ligatures*.

In these early versions of polyphony, pitches an octave apart and four and five notes apart were considered to be consonant. These intervals are the same ones Pythagoras considered to be consonant, and they are the most prominent ones in the overtone series. The interval of a third, which has been the basis for most harmony for the past several hundred years, was regarded as dissonant. That interval was, however, found in the secular music of the time, especially in England. It would be nearly 350 years after Léonin before chords containing thirds would be considered consonant enough to appear in the important final chord of a musical work.

LISTENING GUIDE

PÉROTIN
"Alleluia, Diffusa est gratia" (c. 1190)

Genre: Organum

Download 12

4 minutes 40 seconds

0:00	Chant	*Alleluia, Alleluia —*	Hallelujah
0:37	Organum	*Diffusa, est gratia in labiis tuis; proterea benedixit te deus*	Grace has been poured upon your lips; therefore, God has blessed you
3:40	Chant	*in aeternum.*	eternally.
4:11	Chant	*Alleluia, Alleluia*	Hallelujah, Hallelujah

LISTEN TO... this selection streaming online.

WATCH... an Active Listening Guide of this selection online.

WATCH... a performance of a similar selection online.

DO... an online Listening Practice Activity related to this selection, which your instructor may assign for a grade.

Léonin and Pérotin

GARGOYLE ON NOTRE DAME CATHEDRAL IN PARIS

Léonin and Pérotin had at least three things in common. First is that we know very little about them. Humility was a virtue during medieval times, as was mentioned in the discussion of Hildegard's *Ordo virtutum*. Artists and musicians believed that their efforts were for the glory of God. Personal recognition was not considered proper or important. Thus, we know little about them as individuals.

Second, much of what we do know comes from one source, Anonymous IV, who was a student from England at the University of Paris with a particular interest in music. Third, they were very important composers at the Cathedral of Notre Dame in Paris.

Not only are we unsure of when they were born and when they died, but even their names had varied forms. Léonin was also known as Leoninus, Magister Leoninus, Magister Leonius, and Leo. The word *magister* is a title indicating that he had earned a master's degree. He was also a priest, poet, and high-ranking official in the cathedral. He was active there from about 1150 until 1201.

His book of organum, *Magnum liber organi*, contains about one hundred pieces of two-part organum. He composed this music to make the worship services on special days such as Christmas and Easter more outstanding. This music also provides evidence that sometimes the notes were organized into units of twos or threes—the rhythmic modes mentioned in conjunction with the presentation of Pérotin's "Alleluia." Although these were not measures as we know them today, this was an important first step in organizing rhythm.

Pérotin (c. 1160–1236) was also known as Perrotinus, Perotinus Magnus, and Magister Perotinus. He was probably Léonin's successor at Notre Dame. Anonymous IV names seven compositions by him, but undoubtedly there were many more. Whereas Léonin composed for only two voices, Pérotin wrote for three or four voices, something that had almost never been done before. To keep that many parts together required the further development of rhythm. Although the chant-based tenor part usually retains its long notes, the upper two or three parts follow strict rhythmic patterns. His works tend to be more sectional, with shorter complementary units. The tenor also moves in strict rhythm in some of these short sections.

Léonin, Pérotin, and their colleagues created a huge body of music, probably more than one thousand pieces, which historians later labeled the "Notre Dame School." The University of Paris attracted many students, who learned not only theology but also the music sung in the cathedral. They then spread its features throughout France and the rest of Europe.

THE MOTET

Polyphony also found its way into secular music in the form of the **motet**. Actually, the motet was a combination of Gregorian chant and secular music that was sung in the courts, not churches. Its religious component was the use of phrases from Gregorian chant in one of its lines of melody as the **cantus firmus**, or base.

The secular element in the motet was its use of texts, often about love, that were in vernacular languages, usually French. In contrast to the cantus firmus, these voice parts were quite rhythmic and not based on Gregorian chant. The structure consisted of the cantus firmus and two or more lines sounding at the same time.

The lines above the cantus firmus included many sophisticated composing techniques. For example, twice as many notes might be used in one of the added voice parts as in another part. A musical phrase might be split up so that one part would sing a couple of notes and then the other part would take up the next couple of notes, only to return to the first voice part and back to the other part in order to complete a melodic phrase. This device was called a *hocket*. Another compositional technique was the use of identical rhythms with different melodies, which is called *isorhythm*. Such complexities are difficult to hear in the music. Actually, they can usually be observed only by examining the written notation. It was a highly intellectual approach to composing music.

The best-known composer of isorhythmic motets in the fourteenth century was Guillaume de Machaut (ma-SHOW, c. 1300–1377). His motet "Quant en moi" (see Listening Guide) is typical of the genre. The cantus firmus is sung in long note values. Each of the two voice parts sings a different poem. Machaut composed different music for each stanza of the poem. He also used several hockets, and the first voice part has twice the number of notes the second voice part has. The motet also contains some short, abrupt starts and stops.

LISTENING GUIDE

GUILLAUME DE MACHAUT
"Quant en moi"

Genre: Medieval motet

Download 13

1 minute 45 seconds

The two singers begin together, and they sing the words for their stanzas at the same time. The examples of hocket are indented and positioned in the same order in which they are sung.

0:00

Stanza 1: Voice 1

Quant en moi vint premierement	When I was first visited by
Amours, si tres doucettement	Love, he so very sweetly
Me vost mon cuer enamourer	Captured my heart;
Que d'un regart me fist present,	A glance at what he gave me as a gift,
Et tres amoureus sentiment	And along with loving feelings
Me donna avuec doulz penser,	He presented me with this thought:

Espoir	*d'avoir*	To hope	to have

Merci sans refuser	Grace, and no rejections
Mais onques en tout mon vivant	But never in my entire life
Hardement ne me vost donner.	Was confidence a gift he meant for me.

Voice 2

Amour et biauté parfaite.	Thanks to love and ultimate beauty.

Doubter	*celer*	Fearing	acting

Me font parfaitement.	Are what consume me completely.

0:55

Stanza 2: Voice 1

E si me fait en desirant	And if, in my passion,
Penser si amoureusement	He makes me think so amorously
Que, par force de desirer,	Thanks, to desire
Ma joie convient en tourment	My joy turns into torment—
Muer, se je n'ay hardement.	Must turn, since I am not confident.
Last et je n'en puis recouvrer,	Alas! I cannot save myself—

Qu'amours	*secours*	For Love	no help

Ne me vuer nul prester,	Will lend me—
Qui en ses las si durement	Love, who holds me so tightly
Me tient que n'en puis eschaper.	In his grasp that I cannot escape.

Voice 2

Et vrais desire, qui m'a a fait	And true desire, that has made me

De vous	*cuer doulz*	Love you	dear heart

Amer sans finement.	For ever and ever.

LISTEN TO... this selection streaming online.

WATCH... an Active Listening Guide of this selection online.

WATCH... a performance of this selection online.

DO... an online Listening Practice Activity related to this selection, which your instructor may

assign for a grade.

Guillame de Machaut

Machaut was born about 1300 near Rheims, France. For twenty years he served as secretary to the count of Luxembourg and then King John of Bohemia; he also became a priest. After King John was killed in battle, Machaut, whose services were in much demand by then, worked for various aristocrats and rulers. He was released from priestly duties by Pope Benedict II in 1346.

He survived the plague that swept through Europe in the middle of the fourteenth century and lived the remainder of his life in Rheims, composing music and writing more than four hundred poems. He may have composed the first complete setting of the Ordinary of the Mass. His influence was extensive in the many forms of sacred and secular music he composed. His death in 1377 was recognized in elegies by several composers.

Snark/Art Resource, NY

SECULAR MUSIC

Much of the secular vocal music was performed by wandering musician-entertainers who traveled from place to place singing songs, reciting poems, and even exhibiting trained animals. Later, troubadours dominated secular vocal music in France. They were noblemen who were poets and composers, but usually not performers; they hired minstrels to sing their songs. About 4,000 poems and 1,600 melodies have been preserved. They were for solo voice and may have been accompanied by a mandola, or similar instrument, shown in the *The Goddess Music* painting (Figure 8.2) from a medieval manuscript.

Most troubadours were men, but a few were women, with *trobairitz* used to designate females. One of these was Beatrix de Dia. What little is known about her is that she became Countess of Dia as the wife of the Count of Poitiers. Almost all marriages at the time were arranged by the families of the bride and groom. Brides were usually in their middle teens. She was also a lover of a troubadour gentleman, Raimbaut d'Orange. She composed a number of poems and songs in Occitan (Provençal), of which only a few have survived.

The text of "A chantar" ("I must sing"; see Listening Guide) tells of a frustrated love, which was a popular topic of troubadour poems. For that reason, Beatrix de Dia may not have been expressing her own personal feelings in this song. The music is strophic, with its five stanzas of the poem. The basic pitches, the ones that Beatrix composed, are freely decorated by the singer on the recording. Troubadours in the twelfth century often exercised liberties

Scala/Art Resource, NY

FIGURE 8.2

THE GODDESS MUSIC, SEATED AT CENTER, PLAYS A PORTATIVE (PORTABLE) ORGAN ACCOMPANIED BY (CLOCKWISE FROM TOP CENTER) THE "PIG SNOUT" PSALTERY, A MANDOLA, CLAPPERS, LONG TRUMPETS, KETTLEDRUMS TIED AROUND THE WAIST, BAGPIPE AND SHAWM (BOTH REED INSTRUMENTS), A TAMBOURINE-LIKE JINGLE DRUM, AND A VIELLE (VIOL).

in performing their songs. "A chantar" has no metrical rhythm, with the basic pitches of the melody being about equal in length. The recording presents the initial lines of "A chantar."

LISTENING GUIDE

BEATRIX DE DIA
"A chantar" (excerpt)

Genre: Troubadour song

Form: Strophic

Download 14

1 minute 17 seconds

0:00   Vielle (a medieval bowed string instrument) plays introduction.

0:25   The singer begins:

A chantar m'er de so q'ieu no voldria,	I must sing, whether I want to or not,
Tant me raneur de lui cui sui amia.	I feel such pain from him whose friend I am,

0:52   [Melody repeated]

Car eu l'am mais que nuilla ren que sia;	For I love him more than anyone,
Vas lui nom val merces ni cortesia.	But neither grace nor courtesy has any effect on him.

LISTEN TO... this selection streaming online.

WATCH... an Active Listening Guide of this selection online.

DO... an online Listening Practice Activity related to this selection, which your instructor may assign for a grade.

The tradition of the troubadours was soon adopted in northern France, where they were called *trouvères*. The tradition then spread to Germany, where they were known as *minnesingers*. Later troubadour music influenced Church music and other forms of secular music.

The **estampie** (see Listening Guide) was a twelfth-century dance in triple meter and a clear, fast tempo. Only a single line of music was written down, and no instruments were specified. Performers at that time, as well as those today who perform this music, are free to decide which instruments to use for both the melody and the accompanying parts, including a drone, which is a continuous sound throughout the piece of music.

ANONYMOUS
Estampie (twelfth century)

Genre: Dance music

Form: *a a a' a*

Download 15

1 minute 14 seconds

0:00 A simple flute and violinlike instrument play a lively melody as a drone part is plucked by a string instrument.

0:15 Melody repeated

0:47 Varied version of the melody

1:00 Opening melody returns somewhat varied.

 LISTEN TO... this selection streaming online.

 WATCH... an Active Listening Guide of this selection online.

 DO... an online Listening Practice Activity related to this selection, which your instructor may assign for a grade.

MUSIC IN THE REST OF EUROPE

While the medieval motet was reaching its acme with the compositions of Machaut, interest was waning in this style of music. Medieval motets were developed mainly in France (Figure 8.3). Composers in other parts of Europe evidently didn't care much for the style or were not advanced enough to attempt composing in it. A blind Italian musician named Francesco Landini (Lahn-DEE-nee, 1325–1397) and an English composer named John Dunstable (c. 1385–1453) were writing music that was simpler and easier to listen to. Both men and their successors often used the same text for all parts, which made it possible for the words to be sung about the same time so that they could be understood by listeners.

These composers also avoided harsh dissonances. A significant contribution of Dunstable and other English composers was the use of simultaneous pitches three and six notes apart. These intervals gave the music a richer sound than the fourths and fifths of Léonin and Pérotin.

MAIN POINTS OF CHAPTER 8

1. The medieval period was the time of Scholasticism and the construction of many of the great cathedrals. It also featured chivalry, guilds, and the founding of universities. Many works of music and art were created anonymously.

2. Polyphony developed in the Cathedral of Notre Dame in Paris. Composers added a third and fourth line to music in organum, which consisted of parallel lines of melody a fourth or fifth apart. Polyphonic religious works were based on phrases from Gregorian chant.

 PRACTICE...
your understanding of this chapter's concepts by working once more with the chapter's Active Listening Guides online.

FIGURE 8.3
THE WINDOWS OF THE CHOIR
SECTION OF THE CATHEDRAL AT
REIMS.

JTB Photo Communications, Inc./Alamy

DO...
online quizzes that your
instructor may assign for
a grade.

3. Rhythmic modes, similar to those found in poetry, were used to keep the different lines together.

4. The motet was built over a phrase of Gregorian chant, which was sung in Latin in long notes. Two or more different lines of music were added with words in vernacular languages on secular topics. Complicated rhythmic and melodic schemes were worked into the music. Motets were performed in the courts, not churches.

5. Secular music also existed in instrumental dance music and the songs of the troubadours. These were solo songs based on romantic poems.

Features of Medieval Music

Melodies	Mostly chantlike within a limited range; some pieces with several short flowing notes on a word or syllable
Rhythm	No definite meter; some pieces use rhythmic modes

Textures	Monophonic and polyphonic
Dynamic levels	Restrained and rather soft
Performance media	Small groups of unaccompanied voices; some in two, three, or four parts; a few solos in secular music; very little instrumental music
Forms	Phrase by phrase; a few pieces in sectional form (e.g., *a a b b*)
Genres	Organum Medieval motet Dance music

Renaissance Music

START...

experiencing this chapter's topics with an online video activity that your instructor may assign.

Learning Objectives

1 Describe the general characteristics of the Renaissance period and its music.
2 Explain the settings of the Mass during the Renaissance period.
3 List the characteristics of the motet during the Renaissance.
4 Outline the features of a Renaissance madrigal, especially text painting.
5 Tell about the characteristics of the lute used in Renaissance instrumental music.

READ...

the complete chapter text in a rich interactive eBook!

The word *Renaissance* means "rebirth" in French. Historically, it referred to a revival of interest in the philosophy and arts of ancient Greece and Rome, although there was much more to it than just the admiration of an earlier civilization. Because music had no ancient models to resurrect, for music the term *Renaissance* refers only to the style that predominated from about 1450 to 1600.

THE RENAISSANCE OUTLOOK

The intense interest of Renaissance artists and scholars in the earlier Greek and Roman civilizations led to a curious mixture of Greek and Christian belief. Michelangelo expressed this union of the pagan and Christian by decorating the ceiling of the Sistine Chapel in the Vatican in Rome with alternating figures of prophets (Christian) and sibyls (pagan). Erasmus, the great philosopher, regarded the ancient Athenian Socrates as a pre-Christian saint.

Certain intellectual viewpoints emerged during the Renaissance that are still common in Western civilization today. Among them are optimism, worldliness, hedonism, naturalism, and individualism. But the most important of these is *humanism*, which is an emphasis on the human and natural as opposed to the otherworldly or divine. For example, pride, which was considered a sin in the Middle Ages, was elevated to a virtue.

The humanistic view can be seen by comparing the two treatments of the human body shown here. Figure 9.1A is a sculpture from the great medieval cathedral at Chartres in France. This figure has a spiritual, otherworldly quality; the head and eyes seem serene, and the position of the body is erect and formal. The proportions of the body are exaggerated to make the figure appear longer; the feet seem to dangle as though they were merely attached to the robes. As with most artworks of the medieval period, the artist is unknown.

Michelangelo's *David* (Figure 9.1B), on the other hand, looks like a magnificent Greek god. Standing about 13½ feet high, the sculpture suggests confidence and an admiration of the human body. David looks natural, almost casual, and free.

With increasing interest in the value of life on earth, there was a corresponding interest in the fine arts. Art was valued for its own sake, not just as a means of religious devotion. The result of this new interest in the arts was a long list of outstanding sculptors and painters: Botticelli, Leonardo, Michelangelo, Dürer, Raphael, Titian, Brueghel, and Tintoretto, to name but a few.

Sandro Botticelli's *The Adoration of the Magi* (Figure 9.2) depicts the three wise men or kings paying homage to the infant Jesus. It reveals the fondness of artists of the time for order and balance. A group of figures at the left of the painting is balanced by a group

Christ in Majesty, figure on the south door, c.1250 (stone)/Chartres Cathedral, Chartres, France/The Bridgeman Art Library

Roger Antrobus/Taxi/Getty Images

FIGURE 9.1A

FIGURE 9.1B

MEDIEVAL AND RENAISSANCE INTERPRETATIONS OF THE HUMAN FORM ILLUSTRATE THE ADVENT OF HUMANISM, A PHILOSOPHY THAT ASSERTS THE DIGNITY AND WORTH OF HUMANKIND AND EMPHASIZES SECULAR RATHER THAN SPIRITUAL CONCERNS.

Courtesy National Gallery of Art, Washington

FIGURE 9.2

THE ADORATION OF THE MAGI BY BOTTICELLI PRESENTS THE LOGICAL, PLANNED QUALITIES ALSO FOUND IN RENAISSANCE MUSIC.

FIGURE 9.3
A SKETCH FROM LEONARDO'S NOTEBOOKS AS CAN BE SEEN HERE, LEONARDO WROTE SO THAT THE WORDS READ FROM RIGHT TO LEFT WITH THE LETTERS REVERSED. HIS WRITING IS MOST EASILY READ USING A MIRROR.

on the right, with the Madonna and Child in the center. The painting has a "staged" look. The converging lines of the Greek and Roman ruins add linear perspective to the painting and indicate a renewed interest in these ancient civilizations. Botticelli gives many of his figures brightly colored clothing. In addition, the sky is bright and clear.

Not only were works of art being enjoyed in a new climate of acceptance, but improving economic conditions meant that money was available to hire artists and musicians. The Church sought rich adornment for its buildings, which was one of the practices that led to the Reformation started by Martin Luther in 1517.

An event that affected education, commerce, and religion was Johann Gutenberg's invention of printing using movable type. His invention made possible the wide dissemination of music, beginning with the appearance of the first printed music books in 1501.

The spirit of the time was one of optimism and discovery. The voyages of Columbus, Cabot, Balboa, and Magellan took place during the Renaissance. Copernicus was announcing his discoveries about the universe. Rabelais, Machiavelli, Boccaccio, Montaigne, More, Bacon, and Erasmus were exploring new ideas in literature and philosophy.

Perhaps the Renaissance is best epitomized by Leonardo da Vinci (1452–1519). It seems there was little that this genius did not do extremely well: design weapons and other devices, recite stories, paint, depict human anatomy, plan cities, make maps, and analyze proportions and things mathematical. He was interested in everything and left seven thousand pages of notebooks (Figure 9.3)!

FEATURES AND TYPES OF RENAISSANCE MUSIC

Musically, the Renaissance started in the Netherlands. The composers there had reached a level of achievement that was the envy of Europe. Many were eventually lured away from their homeland to better-paying jobs in Spain, Bohemia, Austria, Germany, and especially the cities of northern Italy.

The style and techniques of the Netherlanders became internationally known and imitated. Many composers became so cosmopolitan that they thought of themselves as musicians first and citizens of a particular country second.

One composer who shaped the period known as the High Renaissance was Josquin des Prez. Like composers before him, Josquin used the device of *imitation*, in which one line of melody appears in another part a measure or two later, somewhat like a round. But instead of having all parts singing continuously, as composers before him did, he had each voice enter one after another. This emphasized the imitation and made the words sung by each entering part easier to hear.

Josquin des Prez

Josquin des Prez ("JZHOSS-can deh PRAY"), the most esteemed composer of the middle Renaissance, lived from about 1440 to 1521. Born in Flanders (now part of Belgium), Josquin was a choir singer in Milan, a musician in the service of the Sforza family, a member of the Papal Choir, a choirmaster, and finally a musician in the service of Louis XII of France. His composing skill was much admired by his contemporaries, including Martin Luther. Josquin composed what and when he wanted, not what his patron wanted. He was known for his motets

and chansons, which were French polyphonic songs. He also demanded a salary much higher than that of most of his contemporaries, which could explain why he changed jobs rather often. He was also very particular about his music and would become angry if singers tried to make any changes in it.

Best-Known Works

Choral
- *Missa Ave Maria Stella*
- *Missa de Beata Virgine*

UniversalImagesGroup/Getty Images

THE RENAISSANCE MASS

It was the custom among composers during the Renaissance to compose music for the Ordinary of the Mass using a phrase from a chant as a *cantus firmus*. The Mass usually acquired the name of the phrase or chant. For example, Josquin wrote eighteen different settings of the Mass. His *Pange lingua Mass* has many melodies from a Gregorian hymn called "Pange lingua." A portion of both the hymn and the Kyrie section of Josquin's Mass (see Listening Guide) is shown here.

Plainsong hymn, "Pange lingua"

LISTENING GUIDE

JOSQUIN DES PREZ
Kyrie from *Pange lingua Mass* (c. 1500)

Genre: Mass, "Kyrie"

Download 16

3 minutes 15 seconds

0:00   Tenors enter singing "Kyrie eleison."

0:03   Basses enter singing "Kyrie eleison" in imitation.

0:12   Sopranos enter singing "Kyrie eleison" in imitation.

0:20   Altos enter singing "Kyrie eleison" in imitation.

0:24   Basses enter again, followed by tenors and then sopranos.

0:50   Basses sing "Christe eleison." Altos soon follow.

1:07   Tenors sing "Christe." Sopranos soon follow.

2:16   Sopranos sing "Kyrie eleison," but the melody differs from the first Kyrie. Altos, tenors, and basses follow.

3:10   After an extended cadence, the Kyrie concludes.

LISTEN TO... this selection streaming online.

WATCH... an Active Listening Guide of this selection online.

DO... an online Listening Practice Activity related to this selection, which your instructor may assign for a grade.

More than any previous composer, Josquin was aware of a consistent organization of harmonies. Closely related to more-sophisticated harmony was the development of the bass line. Prior to Josquin, when composers started adding melodies to chant; they placed the chant around middle C and put the additional melodies above it. But this did not provide a convincing sense of chord movement. Therefore, around the year 1450, composers began to add another line *below* the chant to give the music a more solid foundation. Even today this arrangement of voice parts (Figure 9.4) remains the standard for a choral group containing men's and women's voices. At the time, the sections were called *superius, altus, tenor,* and *bassus;* today they are called soprano, alto, tenor, and bass.

Singing angels, relief from the Cantoria by Luca della Robbia (1400-82), c.1435 (marble), Della Robbia, Luca (1400-82)/Museo dell' Opera del Duomo, Florence, Italy/The Bridgeman Art Library

FIGURE 9.4
SINGING ANGELS, FROM THE *CANTORIA,* OR SINGERS' PULPIT, BY THE RENAISSANCE SCULPTOR LUCA DELLA ROBBIA.

The most esteemed composer of the late Renaissance was Giovanni Pierluigi da Palestrina. Historical circumstances encouraged him to be a conservative reformer, musically speaking. The Council of Trent was held intermittently between 1545 and 1563. The Church felt threatened by the Protestant Reformation, so the council met to respond to that situation and to acknowledge the need for some reform within the Church.

One aspect that was under attack was its music, which over the centuries had strayed far from the ideals of Gregorian chant. Complaints were voiced about the use of secular tunes, the complicated polyphony that made the words nearly impossible to understand, the use of noisy instruments, and the irreverence of the singers. The council directed that the music be purged of "barbarism, obscurities, contrarieties, and superfluities" so that "the House of God might rightly be called a house of prayer." To his credit, Palestrina achieved a return to the purity and reverence of earlier music without discarding the highly developed style of his predecessors.

THE RENAISSANCE MOTET

The Renaissance motet is very different from the medieval motet. The **Renaissance motet** is a unified piece with all voices singing the same Latin text. It borrows some phrases from chant, and it conveys the desired spirit of reverence. Above all, the Renaissance motet is serious, restrained, and designed for inclusion in the worship service. In addition, it avoids the complicated musical complexities of the Gothic motet.

Palestrina's "Sicut cervus"

Palestrina's works have a pure, celestial quality. His "Sicut cervus" (see Listening Guide) is a good example of a Renaissance motet for the following reasons:

* The text is in ecclesiastical (church) Latin. It is a portion of Psalm 42, with Part I using only the first two lines. It likens a person's soul to a hart, which is a male deer, a stag.

   As a hart longs for flowing streams,
   So longs my soul for Thee, O God.

My soul thirsts for God, for the living God.
When shall I come and behold the face of God?
My tears have been my food day and night,
While men say to me continually, "Where is your God?"

- The music is polyphonic. All the lines are given equal attention, and each has melodic character.

- Each voice usually enters in imitation of another when new text is introduced.

- The music does not have a strong feeling of chord progression.

- "Sicut cervus" does not have a strong meter or beat. Although it moves along steadily, it certainly is not toe-tapping music. Today's versions of the music have bar lines, but these have been added by modern editors so singers can more easily keep their place. The bar lines do not imply a metrical pattern.

LISTENING GUIDE

GIOVANNI PIERLUIGI DA PALESTRINA
"Sicut cervus," Part I (c. 1577)

Genre: Motet

Download 17

3 minutes 32 seconds

0:00   Tenors sing "Sicut cervus."

0:07   Altos follow with "Sicut cervus" five notes higher.

0:12   Sopranos sing "Sicut cervus" one octave higher than tenors sang the phrase.

0:18   Basses sing "Sicut cervus" on the same pitch on which the tenors started.

1:18   Basses sing "ita desiderat." Tenors, sopranos, and altos follow in imitation.

2:10   Sopranos sing "anima mea ad te Deus." Altos, tenors, and basses follow in imitation.

3:21   After the voice parts have sung "ad te Deus," Part I of the motet concludes.

LISTEN TO... this selection streaming online.

WATCH... an Active Listening Guide of this selection online.

WATCH... a performance of this selection online.

DO... an online Listening Practice Activity related to this selection, which your instructor may assign for a grade.

Giovanni Pierluigi da Palestrina

IOANNES PETRALOYSIUS PRAENESTINUS

Imago secundum prototypum in Archivo musico
Basilicae Vaticanae conservatum.

Josia picturi

Science Source

Palestrina (c. 1526–1594) was born in the small town of Palestrina outside Rome, which provided him with the name by which he is known today. He began his career as chorister at Santa Maria Maggiore in 1537 in Rome. In 1544 he returned as organist and choirmaster to his native town, where he married and had two sons.

In 1550 the bishop of Palestrina was elected pope, assuming the name Julius III. A year and a half later, he summoned Palestrina back to Rome to become choirmaster of the Cappella Giulia in the Vatican. Soon Palestrina was to publish his first book of Masses.

Pope Julius III died and was succeeded by Pope Paul IV, who was determined to reform what he considered the excesses in Church music. In 1555 Palestrina was dismissed from his job because he was married. He was soon appointed choirmaster at the Church of Saint John Lateran in Rome, where he stayed for five years. He then returned to Santa Maria Maggiore and published his first book of motets. In 1571 he returned to Cappella Giulia, but misfortune struck when his two eldest sons and wife died of various diseases.

Palestrina married again and entered the fur business, and he proved to be a highly successful businessman. His more than adequate funds allowed him to publish about sixteen collections of music. He died in 1594, leaving a wealth of beautiful and finely crafted music and the distinction of creating the finest church music of his time.

Best-Known Works

Choral
- *Pope Marcellus Mass*
- "Sicut cervus"

- Motets today are almost always sung without accompaniment. During the Renaissance, however, the voices were sometimes doubled by a few instruments. But the ideal was a purity of sound, which implies no accompaniment or, in musical terms, **a cappella.** The term actually means "for the chapel."

- A small group of singers is the authentic performance medium for Renaissance motets. Probably no more than two or three singers were originally assigned to each part. Boys, or men singing in falsetto, sang the upper voice parts. Women were not permitted by the Church to celebrate the Mass or to sing in choirs at Masses.

- The lines of melody are very singable. The range for any one voice part does not exceed an octave, except for the bass. Furthermore, the lines do not move far from one pitch to the next. The melodies are quite smooth and conjunct.

- The form of a motet is usually based on the structure of the text, which in this case is a psalm, so each verse has its own polyphonic setting.

- The music has a restrained quality. Bombast and showmanship were considered not in keeping with the attitude of reverence and awe that should prevail in worship.

- The melodic lines are woven together with great skill and beauty. That is the main reason Palestrina's music is so highly esteemed and still sung today.

THE MADRIGAL

The Renaissance also had a distinctly worldly side, as was noted earlier. Many types of secular music were composed and performed, and some of this music contained features of the musical style of a particular country. The most significant type of secular music at this time was the madrigal.

Madrigals are both similar to and different from motets. They are similar in that they were written for a small group of singers. They also have some imitative entrances of new phrases of text, contain singable vocal lines, and are generally more polyphonic than homophonic. But there are some important differences.

- Madrigals are in vernacular languages, and their texts often deal with sentimental and sometimes erotic love.
- Madrigals tend to have stronger and more regular rhythm, and most of them are composed to be performed at a faster tempo.
- Madrigals were sung at courtly social gatherings and meetings of learned and artistic societies, so they were not the popular or folk music of the day. They were very popular, however, among the aristocratic, educated class, and an enormous number of them were composed. In England madrigal singing—with its implied requirement of music reading—was expected of educated persons.
- Madrigals often contain **text painting**, or **word painting**, in which the music attempts to depict the words being sung.

Because madrigals were written for secular situations, they were not limited by religious traditions. They therefore contained more innovative musical ideas, such as word painting. This practice is especially evident in the madrigal "As Vesta Was from Latmos Hill Descending" (see Listening Guide).

The madrigal was originally an Italian development associated with such composers as Cipriano de Rore and Luca Marenzio. By the mid-1500s madrigals had spread to other countries. Interest in madrigals reached England late in that century. English madrigals are especially enjoyable to listeners today for three reasons:

- Their texts are in English, so no translation is necessary for English-speaking people.
- English composers had a knack for making the lines of music tuneful and singable.
- The English had the delightful trait of not taking themselves too seriously. No matter how sad a song may be, the listener senses a detached quality.

Weelkes's "As Vesta Was from Latmos Hill Descending"

Thomas Weelkes was one of England's finest composers of madrigals. "As Vesta Was from Latmos Hill Descending" is from an anthology of madrigals, *The Triumphs of Oriana*. It was composed in honor of Queen Elizabeth I, who was often called "Oriana." She never married and was often referred to as the "maiden" or "virgin" queen.

This madrigal is written for six voice parts instead of the usual four. Vesta is the Roman goddess of the hearth and home, and Diana is the goddess of the hunt, chastity, and the moon. The text tells about Vesta coming down a hill with her attendants, who are referred to as "Diana's darlings." At the same time, Oriana, the "maiden queen," climbs the hill with her shepherd attendants. Vesta's attendants leave her and hurry down to join Oriana.

When the text tells about Vesta's attendants and male admirers (swain) leaving her to run down the hill, Weelkes has the appropriate number of singers singing—two, then three, and then one. Later in the piece, the word *long* is the longest note in that portion of the madrigal.

Weelkes fits the words and rhythm of the music together in a way that would be natural if they were spoken. Often the rhythmic setting of the words contributes to their expressiveness.

THOMAS WEELKES

"As Vesta Was from Latmos Hill Descending" (1590)

Genre: Madrigal

Download 18

3 minutes 7 seconds

0:00	As Vesta was from Latmos hill descending,	*Descending scales*
0:12	she spied a maiden queen the same ascending,	*Ascending scales*
0:33	attended on by all the shepherds swain,	
0:49	to whom Diana's darlings came running	
	down amain.	*Rapid descending notes*
1:12	First two by two, then three by three together,	*Two voices, three voices, then all voices*
1:21	leaving their goddess all alone, hasten thither,	*One voice*
1:34	and mingling with the shepherd of her train	
1:41	with mirthful tunes her presence entertain.	*Short, happy phrase in imitation*
1:55	Then sang the shepherds and nymphs of Diana,	*Flowing melody*
2:06	Long live fair Oriana!	*Long notes in the bass part*
3:03	Madrigal concludes with sustained notes.	

 LISTEN TO... this selection streaming online.

 WATCH... an Active Listening Guide of this selection online.

 DO... an online Listening Practice Activity related to this selection, which your instructor may assign for a grade.

Thomas Weelkes

Thomas Weelkes (c. 1576–1623) was one of several excellent composers of choral music who flourished in England at the end of the sixteenth century and the early part of the seventeenth. His contemporaries included William Byrd (1543–1623), John Dowland (1562–1626), Thomas Morley (c. 1557–1603), Thomas Tallis (c. 1501–1585), and John Wilbye (1574–1638). Although

(continued)

madrigals were slow in coming to England, interest in them seemed to explode once they finally arrived.

Weelkes was organist first at Winchester College, but spent most of his career in Chichester. There he married the daughter of a wealthy merchant, and they had three children. His most musically productive years were the early ones in Chichester. As the years went by, he became more negligent in his church music duties and drank heavily. He was reported to the bishop as being "noted and famed for a common drunkard and notorious swearer and blasphemer." By 1617 he was fired from his job and apparently was employed only sporadically after that.

Whatever Weelkes's personal foibles, he composed some of the finest church music and madrigals during that period of English history. Typical of most of his contemporary composers, he wrote madrigals that were lighter and more experimental than his church music.

RENAISSANCE INSTRUMENTAL MUSIC

Composers during the Renaissance devoted most of their efforts to vocal music. Instruments did often accompany the singing of secular music, especially a lute or harpsichord. Instrumentalists simplified the written parts by reducing the polyphony to chords. The pieces are shorter, seldom lasting more than a couple of minutes. The rhythms are straightforward and clearly in two- or three-beat meter.

The lute was the most popular instrument of the Renaissance. As can be seen in Figure 9.5, it has a pear-shaped body, several strings, and frets. **Frets** are metal strips

WATCH...
Renaissance instrumental music online.

Isabella Stewart Gardner Museum Boston

FIGURE 9.5

A GIRL WITH A LUTE, AN OIL PAINTING ON WOOD BY BARTOLOMEO VENETO. THE LUTE REACHED ITS PEAK OF POPULARITY DURING THIS TIME, BOTH AS A SOLO INSTRUMENT AND AS ACCOMPANIMENT TO SINGING.

placed across the fingerboard to help the player in accurate finger placement. Its pegbox is slanted back sharply away from the body. It is played by plucking, and intricate music can be performed on it.

Instruments were used extensively for dance music. One of the most popular dances of the time was the *pavane* ("pa-*vahn*"), a solemn dance in two beats to the measure with the dancers moving in a formal way. The pavane was often paired with the *galliard*, which had three beats to the measure. These and other dances are made up of clearly identifiable sections that produced forms such as *A A B B* and *A A B B C C*.

 WATCH...
a Renaissance instrumental performance online.

MAIN POINTS OF CHAPTER 9

1. The word *Renaissance* means "rebirth" and is the name given to the period that lasted from about 1450 to 1600, when there was a revival of interest in the culture of the ancient Greeks and Romans. It was also the age of explorers and the introduction of the printing press.

2. The bass voice part became an important addition to choral music.

3. The Renaissance motet had a sacred text sung in Latin with all parts singing the same text. New phrases of text were often introduced in imitation. Its mood was reverent and restrained, with no strong feeling of meter.

4. Madrigals were the most popular genre of secular vocal music. They were similar to motets in that they were usually sung without accompaniment by a small group of singers. But madrigals have secular texts in a vernacular language, were performed at social gatherings, often contained text painting, and generally are more lively.

5. Instrumental music during the Renaissance featured the lute. Most instrumental music was created as dance music.

 PRACTICE...
your understanding of this chapter's concepts by working once more with the chapter's Active Listening Guides online.

 DO...
online quizzes that your instructor may assign for a grade.

Features of Renaissance Music

Melodies	Flowing to adjacent notes within a somewhat limited range
Rhythm	Even, steady flow without a clear sense of beat
Texture	Mostly polyphonic
Dynamic levels	Restrained and rather soft
Performance media	Small, unaccompanied groups of singers, some with soprano, alto, tenor, and bass voice parts
	A small amount of lute and keyboard music
Forms	Phrase by phrase; a few pieces in sectional form
Genres	Mass Renaissance motet Madrigal Dance music

PART 3

Baroque Music

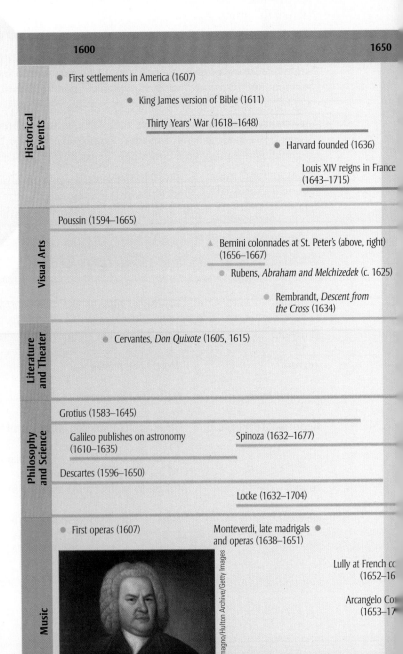

	1600	1650
Historical Events	● First settlements in America (1607)	
	● King James version of Bible (1611)	
	Thirty Years' War (1618–1648)	
		● Harvard founded (1636)
		Louis XIV reigns in France (1643–1715)
Visual Arts	Poussin (1594–1665)	
		▲ Bernini colonnades at St. Peter's (above, right) (1656–1667)
		● Rubens, *Abraham and Melchizedek* (c. 1625)
		● Rembrandt, *Descent from the Cross* (1634)
Literature and Theater	● Cervantes, *Don Quixote* (1605, 1615)	
Philosophy and Science	Grotius (1583–1645)	
	Galileo publishes on astronomy (1610–1635)	Spinoza (1632–1677)
	Descartes (1596–1650)	
		Locke (1632–1704)
Music	● First operas (1607)	Monteverdi, late madrigals ● and operas (1638–1651)
		Lully at French co (1652–16
		Arcangelo Co (1653–17

Imagno/Hulton Archive/Getty Images

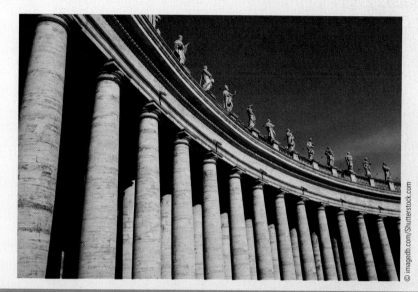

© imagedb.com/Shutterstock.com

1700 **1750**

- Ottomans seize Vienna
  - Salem witchcraft trials (1692)

Boucher (1703–1770)

Gainsborough (1727–1788)

Fragonard (1732–1806)

Watteau (1684–1721)

- Milton, *Paradise Lost* (1667, 1674)
  - Defoe, *Robinson Crusoe* (1719)

Swift, *Gulliver's Travels* ● (1735) ● Fielding, *Tom Jones* (1749)

- Newton's laws of physics

Voltaire (1694–1778)

Hume

- Purcell, *Dido and Aeneas* (1689) ● Handel, *Messiah* (1741)
  - Fugues (c. 1700) ● Vivaldi, *The Four Seasons* (1723)

Lebrecht/The Image Works

◀ J. S. Bach (left) and ▲ Handel (above), instrumental and choral works
(1685–1750) (1685–1759)

10

The Baroque Period

START...
experiencing this chapter's topics with an online video activity that your instructor may assign.

Learning Objectives

1 Describe the main characteristics of Baroque style, in art, intellectual activity, and music.

2 Enumerate the main characteristics of Baroque music.

3 Explain how the recitative contains most of the features of Baroque music.

4 List the key features of Baroque instrumental music.

READ...
the complete chapter text in a rich interactive eBook!

Even before 1600, the approximate beginning of the Baroque period, a new style had been emerging. The Renaissance ideals of restraint and balance had begun to fade. The change could be seen in the growing emotion displayed in the later sculptures of Michelangelo, as well as in Giovanni Gabrieli's massive works for instruments and two choruses. The initial reaction to the new style can be seen in the word *baroque* itself, which was probably derived from a Portuguese word meaning "irregularly shaped pearl."

Sometimes *baroque* means extravagant, grotesque, and in bad taste, which is perhaps a carryover from its original meaning. In discussions of music, however, **Baroque** refers only to the style that prevailed from about 1600 to 1750. And that style was certainly not grotesque or in bad taste.

STYLES IN MUSIC

What do we mean by a musical style? Simply that the elements in a particular style are generally treated in a similar way. In some styles, for example, there is little sense of meter, in other styles it is very pronounced, and in yet others the metrical patterns are often irregular. The same is true of melodies, size and nature of performing groups, texture, type of harmony, and so on. Many of these similarities can be partly described in words. Sometimes a style is recognized "just because it sounds like it." But a clear understanding of the characteristics of a style can come only from listening for them.

When a large amount of music over a long span of time has used musical elements in a similar way, it has been grouped by scholars and given a name—Renaissance, Baroque, and others. These names are usually designated quite a few years *after* the years in which a style was dominant. No one got up on the morning of January 1, 1600, and thought, "Good, the Baroque period has finally arrived." People have always thought of themselves as modern and up to date, which, of course, at the time they were. But they did not think they had entered a new style period.

Why do writers and scholars designate periods in music and history? Just as it helps to divide a book into units and chapters, it helps to divide the thousands of years of human history into periods. The idea of style periods permits us to organize topics according to similarities and to talk, think about, and remember them more easily.

What you hear in a piece of music and what you know about it reinforce each other, as was stressed in Chapter 1. An understanding of styles in music also clues us in on what to listen for, as well as what not to expect. For instance, you seldom encounter an accompanied solo singer in music written before 1600. So, when you hear such a work, you will know that it's not in Renaissance style. Being able to recognize the differences between styles from listening is an excellent indicator of how well you are connecting what you hear with what you know.

CHARACTERISTICS OF BAROQUE STYLE

It is difficult to summarize in a few paragraphs a period of 150 years in which major changes took place and contrasting forces were at work. Three general characteristics, however, mark the Baroque style: grandiose dimensions, love of drama, and religious intensity.

Grandiose Dimensions

The artists and musicians of the Baroque period were fond of the large and grandiose. In music this characteristic is evident in the prominent place given the pipe organ—the largest and most powerful instrument of the time. In architecture the love of grandeur can be seen in Gian Lorenzo Bernini's monumental colonnades encompassing the vast piazza (Figure 10.1) in front of Saint Peter's Basilica in Rome. The huge columns reach out before Saint Peter's like giant arms seeking to draw everyone into the building. Four rows of columns run parallel to one another. But when standing in the center of the piazza, viewers can see only a single row of columns, because the other three rows are perfectly blocked out. The colonnade is made up of 284 different columns, and statues of 140 saints are placed on top of the columns.

Love of Drama

Baroque artists and musicians were fond of drama. Three major dramatic genres were developed in music: opera, oratorio, and cantata. Drama can also be seen in the twisted lines and struggling subjects in artworks. Both size and twisting motion are evident in the ceiling paintings and many other Baroque works of art.

Religious Intensity

The years of the Baroque period were a time of strong religious feelings—and conflicts. The Protestant churches established themselves generally in northern Europe and on the British Isles. Protestant worship was devout, plain, and dead serious. John Milton's *Paradise Lost* and John Bunyan's *Pilgrim's Progress* were two monumental writings containing the Protestant viewpoint.

The Catholic faith was generally found in southern Europe. The Catholic Counter-Reformation developed in response to the Protestant Reformation and a sense that the Catholic Church was in need of reform. The times were marked by a series of tragic religious wars between Protestants and Catholics. A positive by-product of this religious intensity, however, was the creation of many great pieces of art and music.

MASSIMO SESTINI/AFP/Getty Images/Newscom

FIGURE 10.1
BERNINI'S PIAZZA SAN PIETRO IS LARGER THAN THE LENGTH OF TWO FOOTBALL FIELDS AND TOOK ELEVEN YEARS TO COMPLETE.

BAROQUE ART

Baroque artworks are very different from those of the Renaissance. Consider Peter Paul Rubens's *The Meeting of Abraham and Melchizedek*, which was painted about 1625 (Figure 10.2). Originally designed for a tapestry, this work is the opposite of the calm, posed quality of Giotto's *Madonna and Child* (Figure 8.1). The painting looks as though a movie director had shouted "Action!" to the figures; even the horse on the left side of the picture appears to have responded to the command. The bodies of the figures are often twisted to add to the dramatic effect. Abraham and Melchizedek lean actively toward each other. The men on each side are set in a tight design of profiles and frontal poses. Their bodies look natural and robust. The edges of the painting show a luxurious carpet piled up on a ledge, and the scene is anchored by the columns on the right and clamped into place by the servants in the foreground.

Rembrandt van Rijn's *Descent from the Cross* (Figure 10.3) shows another side of Baroque painting. It features the dramatic treatment of light on the faces of people, much as a spotlight in a stage production centers attention on a particular character. The light focuses on two parts of the painting. One is the body of Jesus and the face of the man helping lower his body. The other, weaker spotlight is on the woman, presumably Mary, on the right-hand side. The light in this painting seems to be coming from the candle shielded by a man's hand, which gives the scene an eerie pall. To increase the spotlight effect, Rembrandt painted an almost black background.

Another Baroque characteristic of Rembrandt's painting is the twisted, almost corkscrew design. Notice that Jesus's body is turned, as are most of the other figures in the painting; none is facing straight ahead or sideways. And the cross is not in the center of the painting, as it probably would have been if this were a Renaissance work. As if the spotlighting and twisted figures were not enough, you can also see the tenderness and grief in the faces of the people. It's a very dramatic painting.

The Baroque love of size and grandeur is evident in the ceiling painting *Apotheosis of Saint Ignatius* by Andrea Pozzo, which adorns the San Ignazio (St. Ignatius) Church in Rome (Figure 10.4). The work is a fresco; that is, it was painted right into

FIGURE 10.2

THE MEETING OF ABRAHAM AND MELCHIZEDEK BY PETER PAUL RUBENS. THE PAINTING IS FILLED WITH THE SENSE OF DRAMA THAT BAROQUE MUSICIANS AND ARTISTS CREATED IN THEIR WORKS.

Print Collector/Hulton Fine Art Collection/Getty Images

FIGURE 10.3
DESCENT FROM THE CROSS BY REMBRANDT VAN RIJN. THE PAINTING ADDS TO THE SENSE OF DRAMA BY SPOTLIGHTING THE FACES OF THE FIGURES IN THE SCENE, SIMILAR TO THE WAY THAT SINGERS AND ACTORS ARE SPOTLIGHTED ON A STAGE.

Scala/Art Resource, NY

FIGURE 10.4
APOTHEOSIS OF ST. IGNATIUS BY ANDREA POZZO. THE PIPE ORGAN WAS THE MOST POWERFUL INSTRUMENT DURING THE BAROQUE, AND THE CEILING PAINTING WAS THE MOST MASSIVE TYPE OF PAINTING.

the ceiling plaster while it was still fresh. It is one of a number of ceiling paintings completed during the Baroque period, the most famous of which are Michelangelo's frescoes for the Sistine Chapel in the Vatican in Rome. It seems that Baroque artists (and/or their patrons) thought that bigger was better. Works of music became much longer and involved more performers, and artwork became larger, both in concept and in actual size. This fresco tries to exceed its physical limits by creating the illusion that the viewer is gazing into heaven. The scene depicts saints, angels, and sinners all overwhelmed by what they see.

BAROQUE INTELLECTUAL ACTIVITY

Although it was marked by religious fervor, the Baroque period was also a time of important advances in science.

- Sir Isaac Newton developed the theory of gravity.
- Johannes Kepler and Galileo Galilei developed Copernicus's theories about the movements of the planets.
- William Gilbert introduced the word *electricity* into the language.
- Robert Boyle helped develop chemistry into a science.
- Robert Hooke first described the cellular structure of plants.
- William Harvey described the circulation of blood in the human body.
- Newton and Gottfried Wilhelm von Leibniz developed infinitesimal calculus.
- René Descartes founded analytical geometry. He is also remembered for his philosophical statement "I think, therefore I am."

EARLY BAROQUE MUSIC

No musical style is ever fully uniform, and this is especially true of the Baroque. Some scholars have divided the period into three subperiods: early, middle, and mature. Music in the early years of the Baroque was more experimental; the style usually associated with this period developed during the middle and mature years.

The transition from the Renaissance to the Baroque style resulted in some powerful music by a number of composers. An important group worked in Venice, which was a major cultural center throughout the sixteenth and into the seventeenth century. Venice's musical activity centered in the Basilica of Saint Mark. The position of organist-choirmaster there was the most sought after in all of Italy. Over the years the distinguished musicians who held that post composed more and more for two choruses placed with the two organs on each side of the church. And not only were there singers and pipe organs; there were also trombones, cornets, and viols. Viols are string instruments that look something like cellos, but have frets, flatter and less curving bodies, and more strings.

The result was a powerful and exciting stereophonic sound with one group of performers answering the other. This technique was known as *polychoral* or *antiphonal singing*. Giovanni Gabrieli (1555–1612) brought antiphonal music to a peak in the early years of the seventeenth century. He was also the first composer to specify particular instruments for a part and the first to indicate dynamics in music notation.

Patronage System

During the Baroque period, Europe consisted of many small principalities and states, including three hundred principalities in what is present-day Germany. As expensive cars and designer clothing are used today in establishing social status, music and art became symbols among the nobility and wealthy merchants. Composers often worked under a patronage system in which they composed music exclusively for their employer. George Frideric Handel (1685–1759), for example, was employed by the elector of Hanover in Germany (where his name was Händel) and was on leave for a second time in England when the elector was crowned King George I of England.

The patronage system had its good and bad points. It could provide a composer steady employment, but the position also demanded that he please his employer or else he would need to find another job. And the job often involved teaching singers, rehearsing instrumentalists, and even quelling squabbles among the musicians, as well as writing music "on demand."

Family Tradition

Sons often followed their fathers' occupation. For example, the Bach family tree contains about sixty outstanding musicians, including thirty-eight composers. Education beyond the elementary school level was limited to those who were rich or born into noble families. Learning to be a composer often consisted of copying music when young and later studying as an apprentice with a master composer. A few musicians studied an instrument or voice at one of the newly emerging conservatories, but rarely was composition taught there during the Baroque.

Need for New Music

There was no established body of music such as we have today. Almost all music was expected to be, and was, new. For this reason, many Baroque composers wrote huge amounts of music. Georg Phillip Telemann (1685–1767), for example, composed more than three thousand pieces, and many other Baroque composers produced prodigious amounts of music. How did they do it?

1. They must have worked very hard.
2. They used a shorthand system called *figured bass* in which they did not have to write in every note in a chord.
3. They used some of their own themes (and once in a while a theme by another composer) in more than one of their works.
4. They had young boys (future musicians) copy a lot of the parts for the instrumentalists and singers.
5. They didn't fuss over details, often because they were going to perform a work themselves. They never dreamed (at least as far as anyone can determine) that people hundreds of years later would be performing and listening to their music! They probably thought of themselves as skilled craftsmen, not artists who were creating music that future generations would understand and appreciate.

Performance of Baroque Music

There were no professional orchestras during the Baroque. The only orchestras were associated with courts and employed part-time performers. The orchestras were also small (about twenty players), and there was no need for a conductor. Usually the keyboard player would simply nod his head to indicate when the music was to begin. Public performances were rare; usually they were held in churches or palaces. Opera companies were a different matter. A number of cities in Italy had them. Performances took place in opera houses and were attended by the public. At one time in the seventeenth century, Venice, which had at the time a population of 125,000, supported six opera houses.

The quality of playing on most orchestral instruments was probably not at all impressive compared to the quality of performers today. Most players held other jobs, often not associated with music, and the development of playing skills was limited. Many of the instruments were not fully developed. Woodwinds had few keys, and brasses had no valves with which to produce pitches not in their basic overtone series. However, some organists and harpsichord players were outstanding performers. It was different in the case of singers. Some of them were reputed to possess sensational ability.

Improvisation

Creating music "on the spot" was an important feature in Baroque music. An organist was expected to be able to improvise intricate and complex music. During their lifetimes Bach, Handel, and several other Baroque composers were known as much for their ability to improvise as for their compositions. Handel continued to give organ concerts in which he improvised even after he became blind. Singers and instrumentalists frequently added ornaments to a melody, so what is seen in the notation of Baroque music was sometimes only a skeleton of what was actually performed.

CHARACTERISTICS OF BAROQUE MUSIC

The differences between the Renaissance music of composers such as Josquin and Palestrina and the Baroque music of J. S. Bach, Handel, and Vivaldi are immense.

Homophony

From the monophonic texture of Gregorian chant, music moved to simple organum and then to highly complex polyphonic music of medieval times and the Renaissance. Polyphonic music can be beautiful and interesting, but it does have drawbacks. When several different voice parts are singing at the same time, the words tend to be obscured by other voice parts. It's somewhat like trying to listen to two or more different conversations at the same time. What's more, because they need to fit with other lines of music, it is difficult for the lines in polyphonic music to be expressive of the words.

Although there are moments in Renaissance music in which all the voice parts move together, these places are not truly homophonic in the sense that one melody predominates and the other parts are supportive of it. Near the beginning of the Baroque period, several composers in and around Florence, Italy, decided to have a singer sing one line and make that line of music expressive of the text being sung, while the other parts became just accompaniment. In this way, the music could be much freer and more dramatic, a characteristic of Baroque music. Homophony developed from these efforts, and over the years it was to become as important as polyphony. The type of homophony consisting of a solo line with instrumental accompaniment that flourished in the early seventeenth century is often called *monody*.

The transition from the polyphony of the Renaissance to the homophony of the Baroque can be seen in the books of madrigals by Claudio Monteverdi (1567–1643). Between 1587 and 1603, he published four books of polyphonic madrigals in Renaissance style. In 1605, however, he published a book of homophonic pieces, some of which have accompaniments. By the eighth book in 1638, Monteverdi's music also contained works for small vocal and string ensembles.

Recitative

The early efforts to have a single expressive line of melody were almost entirely in a singsong style called **recitative** (REH-si-tah-TEEV). During some early recitatives, singers went so far as to grimace, act, and imitate inflections of crying and gasping. Whatever the merits of such attempts at artistic expression, they did open up a new dimension in vocal music. The single melody could have a wider range, more movement by half steps, and more rhythmic freedom than a line in a traditional Renaissance motet.

Because the main objective of recitatives was to express the text, composers did not attempt to write memorable melodies for them. They would save such melodies for other pieces of music. They seldom repeated words in recitatives because they wanted to cover the text in as direct and expressive a way as possible.

Metrical Rhythm

Renaissance music usually has a sense of even flow. It does not, however, provide a sense of metrical pattern. That was to change in Baroque music. Regular metrical patterns became the norm. In fact, Baroque music seemed to be subject to what was sometimes referred to as "the tyranny of the bar line." And bar lines began to appear in music notation during this time. Because of its regular beat, and because most Baroque orchestras and choral groups were small, musical works were performed without a conductor.

There is one exception to the strict metrical quality of Baroque rhythm: recitatives. Although the notation of recitatives contains bar lines, musicians understood then, and still understand today, that the music is to be performed very flexibly. The accompanying orchestra or keyboard player follows whatever changes singers make in the flow of the music.

Major/Minor Keys

Prior to the Baroque period, musicians had used scale patterns called **modes**. The modes followed patterns of whole and half steps that can be seen by the beginning and ending scales on each of the white keys on the piano—C to C, D to D, and so on. Two of those patterns were retained in Baroque music: the one from C to C, which is major, and the one from A to A, which is minor. The other five patterns were almost never used again until the twentieth century, although they continued prominently in folk music.

Tonal Center

The Baroque period saw the establishment of music with a **tonal center**, or **key center**, and the systematic use of harmony. Prior to that time, composers concentrated on fitting the lines of music together well. Now composers began to think much more about how the progression of chords affected the music. They based their use of chords around the "magnetic pull" of the tonal center.

Modulation

Having established a key center, Baroque composers then devised ways of changing it during a recitative or other musical work. Today, listeners are so used to hearing music modulate that they are not aware of how monotonous music would sound without it. Music with no modulations is like a room with beige carpeting, beige draperies, beige walls and ceiling, and beige furniture. Changes of key center, or **modulations**, make music more interesting.

Doctrine of Affections

The distinctive treatment of the words in recitatives and other vocal music illustrates the belief of Baroque composers in projecting the ideas of the text in the music. Called the **doctrine of affections** or **doctrine of affects**, this belief is often evident in Baroque music. Because the type of music associated with particular moods or ideas is often not known by listeners today, this doctrine is largely of historical interest. However, the concept of music expressing the text certainly is not. The doctrine of affections is also reflected in the consistent mood that is maintained throughout an entire section of a work.

HANDEL'S "THE VOICE OF HIM THAT CRIETH IN THE WILDERNESS" FROM *MESSIAH*

The recitative "The Voice of Him That Crieth in the Wilderness" (see Listening Guide) contains all the features of Baroque music discussed thus far, except metrical rhythm. It is for a tenor and appears early in Handel's oratorio *Messiah*, which is presented in the next chapter. It is typical for the following reasons:

- It is very expressive of the text. Notice the treatment of the word *crieth* in the first phrase, the word *straight* in the third phrase, and the word *highway* in the fourth phrase. Listen to how the singer brings out these words.

- It features a single melodic line with accompaniment; it is clearly homophonic in texture. Almost all the musical interest is in the melodic line; while the accompanying part is limited to a few chords.

- Its melody is not very distinctive. The more memorable melodies are found elsewhere in Baroque music.

- The singer sings the rhythm freely, even though it has bar lines and a meter signature.

- It begins with a tonal center, B major.

- It modulates and concludes with a different tonal center, A major, which is firmly established with a V-I cadence in the final two chords of the accompaniment.

- It demonstrates the doctrine of affections by the emphasis it places on words such as *crieth* and *highway*.

GEORGE FRIDERIC HANDEL

"The Voice of Him That Crieth in the Wilderness" from *Messiah* (1741)

LISTENING GUIDE

Genre: Recitative, oratorio

Download 19

27 seconds

0:00	Accompanied by a few chords, the tenor sings:
	The voice of him that crieth in the wilderness,
	Prepare ye the way of the Lord,
0:15	*Make straight in the desert*
	A highway for our God.
0:27	Recitative ends with simple V-I cadence.

LISTEN TO... this selection streaming online.

WATCH... an Active Listening Guide of this selection online.

WATCH... a performance of this selection online.

DO... an online Listening Practice Activity related to this selection, which your instructor may assign for a grade.

FEATURES OF BAROQUE INSTRUMENTAL MUSIC

Tuning

A significant breakthrough was made during the Baroque period in how instruments were tuned, a problem that had plagued musicians since the time of Pythagoras around 555 BC. Pythagoras's discovery of certain basic intervals did not solve the problem of precisely where the intervening notes should be placed. The situation was made much more difficult by a caprice of nature. Theoretically, if you play a series of intervals of a fifth, ascending from a given note, the thirteenth note should duplicate the original pitch. But if the Pythagorean ratio for the fifth is used, and if the fifths are computed upward, the thirteenth note is noticeably higher than it should be! This phenomenon is known as the *Pythagorean comma*.

This pitch problem did not bother singers or string players, because they could easily make slight pitch adjustments to account for it. But it was quite different for keyboard instruments, which have fixed pitches. To get perfect tuning in some keys, people who tuned keyboard instruments had to sacrifice the pitch accuracy in others. Keys with several sharps or flats were therefore usually avoided, because keys with few sharps or flats were normally favored in the tuning process. These tuning complications meant that the only modulations likely on keyboard instruments were those to nearly related keys.

The problem was resolved through a compromise: Make all the intervals slightly off so that the distance between all half steps is equal. The term for this tuning practice is **equal temperament**, and it is the system of tuning still used today. To promote better systems of tuning and to help develop a player's technique for playing in all keys, a few composers, including Bach, wrote a series of pieces in all twenty-four major and minor keys.

Terraced Dynamics

A gradual increase or decrease in dynamic levels was not common in Baroque music. Renaissance composers placed no dynamic markings in their music at all, and Baroque composers wrote very few. Often composers rehearsed and performed their own music, so extensive markings were not necessary. The few indications that are present, however, call for abrupt changes of dynamic level. A *forte*, or loud level, changed suddenly to a *piano*, or soft level, and vice versa. These abrupt changes are called **terraced dynamics**. They were probably made in this way because Baroque artists and musicians were interested in dramatic contrasts. Also, the keyboard instruments of the time could not make gradual changes. The organ and harpsichord could change dynamic levels only by coupling manuals, adding pedals, or pulling out stops.

Continuo

The harmonies in Baroque music became so well standardized that musicians devised a shorthand system called **figured bass** to notate chords. The composer provided a bass line that contained cues in the form of numbers and an occasional sharp, flat, or natural to indicate the parts between the highest and lowest notes. Keyboard players were expected to read these symbols while performing the music, a process called **realization**.

The highest and lowest parts became the two important lines, with the melody being the most important. The bass part provided a foundation to the music. Because it sounded nearly all the time, it came to be known as the **basso continuo** (continuous bass), which for convenience is usually shortened to **continuo**. A cello, gamba, or bassoon usually played the continuo line along with the keyboard player.

The long list of significant changes that occurred in both vocal and instrumental music during the Baroque are evidence of how different it was from the music of the Renaissance. In fact, it requires four more chapters just to provide a useful sample of it.

MAIN POINTS OF CHAPTER 10

PRACTICE...
your understanding of
this chapter's concepts
by working once more
with the chapter's Active
Listening Guide online.

DO...
online quizzes that your
instructor may assign for
a grade.

1. The Baroque style had three predominate characteristics:

   • Grandiose size and concept—The pipe organ, the mightiest instrument of the time, reached the acme of its development.

   • Religious fervor—The result was the creation of some great works of art but also a series of tragic wars.

   • Drama—Three major genres of musical drama developed during that time: oratorio, cantata, and opera.

2. Many Baroque composers worked under a system of patronage in which they were employed exclusively for one person or institution, often a church. Several of them were outstanding performers in addition to being excellent composers. They were also very good at improvising music at the keyboard.

3. Homophony developed during this time, especially in vocal music. The accompanying parts are based on the system of major and minor chords that still prevails in music today. A tonal center was established for a work, but temporary modulations to different keys became common.

4. Rhythm was marked by regular metrical patterns of strong and weak beats.

5. Recitatives were developed to allow the music to express more effectively the words being sung by the singer. Recitatives are sung with flexible rhythm. Usually they are rather short and do not repeat words. Their accompaniments are simple, with occasional places in which they enhance the words being sung.

6. The Doctrine of Affections (or Affects) was the belief in the emotional or affective qualities of music. It is present in vocal music by sometimes linking a melodic pattern to the particular words being sung.

7. Equal temperament was developed for tuning keyboard instruments. It solved an acoustical caprice of nature by making all intervals slightly less than perfect.

8. During the Baroque period harpsichords and pipe organs could not make gradual changes in dynamic levels. Therefore, these changes tended to be abrupt, or what is termed terraced dynamics.

9. The accompanying bass line in much Baroque music usually has a continuous, steady quality. In fact, it was called basso continuo, or, more commonly, continuo.

Oratorio *and* Cantata

11

Learning Objectives

1 Differentiate recitatives, arias, and choruses.
2 Discuss the role of the chorale in worship services.
3 Distinguish oratorios from cantatas.

 START...
experiencing this chapter's topics with an online video activity that your instructor may assign.

 READ...
the complete chapter text in a rich interactive eBook!

Three dramatic genres of music were developed during the Baroque period: oratorio, cantata, and opera. This chapter concentrates on the oratorio and the cantata. Opera is presented in Chapter 12.

ORATORIO

An **oratorio** is a lengthy musical work for voices and orchestra. It consists of many arias, recitatives, and choruses, plus a few sections for the accompanying orchestra. When oratorios first appeared on the musical scene early in the Baroque, they were more like operas on religious topics, complete with scenery, costumes, and actions. Long before the end of the Baroque, however, the stage elements had been discarded, but the idea of drama remained. Soloists still represented specific characters, the text related a story, and the music exploited the dramatic situation. The Old Testament, with its dramatic stories, was an especially rich source for oratorio texts.

Although oratorios are on religious topics, they are not intended for use in worship services. They are too long and require too many performers. Instead, they were created for performance in concert halls or special occasions in churches. Because of the cost of hiring an orchestra, oratorios are usually performed with an organ.

Handel's *Messiah*

Probably the most famous oratorio of all time is *Messiah* by George Frideric Handel. It consists of fifty-three sections: nineteen choruses, sixteen arias, sixteen recitatives, and two sections for orchestra alone. It is typical in terms of its length and distribution of sections. Nearly two and a half hours are required to perform all the music in *Messiah*. Today, conductors usually select which sections they wish to perform.

It is not so typical, however, in that its text is taken entirely from the Bible. Although based on biblical stories, oratorios normally were not confined to scripture. *Messiah* also lacks a role for a narrator, usually a tenor, who relates the story. It is primarily a contemplation on Christian belief in three parts: the prophecy and Christ's birth, his suffering and death, and the Resurrection and Redemption.

Messiah is also atypical in terms of its success with audiences over the more than 270 years since it was written, as evidenced in its many translations into other languages and a multitude of recordings. Word of the new work spread before its premiere. Because only seven hundred people could be squeezed into the hall—even though they stood because the hall had no seats—advertisements requested that ladies avoid wearing dresses with hoops and that men come without swords.

ARIA

In addition to recitative, a second type of music for one singer with accompaniment that developed during the Baroque was the **aria** (AR-ee-ah). They are very different from recitatives in a number of ways.

1. Arias are much longer than recitatives. For example, "Ev'ry Valley Shall Be Exalted" from Handel's *Messiah* is eight times as long as the recitative "The Voice of Him."

2. The accompanying orchestra has a much larger and more important role in the aria. The accompaniments usually have some musically interesting passages, which they often perform without the soloist. The orchestra may also reiterate a figure that the soloist has sung, or it may play musical material of its own.

3. In arias the soloists frequently sing rapidly moving notes or perform long phrases on one word or syllable, a feature that is prominent in "Ev'ry Valley Shall Be Exalted."

4. Although most arias are much longer than recitatives, often their texts are shorter. Arias are usually longer because they often repeat words and phrases, as well as contain passages for the accompanying instruments.

5. The texts of arias dwell on a single idea. Sometimes they are like sung soliloquies that offer reactions to situations. They seldom advance the story by describing an event. The mood of "Ev'ry Valley Shall Be Exalted" is filled with a sense of anticipation.

6. Arias often have a formal pattern, and sections of them are generally repeated. "Ev'ry Valley Shall Be Exalted" follows a binary *A B A B* form.

7. Arias follow the strict metrical rhythm and steady beat found in most Baroque music. Except for unmetered recitatives, Baroque rhythm is very straightforward. Changes of tempo in arias and other works are permitted only near the conclusions of sections in a long work.

8. Composers intended arias to stand on their own musical merits to a much greater extent than recitatives, which often serve mainly to advance the story or to be a bridge between sections. For this reason, they gave arias more memorable melodic and vocal qualities.

"Ev'ry Valley Shall Be Exalted" from *Messiah*

The upbeat mood of "Ev'ry Valley" (see Listening Guide) allowed Handel to write music that shows off the singer's vocal prowess through long series (called **runs** by musicians) of sixteenth notes on the word "exalted":

These runs are examples of the Baroque practice of *virtuoso singing*. A **virtuoso** is someone who has outstanding skill in performing. The word *virtuoso* is not restricted to music. It can also describe performances by very skilled athletes, dancers, and others.

Much attention was given to soloists in the Baroque period. Vocalists competed with one another for the favor of audiences by adding flashy runs and ornaments to the music. This custom grew until the music became merely a framework for soloists to build on as they wished. Some astonishing singing skill was the result, but the quality of the music often suffered. Although the situation had been somewhat moderated by Handel's time, the virtuoso style was still very much alive, and audiences expected to hear some vocal displays.

In "Ev'ry Valley" the runs do more than show off the skill of the singer. Handel integrates them into the overall musical fabric so that they enhance the effect of the music and emphasize the message of the words.

GEORGE FRIDERIC HANDEL
"Ev'ry Valley Shall Be Exalted" from *Messiah* (1741)

Genre: Aria, oratorio

Form: *A B A B*

Download 20

3 minutes 40 seconds

0:00   The orchestra plays a *ritornello* (refrain).

0:22   The tenor soloist sings "Ev'ry valley shall be exalted" (A).

0:35   First long run on "exalted."

0:50   Second long run on "exalted."

0:58   Aria continues "and ev'ry mountain and hill made low."

1:04   *B* portion begins with "the crooked straight" and continues with "and the rough places plain."

1:45   *A* returns with some changes.

2:28   *B* returns with some changes.

2:58   Tempo slows, and some decorative notes are added.

3:17   The orchestra repeats the ritornello.

LISTEN TO... this selection streaming online.

WATCH... an Active Listening Guide of this selection online.

WATCH... a performance of this selection online.

DO... an online Listening Practice Activity related to this selection, which your instructor may assign for a grade.

LISTENING GUIDE

The text of "Ev'ry Valley" says basically that things are going to be turned upside down when the Messiah comes. The valleys will be raised up—they will be exalted. By having the soloist sing long runs on "exalted," Handel emphasizes that thought.

Virtuoso passages in Baroque vocal music are sometimes baffling to people who are not familiar with them. At first glance, it is difficult to understand why one syllable or word is stretched out over forty or more notes. "Exalted" could be sung with just three notes, of course. In everyday practical terms, it seems pointless to use forty notes to sing one syllable or word. But the music would not have nearly so much impact and interest. It is impressive to hear a skilled singer execute long runs and to hear them fit so well into the music.

Handel follows the doctrine of affections in the aria as well as the chorus. The words "The crooked straight" are set to pitches that rock back and forth one step apart, except the word "straight," which is a steady long note. The word "mountain" is high, and the word "low" is low. The word "plain" is set in a sequence of smooth planes.

What is it about the arias from Handel's *Messiah* that motivates people to listen to them hundreds of years after they were written? They feature several exceptional qualities:

- They demonstrate the expressive impact when words and music are combined so skillfully. When a sensitive recitative or a tender aria is sung well, the music has much expressive power.

- They exhibit the virtuoso techniques of a good singer. Hearing a virtuoso singer executing the difficult or showy passages of an aria is similar to watching a champion figure skater flawlessly execute a difficult routine.

- They contain the qualities of Baroque music that help it "wear well" with listeners.

CHORUS

The word **chorus** has two meanings in music. One is a group that sings choral music. The other meaning refers to the choral sections of a large choral work such as an oratorio. So a chorus sings a chorus.

Choruses can vary a lot in size. They can have as few as sixteen singers, although that is unusual, or they can have several hundred singers, but that also is unusual. More typical is that they contain approximately an equal number of men and women, unless they are specifically limited to men or women. The choruses that sang Handel's *Messiah* during his lifetime were definitely on the small side; only eighteen singers made up the chorus at its premiere performance.

The following are characteristics of choruses in Baroque choral works:

- They are somewhat lengthy and often repeat words.

- The rhythm is strictly adhered to, unlike what happens in recitatives.

- The accompanying part plays an important role.

- The music for choruses normally requires more than average singing skill. In fact, some of them are quite challenging and contain virtuoso-like passages.

- They are often contrapuntal. The various sections often enter in imitation.

"Hallelujah Chorus" from *Messiah*

The "Hallelujah Chorus" (see Listening Guide) is familiar to most people and is traditionally performed at Christmas. In fact, at the first performance of *Messiah* in London, King George II was so impressed when he heard the "Hallelujah Chorus" that he stood up. In those days, when the king stood, everyone stood. King George's spontaneous action started a tradition that is still honored today.

George Frideric Handel

Lebrecht/The Image Works

George Frideric Handel (1685–1759) was a German by birth, born in the city of Halle, in Saxony, to a well-to-do barber-surgeon who never wanted his son to pursue music as a career. Young George showed talent in composing and playing the harpsichord and organ. His father's early death removed the obstacle to pursuing a career in music. After a year of college, he went to Hamburg, where he got a job playing in an orchestra.

Handel soon moved to Italy, which was the center for music at that time. He studied composition and culti-vated friendships with music patrons. At the age of twenty-five, he returned to Germany as music director of the Electoral Court at Hanover. In two years he managed to take two leaves of absence to go to London, where his operas (in Italian) were very successful. He was in London when the elector of Hanover was proclaimed King George I of England.

Handel stayed in London for the remainder of his life. For eight years he held an important position as director of the Royal Academy of Music, which was founded to present Italian opera. The job was not an easy one. The musicians were temperamental and engaged in much infighting, and the situation was not helped by Handel's stubborn and over-bearing personality. One hair-pulling and shouting fight between singers took place at a performance when Princess Caroline (for whom North and South Carolina were named) was in the audience.

In time, another type of musical the-ater became fashionable with English audiences. Called *beggar's opera*, it was more like a play with politically satirical songs inserted. Handel refused to aban-don his Italian operas, however. After nine more years of writing and losing money in that endeavor, his health broke, and he was heavily in debt. He went abroad to recover.

And recover he did. After a few more futile tries at reviving Italian opera, he turned to oratorios. Within a few years, he was again at the top of the English musical world. He wrote more than twenty-six oratorios, but none is heard as often today as *Messiah*. Handel composed this monumental work in 1741 in a little more than three weeks! He worked at it almost constantly and paid little atten-tion to the meals servants left at his door. Its first performance was a benefit concert in Dublin, Ireland. It was a tremendous success, although later performances in London were received more coolly.

In 1759 Handel collapsed after con-ducting a performance of *Messiah*. He died eight days later and was interred with state honors in Westminster Abbey.

Best-Known Works

Oratorios
- *Messiah*
- *Israel in Egypt*
- *Samson*
- *Saul*

Operas
- *Acis and Galatea*
- *Giulio Cesare (Julius Caesar)*
- *Semele*
- *Hercules*

Instrumental suites
- *Water Music*
- *Fireworks Music*

As you listen to this chorus, notice how skillfully Handel has placed the words in terms of their rhythmic emphasis. The word *Hallelujah* is written as one would say it when really pleased. In phrases such as "and He shall reign forever and ever," the impor-tant words in the phrase land on the important beats and parts of the beats in the rhythm pattern. The important words in the phrase are *He, reign,* and *ev-* of *forever,* because it is

LISTENING GUIDE

GEORGE FRIDERIC HANDEL
"Hallelujah Chorus" from *Messiah* (1741)

Genre: Chorus, oratorio

Download 21

3 minutes 37 seconds

0:00   Orchestra plays a short introduction.

0:06   Chorus sings "Hallelujah" five times, then five more times at a different pitch level.

0:24   Chorus sings "for the Lord God Omnipotent reigneth," followed by four "Hallelujahs."

0:35   Altos, tenors, and basses repeat "for the Lord God ...," followed by four "Hallelujahs."

0:46   Sopranos sing "for the Lord God ...," with chorus singing "Hallelujah" in counterpoint.

0:53   Tenors and basses sing "for the Lord God ..." while sopranos and altos sing contrasting "Hallelujahs."

1:02   Altos and tenors sing "for the Lord God ..." while sopranos and basses sing contrapuntal "Hallelujahs."

1:12   Chorus sings together "The kingdom of this world is become the Kingdom of our Lord and of His Christ."

1:30   Basses begin new melodic phrase and text, "and He shall reign forever and ever," followed in imitation by tenors, altos, and sopranos.

1:52   Sopranos and altos sing alternately "King of Kings" and "Lord of Lords" while basses and tenors sing "forever and ever, Hallelujah." Same pattern repeated four times, each time at a higher pitch level.

2:33   Basses begin "and He shall reign ..." as other sections sing contrasting material.

2:44   Tenors sing "King of Kings" and "Lord of Lords" while other sections respond with "forever and ever" and "Hallelujah."

2:53   Chorus sings together, with basses singing "and He shall reign ...,"

3:00   "King of Kings" sung again.

3:09   "And He shall reign ..." sung again.

3:25   "Hallelujah Chorus" ends after four "Hallelujahs" and one long final "Hallelujah."

LISTEN TO... this selection streaming online.

WATCH... an Active Listening Guide of this selection online.

WATCH... a performance of another outstanding chorus online.

DO... an online Listening Practice Activity related to this selection, which your instructor may assign for a grade.

the emphasized syllable in that word. It would be much more difficult to sing the phrase, "*and* he *shall* reign *for-ev-er*," and it would sound awkward and unmusical. To realize how important the placement of emphasis in words is, try saying "Hallelujah" in different ways: "*HAL-le-lu-*jah," "Ha-*le-*lu-*JAH*," and so on. Handel's success in matching words and music is especially interesting because he never learned to speak English well after emigrating from Germany in his late twenties.

Handel did a lot of things right in the "Hallelujah Chorus" in addition to matching words and music so well. In the first part, he contrasts quick "Hallelujahs" with the steady, solid-sounding "For the Lord God Omnipotent reigneth." He uses text painting when he has the first four notes of that phrase ascend by step up to the word "God." In the middle section, the words "The Kingdom of the world" are sung softly at a low pitch level. Then they become much louder and higher as the words progress: "is become of the Kingdom of our Lord …." At one point in the third section, he builds on the words "King of Kings, and Lord of Lords" by repeating them several times in succession, each time at a higher level of pitch. Finally, the trumpets enter to bolster the dramatic impact of the music at that point. Especially important is the sense of power and grandeur that this chorus conveys.

CHORALE

The chorale was a product of early Protestant belief and practice in the sixteenth century, when Martin Luther's break from the Roman Catholic Church became final. Luther and some of his colleagues set about providing music suitable for worship in the newly developed services. They wanted the members of the congregation to be partici-pants in the service, not just observers.

One way to involve them was to have them sing. But what should they sing? Chant was associated too strongly with the rejected Roman Catholic Church. Also, its style and subtleties are difficult for untrained singers to perform properly. The answer was to create a new body of religious music that had strong, simple melodies. So from German religious songs, from adaptations of chant and secular tunes, and from the pen of Luther himself and others came the **chorale** (cor-AL), which is basically a German Lutheran hymn. It is very likely that Luther himself composed the words and music for the chorale "A Mighty Fortress Is Our God."

Luther believed not only that worshipers should sing, but also that their music should encourage the proper religious attitude. So the purposes of the chorale were to proclaim beliefs and contribute to the spirit of worship. The Protestant attitudes of that time are clearly expressed in "A Mighty Fortress Is Our God." Here is a translation of one of its verses:

> *Though devils all the world should fill,*
> *All eager to devour us;*
> *We tremble not, we fear no ill,*
> *They shall not overpower us.*

As his metaphor for God, Luther chose the German word *Burg*, a medieval stone fortress, a symbol of austere strength. The chorale reflects the serious religious outlook of the early Protestants. Each note in its melody stands like a block of stone in a fortress.

What are the significant characteristics of a chorale?

- It has a regular, steady rhythm.
- It is in German or other vernacular language.
- It has several verses of words for the same melody.
- It can be accompanied by organ or other instrument.

On first hearing, a chorale, like Gregorian chant, may seem dull. It's true; both lack novelty and flashiness. But religious music seeks to express what the faithful believe to be the ultimate and eternal. Theological beliefs and the music need to be congruent, with one reflecting the other. Furthermore, both the chorale and the chant provide devout worshipers with a sense of communion with believers who have gone before, as well as suggest the timeless nature of their beliefs.

CANTATA

Because of their strong, simple qualities, chorale melodies are well suited for use as themes for other musical works. These melodies are often found in cantatas. Originally, the word **cantata** meant any sizable work, sacred or secular, that was sung. By the time of Johann Sebastian Bach (1685–1750), the cantata had become a short oratorio, with an instrumental accompaniment, arias, recitatives, and choruses. A cantata is much shorter than an oratorio, and it is written to be performed in a worship service. A cantata typically has between five and eight sections and incorporates a chorale melody into some of its sections. It often ends with the chorale on which it is based.

There was plenty of time in worship services at Bach's church in Leipzig, Germany (Figure 11.1), for a twenty-minute cantata. The main service began at 7 am and could last until noon! There were also three other short services on Sunday, as well as daily services and special religious celebrations. Altogether, Leipzig's Lutheran churches required fifty-eight cantatas each year, as well as other types of music for special occasions. Bach composed about one cantata per month during most of his time in Leipzig. About two hundred of the three hundred cantatas he composed have been preserved.

Bach's Cantata No. 140

One of Bach's best-known cantatas is *Wachet auf, ruft uns die Stimme* (*Wake Up, Call the Voices*), Cantata No. 140. It was written for the Sunday before Advent, which is four Sundays before Christmas. The text, based on Matthew 25:1–13, tells the parable of the five wise and five foolish maidens. The cantata had this message for the congregation: Be prepared and vigilant, because you never know when you will be called to be with God.

FIGURE 11.1

THE INTERIOR OF ST. THOMAS IN LEIPZIG, WHERE BACH SERVED THE LAST TWENTY-SEVEN YEARS OF HIS LIFE.

Michael DeFreitas/Robert Harding World Imagery/Getty Images

Cantata No. 140 is divided into seven sections. The chorale melody appears in the first, fourth, and seventh sections. The first section is the longest and most complex. It is a chorus that features the driving, uneven rhythm of dotted-eighths and sixteenths played against a contrasting part. The chorale melody appears in long notes in the soprano part. As these notes are sung, the alto, tenor, and bass parts sing contrasting musical lines.

This chorus illustrates the interest of Baroque composers in the doctrine of affections. For example, in Bach's cantata the words *wach' auf* (wake up), *wohl auf* (cheer up), and *steht auf* (get up or arise) are sung to notes that move from lower to higher pitches.

The second section of Cantata No. 140 is a recitative for tenor. It sets forth the image of Christ as the Heavenly Bridegroom and tells about his coming. Many cantatas use the analogy of Christ as the groom and the Church as his bride.

The third section is a duet between an anxious soul (sung by the soprano soloist) and Jesus (sung by the bass soloist). This section also features a florid violin solo.

JOHANN SEBASTIAN BACH
Chorale (Section 7) from Cantata No. 140 (melody c. 1600; harmonized 1731)

LISTENING GUIDE

Genre: Chorale, cantata

Download 22

1 minute 23 seconds

0:00 | *Gloria sei dir gesungen* | Glory now be sung to praise Thee
mit Menschen und englischen Zungen, | with tongues of all mankind and angels,
mit Harfen und mit Zimbeln schon. | with harps and cymbals sounding forth.

(continued)

0:24	*Von zwölf Perlen sind die Pforten*	Of twelve pearls are built the portals of
	an deiner Stadt; wir sind Konsorten	thy fair city, we have joined hosts of
	der Engel hoch um deinen Thron.	angels high around thy throne.
0:47	*Kein Aug' hat je gespürt,*	No eye hath ever seen,
	kein Ohr hat je gehört	no ear hath ever heard
	solche Freude.	such wondrous joy.
	Dess sind wir froh,	Thus we rejoice,
	Io, io!	io, io!
	ewig in dulci jubilo.	for evermore in sweetest praise.
1:20	Chorale concludes.	

 LISTEN TO... this selection streaming online.

 WATCH... an Active Listening Guide of this selection online.

 DO... an online Listening Practice Activity related to this selection, which your instructor may assign for a grade.

In the fourth section, "Zion Hears the Watchmen" (see Listening Guide), a gentle melody is played by the strings while the tenor section in unison sings the chorale melody.

The fifth section is a recitative for bass in which Jesus tenderly greets the bride.

The sixth section is a duet between the soprano (the soul) and the bass (Jesus).

The seventh and final section of Cantata No. 140 (see Listening Guide for Section 7) is a harmonization of the chorale melody in which the worshipers praise God and rejoice. It was customary for the congregation to join in singing the final chorale. The chorales were familiar to the congregation and were sung in their native language. The chorale melody appears in the soprano (top part in the treble clef). Bach did not compose the melody. He added the alto, tenor, and bass parts to complete the harmony.

The idea of chorale singing by the congregation was also influenced by the educational level of the worshipers. Many people in the Baroque period could not read or write, so pictures, statues, and music in churches were intended to be educational as well as beautiful. A text for a chorale was selected for reasons of instruction as well as worship.

OTHER TYPES OF BAROQUE VOCAL MUSIC

The cantata is only one of several types of vocal music composed for Protestant worship services in the Baroque period. Another type is the **passion**, which is like an oratorio except that its subject is the suffering of Christ on the cross. Bach's *St. Matthew Passion* was rediscovered and performed seventy-nine years after his death, and that performance renewed interest in other music by Bach. Like the cantatas, the *St. Matthew Passion* gives a prominent place to a chorale, "O Sacred Head Now Wounded."

There is also a Baroque motet. It is an unaccompanied, religious, and polyphonic work. In the Baroque, however, the music had a strong sense of metrical rhythm and systematic harmony. It was also written in a vernacular language.

JOHANN SEBASTIAN BACH

"Zion Hears the Watchmen" (Section 4) from Cantata No. 140 (1731)

Genre: Cantata

Download 23

4 minutes 15 seconds

0:00   Upper strings play a flowing melody above a steady bass:

Violins, Violas

0:43   Tenors sing the first three phrases of the chorale in unison.

Zion hört die Wächter singen,   Zion hears the watchmen calling,
das Herz thut ihr vor Freuden springen, her heart within her leaps for gladness,
sie wachet, und steht eilend auf,   she wakes and stands to hasten forth,

1:11   The flowing melody is repeated by upper strings.

1:52   The first three phrases of the chorale are repeated, but with different words.

Ihr Freund kommt vom Himmel prächtig,   Her friend comes from Heaven in splendor,
Von Gnaden stark, von Wahrheit mächtig, In mercy strong, in truth almighty,
Ihr Licht wird hell, ihr Stern geht auf. Her light grows bright, her star appears.

2:22   The flowing melody is repeated by upper strings.

2:47   The fourth, fifth, and sixth phrases of the chorale are sung.

Nun komm, du werthe Kron',   Now come, thou precious crown,
Herr Jesu, Gottes Sohn,   Lord Jesus, God's Son,
Hosianna!   Hosanna!

3:10   The flowing melody continues, but in minor.

3:28   The seventh and eighth phrases of the chorale are sung.

Wir folgen all' zum Freudensaal,   We follow all to the festive hall,
und halten mit das Abendmahl.   and share in our Lord's Supper there.

3:55   Orchestra repeats some of the opening music.

LISTEN TO... this selection streaming online.

WATCH... an Active Listening Guide of this selection online.

WATCH... a performance of this selection online.

DO... an online Listening Practice Activity related to this selection, which your instructor may assign for a grade.

MAIN POINTS OF CHAPTER 11

PRACTICE...

your understanding of this chapter's concepts by working once more with the chapter's Active Listening Guides online.

DO...

online quizzes that your instructor may assign for a grade.

1. An oratorio is a lengthy work for soloists, chorus, and orchestra. Its many sections are divided into recitatives, arias, and choruses, with an occasional work for orchestra alone. Although their stories are dramatic, often drawn from the Old Testament, oratorios are performed without scenery, costumes, or actions.

2. Arias are sizable vocal solos accompanied by an orchestra. They are much more melodic than recitatives and repeat lines of text. Often their texts are reflective; they do not necessarily advance the story. They usually follow a form, with A B A being the most common one.

3. Arias often contain virtuoso passages that show off the singer's ability. These passages of rapidly moving notes add to the musical impact of an aria.

4. A chorus is sung by a chorus. It has many of the features found in an aria, but is sung by a group of singers. It is also different in that it often contains imitation among the voice parts.

5. A chorale is a Lutheran hymn. It features a strong, simple melody that was created to be sung by the congregation. These melodies were used many times as themes in other Baroque works such as cantatas and organ music.

6. In one sense, a cantata is a short oratorio. It is different in that it uses a chorale melody in some of its parts. Cantatas were composed to be performed during worship services, and they usually contain a religious message.

Opera *in the* Baroque

12

Learning Objectives

1 Outline the various elements of opera.
2 Discuss the artistic conventions found in operas.
3 List some reasons why operas are a pleasure to see and hear.
4 Trace the elements of opera at work in two Baroque operas.

START...

experiencing this chapter's topics with an online video activity that your instructor may assign.

Drama was one of the main features of Baroque style. The carefully planned figures in Renaissance paintings were replaced with twisting lines and energetic poses, and restrained polyphonic motets and madrigals gave way to recitatives and arias that projected emotion and feelings. The goals of artists and composers had changed—dramatically.

Opera was one result of the desire to make music more expressive. It was founded as an attempt to re-create the dramas of ancient Greece. Around 1600 a group of noblemen in Florence, Italy, believed that a single line of melody with simple accompaniment would be much more expressive of the words. The result was the development of recitative, which was presented in Chapter 10. In fact, the earliest operas consisted almost entirely of recitatives.

READ...

the complete chapter text in a rich interactive eBook!

But do audiences enjoy listening to a couple of hours of nothing but one recitative after another? Soon composers began to realize that the answer to that question was no. Something more was needed. By the time the first opera house opened in Venice in 1637, the artistic goal of a musical version of ancient Greek drama had been largely forgotten. The stories became burdened by the addition of irrelevant incidents, spectacular scenes, and incongruous comedy episodes. But other changes were more constructive. Arias, duets, and ensembles evolved, and the accompanying orchestra took on more importance.

As opera spread throughout Europe, its dramatic elements were largely absent. The singers reigned supreme. In their desire to hold the attention of the audience, soloists added all sorts of embellishments to a melody to show off their singing prowess.

Although opera was a child of the Baroque, the operas of that period are not often performed today in opera houses in Europe or America. The reason is not that the Baroque operas lack musical merit but that opera companies can produce only a limited number of operas, and subsequent operas have found greater favor with audiences. Nevertheless, the operas of a few Baroque composers stand out, especially those of Claudio Monteverdi and Henry Purcell, which are presented later in this chapter.

THE ELEMENTS OF OPERA

Each element in the amalgam that is opera makes a particular contribution, and each merits further discussion, beginning with singers and their voice ranges and types.

Voices and Roles

Opera has acquired a number of traditions regarding the types of voices and characters portrayed. The heroine is almost always a soprano. In most operas, she is young

B. Rafferty/Lebrecht/The Image Works

FIGURE 12.1
TENOR NIGEL ROBSON AND
SOPRANO MARIE ANGEL
PERFORM IN AN OPERA FACTORY
PRODUCTION OF MONTEVERDI'S
THE CORONATION OF POPPEA.

and beautiful, so a high, lighter voice is appropriate. Often the heroine's part calls for virtuoso singing. Some female parts are written for lower or heavier voices such as mezzo-soprano or contralto. These roles often portray older women, servants, rivals, or villainesses.

The leading male role is often for a tenor (Figure 12.1). He is young and frequently sings duets with the leading soprano, often doubling her pitches one octave lower. This puts his notes near the top of the male voice range and gives the singing more brilliance. Other male parts may be sung by a baritone, a voice that is lower and heavier than the tenor. The bass, which is the lowest and heaviest male voice, is often used to portray villains, older men, or authority figures such as kings. In Western civilization there seems to be an association in people's minds between age and the pitch level of the voice: the older a person is, the lower the voice.

The vocal and dramatic demands for singing operatic roles are great. Almost all roles require extensive training in the use of the voice to achieve the necessary breath control, endurance, wide pitch range, richness of tone quality, control of dynamic levels, and technical know-how, not to mention the ability to project the singing over an orchestra all the way to the last row of the balcony. This fact is important because operas are usually performed without amplification.

Not only do opera singers sing, but they must also be actors in a drama. They must make their efforts sound and look convincing, sometimes as they sing difficult music.

Ensembles

Most operas have parts for small ensembles and choruses. **Ensembles** frequently consist of several characters singing different words and music expressing their particular feelings, creating a kind of musical and emotional counterpoint.

Operatic choruses usually appear in scenes with many people—a wedding, a coronation, a crowded tavern. To a degree, the chorus participates in the stage action, but usually from behind the soloists. Often the words the chorus sings are a commentary on the situation.

The Orchestra

The orchestra is placed largely out of sight in a pit in front of the stage. Although unseen, it has an important role in opera. Not only does the orchestra accompany the singers, it also sets moods, enhances the actions onstage, and performs overtures and preludes while the curtain is closed. The orchestral music written for operas by some nineteenth-century composers is so complete that today portions of it are frequently performed as concert works without any singing at all.

The Libretto

The script or text of an opera is called the *libretto*, which means "little book" in Italian.

The composer of the music usually does not write the libretto for the opera. Instead, a librettist generally creates a version of a play, historical event, or story. Often the libretto is set in poetic form, especially the portions that are likely places for arias or choruses. Once the libretto has been written, the composer takes over and sets the words to music.

Staging

Visual elements are an integral part of opera. The quality of acting, costumes, scenic design, lighting, and dancing makes a great difference in the success of an opera. The lighting and stage effects that can be achieved in a first-rate opera house are truly amazing and at times dazzling. For example, if a character is to be demolished in smoke and fire, this can be done in quite a convincing and dramatic way.

The need for set designers, costumers, electricians, and stagehands in addition to singers, orchestral musicians, and sometimes dancers is one of opera's greatest obstacles: It is a very expensive art form. A large opera can require the services of a hundred highly skilled technicians and instrumentalists, who often are paid more than most of the performers. These requirements are reflected in the high ticket prices and the chronic financial problems of opera companies. A lack of funds also discourages touring by opera companies and presentations of new operas.

One recent positive development in making opera more available and less expensive is the projection of performances on large screens in theaters and auditoriums. Not only do these performances cost operagoers a fraction of live performances, they also provide close-up shots of the singers and actions on stage. The sound is sometimes clearer than at a live performance, depending on one's seat, of course. Although they lack the sense of presence that live performances provide, they are an excellent next-best choice.

The fact that opera is still active and vital in American musical life, in spite of its high costs and lack of familiarity to much of the population, is eloquent testimony to its musical and dramatic value.

OPERATIC CONVENTIONS

All forms of theater have conventions and customs that audiences accept. For example, in films an orchestra is often heard in the background, adding to the suspense as an actor is about to be attacked in a dark, deserted house. What's an orchestra doing there? No one wonders about that, because viewers are accustomed to the convention of background music. Nor is anyone bothered when a scene changes in a few seconds to one that supposedly occurs hours or even years later, or that the stage in a theater is like a room with one wall removed so that the audience can see what's taking place.

The reason people are not bothered by these conventions is simple: They are used to them. On the other hand, most people are not familiar with operatic customs, and so such customs often hinder their enjoyment.

All Singing

What are the more obvious conventions associated with opera? One is the replacement of speaking with singing. In everyday life a phrase such as "Robert will be here at three o'clock" is spoken. Furthermore, sometimes rather robust singing takes place when logically it does not make a lot of sense—such as when a character is dying or very sick.

Style of Singing

Not only are all the words sung but they are also sung in a highly trained style, which is another operatic convention. Most operas have a "bigger than life" quality about them, and that is one of their attractive features. The style of singing, therefore, needs to be bigger than life. It must have enough power to be heard over an orchestra in a large hall, and it should have a quality that moves listeners emotionally. Folk singers can sing their ballads in a simple, unaffected style because they usually perform in a small room accompanied by a guitar, and even then their singing is often amplified. Neither singing style is more musical than the other, because each is appropriate for a particular type of music and setting.

Foreign Languages

Another convention concerns the words. Even when sung in English, they are not easily understood. The problem is increased by the large number of operas in foreign languages. These operas can be translated and sung in English, but should they be?

Claudio Monteverdi

Portrait of Claudio Monteverdi (1567-1643) (oil on canvas), Fetti or Feti, Domenico (1589-1624) / Galleria dell' Accademia, Venice, Italy/Cameraphoto Arte Venezia/The Bridgeman Art Library

Claudio Monteverdi (1567–1643) was the most influential composer of the early Baroque period. He was born in Cremona, Italy, which was famous for its violin makers, and his early musical training included learning to play the violin. His father was a chemist/physician who wanted his son to have a good education in music. Monteverdi was first employed as a court musician at Mantua and later was appointed to be in charge of the music there. He left when the duke failed to pay him some of the wages due him. At the age of forty-five, he was awarded the coveted position as music master at Saint Mark's in Venice.

Monteverdi began writing madrigals in the Renaissance, but slowly his madrigals began to change. Instrumental parts were added, and they became more homophonic in texture. In a real sense, he bridged the Renaissance and Baroque periods and helped bring about major changes in music.

Although his position in Venice was to produce music for the Church, he never stopped composing operas. *L'Orfeo* (*Orpheus*), written in 1607, was his first successful opera and one of the most important in the development of Western music. *L'incoronazione di Poppea* (*The Coronation of Poppea*), composed in 1642, was his last. He was very effective in injecting emotional qualities into his music. He was also probably the first composer to ask the violinists for effects such as *tremolo* (rapidly moving the bow back and forth on the string) and vibrato to add warmth to the tone quality.

Best-Known Works

Opera
- *Combattimento di Tancredi et Clorinda*
- *L'incoronazione di Poppea*
- *L'Orfeo*

Although translations are not easy, involving correct numbers of syllables, natural accents, shades of meaning, and rhyme schemes, the answer is probably yes, at least for people who are not familiar with opera. When operas are sung in languages other than English, listeners need to follow a translation or observe the words projected in English, if available. Actually, it is almost impossible to translate the lines of an opera without losing some of the original meaning.

Amount of Time

A fourth convention involves the element of time. In addition to the usual flexibility in the treatment of time in films and dramas, operas have to deal with the impact of singing on the amount of time available. If the words "Robert will be here at three o'clock" are spoken, they don't require much time. If those words were set to a nice melody, however, they would take much more time. The difference would be some pleasant music, but an interruption of the story. If the words were to be sung in about the same amount of time as when spoken, they would not be of much musical interest.

Operagoers accept the distortions of time caused by the addition of the music because of the heightened overall musical and dramatic impact. The increased impact of music on words can be demonstrated by reading the words of an aria or a chorus aloud and then hearing those same words as they have been set to music by a great composer.

ENJOYING OPERA

When the conventions of opera are accepted, most people find that they enjoy attending an opera. This is true for several reasons:

- The music is often stunning and beautiful. Operas offer listeners a rich source of flowing melodies, impressive tonal effects, and sensuous harmonies. In addition, there is a great deal of outstanding singing.
- The combined expressiveness of words and music is a pleasure to hear. Opera sets up situations in which the combination of the two can have even greater emotional impact than music apart from the dramatic situation. While the singing of the text may slow down the action on stage, it adds much to the overall drama. Some operatic I-love-yous, for example, can cause chills to run up one's spine.
- Opera appeals to both the ears and the eyes. Looking at an opera without hearing the music is an incomplete experience, just as it would be when listening to the music without seeing what takes place onstage.
- Opera lets people see and hear experiences that are beyond ordinary life. For some rather deep-seated psychological reasons, people enjoy stories, films, television shows, and the like that take them temporarily out of their own everyday existence. In soap operas, for example, the actors undergo traumatic experiences with a frequency and an intensity that (fortunately) far exceed what most people encounter in their lives. Soap operas were given that name because originally they were often sponsored by soap companies, and also because the characters' lives are much more crisis-ridden than those of ordinary people.

MONTEVERDI'S *THE CORONATION OF POPPEA*

Monteverdi was the most important composer of the early Baroque, and especially of opera. His last opera was *The Coronation of Poppea* (*L'incoronazione di Poppea*). The story is based very loosely on the Roman emperor Nero, who reigned from AD 54 to 68 and who is remembered throughout history for fiddling while Rome burned. He was a weak, vain man who pursued many women. Poppea knew how to play up to Nero's passions, and by careful scheming she was able to dispose of his wife so that Nero would marry her and make her empress.

The plot of Monteverdi's opera is characterized by much intrigue among the characters. Poppea is spared from an assassin by the intervention of the god Cupid, and she achieves her goal of becoming empress of the Roman Empire. Poppea's success in real life was actually short-lived. She was murdered, possibly by Nero himself, after only a few years as empress.

Many characteristics of recitative can be heard in a portion of Monteverdi's *The Coronation of Poppea* (see Listening Guide). In the excerpt presented here, dawn has just broken, and the scheming Poppea, having enticed Nero to spend the night with her, tries to delay his departure as long as possible and make him promise to return. Several times she sings the word "Tornerai?" ("Won't you return?") in a seductive way. Notice how the singers' lines follow the natural rise and fall and changes of speed and inflection as the words would if spoken. The recitative style is broken only by a short solo in which Nero sings passionately that he cannot live without her.

CLAUDIO MONTEVERDI

Recitative from *The Coronation of Poppea,* Act I, Scene 1 (1642)

LISTENING GUIDE

Genre: Recitative duet, opera

Download 24

2 minutes 44 seconds

0:00	**POPPEA:** *Tornerai?*		Won't you return?
	NERO: *Se ben io vò*		I leave you only
	Pur teco io stò, pur teco stò . . .		to be with you all the more . . .
	POPPEA: *Tornerai?*		Won't you return?
	NERO: *Il cor dalle tue stella*		My heart can never be torn away
	Mai mai non se divelle . . .		from your beautiful eyes . . .
	POPPEA: *Tornerai?*		Won't you return?
0:32	**NERO:** *Io non posso da te, non posso da te*		I can never really live away from you
	da te viver disgiunto		
	Se non si smembra la unità del punto . . .		no more than a soul can be severed from itself . . .
	(Line repeated)		
1:03	**POPPEA:** *Tornerai?*		Won't you return?
	NERO: *Tornerò.*		I will return.
	POPPEA: *Quando?*		When?
	NERO: *Ben tosto.*		Very soon.
	POPPEA: *Ben tosto, me'l prometti?*		Very soon, you promise?
	NERO: *Te'l giuro.*		I swear it.

1:18   **POPPEA:** *E me l'osserverai?*   And you will keep your promise?

            NERO: *E s'a te no verrò, tu a me verrai!*   If I do not come, you'll come to me!

(Two lines repeated)

            POPPEA: *Addio...*   Goodbye...

            NERO: *Addio...*   Goodbye...

            POPPEA: *...Nerone, Nerone, addio...*   ...Nero, Nero, goodbye...

            NERO: *...Poppea, Poppea, addio...*   ...Poppea, Poppea, goodbye...

            POPPEA: Addio, Nerone, addio!   Goodbye, Nero, goodbye!

            NERO: *Addio, Poppea, addio!*   Goodbye, Poppea, goodbye!

 LISTEN TO... this selection streaming online.

 WATCH... an Active Listening Guide of this selection online.

 WATCH... a performance of another part of this opera online.

 DO... an online Listening Practice Activity related to this selection, which your instructor may assign for a grade.

PURCELL'S *DIDO AND AENEAS*

Purcell composed *Dido and Aeneas* for a private girls' school in Chelsea, outside London. The story comes from Virgil's *Aeneid*, one of the masterpieces of classical Latin literature. Aeneas, the hero of Troy, is fleeing from his conquered homeland. He sets sail to found the city of Rome but is blown off course onto the shores of Carthage, where Dido is the widowed queen. They meet and fall in love, but soon the gods order Aeneas to continue on to found Rome. Feeling very alone and betrayed, Dido expresses her feelings in the tender and beautiful aria "When I am laid in earth," which is often called "Dido's Lament" (see Listening Guide). Dido and her servant, Belinda, are alone onstage, and only Dido sings.

The term **ostinato** comes from the Italian word for stubborn, and indeed ostinatos are persistently repeated musical phrases. Dido sings her moving melody over the ostinato, and the combination gives the aria the qualities of both unity and variety.

Notice that Dido's phrases are incomplete, as though she were consumed in her thoughts. The exclamation "ah" is sung four times in the aria on a major chord but is followed by a minor chord, as if it cannot shake the shadow of death. Six times she asks to be remembered. She dies as the orchestra plays its closing appearances of the ground bass.

LISTENING GUIDE

HENRY PURCELL
"Dido's Lament" from *Dido and Aeneas* (1689)

Genre: Recitative and aria, opera

Download 25

4 minutes 30 seconds

0:00   Music opens with a short recitative accompanied by lute and low strings. Dido sings, "Thy hand, Belinda! Darkness shades me; on thy bosom let me rest. More I would—but Death invades me: Death is now a welcome guest."

0:47   Lute plays the basso ostinato (ground bass).

1:01   Strings join ground bass. Dido sings, "When I am laid in earth, may my wrongs create no trouble in thy breast. Remember me, but ah! forget my fate."

1:21   Ground bass continues appearing seven more times as words of aria are sung.

3:45   Instruments play final two appearances of ground bass.

LISTEN TO... this selection streaming online.

WATCH... an Active Listening Guide of this selection online.

WATCH... a performance of this selection online.

DO... an online Listening Practice Activity related to this selection, which your instructor may assign for a grade.

Henry Purcell

Henry Purcell (c. 1659–1695) was born and lived in England. Despite his short life, he composed an enormous amount of excellent music. Trained as a choirboy, he began composing when he was eight. His voice changed early, so he worked as an assistant in caring for the king's keyboard and wind instruments. He was later appointed organist at Westminster Abbey and composed much music. He probably died of pneumonia. Purcell was buried in Westminster Abbey in recognition of his great contributions to English music.

Purcell was especially adept at writing music for the stage. Although *Dido and Aeneas* was his only true opera, he composed a number of works that combined spoken words with music, as well as music for royal occasions, including the funeral of Queen Mary the year before his own death.

Henry Purcell (engraving), Kneller, Sir Godfrey (1646-1723) (after)/ Private Collection/The Bridgeman Art Library

Best-Known Works

Opera and Stage Works
· *Dido and Aeneas*
· *The Fairy Queen*

MAIN POINTS OF CHAPTER 12

1. Opera was founded at the beginning of the Baroque period by a group of noblemen in Florence, Italy, who wanted to recapture the drama believed to have existed in ancient Greece. The first operas consisted entirely of recitatives.

2. As is true of oratorios and cantatas, operas consist of recitatives, arias, and choruses accompanied by an orchestra. They differ in that operas are performed with costumes, actions, and scenery.

3. Operas are much more enjoyable if certain conventions are accepted:

   * All the words are sung.
   * The style of singing is powerful and dramatic.
   * Often the words of an opera are not in English.
   * The progress of the story almost stops while an aria or chorus is sung. At other times, significant events happen very quickly.

4. Good opera is good theater. Therefore, it must be both seen and heard to realize its full impact. It has a "bigger than life" quality about it.

5. The text of an opera is called the libretto. It is prepared before the composer sets the words to music. Most composers did not write the librettos for their operas.

6. Several traditions exist regarding the types of voices and the roles they sing. Sopranos and tenors often get the lead roles, while altos and basses sing the roles of older persons, villains, or authority figures such as a king.

7. An ostinato is a short phrase of music that is repeated again and again. When it's in the bass part, as it is in "Dido's Lament," it is referred to as a basso ostinato.

 PRACTICE...
your understanding of this chapter's concepts by working once more with the chapter's Active Listening Guides online.

 DO...
online quizzes that your instructor may assign for a grade.

13 Baroque Instrumental Music: Suite *and* Sonata

START...
experiencing this chapter's topics with an online video activity that your instructor may assign.

READ...
the complete chapter text in a rich interactive eBook!

Learning Objectives

1 Identify the ostinato bass and imitation in Pachelbel's Canon in D.
2 Describe the characteristics of a Baroque suite.
3 List the features of a Baroque sonata.
4 Name two composers of Baroque music in addition to Bach and Handel.

Some important differences developed between instrumental and vocal music during the Baroque period. Until the Baroque, a piece of music was not composed specifically for a particular instrument, with the exception of works for lute or keyboard instruments. In fact, many works could be performed by instruments or voices or both.

The eventual distinction between vocal and instrumental styles was probably inevitable. Instruments and voices do not produce music in the same ways; certain types of music are more suitable for the voice, while others lend themselves better to instruments. For example, a violin or flute can easily produce sounds that are higher than the upper limits of the human voice. Performers on most instruments can also play notes with a speed and clarity that are almost impossible for a singer to achieve.

In general, Baroque instrumental music tended to be more contrapuntal than homophonic, but the opposite tended to be true for vocal music. There is a logical explanation for this. In vocal music, composers tried to project a message; recitatives and arias were developed as a means of giving expression to the ideas contained in the text. Instrumental music is, of course, not affected by a text.

BAROQUE INSTRUMENTS

Two keyboard instruments were important in the Baroque period: the pipe organ and the harpsichord (both described in Chapter 6). The organ had existed in a rudimentary form for fifteen hundred years, but it reached its height of development during the Baroque (Figure 13.1). In fact, some organs built today attempt to replicate those of the eighteenth century. During the late nineteenth and early twentieth centuries, several ranks of pipes were added to organs, especially those built for use in movie theaters in the early decades of the twentieth century, to imitate the sound of trombones and other instruments. But these synthesized sounds were seldom musically satisfying.

The harpsichord was frequently played during the Renaissance, and it became even more important in the Baroque. When the Baroque period ended, the harpsichord receded in significance, and it was seldom heard from until the twentieth century. There was then a revival of interest in the harpsichord, and new ones were constructed.

Several orchestral instruments are featured prominently in Baroque music. One is the "whistle" flute, or *recorder*, which is played straight forward from the player's mouth, rather than sideways to the right as flutes are today. This flute was made of wood and had a lighter, less brilliant tone quality.

The trumpet, too, was given important roles during that period. It had no valves, so pitches had to be controlled entirely by the player's lips. Many Baroque trumpets were

FIGURE 13.1
THE ORGAN AND CHOIR LOFT OF
ST. THOMAS CHURCH IN LEIPZIG,
GERMANY, WHERE J. S. BACH
SERVED FOR MANY YEARS.

smaller and had narrower bores, which made it easier for players to reach the high notes found in some Baroque compositions.

The violin also played a major role in the Baroque period. It looked similar to the violins of today. The fingerboard was shorter, because the players did not play very high notes. The bow curved slightly away from the hair, with a shape somewhat resembling an archer's bow, from which it got its name. The tension on the bow hair was looser, too. The strings of the instrument were set on a flatter plane, making it easier for violinists to play more than one string at a time. Gut strings were used instead of the metal strings generally in use today.

PACHELBEL'S CANON IN D

Pachelbel's Canon in D (see Listening Guide) is an unusual work. To begin with, although it was composed around 1680, it was largely forgotten until the latter half of the twentieth century. Suddenly, it seemed to have been "found" by many musicians and has enjoyed enormous popularity since, at least in terms of concert music. More than two hundred versions of it have been recorded, including a few in rock style, and it has found its way into many television commercials and several motion pictures. It has served as background music for commercials ranging from GE lightbulbs to Taster's Choice coffee, and in the Academy Award–winning film *Ordinary People*, as well as *Father of the Bride*. It was also played at Princess Diana's funeral and the wedding of Prince William and Kate Middleton.

Canon in D is unusual in that it combines two different approaches to composition. It is built on a ground bass of eight notes, all of equal length, with every other note a fourth apart. In addition, melodic variations are played over the ground bass twenty-seven times. They appear in three instrumental parts, one following the other eight beats apart in strict imitation—thus the name *canon*. Originally for three violins and continuo, today it is often played by a string orchestra and continuo.

JOHANN PACHELBEL
Canon in D (c. 1680)

Genre: Canon

Download 26

3 minutes 54 seconds

0:00   Continuo part sounds alone.

0:09   First violin plays one note to the beat. Second violin follows eight beats later, and third violin eight beats later than the second.

0:26   First violin plays two notes to the beat. Then it plays:

0:43   —four notes to the beat

1:00   —one and two notes to the beat in higher range

1:16   —part with many notes at the speed of eight to the beat

1:32   —one short note on the beat, and then off the beat

1:48   —four notes to the beat that alternate between higher and lower pitch levels

2:04   —four repeated notes on many beats

2:19   —line with two fast notes in each beat

2:34   —long notes

2:49   —a contrasting melody

3:06   —long notes, some starting in the middle of the beat

3:23   —notes that move one octave to another

3:52   Canon concludes.

LISTEN TO... this selection streaming online.

WATCH... an Active Listening Guide of this selection online.

WATCH... different performances of this selection online.

DO... an online Listening Practice Activity related to this selection, which your instructor may assign for a grade.

LISTENING GUIDE

Johann Pachelbel

Johann Pachelbel (1653–1706) was born and died in Nuremberg, Germany. He was a church organist and teacher, counting among his pupils J. S. Bach's teacher. He held several positions as organist and choir director, including one in Stuttgart from which he had to flee because of the French invasion. His longest position was in his native Nuremberg. He composed a great deal of religious choral music and works for organ, which were much admired by J. S. Bach. It's ironic that today he is remembered mostly for just one work, Canon in D.

Best-Known Works

- Fugues on the *Magnificat*
- Canon in D

THE SUITE

The word **suite** (pronounced "sweet") as used in music refers to a series or set of musical works that belong together. During the Baroque period, a suite was a collection of dances that were intended for performance as a group. Suites were usually written for keyboard instruments. A contemporary composer might do the same thing by taking a popular dance of a generation or more ago and writing similar music with more interesting harmonies while retaining the essential rhythm and style of the original.

The dances included in the suites of Handel and other composers of the time were *stylized*. That is, they were "dressed up" to make them interesting pieces for listening. Composers wrote their own music for them, but the meter, tempo, and other characteristics were derived from various types of dances that had previously been in fashion.

Handel's "Hornpipe" from *Water Music*

Not all suites were written for keyboard instruments. Handel and others composed collections of stylized dance music for wind and string groups as well. Handel's *Water Music*, HWV 348–350, consists of an overture and about twenty dances. It was written in 1717 for an excursion by King George I as he and his large party floated down the River Thames on barges (Figure 13.2). The king reportedly liked the music so much that he had it played three times. It was performed by a total of fifty instruments of different types.

A hornpipe (see Listening Guide) is an energetic, jaunty dance in three beats to the measure. It is in binary form, and the theme is repeated by different groups of instruments.

THE SONATA

The word **sonata** is used often in music. It first appeared in the Baroque period, and it simply referred to an instrumental work for one or a few instruments. At that time there were two types of sonatas—one was the church sonata (*sonata da chiesa*), and the other was the chamber sonata (*sonata da camera*). The former was more serious and included some thoughtful music and quite a bit of imitation among the melodic lines. The chamber sonata consisted largely of stylized dance music and was lighter in character.

Probably the most prominent type of sonata during the middle of the Baroque was the *trio sonata*. Actually, the designation is not accurate, because it includes two violins

FIGURE 13.2
VIEW OF THE THAMES RIVER AND LONDON WITH ST. PAUL'S CATHEDRAL BY CANALETTO (1697–1768). THE BARGES ARE MUCH MORE ELEGANT THAN WHAT WE THINK OF AS BARGES TODAY.

Bridgeman-Giraudon/Art Resource, NY

LISTENING GUIDE

GEORGE FRIDERIC HANDEL
"Hornpipe" from *Water Music* (1717)

Genre: Suite

Form: Binary

Download 27

2 minutes 27 seconds

0:00   Strings play A theme and then repeat it.

0:24   Strings play B theme and then repeat it.

0:47   Woodwinds play A theme and then repeat it.

1:10   Woodwinds play B theme and then repeat it.

1:34   Strings play A theme and then repeat it.

1:57   Strings play B theme and then repeat it.

2:20   The hornpipe ends quietly.

LISTEN TO... this selection streaming online.

WATCH... an Active Listening Guide of this selection online.

DO... an online Listening Practice Activity related to this selection, which your instructor may assign for a grade.

and one lower instrument (gamba or cello) plus the continuo, which was usually played by a keyboard instrument.

Almost all sonatas were divided into *movements*, a term introduced in Chapter 2. Four movements were typical, and they were often arranged so that their tempos contrasted with one another.

Corelli's Trio Sonata

The Trio Sonata in F, Op. 3, No. 1, is one of the twelve sonatas published together as "Op. 3." The abbreviation **Op.** is from the Latin word **opus**, meaning "work," and is used to identify individual instrumental works. Generally, the numbers indicate the order in which a composer wrote his or her music, but opus numbers were not employed consistently until early in the nineteenth century. Sometimes publishers attached opus numbers to works composed before then. In some instances, scholars have cataloged the works of composers such as Bach, Schubert, and Mozart, in which cases the name or initials of the cataloger appear along with a catalog number. Numbers are rarely used for works of vocal music because they can be identified by the words in their texts.

Corelli's trio sonata has four movements; only the second movement is presented here (see Listening Guide). The first movement of this church sonata is typically a slow, solemn movement marked *Grave* (pronounced "*grah-vay*"). The cello sounds a steady stream of low notes while the two violins play higher notes for the first half of the movement.

Arcangelo Corelli
Trio Sonata in F, Op. 3, No. 1, Second Movement (1681)

Genre: Trio sonata

Download 28

1 minute 11 seconds

0:00 First violin enters, second violin follows, and then cello.

0:17 Free counterpoint follows.

0:42 Opening theme appears twice as rapidly moving notes are played.

1:05 Opening theme played one more time before movement concludes.

LISTEN TO... this selection streaming online.

WATCH... an Active Listening Guide of this selection online.

DO... an online Listening Practice Activity related to this selection, which your instructor may assign for a grade.

LISTENING GUIDE

FierceAbin/E+/Getty Images

Arcangelo Corelli

Arcangelo Corelli (1653–1713) lived at a time when the violin was replacing the viol. He was one of the first great violinists, a teacher, and a composer, and he promoted the technical and tonal capabilities of the violin. He spent most of his life in Rome in the service of Cardinal Ottoboni, whose concerts he directed. His "Christmas" concerto was completed shortly before he died. Unlike many composers, he died having amassed a large fortune. In return, he left the world a fortune in string music.

Best-Known Works

- Violin Sonatas (12)
- Concerti Grossi (12)

The second movement has a fast tempo and contains much imitation among the three instruments. After each instrument enters in imitation, it continues with free contrapuntal material. The opening theme appears four more times in the movement, including a shortened version near the end of the movement.

The third movement has a waltzlike character with its three rapid beats in each measure. Several times Corelli presents a melody consisting of two phrases, each four measures long, and then repeats it accompanied by decorative notes played by the violins.

The fourth movement is similar to the second. It has a rather fast tempo and contains much imitation.

OTHER BAROQUE COMPOSERS

GIOVANNI GABRIELI (1557–1612) studied music with his uncle Andrea in Venice; later he probably studied with Orlando di Lasso in Munich. In 1585 he succeeded his uncle as organist at Saint Mark's, a position that he held until his death twenty-seven years later. Until about 1600, his compositions were in the Renaissance style. His later compositions were in the then-new Baroque style.

Although an organist and master at writing choral music, he is remembered more today for his use of instruments, especially brasses. They included trombones (which were puny instruments compared with the modern versions) and cornetto. The cornetto was a wooden instrument that bears little resemblance to the present-day cornet. Corelli's *Sonata pian'e forte* is recognized as probably the first work to specify dynamic levels.

JEAN-BAPTISTE LULLY Though Italian by birth, Jean-Baptiste Lully (1632–1687) made his way into the court of French kings by wit and luck. He changed his name from the Italian *Lulli* to the French version by which he has been known throughout history. Lully was a supreme entertainer in what was the most sumptuous court in Europe. There he staged dance spectaculars and other performances. He developed the *French overture*. It had a slow introduction with many dotted rhythms, a fast middle section with imitation of a short melody, and usually a third section in a slow tempo like the first.

The story of Lully's death is probably true. To keep the performers together, he would mark the beat by pounding a stick on the floor. One day he hit his toe, which later became infected. He died from the infection.

GEORG PHILLIP TELEMANN One of the best-known composers of the first half of the eighteenth century, Georg Phillip Telemann (1685–1767) spent most of his life near Hamburg, Germany. He left a huge amount of music—forty operas, forty-four passions, twelve

Lutheran services, and more than three thousand works of other types! He was adept at composing instrumental music, especially for the flute.

MAIN POINTS OF CHAPTER 13

1. The important keyboard instruments during the Baroque period were the harpsichord and pipe organ, which reached their acme during that time. Flutes were often like recorders. Many trumpets, which had no valve mechanisms, were smaller than today's versions, which allowed them to play high pitches more easily. Violins used gut strings, had a flatter bridge, and were played with a more curved bow.

2. Ostinato and ground bass were used in some instrumental works. Pachelbel's Canon in D uses both of these techniques.

3. Suites consisting of stylized dance music were popular. They were composed for harpsichord or small instrumental ensembles.

4. Sonatas were first composed in the Baroque period. The church sonata (*sonata da chiesa*) was more serious, whereas the chamber sonata (*sonata de camera*) consisted of stylized versions of dance music.

5. The trio sonata was a feature of Baroque instrumental music. It actually required four players: two violins, one cello, and a continuo part played on the harpsichord and/or other bass instrument. The short movements of the trio sonata were arranged in contrasting tempos and often contained imitation among the parts.

6. Because instrumental works do not have words, they are usually given generic titles such as sonata or suite. In addition, they are frequently identified further by an opus number.

PRACTICE...
your understanding of this chapter's concepts by working once more with the chapter's Active Listening Guides online.

DO...
online quizzes that your instructor may assign for a grade.

14 Baroque Instrumental Music: Concerto *and* Fugue

START...

experiencing this chapter's topics with an online video activity that your instructor may assign.

READ...

the complete chapter text in a rich interactive eBook!

Learning Objectives

1 Describe the characteristics of a concerto grosso.
2 Define the terms associated with fugues.
3 Recognize sequences, suspensions, and use of the pedal.
4 List some other Baroque keyboard forms.

In a sense, the concerto grosso, the solo concerto, and the fugue represent the more mature instrumental works composed during the Baroque. They were generally written in the eighteenth century by composers whose music is performed frequently today. The examples of concerto grosso and fugue represent a high point for their particular type of music, and some of the solo concertos of that time are still staples of concert music today.

THE CONCERTO GROSSO

A favorite musical effect during the Baroque period was the contrast between groups of instruments, or what is called **concerted style**. There are two types of **concerto grosso**. One featured the contrast between different types of instruments, such as woodwinds and strings. The other, more common, type presented contrast between a few instruments and the orchestra. The contrast between groups is more than just a case of taking turns in answering each other, especially in the later concertos. They are more subtle and complex than that, but the basic idea of contrast is present. The idea of contrast also carried over to the movements of the concertos. Typically, they consisted of three movements: fast–slow–fast.

There is little difference in the difficulty of the music that the small group and the larger group (called the *tutti*) perform. No attempt was made to have one group show off, as is true in later concertos. The players in the small group are usually the first-chair players in their respective sections. The small group remains in (either seated or standing) place and often plays along in unison with the *tutti*. Usually, concerti grossi are composed for strings, with a harpsichord filling in the harmonies. A few wind instruments are sometimes included in the small group.

The fact that the same or similar instruments play the same music sometimes makes it difficult to distinguish which group is playing at a particular moment. Orchestras during the Baroque period were small, so the larger group really wasn't large by today's standards. Also, three or four good string players can produce a quite vigorous sound. Recordings tend to make the groups less distinguishable by taking away most of the physical distance of live performances.

The most common form of the movements in a concerto grosso is **ritornello form**. It presents a pattern in which the main theme alternates with a contrasting section, with modifications as the movement progresses.

Bach's Brandenburg Concerto No. 5

The margrave of Brandenburg was one of the more important rulers in what is Germany today. In 1717 Bach was court composer at Cöthen and had a chance to perform for the margrave, who was visiting there. The margrave was so impressed with Bach's music that he asked him to write some music for his orchestra. In 1721 Bach sent him six concertos, complete with dedication to "His Highness," that contrasted a variety of small instrumental groups with the orchestra. Later they became known as the Brandenburg Concertos. Bach may have hoped that his gift of six concertos with its glowing dedication would lead to a job offer from the margrave. None ever came.

Whether the margrave ever responded to Bach's gift is not known. In fact, the concertos were placed in the margrave's library and were never performed by the musicians at his court. They were probably performed by Bach during his tenure at Cöthen, and perhaps while he was in Leipzig.

The Brandenburg Concerto No. 5 calls for a flute, violin, and harpsichord contrasted with a string orchestra and continuo. (Actually, the harpsichord has a dual role. It is part of the small group, but it also contributes to the continuo part as part of the *tutti*.) The harpsichord had seldom been given such importance in the concerti grossi of earlier composers. Bach may have given it a prominent place in this concerto because the prince at Cöthen had just purchased a new harpsichord, and Bach was an outstanding keyboard player. The concerto contains much counterpoint throughout and musical "conversations" among the three instruments and between them and the orchestra.

The first movement (see Listening Guide) is the longest and contains a stunning harpsichord cadenza. It is in D major and is marked *Allegro*.

The first movement consists of the main theme (ritornello), which is played by the strings in the orchestra and the harpsichord realizing the figured bass line. It's called the

JOHANN SEBASTIAN BACH
Brandenburg Concerto No. 5, First Movement

LISTENING GUIDE

Genre: Concerto grosso

Form: Ritornello

Download 29

9 minutes 59 seconds

0:00   Strings play the vigorous first theme. It's in major and features repeated notes.

0:22   Flute and violin exchange melodic lines, and are then joined by the harpsichord.

0:46   Strings return, playing part of the ritornello theme.

0:52   Flute, violin, and harpsichord play a varied fragment of the ritornello.

1:17   Violin, flute, and harpsichord play.

1:38   Strings play a fragment of the ritornello in minor.

1:44   Harpsichord, flute, and violin heard again.

2:25   Strings play ritornello in major.

2:32   Flute, harpsichord, and violin softly play a varied version of the ritornello

(continued)

2:57 New theme in minor is softly traded between flute and violin.

4:14 Strings play a fragment of the ritornello at a forte level.

4:19 Violin, flute, and harpsichord return.

4:22 Strings play a longer fragment of the ritornello.

4:37 Violin, harpsichord, and flute play a varied fragment of the ritornello.

5:03 Strings play the ritornello.

5:49 Violin and flute play a freely adapted version as harpsichord plays rapid scales in the background.

6:28 Harpsichord plays a cadenza with many virtuoso passages.

8:50 Tension gradually increases, leading to—

9:35 a return of the ritornello and the conclusion of the movement.

LISTEN TO... this selection streaming online.

WATCH... an Active Listening Guide of this selection online.

WATCH... a performance of another movement of this selection online.

DO... an online Listening Practice Activity related to this selection, which your instructor may assign for a

grade.

tutti, an Italian term meaning *all.* It alternates with the solo part played by flute, violin, and harpsichord. It is the longest of the three movements of the concerto and leads up to a stunning harpsichord cadenza that Bach wrote.

The tutti theme has a straightforward melody, while the solo instruments have more playful lines that they exchange with each other. The tutti sections tend to be louder, partly because more instruments are playing. But the nature of the melodic material also differs. Much of the movement is in major, but about three minutes into the movement a new theme in minor is introduced.

The second movement is in D minor and has a slow tempo.

The third movement is in major and has a happy, dancelike character that moves rapidly with many notes played by the harpsichordist. Its short main theme is imitated and exchanged among the solo instruments alone and then repeated while accompanied by the orchestra.

Vivaldi's Concerto "Spring" from *The Four Seasons*

Antonio Vivaldi's "Spring" from Concerto for Violin and String Orchestra, Op. 8, No. 1 (see Listening Guide), is from a collection of four concertos often called *The Four Seasons.* Each concerto contains elements of a concerto grosso but is more of a solo concerto in

ANTONIO VIVALDI

"Spring" from *The Four Seasons*, First Movement (1725)

Genre: Solo concerto

Form: Ritornello

Download 30

3 minutes 28 seconds

0:00   Entire string orchestra plays the main theme (ritornello) and then repeats it softly. The words in the score can be translated "Spring with all its happiness is here."

0:16   Orchestra plays second half of ritornello theme and then repeats it.

0:33   Violins play chirping, birdlike sounds: "And the birds welcome it with happy songs."

1:10   Orchestra repeats second half of ritornello.

1:18   Orchestra plays short, flowing, rapidly moving notes: "And the brooks, touched by the breezes, flow with sweet murmurings."

1:43   Second half of ritornello is repeated.

1:52   Music changes to minor. Orchestra plays rustling, nervous sounds (tremolos), and violins zip up notes of the scale: "Dark clouds fill the sky announced by lightning and thunder."

2:20   Orchestra plays second part of ritornello again but in minor.

2:28   Violins play birdlike sounds: "But when everything is quiet, the birds begin to sing again their enchanting song."

2:45   Orchestra plays first part of ritornello in major, and then solo violin enters.

3:11   Orchestra again plays second part of ritornello and then repeats it softly.

3:28   "Spring" concludes.

LISTEN TO... this selection streaming online.

WATCH... an Active Listening Guide of this selection online.

DO... an online Listening Practice Activity related to this selection, which your instructor may assign for a

grade.

LISTENING GUIDE

Antonio Vivaldi

Antonio Vivaldi (c. 1675–1741) is much admired by musicians today, but is not as well known to the general public. He was born in Venice, Italy, the son of a violinist. As a young man, he was ordained a priest, but he did not live the typical life of a cleric. He concertized throughout Europe, wrote and produced almost fifty operas, made a good deal of money, and lived with a French soprano for many years.

From 1703 to 1740 he taught at the Ospedale della Pietà in Venice. It was an orphanage for about four hundred young women. According to accounts written at the time, each Sunday afternoon the girls offered public performances of an exceptionally high quality. His lifestyle got him in trouble with Church authorities, however, and he was forbidden to continue his music-making activities in areas controlled by the pope. The ban drastically reduced his income and seemed to drain him of his creative juices. He died in Vienna, poor and virtually unknown.

Vivaldi was a prolific composer who wrote an enormous amount of music of practically every kind. He wrote many works for the girls at the school to play or sing, including concertos for violin (about three hundred of them!), flute, bassoon, guitar, mandolin, and piccolo—more than 450 in all. His music was much admired during his lifetime but had fallen from favor by the time he died. It has enjoyed a rebirth of interest. For example, more than 150 recordings have been made of *The Four Seasons* alone.

Best-Known Works

Concertos
· Concerto for Two Violins, Strings, and Continuo (*L'estro armonica*)
· Concertos for Violin, Strings, and Continuo (*The Four Seasons*)

Choral
· *Gloria*

that the principal violinist is given a virtuoso part to play. The four concertos each have three movements arranged in a fast–slow–fast order of tempos.

The title of the work comes from the fact that Vivaldi associated each concerto with a different season of the year by its title and by the insertion of lines of poetry in the orchestral score. Such nonmusical associations were unusual in instrumental works during the Baroque period, although they are encountered occasionally. Instrumental works associated by the composer with nonmusical ideas are known as **program music** and became very popular during the nineteenth century.

THE FUGUE

Because a pipe organ can produce a wide variety of tone colors with tremendous power and range, Baroque composers began to write music specifically for it. In the process they developed several forms of organ compositions. The **fugue** (pronounced "fewg") is the most important of these forms.

The fugue, as is true of most musical forms, did not appear fully developed. It evolved from less complex types of keyboard music. The fugue and its predecessors have one thing in common: They are contrapuntal, with the lines of music often imitating one another.

What makes fugues interesting to listen to? At least three things:

1. Fugues are built around one main theme, which helps give the work a strong sense of unity. This theme is featured alone at the beginning and then repeated often during the work.

FIGURE 14.1
TYPICAL FOUR-VOICE FUGUE

2. Contrasting lines of counterpoint give the work variety and make it more interesting. These lines fit together with the theme and with one another.

3. The entire work is crafted so that it evolves in a wonderfully logical manner. The musical process of a fugue is somewhat like a complicated mathematical formula working itself out to a beautifully correct conclusion.

Fugues have their own vocabulary. The various lines are called **voices**, even though they are actually played on an instrument, not sung. The main theme is called the **subject**, and the contrasting theme is called the **countersubject**. The opening section that presents the subject in each voice is termed the **exposition;** the remainder of the fugue is known as the **development**. Sections of the fugue following the exposition in which the subject does not appear are called **episodes**.

The pattern of a typical four-voice fugue is shown in Figure 14.1.

The typical fugue has four voices, but it could have two, three, or five. The order in which the voices enter is a matter of choice for the composer. Each fugue is structured somewhat differently.

Bach's Toccata and Fugue in D Minor

Toccata and Fugue in D Minor by Bach (see Listening Guide) presents a fugue surrounded by a **toccata**, which is a free-sounding virtuoso work, usually for keyboard. Both the fugue and the toccata offer the organist plenty of chances to show off the tremendous tonal possibilities of the instrument, as well as his or her virtuoso skill as a performer. The third and concluding section of this work is another toccata that Bach labels *recitativo.* The word refers to the free and expressive style of singing described in Chapter 10. It is a work filled with drama.

Three features of Baroque instrumental music are prominent in this fugue as well as fugues in general. One is the use of **sequence**. A sequence is a pattern of notes repeated several times in succession, but each time at a different pitch level. Sequences are a staple of Baroque music, and Toccata and Fugue in D Minor contains many of them.

Second is the use of repeated notes in a theme. The subject of the fugue contains a lot of notes, which gives the music more energy. But only half of the notes form the basis of the subject. Only the circled notes in the music example change; the others do not.

For this reason, you should focus on the notes that change as you listen to the subject of this fugue.

The third feature is a bit more complicated. Composers, especially in the Baroque period, created a pattern of tension and release by holding a consonant note from one chord over into the next chord, where it was dissonant, and then resolving that note to a consonant note in the new chord. This compositional device is called a **suspension**. Suspensions are more frequent in cadences near the conclusion of phrases. At the end of the entire Toccata and Fugue, it may sound as if Bach is simply holding a long chord. But listen carefully as notes in the middle of the chords change and finally resolve. The interplay of consonance and dissonance makes for some very interesting and challenging listening.

JOHANN SEBASTIAN BACH

Toccata and Fugue in D Minor, BWV 565 (before 1708)

Genre: Fugue with toccata and recitative

Download 31

7 minutes 47 seconds

Toccata

0:00   Toccata opens at loud dynamic level with dramatic ornamented figure followed by a pause and then rapidly moving notes. Figure is played three times, each time one octave lower.

0:17   Long chord is built note by note in an ascending pattern, resolving to a massive chord in major tonality.

0:28   Series of rapidly moving triplets ascends.

0:34   Series of triplets is repeated with a different timbre at a higher pitch level.

0:40   Rapidly moving triplets sound in a descending pattern.

0:47   Another massive chord is built, but this time a short decorative pattern appears before it resolves.

0:58   Passage with many rapidly moving notes features one note that is repeated persistently.

1:12   Four passages of rapidly moving triplets are followed by four descending chords.

1:22   Free-sounding passage of rapidly moving notes leads to …

1:33   … a massive chord followed by a string of rapidly moving triplets.

1:51   Series of full-sounding chords sounds at loud dynamic level.

1:57   Low notes of the pedal heard, followed by more massive chords leading to the conclusion of the opening toccata section in minor tonality. Listen for the changing notes in the middle of the chords.

Fugue: *Exposition*

2:11   Subject of the fugue opens in the first voice. Its more important notes move mostly by step as the repeated notes add energy and brilliance.

2:16   Subject follows in the second voice four notes higher. First voice continues with countersubject consisting of steady, even notes.

2:20   Two voices continue in free counterpoint, with the same figures appearing sequentially.

2:34   Subject appears in the third voice in high notes in the same key as the first voice.

2:38   Fugue continues in free counterpoint with the same material played in sequence.

2:49   Same melodic figures appear in sequence, sometimes appearing to answer each other.

3:06   Subject is played on the pedals at a low pitch level as the countersubject appears in another voice.

3:11   Exposition of the fugue concludes as all voices continue in free counterpoint, again with much use of sequence.

Fugue: *Development*

3:20 Subject appears again in the third voice, with the countersubject at a higher pitch.

3:25 Descending scale passages appear in sequence.

3:31 Two measures of continuously moving notes are played and then repeated exactly, except for organist's change of timbre and terraced dynamics.

3:42 Statement-response of idea of melodic figures continues in sequence with change of timbre.

3:53 Subject sounds in high notes, again with the countersubject.

4:00 More sequential figures appear in statement-answer pattern(s), with changes of timbre of the answering figure.

4:34 Subject played on pedalboard, along with trilled note and countersubject played at higher pitch level.

4:41 Subject sounds in middle voice with trilled note and countersubject in pedal part.

4:46 Fugue continues with same melodic figures in sequence.

4:53 Subject appears again in middle voice as pedal holds a long note.

5:00 Fugue continues with free counterpoint.

5:22 Portion of the subject in inversion in lower notes while countersubject is played in higher notes.

5:28 Subject appears in middle voice while countersubject is heard above it as a long note is held.

5:38 Subject appears alone in pedal part.

5:54 Upper voices repeat a melodic figure in sequence as pedal part sounds same note on every other beat.

6:07 Portion of the subject appears several times in pedal part.

6:18 Subject again in middle voice, with countersubject above it and pedal part holding long note.

6:25 Fugue concludes with cadence that gives feeling that music is not ending.

Recitativo

6:30 Free "recitativo" section opens with many short phrases of fast notes.

6:39 Three loud, very slow chords give the feeling music has not concluded.

6:47 Series of notes sounded on pedalboard lead to another cadence, giving feeling work has not concluded.

6:58 Another series of fast notes

7:09 Two slow chords are followed by eight appearances of fast notes alternating with two short chords.

7:27 Series of slow, loud chords follows. Three times a consonant note within chord is held into next chord, creating a dissonance for one beat before resolving to consonant note.

7:39 Work concludes with long, powerful minor chord.

 LISTEN TO... this selection streaming online.

 WATCH... an Active Listening Guide of this selection online.

 WATCH... a performance of this selection online.

 DO... an online Listening Practice Activity related to this selection, which your instructor may assign for a grade.

Johann Sebastian Bach

Imagno/Hulton Archive/Getty Images

Johann Sebastian Bach (1685–1750) is a name that appears in nearly every discussion of Baroque music. And well it should! Bach ranks as one of the musical giants of all time.

Bach lived an uneventful life, not very different from that of many gifted musicians of his time. The most notable feature about him was his lineage. Over a period of about six generations, from 1580 to 1845, more than sixty Bachs were musicians of some repute, and at least thirty-eight of them attained eminence as musicians. Included among the latter were Johann Christoph (1642–1703), who was a cousin of Johann Sebastian's father, and several of J. S. Bach's own sons: Wilhelm Friedemann (1710–1784), Carl Philipp Emanuel (1714–1788), Johann Christoph Friedrich (1732–1795), and Johann Christian (1735–1782).

J. S. Bach was born the son of a town musician in Eisenach, Germany. When he was ten, his father died. Johann's musical training was taken over by his elder brother, Johann Christoph, who was an organist. During his early career, Bach was known more as an organist than as a composer. After two brief positions as organist, Bach was appointed to his first important post as court organist and musician to the duke of Weimar. He stayed nine years, during which he concentrated on organ, as both a composer and a performer.

When the duke failed to advance him, Bach accepted a position at Cöthen. The prince there wanted music for instrumental groups, so the versatile Bach turned to composing for instruments other than organ. During this time he wrote the Brandenburg Concertos. After the sudden death of his wife, Maria Barbara, he married Anna Magdalena and immortalized her by writing a book of keyboard music for her. Piano students today often play pieces from this book.

The third and final portion of Bach's life began with his appointment in 1723 as organist-teacher at Saint Thomas Church in Leipzig. The position called for him to compose, teach the boys in the choir school, and prepare the music for worship services. His contract also required him to walk with the boys at funerals, not to leave town without permission, and to "chastise them with moderation" if the boys disobeyed. His salary was low, and he had to pay for a substitute in case he couldn't perform a duty.

Ironically, Bach was not the first choice for the position. In spite of the annoyances of the position and tragedies in his personal life (six of his eight children born in Leipzig died), Bach continued his vast stream of great music. Later in life he suffered a stroke and became blind. In 1750 he died, with his true stature still unknown.

Except for a few brief journeys in Germany, Bach knew little of the world beyond where he lived and worked. He created no new musical forms and instituted no new compositional techniques. His music was seldom heard outside Leipzig during his lifetime, and even there it was probably not performed well.

Why, then, is Bach so dominating a figure in music? The answer is that he wrote with such skill and effectiveness. Especially remarkable was his ability to write counterpoint. Words are inadequate to describe his genius. Perhaps the late Dag Hammarskjöld, former secretary-general of the United Nations, expressed it best. In speaking of Bach and Vivaldi, he said, "Both have a beautiful way of creating order in the brain."

Best-Known Works

Choral
- *St. Matthew Passion*
- *Christmas Oratorio*
- *Mass in B Minor*
- *Magnificat*
- Cantatas Nos. 4, 84, and 140

Keyboard
- French Suites (6)
- English Suites (6)
- *The Well-Tempered Clavier*

Orchestra
- Brandenburg Concertos (6)
- Suites for Orchestra (4)

OTHER KEYBOARD FORMS

The fugue was not the only musical form composed for keyboard instruments during the Baroque period. Two forms based on the chorale are chorale variations and chorale prelude. In *chorale variations*, a chorale melody is repeated several times in succession but with changes each time. The *chorale prelude* is usually a contrapuntal piece for organ built on a chorale melody.

A third type of keyboard music, one that is especially suited to the organ, is the **passacaglia** (pah-sah-CAHL-ya). It begins with a statement of the theme in the lower notes. In a passacaglia, this melody is repeated over and over in its original form, but variations are added in other voices each time. The melody usually remains in the bass throughout. The pedals are ideal for maintaining the rather slow-moving melody, leaving the player's hands free to play the faster, higher-pitched lines. Continuous repetition combined with continuous variation provides both unity and variety in the music. One of Bach's greatest organ works is his Passacaglia in C Minor.

The **prelude** was another common work for keyboard instruments. In the Baroque period, this title simply meant a short piece of instrumental music.

MAIN POINTS OF CHAPTER 14

1. The Baroque concerto grosso is based on the idea of contrast, usually between a small instrumental group and the orchestra. The players in the small group do not play music that is more showy than what is played by the orchestra.

2. Typically, the three movements of a concerto are arranged in a fast–slow–fast tempo order. Ritornello form, with its recurring theme and contrasting sections, is used for many movements.

3. Program music is instrumental music that is associated by the composer with a non-musical idea or situation. An early example is Vivaldi's *The Four Seasons*.

4. A fugue is an instrumental work, often for organ, that is based on a recurring theme and contrasting theme, which appear between sections of free contrapuntal music. Often a fugue has four lines or voices. The opening section of a fugue is called the exposition, and the remainder is termed the development.

5. Sequence is a music technique encountered frequently in Baroque music. It occurs when a pattern of notes is repeated several times in succession, each time at a different pitch level.

6. Other types of keyboard music composed during the Baroque period include toccata, chorale variations, prelude, and passacaglia.

 PRACTICE...
your understanding of this chapter's concepts by working once more with the chapter's Active Listening Guides online.

 DO...
online quizzes that your instructor may assign for a grade.

Features of Baroque Music

Melodies	Expressive "reciting style" (recitative) in vocal music
	Quite a few virtuoso passages in vocal and instrumental music
	Many instrumental melodies have a continuous, "spinning out" quality
Rhythm	Strongly metrical with regular patterns of beats (except in recitatives)
Textures	Polyphonic (contrapuntal) and homophonic

(continued)

Harmony	Tonal in major and minor; tonal center can modulate
	Continuo (basso continuo) part in many works
Dynamic levels	Loud and soft; terraced dynamics in instrumental music
Performance media	Accompanied vocal solos and choral pieces
	Harpsichord and pipe organ
	Small instrumental ensembles
Forms	*A B* (binary)
	A B A (ternary)
	Ritornello
	Fugue
Genres	Oratorio, Cantata
	Recitative
	Aria
	Chorus
	Chorale
	Opera
	Suite
	Sonata, trio sonata
	Concerto grosso
	Solo concerto
	Fugue
	Short organ works

PART 4

Classical Music

	1750		1775
Historical Events	● Factory system begins (1770s)		American Revolution (1775–1781)
		● Watts develops steam engine (1763–1775)	
Visual Arts	Boucher (1703–1770)		
	Fragonard (1732–1806)		
Literature and Theater		● Voltaire, *Candide* (1759)	
			Wordsworth (1770–1850)
		Robert Burns (1721–1784)	
			Coleridge (1772)
		Schiller (1759–1805)	
Philosophy and Science	Kant (1724–1804)		
		● Rousseau, *Social Contract* (1762)	
Music	C. P. E. Bach (1714–1788)		
		Haydn composer for Esterházys (1761–1799)	
	J. C. Bach (1735–1782)		
	Mannheim Orchestra thrives (c. 1720–1800)		

1800   **1820**

French Revolution (1789–1799)   ● Louisiana Purchase (1803)   ● Napoleon defeated (1815)

● David, *Death of Socrates* (1787)   ● Goya, *The Third of May* (1814)

● Goethe, *Faust*   ● Scott, *Ivanhoe* (1819)
(1808, 1832)

● Jenner, smallpox vaccine (1796)

▲ Mozart symphonies and operas (above) (1770–1791)

▶ Beethoven symphonies (right) (1799–1824)

Schubert songs (1823–1828)

15 Classicism *and* Classical Music

 START...
experiencing this chapter's topics with an online video activity that your instructor may assign.

 READ...
the complete chapter text in a rich interactive eBook!

Learning Objectives

1 Describe the intellectual and philosophical principles of the Classical period.
2 Explain how these principles manifested themselves in the art of the period.
3 Discuss how the rational outlook of the Classical period affected the music.

When most people use the word *classic* to describe something, they mean that it has an enduring quality of excellence. *The Wizard of Oz* is a classic motion picture, and *Moby Dick* is a classic novel, to give two examples. That use of the word is close to the original Latin *classicus*, meaning "something of highest quality."

When most people use *classical* with regard to music, they mean concert or art music, music that is not popular or folk. On the other hand, when musicians use the word *Classical* (written with a capital C), they are talking about the musical style that prevailed from about 1750 to around 1820.

CULTURAL SETTING

Although the approximate dates of the **Classical period** give it a life span of only about seventy years, it produced a great deal of wonderful and enjoyable music. Instrumental music developed and equaled or exceeded vocal music in importance. The symphony, solo concerto, and chamber music and musical forms associated with them were developed. Opera also continued to flourish.

The center of music moved from the cities of Italy to Vienna, the capital of the Austrian Empire. Four master composers lived there—Mozart and Haydn during the Classical period and then Beethoven and Schubert, whose music bridged into the nineteenth-century style.

Among the educated population during the eighteenth century, there was a widespread interest in intellectual accomplishments in the philosophy, science, and arts of the ancient Greeks. Therefore, these years are often referred to as the Age of Enlightenment or the Age of Reason. This interest can be seen in the publication of Denis Diderot's *Encylopédie* in France and the *Encyclopœdia Britannica* in England. These books sought to break away from the religious restrictions of the past and promote reason and scientific thinking.

Four Leaders

Four persons are especially representative of the spirit of the time. One was Frenchman François Marie Arouet (1694–1778), who called himself Voltaire. His writings spoke out for justice and challenged the government and religion of France at that time, even to the point where he spent a year in prison for his beliefs. But he had his weak and inconsistent side, too. He was shrewd at business and lived comfortably, and some of his writings were published anonymously. Later when questioned about them, he continued to deny having written them. But in the end, his influence toward an enlightened outlook was enormous.

The Swiss-French Jean-Jacques Rousseau (1712–1778), like Voltaire, sought to reform the moral climate and governmental policies. In his writings he strongly urged a less dogmatic, formal system of government. He believed that people were naturally good and that they had been corrupted by civilization, education, and governments, beliefs that are still very much alive in the United States today. Rousseau was a skilled musician who advocated a new system of music notation. He composed music and wrote comedies. His music was simple and folklike in comparison with the highly decorated style of the other French composers of the time.

A third person representative of the spirit of the Age of Enlightenment was the American Benjamin Franklin (1706–1790). In spite of his rather unkempt appearance, he was a brilliant and well-read man who published books and magazines, promoted education, was pivotal in bringing about the Constitution of the United States, contributed much to the understanding of electricity, invented the Franklin stove and bifocal glasses, and developed a musical instrument called the "glass armonica," which was mentioned in Chapter 6.

Thomas Jefferson (1743–1826), the fourth representative of the outlook of the period, was not only author of the Declaration of Independence and third president of the United States but also an outstanding scholar and architect. His ideas can be seen in his home (which he named Monticello) at Charlottesville, Virginia; the University of Virginia (which he founded); and the Library of Congress (which he also founded—his books served as the nucleus of its original holdings). He was also a competent violinist and singer. The music stand he used for string quartet playing is on display today at Monticello.

Architecture

Admiration for the ancient Greeks and Romans can also be seen in architecture and art. Greek pillars and symmetrical, balanced designs are found in many public and private buildings in America today. The front of the U.S. Supreme Court Building in Washington, D.C., is very much in the Greek tradition (Figure 15.1). Note the sensible proportions of the triangle above the pillars; it is neither too tall nor too low from the baseline to the peak. Notice also the symmetry of the columns to each side of the center of the roof.

© Mesut Dogan/Shutterstock.com

FIGURE 15.1
Supreme Court Building

Philosophy

The philosophical approach of eighteenth-century thinkers was founded on three basic propositions:

1. Reason and logic are the way to truth. Emotions are false and misleading.
2. The universe is governed by permanent laws that people cannot alter. What is true is true throughout the world and for all time. It is universal and eternal.
3. Therefore, the intellect should control people's activities, including art and music.

These philosophical ideas began with Socrates and Plato in ancient Athens, but they were refined and applied to many areas of culture and scholarship by thinkers in the eighteenth century. One of the many areas affected by the Classical outlook was music, which is explored later in this chapter.

THE ROCOCO STYLE IN ART AND MUSIC

A forerunner of sorts of the more typical Classical style in the arts was the **Rococo** or **galant style**, which was popular mainly in France during the first half of the eighteenth century. With a name coming from the French word *rocaille*, meaning "shellwork," the Rococo style marked the acme of the highly decorative, almost frivolous French style of the Court of Versailles. It can be seen in the paintings of François Boucher (1703–1770), Antoine Watteau (1684–1721), and Jean Honoré Fragonard (1732–1806).

Boucher's *Venus and Cupid* (Figure 15.2) is a good example of Rococo art, which was strongly associated with the court of the French kings at Versailles. Boucher was trained as a decorator by his father, who designed embroideries. That influence can be seen in the exquisite lightness and decorative qualities of his paintings. The aristocracy of the time demanded a type of art and music that was pretty and decorative, even if it was superficial. A wide range of colors was used. Often the subjects of Rococo art were mythological or allegorical. The protagonist almost always appears as a young, elegant, and sensually abandoned woman. Cupids, nymphs, and doves are found in many paintings, which are frequently set in beautiful gardens or forests.

Two Rococo composers who merit mention are François Couperin (1688–1733) and Jean-Philippe Rameau (1683–1764). The happy tunes and almost frilly quality in Rameau's music seem perfectly suited for the powder-and-wig world of the Court of Versailles at the time of Louis XIV. Rameau is also important in music history for a book

FIGURE 15.2

VENUS AND CUPID, BY FRANÇOIS BOUCHER. THE ROCOCO SUBPERIOD FAVORED DECORATIVE WORKS OF ART AND MUSIC, INCLUDING MELODIES WITH MANY ORNAMENTS.

Venus and Cupid, 1754 (oil on canvas) by Boucher, Francois (1703–70) © Wallace Collection, London, UK/The Bridgeman Art Library

FIGURE 15.3

THE DEATH OF SOCRATES, BY JACQUES-LOUIS DAVID. THIS PAINTING SHOWS THE FORMAL PROPERTIES OF BALANCE AND RESTRAINT THAT ARE FOUND IN MUCH OF THE MUSIC OF MOZART AND HAYDN.

he wrote on harmony. In it he outlined principles of chord structure and progressions that have prevailed for hundreds of years. Much of Rameau's and Couperin's music is for a French version of the harpsichord called the *clavecin.*

CLASSICAL ART

The Death of Socrates by Jacques-Louis David (Figure 15.3) depicts the great philosopher of ancient Greece just about to drink the poisonous cup of hemlock. His students grieve while he remains composed and upright. In spite of the anguish of the scene, the figures seem almost frozen or posed. There is a detached quality about the picture. The admiration of the culture of ancient Greece and Rome can be seen in its symmetrical, balanced design. Groups of men are placed on each side of Socrates, who is the focus of attention. The colors are somewhat muted, in keeping with the overall nature of the scene. The arches of the building add a linear perspective to the painting.

CHARACTERISTICS OF CLASSICAL MUSIC

The overall impression of Classical music is that it is light, airy, elegant, and well thought out. It is music in which reason prevails over feelings. Composers thought more about creating beautiful and interesting works of music than pouring out their personal feelings in their music, which is a huge difference from the music of the century that followed.

Much music of the time was written under a patronage arrangement. The patronage system during the Classical period, therefore, produced a quite homogeneous style of music. For example, although there are subtle differences between the music of Haydn and Mozart, their works tend to sound quite similar. In fact, using themes of other composers was an accepted practice at the time. The original composer of the theme considered its appropriation by another composer a compliment, not a case of plagiarism. One theme called the "Mannheim rocket," for example, was used by Mozart, Beethoven, and many other composers.

People in the Classical period, including composers, seemed to attribute little mystery to the act of creating music, an attitude that would change radically in the nineteenth century. For example, a game attributed to Mozart consisted of a booklet with which anyone with a pair of dice could "compose" a piece of music. The booklet contained a short work for two violins, flute, and bass with each edition. When the instructions are followed, the result is a pleasant short piece of music.

FEATURES TO LISTEN FOR IN CLASSICAL MUSIC

Melody

For the most part, the themes are pleasant and tuneful. Most of them can be sung, if put in the right range. These melodies are made up of short phrases of two and four measures in length. And the phrases often are arranged in a statement–answer pattern. They form a musical equivalent of "How do you do?" and "Very well, thank you." Such paired patterns are balanced and symmetrical, and they contribute to the clear, logical quality of the music.

Homophony

The music of the Classical period was usually homophonic—melody plus accompaniment. There is some counterpoint in Classical music, but it is more the exception than the rule.

Harmony

Classical composers used essentially the same system of harmony as Baroque composers, but they made two important changes: (1) They abandoned the continuo part and the filling in of chords from figured bass, and (2) they changed chords less frequently. Sometimes Classical composers would keep the same chord for a measure or two before making a change, and then they might change chords several times in a rather short span of time. Classical harmony has the role of providing a backdrop for the melodies and does not draw attention to itself.

Rhythm

Classical music follows regular metrical patterns with few fluctuations in steadiness of the beat, except for recitatives in operas and oratorios. But it lacks the persistent quality of the rhythm of many Baroque works. Part of the reason for this difference is the result of abandoning the continuo and its steady stream of notes.

Dynamic Levels

The gradual **crescendo** and **decrescendo** developed during the Classical period. These gradual changes in dynamic level were considered quite dramatic at the time. They were an important contribution of that period to the development of music.

Performance

The orchestras of the Classical period grew somewhat but did not come close to the size of the symphony orchestras of today. When orchestras today perform a symphony by Haydn or Mozart, they often reduce the size of the string section by about one-fourth. Orchestras during the Classical period used only pairs of woodwinds and brasses. No trombones or tubas were included, and the percussion section usually consisted of the timpani player. There were no permanent orchestras in the Classical period. Orchestra players were part-time musicians who also held other jobs, so the level of performance was probably not high by today's standards.

Public concerts began during this time in the sense that performances were not always closed to all except invited guests in a palace. Public concerts were available in a few large cities such as Paris, London, and Leipzig, and they were within the financial means of the prosperous merchant class.

Forms

An important feature of Classical music is the development and refinement of various forms of instrumental music. Such music is referred to as **absolute music**. It has no association with any object, idea, or event outside itself. It is the opposite of *program music*, which was presented in conjunction with Vivaldi's *The Four Seasons*. The rational outlook of the time encouraged the creation of music that was well ordered and planned, as well as in good taste. Writing music (especially instrumental music with its lack of a story and text) that spans more than a few minutes generally requires some means of organization, some plan. Classical composers continued to use the sectional forms of the Baroque period, but they also developed and expanded sonata, rondo, and theme-and-variation forms. These forms contributed to the creation of symphonies, concertos, and chamber works.

MAIN POINTS OF CHAPTER 15

1. The Classical period lasted from approximately 1750 to 1820, and its artistic center was Vienna. Four persons stand out as representing those years: Voltaire, Jean-Jacques Rousseau, Benjamin Franklin, and Thomas Jefferson.

2. Because of its interest in intellectual endeavors, the Classical period is sometimes referred to as the Age of Reason or the Age of Enlightenment. During those years intellectuals believed that certain laws of nature and humanity were universal and eternal.

3. The Rococo style predated the Classical period. It existed largely in France, and its decorative and ornate works of art and music reflected the outlook of the aristocracy.

4. Many composers of that time worked under a patronage arrangement in which they composed exclusively for one person such as a count, duke, or king.

5. The Classical style differs from the Baroque style in several ways:

   • Its melodies often consist of short, tuneful figures.

   • Homophonic texture clearly predominates.

   • The continuo part has been abandoned.

   • Gradual changes in dynamic levels are present.

   • The chords that accompany a melody change less frequently.

   • Several important forms of instrumental music are developed.

 DO...
online quizzes that your instructor may assign for a grade.

16 Sonata Form

START...
experiencing this chapter's topics with an online video activity that your instructor may assign.

READ...
the complete chapter text in a rich interactive eBook!

Learning Objectives

1 Describe the development of themes in the Classical period.
2 Outline the characteristics of sonata form.
3 Describe the accomplishments of Mozart.

The most important form developed during the Classical period was **sonata form**, which is also called *first movement form* or *sonata–allegro form*. It became the expected form for the first movements of symphonies, concertos, and chamber music works in the last part of the eighteenth century and, with modifications, in the nineteenth century as well. And it is still used in compositions today. Sonata form was also found in other movements of multimovement works. Although the same word is used, *sonata form* and a *sonata* are different. One is a form, but a sonata is a genre of instrumental music.

DEVELOPMENT IN MUSICAL WORKS

Sonata form is more than just a plan or schema, however. It features a fundamental idea in concert music: *the development of themes*. True, sonata form contains themes, which are of interest, but what a composer does with the themes makes the music even more interesting and enjoyable to listen to. As the word is used in music, *development* does not mean "building up" or "finishing," but rather "working with." The themes are at best only half of what music in sonata form has to offer. The other half is the way the themes are developed.

Several years ago, people in a small town in Ohio realized that zucchini grew abundantly in their gardens and farms. In fact, the conditions one summer were so good that they could never use all of it, and a lot of zucchini would rot unused on the vine. What to do? They decided to hold a "Zucchini Festival," complete with crafts, dancing, music, and, of course, zucchini. Sure enough, it was chopped, sliced, and ground up and incorporated in all sorts of vegetable dishes, made into preserves and pickles, and blended in bread and muffins. Even the arts were included, as many fine pieces of zucchini sculpture were carved.

It's a bit like that with the development of themes in sonata form. Composers take a theme and work with it in all sorts of ways. The themes—or at least parts of them—are still there, but they have been given a variety of treatments.

SONATA FORM IN MOZART'S SYMPHONY NO. 40, K. 550

As his biographical sketch points out, Mozart was perhaps the greatest musical genius of all time. He wrote a huge amount of music, much of which is still performed today. His Symphony No. 40 was composed in 1788. Why he composed it and two other symphonies that year is not known. It is unlikely that he ever heard them performed. The score calls for the typical orchestra of the time: violins, violas, cellos (doubled by string basses in performance), a flute, two oboes, two bassoons, and two French horns. Later, Mozart revised the score to include two clarinets.

The first movement, in sonata form, is explored in depth here (see Listening Guide). It has three other movements. The second has a slow tempo and features beautifully crafted melodies. The third is a stylized minuet. The fourth provides a lively conclusion to the symphony. Not typical of symphonies of the Classical period is the fact that three of its four movements use sonata form.

Wolfgang Amadeus Mozart

Imagno/Hulton Archive/Getty Images

Wolfgang Amadeus Mozart (MOHT-zart, 1756–1791) is certainly one of the greatest musical geniuses of all time. He was born in Salzburg, Austria, where his father was a recognized violinist and composer in the court of the archbishop. The elder Mozart was quick to realize that his son was a musical prodigy, and he set out to have him bring the family extra income. By the age of five, young Mozart composed his first pieces; at the age of six, he and his sister, who was four years older, toured Europe. By the age of thirteen, he had composed concertos, symphonies, sonatas, religious music, and an opera. At fourteen, he was knighted by the pope.

Mozart had a phenomenal memory for music and the ability to work out entire pieces in his head. When he committed the music in his mind to paper, he said that it rarely differed from what he had imagined. He was an excellent pianist and a competent violinist.

His great talent did not bring him financial success, however. He never had a steady appointment as a composer to a patron. He tried to work for the prince-archbishop at Salzburg, but the archbishop was a difficult man to please. Mozart did not get along with him, so he was dismissed. At the age of twenty-five, he moved to Vienna, where he spent the last ten years of his life. There he married, but had trouble supporting himself and his wife.

As he put it, his existence consisted of "hovering between hope and anxiety." He managed by teaching, giving concerts, composing, and borrowing from friends. During some of those years, he was able to earn a reasonable income, but he was overly generous and not good at managing money. At the age of thirty-five, Mozart died, probably of complications from rheumatic fever. He was buried on a cold, rainy December day in a common grave, which was customary in those days. The motion picture *Amadeus* contains many inaccuracies about Mozart's life and death. The probability that he was poisoned by his competitor Salieri was one such inaccuracy.

During his short life, he composed more than six hundred works, including many sizable compositions such as symphonies, concertos, and operas. He never assigned opus numbers to his music, but some were added by publishers. All his works were later cataloged by a Viennese botanist and amateur musician named Ludwig Köchel, which is the reason for the *K.* in the listings of his music.

Best-Known Works

Chamber music
- Clarinet Quintet
- String Quartet No. 17

Choral
- Requiem

Orchestra
- *Eine kleine Nachtmusik*
- Symphonies Nos. 39, 40, and 41 ("Jupiter")
- Clarinet Concerto
- French Horn Concerto No. 3
- Piano Concertos Nos. 20, 21, 24, and 26
- Violin Concertos Nos. 3, 4, and 5

Opera
- *Don Giovanni*
- *The Magic Flute*
- *The Marriage of Figaro*

Sonata form itself is divided into three large sections: exposition, development, and recapitulation. Each section has a number of characteristics and features.

Exposition

In the exposition of sonata form, the composer presents or exposes the themes for the movement. The first theme is heard immediately:

Several features can be pointed out about these eight measures:

- The theme is divided into two equal halves, with the second being nearly identical to the first, but one note lower. Each half is further divided in half, with the first portion sounding like a melodic statement and the second like its musical answer.

- The theme is actually simpler than it seems. The same rhythmic pattern appears on each of the four pitches. The quarter notes (♩) suggest chords: D D D B-flat (G minor) and C E-flat C (C minor) in the first four measures and so on. To this uncomplicated basic structure Mozart adds some musical spice—a little dissonance. The eighth notes marked with an X in the example are not in the harmony of the chord. Because they are short and do not occur on the beat, the effect is not harsh. Instead, it is more like a quick nudge.

- The repeated three-note figure that leans upward creates a sense of forward movement, a necessary quality in concert music. It's somewhat like saying words several times for emphasis.

- The theme is in a minor key, which is unusual among Mozart's symphonies. The minor mode adds its own particular mood to the music. Many composers in the nineteenth century used the minor mode to suggest gloomy music, but not Mozart. His use of minor in this symphony adds only a tinge of color; never does the music become sticky or sentimental.

- In a sense, the theme is a collection of several melodic fragments. It is not a sweeping, arching series of pitches but instead contains neat and concise phrases that are clearly delineated from each other. This quality makes it easier to develop.

After a few closing chords, the theme starts to repeat. But this time, halfway through, the music shifts to some solid-sounding chords and rapidly moving scales. A transition has begun. Transitions may or may not have much musical character of their own. They can (1) help the music modulate smoothly, (2) make a gradual change to a new theme, and (3) provide new musical ideas. Mozart's transition does all three of these things. Two chords followed by a rest mark the end of the transition. Such clear-cut points marking out the form are typical of music in the Classical period.

The second theme is divided between the violins and the woodwinds:

Exposition

First theme	Transition	Second theme	Transition	Codetta
In tonic key		In dominant key or relative major		

© Cengage Learning®

FIGURE 16.1
EXPOSITION

It differs from the first theme in several ways:

- It has longer note values.
- It has no frequently repeated rhythm pattern.
- It contains few skips up or down to other notes.
- It is more difficult to remember than the first because of its chromatic movement, which is movement by half steps. Usually it can be seen in the added sharps and flats.
- It is in a different key from the first theme, which is usually true of the themes in expositions in the Classical period. If a movement begins in a minor key, the second theme is generally in the relative major key. If the movement is in major, the second theme often is in the major key five notes higher.

Following the second theme, another transition appears. Fragments of the first theme are interspersed in it. At this point in sonata form, composers have some options. They can introduce a third theme (sometimes called the *closing theme*), they may write an extended transition, or they may borrow a fragment from one of the themes, which is what Mozart did here.

The transition concludes with a *codetta*, which is a short concluding section. Sometimes codettas have a brief melody of their own.

So far, only the first of the three sections that sonata form comprises has been presented. The exposition can be depicted as in Figure 16.1.

Classical composers usually indicated that the entire exposition was to be repeated. In performances today the repeat sign is sometimes ignored, and the music moves directly into the next section. It is repeated in the recording that is available in this edition's music collection.

Development

Logically, the **development** section is where much of the development of themes described earlier in this chapter takes place. What does Mozart do in the development section of the first movement of Symphony No. 40? Essentially, he treats the first theme in three ways:

1. The first half of the first theme is played three times, each time in a different key.
2. Counterpoint is introduced. While the lower strings play the first theme in a different key, the violins begin a countermelody of rapidly moving notes:

When the lower strings finish the first half of the first theme, they take up the countermelody while the violins play the theme. A similar exchange occurs two more times, each time one note lower than its preceding phrase.

3. The first theme is fragmented even further. The first few notes are tossed back and forth among the flute, clarinet, and violins. The music modulates often, but this section is quiet compared with the busy, vigorous exchanges between low and high strings that preceded it. Soon the answer in the woodwinds is shortened again to

include only its first three notes. Several times the melodic figure is inverted, so it ascends in pitch rather than descends:

Fragments of the first theme appear in *all but the first two measures* of the development section. Fragments of the theme also appear in the transition leading from the development into the next main section of sonata form.

In this particular development, Mozart works with only the first theme. He breaks it apart, modulates frequently, adds countermelodies, and inverts it. Such treatments of the theme are typical of development sections in sonata form. He could have done other things as well. He could have developed the second theme, or he could have introduced a new theme. He might have altered the rhythm, written different chords for it, or combined two themes in a contrapuntal manner. The means of development are endless.

WOLFGANG AMADEUS MOZART
Symphony No. 40, First Movement (1788)

LISTENING GUIDE

Genre: Symphony

Form: Sonata

Download 32

8 minutes 11 seconds

Exposition

0:00   First theme begins in violins and is repeated. (Repeats at 2:02)

0:33   Transition containing short motive and many scalewise notes. (Repeats at 2:34)

0:51   Violins and woodwinds play second theme. (Repeats at 2:53)

1:01	Woodwinds and violins repeat second theme; then transition begins. (Repeats at 3:04)
1:47	Codetta begins with fast notes by violins. (Repeats at 3:49)
2:00	Codetta concludes with a solid chord. (Repeats at 4:01)

Development

4:02	Development section begins with two short chords and notes by woodwinds.
4:07	First theme appears three times in sequence, each time one note lower.
4:22	Upper and lower strings alternate portion of first theme and rapidly moving notes.
4:50	Motive from first theme alternates between violins and flute.
5:07	Fragment of first theme played forcefully several times by violins

Recapitulation

5:22	First theme returns, played by violins in the tonic key, and is repeated.
5:55	Transition begins but is longer and more complex than in the exposition.
6:37	Woodwinds and strings play second theme.
6:49	Second theme repeated; then transition begins.
7:21	Clarinet and bassoon exchange the motive from the first theme.
7:39	Coda begins with fast scalewise passages.
7:51	Strings and woodwinds play motive from first theme several times.
8:06	Movement closes with three solid chords.

🎵 **LISTEN TO...** this selection streaming online.

🎵 **WATCH...** an Active Listening Guide of this selection online.

🎵 **WATCH...** a performance of this selection online.

🎵 **DO...** an online Listening Practice Activity related to this selection, which your instructor may assign for a grade.

Recapitulation

The term for the third section of sonata form is **recapitulation**. The first five letters of the word *recapitulation* form the word *recap*. And, sure enough, Mozart comes back to the first theme. It is played by the same instruments and with the same accompanying music. This literal repetition doesn't last long, however. Changes are introduced gradually as the bassoon adds a few notes in contrast.

More changes occur as the music moves into the transition heading toward the second theme. The transition is longer than it was in the exposition. In fact, for a short time it sounds almost as if another development section has begun. While the second

Sonata Form

Exposition

Introduction (optional)	First theme	Transition	Second theme	Transition	Codetta
	In tonic key		*In dominant key or relative major*		

Development

Working over of musical ideas; sometimes new melodies introduced

Recapitulation

First theme	Transition	Second theme	Transition	Codetta
		In tonic key		

© Cengage Learning®

FIGURE 16.2

SONATA FORM

violins play rapidly moving notes, the short fragment heard just briefly in the exposition is exchanged between the first violins and the low strings:

There is another difference. The second theme is not in a new key; it stays in the tonic or home key. If the second theme were in a different key, the composer would have to have the music modulate quickly back to the tonic before the movement ends and sound convincing about it. That is not an easy thing to do. Following the second theme, the transition uses music similar to what was played at the comparable place in the exposition.

The movement ends with a *coda*, which means "tail" in Italian. It is like the codetta, except that it is longer so that it can provide a convincing conclusion to the entire movement. In this coda, Mozart again uses a fragment from the first theme. Dominant (V_7) and tonic (I) chords alternate in typical Classical style to give the movement a solid ending.

No two movements in sonata form are exactly alike; each is unique. In general, however, sonata form can be diagrammed as shown in Figure 16.2.

OTHER ASPECTS OF SONATA FORM

The key of the music was important in the Classical period. It is usually provided along with the title of the work: Symphony No. 40 in G Minor by Mozart. Sometimes a work is referred to by its key, for example, Mozart's G Minor Symphony. Today, however, the key of a work is not particularly important to listeners. Music of the nineteenth century modulated so often and so far from the tonic that the impact of key change has been greatly reduced. And music in the twentieth century continued this trend, even to the point where some music has no key center at all.

Keep in mind that *everything* in a movement matters. It is not that the themes are the really good stuff and the transitions are just filler around them. As in doing a puzzle, every piece of it is needed for the complete picture.

Many movements in sonata form have introductions, although Mozart's Symphony No. 40 does not. They are usually in a slow tempo and seldom have much musical relationship with the rest of the movement in terms of their themes.

MAIN POINTS OF CHAPTER 16

1. The most important form developed during the Classical period was sonata form. It consists of three large sections: exposition, development, and recapitulation. A coda usually concludes a movement in sonata form.

2. The exposition consists of the first theme, a transition to a second theme, and a transition leading to a codetta.

3. In the development section, composers could work with fragments of either or both themes, change keys often, invert a motive from a theme, add counterpoint or different chords with the theme, or any combination of these possibilities.

4. The recapitulation returns to the music of the exposition, but usually with small changes as the music progresses. It concludes with a coda.

5. Mozart was one of the greatest musical geniuses of all time. In his short life he composed 626 pieces of music, many of them sizable works such as symphonies, concertos, operas, and chamber and choral works.

 PRACTICE...
your understanding of this chapter's concepts by working once more with the chapter's Active Listening Guides online.

 DO...
online quizzes that your instructor may assign for a grade.

17

The Concerto

START...

experiencing this chapter's topics with an online video activity that your instructor may assign.

READ...

the complete chapter text in a rich interactive eBook!

Learning Objectives

1   Distinguish the features of a concerto of the Classical period.
2   Discuss the patterns of themes that make up rondo form, in the context of a third movement of a concerto.

Neil Simon, the highly successful playwright, has written two plays consisting of three short acts that take place in the same location. But each play has characters and stories not found in the other plays. The location of *Plaza Suite* is New York's Plaza Hotel; *California Suite* utilizes a hotel setting in California. The only connection among the acts of each play is the suite of rooms.

It is somewhat like that with the multimovement works composed during the Classical period. Instead of a single location, however, Classical composers related the movements only in terms of tempos and keys. They planned for contrast among the movements in terms of forms, melodic character, amount of development, tempo, and so on. In this chapter we look at how composers during the Classical period achieved contrast among movements in the solo concerto.

THE SOLO CONCERTO

The concerto grosso of the Baroque period went out of fashion in the Classical period and was replaced by the solo concerto. Since the Classical period, the word *concerto* almost always refers only to a solo concerto. The advent of the solo concerto parallels to some degree the beginning of public concerts, for which the composer organized and managed most of the administrative details.

There are important differences between the two types of concertos. The most obvious one is the fact that the Classical concerto is a solo concerto that features one player. The soloist stands while the players in the orchestra sit. He or she is given special status in terms of stage protocol by entering and leaving with the conductor and the chance to bow and acknowledge the applause of the audience. The soloist usually memorizes the music and is given special attention in the printed program and in the advertisements for the concert. Yes, the soloist is paid more than the members of the orchestra, sometimes quite a bit more.

There is one more important difference. The music the soloist plays is more technically demanding and showy than the music for the other players in the orchestra. It provides the soloist a chance to demonstrate his or her outstanding prowess as a performer. Audiences are attracted by the opportunity to hear an outstanding performer.

Most concertos are for the piano or violin, which are the most frequently featured instruments for concertos. Both Haydn and Mozart also composed concertos for less typical instruments such as clarinet, trumpet, bassoon, and French horn. The concertos for these instruments are amazing in terms of overcoming or working around the limitations of the wind instruments at the time. The works are of such high quality that they are still performed often today.

Mozart's Piano Concerto No. 21 in C Major, K. 467

Mozart must have liked, or thought his listeners would like, solo concertos, because he certainly wrote a lot of them: about twenty-seven for piano, seven for violin, four for French horn, two for flute, and one each for bassoon, clarinet, and oboe. In addition, he composed a number of concertos for two violins and other combinations of instruments.

Three features characterize the first movements of Classical concertos. They are:

DOUBLE EXPOSITION Although the first movement is in sonata form, a second or **double exposition** is incorporated in the form. The first exposition is played by the orchestra; the second by the orchestra and the soloist. Because the second exposition usually includes music that shows off the soloist's prowess on the instrument, it tends to be longer than the first exposition.

CADENZA Neither of the movements selected for this chapter happens to include a cadenza. Usually, a Classical concerto had one in its three movements. The difference between the cadenzas in Classical concertos and the cadenzas in Rodrigo's *Concierto de Aranjuez* and Bach's Brandenburg Concerto No. 5 is that Rodrigo and Bach wrote out every note for the performer to play. In the Classical period, composers just wrote the word *cadenza* or its abbreviation *Cad.* at the appropriate place in the music. The performer was expected to make up a technically impressive paraphrase of the themes in the movement.

Whether soloists actually did so onstage is open to question. Improvisation was a much more common practice during the Baroque and Classical periods than it is today. Performers at that time probably worked at being good improvisers, but one wonders about doing so before an audience without prior preparation. For this reason, concerto programs today will sometimes indicate who wrote the cadenza for a particular Classical concerto, and the cadenzas will differ depending on the preferences of the soloist.

The Second Movement of Concertos

The second movement of almost all concertos composed in the Classical period features beautiful melodies and a slow tempo. The second movement to Mozart's Piano Concerto No. 21 (see Listening Guide) is no exception. It has the well-deserved reputation as one of the most beautiful works ever written. Part of its fame is the result of its use in the soundtrack of a very romantic movie of fifty years ago, *Elvira Madigan*.

The movement is in an overall *A B A* form. Parts of its melody have the quality of an operatic aria as the melody soars above a simple, throbbing accompaniment played mainly by the strings in the orchestra. It seems so simple, so superbly simple. Its overarching melody is accompanied by throbbing muted sounds played quietly, three notes to the beat, by the upper strings. The low strings play pizzicato one note on each beat.

Throughout the movement the melody often contains a note that doesn't fit with its accompanying chord for half or an entire beat. It soon resolves to a consonant member of the chord. It's somewhat like a musical sigh, and it adds much to the character of the music.

WOLFGANG AMADEUS MOZART
Piano Concerto No. 21, Second Movement (1785)

Genre: Concerto

Form: *A B A*

Download 33

7 Minutes 20 Seconds

A Section

0:00   Movement begins with muted first violins playing the melody and second violins and violas playing three notes to the beat as cellos and basses pluck a single note on the beat.

0:31   Contrasting phrases with abrupt dynamic changes. Wide leaps follow.

1:12   Pair of phrases by oboe and violins. Flute and bassoon join in.

1:42   Piano enters and plays first phrase of *A* section.

1:56   Second phrase played by piano

2:31   Accompanying triplets move into *B* section.

B Section

2:40   Music changes to minor key. Piano soon plays some faster notes.

3:15   Some of the free material returns in descending sequence.

3:36   Piano and woodwinds play pairs of phrases from *A* section.

4:03   Piano and woodwinds exchange sustained phrases.

4:45   Music leads to return of *A* section.

A Section

5:17   *A* section returns with its melody more ornamented.

6:03 Free material played again in descending sequence

6:23 Music returns to tonic key as movement ends quietly.

LISTEN TO... this selection streaming online.

WATCH... an Active Listening Guide of this selection online.

WATCH... a performance of this selection online.

DO... an online Listening Practice Activity related to this selection, which your instructor may assign for a grade.

RONDO FORM

Most third movements of Classical concertos are written in rondo form. The basic idea of a **rondo** is the return of the same theme several times after other themes have been inserted among its various appearances. A rondo can be represented *A B A C A D A* and so on. Theoretically, there is no limit to the number of sections possible in a rondo, but five is the minimum number. The pattern does not need to alternate as indicated by the foregoing example. They can be juggled *A B A C A B A*, or *A B A C D A*, or the shorter *A B A C A*, and so on, as long as the principle of the return of the *A* theme is followed.

The themes used in rondos tend to be shorter, less complicated, and happier sounding than those in the first or second movements. Because the sections of a rondo are not usually long, composers do not have much room in which to develop themes or introduce complex musical ideas. Movements in rondo form seem especially suited to the final movements of concertos and symphonies because they leave the listeners in an upbeat mood. The principle of the rondo is found in the final movement of most multimovement works composed during the Classical period and many such works since then.

Haydn's Trumpet Concerto

Haydn composed his Trumpet Concerto in E-flat (see Listening Guide) in 1796 for a keyed (not a valve) trumpet (Figure 17.1). Keys were added to the sides of the instrument somewhat like keys on a clarinet or saxophone. Valves, which are clearly superior, replaced keys on the trumpet about 1813.

The Sterns Collection of Musical Instruments, the School of Music, Theatre and Dance, the University of Michigan.

FIGURE 17.1
THE KEYED TRUMPET

FRANZ JOSEPH HAYDN

Concerto for Trumpet in E-flat, Third Movement (1796)

Genre: Concerto

Form: Rondo

Download 34

4 minutes 10 seconds

0:00   Violins play main theme (A) softly and at a rather fast tempo.

0:20   Violins play first contrasting theme (B).

0:36   Solo trumpet enters playing A theme.

1:05   Trumpet and violins alternate playing B theme in a new key.

1:23   Violins and trumpet play second contrasting theme (C) in minor.

1:45   Trumpet plays A theme.

1:54   Trumpet and orchestra play short development of A theme as music changes key several times.

2:31   Trumpet plays first portion of A theme.

2:46   Violins and trumpet play part of B theme.

3:17   Trumpet plays short segment of A theme.

3:27   Trumpet plays a descending series of trilled notes that evoke C theme.

3:54   Coda begins as trumpet plays part of A theme softly.

4:10   Rondo closes with a crescendo and a full-sounding chord.

LISTEN TO... this selection streaming online.

WATCH... an Active Listening Guide of this selection online.

WATCH... a performance of this selection online.

DO... an online Listening Practice Activity related to this selection, which your instructor may assign for a grade.

What makes Haydn's Trumpet Concerto enjoyable to listen to?

- The trumpet has a brilliant, full sound.
- The music has a truly happy quality and a bubbling personality.
- Rondo form gives listeners the expectation that the main theme will return. When it does, they have the satisfied feeling of being right.
- Rondo form contains both something old and something new. The main theme appears a number of times with new material interspersed.

Often the contrasting sections in a rondo do not have memorable themes. Also, occasionally the composer works the material into a short development section, as Haydn does in this concerto. The movement concludes with a coda that contains two brief statements of the main theme.

Franz Joseph Haydn

Science Source

Franz Joseph Haydn (1732–1809) was born in eastern Austria the same year as George Washington. An uncle with whom Haydn went to live at the age of six gave him his first instruction in music. At eight he became a choirboy at the Cathedral of Saint Stephen in Vienna. When his voice changed, he was dismissed. For the next few years, he managed to exist doing odd jobs and teaching, as well as studying music theory. At the age of twenty-nine, he was taken into the service of Prince Paul Anton Esterházy, head of one of the richest and most powerful noble families in Hungary.

The next year Nicholas Esterházy succeeded his brother Paul. Nicholas was a connoisseur of music. Most of the time, the Esterházys lived at a country estate that rivaled the French court at Versailles (Figure 17.2). On the estate were two concert halls and two theaters, one for opera and one for marionette plays. Prince Nicholas was also an amateur performer on a string instrument called a baryton, which looks something like a cello.

As was typical of the time, Haydn not only composed but also conducted the performances, trained the musicians, and kept the instruments in repair. Fortunately, he had twenty-five good instrumentalists and a dozen or so fine singers. His contract was typical in that it required him "to produce at once any composition called for" and to smooth out all difficulties among the musicians. He was expected to present himself twice daily to await orders. For the most part, Haydn's experience with the Esterházy family represented the patronage system at its best.

After Haydn had been with the Esterházys for thirty years, Prince Nicholas died. Haydn subsequently made two visits to London in the 1790s. For each trip he composed six symphonies. After the London visits, he returned to work for a while for Nicholas Esterházy II, who was not as interested in music as his father had been. Haydn gradually retired from composing and died in 1809, the same year Abraham Lincoln was born.

Haydn is sometimes referred to as the "father" of the symphony, the string quartet, the modern orchestra, and instrumental music in general. Although such claims are exaggerated, they give an indication of his importance. What Haydn actually did was work out a better balance for the new forms. For example, he developed the finale of the symphony. Before him, the fourth movement had been no more than a light little section.

Best-Known Works

Chamber music
- String Quartets (6) Op. 76
- Piano Trios Nos. 27, 28, and 29

Concertos
- Concerto No. 1 for Cello
- Concerto for Trumpet

Choral
- *The Creation*
- *Lord Nelson Mass*
- *The Seasons*

Orchestra
- Symphonies No. 92 ("Oxford"), 94 ("Surprise"), 100 ("Military"), 101 ("Clock"), and 104 ("London")

FIGURE 17.2
Esterházy Palace, the "Hungarian Versailles," where Haydn was court musician for thirty years

© Maran Garai/Shutterstock.com

 PRACTICE...
your understanding of this chapter's concepts by working once more with the chapter's Active Listening Guides online.

DO...
online quizzes that your instructor may assign for a grade.

MAIN POINTS OF CHAPTER 17

1. The solo concerto for soloist and orchestra replaced the concerto grosso of the Baroque period as the main type of concerto. The solo part became more technically difficult and showy than the orchestra part, and soloists were placed in front of the orchestra.

2. The first movements of most concertos are in sonata form that consists of an exposition for the orchestra alone followed by a second exposition for the soloist accompanied by the orchestra.

3. At least one of the three movements of a concerto usually includes a cadenza. During that time, the cadenzas were not written by the composers. Instead, they merely indicated where a cadenza should occur, and the soloist was expected to improvise it.

4. At least five sections are required for rondo form: the main theme with two contrasting themes inserted between its appearances to give the movement an *ABACA* form. The A theme is in the same key, and the contrasting sections are usually in different keys. Many rondos contain more than five sections.

5. Rondos usually have a bright, happy quality, and are often the final movement of instrumental works in the Classical period.

Classical Opera

Learning Objectives

1 Discuss the features of opera in the Classical period.
2 Differentiate opera seria and opera buffa.
3 Characterize Mozart's operas in the context of *Don Giovanni*.

 START...
experiencing this chapter's topics with an online video activity that your instructor may assign.

 READ...
the complete chapter text in a rich interactive eBook!

A span of about 185 years passed between the first Baroque operas and Mozart's highly successful operas. In some ways, the genre had changed somewhat during that time, but in other ways it was similar. It was still the great amalgamation of the arts that brought together vocal and instrumental music, theater, and sometimes dance. And the music still consisted of accompanied recitatives, arias, and choruses that are clearly distinguishable from one another. But changes were taking place.

THE DEVELOPMENT OF OPERA

Although around 1600 operas began consisting largely of dramatic singing in recitative style, that soon became much less important than arias displaying virtuoso singing. The combination of music and drama had grown so out of balance that near the end of the Baroque, the composer Christoph Willibald Gluck (1714–1787) felt compelled to lead a reform movement. Gluck had composed many operas himself, so he knew the genre well. He tried to bring back its dramatic integrity by making the music serve the text. Everything in opera, including ballet, was to be an integral part of the drama. Gluck composed several operas that demonstrated his reforms.

In the decades following the opening of the first opera house in Venice, opera divided into two rather distinct styles. **Opera seria** had a serious nature and was closer to the original dramatic intent of the first operas. **Opera buffa** ("*boo*-fah") was a light style that was often comic. "The War of the Buffoons" between those who favored opera buffa and those who favored the more serious court opera occurred around the middle of the eighteenth century in Paris. The word *buffoon* is derived from *buffa*.

MOZART'S OPERAS

Mozart's operas differed from Baroque operas in several ways. For one thing, his more successful ones were not based on historical or mythological characters such as those in Purcell's *Dido and Aeneas* (mythological) or Monteverdi's *The Coronation of Poppea* (historical). In short, they were much more human. They were often about the nobility, who sometimes came off looking less than noble. For example, the play on which Mozart's *The Marriage of Figaro* is based has a servant outwitting a count. The play was originally forbidden in Vienna. The libretto was made less offensive and was acceptable because it was sung, not spoken.

Another difference was that Mozart composed in both the seria and buffa types. His biggest successes were of the buffa type, which were in German, his native language. His seria operas were in Italian, a language that Mozart knew quite well because of his visits to Italy. Opera audiences in Vienna at the time were used to hearing operas in Italian and were fond of that style.

Mozart's operas also differed from Baroque operas because he was such a gifted composer. His arias are usually of exceptional musical quality, so much so that many of them are often sung at performances apart from the opera. Several of the orchestral overtures to his operas enjoy similar status.

Mozart's *Don Giovanni*

Don Giovanni (*Don Juan*) is a legendary Spanish nobleman whose appetite for women attracted many composers and playwrights before Mozart. Don Juan's exploits seemed to provide a source for artistic ideas. Mozart received a commission for the opera from an opera company in Prague, largely because of the huge success a year earlier of his opera *The Marriage of Figaro*. The libretto for both operas was written by the Italian Lorenzo da Ponte, the most recognized librettist of his day. *Don Giovanni* was warmly received in Prague but was less successful in Vienna. Apparently, the Viennese did not take to what seemed to them the opera's heavier qualities.

For the most part, *Don Giovanni* is opera seria. It contains some humorous moments, but its outlook is serious. Because of the opera's length, the discussion here is limited mainly to the last portion. The plot is intricate, so the opera should be listened to with the aid of an English translation of the libretto.

Don Giovanni opens with a typical overture. The stage action starts as Don Giovanni begins his adventures with Ottavio's fiancée, Donna Anna. She refuses his advances, and her father, the Commendatore (the Commandant), is killed by Don Giovanni in a duel while defending his daughter's virginity. At an engagement party, Don Giovanni attempts to seduce Zerlina, the bride of the peasant Masetto.

Later, Don Giovanni plays a cruel trick on Donna Elvira, whom he had seduced long ago and then deserted, and pursues other sexual adventures and pleasures. During one of his escapades, he takes refuge in a cemetery, where he discovers the statue of the Commandant and mockingly invites it to dinner. The statue nods its head to accept the invitation.

The final scene (see Listening Guide) is set in the banquet hall in Don Giovanni's palace. The light, bouncy music lets the audience know immediately that the Don isn't worried. In fact, he seems to have forgotten all about the graveyard and the statue. He commands his private orchestra to play some dinner music. A wind ensemble plays a song from a popular opera of the day.

Leporello serves the table and looks hungrily at the food. "What a greedy appetite," he complains as he watches Don Giovanni down one mouthful after another. A second piece is then heard from the wind ensemble. Leporello pours the Don some wine and, thinking that he won't be seen, stuffs some food in his mouth. Leporello helps himself to more food as the third number begins—"Non più andrai" from Mozart's own *Marriage of Figaro*.

The Don, realizing that Leporello's mouth is full, asks him to whistle along with the music from *Figaro*. Poor Leporello is forced to admit that he has been snitching. The whole scene bubbles along like champagne.

Donna Elvira breaks the mood as she rushes in and throws herself at Don Giovanni's feet. She begs her former lover to give up his immoral ways. Leporello is moved, but not Don Giovanni. He mocks Donna Elvira by proposing a toast to her ("Long live women and good wine!"). Angered and humiliated, she turns and runs out the door. As she is leaving, she screams as she sees the statue of the Commandant.

The music reflects the lines of the characters—the sternness of the Commandant, the cowardice of Leporello, and the cockiness of Don Giovanni. At several points in the music, Mozart has the singers repeat words or phrases. In this book, those repetitions appear only the first time they are sung, which makes the libretto less cluttered.

WOLFGANG AMADEUS MOZART
Don Giovanni, excerpt from Act II, Scene 5 (1778)

LISTENING GUIDE

Genre: Opera

Download 35

8 minutes 52 seconds

Donna Elvira screams.

0:00 DON GIOVANNI: *Che grido è questo mai?*

DON GIOVANNI: What's that scream about?

LEPORELLO: *Che grido è questo mai?*

LEPORELLO: What's that scream about?

DON GIOVANNI: *Va a veder che cosa è stato.*

DON GIOVANNI: (*to Leporello*) Go and see what's happened.

Leporello goes to the first door, looks out, screams, and returns.

LEPORELLO: *Ah!*

LEPORELLO: (*screaming*) Ah!

DON GIOVANNI: *Che grido indiavolato! Leporello, che cos'è?*

DON GIOVANNI: What a devilish scream! Leporello, what is it?

LEPORELLO: *Ah! Signor! per carità! non andate fuor di quà! L'uom di sasso, l'uomo bianco, ah! padrone! io gelo, io manco, se vedeste che figura, se sentiste come fa ta, ta, ta, ta!*

LEPORELLO: Ah! Sir! For pete's sake! Don't go out there! The man of stone, the white man. Master! I'm cold; I'm shaking. If you had seen that form; if you had heard how it goes—ta, ta, ta, ta!

DON GIOVANNI: *Non capisco niente affatto.*

DON GIOVANNI: I don't understand this.

LEPORELLO: *Ta, ta, ta, ta!*

LEPORELLO: (*imitating the statue*) Ta, ta, ta, ta!

DON GIOVANNI: *Tu sei matto in verità, in verità, in verità!*

DON GIOVANNI: Really, you're crazy!

A knock is heard.

LEPORELLO: *Ah! sentite!*

LEPORELLO: Ah! Do you hear!

DON GIOVANNI: *Qualcun batte! Apri!*

DON GIOVANNI: (*impatiently*) Someone's knocking! Open it!

LEPORELLO: *Io tremo!*

LEPORELLO: I'm trembling!

DON GIOVANNI: *Apri, dico!*

DON GIOVANNI: Open it, I say!

LEPORELLO: *Ah!*

LEPORELLO: (*pleading and terrified*) Ah!

DON GIOVANNI: *Apri!*

DON GIOVANNI: Open it!

LEPORELLO: *Ah!*

LEPORELLO: Ah!

DON GIOVANNI: *Matto! Per togliermi d'intrico ad aprir io stesso andrò.*

DON GIOVANNI: Madman! In order to clear this up, I'll open the door myself!

Don Giovanni takes one of the candle stands from the table and goes to the door. Leporello crawls underneath the table.

LEPORELLO: *Non vo' più veder l'amico, pian, pianin, m'asconderò!*

LEPORELLO: I don't want to see my friend again. Quietly, very quietly, I'll hide!

(continued)

With a rumbling of timpani, the marble statue of the Commandant enters the room.

1:30   STATUE: *Don Giovanni! a cenar teco m'invitasti! e son venuto!*

STATUE: Don Giovanni! You invited me to dine with you! And I have arrived!

Don Giovanni is somewhat startled but conceals his surprise under an air of cockiness.

DON GIOVANNI: *No l'avrei giammai creduto; ma farò quel che potrò. Leporello! un'altra centa! fa che subito si porti!*

DON GIOVANNI: I can hardly believe this. But I'll do what I can. Leporello, another dinner! Bring it immediately!

Leporello peers out from under the table with a bewildered look on his face.

LEPORELLO: *Ah, padron! siam tutti morti!*

LEPORELLO: Ah, master! We're as good as dead!

DON GIOVANNI: *Vanne, dico!*

DON GIOVANNI: Get to it, I say!

Leporello begins to crawl out.

STATUE: *Ferma un po'! Non si pasce di cibo mortale, chi si pasce di cibo seleste! Altre cure più gravi di queste, altra brama quaggiù mi guidò.*

STATUE: Wait a minute! One who partakes of heavenly food does not partake of mortal food. Things more serious than these brought me down here.

Leporello crawls back under the table.

LEPORELLO: *La terzana d'avere mi sembra, e le membra fermar più non sò.*

LEPORELLO: I have the chills and I can't stop shaking.

DON GIOVANNI: *Parla dunque! che chiedi? che vuoi?*

DON GIOVANNI: (to the Statue) Speak, then! What do you ask? What do you want?

STATUE: *Parlo: ascolta! più tempo non ho.*

STATUE: I speak—listen! I don't have much time.

DON GIOVANNI: *Parla, ascoltando ti sto.*

DON GIOVANNI: Speak! I am listening.

LEPORELLO: *Ah le membra fermar più non sò. la terzana d'avere mi sembra, le membra fermar più non sò!*

LEPORELLO: Ah! I can't stop shaking. I have the chills.

STATUE: *Parlo: ascolta! più tempo non ho.*

STATUE: I speak—listen! I don't have much time!

Don Giovanni becomes more defiant.

DON GIOVANNI: *Parla, ascoltando ti sto.*

DON GIOVANNI: Speak! I am listening!

STATUE: *Tu m'invitasti a cena, il tuo dover or sai, rispondimi, verrai tu a cenar meco?*

STATUE: You invited me to dinner. Do you know your obligation? Answer me! Will you come to dine with me?

Leporello shakes with fear beneath the table.

LEPORELLO: *Oibò, tempo no ha, scusate.*

LEPORELLO: Oh! He doesn't have time, sorry.

DON GIOVANNI: *A torto di viltate tacciato mai sarò.*

DON GIOVANNI: (coolly) I will never be accused of being a coward.

STATUE: *Risolvi!*

STATUE: Decide!

DON GIOVANNI: *Ho già risolto!*

DON GIOVANNI: I have already decided!

STATUE: *Verrai?*

STATUE: You will come?

LEPORELLO: *Dite di no! dite di no!*

LEPORELLO: Say no. Just say no!

DON GIOVANNI: *Ho fermo il core in petto, non ho timor, verrò!*

DON GIOVANNI: My heartbeat is steady. I am not afraid! I will come!

The statue extends a hand toward Don Giovanni.

6:10   STATUE: *Dammi la mano in pegno!*

STATUE: Give me your hand as a pledge!

Still defiant, Don Giovanni gives the statue his hand.

DON GIOVANNI: *Eccola! Ohime!*

DON GIOVANNI: Here it is! Ah!

STATUE: *Cos'hai!*

STATUE: What's the matter?

DON GIOVANNI: *Che gelo è questo mai?*

DON GIOVANNI: It's freezing cold!

STATUE: *Pentiti, cangia vita, è l'ultimo momento!*

STATUE: Repent! Change your life! It's your last chance!

Don Giovanni tries to withdraw his hand.

DON GIOVANNI: *No, no, ch'io non mi pento, vanne lontan da me!*

DON GIOVANNI: No, no. I will not repent! Get away from me!

STATUE: *Pentiti, scellerato!*

STATUE: Repent, villain!

DON GIOVANNI: *No, vecchio infatuato!*

DON GIOVANNI: No, you stupid old man!

STATUE: *Pentiti!*

STATUE: Repent!

DON GIOVANNI: *No!*

DON GIOVANNI: No!

STATUE: *Pentiti!*

STATUE: Repent!

DON GIOVANNI: *No!*

DON GIOVANNI: No!

STATUE: *Sì!*

STATUE: Yes!

DON GIOVANNI: *No!*

DON GIOVANNI: No!

STATUE: *Sì!*

STATUE: Yes!

DON GIOVANNI: *No!*

DON GIOVANNI: No!

With a desperate effort, he wrests his hand away from the statue.

STATUE: *Sì! Sì!*

STATUE: Yes! Yes!

DON GIOVANNI: *No! No!*

DON GIOVANNI: No! No!

The Commandant's statue begins to move toward the door. Roaring flames begin to surround Don Giovanni.

STATUE: *Ah! tempo più non v'è!*

STATUE: Ah! There is no more time!

DON GIOVANNI: *Da qual tremore insolito sentoassalir gli spiriti! dond'escono quei vortici di foco pien d'orror?*

DON GIOVANNI: I feel my strength afflicted by really unusual trembling! Where are those horrible whirlpools of fire coming from?

A chorus of ghostly demon voices sounds from below.

7:45   **DEMON VOICES:** *Tutto a tue colpe è poco! Vieni! c'è un ma! peggior!*

DEMON VOICES: This is nothing compared to your crimes! Worse things await you!

DON GIOVANNI: *Chi l'anima mi lacera? Chi m'agita le viscere? Che strazio, ohimè, che smania! Che inferno, che terror!*

DON GIOVANNI: Who rips my spirit? Who shakes my innards? What twisting, alas, what frenzy! What hell! What terror!

LEPORELLO: *Che ceffo disperato! Che gesti da dannato! Che gridi! Che lamenti! Come mi fa terror!*

LEPORELLO: What a terrible look on his face! What gestures of a damned soul! What shouts! What wailing! It terrifies me!

DEMON VOICES: *Tutto a tue colpe è poco!*

DEMON VOICES: All this is nothing compared to your crimes!

DON GIOVANNI: *Chi l'anima mi lacera?*

DON GIOVANNI: Who rips my spirit?

LEPORELLO: *Che ceffo disperato!*

LEPORELLO: What a terrible look on his face!

DEMON VOICES: *Vieni! c'è un mal peggior!*

DEMON VOICES: Come! Worse things await you!

DON GIOVANNI: *Chi m'agita le viscere? che strazio, ohimè, che smania! Ah! che inferno! che terror!*

DON GIOVANNI: Who shakes my innards? What twisting, alas, what frenzy! Ah! What hell! What terror!

LEPORELLO: *Che gesti da dannato! che gridi! che lamenti! Come mi fa terror!*

LEPORELLO: What gestures of a damned soul! What shouts! What wailing! It terrifies me!

DEMON VOICES: *Vieni! vieni! vieni! c'è un mal peggior!*

DEMON VOICES: Come! Worse things await you!

DON GIOVANNI: *Ah!*

DON GIOVANNI: (screaming) Ah!

(continued)

Don Giovanni utters his final sound, is enveloped by flames, and sinks to hell.
Leporello echoes the Don's shout.

LEPORELLO: Ah!   LEPORELLO: Ah!

8:43   Orchestra concludes with a flourish.

 LISTEN TO... this selection streaming online.

 WATCH... an Active Listening Guide of this selection online.

 WATCH... a performance of this selection online.

 DO... an online Listening Practice Activity related to this selection, which your instructor may assign for a grade.

Following the immolation of Don Giovanni (Figure 18.1), the mood suddenly changes to something more lighthearted. Donna Anna, Donna Elvira, and Zerlina rush in, followed by Ottavio and Masetto. They find Leporello crawling about on the floor and demand to know what has happened. Leporello stammers out the story of what he just witnessed.

The music is again filled with wit and sparkle. Don Giovanni is already just a memory. In a brief duet, Donna Anna and Ottavio tell of their plans to marry after her year of mourning for her father is over. Donna Elvira pledges to end her days in a cloister. Zerlina and Masetto are anxious to be off so they can have dinner. And Leporello sets about finding himself a new master. As the six singers face the audience, they deliver the

FIGURE 18.1
DON GIOVANNI ON STAGE IN LONDON GERALD FINLEY (AS DON GIOVANNI) AND ROBERT LLOYD (AS COMMANDANT) IN THE PRODUCTION *DON GIOVANNI* AT THE ROYAL OPERA HOUSE IN COVENT GARDEN.

moral of the opera. The whole scene is so mischievous that one wonders whether Mozart was not really attempting to have the last laugh with the moralizing. The sextet sings:

> *Such is the end*
> *Of those who do evil.*
> *The death of the wicked*
> *Always matches their life.*

This last scene containing moralizing by the sextet has often been omitted from the opera. In the nineteenth century, it was thought out of place after the damnation of *Don Giovanni*. Mozart himself approved the deletion the second time it was staged.

MAIN POINTS OF CHAPTER 18

1. Opera developed at the beginning of the Baroque period as an attempt to recreate the drama of the Ancient Greeks. Over the years, however, dramatic quality had given way to displays of virtuoso singing in operas with flimsy plots and little dramatic impact. Christoph Willibald Gluck began the reform of opera by integrating all of its components into a unified entity.

2. Two types of opera were important in the Classical period: opera seria and opera buffa. Opera seria are usually tragic and feature stories about ancient gods and heroes. Opera buffa are filled with fun and frivolity, including the occasional use of popular tunes.

3. Mozart composed both opera seria and opera buffa. His seria operas were in Italian, and his buffa operas were in German. Many of his operas involved human rather than mythological characters. Many of his opera arias and overtures are often performed as concert works apart from the opera.

 PRACTICE...
your understanding of this chapter's concepts by working once more with the chapter's Active Listening Guide online.

 DO...
online quizzes that your instructor may assign for a grade.

19 Chamber Music

START...

experiencing this chapter's topics with an online video activity that your instructor may assign.

READ...

the complete chapter text in a rich interactive eBook!

Learning Objectives

1 List the features of chamber music and its movements in the Classical period.

2 Describe minuet and trio form in the context of a string quartet.

3 Characterize theme and variations in the context of a clarinet quintet.

Until the Classical period, most instrumental music (except for keyboard) did not clearly indicate the size of the group for which it was written. As the orchestra became more standardized, composers began to specify the type of group for which they were writing. Apparently they felt that music for an orchestra was not as suitable for music created with a small group in mind, and vice versa. The music they created for small groups is known as **chamber music**.

Musicians to this day have continued to value chamber music, primarily because it permits a refinement and intimacy of expression that cannot be derived from a large musical organization. An orchestra has power and color; a string quartet provides a sense of involvement and clarity. One medium can be as musically satisfying as the other in the hands of skilled composers and performers.

THE NATURE OF CHAMBER MUSIC

The chief characteristic of chamber music is one player on each part. This definition refers to parts, not instruments. For instance, a string quartet consists of two violins, one viola, and one cello, but there are two *different* violin parts. So long as each has a different part, there could be three or more violins, and the work would still be considered chamber music.

Voices are not usually involved in chamber music, although early chamber works were influenced by vocal style. In fact, during the Renaissance, madrigals could be either sung or played on string instruments. In the twentieth century, Igor Stravinsky, Arnold Schoenberg, and others composed for voices in chamber compositions. Since the Renaissance, however, and particularly during the Classical period, chamber music has consisted of instrumental music.

The players perform chamber music while looking at their music notation; only soloists play from memory. In chamber music, the individual must be subordinate to the group, so memorizing is not called for. Furthermore, the undistinguished quality of the parts when providing harmony and the number of players involved make the memorized performance more susceptible to error.

The formal patterns found in chamber music in the Classical period are the same as those presented in earlier chapters in conjunction with the symphony and the concerto. Not only are the same forms used for individual movements but also the pattern of movements is the same. The first movements of sonatas, string quartets, and other chamber works are in sonata form. The second movements have slow tempos and emphasize melody; often they are in a three-part form. The third movements of four-movement works are usually in the form of a minuet and trio. The fourth or last movements generally have a fast tempo and often are rondos. This arrangement of forms and movements tends to be true regardless of the particular combination of instruments used in a work.

Listening to Chamber Music

The methods for listening to chamber music are essentially the same as those for listening carefully and thoughtfully to music of any type. But because chamber music is performed by a small group, it lacks the tonal power and the lush, colorful sounds of a full orchestra or chorus. Listeners must therefore concentrate on what is happening in the music itself. The composer's musical ideas and treatment of them in a composition are the heart of chamber music.

The fewer players there are, the easier it is to hear small errors in playing, so the performers must execute their parts with accuracy and unity. This feeling of oneness in musical performance is called *ensemble*. Chamber music is usually performed without a conductor, so the sensing of tempos, phrasing, and dynamics is the responsibility of each player. However, the person who plays the first violin part is usually considered the leader.

Although one person is acknowledged to be the leader, the cues and nods that start and stop the group are so subtle that the audience sees them only by watching carefully. This explains why the word *ensemble* refers both to the sense of unified performance by the players and to the chamber music group itself.

When a chamber music group is heard live in a home or small recital hall, something is added to the listeners' enjoyment. Perhaps the closeness of the performers provides a sense of involvement that makes listening to chamber music enjoyable. In any case, chamber music is best heard in a live performance in small recital halls or the living rooms of large homes.

Music for orchestra is generally far better known than chamber music, probably because more knowledge and attention are required for successful chamber music listening. Because there is a limited audience, few chamber groups can earn a living solely from performing. Today, chamber ensembles are found in residence at a number of universities.

Chamber Music in the Classical Period

Chamber music thrived in the Classical period, because the social setting encouraged its creation and performance. Most performances of music were still for private audiences. When hosts wished to provide after-dinner music for guests in their palatial homes, they often thought of a chamber group.

Haydn's experience with chamber music indicates its use during the Classical period. As mentioned in Chapter 17, his patron, Prince Nicholas Esterházy, happened to enjoy playing the baryton. The instrument looks something like a cello but has sloping shoulders and more strings that vibrate sympathetically. Haydn composed a great deal of music for his patron to play: 125 trios, 12 short divertimentos, and 2 duets. But he wrote many chamber pieces in addition to those involving the baryton (Figure 19.1).

In addition, musicians such as Mozart and Haydn and competent amateurs engaged in playing chamber music on an informal social basis. It was a fashionable thing to do during the Classical period.

THE SONATA

From the Classical period forward, the *sonata* became a sizable instrumental work in three or four movements. Classical sonatas are divided into two categories. The *ensemble sonata* is usually a composition for two instruments: piano and one other instrument. The *solo sonata* is for a single instrument. Note: A sonata frequently has one or more of its movements in sonata form. It's logical, but it can seem confusing.

The Metropolitan Museum of Art The Crosby Brown Collection of Musical Instruments 1889. (89.4.1851) Baryton Bohemia 1779 Wood Body length 66.4 cm Body width upper bout 15.2 cm © The Metropolitan Museum of Art

FIGURE 19.1

THE BARYTON IS A VERY DIFFERENT INSTRUMENT FROM THE BARITONE HORN. IT IS A MEMBER OF THE VIOL FAMILY.

The two instrumental parts are considered to be of equal importance in the ensemble sonata. In no sense is the piano accompanying the other instrument. As a matter of fact, some of the time the piano part contains a more important musical idea, while the other instrument plays accompanying material. Because the presence of the piano is assumed, the sonata is called by the name of the other instrument. So, a violin sonata is for violin and piano.

Unlike other ensemble works, a solo sonata is usually played from memory. Although a few solo sonatas have been written for violin or other instruments, the solo sonata is most associated with the piano. Solo sonatas for piano are presented in Chapter 20.

THE STRING QUARTET

With its instrumentation of two violins, a viola, and a cello, the **string quartet** (Figure 19.2) is probably the most significant chamber ensemble. Early in the eighteenth century, compositions called **divertimentos** were common. As the name implies, they were diversionary, innocuous pieces. They could be played by either a quartet or a string orchestra. Haydn took the divertimento, deleted one of its two minuets, and gave it more musical substance. He called these new works *quartets* rather than divertimentos. The change did not occur quickly; it was stretched out over much of Haydn's adult life.

Haydn's String Quartet, Op. 76, No. 3 ("Emperor")

Haydn's Op. 76, No. 3, is known as the "Emperor Quartet" because its second movement uses as its theme "The Emperor's Hymn," a melody based on a folk song that Haydn composed for Emperor Franz II a year before the quartet in 1796. This melody is the national anthem of both Austria and Germany today and is a hymn in several mainline Protestant churches.

The six quartets in Op. 76 were commissioned and dedicated to a Count Endödy for a fee of a hundred ducats. They were the exclusive property of the count "for a certain number of years" before being published in 1799 and selling well. They were composed late in Haydn's career, and he finished only two more quartets during the remainder of his life.

The first movement is in sonata form. The second movement features "The Emperor's Hymn," and the fourth is lively and in sonata form. The third movement (see Listening Guide) is a minuet and trio, which is a stylized version of a popular dance of the time. Third movements of Classical symphonies and quartets usually follow a form more closely than other movements do. Essentially, the form is a large three-part *A B A* form, with each large part having subsections (Figure 19.3).

The music is in a clear three-beat meter, with the first violin being responsible for most of the themes. The second violin, viola, and cello generally have accompanying parts that occasionally contain a melodic figure. The minuet is in major, whereas the trio begins in minor, but its *b* theme is in major. The term *trio* is the result of a tradition in which the contrasting parts of a minuet were played by two instruments plus accompaniment.

FIGURE 19.2
Title Page for the French publication of three of the six quartets that Mozart wrote and dedicated to Haydn. Mozart offered them "as children" to his friend.

Lebrecht Music & Arts/The Image Works

 WATCH... a performance of a minuet.

FIGURE 19.3
Minuet and trio form

	Minuet	Trio	Minuet
	A	*B*	*A*
	a a b a' b a'	*a a b a' b a'*	*a b a'*

LISTENING GUIDE

FRANZ JOSEPH HAYDN
String Quartet in C Major, Op. 76, No. 3, "Emperor," Third Movement (1797)

Genre: Chamber Music

Form: Minuet and Trio

Download 36

5 minutes

Minuet

0:00   First violin plays the *a* theme of the minuet in a major key and three-beat meter.

0:22   The *a* theme is repeated.

0:44   The *b* theme of the minuet begins.

0:57   The *a* theme is extended.

1:23   The *b* theme is repeated.

1:37   The extended *a* theme is repeated.

Trio

2:04   First violin plays the *a* theme of the trio in a minor key.

2:14   The *a* theme of the trio is repeated.

2:23   First violin plays a link to the next theme.

2:40   First violin plays the *b* theme of the trio in a major key.

2:48   The *b* theme is repeated as cello plays contrasting phrases.

2:58   The *a* theme of the trio is extended.

3:08   The *b* theme is repeated.

3:26   The *a* theme is extended.

Minuet

3:55   The *a* theme of the minuet returns.

4:09   The *b* theme of the minuet returns.

4:31   The extended *a* theme of the minuet returns.

4:50   The minuet concludes quietly.

LISTEN TO... this selection streaming online.

WATCH... an Active Listening Guide of this selection online.

WATCH... a performance of this selection online.

DO... an online Listening Practice Activity related to this selection, which your instructor may assign for a grade.

OTHER TYPES OF CHAMBER MUSIC GROUPS

Almost every conceivable combination of instruments has had chamber music written for it, but certain types of chamber groups are more common, including the sonata and the string quartet. Another likely string group is the *string quintet* (two violins, two violas, and one cello). The *piano trio* (violin, cello, and piano) is another ensemble for which a lot of music has been composed. The *woodwind quintet* (flute, oboe, clarinet, French horn, and bassoon) was not common in Haydn's time, but it has become a standard chamber ensemble in the twentieth century. Brass ensembles have the least standardized instrumentation. Perhaps the *brass quintet* (two trumpets, a French horn, a trombone, and a tuba) has most frequently drawn the attention of composers.

It is not unusual to find one nonstring instrument added to a string quartet. For example, Mozart's work for clarinet and string quartet has the title Clarinet Quintet in A Major, although only one clarinet is present. If a piano plus a string quartet is called for, the work is a piano quintet. Apparently, the presence of strings is taken for granted in such ensembles, so the added instrument is cited in the name of the group.

Mozart's Clarinet Quintet

The Clarinet Quintet in A Major, K. 581 is a relatively late work by Mozart, written after his Symphony No. 40. It is in the best polished style of the eighteenth century. The form is clearly delineated, the instrumental parts are well balanced, and everything is neat and enjoyable.

The Clarinet Quintet by Mozart is for clarinet in A, not B-flat, the key of most clarinets today. There is a subtle difference in timbre between the two clarinets, and this quintet is a bit easier for the A clarinet because it is in the key of A major. This means that the clarinetist is looking at notes in C major, but, of course, sounding pitches a third lower.

FIRST MOVEMENT The first movement is in sonata form. Its first theme consists of a simple, songlike portion played by the four string instruments. The clarinet follows playing a florid passage containing many rapidly moving notes.

The development begins quietly with the first theme presented in a different key. Other figures from the exposition are also heard. The recapitulation is very similar to the exposition, except for small changes. The movement closes, as did the exposition, with a statement of the opening theme.

SECOND MOVEMENT In the second movement, the clarinet plays a beautiful melody that could easily be an aria in a Mozart opera. The B portion of the movement contains contrasting melodic material played by the violin, with the clarinet adding decorative melodic comments from time to time, which are later taken up by the violin. The opening melody returns, again played by the clarinet.

THIRD MOVEMENT The third movement is an elegant-sounding minuet and trio. This minuet is unusual because it has two trios, one for the strings and a second one giving the clarinet a chance to show off its capabilities at playing notes over a wide range along with its varied timbre.

FOURTH MOVEMENT The fourth movement (see Listening Guide) is both a form and a musical process: *theme and variations*. The basic idea of a theme and variations movement is simple: Take a melody and cast it in different settings. The process is something like taking a number of pictures of a house, but each time under different conditions and from different angles. One picture might be at daybreak, another during a rainstorm, another from ground level, and so on.

The difference between varying and developing a theme can be made clearer by thinking about what Mozart did in developing themes in his Symphony No. 40 and contrasting that with what he did in varying the theme in his clarinet quintet. *Development* involves fragmenting and remolding a theme. **Variation** consists of placing the theme in a new setting or giving it a new harmonic, rhythmic, or melodic costume.

WOLFGANG AMADEUS MOZART

Clarinet Quintet in A Major, Fourth Movement (1789)

LISTENING GUIDE

Genre: Chamber Music

Form: Theme and Variations

Download 37

9 minutes 37 seconds

Theme

0:00   Violins play *a* part of the theme and then repeat it.

0:29   They continue with *b* part of the theme and then repeat it.

Variations

0:59   Variation 1. Clarinet plays freewheeling melody as violins play *a* half of theme. Each half of each variation is repeated throughout movement.

(continued)

| 1:28 | Clarinet and violins play *b* part of theme. |
| 1:58 | Variation 2. Violin plays ornamented version of theme as second violin and viola play repeated notes. |

| 2:30 | Violins continue *b* portion of theme. |
| 3:02 | Variation 3. Viola "sobs" out its variation of theme in minor key. |

| 3:40 | Violin plays chromatic notes before viola returns with its variation. |
| 4:17 | Variation 4. Clarinet and violin play fast notes, and music returns to major. |

4:47	Clarinet plays wide leaps as violin plays rapidly moving notes.
5:16	Transition begins to next variation.
5:33	Variation 5. Violins play a slow-moving figure heard in second variation. Clarinet joins in halfway through.
6:50	The *b* portion of variation is played.
8:10	Soft, slow chords link to coda.
8:41	Coda. Violins and clarinet energetically play *a* portion of theme.
9:33	Movement ends with two short, solid chords.

LISTEN TO... this selection streaming online.

WATCH... an Active Listening Guide of this selection online.

WATCH... a performance of this selection online.

DO... an online Listening Practice Activity related to this selection, which your instructor may assign for a grade.

MAIN POINTS OF CHAPTER 19

1. Chamber music is played by small groups of instrumentalists with only one player on each part.

2. Chamber music is an important feature of Classical music. Composers wrote enormous amounts of music for performances in large rooms, not concert halls.

3. Chamber works use the same forms as the other instrumental music of the time. Although chamber works with four movements were not uncommon, many chamber works omit the minuet and trio movement found in symphonies.

4. If a string ensemble includes a nonstring instrument, then the ensemble is referred to by the name of that instrument. So an ensemble consisting of a violin, cello, and piano is called a "piano trio."

5. A sonata is a chamber work in three or four movements for solo piano or piano and another instrument. When another instrument is involved, the role of the piano is as important as that of the other instrument.

6. Theme and variations are an important type of music, both as movements in multi-movement works and stand-alone works. The concept of theme and variations is to treat a theme in a variety of settings.

7. A minuet and trio is a three part (*A B A*) form based on the minuet. It has a clear triple meter and is often used as a third movement of symphonies and string quartets.

 PRACTICE...
your understanding of this chapter's concepts by working once more with the chapter's Active Listening Guides online.

 DO...
online quizzes that your instructor may assign for a grade.

20 Piano Sonatas

START...
experiencing this chapter's topics with an online video activity that your instructor may assign.

READ...
the complete chapter text in a rich interactive eBook!

Learning Objectives

1 Describe the characteristics of Classical piano sonatas, including the development of music for the piano because of the technical improvements in it.

2 Differentiate piano sonatas by Mozart and Beethoven.

The harpsichord was the keyboard instrument of choice during the Baroque period, except for music in churches. But in the latter half of the eighteenth century, the instrument fell out of favor and was replaced by the piano. Because of the piano's increasing popularity, composers wrote music for it using the same forms that were in vogue for orchestral and chamber groups. These works for solo piano, called *sonatas*, continue to be a vital part of the music played by pianists today.

THE SONATA

As was pointed out in Chapter 19, a sonata is for either solo piano or for piano plus one other instrument. In either case, sonatas are similar to the orchestral works by the particular composer. The first movement is in sonata form, with the same general use of keys and development of themes and motives. The second movement is slow and features melody. It is often in *A B A* form, but other forms are also used. The main difference between sonatas and symphonies is that the third movement of a sonata is not the usual minuet and trio. That movement is eliminated, and the third movement becomes the final movement. Usually it is in rondo form.

The piano sonatas of the Classical period are not just miniature versions of larger works. Indeed, sometimes they are longer and occasionally seem more serious. Composers during this time also composed many of them: Mozart wrote seventeen, and Haydn thirty-one. Beethoven composed thirty-two for piano, and they represent a major contribution to the music pianists play.

THE PIANO

In Mozart's time, the piano was essentially a drawing-room instrument. Its tone was light and delicate, and composers wrote for it accordingly. During Beethoven's lifetime many improvements were made to the piano, probably the most important of which was the addition of metal braces to the frame across which the strings were strung. These braces permitted heavier strings, because the frame could now withstand the greater tension required to bring such strings up to pitch. In turn, the greater tension and heavier strings gave the piano a more powerful sound. Later the entire frame was made of cast iron, which is an absolutely rigid material. The combination of Beethoven's forceful music and a more powerful instrument inevitably enabled the piano to gain a prominent place in the concert hall.

The piano of today has changed only slightly since the beginning of the nineteenth century. The key action has been made a bit more responsive, and a pedal has been added to permit certain sustaining effects, but these improvements are relatively minor.

The type of piano construction affects the musical results. The grand piano is superior to the upright in structural design. In order to fit inside the case of an upright, the low strings have to be shortened and tuned with less tension. So the upright or spinet lacks the volume and consistency of tone found in the grand piano. The smaller the instrument, the more serious the loss of tone quality. Concert music such as a Beethoven sonata is understandably best appreciated when performed on a high-quality grand piano.

MOZART'S PIANO SONATA NO. 11

Mozart composed his eleventh piano sonata (K. 331) in the summer of 1778 while in Paris with his mother. It is one of the four piano sonatas that he wrote that summer, probably as a way of publicizing his abilities as a composer and performer. It is likely that he had hopes for a high-paying position in a prominent court. Like Bach sixty years earlier, Mozart was not successful at finding a high-paying court position.

Sonata No. 11 is typical in that the first movement is in sonata form, but the second is different from most second movements in sonatas. In an effort to appeal to the lighter tastes of Paris audiences, he substituted a minuet and trio.

The third movement, "Rondo alla Turca" (see Listening Guide), follows the usual practice by being in modified rondo form. But it is certainly not typical in terms of its appeal to audiences. It is one of Mozart's most frequently played piano works. By the way, Mozart's music is hardly Turkish. It was a fad in Paris at the time to refer to any music that sounded even slightly Middle Eastern as "Turkish."

The movement opens with music that consists of many rapidly moving notes. It is repeated, as are almost all the sections in this movement.

The B portion of the rondo switches to major and is the theme that is more easily remembered.

The music moves to the C section, then back to B, then A, and one more time for a somewhat more active-sounding B. The movement ends with a short coda.

WOLFGANG AMADEUS MOZART

Piano Sonata No. 11 in A Major, K. 331, Third Movement, "Rondo alla Turca" (1778)

Genre: Solo sonata

Form: Rondo

Download 38

3 minutes 15 seconds

0:00	First part of A section features a lively melody in minor; is repeated.
0:14	Second half of A section, which concludes with opening music; is repeated.
0:41	B section is in major and presents an energetic melody; is repeated.
0:55	C section features moving, even notes in minor.
1:09	Second half of the C section. Section is repeated.

(continued)

1:36	B section returns; is repeated.
1:51	First part of A section returns; is repeated.
2:04	Second part of A section returns; is repeated.
2:32	A vigorous version of B section returns; is repeated.
2:45	Coda begins. Contains repeated notes and chords.
3:11	Movement concludes with three solid chords.

LISTEN TO... this selection streaming online.

WATCH... an Active Listening Guide of this selection online.

WATCH... a performance of this selection online.

DO... an online Listening Practice Activity related to this selection, which your instructor may assign for a grade.

BEETHOVEN'S PIANO SONATA NO. 8 ("PATHÉTIQUE")

Beethoven's instrument was the piano, and his compositions for the instrument constitute some of his greatest contributions to music. His piano sonatas are known by their number as well as their key or nickname. The thirty-two sonatas are numbered in the order in which they were published.

Ludwig van Beethoven

Fine Art Images/SuperStock/Getty Images

Ludwig van Beethoven ("*Bay*-toe-ven," 1770–1827) was born in Bonn, Germany. His father was an alcoholic musician who hoped that young Ludwig would be a prodigy like Mozart and bring in lots of money. Although talented, young Beethoven never became the prodigy his father hoped for. At the age of twenty-two, he set off for Vienna, which was to be his home for the remainder of his life.

Beethoven had little formal schooling. He studied composition with several teachers, including a few lessons with Haydn, and made a name for himself as a pianist. He was able to win the support and admiration of the aristocracy and over a period of ten years established himself as a composer and performer. Although he was trained in the formal style of the Classical period, other events left a lasting impression on Beethoven. One was the revolutionary spirit that was

awakening in Europe, which erupted in the French Revolution in 1789.

Then there was Beethoven's own personality. Were he alive today, he would probably identify himself with humanitarian causes and social protest groups. For example, as early as 1792 he had thought of setting German dramatist-poet Friedrich von Schiller's "Ode to Joy" to music. The ethical ideals of the universal human race and its basis in the love of a heavenly Father expressed in the poem appealed to Beethoven, and he used it as the text for the last movement of his Ninth Symphony. He was probably the first composer in history to be considered a "personality." His mature works sound like no one else's music, a situation that still exists today.

Beethoven's personality was also affected by a gradual loss of hearing that eventually led to complete deafness. The condition was evident by the time he

ONE OF BEETHOVEN'S EAR TRUMPETS, AN EARLY TYPE OF HEARING AID. THE MECHANIST J. N. MÄLZEL, INVENTOR OF THE METRONOME, MADE A VARIETY OF EAR TRUMPETS FOR THE INCREASINGLY DEAF COMPOSER.

Courtesy Gesellschaft der Musickfreunde in Wien

was twenty-eight, and it caused him to lose contact with others and to withdraw into himself. His final compositions were products of this time in his life, and they tend to be more personal, meditative, and abstract.

How was it possible for Beethoven to write entire symphonies when he was deaf? The process can be understood if you think about your own experience. You can recall melodies and the sounds of people's voices in your memory, even though you aren't actually hearing them. Trained musicians can think out a large amount of music in their minds, and Beethoven was clearly a well-trained musician with outstanding abilities!

There is a second reason for his ability to compose while deaf. It was his custom to write down themes in a sketchbook. Then he would work over these themes, revising and rewriting them, and trying them out to determine their suitability for the piece he had in mind. This process went on over a period of years, so the themes for many of his later compositions had actually been worked out when he was still able to hear fairly well.

Beethoven was not a "natural" composer as Mozart was. He poured much effort into each measure he wrote, as is evident from the manuscript in Figure 21.1. As someone once said, his manuscripts look "like a bloody record of a tremendous inner battle."

Beethoven was more successful in writing instrumental music than vocal music. He composed much excellent chamber music, with his string quartets representing a high point for that ensemble. His five piano concertos and one violin concerto are staples in the music performed in concert halls today. His overtures to dramas and his opera are also performed often. He was not as at ease with music for singers. He composed only one opera, *Fidelio*, and compared its writing to the process of childbirth. He did compose two major religious works, however, and his Ninth Symphony features a chorus and soloists in the fourth movement.

Beethoven's death from jaundice and cholera occurred during a thunderstorm, a coincidence that seems appropriate to the man and his life.

Best-Known Works

Chamber music
- String Quartets Nos. 7 and 14

Choral
- *Missa Solemnis*

Orchestra
- Piano Concertos Nos. 3, 4, and 5 ("Emperor")
- Violin Concerto
- *Egmont Overture*
- *Overture to Leonore No. 3*
- Symphonies Nos. 3 ("Eroica"), 5, 6 ("Pastoral"), 7, 8, and 9 ("Choral")

Opera
- *Fidelio*

Piano
- Sonatas Nos. 8 ("Pathétique"), 14 ("Moonlight"), 21 ("Waldstein"), and 23 ("Appassionata")

He wrote a piano sonata about 1798 that he named "Pathétique." The name seems to fit the music's dramatic introduction to the first movement. It's marked *Grave*, meaning "solemn," and it does sound very serious. The symbol *fp* at the beginning of each measure in the example calls for a loud chord, which is then followed by quiet notes in a dotted rhythm.

The remainder of the first movement, however, has a lively tempo and an energetic quality. It is in sonata form, with the first theme in minor, as is the second theme. Even by Beethoven's time, composers were changing key more liberally than Mozart and Haydn did only a generation earlier. Before the end of the movement, the slow introduction appears two more times, adding a sense of drama to the entire movement.

WATCH...
a performance of the first movement online.

The second movement is songlike. Its melody is heard over a typical accompaniment figure found in eighteenth-century music. The melody is repeated one octave higher, and then contrasting sections are presented.

The overall form of the movement is A B A C A, which gives it the form but not the spirit of a rondo. The C section is especially dramatic, with sudden changes of dynamic level and a triple meter.

Third Movement

The third movement (see Listening Guide) is typical in that it is in rondo form: A B A C A B A. The pattern reveals the eighteenth-century fondness for symmetry. There is a codetta at the end of the B section and a coda at the end of the movement. Its form combines rondo and sonata, which logically is often called sonata–rondo.

LUDWIG VAN BEETHOVEN
Piano Sonata No. 8, Op. 13 ("Pathétique") Third Movement, 1799

Genre: Solo sonata

Form: Sonata–rondo

Download 39

3 minutes 44 seconds

0:00   The A theme opens in minor in the upper notes.

0:20   A theme extended following a short silence and two decisive chords.

0:38   Transition consisting of rapidly moving triplets.

0:49   B theme in a major key, followed by a return of the triplets.

1:13   A theme returns softly.

2:06   C theme begins and is repeated numerous times, sometimes in imitation.

2:06   Transition consisting of rapidly moving notes that become triplets.

2:23   A theme returns after a long chord followed by silence.

2:50   Return of transition in triplets.

3:01   B theme returns, changing key several times.

3:24   A theme returns softly.

3:37   Coda begins with triplets and music increases in intensity.

4:02   Following a long, loud chord, part of the A theme returns.

4:14   Movement closes with a series of rapidly moving notes and a short chord.

🎧 **LISTEN TO...** this selection streaming online.

🎧 **WATCH...** an Active Listening Guide of this selection online.

🎧 **WATCH...** a performance of this selection online.

🎧 **DO...** an online Listening Practice Activity related to this selection, which your instructor may assign for a grade.

MAIN POINTS OF CHAPTER 20

PRACTICE...
your understanding of this chapter's concepts by working once more with the chapter's Active Listening Guides online.

DO...
online quizzes that your instructor may assign for a grade.

1. By the beginning of the Classical period, the piano had replaced the harpsichord as the most common keyboard instrument. Composers wrote many sizable works for it, including many sonatas.

2. These sonatas followed the same forms as those used for symphonies, concertos, and chamber works, with the exception that often they had only three movements instead of four.

3. Mozart composed many piano sonatas. They have a light, tuneful character, which was suitable for the piano available during his lifetime.

4. The nature of the piano changed greatly from the time of Mozart to Beethoven. The most important change was the addition of metal braces on the frame, which permitted greater tension on the strings and in turn allowed the instrument to produce louder and more powerful sounds.

5. Beethoven's thirty-two piano sonatas are longer and more profound than Mozart's. His music is also technically more demanding, and it makes greater use of the high and low notes available on the piano.

6. In addition to piano sonatas and symphonies, Beethoven composed many outstanding overtures, chamber music works, concertos, and vocal compositions. Some of his greatest music was written after he became deaf.

The Symphony
and Beethoven

21

Learning Objectives

1 Describe the nature of the music in the four movements of Beethoven's Fifth symphony.

2 Tell about the features of a scherzo.

3 List the general features of Beethoven's music.

 START...
experiencing this chapter's topics with an online video activity that your instructor may assign.

 READ...
the complete chapter text in a rich interactive eBook!

The study of the symphony is presented here in conjunction with one of the biggest names in concert music: Ludwig van Beethoven. He did not develop the genre, but he certainly changed it in a massive way.

The symphony became the most important and largest musical genre during Beethoven's lifetime and for nearly a hundred years afterward. Beethoven composed just nine symphonies, and most of them take about forty minutes or more to perform. Haydn wrote more than a hundred symphonies and Mozart about fifty, some as short as fifteen minutes. But number and length were not the only differences, as will soon become evident.

A **symphony** is a large work composed for an orchestra that is divided into movements, usually four. The four movements present a contrast of tempo and mood.

BEETHOVEN'S SYMPHONY NO. 5

Beethoven composed his Symphony No. 5 in C Minor, Op. 67, between 1804 and 1808, when it received its premiere performance. Less than twenty years passed between when Mozart composed his Symphony No. 40 and Beethoven composed his Symphony No. 5. But what huge changes Beethoven wrought in his symphonies!

The difference might best be described by the word *more*. Mozart and Haydn developed themes and had some contrast in their music, but Beethoven presents much more development and more contrast of mood and character. In some of Beethoven's music, including his Fifth Symphony, he seems to want to burst the limits of musical sound. Musical ideas are worked and reworked and reworked again. Some chords are almost hammered into the listeners' ears, and at other times a quiet interlude is suddenly interrupted with a burst of sound. In addition, he also increased the size of the orchestra, including the addition of trombones and the piccolo.

The result of the sudden contrasts, the many repeated notes, and the extensive development of themes is music infused with more emotion. "The whole is greater than the sum of its parts" applies to all music, but especially to Beethoven's music. He achieved in it an emotional quality that had never existed before. His music often has more—much more—emotional content than the typical symphony or sonata of composers just one generation before him.

Beethoven was fortunate—and so are his listeners—that his music tends to be a bridge from the Classical style to the approaching Romantic style; it contains the best of both worlds. His training was in the style of Mozart and Haydn, as reflected in his early works. But then he added that "more" quality to his music, expanded it, and gave it greater emotional impact. His Fifth Symphony demonstrates these qualities well. From

193

the "Fate knocking at the door" motive in the first movement, to the beautiful and dramatic second movement, to the lively and playful third movement, to the dramatic bridge leading to the monumental fourth movement, this symphony can appropriately be thought of as an emotional musical journey of epic proportions.

First Movement

This movement (see Listening Guide) is a prime example of how Beethoven took what appears to be an ordinary theme and built something monumental out of it. It begins with a four-note motive. These four notes are repeated again and again, and they become the basis for the main theme:

LISTENING GUIDE

LUDWIG VAN BEETHOVEN

Symphony No. 5 in C Minor, First Movement (1808)

Genre: Symphony

Form: Sonata

Download 40

7 minutes 32 seconds

Exposition

0:00 Orchestra vigorously plays the four-motive from the first theme in minor. (Repeated at 1:27)

0:07 First theme followed by motive in sequence. (Repeated at 1:34)

0:22 Transition built around repeated fragments of first theme. (Repeated at 1:49)

0:44 French horn expands on four-note motive and creates two-note motive. (Repeated at 2:12)

0:47 Strings and woodwinds softly play second theme in a major key. Inverted version of four-note motive is soon heard on low strings. (Repeated at 2:15)

1:07 Codetta based on four-note motive. (Repeated at 2:34)

Development

2:54 French horns, then strings play first theme. Four-note motive, sometimes inverted, is passed sequentially among sections.

3:23 Winds and strings play full-sounding chords followed by silences.

3:31 Strings play first theme.

3:41 Winds and strings alternate playing the two-note motive derived from first theme. Soon reduced to one note.

4:04	Orchestra plays portion of first theme loudly, followed by soft notes in the woodwinds.
4:12	Motive repeated five times leading to …

Recapitulation

4:17	First theme.
4:37	Short oboe cadenza.
4:51	Transition.
5:12	French horn plays expanded motive.
5:15	Violins and woodwinds play second theme, again in major, followed by transition.
5:41	Violins outline chords based on first theme.

Coda

5:59	Strings vigorously play many repeated notes.
6:15	Expanded and extended treatment of four-note motive.
6:41	Woodwinds and strings alternate four-note motive. It is then fragmented to two notes.
7:05	Orchestra forcefully repeats first theme.
7:22	The movement closes with brusque chords.

LISTEN TO... this selection streaming online.

WATCH... an Active Listening Guide of this selection online.

WATCH... two YouTube videos that spotlight this selection online.

DO... an online Listening Practice Activity related to this selection, which your instructor may assign for a grade.

There have been several attempts to explain the origin of this motive. One is that it is Fate knocking at the door; another claims that the three dots and a dash stand for the letter V in Morse code. Neither of these theories has been substantiated. The latter is especially doubtful because Morse code was developed years after the writing of the symphony!

And what happens to that theme? It is treated as a germinal idea. For example, right after the first theme is presented, it is developed somewhat in the transition leading to the second theme:

Most of the development section is an outgrowth of the original theme. Beethoven does such things as fill in the interval of the original motive:

Sometimes to the filled-in interval he adds the inversion—the upside-down version—of the motive:

He reiterates a few simple musical ideas based on the theme:

He also fragments themes. The notes circled in the second example in the Listening Guide are the two middle pitches from the transition played by the French horn. The two pitches are echoed between the woodwinds and the strings, and then the segment is fragmented further until just one note is echoed:

There are also long, gradual crescendos and abrupt changes from loud to soft.

The recapitulation is followed by an extended coda. In fact, the coda in Beethoven's symphonies is almost as important as the other three sections of sonata form. He seemed to regard it as a second development section. A synthesis of the themes of the coda can be seen in this example:

The pitches of the first theme and the rhythm pattern of the transition are combined. The two-pitch fragment emphasized in the development appears again, this time in a downward sequence.

Second Movement

The second movement of Beethoven's Fifth Symphony (see Listening Guide) reveals his ability to write melodies. He is so often thought of for the brusque, forceful qualities in some of his music that it's easy to forget he could write lovely lyric melodies as well.

Several forms can be found in second movements of symphonies. The most common is the large three-part form, **A B A**. Theme and variations are also encountered some of the time, and even sonata form with a shortened development section is used.

This movement of the Fifth Symphony is a theme and variations built on two melodic ideas. The first one contains three shorter melodic sections. During the course of the second movement, these ideas are varied by changing the melody and ornamenting it, and by altering the harmony, rhythm, dynamics, tempo, and type of accompaniment.

LUDWIG VAN BEETHOVEN
Symphony No. 5 in C Minor, Second Movement (1808)

Genre: Symphony

Form: Theme and variations

Download 41

10 minutes

Themes

0:00   Theme 1: major, in three-beat meter with three parts. Part 1: violas and cellos.

0:24   Part 2 of first theme: woodwinds.

0:36   Part 3 of first theme: violins.

0:53   Theme 2: violins and woodwinds.

1:14   Brasses play second theme in an expansive style.

1:30   Music becomes quiet and mysterious.

Variation 1

1:58   Theme 1: Strings play steadily moving notes.

(continued)

2:31	Theme 1: Strings play third part.
2:49	Theme 2: Woodwinds and violins are featured.
3:10	Theme 2: Brasses play in an expansive manner.
3:27	Music becomes quiet and mysterious.

Variation 2

3:52	Theme 1: Lower, then upper strings play rapidly moving notes.
4:28	Theme 1: Lower strings play rapidly moving notes.
5:04	Theme 1: Woodwinds quietly play fragments.
5:50	Theme 2: Orchestra plays in a majestic style.
6:36	Theme 1: Woodwinds play short notes in minor.

Variation 3

7:18	Theme 1: Violins play first part.
7:43	Theme 1: Woodwinds play second part.
7:53	Theme 1: Strings play third part.

Coda

8:09	Tempo increases as bassoons play beginning of first theme.
8:23	Violins play fragments of second theme.
8:37	Woodwinds and strings alternate parts of first theme.
9:26	Low strings begin a crescendo using fragments of first theme.
9:56	Movement concludes with abrupt chords.

 LISTEN TO... this selection streaming online.

 WATCH... an Active Listening Guide of this selection online.

 WATCH... a performance of this selection online.

 DO... an online Listening Practice Activity related to this selection, which your instructor may assign for a grade.

Third Movement

The third movement of the symphonies of Haydn and Mozart was a stylized dance—the minuet. With its graceful ¾ meter, it provided a nice contrast to the lyric, melodious second movement. Even the three-part form of the minuet was followed, with the middle section being called the *trio*. This movement was in the home key of the symphony.

Beethoven made two important changes in the minuet of his predecessors:

- He called for a faster tempo, which gave the movement a more lively, energetic, jovial character. No longer was ¾ felt in three beats per measure; rather, the music is felt in one strong beat per measure.

- He named the movement "Scherzo," a word that means "joke" in Italian. Accordingly, the movement did not just fulfill a formal pattern; it could—and often did—contain surprises for its listeners.

The main theme of the third movement (see Listening Guide) is one that several other composers of the time had also used. In fact, the theme had acquired a name—the "Mannheim rocket." The *Mannheim* part of the name comes from the southern German city that figured prominently in the development of the symphony, and the *rocket* probably came from the fact that it is the ascending notes of a chord.

The trio of the movement is interesting in that it starts out sounding like a lively fugue, but Beethoven does not follow through with a full-blown fugue. In musical terms, he wrote a *fugato*—a fugue-like passage.

Another feature of the movement is its attachment to the fourth movement. A movement normally comes to an end, and a few moments of silence are observed before the next movement begins. Beethoven and composers who followed him occasionally connected two movements.

LUDWIG VAN BEETHOVEN
Symphony No. 5 in C Minor, Third Movement (1808)

Genre: Symphony

Form: Scherzo and trio

Download 42

5 minutes 28 seconds

Scherzo

0:00 Low strings play "rocket" theme softly in minor; music has an "eerie" character.

0:19 French horns forcefully play second theme in major.

0:40 Low strings softly play the "rocket" theme.

1:03 Orchestra plays second theme loudly.

1:24 Strings softly play opening theme.

Trio

1:58 Cellos and basses play a dancelike theme in a major key. Other instruments soon follow in imitation.

2:14 Imitative section is repeated.

2:31 Low strings play a short link to opening theme.

Scherzo

3:28 Low strings quietly play opening theme. More strings enter playing pizzicato.

3:49 Woodwinds play second theme softly.

(continued)

Bridge to Fourth Movement

4:46 Strings quietly sustain a long note as timpani quietly play a slow, steady stream of notes.

4:59 Three-note pattern begins in violins and is repeated many times as music grows louder, key changes to major, and music leads without a break to fourth movement.

 LISTEN TO... this selection streaming online.

 WATCH... an Active Listening Guide of this selection online.

 DO... an online Listening Practice Activity related to this selection, which your instructor may assign for a grade.

Fourth Movement

The fourth movements of Classical symphonies are lively and filled with happy melodies. Apparently, the hope was to have the listeners leave feeling good. Often fourth movements are rondos. They were almost always in the home key of the symphony.

The fourth movement of Beethoven's Fifth Symphony (see Listening Guide) is in sonata form. A rondo would not have accommodated the monumental concept of this movement. Beethoven seems to have wanted to leave a serious but positive impression on his audiences. His optimism had deeper roots than just pleasant, cheery music.

An unusual feature of this fourth movement is the brief appearance of a theme from the third movement. The appearances of themes from other movements would become more common later in the nineteenth century, but it was very rare at the time the Fifth Symphony was composed.

LISTENING GUIDE

LUDWIG VAN BEETHOVEN
Symphony No. 5 in C Minor, Fourth Movement (1808)

Genre: Symphony

Form: Sonata

Download 43

8 minutes 30 seconds

Exposition

0:00 Orchestra, especially the brass section, plays first theme.

0:33 French horns begin transitional theme.

0:59 Strings play second theme.

1:25 Codetta; same phrase appears three times.

Development

2:00 Violins play a portion of second theme.

2:08 Fragment from second theme becomes more prominent as music progresses through different keys.

2:23 Low strings play four-note motive as fragments of second theme continue.

2:59 Climax reached as orchestra loudly plays four-note motive followed by a pause.

3:34 Portion of scherzo theme played softly by violins and woodwinds.

Recapitulation

4:09 First theme played vigorously by orchestra.

4:42 Transition featuring French horns.

5:13 Second theme played by violins.

5:39 Woodwinds play theme for the codetta.

Coda

6:09 Second theme in violins over four-note motive from development in low strings.

6:40 Transition features woodwinds and French horns.

7:23 Tempo suddenly becomes very fast.

7:49 First theme played twice as fast (diminution) by brasses.

8:14 Movement concludes with several V-I cadences and successive soundings of final chord.

LISTEN TO... this selection streaming online.

WATCH... an Active Listening Guide of this selection online.

WATCH... a performance of this and the previous selection online.

DO... an online Listening Practice Activity related to this selection, which your instructor may assign for a grade.

APPRECIATING BEETHOVEN'S MUSIC

The "Pathétique" sonata and the Fifth Symphony provide a good idea of what Beethoven's music is like. What is it about his music that causes people to continue to listen to it today? What about it has contributed to continuing interest in the man himself? Among the many potential reasons, four stand out:

- *Contrast.* Beethoven's music is filled with dramatic contrasts. His themes often seem to be paired by opposites that can be thought of as male/female, rough/smooth, loud/soft, brusque/tender, and so on. A placid passage can be suddenly broken as a *sforzando* chord is sounded, or a raging section can abruptly cease and change to a gentle melody.

- *Motive development.* Beethoven's music is a showcase of developing musical ideas, especially short, simple ones. A theme becomes a seed that grows and takes many shapes, and it is fascinating to follow that musical process.

- *Sense of drive.* Beethoven's music contains a wonderful drive or what has been described as "inevitability." This quality is difficult to put into words, but his music seems always to be heading toward its final destination. Even though it has many changes and stops, the sense of inevitability is still there. Listeners sense that though the music is quiet at a particular moment, that situation will not last. The musical journey will resume and continue on to its inevitable conclusion.

- *Personality.* Beethoven's music has a personality all its own. His mature works don't sound like those of Mozart, Haydn, or any other composer (Figure 21.1).

Lebrecht Music & Arts/The Image Works

FIGURE 21.1

A PAGE FROM BEETHOVEN'S AUTOGRAPH MANUSCRIPT   REVEALS HIS CREATIVE TURMOIL.

A person does not need to be familiar with a lot of concert music to sense that there is something unique about Beethoven's music. It presents listeners with dramatic contrasts, a fiery spirit, huge amounts of thematic development, and an inner sense of musical logic.

MAIN POINTS OF CHAPTER 21

1. The symphony is a large work for orchestra with four movements.

   - The first movement is in sonata form and has a moderately fast tempo.
   - The second movement is often in A B A form, but other forms such as theme and variation are also used. It tends to have a slow tempo and features melody.
   - The third movement was traditionally a minuet and trio, but Beethoven gave it a faster tempo and called it a scherzo.
   - The fourth movement often used rondo form and a lively tempo. Beethoven's fourth movements, however, are sometimes massive and exhilarating.

2. Beethoven was especially fond of developing themes. Some of his music is filled with repeated, inverted, and fragmented motives. He also lengthened the coda section so that it almost became a second development section.

3. Beethoven's music often contains surprising changes in dynamic level and the nature of themes. A forceful, powerful theme can be followed by a tender melody, and a loud chord can suddenly appear in a quiet passage.

 PRACTICE...
your understanding of this chapter's concepts by working once more with the chapter's Active Listening Guides online.

 DO...
online quizzes that your instructor may assign for a grade.

Features of the Music of the Classical Period

Melodies	Often consist of short, tuneful phrases strung together; usually have a light, elegant quality; statement–answer pattern
Rhythm	Metrical with a steady beat, except in recitatives
Texture	Mostly homophonic
Harmony	Tonal with modulations mostly to nearly related keys; continuo part no longer present
Dynamic levels	Gradual crescendo and decrescendo developed
Performance media	Orchestra; chamber music groups; piano replaces harpsichord; vocal music
Forms	Sonata, theme and variations, rondo, and minuet and trio; forms often contain balanced and symmetrical phrases
Genres	Symphony, solo concerto, sonata, chamber music, opera

PART 5

Romantic Music

	1820		1850
Historical Events		● Monroe Doctrine (1823)	California gold rush ● (1848–1855) Revolutions in Europe ● (mid-1800s)
Visual Arts		● Delacroix, *The Bark of Dante* (1822)	
Literature and Theater		Keats (1795–1821) Byron (1788–1824) Poe (1809–1849) Dickens's work (1836–1870) Hugo's work (1824–1885) Longfellow's work (1839–1882)	Hawthorne (1804–1864) Tennyson's work (1829–1892) Dumas (1802–1870)
Philosophy and Science		Schopenhauer (1788–1860) ● Morse telegraph (1840s) Daguerre photography ● (1839)	Kierkegaard's work (1841–18!
Music	Schubert (1797–1828) Liszt (1811–1886)	Mendelssohn's work (1824–1847) Chopin's work (1830–1849) Berlioz's work (1830–1869)	R. C. Schumann's work (1831–1856) Verdi's work (right) ▶ (1830–1901)

AP Images/Michael Dwyer

1875   **1900**

● Franco-Prussian War (1870–1871)   ● First automobiles (1895)

American Civil War (1861–1865)   ● Spanish-American War (1898)

Boer War in South Africa ●
(1889–1902)

Renoir's work (1862–1919)   ● Munch, *The Scream* (1893)

● Corot, *Villa
d' Avray* (c. 1867)   Cezanne's work (1863–1906)

Degas's work
(1852–1912)   ● Monet, *Rouen Cathedral*
(1897)

Dostoevsky's work (1844–1881)   Wilde's work (1878–1900)

Kipling's work (1888–1936)

Twain's work (1869–1910)

Tolstoy's work (1852–1910)

T. H. Huxley's work (1845–1895)   ● Mill's death (1873)   Bergson's work (1877–1941)

● Darwin, *Origin of Species* (1859)   ● Bell telephone (1876)   Marconi radio ●
(1901)

Nietzsche's work (1870–1900) ● Edison light bulb and phonograph (1879, 1877)

Smetana's work (1855–1884)   Debussy's work (1885–1918)

Puccini's operas (1893–1904)

● Wagner,   Dvořák's work (1871–1904)
Bayreuth
Brahms's work   (1872–1883)
(1853–1897)

Mussorgsky's work (1858–1881)

Leemage/Universal Images Group/Getty Images

▲ Tchaikovsky, *The Nutcracker* (top)
(1891–1892)

22 Romance *and* Romanticism

START...

experiencing this chapter's topics with an online video activity that your instructor may assign.

READ...

the complete chapter text in a rich interactive eBook!

Learning Objectives

1 Enumerate the general characteristics of Romanticism.
2 Give examples of the contradictory fascination with beauty and evil in the nineteenth century.
3 Describe the major differences between the Romantic and Classical styles of nineteenth-century music.

To most people, the word *romantic* refers to the emotion of love. To scholars, however, it means much more. It comes from *romance*, which originally referred to a medieval poem written in one of the Romance languages (those that developed from Latin) and dealing with a heroic person or event. Later, the word took on the connotation of something far away and strange or something imaginative and full of wonder. Yes, it also includes the idea of love—romantic love.

Romanticism came of age during the nineteenth century. It began in some of the music of Beethoven and Schubert, and it continued into the early years of the twentieth century, roughly from 1820 to 1900. In fact, elements of romanticism are still encountered in some music being written today. The Romantic outlook affected every type of music, and it brought several kinds of music to their high point of development.

CHARACTERISTICS OF ROMANTICISM

Romanticism was an artistic viewpoint that also predominated in dance, theater, the visual arts, and music throughout the nineteenth century. What were the features of this outlook?

• Romanticists were fascinated by the unknown and stood in awe of the world. They were impressed by the mystery, not the clarity, of the world and its inhabitants. At times, they were almost mystic. They seemed especially fascinated by the mystery and power of evil.

• Romanticists also tended to rely on emotion and imagination rather than rational intellect, which had been central to the Classical outlook. Feelings replaced reason. Truth became what a person *felt* to be true, so it was wrong to deny one's feelings. Poet John Keats wrote in one of his letters: "I am certain of nothing but the holiness of the heart's affections, and the truth of the imagination. What the imagination seizes as beauty must be truth." Inevitably, Romanticism grew to distrust reason and science. To quote Keats again, this time from his poem "Lamia":

> *Do not all charms fly*
> *At the mere touch of cold philosophy?*

(During Keats's lifetime the word *philosophy* was a synonym for *science*.)

• Romanticists were fascinated by the long ago and far away. During the Classical era, intellectuals had thought of medieval times as the "Dark Ages"; the Romanticists

DEA PICTURE LIBRARY/De Agostini/Getty Images

FIGURE 22.1
THE VIRTUES OF RURAL LIFE
WERE CELEBRATED BY ARTISTS OF
THE ROMANTIC PERIOD, AS SHOWN
IN *POTATO PLANTERS* BY JEAN
FRANÇOIS MILLET.

considered them heroic. Literature is filled with examples of this attitude, including Alfred Lord Tennyson's *Idylls of the King*, John Keats's "Eve of St. Agnes," Samuel Taylor Coleridge's "Christabel," and Sir Walter Scott's *Ivanhoe*.

- Not only were the Romanticists impressed by the unknown forces of the world, they also reveled in the struggle against those forces. In Coleridge's poem *The Rime of the Ancient Mariner*, the sailor is "alone on a wide, wide sea."

- Romanticists were enthralled by nature. They had a rural outlook (Figure 22.1) instead of the urban outlook of the Classical period. In Mozart's day the cities—London, Paris, Vienna—were the centers of artistic activity, so they attracted people with creative and artistic interests. To Romanticists, however, nature had more appeal because it represented a world untainted by humans. Sometimes nature was extolled to the point of pantheism—the belief that God and nature are one. The rural interest of the time led to landscape painting, poems on natural phenomena, and works such as Beethoven's Symphony No. 6 ("Pastoral"). He intended the music to convey the moods evoked during his visits to the countryside around Vienna.

- Many Romanticists resented rules and restraints. They regarded the Classical period as cold and formal and were unimpressed by its rational deductions and universal laws. They felt perfectly capable of making their own rules—and proceeded to do so in their artworks. They cherished freedom, limitless expression, passion, and the pursuit of the unattainable. After all, what more glorious struggle could there be than seeking the impossible? This search is perhaps best represented in the legend of the Holy Grail, which was the cup that Jesus used at the Last Supper. It was believed to have special powers.

- Beginning with Jean-Jacques Rousseau and the Earl of Shaftesbury (A. A. Cooper) and continuing through the American Henry David Thoreau in the nineteenth century to the present time, a group of philosophers have expounded the idea of natural goodness. The "artificialities" of civilization are rejected because they corrupt people. William Wordsworth summed up the Romanticists' thinking on nature when he wrote in his poem "The Tables Turned":

> *One impulse from vernal wood*
> *May teach you more of man,*
> *Of moral evil and of good,*
> *Than all the sages can.*

(*Vernal* means springtime, and *sages* refers to wise men.)

- Because Romanticists were highly subjective and individualistic, it is not surprising that they tended to be self-centered. Works of art were no longer objective examples of a person's skill. Instead, they were considered a projection of the person who created them. Romantic artists felt that a bit of their psyche had been given to the world in their poems and preludes. Their works were now created for posterity, for an audience that someday, somewhere, would appreciate their true value.

- Some Romanticists were nonsocial, if not antisocial. They withdrew into a world of their own, surrounded by a close circle of friends and admirers. Yet the Romantic era saw the establishment of the concert hall with its large audiences, and some Romantic musicians thoroughly enjoyed the adulation of the public.

- Romantic musicians were often concerned with the other fine arts as well as with philosophy. They were familiar with the writings of Johann Wolfgang von Goethe and Alphonse Lamartine, and many times they knew the writers personally. Franz Liszt wrote a number of literary works, including books on gypsy music and another entitled *Life of Chopin*. Robert Schumann's literary interests led him to edit a music magazine. Richard Wagner wrote lengthy treatises on music, art, and philosophy. Romantic composers believed strongly in a unity of the arts. This attitude is epitomized in the music dramas of Wagner.

ROMANTIC ART

Eugène Delacroix's *The Bark of Dante* (Figure 22.2) depicts the struggling souls of the wicked people of Florence, Italy, trying to escape from Hell by climbing into the boat with the ancient Roman poet Virgil and the fourteenth-century poet Dante Alighieri, whose best-known work was *The Inferno*. It demonstrates the interest of Romantic artists in subjects from the past and their fascination with evil and its consequences. In the painting the sea and clouds swirl around ominously. The twisted and pained bodies of the Florentines are very much involved in the scene as they struggle hopelessly. There is little symmetry; Dante (in the green cloak) stands about a third of the way from the left. Straight angles are absent, too, as the bodies of the sinners writhe throughout the picture.

The Romanticists' love of nature can be seen in Jean-Baptiste-Camille Corot's *Villa d'Avray* (Figure 22.3). The painting is of a peaceful rural scene filled with flowers, beautiful trees, and a lake. The two figures in the foreground blend in with the scene. The lake is calm and reflects the villa on the other side. The message of the picture could easily be "Nature is good and beautiful."

A *Traveler Looking over a Sea of Fog* by Caspar David Friedrich (Figure 22.4) shows another aspect of Romanticism: the individual-against-all-the-elements attitude, its self-absorbed outlook. Friedrich's belief was that the artist's feeling is his law. The erect, determined posture of the man viewing the fog and mountains is expressed well in the famous nineteenth-century poem "Invictus" by William Ernest Henley, which begins, "I am the master of my fate, the captain of my soul."

The Split Personality of Romanticism

Every era in history seems to carry its contradictions. In the case of the **Romantic period**, those contradictions are massive. On the one hand, it produced much extremely

FIGURE 22.2
THE BARK OF DANTE, BY EUGÈNE DELACROIX. TWO FEATURES OF ROMANTIC ART AND MUSIC ARE EVIDENT IN THIS WORK: LOVE OF DRAMA AND ADMIRATION OF THE MIDDLE AGES.

FIGURE 22.3
VILLA D'AVRAY, BY JEAN-BAPTISTE-CAMILLE COROT. ANOTHER CHARACTERISTIC OF ROMANTICISM WAS LOVE OF NATURE, WHICH IS EVIDENT IN BEETHOVEN'S SYMPHONY NO. 6 AND MANY OTHER MUSICAL WORKS OF THE NINETEENTH CENTURY.

beautiful and tender music and works of art. On the other hand, it showed a fascination with evil and misery. Song after song and opera after opera end unhappily, often with the hero or heroine (or both) dying. For example, in Schubert's "Der Erlkönig" ("The Erl King") the son dies in his father's arms; in Wagner's *Götterdämmerung*, after Brünnhilde rides her horse into the funeral pyre of her beloved Siegfried (Figure 22.5), flames and then a flood engulf the home of the gods, Valhalla.

FIGURE 22.4

A TRAVELER LOOKING OVER A SEA OF FOG, BY CASPAR DAVID FRIEDRICH. THE HEROIC CHARACTER WAS A PART OF ROMANTIC ART AND MUSIC, CULMINATING IN RICHARD STRAUSS'S TONE POEM *EIN HELDENLEBEN (A HERO'S LIFE)*.

DEA PICTURE LIBRARY/De Agostini/Getty Images

The fascination with evil led to the inclusion of the Dies irae chant in several musical works and compositions such as *Mephisto Waltz* (Mephisto being another name for the devil), *Danse Macabre*, and *Totentanz (Dance of Death)*. The disasters of the nineteenth century certainly did not reach the heights of mayhem that can be seen in films or described in books over the past few decades. They did, however, reveal a side of Romanticism that seemed to enjoy being miserable.

Romanticists also had their optimistic and happy side that loved beauty. The music of Brahms, Mendelssohn, Tchaikovsky, Grieg, Schumann, and many others contains

FIGURE 22.5

THE DEATH OF SIEGFRIED, BY HENRI DE GROUX. THE DEATH OF SIEGFRIED IS A SCENE FROM THE NIBELUNGENLIED, THE EPIC POEM MADE FAMOUS BY WAGNER'S "RING CYCLE" OPERAS.

Christie's Images/Fine Art/Corbis

FIGURE 22.6
THE SNOW MAIDENS PERFORMING IN TCHAIKOVSKY'S *THE NUTCRACKER*.

rich harmonies and luscious melodies. Such music is difficult to top in terms of sheer beauty. Many paintings also reveal a love of beauty; Corot's *Villa d'Avray* is one example. Beauty of motion and movement was (and still is) one of the main goals of ballet. Often its stories are pure and lovely fantasy and present beauty that seems to exceed anything in ordinary life. The scene of the Snow Maidens (Figure 22.6) dancing gracefully in *The Nutcracker* to Tchaikovsky's beautiful music as snow falls gently around them seems to be as total an experience of loveliness and beauty as can be conceived.

 WATCH...
a performance from *The Nutcracker* online.

WHAT TO LISTEN FOR IN ROMANTIC MUSIC

What makes music in the Romantic style of the nineteenth century different from the Classical style of Mozart and Haydn? Several things:

1. The melodies are more flowing and passionate. Whereas the melodies of Classical composers many times consisted of short fragments strung together, melodies in Romantic style are often sweeping and expansive.

2. The harmonies are much richer. Chords contain more notes. Also, many more chromatic notes are used. Changes of key occur more often and to keys that are harmonically more distant. Harmony became much more than the functional accompaniment encountered in many works of the Classical period.

3. Rhythm is treated more freely, especially in speeding up and slowing down the tempo. A rather steady beat and metrical rhythm are not abandoned, but they are less structured.

4. Changes in dynamic levels are more frequent, with many of the soft places softer and the loud places louder. Often, the dynamic levels have an almost undulating quality.

5. The tonal qualities are richer. The size of the orchestra increased significantly, and several new instruments, such as the piccolo and English horn, were added.

6. The works, especially those for large ensembles, are often quite a bit longer. Many Romantic composers admired and desired long works.

7. The element of contrast in music begun by Beethoven is a feature of nineteenth-century music. Tender portions are often contrasted with stormy sections, for example.

8. These features of Romantic music often coalesce to produce music of outstanding beauty. Many works remind one of eating an especially rich-tasting dessert.

MAIN POINTS OF CHAPTER 22

1. Romanticism refers to the style that prevailed from roughly 1820 to 1900. The term refers to more than romantic love. It is marked by these characteristics:

   - Fascination with mystery and the unknown, including the power of evil.
   - Reliance on emotion and imagination. Feelings replaced reason as a guide to actions.
   - Fondness for the long ago and far away. A new interest in medieval times emerged.
   - Attraction to the struggle with unknown forces. Many stories involved a struggle against overwhelming and magical forces.
   - Resentment of rules and restraints. Romanticists felt perfectly capable of making their own rules and loved freedom of expression.
   - Fascination with nature. Nature appealed to romanticists because it represented the world untainted by humans.
   - Individualistic view of life. Works of art and music became personal creations.

2. The Romantic period seemed to have a split personality. On the one hand, it loved beauty and passion. On the other, it was fascinated with suffering and the idea of evil.

3. Romantic music represents a significant change from the music of Mozart and Haydn. Its melodies are more warm and flowing, harmonies richer, dynamic levels more extensive, and rhythm more flexible. Many of these works are longer and have a more monumental character.

 DO...
online quizzes that your instructor may assign for a grade.

Early Romantic Music

23

Learning Objectives

1 Describe the characteristics of art songs.
2 Differentiate concertos in the early Romantic period from those of the Classical period, in the context of Mendelssohn's Concerto for Violin in E Minor.
3 List the reasons why few women are recognized as major composers.

 START...
experiencing this chapter's topics with an online video activity that your instructor may assign.

 READ...
the complete chapter text in a rich interactive eBook!

The Romantic attitude and outlook had a massive impact on music. Changes happened not so much in new forms or techniques of composing, although some of them occurred in those areas, but more in what composers tried to accomplish in their works. Their music tended to be much more personal and expressive. They reveled in the qualities of mystery, emotional release, love of nature, and inner feelings that were fashionable during the nineteenth century.

THE ART SONG

The songs Schubert wrote are called art songs. An **art song**, or **Lied**, is a musical setting of a poem. (**Lied**, pronounced "leed," is the German word for "song"; **Lieder** is its plural.)

The order is important here. Composers of art songs began by selecting a suitable poem and *then* composed music that best projected the mood and thought of the text. The idea of preserving and building on the message of the words was fundamental.

Because the setting of the words was so vital, composers were not primarily concerned with writing a lovely melody. They wanted a good melody, of course, but more than that, they wanted the melody to express the words. The idea of expression also carried over to the piano part, which evokes a mood, paints a picture, or enriches ideas beyond what a singer can achieve. For example, through rapidly moving notes and changes of dynamic level, the piano can suggest wind blowing through the trees.

Singers of art songs must project the idea of the song. Sometimes they are called on to convey different roles in the same song. Any mood can prevail in an art song—anger, sadness, anxiety, joy, pity, contentment (Figure 23.1).

The demands on singers of art songs are, therefore, somewhat different from those required of opera singers. In fact, singers tend to specialize in one type of vocal music or another. The art song is less demanding in a technical sense; the vocal range is narrower and there are few virtuoso passages. But singers of art songs must be versatile and able to project the essence of a character or situation. Because art songs are sung in small recital halls, singers must establish a rapport with the audience while maintaining a balance between good taste and expressiveness. In some ways, art songs and chamber music have several musical similarities. Both are intended to produce a sense of intimacy, refinement, and listener involvement.

A sense of involvement is not achieved if the listener does not understand the words. Most art songs are in languages other than English. As was pointed out in Chapter 12, word placement in vocal music is crucial, so translations are difficult. In fact, strictly speaking, something is lost in translation, no matter how carefully it is done. Many words have shades of meaning that cannot be translated. For these reasons, art songs are usually sung in their original languages.

STAN HONDA/AFP/Getty Images

FIGURE 23.1

THE ART SONG COMBINES POETRY, MELODY, THE EXPRESSIVENESS OF THE HUMAN VOICE, AND THE TONAL POWER OF THE PIANO. THE SOPRANO IN THIS PHOTO IS RENÉE FLEMING, AND THE PIANIST IS LEONARD SLATKIN.

Translation difficulties are only part of the language problem. Many of the poems that Schubert and other composers set to music are not of high literary merit. Some of them seem overly sentimental to people today who have grown up with down-to-earth (if not downright earthy) popular songs.

Art songs are a type of music well worth knowing, however.

- They reveal much sensitivity and skill in combining words and music.

- They are very expressive of their texts. For example, when the singer of "Der Erlkönig" sings "My father, my father, can't you see …," listeners can really sense the child's frustration and fear.

- The human voice can be a very expressive and beautiful musical instrument. When coupled with the tonal power of the piano in the infinite variety of the art song, the result can be very moving.

Schubert's "Der Erlkönig"

Schubert wrote "Der Erlkönig" ("The Erl King") when he was only eighteen (see Listening Guide). He chose a text from the great German writer Goethe. The overall mood of the song is one of fear and suspense because of the mythical king of the elves. According to legend, whoever is touched by him must die. The singer is required to represent the narrator, the father, the son, and the Erl King—quite an assignment. The piano sets the mood and helps delineate the characters in the song as well as playing the role of the horse.

Before listening to the song, read over the text to determine which of the four roles the singer is presenting. As you listen, notice how Schubert, the singer, and the pianist treat the different roles. For example, be aware of how "My son, it's only a misty cloud" differs from "You lovely child, come…" and how "My father, my father, now don't you hear…" differs from "My son, my son, all I can see…." Notice not only the difference in the tone quality of the singer's voice for each role but also how the entire mood changes when the Erl King speaks.

None of the music is repeated in "Der Erlkönig." New lines of melody follow one another until the song ends. The term for this type of song is **through-composed**, meaning that no line repeats. The accompaniment adds to the mood with an agitated triplet figure and a foreboding bass pattern, which depicts the urgency of the scene.

FRANZ SCHUBERT

"Der Erlkönig" (1815)

LISTENING GUIDE

Genre: Art song (Lied)

Form: Through-composed

Download 44

4 minutes 5 seconds

0:00   Piano sets an agitated mood.

0:23   NARRATOR: *Wer reitet so spät durch Nacht und Wind?*
   Es ist der Vater mit seinem Kind;
   Er hat den Knaben wohl in dem Arm,
   Er fasst ihn sicher, er hält ihn warm.
  FATHER: *"Mein Sohn, was birgst du so bang dein Gesicht?"*
  SON: *"Siehst, Vater, du den Erlkönig nicht?*
   Den Erlenkönig mit Kron' und Schweif?"
  FATHER: *"Mein Sohn, es ist ein Nebelstreif."*

1:29   ERL KING: *"Du liebes Kind, komm, geh' mit mir!*
   Gar schöne Spiele spiel' ich mit dir;
   Manch' bunte Blumen sind an dem Strand,
   Meine Mutter hat manch' gülden Gewand."
  SON: *"Mein Vater, mein Vater, und hörest du nicht,*
   Was Erlenkönig mir leise verspricht?"
  FATHER: *"Sei ruhig, bleibe ruhig, mein Kind;*
   In dürren Blättern säuselt der Wind."
  ERL KING: *"Willst, feiner Knabe, du mit mir geh'n?*
   Meine Töchter sollen dich warten schön;
   Meine Töchter führen den nächtlichen Reih'n
   Und wiegen und tanzen und singen dich ein."
  SON: *"Mein Vater, mein Vater, und siehst du nicht*
   dort Erlkönigs Töchter am düstern Ort?"
  FATHER: *"Mein Sohn, mein Sohn, ich seh' es genau,*
   Es scheinen die alten Weiden so grau."
  ERL KING: *"Ich liebe dich, mich reizt deine schöne Gestalt,*
   Und bist du nicht willig, so brauch ich Gewalt!"

Who rides so late through the night wind?
 It is a father with his child.
 He holds the boy within his arm,
 He clasps him tightly, he keeps him warm.
"My son, why do you hide your face in fear?"
"See, father, isn't the Erl King near?
 The Erl King with crown and shroud?"
"My son, it's only a misty cloud."

"You lovely child, come, go with me!
 Such pleasant games I'll play with thee!
 The fields have flowers bright to behold,
 My mother has many a robe of gold."
"My father, my father, now don't you hear
 What the Erl King whispers in my ear?"
"Be calm, be calm and still, my child;
 The dry leaves rustle when wind blows wild."
"My lovely boy, won't you go with me?
 My daughters all shall wait on thee,
 My daughters nightly revels keep,
 They'll sing and dance and rock thee to sleep."
"My father, my father, can't you see
 Erl King's daughters in that dark place?"
"My son, my son, all I can see
 Is just the old gray willow tree."
"I love thee, thy form enflames my sense;
 Since thou art not willing, I'll take thee hence!"

(continued)

3:13	SON: *"Mein Vater, mein Vater, jetzt fasst er michan!*	"My father, my father, he's grabbing my arm,
	Erlkönig hat mir ein Leid's gethan!"	The Erl King wants to do me harm!"
	NARRATOR: *Dem Vater grauset's, er reitet geschwind,*	The father shudders, he speeds through the cold
	Er hält in Armen das ächzende	His arms the moaning child enfold,
	Kind, Erreicht den Hof mit Müh' und Noth:	He reaches home with pain and dread:
	In seinen Armen das Kind war tot!	In his arms the child was dead!

The song ends with two solid-sounding chords.

LISTEN TO ... this selection streaming online.

WATCH ... an Active Listening Guide of this selection online.

WATCH ... a performance of this selection online.

DO ... an online Listening Practice Activity related to this selection, which your instructor may assign for a grade.

Franz Schubert

DEA/A. DAGLI ORTI/Getty Images

Franz Schubert (1797–1828) is often considered, along with Beethoven, to be a composer who marked the beginning of the Romantic style in music. And there is much about his life to justify his reputation as the prototype of the Romantic artist. Born into the family of a schoolteacher in a Vienna suburb, the young Schubert displayed creative talent while he was still a boy. After completing school, he tried to follow in his father's footsteps, but he could not accept the routine involved in teaching. He preferred to spend his time composing music.

Schubert did not adjust well to adult life. He never held a real job and made only halfhearted attempts to find one. He had a small circle of friends, who appreciated his talents. They housed and fed him when he was in need, which he often was. He was not good at dealing with publishers, who made hefty profits from his music. Schubert was a versatile composer. He wrote piano works, chamber music, and symphonies. But it is his vocal music, especially his six hundred songs that ensured his place in the world of music.

As the years passed, Schubert became lonelier and more discouraged. He was even unlucky in love and once contracted venereal disease. Schubert's Symphony No. 8 ("Unfinished") was not left incomplete because he was heartbroken over a failed romance, as is sometimes claimed. He simply never got around to finishing it.

He was not in good health the last five years of his short life, but his compositions kept on coming. He died from typhus at the age of thirty-one, leaving almost no worldly goods—except a vast store of beautiful music.

Best-Known Works

Chamber music
· Piano Quintet ("Trout")
· *Arpeggione* Sonata

Orchestra
· *Rosamunde* (incidental music)
· Symphonies Nos. 8 ("Unfinished") and 9 ("The Great")

Songs (more than 600) including
· "Der Erlkönig"
· "Gretchen am Spinnrade"

Song cycles
· *Die schöne Müllerin*
· *Winterreise*

Dissonance is heard as the child expresses fear, and the father's music has a reassuring quality. Notice how effectively Schubert ends the song. The piano stops, and the singer declaims, "In his arms, the child"—a pause to allow anticipation to build up—"was dead."

Art songs provide a kind of music that is not duplicated in arias or folk songs. Those forms of vocal music have other qualities and functions.

SOLO AND CHAMBER MUSIC

Although the Romantic era is noted for large compositions, its composers continued to produce many excellent works for small groups and solo works other than concertos. Schubert composed an enormous amount of chamber music, as did Mendelssohn. Two other early Romantic composers merit mentioning: Carl Maria von Weber (1786–1826) and Robert Schumann. Weber is known for his operas. Schumann is an important name in the world of music and is presented in the next chapter.

Mendelssohn's Violin Concerto in E Minor

Mendelssohn's Violin Concerto in E Minor was probably inspired by his friendship with Ferdinand David, who was concertmaster of his orchestra. In 1844 he wrote to David, "I should like to make a violin concerto for you next winter." He continued, "One in E minor runs in my head and its beginning gives me no rest." David performed its highly successful premiere in 1845. Its popularity with concert audiences continues to this day.

In some ways Mendelssohn was a rather conservative composer, at least compared with a number of his contemporaries. He did, however, make several sizable changes in his violin concerto. For one, he linked all of its three movements together so that there are no breaks in the entire work. Composers in the Classical period always made clean breaks between movements. Beethoven did link the third and fourth movements of his Symphony No. 5, but that was quite unusual for him and other composers at that time.

Mendelssohn's treatment of sonata form was also quite different. Sonata form in concertos during the Classical period had two expositions. The first was for the orchestra, and the second was for the orchestra and the solo instrument. Mendelssohn dropped that idea by having the solo violin start right at the beginning of the first movement, which is in sonata form (see Listening Guide).

It was also the practice of composers in the Classical period to have a cadenza just ahead of the coda. Mendelssohn placed the cadenza in his concerto at the end of the development section just ahead of the recapitulation. By doing this, he integrated the cadenza into the movement much better. No longer does it seem like an appendage to a movement.

He made another important change from the concerto of the Baroque and Classical periods. Bach's Brandenburg Concerto No. 5, with its long cadenza that the composer wrote, was a rare exception. Cadenzas were left to the performer to improvise during the performance. Mendelssohn, probably with David's help, wrote out all the notes for this cadenza. In this way the cadenza could be more integrated with the rest of the music in the movement. The practice of specifying all the notes for cadenzas continues to this day.

The second movement is more typical. It is a slow movement in *A B A* form and has a songlike style. There is a short bridge to the third movement.

The third movement with its rapid tempo gives the soloist many chances to show off his or her playing prowess. The movement is in sonata form with its two main themes. However, Mendelssohn introduced a third theme in the development section. The recapitulation leads to a stunning conclusion of the work.

FELIX MENDELSSOHN

Concerto for Violin in E Minor, OP. 64 (1845), First Movement

Genre: Concerto

Form: Sonata

Download 45

12 minutes 1 second

Exposition

0:00   Solo violin opens, playing first theme in minor, somewhat softly and in duple meter.

0:29   Violin plays faster notes as music becomes louder.

0:32   Pattern of four, then two, orchestra chords played forte. Violin descends, then ascends rapidly.

0:45   Violin plays single ascending octaves, then repeats with rapid triplet figure punctuated by orchestra chords.

0:54   Orchestra forcefully plays the first theme.

1:04   Lower strings play rising phrase propelled by short-short-long (dee-dee-DAH) chords in woodwinds and brass.

1:22   Violins play a bridge theme, then solo violin repeats it an octave higher.

1:35   Solo violin plays many notes moving downward and upward. Flute joins, then music builds to crescendo, then becomes softer.

2:34   Second theme introduced by clarinets and flutes. It is soft and calm as solo violin assumes accompanying role.

2:49   Solo violin expands on second theme, supported by woodwinds and strings.

3:53   Solo violin plays first theme in major.

4:40   Trills played by orchestra as first theme is played again.

Development

5:00   Solo violin plays bridge theme.

5:13   Solo violin plays rapidly moving notes as orchestra plays fragments of first theme.

5:38   Solo violin varies first theme as orchestra crescendos to *ff*.

Cadenza

6:27   Solo violin plays broken chords and trills.

Recapitulation

8:01   First theme played by orchestra as solo violin plays broken chords

8:18   Bridge theme played by orchestra

8:48   Second theme played softly by woodwinds

9:03   Solo violin expands on main theme.

10:09   Solo violin plays fast passages.

10:55   Climactic point reached with trills and reappearance of first theme.

Coda

11:14   Tempo grows faster as fast passages are played leading to a *ff* conclusion by the orchestra and soloist.

LISTEN TO ... this selection streaming online.

WATCH ... an Active Listening Guide of this selection online.

WATCH ... a performance of this selection online.

DO ... an online Listening Practice Activity related to this selection, which your instructor may assign for a grade.

Felix Mendelssohn & Fanny Mendelssohn Hensel

It is appropriate to couple **Felix Mendelssohn** (1809–1847) and his older sister, **Fanny** (1805–1847), in the same biographical sketch. The two were very close during their childhood and remained so throughout their lives. They took music lessons and read Shakespeare's plays together, and their young lives were certainly idyllic ones. Their father was a wealthy banker who hired musicians to come to the Mendelssohn home in Berlin to give concerts and later to play music that one of his children had composed.

In his adult life, Felix became a very successful pianist, composer, conductor, and organizer of concerts. He was one of the first conductors to stand in front of the orchestra, and he was very influential in stimulating an interest in the music of Bach with his performance of the *St. Matthew Passion*. He made ten journeys to England to conduct and perform and was warmly received by Queen Victoria at Buckingham Palace.

And what about Fanny's musical career? She, too, was a gifted composer and pianist, but her father insisted that

FELIX MENDELSSOHN

Leemage/Hulton Fine Art Collection/UIG/Getty Images

(continued)

FANNY MENDELSSOHN HENSEL

Kean Collection/Getty Images

a lady of her social standing should not become a professional musician. As caring a brother as Felix was, that did not keep him from discouraging Fanny's efforts at composing.

Eventually, she married the painter Wilhelm Hensel. She did not completely give up her interest in music, but she refrained from pursuing it as a career. She performed occasionally as a piano soloist and composed more than two hundred works, mostly songs, chamber music, and short piano pieces. Only a few of her compositions have been published.

In May 1847 Fanny died of a stroke during a rehearsal for one of the family concerts. Felix was crushed. Although his own health was failing, he composed a string quartet in her memory. He also journeyed to visit her grave, which was especially hard on him and hastened his death about six months later. He was buried near his sister.

Best-Known Works of Mendelssohn

Orchestra
- Incidental Music for A *Midsummer Night's Dream*
- Symphonies Nos. 3 ("Italian") and 4 ("Scottish")
- Violin Concerto

Oratorio
- *Elijah*

Best-Known Works of Hensel

Choral
- *Gartenlieder*

Songs
- Op.7

Where Are the Women Composers?

You have probably noticed by now a distinct absence of women's names among composers. Shouldn't there be a nearly equal number of men and women? Why such a preponderance of males? Granted, a few women have been successful composers: Hildegard of Bingen and Péronne d'Armentières in early music, Fanny Mendelssohn Hensel and Clara Schumann in the nineteenth century, and others. But the number of women composers and their compositions is small.

As is true of most things in life, there is no single, simple explanation for the paucity of women composers. Several factors very likely contribute to the situation. A major one was the fact that it was a "man's world" until only the past century or so. Women usually could not own property, vote in the few democratic countries that had elections, engage in enterprises outside the home, or travel overnight without an escort. They were generally treated as the property of their husbands. They were often discouraged from composing music by their fathers or husbands, which happened in the case of Fanny Mendelssohn. Such circumstances hardly encouraged women to have the fortitude to compose music and hope to have it published.

An additional impediment to women composers is that it has seldom been easy for *anyone* to have compositions published. Until a composer had achieved a certain degree of name recognition, which made a publisher more confident of sufficient sales, getting a work published was no easy matter, a situation that is still true today. There are a number of works now well regarded for which composers had difficulty finding a publisher. And yet a publisher's cautious approach is understandable. After all, how many sales of a symphony could be anticipated at a time when there were few permanent orchestras and no residuals from the sale of recordings?

Another reason for the lack of women composers was the prejudice they faced in pursuing instruction in harmony, counterpoint, orchestration, and similar subjects. For example, the Paris Conservatory did not permit women in advanced theory classes until the late 1800s.

A few women authors, such as George Sand and George Eliot, were able to break the male dominance by writing under a male pseudonym. An undetermined number of Fanny Mendelssohn Hensel's songs were published under Felix's name! Are there other works by women published under a man's name? We don't know, but if it happened once with Fanny Mendelssohn, it probably happened with other women, too.

Has the situation changed for women in the world of musical composition? Fortunately, in at least two important ways, it has. Much research has recently been conducted on locating compositions by women, and a considerable body of music has been uncovered. The other change is in the acceptance of women composers. Whether the playing field is level between men and women today in terms of recognition for their compositions is difficult to determine. However, Ellen Taafe Zwilich, Joan Tower, Libby Larsen, and others are rightfully being recognized for their works. Perhaps in another hundred years the question about the lack of women composers will no longer be a logical one to raise.

MAIN POINTS OF CHAPTER 23

1. An art song is a musical setting of a poem for solo singer and piano. It developed in Germany and is often called a lied (song) or its plural, lieder. Its main purpose is the musical expression of the text, not necessarily a singable tune.

2. Art songs in foreign languages are seldom translated into English. It is very difficult to match the translated words with the music effectively.

3. In an art song the piano does more than accompany the singer. It plays an equal part in evoking a mood and reinforcing the effect of the words of the song.

4. Because their main purpose is to express the words, many art songs are through-composed. This gives the composer more freedom, since it is not necessary to repeat lines of music if they don't suit the text.

5. The form of the solo concerto deviated significantly from the strict form used in Classical concertos with their double expositions.

6. There were several reasons for the small number of women composers. They included the fact that it was a "man's world," it was difficult for anyone to get their music published, and women were prohibited from gaining advanced instruction in composition.

 PRACTICE...
your understanding of this chapter's concepts by working once more with the chapter's Active Listening Guides online.

 DO...
online quizzes that your instructor may assign for a grade.

24 Romantic Piano Music

START...

experiencing this chapter's topics with an online video activity that your instructor may assign.

Learning Objectives

1 List the names and qualities of character pieces for piano.
2 Describe the features of Chopin's music.
3 Describe the features of virtuoso music, such as Liszt's.
4 Recount the accomplishments of Clara and Robert Schumann.

READ...

the complete chapter text in a rich interactive eBook!

The Romantic period tended to exhibit two different viewpoints regarding piano music. One outlook exploited the power and brilliance of the instrument; the other treated the piano in a more intimate, sensitive way. These two approaches were by no means mutually exclusive, but they were distinctive enough to be noticeable. For example, Liszt composed much piano music that dazzled his audiences with technical display and forceful sounds. Chopin, on the other hand, often wrote piano pieces that sought to enchant listeners with their beauty.

The Romantic period featured piano music. An enormous amount of music was composed for the instrument, not only at the concert level, but for amateur players as well. The piano was the most popular instrument in the home during the nineteenth century. Piano recitals were the only means of hearing concert music for most people, because there were no recordings or radio broadcasts or MP3 players.

Many composers were also pianists themselves and introduced their own works to the public; Liszt, Beethoven, and Frédéric Chopin are among the composers who did this. But gradually a class of virtuoso performers emerged who were known for their interpretative abilities as well as their stunning technical virtuosity.

CHARACTER PIECES

Romantic composers did not want to be confined to the carefully balanced forms that Mozart and Haydn had used so well. To replace the rondo, sonata, and other forms, composers in the nineteenth century created many free, short forms that are often referred to as **character pieces**, such as the ballade, berceuse, étude, prelude, impromptu, fantasia, scherzo, and nocturne.

The **ballade** (bah-LAHD) and **berceuse** (bair-SOOS) are songlike pieces. The ballade is the longer and more complex of the two and is supposed to hark back to the ballad poems of the Middle Ages. An **étude** (AY-tood) is an instrumental piece that develops a particular technique. Études were written for all instruments but were especially popular for the piano. In the hands of Chopin, Liszt, or similarly gifted composers, an étude was transformed into an exciting concert work. A **prelude** is a short work for piano.

An **impromptu** is supposed to convey the spontaneity its name suggests. A **fantasia** or **fantasie** is a free and imaginative work. The **scherzos** by Chopin are not as playful as those by Beethoven. Instead, they are longer and more serious, although the typical triple meter and fast tempo of the scherzo are retained. **Nocturne** was the name given by the Irish composer John Field to his piano pieces with a songlike melody. Chopin adopted the title from Field and wrote many beautiful, lyrical nocturnes. The word *nocturne* refers to night song.

Another type of character piece consisted of stylized dance forms such as the mazurka, polonaise, and waltz. What Romantic composers did was essentially the same as what

Bach had done with his Baroque keyboard suites. The Romantic composers, however, used different dances and wrote in a very different style from their Baroque and Classical predecessors. They expanded the forms so that each dance became a separate piece rather than just one part of a larger suite.

These character pieces were often intended to convey an air of improvisation as if they were an inspiration—a momentary feeling that had been rendered in sound. The impression of improvisation is an illusion, however, because Chopin and his contemporaries labored carefully over each measure they wrote. They worked hard at sounding spontaneous. For example, Chopin was known to spend as long as six weeks on a single page of music, changing note after note, stomping around in frustration, and breaking pens. Sometimes he would return to exactly what he had started with.

There is a feature of Romantic music that cannot be seen in music notation but is used frequently in performing the music. It is known as **rubato** (roo-BAH-toh). Rubato is a style of performance in which the performer deviates slightly from the exact execution of the rhythm. A fraction of time is borrowed from one note to lengthen another. Chopin was occasionally criticized as a performer for his use of rubato. Some listeners charged that he could not keep a steady beat. Undoubtedly he could, but he sometimes chose not to. He wanted the music to have the free expression that the Romanticists admired.

Chopin's Nocturne in D-Flat

Chopin composed about twenty nocturnes. Most of them have an introspective, delicate, lyric quality. The Nocturne in D-flat, Op. 27, No. 2 (see Listening Guide),

FRÉDÉRIC CHOPIN
Nocturne in D-flat Major, Op. 27, No. 2 (1835)

LISTENING GUIDE

Genre: Character piece

Form: Binary (*A B A B A B*)

Download 46

5 minutes 55 seconds

0:00   Accompaniment begins and is soon followed by a tender melody (A):

(continued)

0:42   B melody begins and is repeated and varied several times.

1:17   B melody extended.

1:57   A melody returns and is extended, leading to a climactic moment.

2:40   B melody returns, leading to climactic moment.

3:26   A melody returns. Much use of decorative figures.

3:58   B portion returns and grows more passionate.

4:33   Coda begins with a descending, "sighing" interval.

4:53   Sighing figure repeated.

5:38   Nocturne closes with a simple cadence after an ascending, fading scale.

LISTEN TO... this selection streaming online.

WATCH... an Active Listening Guide of this selection online.

WATCH... a performance of this selection online.

DO... an online Listening Practice Activity related to this selection, which your instructor may assign

for a grade.

is one of the most voluptuous and passionate of these works. It contains rich harmonies and many musical "sighs" consisting of descending intervals and delayed resolutions of phrases and harmonic progressions. The left-hand part is made up of six continuously moving notes for each beat. The notes are actually chords that are sounded in a broken style. The right hand plays a songlike melody that is decorated with grace notes and other melodic figures. Although the music notation makes the rhythm look steady and regular, pianists almost always take liberties with the rhythm, as Chopin himself did in his own playing.

Pianists also use the pedals a great deal in playing Romantic music. The *Ped.* marking in the notation tells the pianist to depress the damper pedal, which lifts the dampers and allows the strings to resonate freely. Richness is added to the music when the dampers are raised. Proper pedaling also contributes to smooth lyric phrasing. The composer and performer must plan carefully for the use of the pedals, because unwanted notes that are allowed to sound create a blurring effect.

As you listen to the nocturne, notice the effect of the long note in the melody and the accompanying notes in the fifth and sixth measures of the opening theme. You can sense that the long note is going to move up a half step, which it finally does. But Chopin makes listeners wait what seems like an extra long time for it to resolve. He is a master at such toying with listeners' expectations.

Frédéric Chopin

Science Source

Frédéric Chopin (SHOW-pan, 1810–1849) was the son of a French father and a Polish mother. He exhibited much talent at an early age and received his musical education at the Conservatory in Warsaw. Before he was twenty, he was on his own in the world. He left Poland and traveled awhile before settling in Paris. Shortly after his departure from Poland, the Poles revolted against the Russians and their czar. In time the Russians crushed the revolt, which caused Chopin much anguish. Chopin's loyalty to Poland remained strong throughout his life.

His abilities as a composer and pianist made him a sought-after musician in Paris. Soon he acquired a circle of artistic friends—the painter Eugène Delacroix, musicians Franz Liszt and Hector Berlioz, and writers Victor Hugo, Honoré de Balzac, Alphonse de Larmartine, Alexandre Dumas (père), and Heinrich Heine. Through this group of friends, Chopin met George Sand, and they lived together for nine years.

George Sand was the pen name of Amandine Aurore Lucie Dupin, Baroness Dudevant, who was one of the more outstanding writers of the time with over a hundred books to her credit. She favored novels in which love transcended the obstacles of convention and social class. She had liaisons with a number of famous men, but her most lasting relationship was with Chopin.

When they first met, Chopin, who had always been drawn to beautiful women and loved the polished and elegant life, was repelled by her: She had adopted a number of masculine attitudes and habits, including wearing men's clothes and smoking cigars. And she was not conventionally attractive. Yet in time he was drawn to her. Her fame as a writer and her strong personality seemed to be a good balance for his not very forceful ways. When they separated, she did not seem to be affected. But Chopin lived only another two years before his death from tuberculosis. Liszt wrote of the separation: "In the breaking of this long affection, this powerful bond, he had broken his life."

Most composers before Chopin wrote well in a variety of types of music. Chopin was different. He was one of the first major composers to limit his writing to one or two areas. He wrote almost exclusively for the piano, and it is this music that made a place for him in the world of music. He is often referred to as "the poet of the piano."

Best-Known Works

Orchestra
- Piano Concertos Nos. 1 and 2

Piano—character pieces
- Études (24), including "Black Key," "Winter Wind," and "Revolutionary"
- Fantasies, including *Fantasie-Impromptu*, Op. 66
- Nocturnes (21)
- Preludes (24, one in each major and minor key)
- Scherzos (4)

Piano—stylized dances
- Polonaises, including Op. 53
- Mazurkas
- Waltzes, including "Minute Waltz"

Piano—sonatas (3)

VIRTUOSO MUSIC

Another type of piano music was for the virtuoso performer. Audiences during the nineteenth century were fond of dazzling, showy music and stunning performances by musical idols such as the pianist Franz Liszt (Figure 24.1) and the violin virtuoso Niccolò Paganini.

Liszt's *La Campanella*

Liszt admired the virtuoso skills of Paganini on the violin. This admiration led to Liszt's transcribing six of Paganini's violin works for piano under the title *Transcendental Études after Paganini*. *La Campanella* (*The Little Bell*) is the third of these pieces (see Listening Guide). Liszt retains the bell effect by sounding a high D-sharp repeatedly throughout the piece.

FIGURE 24.1
A CONTEMPORARY CARICATURE OF LISZT LAMPOONS HIS EXTRAORDINARY VIRTUOSITY.

Mary Evans Picture Library/The Image Works

Transcriptions were popular in the Romantic era. They offered the new public audience the opportunity to hear technically stunning variations on operatic melodies and other works not originally written for piano. Liszt arranged many of the transcriptions in the form of duets for two persons playing at the same keyboard.

La Campanella is a typically Romantic composition, for several reasons:

- It is virtuoso music; even a professional pianist does not undertake it lightly.
- It demands of the player the full range of techniques developed in the Romantic period.
- It is an attempt to make the piano more orchestral in sound and concept. The very name of the piece suggests that the piano is to be descriptive of something more than itself.

Even though *La Campanella* is technically challenging, it is musically rather simple. It is a set of scintillating variations on a simple melody in which the opening two-measure phrase is stated and then repeated twice with a concluding phrase. After the main theme is presented again, there is a contrasting section. It, too, is composed of short, repeated phrases. The piece has a form of *a a b*.

The technical devices of piano playing are too numerous to cover fully here. A few examples provide an idea of what Liszt did in the way of virtuoso display. One involves rapidly repeated notes, which Liszt used often. It may seem that the pianist is simply rapping his or her finger repeatedly on the key with tremendous speed. Not so. It is much easier to play notes rapidly in succession if the key is struck with a different finger for each sound. Here is an example of where that technique is used. The *8va* sign tells the performer to play the notes one octave higher than written.

Liszt also calls for very fast playing of the chromatic scale:

Alternating hands gives the pianist more speed and power:

FRANZ LISZT

La Campanella (1851)

Genre: Virtuoso piano work

Form: Theme and Variations (*a a b*)

Download 47

4 minutes 17 seconds

0:00	Introduction based on motive from the theme.
0:09	The *a* theme with a few decorative notes.

0:25	The *a* theme repeated with more decorative notes one octave higher.
0:40	The *b* portion of theme built on a sequential figure; leads to a fragment of *a* in sequence.
1:16	The *a* theme played in high notes that alternate an octave apart; then repeated.
1:44	The *b* theme with rapidly repeated notes; leads to sequence on *a* theme with trill on high notes.
2:39	The *a* theme returns softly and is repeated with many fast, high notes.
3:09	The *b* theme returns with a freer tempo and much contrast between high and low notes.

(continued)

| 3:44 | Coda begins as *a* theme is repeated at a faster tempo. |
| 4:15 | *La Campanella* closes with a soft but accented chord. |

LISTEN TO... this selection streaming online.

WATCH... an Active Listening Guide of this selection online.

WATCH... a performance of this selection online.

DO... an online Listening Practice Activity related to this selection, which your instructor may assign for a grade.

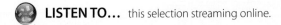

Niccolò Paganini & Franz Liszt

NICCOLÒ PAGANINI

FRANZ LISZT

Niccolò Paganini (1782–1840) and **Franz Liszt** (1811–1886) had much in common. First, they were the supreme virtuoso performers of the nineteenth century on their respective instruments: Paganini on the violin and Liszt on the piano. Second, they both came from modest circumstances. Third, for what it's worth, both successfully pursued many women over the course of their lives.

Paganini had the more interesting reputation. Part of his fame was the result of his appearance and character. He had a pale, long face with hollow cheeks and thin lips that seemed to curl in an evil smile, and his eyes had a piercing quality. There were also popular suspicions that he was influenced by the devil. Paganini was even forced to publish letters from his mother to prove that he had human parents!

His ability to play the violin was legendary, and he added a new dimension to the playing of the instrument. He developed a repertoire of violin tricks and technical maneuvers that he guarded jealously, refusing to have much of his music published for fear that others might find out exactly what he was doing.

On the night of March 9, 1831, Liszt attended a recital by Paganini. The dazzling virtuoso left an indelible impression on the nineteen-year-old Liszt, who became consumed with the idea that he could do for piano technique what Paganini had done for the violin. Liszt

canceled all of his concerts for two years and began to retrain himself. He spent hours practicing techniques such as octaves, trills, scales, and arpeggios (playing notes of a chord successively rather than simultaneously). Liszt's exploitation of the range of the piano can be heard in *La Campanella* with the long trill on the high D-sharp. This trill is only a few notes from the top of the keyboard.

He returned again and again to hear Paganini and take notes on what he did. He even imitated some of the visual effects of Paganini's appearance: his black, tight-fitting clothes, tossing hair, and facial expressions.

Traditionally, pianists had performed with their backs to the audience and played with the music in front of them. Liszt was one of the first to turn the piano to its now-familiar sideways position and to memorize his music. His chiseled profile fascinated the audience, especially the women, as he crouched over the keys, alternately caressing and pounding them.

Behind the image of the sensational artist, which Liszt did not discourage, there was a musician of depth and a man of generous heart who helped many young musicians. Toward the end of his life, Liszt took minor religious vows and had the title Abbé Liszt.

He was also a prolific composer. Although he is especially known for his piano music—and many more piano transcriptions—he also composed many works for orchestra as well as about sixty religious works.

Best-Known Works of Liszt

Orchestra
· *Hungarian Rhapsodies* Nos. 2 and 14
· *Les Préludes*

· Piano Concertos Nos. 1 and 2
· *Totentanz* for Piano and Orchestra

Piano
· *Harmonies poétiques et religieuses*
· Sonata in B Minor
· *Transcendental études* (6)

Perhaps virtuoso compositions are not considered as intellectually challenging as other types of musical works. But most of them—and *La Campanella* is certainly one—contain some really imaginative writing. The high notes of the piano are used in a way that is not found in Mozart or Beethoven sonatas or other piano music. And the variations are fresh and attractive. One must be a virtuoso pianist to play these works well. Technical virtuosity, or any artistic endeavor, whether achieved by an Olympic figure skater or a fine pianist, demands exceptional dedication and talent. It is a pleasure to observe such performances, especially if the observer has tried some skating or piano playing and therefore can appreciate better the skill demanded.

CLARA SCHUMANN'S SCHERZO, OP. 10

As seems true of many recognized composers in the eighteenth and nineteenth centuries, Clara Schumann composed successful musical works before the age of twenty. Her Op. 10, a scherzo for piano (see Listening Guide), was written when she was nineteen.

CLARA SCHUMANN
Scherzo, Op. 10 in D Minor (1838)

LISTENING GUIDE

Genre: Character piece

Form: Scherzo with two trios

Download 48

4 minutes 57 seconds

0:00   Introduction.

0:08   Scherzo begins; very rhythmic with accented chords.

(continued)

0:36	Scherzo repeated.
1:04	Scherzo varied, growing softer leading to trio.
1:30	Trio 1; slower and smoother.

| 2:13 | Scherzo returns forcefully. |
| 2:42 | Trio 2; melody in clearly marked style but gentler than scherzo. |

| 4:12 | Scherzo returns and builds to fiery ending. |

LISTEN TO... this selection streaming online.

WATCH... an Active Listening Guide of this selection online.

DO... an online Listening Practice Activity related to this selection, which your instructor may assign for a grade.

Robert Schumann & Clara Wieck Schumann

Leemage/Universal Images Group/Getty Images

Robert Alexander Schumann (1813–1856) and **Clara Wieck Schumann** (1819–1896) were husband and wife. Robert's father was a bookseller and writer, who encouraged his son's musical interests. Robert entered law school at the University of Leipzig in Germany but gave it up to pursue his ambitions to become a piano virtuoso. However, he permanently injured his hands in an attempt to develop finger strength with a mechanical device. His interests moved on to the founding of an important music magazine and to composing. Besides a great deal of piano music, he wrote chamber music, concertos, and symphonies. He composed about 150 songs, many of them written the year after he married Clara.

Clara Wieck was the daughter of Robert's piano teacher, and he fell in love with her when she was sixteen. At that time she was already well on her way to becoming an outstanding concert pianist. Her father strongly opposed their marriage, so the couple had to wait until she was twenty-one (minus one day) before getting married. In nineteenth-century Germany, children seldom could or would go against their father's wishes. Their marriage was a happy one, and they had eight children. In spite of Robert's bouts with mental illness, Clara continued her career as a concert pianist, although her family demanded more and more of her time.

Two years before his death, tormented by hallucinations, Robert leaped into the Rhine River. He was saved, but he spent the remainder of his life in an asylum. Those were difficult years for Clara. At the age of thirty-seven, she lost her husband, to whom she was devoted. She later found herself attracted to the twenty-two-year-old protégé of her husband, Johannes Brahms. Brahms remained a bachelor and Clara never remarried, but they did remain close friends and admirers.

For the last forty years of her life, Clara continued to teach and give concerts. Clara went on tour again after Robert's death. She gave the last of her thirteen hundred public concerts at the age of seventy-two. Although she was a promising composer, she was not able to devote much time to this aspect of her great talent. She did write a few works for piano and a piano trio, however. Throughout her adult life, she promoted Robert's music through her performances.

Best-Known Works of Robert Schumann

Chamber music
• Piano Quintet

Orchestra
• Piano Concerto
• Cello Concerto

Piano, many character pieces, plus
• *Carnaval*
• *Fantasia in C*
• *Kinderscenen*

Song cycle
• *Frauenliebe und Leben*

Best-Known Works of Clara Wieck Schumann

Piano
• *Romances*
• *Soirées Musicales*

Violin and piano
• *Three Romances*

It reveals her inclination toward virtuoso music with its tempo marking: *Presto, Scherzo con passione* (Very fast, Scherzo with passion). Audiences at that time liked such music. Clara wrote to her husband, Robert, from Paris: "It is extraordinary to me that my Scherzo is so well liked here. I always have to repeat it."

The form is clear: a scherzo and two trios that are not quite as passionate as the scherzo. Sudden accented chords and trills help make the music dramatic. In true virtuoso style, the notes come in rushes of sound, which build to a climactic point. The two trios are more melodic. It is a work worthy of her outstanding abilities as one of the finest pianists of her day.

MAIN POINTS OF CHAPTER 24

1. The Romantic period is sometimes called the "Golden Age of the Piano." The piano was easily the most popular keyboard instrument of the time.

2. There were no recordings in the nineteenth century, so piano transcriptions and arrangements of symphonies and opera arias were the only way most people heard those works.

3. Numerous short, solo works were composed for piano. They are often referred to as "character pieces." Some were intended to sound like the inspiration of the moment (fantasie and impromptu), whereas others were intended to project a mood (nocturne and ballade). Some consisted of stylized dance music (polonaise and waltz).

PRACTICE...
your understanding of this chapter's concepts by working once more with the chapter's Active Listening Guides online.

DO...
online quizzes that your instructor may assign for a grade.

4. Pianists use the pedals to contribute to smooth, lyrical phrasing of the music and other artistic effects.

5. The word "rubato" is the term for taking small liberties with the tempo in order to achieve greater artistic expression.

6. Chopin wrote almost exclusively for the piano. He is sometimes referred to as the "poet of the piano."

7. Liszt was very likely the greatest pianist of his day in terms of playing and creating technically demanding music. He was greatly influenced by Niccolò Paganini's accomplishments in advancing techniques for playing the violin.

8. Clara and Robert Schumann were important in the creation and performance of Romantic music, especially piano music.

Program *and* Ballet Music

Learning Objectives

1 Describe the features and types of program music.
2 Identify the characteristics of theme transformation, in the context of Berlioz's program symphony.
3 Discuss the development of ballet.
4 Tell the general story of *The Nutcracker* ballet.

START...
experiencing this chapter's topics with an online video activity that your instructor may assign.

Program music and ballet music have several things in common. The most significant similarity is their association with something not musical—a story, event, or place. Because the music is based on something nonmusical, composers did not need to follow the forms that had prevailed in the Classical period. Although the result might be the general pattern of a form, composers of program and ballet music were much more interested in writing imaginative music.

READ...
the complete chapter text in a rich interactive eBook!

THE NATURE OF PROGRAM MUSIC

Instrumental works that composers consciously associate with nonmusical ideas are called *program music*. The particular associations are often indicated in the title, or in some cases by an explanation included in the score—the "program." The term **program music** refers only to instrumental music. Vocal music usually has specific references through words. Works that have been named by a publisher or other person are not really program music. Sometimes they give a work a name because names are easier to remember than numbers.

Program music became especially important in the nineteenth century. It provided one type of "form" for a major work. Some program works, however, actually follow one of the traditional forms, even if the composer does not admit doing so. And the opposite can also be true: A composer may compose a work with a title such as Sonata No. 2 that was sparked by some nonmusical association.

Musical sounds cannot really tell specifically about an event or a person. Only a song and its words can do that in music. Musical sounds can, however, convey an atmosphere, a general feeling. Listeners may hear some massive chords and assume that they signify something great or big—the coronation of a king or a large animal walking. The idea of largeness or importance is there, but not the specifics. It is possible to make up a story to go with a musical work, of course, but that story may not be what the composer had in mind. Furthermore, instrumental music that tries to tell a story in detail becomes almost comic. It loses its value as musical expression and becomes something closer to sound effects.

Identifying the nonmusical association is not really all that important anyway. Good program music has substance in and of itself. It can stand without the story because of its musical qualities.

TYPES OF PROGRAM MUSIC

There are several types of program music: concert overtures, incidental music, tone poems (also called symphonic poems), and program symphonies.

Concert Overture

An **overture** to an opera is an instrumental introduction that incorporates programmatic ideas from the story that follows. A **concert overture** is similar, but it is an independent one-movement work that is not associated with an opera. Sometimes it is in sonata form. Several overtures of this type were composed in the nineteenth century. Examples include Felix Mendelssohn's seascape *Hebrides* (*Fingal's Cave*) and Piotr Ilich Tchaikovsky's *Festival Overture "1812."*

Incidental Music

Early in the nineteenth century, composers were often asked to write **incidental music** for a drama or play. They would compose an overture and five or six other pieces to be performed during the play or between various acts. Although strictly instrumental music, these works are associated with a particular drama. Beethoven wrote a number of incidental works, including some of his better-known overtures, such as *Egmont* and *Coriolan*. Mendelssohn composed incidental music for Shakespeare's *A Midsummer Night's Dream*. Georges Bizet wrote *L'Arlésienne* for a drama, as did Edvard Grieg (1843–1907) for Ibsen's drama *Peer Gynt*.

Today the music composed as incidental music for plays is usually heard in suites extracted from the complete works.

Tone Poem

The most important type of program music is the **tone poem**, or **symphonic poem**. It is a rather long, complex orchestral work in one movement that develops a poetic idea, creates a mood, or suggests a scene. It differs from the concert overture in that it is much freer in its structure. The symphonic poem was developed by Liszt and Berlioz and expanded later by Richard Strauss.

One of the best-known tone poems is *Les Préludes* by Liszt. Its programmatic association is a philosophical poem by Alphonse de Lamartine. The poem begins:

> *What else is life but a series of preludes to that unknown song*
>   *whose first solemn note is intoned by Death?*
> *Love is the enchanted dawn of all existence;*
>   *but what destiny is there whose first delights of love*
>   *are not interrupted by some storm?*

Notice the fascination with the unknown and the heroic sentiments of these lines of Romantic poetry.

Program Symphony

The main difference between a tone poem and **program symphony** is the presence of more than one movement in a program symphony. Some of the themes usually appear in more than one movement.

Berlioz's *Symphonie Fantastique*

Berlioz's *Symphonie fantastique* (*Fantastic Symphony*) is a program symphony. And what a program it has! Berlioz had become infatuated with the actress Harriet Smithson. To ease his pain and indulge his fantasies, he decided to compose a symphony. He wrote this about the music:

> *A young musician of morbid sensibility and ardent imagination in a fit of lovesick*
> *despair has poisoned himself with opium. The drug, too weak to kill, plunges him into*

a heavy sleep accompanied by strange visions. The sensations, feelings, and memories are translated in his sick brain into musical images and ideas. The beloved one herself becomes for him a melody, a recurrent theme that haunts him everywhere.

The recurrent theme is a **fixed idea**, or in French ***idée fixe,*** that becomes a melodic fragment associated with a particular person or object. The fixed idea, then, is subject to changes in rhythm, harmony, tempo, meter, and elaboration with other tones, but its characteristic pattern of intervals is retained. This technique is called **theme transformation**. Listeners may not be aware of the retained pattern of pitches, but they can usually sense its presence.

Theme transformation should not be confused with theme development or theme and variations. Variation involves keeping the theme intact to some extent and arranging the variations so that they contrast with one another. Development involves retaining the theme but manipulating it, often by breaking it into fragments. Transformation is a looser concept in which a few characteristic intervals are preserved, sometimes with new material interspersed. The retained intervals give the music a sense of unity, and the transformations provide variety. Composers in addition to Liszt and Berlioz exploited this technique; Brahms was masterful in its use.

What are the strengths of Berlioz's music, especially his *Symphonie fantastique*? At least two features stand out:

- His fertile and vivid imagination (Figure 25.1). Not only is the program associated with the work a bit extreme, but the music also builds on those sometimes bizarre scenes into a wonderfully imaginative "soundscape." No one can accuse Berlioz of composing run-of-the-mill music!

Bettmann/Corbis

FIGURE 25.1

AUDIENCES OF BERLIOZ'S TIME WERE SOMETIMES TAKEN ABACK BY THE POWER OF HIS MUSICAL VISION. THIS CARTOON SATIRIZES BERLIOZ'S WILLINGNESS TO EXPAND THE ORCHESTRA AND EXPERIMENT WITH NEW INSTRUMENTS, SUCH AS THE ENGLISH HORN. THE CANNON IS MEANT HERE AS AN OUTRAGEOUS JOKE.

- His masterful use of instruments. Berlioz's expertise in orchestration shows in his ability to get the best out of each instrument and combine their sounds to get the effects he wants to achieve.

Symphonie fantastique contains five rather long movements. Berlioz provided a descriptive commentary for each movement.

I. REVERIES, PASSIONS "He remembers the weariness of the soul, the indefinable yearning he knew before meeting his beloved. Then, the volcanic love with which she at once inspired him, his delirious suffering."

A slow introduction establishes a reverent atmosphere. Soon the *idée fixe* is heard. Brackets have been placed over the fixed idea in the music examples.

The orchestra builds up to mighty climactic moments of sound, which is typical of Berlioz's Romantic style.

II. A BALL "Amid the tumult and excitement of a brilliant ball, he glimpses the loved one again."

This movement is a waltz. Its introduction features the harp playing in contrast to rapidly repeated notes in the strings. A waltz is marked to be played sweetly and tenderly. This movement is in a three-part form, with the middle section containing the fixed idea.

The themes from the first and second movements may look different in the examples because they are in different meters and keys, but the pattern of pitch intervals is the same in each.

III. SCENE IN THE FIELDS "On a summer evening in the country, he hears two shepherds piping. The pastoral duet, the quiet surroundings ... all unite to fill his heart with a long absent calm. But *she* appears again. His heart contracts. Painful forebodings fill his soul. The sun sets—solitude—silence."

The movement begins slowly. It features the English horn, which had only recently been included in the orchestra when Berlioz composed the work. The *idée fixe* appears in the middle section of the movement, which is in a three-part form. Before the movement concludes, a distant rumble of thunder can be heard played by the timpani as the English horn plays a melancholy melody.

IV. MARCH TO THE SCAFFOLD "He dreams that he has killed his beloved that he has been condemned to die and is being led to the scaffold. The procession moves to the sound of a march somber and wild, now brilliant and solemn ... at the very end the fixed idea appears for an instant like the last thought of love interrupted by the fall of the ax."

The movement is basically a march. Also, in spite of Berlioz's desire to write program music, this movement is essentially in sonata form.

V. DREAM OF A WITCHES' SABBATH "He sees himself at a witches' sabbath surrounded by a host of fearsome specters who have gathered at his funeral. Unearthly sounds, groans, shrieks of laughter ... the melody of his beloved is heard, but it has lost its noble and

FIGURE 25.2
WITCHES' SABBATH (DETAIL) BY FRANCISCO GOYA. IN THIS PAINTING GOYA CAPTURED THE SAME GHOULISH QUALITY THAT BERLIOZ WAS ABLE TO PUT INTO THE "WITCHES' DANCE" PORTION OF HIS *SYMPHONIE FANTASTIQUE*.

reserved character. It has become a vulgar tune, trivial and grotesque. It is *she* who comes to the infernal orgy. A howl of joy greets her arrival. She joins the diabolical dance. Bells toll for the dead. A burlesque of the Dies irae. Dance of the witches. The dance and the Dies irae combined."

The movement (see Listening Guide) opens in a slow tempo. There are flickering scales played softly on muted violins and violas to create an eerie, unearthly quality. In the allegro portion that follows, the theme of the beloved is transformed into a grotesque dance played by the clarinet. It is as if everyone is mocking him. Laughter can be heard in the bassoon part that accompanies the fixed idea. Soon bells toll for the dead (himself), followed by the traditional religious Dies irae ("Day of Wrath") motive, taken from the medieval Mass for the dead, played by the bassoons and tuba.

In the "Ronde du sabbat" ("Witches' Dance") portion of the movement (Figure 25.2), a driving rhythm first heard in the cellos and basses is taken up by other instruments. The combination of the various lines creates an intricate fabric of sound.

Hector Berlioz

Hector Berlioz (1803–1869) was born in a small town near Grenoble, France. His father was a well-to-do physician who expected his son to follow in his footsteps. Hector was even sent to Paris to attend medical school, but he was much more interested in the musical life of the city, so he gave up medicine for music.

Berlioz soon found himself part of a group of artists and writers, including the painter Delacroix and the writer Hugo. His parents cut off his funds, so he gave music lessons, sang in a theater chorus, and did other odd jobs of a musical nature. He became fascinated with the music of Beethoven and the dramas of Shakespeare. While attending one

of these plays, he first saw the actress Harriet Smithson and became obsessed with her. He made no attempt to meet her but was content to visit rehearsals of her plays. During one rehearsal Berlioz saw Harriet in the arms of a stage lover. He emitted a loud shriek and ran from the theater. He would take solitary midnight walks around Paris and write letters with lines such as, "Trust me, Smithson and Berlioz will be reunited in the oblivion of the tomb."

In 1830 Berlioz was awarded the coveted Prix de Rome, which provided an allowance and an opportunity to work in Rome. During that year he composed *Symphonie fantastique*. When he

(continued)

returned to Paris, a hectic courtship with Harriet Smithson followed. Both families objected, but the two married anyway. It was a stormy marriage, and it lasted until Hector left about nine years later to live with an Italian opera singer.

Like several other composers of the nineteenth century, Berlioz also wrote reviews and articles. He was the author of an important book on orchestration. His literary efforts earned him income and allowed him to promote his ideas about music. He tried his hand at several operas and wrote a gigantic requiem, but he was at his best with programmatic works.

Best-Known Works

Choral
· *Requiem*

Orchestra
· *Harold in Italy*
· *Roman Carnival Overture*
· *Symphonie fantastique*

Hector Berlioz
Symphonie fantastique, Op. 14, Fifth Movement (1830)

LISTENING GUIDE

Genre: Program music

Download 49

9 minutes 47 seconds

0:00   Muted strings and eerie music give impression of unearthly sounds.

1:21   Clarinet shrilly plays distorted version of *idée* fixe.

1:38   Woodwinds, then orchestra, play loud, grotesque version of *idée* fixe.

2:55   Funeral bells sound three times interspersed with a fragment of the music used for Witches' Dance.

Dies irae

3:22   Dies irae sounds in low brasses.

3:44   French horns and trombones play Dies irae with note values cut in half (diminution). Funeral bells interspersed throughout this section.

3:54   Woodwinds play fast, distorted version of Dies irae.

4:00   Second phrase of Dies irae played by French horns. Then woodwinds play fragments of fixed idea while brasses play the chant.

Witches' Round Dance (Fugato)

5:15   Theme enters four times in low strings and woodwinds. A short episode follows.

6:03   Theme enters three more times in woodwinds, low strings, then orchestra. Another episode containing the "laughing motive" follows.

7:00	Low strings play fragments of Dies irae. Then portions of the Witches' Dance build slowly to a climactic moment with syncopated chords.
8:00	Violins play Witches' Dance as low brasses sound Dies irae.
8:32	Woodwinds play Witches' Dance again.
9:05	Dies irae returns in low brasses and percussion as music begins to build.
9:22	Movement ends in a burst of sound.

LISTEN TO... this selection streaming online.

WATCH... an Active Listening Guide of this selection online.

WATCH... a performance of this selection online.

DO... an online Listening Practice Activity related to this selection, which your instructor may assign for a grade.

Richard Strauss

Another major nineteenth-century composer of program music was Richard Strauss. His tone poems are monumental in size and sound. At least four or five are performed frequently: *Don Juan, Death and Transfiguration, Till Eulenspiegel's Merry Pranks, Don Quixote,* and *Also Sprach Zarathustra.* A portion presenting majestic chords from *Also Sprach Zarathustra* achieved popularity from its use in the sound track of the film *2001: A Space Odyssey.* Strauss also composed three successful operas, plus songs and two concertos for French horn and orchestra, but today he is best remembered for his programmatic works.

Ballet and Ballet Music

Ballet is an art form in which music and the visual aspects of body movement, costumes, and scenery are combined for the psychological and artistic satisfaction they provide. Ballet is to dance as concert music is to music—an intellectually and emotionally satisfying creation.

There is no clear distinction between concert music and ballet music. Composers originally wrote music specifically to be danced to. But in the past one hundred years, every style of music has also featured ballets. Some ballet music is heard more often today as concert music than in conjunction with a ballet.

Traditionally, the music for a ballet was the result of a collaboration between a composer and a choreographer. Sometimes the choreographer is quite explicit about the type of music desired; at other times only a vague outline is provided for the composer. In a few instances in this century, the dance has been created first, and then the composer has written the music to fit the dance. But the opposite procedure has happened more often, when a ballet was created for an existing piece of music.

Like opera, early ballet stories were based on mythological subjects. During the nineteenth century, many plots of ballets had a fairy-tale quality, which is true of Tchaikovsky's *Swan Lake, Sleeping Beauty,* and *The Nutcracker.*

The Development of Ballet

Classical ballet began in the courts of Europe, especially France, about three hundred years ago. Its main goal was to achieve grace and courtliness, not artistic expression. Deportment and etiquette were supreme virtues among the aristocracy. In the court of Louis XIV of France, everyone took dancing lessons, and this dancing was not a type in which they just shuffled around. One feature of such dancing was proper ballet posture; another was a balance of footwork and elevation—the ability to rise on the toes and to leap gracefully. Ballet posture was based on a straight and quiet spine; a stiffened, straight knee; and a level hip line. The hips were not to lift, thrust out, or rotate; and the shoulders were not to ripple.

From such principles and practices there developed a systematic set of positions and steps that are basic in classical ballet. From these and other movements, which often carry French names, the **choreographer** (the designer of dances) plans routines and sequences for a complete scene. The choreography is carefully designed to fit with the music and its story, if there is one. (Not all ballets are developed around a story.)

The first truly Romantic ballet was *La Sylphide* (1832) by Jean Scheitzhöffer. Its story was one of love between a supernatural being and a human. If not remembered for its music, this ballet can make two claims to fame: (1) The female lead wore a tight-fitting costume with a short, flared skirt that became the standard for women in all Romantic ballets. (2) It was the first ballet in which the leading ballerina danced on the points of her slippers, which created the technique for dancing on the toes referred to as *en pointe*.

Other ballets that followed in the Romantic tradition are *Giselle* by Adolphe Adam, *Coppélia* by Leo Délibes, and the three ballets by Tchaikovsky mentioned in this chapter.

The art of ballet remained relatively unchanged until the twentieth century. Ballet is a beautiful art form, but it is also artificial. The first reaction against these artificialities occurred near the turn of the twentieth century, when Isadora Duncan threw off her corset and shoes and danced barefoot throughout Europe. She believed that dancing should be harmonious and simple, with no ornaments. Although she devised no new techniques, she gave ballet a more natural look. Her ideas were adopted by Michel Fokine, Ruth St. Denis, Martha Graham, Agnes de Mille, and others. To some extent, the separation between classical ballet and modern dance still exists.

The music for ballet also changed greatly in the twentieth century. One of the most important landmarks in ballet is *The Rite of Spring*, with music by Stravinsky, which is presented in Chapter 32. Other well-known twentieth-century American ballets are *Rodeo*, *Appalachian Spring*, and *Billy the Kid*, all with music by Aaron Copland.

FIGURE 25.3

The Nutcracker looks like an old-fashioned soldier in dress uniform. A lever in its back caused the jaw to move up and down. It would crack a nut that had been placed in its mouth.

© Nicole Gordine/Shutterstock.com

Tchaikovsky's *The Nutcracker*

Tchaikovsky was already a famous composer by the time he composed the music for *The Nutcracker* (see Listening Guide) in 1891, only two years before his death. It is the shortest and best-known of his three ballets, consisting of fifteen musical works and an overture. A suite of eight pieces from the ballet was organized and presented in 1892, the same year that the ballet itself was given its premiere performance at the Mariinski Theater before the czar and his court.

The story is filled with fantasy and magic, as are many ballet stories. At a Christmas party, Clara receives a gift of a Nutcracker (Figure 25.3) from the eccentric Drosselmeyer. Her brother, Fritz, breaks her new gift. Sadly, she cradles the broken Nutcracker and puts it to sleep in a toy cradle before she goes to bed.

After everyone has fallen asleep, she sneaks back into the room to look at the Nutcracker. Magically, the Christmas tree begins to grow to enormous size. Large mice appear from the corners of the room and challenge the toy soldiers, who are led by the Nutcracker. The soldiers are about to lose the fight when Clara throws a shoe at the Mouse King, and the invading mice flee. The Nutcracker is then transformed into a handsome Prince. The Prince invites her to go with him to his kingdom. On the way, they stop in a snow-covered pine forest and then go to the Kingdom of the Sweets, where Clara is treated to a lavish banquet, complete with entertainment and dancers from several different lands—Arabia, China, Spain, Russia—as well as by the Reed Flutes.

PIOTR ILICH TCHAIKOVSKY
"Waltz of the Flowers" from *The Nutcracker* (1891)

Genre: Ballet music

Form: Rondo (*A B A B C A B*)

Download 50

6 minutes 52 seconds

0:00 Woodwinds and harp open with fragment of *A* theme.

0:21 Harp cadenza.

1:08 *A* theme played by French horns with flowing notes in clarinet.

1:24 *A* theme repeated.

1:40 *B* theme enters in violins and then repeated.

2:12 *A* theme played by French horns and clarinets.

2:43 *B* theme played by violins and then repeated.

3:15 *C* theme enters in oboe, with contrasting line in violins.

3:31 *C* theme repeated.

3:45 *C* theme extended by cellos, then violins with contrasting line in woodwinds.

4:41 *A* theme returns played by the French horns as violins play flowing notes.

5:11 *B* theme returns in violins and is repeated one octave higher.

5:51 Coda begins softly but then starts to build as fragments of *B* are heard.

6:21 Music suddenly becomes softer with a short passage in two-beat meter.

6:47 "Waltz of the Flowers" concludes with full-sounding chords.

 LISTEN TO... this selection streaming online.

 WATCH... an Active Listening Guide of this selection online.

WATCH... a performance of this selection online.

DO... an online Listening Practice Activity related to this selection, which your instructor may assign for a grade.

The Nutcracker ends as Clara awakens to find that she has had only a vivid dream.

The music for *The Nutcracker* is not heavy and serious. That would not be in the character of the story. All of it is beautiful and very listenable. The eight parts of the *Nutcracker Suite* are:

1. Miniature Overture

2. March

3. Dance of the Sugar Plum Fairy

4. Russian Dance, "Trepak"

5. Arab Dance

6. Chinese Dance

7. Dance of Reed Flutes

8. Waltz of the Flowers

Piotr Ilich Tchaikovsky

Library of Congress Prints and Photographs Division [LC-US-B2-433571]

Piotr Tchaikovsky (Chy-KOFF-skee, 1840–1893), until early adulthood, seemed destined to follow in his father's footsteps by working in a government position. At the age of twenty-three, however, he decided to become a musician, resigned his job, and entered the newly founded Conservatory of Music in St. Petersburg. He did well, and in three years he had finished his course of study. He was recommended for a teaching position in the new Conservatory in Moscow, where he taught harmony for twelve years.

Throughout his life Tchaikovsky was plagued by the fact that he was a homosexual. He once described his existence as "regretting the past, hoping for the future, without ever being satisfied with the present." He married a Conservatory student, a rather unstable girl who was madly in love with him. The marriage was a disaster. Finally, on the verge of a complete mental breakdown, he went to live with his brothers in St. Petersburg.

Nadezhda von Meck entered his life at this point. She was a wealthy widow who, though a recluse, successfully ran her inherited business empire and the lives of her eleven children. She was impressed by the beauty of Tchaikovsky's music and decided to support him financially. There was, however, one unusual stipulation: So that she could be sure she was supporting a composer, not a personal friend, she required that they should never meet. And so it was. For thirteen years, they carried on an intense and devoted relationship—all by letters.

In 1893 while in St. Petersburg to conduct his Sixth Symphony, Tchaikovsky contracted cholera and died. Although he was born and lived in Russia, his music is not particularly nationalistic, especially in contrast to the music of some of his contemporaries, who are discussed in subsequent chapters.

Best-Known Works

Ballet
- *The Nutcracker*
- *Sleeping Beauty*
- *Swan Lake*

Opera
- *Eugene Onegin*

Orchestra
- Piano Concerto No. 1
- Violin Concerto
- *Romeo and Juliet*
- Festival Overture "1812"
- Symphonies Nos. 4, 5, and 6

MAIN POINTS OF CHAPTER 25

1. Program music is instrumental music that the composer associates with a nonmusical idea. It cannot tell a specific story, but it can convey general impressions. The program for such a work is indicated in its title, which is sometimes accompanied by a poem or other descriptive material.

2. For Romantic composers, program music became a means of organizing a work without resorting to the forms developed during the Classical period. It was also a source of musical material that had hardly been tapped.

3. Four types of program music were composed:

   - Concert overture—an independent piece in one movement with programmatic associations
   - Incidental music—written to be performed in conjunction with a play or drama

- Tone poem (or symphonic poem)—a large, one-movement work for orchestra that develops a poetic idea, suggests a scene, or creates a mood
- Program symphony—a multimovement work that is built around an idea or story

4. Berlioz's *Symphonie fantastique* represents his fantasies about his beloved in five different situations. The work is unified through a theme (fixed idea) that is transformed. The basic pitches of the fixed idea are retained while its rhythm, harmony, and timbre are changed.

5. Ballet is an art form that combines body movement, costumes, scenery, and music in an artistic way. It began in the courts of France about three hundred years ago, where its main goal was grace and courtliness.

6. Choreographers usually create the dance movement to go with a particular musical work. Composers sometimes arrange suites consisting of music from the complete ballet.

 PRACTICE...
your understanding of this chapter's concepts by working once more with the chapter's Active Listening Guides online.

 DO...
online quizzes that your instructor may assign for a grade.

26 Romantic Opera

START...

experiencing this chapter's topics with an online video activity that your instructor may assign.

Learning Objectives

1 Describe Italian operas in the Romantic period, in the context of Verdi's *Rigoletto* and Puccini's *La bohéme*.

2 Characterize the features of Wagner's music dramas through studying a scene from *Götterdämmerung*.

READ...

the complete chapter text in a rich interactive eBook!

Italian opera dominated the opera world until the nineteenth century. But that situation was about to change. Several other distinct styles of opera developed during the Romantic period. One was the German style, followed later in the century by the French and Russian styles. Italian opera also changed, but less dramatically.

THE ITALIAN STYLE

At the beginning of the nineteenth century, Italian opera was still in the style of Mozart's *Don Giovanni*, discussed in Chapter 17. Gioacchino Rossini (1792–1868) even based his opera *The Barber of Seville* on the characters in Mozart's *The Marriage of Figaro*.

With Vincenzo Bellini (1801–1835) Italian opera reached a high point of interest in melody. The arias in his operas, such as those in *Norma*, emphasize beautiful singing through technically demanding melodic lines, cadenzas, and ornamentation. This style of opera is termed **bel canto**, which means "beautiful singing" in Italian. Gaetano Donizetti (1797–1848) also contributed to the bel canto style of opera. Although these early operas often lack convincing dramatic qualities, the brilliance of the soloists' lines and the beauty of the melodies make for highly enjoyable listening.

The two most important names in Italian opera in the nineteenth century were Giuseppe Verdi and Giacomo Puccini. Both composed operas that contained the beauty of bel canto melodies, but they added much more to their music.

Verdi's *Rigoletto*

Rigoletto is hardly the typical hero—he is a hunchbacked court jester. And he isn't even a nice guy. His one redeeming virtue is his love for his daughter, Gilda. Rigoletto's master, the womanizing Duke of Mantua, is able to get Gilda to fall in love with him while he pretends to be a poor student. He manages to seduce Gilda, which motivates Rigoletto to plot the Duke's murder. But Gilda really loves the Duke, even when she finds out that he is a liar and a cheat. In the end, she sacrifices her own life to save his. As often happens in Romantic opera, evil overcomes good.

The Duke's aria "La donna è mobile" ("Woman is fickle") expresses the Duke's pleasure-seeking personality (see Listening Guide). It also shows Verdi's ability to compose rousing music. He knew that the aria would be a hit, and he didn't want it to leak out of rehearsals and have everyone singing it before the opera opened. Therefore, he waited until as close as possible to the premiere to give the music to the tenor who had the Duke's role. It achieved a popular status in the United States in the 1950s as recorded by a tenor named Mario Lanza.

GIUSEPPE VERDI
"La donna è mobile" from *Rigoletto* (1851)

Genre: Aria, opera

Form: Strophic

Download 51

2 minutes 4 seconds

0:00	Orchestra plays short introduction.	
0:13	La donna è mobile Qual piuma al vento, Muta d'accento E di pensiero.	Woman is fickle Like a feather in the breeze, She changes her words And her thoughts.

0:22	Sempre un amabile Leggiadro viso, In pianto o in riso, é menzognero.	Always a lovable And beautiful face, Crying or laughing, Is lying.
0:32	La donna è mobile, ecc.	Woman is fickle, etc.
1:08	é sempre misero Chi a lei s'affida, Chi le confida Mal cauto il core! Pur mai non sentesi Felice appieno Chi su quel seno Non libra amore!	The man's always miserable Who believes in her, Who carelessly trusts His heart to her! And yet one who never Enjoys love on that breast Never feels Really in love!
1:27	La donna è mobile, ecc.	Woman is fickle, etc.
1:56	Aria concludes with tenor singing high note and decisive chords by the orchestra.	

LISTEN TO... this selection streaming online.

WATCH... an Active Listening Guide of this selection online.

WATCH... a performance of this selection online.

DO... an online Listening Practice Activity related to this selection, which your instructor may assign for a grade.

LISTENING GUIDE

Giuseppe Verdi & Giacomo Puccini

GIUSEPPE VERDI

GIACOMO PUCCINI

Giuseppe Verdi (VAIR-dee, 1813–1901) was born in a small town in northern Italy, the son of a poor innkeeper. He probably would not have had a musical education had it not been for the support of a prosperous merchant who paid for two years' study in Milan. When Verdi returned, he fell in love with the merchant's daughter. The marriage was a happy one, but misfortune struck. His two children and his young wife died within a three-year span.

Although Verdi's first opera had been moderately successful, the next one was not. That failure, coupled with the tragedies in his family, caused him to give up composing for a year. He was finally persuaded to write another opera on the story of Nebuchadnezzar, the biblical king of Babylon. It was an immediate success and it launched Verdi on a career that spanned more than fifty years. Part of his success lay in his selection of high-quality libretti. He was also an excellent dramatist and sensed what would be effective onstage.

Verdi's career was helped by the strong nationalistic feelings of the Italians, who were attempting to free themselves from the control of Austria. Cries of "Viva Verdi" rang out in Italian opera houses, both in admiration of Verdi and in allegiance to Italy. To many patriots, the letters of his name represented "Victor Emmanuel, *Rex d'Italia*." The phrase means "Victor Emmanuel, king of Italy." Victor Emmanuel became Italy's first king.

In spite of his fame, Verdi remained a simple man who preferred the quiet of his farm to the pressures of society. His second wife was a sensitive and intelligent woman who encouraged him in his work. Verdi was able to produce one masterpiece after another. He wrote his last operas when he was nearly eighty years old.

Best-Known Works of Verdi

Opera
- *Il trovatore*
- *La traviata*
- *Rigoletto*
- *A Masked Ball*
- *Aïda*
- *Otello*
- *Falstaff*

Giacomo Puccini (Poo-CHEE-nee, 1858–1924) was a generation younger than Verdi and perhaps not so sophisticated a composer. He possessed a wonderful gift of melody, however, and an instinct for successful theater. These attributes made his operas very popular.

Puccini belonged to a group of opera composers who stressed *verismo* (realism). Their characters came from everyday life, and they rejected heroic or exalted themes from mythology and history. In *La bohème*, for example, four young men occupy a shabby, cold apartment and have trouble meeting the rent and finding enough to eat.

Best-Known Works of Puccini

Opera
- *La bohème*
- *Tosca*
- *Madame Butterfly*
- *Turandot*

Puccini's *La Bohème*

La bohème (*The Bohemian*) is a story of the artsy life on the Left Bank of the Seine in Paris. The curtain rises on the run-down small apartment where four young men live: the poet Rodolfo, the painter Marcello, the philosopher Colline, and the musician Schaunard. It's Christmas Eve, and they can't afford fuel for a decent fire. Colline and Schaunard come back and flourish some of that rare item—money. The landlord, who seems to have heard of their good fortune, soon comes to ask for the rent. By the use of a little trickery, they are able to get rid of him. (The young men's break comes when the landlord brags about his virility with women, and they threaten to tell his wife.) They decide to celebrate at the Café Momus, and everyone except Rodolfo leaves; he is finishing some writing and plans to join them shortly.

Soon there's a knock at the door. It is Mimi, who has not met Rodolfo before. Her candle has gone out, and she can't see to get up the stairs to her apartment. She is also weak and out of breath, so Rodolfo gives her a little wine and offers her a chair. As he helps her search for the key she has dropped on the floor, a draft of wind blows out their candles. (How fortunate for the plot that the wind just happened to come along at that moment!)

They grope in the dark for her key. He finds it and, thinking quickly, slips it into his pocket without telling her. As they continue feeling along the floor, Rodolfo's hand meets hers and he exclaims, *"Che gelida manina!"* ("How cold your little hand is!"). Then begins one of those glorious arias and a duet that show Romantic opera at its best (see Listening Guide).

In good operatic tradition, Mimi and Rodolfo fall in love very quickly. Musically, it all works very well, even if it isn't quite realistic. The scene would not be effective opera if their relationship were allowed to grow more naturally over several hours or days.

The rest of *La bohème* is equally beautiful and not long, as least by the standards of nineteenth-century opera. Act II is a delightful scene at the Café Momus in which Musetta, Marcello's former love and a notorious flirt, sings a tantalizing waltz. In Act III, Mimi and Rodolfo have had a falling out. There is a hint of impending doom because of Mimi's deteriorating health from tuberculosis.

In Act IV the setting is again the apartment, and there are several musical dramatic parallels to the first act. This time Musetta enters, saying that Mimi is downstairs, too weak to climb up them—an ironic parallel to the events of the first act. Mimi is helped into the room, and the friends leave quickly to get medicine and a doctor. Rodolfo and Mimi recall their first meeting. The old themes are heard, but the music is no longer robust. It is weak and shattered. The friends return. They talk quietly among themselves, hoping Mimi can sleep. Suddenly, they realize that she has died (Figure 26.1). "Mimi! Mimi!" Rodolfo cries out. The orchestra strikes the same chords heard in the love music from Act I. This time, however, the music is heavy with grief. The curtain falls.

Clive Barda/ArenaPal/Topham/ The Image Works

FIGURE 26.1
The Final Act of La Bohème ends with the death of Mimi in the arms of Rodolfo. Often the duet is staged so that it is sung with a soft spotlight shining on the couple.

GIACOMO PUCCINI
La Bohème, Act I (excerpt; 1896)

Genre: Opera

Download 52

9 minutes 5 seconds

0:00   (Rodolfo holds on to Mimi's hand.)

Rodolfo

Che ge-li-da ma-ni-na, se la la-sci ri-scal-dar. Cer-
How cold your lit-tle hand is! Let me warm it in my own. Your

-car che gio-va? Al bu-io non si tro-va.
key, don't mind it, it's far too dark to find it.

Ma per fortuna,	But soon the light
è una notte di luna	of the moon will help us,
e qui la luna	and in the moonlight
l'abbiamo vicina.	we'll look by the window.
Aspetti signorina,	So listen pretty maiden,
le dirò con	while I tell you
due parole chi son,	in a few words
chi son,	just who I am,
e she faccio, come vivo.	what I do and how I live.
Vuole?	Can I?
Chi son, chi son?	I am, I am?
Sono un poeta,	I am a poet,
Che cosa faccio?	What is my work?
Scrivo. E come vivo?	Writing. Is it a living?
Vivo.	Barely.
In povertà mia lieta	In poverty I gladly
scialo da gran signore	lavish on lonely ladies
rime ed inni d'amore.	rhymes and hymns of love.
Per sogni e per chimere	In dreams and flights of fancy
e per castelli in aria	and castles in the air
l'anima ho milionaria.	truly I am a millionaire.

Ta-lor dal mio for-zie-re ru-ban tut-ti i gio-
And now two eyes have stol-en ev-'ry price-less pos-

-iel-li due la-dri gli oc-chi bel-li.
-ses-sion of my es-teemed pro-fes-sion.

V'entrar con voi pur ora,	You've been here just a short time,
ed i miei sogno usati	but all my usual day dreams
e i bei sogni miei	and all my other fancies

	tosto si dileguar!	now they have disappeared!
	Ma il furto non m'accora	But still the theft doesn't grieve me
	poiché, poiché v'ha preso	because, because here at last
	stanza la dolce speranza!	sweet hope has seized my heart and being!
	Or che mi conoscete	Now that you know about me,
	parlate voi,	tell about you.
	deh! parlate, chi siete?	Won't you tell me who you are?
	Vi piaccia dir!	Please say you will!

Mimi

4:29	*Si. Mi chiamano Mimi*	Yes. They call me Mimi,
	ma il mio nome è Lucia.	but my name is Lucia.
	La storia mia è breve,	My story is a short one,
	A tela o a seta ricamo	I do embroid'ry on silk
	in casa e fuori.	inside and outside.
	Son tranquilla e lieta	I'm content and happy;
	ed è mio svago far gigli e rose.	for leisure I make lilies and roses.

	Che parlano di sogni	They speak to me of fancies
	e di chimere,	and illusions,
	quelle cose che han nome poesia.	of such pleasures as only poets know.
	Lei m'intende?	Are you listening?

Rodolfo

6:12	*Si.*	Yes.

Mimi

6:18	*Mi chiamano Mimi,*	They call me Mimi,
	il perché non so.	but I don't know why.
	Sola, mi fo il pranzo	Living alone, I eat
	da me stesea,	a simple dinner.
	Non vado sempre a messa	I seldom go to Mass,
	ma prego assai il Signor.	but often pray to God.
	Vivo sola, soletta,	I'm alone and it's lonely,
	là in una bianca cameretta;	up there in my one-room apartment;
	guardo sui tetti e in cielo.	looking at the rooftops and sky.
	Ma quando vien lo sgelo	But when the frost is over,
	il primo sole a mio,	sunshine's first rays are mine,
	il primo bacio dell'aprile è mio!	then comes the first sweet kiss of April
	il primo sole è mio!	The first bright sunshine is mine!
	Germoglia in un vaso una rosa,	A rose starts to bud in its vase,
	Foglia a foglia la spio!	leaf by leaf it opens!
	Così gentil il profumo d'un fior	How tender then is the scent a flower
	Ma i fior ch'io faccio, ahimè!	But the flowers I make,
	i fior ch'io faccio, ahimè,	the flowers I fashion, too bad,
	non hanno odore!	they have no fragrance!
	Altro di me non le saprei narrare:	Other than that, there's not much more
	sono la sua vicina che la vien	to tell you, I am merely a neighbor
	fuori d'ora a importunare.	who intruded and came at a bad time.

(continued)

THE FRENCH STYLE

The French did not develop quite as distinct a style of opera as the Italians or the Germans did. Yet their operas do sound different. The more distinctive French quality would flourish at the turn of the century in the impressionistic music of Debussy and Ravel.

Three French opera composers merit attention. One is Charles Gounod ("Goo-noh," 1818–1893). His best-known work is *Faust*, in which a man named Faust sells his soul to the devil in exchange for eternal youth. Another composer of French opera was Jules Massenet ("Mass-en-nay," 1842–1912). His best-known operas are *Manon* and *Thaïs*; the "Meditation" from *Thaïs* is often heard as a solo for violin or singer.

The opera that nearly everyone has heard about, and most people find very attractive, is *Carmen* by Georges Bizet. Actually, *Carmen* was first presented at the opéra comique with spoken lines instead of sung recitatives. It is not as long and serious as the operas usually presented at the Opera House in Paris. Ironically, it was not initially very well received. The opéra comique was more of a family theater, and the femme fatale role of Carmen was probably disturbing to its patrons. This seemed to break Bizet's spirit, and he did not live long after its premiere. Today *Carmen* is the most popular opera in the Western world. By the way, although *Carmen* takes place in Spain and contains much Spanish-sounding music, it is in French and was composed by a Frenchman.

THE GERMAN STYLE

German opera differs from Italian opera in a number of ways. To begin with, the languages are very different. Italian words end in one of the five vowel sounds of the language. German words often conclude with consonants, many of them with hard *t*'s and *k*'s. The subjects are no longer ancient Greek gods but rather the Nordic gods of northern Europe. And the music is different, too. German opera tends to sound heavier and less lighthearted than that of Italy or France.

In 1821, the German composer Carl Maria von Weber ("Vay-ber," 1786–1826) wrote *Der freischütz* (*The Freeshooter*), an opera based on German folklore. The story involves a marksman who receives from the black huntsman, who is the devil, seven magic bullets. Six of the seven do as he wills, but the seventh does as the devil wills. The devil also gets the soul of the one who is hit by the bullet. Besides mysticism, the opera features peasants, rustic scenes, and hunting horns.

Weber completed two more operas before his early death. Although they are seldom performed today, they exerted a significant influence on Richard Wagner, one of the musical giants of the nineteenth century.

Wagner's Music Dramas

More than any previous opera composer, Richard Wagner consciously tackled the dilemma of balance between music and drama. In his lengthy philosophical discourses, he often indicated his belief that poetry and music should be one. To meet his artistic goals, he created a different kind of opera, one that he called **music drama**. Each of his operas has a score the size of a large book.

Music dramas required a new and different approach to the concept of libretto, so Wagner wrote his own texts. The topics were mythological because he felt that such stories appealed best to the emotions. Wagner's favorite libretto themes were also rich with philosophical overtones—the struggle between good and evil, the contest between the physical and the spiritual, and the idea of redemption through love. Because these overarching themes are present, the characters in the music dramas are not personalities but more like symbols or pawns being pushed about by uncontrollable forces. In this respect, Wagner approaches the drama of the ancient Greeks.

Wagner frequently associates a musical motive with a particular character, emotion, or idea. In his music such a motive is called a **leitmotiv**, or leading motive. As soon as various leitmotivs are established, Wagner weaves them in and out of the music at appropriate times to enhance the intrigue of the plot and to provide unity in the work. Such use of motives permits the orchestra to assume a much more vital role in the music drama, because it can expand on the people and ideas referred to in the text.

Because the division of music into recitatives, arias, and choruses interrupts the forward motion of the drama, Wagner eliminated these forms as independent sections. Instead, he created a flowing, melodious line to serve as an unending melody. The vocal line emphasizes the expression of the words being sung. With its continuous interweaving of motives, the orchestra contributes to the impression of never-ending motion.

To increase the impression that a musical work is seamless, Wagner used much chromatic harmony. By making half-step alternations in the chords, he weakened the magnetic pull of the harmony toward the tonic. The absence of a strong tonic means that sometimes the music seldom arrives at a cadence point, so the feeling of key becomes nebulous.

Wagner did not treat the orchestra as mere accompaniment for the singers. The importance of the orchestra in his works equals, or perhaps exceeds, that of the singers. In a real sense, his orchestra is symphonic, both in size and in its ability to stand almost without the vocal parts.

Wagner's *Götterdämmerung*

Wagner's most ambitious achievement was a cycle of four complete operas titled *Der ring des Nibelungen* (*The Ring of the Nibelung*). The four operas in the cycle are *Das Rheingold* (*The Gold of the Rhine*), *Die Walküre* (*The Valkyries*), *Siegfried*, and *Götterdämmerung* (*The Twilight of the Gods*).

The story of the cycle revolves around gold that had been fashioned into a ring and is guarded by the Rhine maidens in the Rhine River. The gold is stolen and a curse put on it. The curse states that if the possessor will renounce love, he will rule the world. The result is a chain of misfortunes affecting all the characters in the drama.

In an earlier opera in *The Ring* cycle, Wotan, king of the gods, made his favorite daughter, Brünnhilde, mortal because she disobeyed him. She falls into a deep sleep, surrounded by a wall of fire. Siegfried passes through the flames and awakens her. Siegfried and Brünnhilde fall in love and become husband and wife.

While on one of his adventures, Siegfried gains possession of the ring. Unfortunately for him, he does not know about the curse. In Romantic operas, the course of events often hinges on curses or magic potions. He is subsequently murdered by the evil Hagen, who lusts after the gold.

The immolation scene (see Listening Guide) concludes *Götterdämmerung*. It takes place in front of a castle on the Rhine River. In this scene, Brünnhilde sings her farewell before joining Siegfried in death by riding her horse into his funeral pyre. Before ending

Johan Elbers/The LIFE Images Collection/Time & Life Pictures/Getty Images

FIGURE 26.2
GÖTTERDÄMMERUNG ENDS WITH
FLAMING DEATH, FLOOD, AND
UTTER DESTRUCTION. BUT BECAUSE
OF THE POWER OF LOVE, A NEW
WORLD WILL EMERGE.

her life, she takes the ring from Siegfried's finger and puts it on. She also bequeaths it to the Rhine maidens upon her death. After she disappears into the flames, a flood engulfs the stage. The flood is followed by a fire. Valhalla, the home of the gods, is destroyed, along with its inhabitants. *Götterdämmerung* ends in tragedy for all except the Rhine maidens.

Although *Götterdämmerung* ends tragically, the final leitmotiv is "Redemption by love" (Figure 26.2). The philosophically minded Wagner is saying through this leitmotiv that the most powerful force of all is love and that, in spite of all that had happened, a new world will emerge through its power.

LISTENING GUIDE

RICHARD WAGNER
Immolation scene from *Götterdämmerung* (1874)

Genre: Opera

Download 53

7 minutes 54 seconds

0:00   The trumpets and trombones play the leitmotiv for "Law" at a loud dynamic level.

Lebhaft (Lively)

f

*Brünnhilde, the ring on her finger, takes a torch from one of the men.
She then sings to a pair of ravens, which are Wotan's messengers.*

0:13   *Fliegt heim, ihr Raben! raunt eurem Herren,*   Fly home, you ravens! Tell your master *was hier am Rhein ihr gehört!*   what you have heard here on the Rhine!

0:29   The orchestra plays the "Magic fire" and "Loge, god of fire" leitmotivs.

Brünnhilde continues singing to the ravens.

An Brünnhildes Felsen fliegt vorbei: Fly past Brünnhilde's rock,
der dort noch lodert,   where Loge is still burning,
weiset Loge nach Walhall!   and tell him to go to Valhalla!
Denn der Götter Ende dämmert nun auf: Because the end of the gods now is dawning.

She throws the torch onto the pyre. The two ravens fly into the background.

so—werf' ich den Brand   See—I throw the torch
in Walhalls prangende Burg.   into Valhalla's glorious fortress!

1:16   Strings play many notes to represent fire.

The pyre bursts into flames. Brünnhilde turns to her horse.

1:37   *Grane, mein Ross.*   Grane, my steed,
sei mir gegrüsst!   Greetings to you!

1:56   The French horns and other instruments sound the "Ride of the Valkyries" leitmotiv.

Weisst du auch, mein Freund,   My friend, do you know
wohin ich dich führe?   where I am leading you?
Im Feuer leuchtend.   Into the blazing fire.

2:07   The flute and Brünnhilde sound the "Redemption by love" leitmotiv.

liegt dort dein Herr, Siegfried, mein seliger Held.   Your master lies in there, Siegfried, my blessed hero.
Dem Freunde zu folgen,   Are you eager to follow your friend?
wieherst du freudig?   Are you neighing?
Lockt dich zu ihm die lachende Lohe?   Are you attracted by the laughing flames?

2:45   *Fühl' mein Brust auch, wie sie entbrennt;*   Notice my breast also, how it is burning;
helles Feuer das Herz mir erfasst.   bright flames consume my heart.
Ihn zu umschlingen, umschlossen, von ihm,   To hold him, to be held by him,
in mächtigster Minne vermählt ihm zu sein!   to be united with him by the power of love!

3:17   *Hei-a-ja-ho! Grane! Grüss deinen Herren!*   Hei-a-yo-ho! Grane! Greet your master!
Siegfried! Siegfried! Sieh!   Siegfried! Siegfried! See!
selig grüsst dich dein Weib!   Joyfully your wife greets you!

Brünnhilde mounts her horse and rides it into the flaming pyre.

3:40   The orchestra plays the "Magic fire" leitmotiv at a loud dynamic level.

Flames engulf the area in front of the castle, which also soon catches fire.

(continued)

The "Magic sleep" leitmotiv is heard.

When everything seems to be burning, the glow is extinguished. Soon only a cloud of smoke is seen. The Rhine begins to rise, and its waters pour over the fire. Three Rhine maidens ride the waves and appear by the funeral pyre. Hagen, Siegfried's murderer, panics when he sees them. He tosses down his spear and shield, and then plunges into the waters, crying:

Two Rhine maidens grab Hagen and drag him down under the water. Another Rhine maiden triumphantly holds up the recovered ring.

5:11   The oboes and clarinets play the "Rhine maidens" leitmotiv.

5:20   The brasses sound the solemn "Valhalla" leitmotiv.

The Rhine gradually returns to its banks, and the Rhine maidens play with the ring in its calm waters.

5:30   "Rhine maidens" motive and "Redemption by love" motive are played together. Brasses play "Valhalla" motive.

From the ruins of the burned castle, the men and women see the red glow in the heavens. In that glow appears Valhalla, with gods and heroes sitting together.

7:08   The music grows louder as the brasses sound the "Siegfried" leitmotiv.

Flames overcome Valhalla. The gods disappear in the flames.

7:34   Strings sound "Redemption by love" leitmotiv.

8:39   The curtain falls after a long chord.

LISTEN TO ... this selection streaming online.

WATCH ... an Active Listening Guide of this selection online.

WATCH ... a performance of this selection online.

DO ... an online Listening Practice Activity related to this selection, which your instructor may assign for a grade.

Richard Wagner

Time Life Pictures/The LIFE Picture Collection/Getty Images

Richard Wagner (REE-card VAHGH-ner, 1813–1883) was an artistic phenomenon. Born in Leipzig, Germany, he was the son of a minor police official, who died when Richard was still an infant. His mother married an actor and playwright, who encouraged his stepson along similar lines. For most of his career, Wagner was largely self-taught. At the age of twenty, he became a chorus master in a small opera house in Leipzig and produced his first operas.

Success was slow in coming, and for the next ten years it seemed that Wagner would spend his life hovering on the edge of poverty. His first successful opera was *Rienzi*, which earned him a position as conductor for the king of Saxony. Other successful operas followed in the 1840s.

In 1848 Wagner became associated with the political uprisings that were taking place in Europe. He even published two articles in a magazine that advocated anarchy. A revolution broke out in Dresden in 1849, and the king and his court fled. Wagner was forced to escape to the home of his friend Franz Liszt in Weimar. Because there was a warrant out for his arrest, Wagner soon fled over the border into Switzerland. At that point, he seemed a ruined man. But he was helped by some willing patrons, and the years in Switzerland were some

of his most productive. During this time he began work on *The Ring of the Nibelung.*

Wagner became estranged from his wife, who had grown unsympathetic to his artistic aims and desires. He became involved with a succession of married women. In 1864, again, all seemed lost. At that point, fate seemed to step in. A nineteen-year-old admirer of Wagner's music ascended to the throne in Bavaria, which at that time was an independent country. He was Ludwig II, known as "Mad Ludwig." He summoned Wagner to Munich, where Wagner resumed work on *The Ring of the Nibelung.*

By 1876 Wagner had reached the top of the operatic world. That year he opened his first Bayreuth (BY-royt) festival. He later built an opera house there, and the Bayreuth festivals continue today. It is the only theater in the world devoted exclusively to the music of one person. He is buried at Bayreuth, which in a sense is his monument.

Best-Known Works

Opera
- *The Flying Dutchman*
- *Tannhäuser*
- *Lohengrin*
- *Tristan and Isolde*
- *The Meistersingers of Nuremberg*
- *The Ring of the Nibelung*

MAIN POINTS OF CHAPTER 26

1. Romantic opera can be divided into three national groups: Italian, French, and German. Each has its own distinctive style.
2. Italian opera features beautiful singing (bel canto) and realism (verismo). Its best-known composers are Giuseppe Verdi and Giacomo Puccini.
3. French opera was often more serious, like those of Charles Gounod. A lighter type of French opera was the opera comique. Bizet's *Carmen* is an example, although it ends tragically.

PRACTICE...
your understanding of this chapter's concepts by working once more with the chapter's Active Listening Guides online.

DO...
online quizzes that your instructor may assign for a grade.

4. German opera tended to be longer and heavier than Italian and French operas. It was begun by Carl Maria von Weber, but the giant of German opera was Richard Wagner.

5. Wagner developed his plots around characters from Nordic mythology. He wrote his own librettos and directed his own staging. He called his operas "music dramas." His most ambitious achievement was a series of four operas titled "Der ring des Nibelungen."

6. Wagner no longer divided the music into recitatives, arias, and choruses, because he thought such divisions interrupted the flow of the drama. He created motives to represent characters and ideas. The orchestra then had an important role because it could play the leitmotiv even when the singer was not on stage.

Late Romantic Music

27

Learning Objectives

1 Describe how Brahms uses sonata form in a symphony first movement.
2 Identify a different sonata-form first movement in the folklike music of Dvořák.
3 Describe how Tchaikovsky altered sonata form and brought back a theme from an earlier movement.

 START...
experiencing this chapter's topics with an online video activity that your instructor may assign.

 READ...
the complete chapter text in a rich interactive eBook!

The works created in the century after the Classical period do not sound like their predecessors. They are noticeably different, for the reasons mentioned in Chapter 22. They are not better, just different. However, the music composed between about 1785 and 1910 still constitutes the heart of the repertoire for the symphony orchestra today.

The composers of the Romantic period never completely abandoned the forms used by Mozart and Haydn in the Classical period. In fact, some composers, especially in the last half of the nineteenth century, used traditional forms extensively. Most of these compositions were for orchestra, although quite a few of them involved piano, chamber music, and choral groups.

BRAHMS'S SYMPHONY NO. 4

Brahms composed only four symphonies, but each has a prominent place in the repertoire of the symphony orchestra. By the second half of the nineteenth century, composers were treating symphonies as monumental efforts. Brahms was so awed by the symphonies of Beethoven that he waited to complete his first symphony until he was forty-three years old. An earlier aborted attempt at writing a symphony became his First Piano Concerto. He completed his Fourth Symphony nine years later in 1885.

Of all the Romantic composers, Brahms liked to use traditional forms the most. In fact, during his lifetime he was considered by many musicians to be an outmoded conservative. But conservative, Romantic, or whatever, he composed much music of extraordinary quality.

First Movement

The first movement (see Listening Guide) is in sonata form. It begins with a theme that has the sweeping, Romantic quality of many of Brahms's melodies:

LISTENING GUIDE

JOHANNES BRAHMS
Symphony No. 4 in E Minor, First Movement (1884–1885)

Genre: Symphony

Form: Sonata

Download 54

13 minutes 22 seconds

Exposition

0:00   First theme, which contains two motives (circled), played by violins.

0:37   First theme repeated.

1:11   Transition.

1:39   Second theme, also containing a motive, begins in woodwinds.

1:46   Second part of second theme sounded by cellos and French horns with a rhythmic accompaniment. Violins repeat theme in high notes.

2:00   Violins and woodwinds exchange fragments of second theme.

2:51   Third theme introduced by French horn and flute, then oboe.

3:18   Modified second theme returns in woodwinds.

4:02   Codetta begins in woodwinds with fragments of first theme.

Development

4:19   First theme played by violins; then motive from it modulates several times.

5:06   Three accented notes from first theme are exchanged among strings.

5:37   Motives from second and first themes played softly by woodwinds.

6:18	First part of second theme played forcefully by strings and French horn.
6:55	Second theme played by woodwinds as violins play fragments of first theme pizzicato.
7:10	Motive from first theme alternates between violins and woodwinds.
7:37	First theme returns in augmentation in woodwinds.

Recapitulation

8:05	First theme returns in violins at the original tempo.
8:35	First theme repeated accompanied by rippling notes in woodwinds.
9:18	Second theme returns in woodwinds and French horn, followed by cellos over rhythmic accompaniment.
9:37	Violins repeat second theme.
9:50	Motive from first theme exchanged between woodwinds and violins.
10:27	Third theme played by oboe and French horn.
10:54	Motive from second theme played softly by woodwinds, then loudly by strings.
11:58	Coda contains two-note fragment from first theme played in imitation between strings and French horns.
12:19	Violins continue playing two-note fragment from first theme as intensity of music increases.
13:06	Movement concludes after five abrupt chords and final cadence of two long chords.

LISTEN TO... this selection streaming online.

WATCH... an Active Listening Guide of this selection online.

WATCH... a performance of this selection online.

DO... an online Listening Practice Activity related to this selection, which your instructor may assign for a grade.

The theme is worked with and manipulated throughout much of the movement. For instance, in the next few measures the same idea appears at *twice* its original speed—**diminution**. The notes don't follow the theme exactly, but the general idea is present:

At the end of the development section, the same idea appears at *half* its original speed—**augmentation**. At this point in the movement, Brahms retains the melodic line but alters the rhythm:

At another place, the theme is varied and exchanged between the first and second violins:

Elsewhere it is exchanged between the strings and woodwinds:

One could go on for pages showing the many ways Brahms fragments, varies, develops, and transforms the theme. Almost from the time the theme appears, he is developing it and blending it into the structure of the music in such a way that throughout the symphony he maintains the warm sounds of the Romantic style. From it he extracts two motives, circled in the Listening Guide, that appear often in the movement. The second theme combines two melodic ideas. One is played by the horns and a few woodwinds. It sounds somewhat like introductory music—and perhaps it is, because soon a passionate melody starts in the cellos and horns. A portion of the theme, including the triplets, is also used as a unifying motive in the movement. Sometimes it is exchanged with the first motive. A third theme appears later in the movement, but it is not developed.

Four qualities stand out about Brahms's music in general and his Fourth Symphony in particular:

- The sheer beauty of the music. Listening to the rich sounds of its melodies and harmonies could be compared to eating a piece of a perfectly baked German chocolate cake.

- The skill with which themes are organized and developed. This is much more than sensual pleasure in listening to this symphony. Brahms is masterful in working with themes and utilizing forms.

- The quality of optimism and good feeling. This is a subjective judgment, of course, but there is something about Brahms's music that gives the feeling that things are right and will continue to turn out right. There is no sense of hand-wringing or self-pity in the music.

- The noble quality of the music. The word *noble* doesn't do justice to the music of Brahms and many other composers, but it comes as close as any. It means "possessing outstanding or superior qualities." There is something extraordinary about the music of Brahms and many other composers, something that is beyond or better than what we usually encounter in everyday life.

In short, you can listen to Brahms's music with your heart, or your head, or both, which is clearly the best way.

Second, Third, and Fourth Movements

Brahms is especially gifted in writing melodious second movements, and his Fourth Symphony is no exception. It is built around two themes. The first consists of a short pattern that is immediately followed in inversion and repeated several times. The second theme is a warm, flowing melody first played by the cellos.

The third movement is filled with an optimistic, jovial spirit. Its theme appears in two versions at the same time, with one being the inversion of the other.

Johannes Brahms

Johannes Brahms (1833–1897) was the son of a rather shiftless double bass player in Hamburg, Germany. Johannes started his musical career by playing piano in the notorious waterfront area of the city. He was highly talented and by the age of twenty-five became the accompanist for one of the finest violinists of the day. He studied composition with Robert Schumann, and the Schumanns took the shy young man into their home. Brahms grew fond of Clara, and he was much help to the family during Robert's illness.

Brahms was aware that he had extraordinary talent as a composer and, for this reason, never accepted a position that made heavy demands on his time. Unlike Beethoven, he left no rejected versions of his music for posterity to find. He wanted the world to know only his best work, so his rough sketches were deliberately destroyed. It was said that Brahms burned as many of his works as he allowed to be published.

Brahms never composed an opera or a tone poem. His coolness toward opera may be due to the overblown competition between his admirers and those of Wagner. The division concerned artistic philosophy as much as it did personalities. The Wagnerites believed that music was a means for communication of emotions and ideas. The admirers of Brahms viewed music as an end in itself and therefore favored absolute music. Brahms ignored the controversy as best he could and went about his composing. Because there is some truth in both views, the dispute has never been resolved.

Keystone Features/Hulton Archive/Getty Images

Best-Known Works

Chamber music
- Clarinet Quintet
- Trio in E-flat for Horn, Violin, and Piano

Choral
- *A German Requiem*

Orchestra
- Concerto for Piano No. 2
- Concerto for Violin
- Symphonies Nos. 1, 2, 3, and 4

The slur marks (⌢) cause the rhythmic emphasis to occur off the beat in the first and third measures. Portions of the melody appear throughout the movement.

The fourth movement is one of the most unusual and musically interesting in the symphonies of the nineteenth century. It is a massive **chaconne**, which is a set of variations on a short theme. The theme for this movement is only eight measures long with only one note per measure. It is very plain and solid.

Thirty-five variations and a coda follow. At the beginning of the thirteenth variation, the speed of the notes of the theme is slowed to half their original speed. During this middle section of the movement, the theme is only implied in the harmony. It is easy to tell when the theme returns, because it is played forcefully again, as it was at the opening of the movement. The return of the original theme gives the movement an overall three-part form in addition to the variations of the chaconne. The continually repeated pattern provides unity to the music, while the variations provide contrast.

DVOŘÁK'S AMERICAN STRING QUARTET IN F MAJOR

The quartet Op. 96 (No. 12) by Antonín Dvořák is often called the *American Quartet* because he wrote it in the town of Spillville, Iowa. For three years in the 1890s, Dvořák was director of the Conservatory of Music in New York City. He was homesick for his native Bohemia, so he spent his summers living among the Czech-Bohemian people of that town. But this quartet is largely Bohemian in character, not American.

The *American Quartet* contains the traditional four movements, with the same pattern of forms and tempos found in most symphonies, concertos, and chamber works of the Classical and Romantic periods. And because the Romantic period is noted for its large works, it is worth remembering that nineteenth-century composers also wrote much excellent chamber music. Dvořák's *American Quartet* is only one example of this fact.

First Movement

The first movement of this quartet is in the traditional sonata form (see Listening Guide). The first theme is built around four one-measure phrases. These one-measure phrases become the germinal ideas for much of the movement. Dvořák uses many dotted-note figures in his music.

Several features stand out about Dvořák's music, specifically the first movement of this string quartet:

- The energy and vitality of the music
- The good-natured quality of the music
- The skill with which Dvořák worked with the four melodic ideas that make up the first theme
- The songlike beauty of the second theme

ANTONÍN DVOŘÁK

American Quartet, First Movement (1893)

Genre: Chamber music

Form: Sonata

Download 55

7 minutes 12 seconds

Exposition

0:00 First theme played by viola, then repeated by first violin.

(Notation for the viola part uses alto clef for the viola. Middle line is middle C.)

0:20 Transition based on measures 3 and 4 of first theme.

1:33 Second theme played softly by first violin.

2:00	Transition using first three notes of second theme.
2:28	Codetta based on measures 1 and 2 of first theme begins softly.

Development

2:37	Viola plays altered version of first theme.
3:48	New melodic idea played by second violin is imitated by first violin, viola, and cello.

Recapitulation

4:22	First theme played by viola and repeated by first violin.
4:46	Cello plays short countermelody.
5:19	Violins play fragments from first theme.
5:59	Second theme played by first violin, then repeated by cello as music begins to build.
6:55	Coda begins with first part of first theme.
7:06	Movement closes with loud chords.

LISTEN TO... this selection streaming online.

WATCH... an Active Listening Guide of this selection online.

WATCH... a performance of this selection online.

DO... an online Listening Practice Activity related to this selection, which your instructor may assign for a grade.

Antonín Dvořák

Hulton Archive/Getty Images

Antonín Dvořák (1841–1904) was born into the family of a Bohemian innkeeper and amateur musician. He grew up listening to the folk music of his native land. After several years of conflict between Dvořák's music teacher and his father, an uncle provided him with the funds needed for a year of music study in Prague. When the money ran out, he earned his living playing in café bands and the National Opera Orchestra.

When Dvořák was about forty, his fortunes changed. He submitted a composition to the Austrian Commission. Although the prize he won was small in monetary terms, it gained for him

the devoted friendship and unsparing help of committee member Johannes Brahms. Brahms opened many doors to publishers and conductors for Dvořák, who was genuinely grateful. Dvořák once expressed his gratitude in a letter to Brahms: "All my life [I] owe you the deepest gratitude for your good and noble intentions toward me, which are worthy of a truly great artist and man."

By 1885 Dvořák was recognized throughout the world. A few years later, he accepted the directorship of the Conservatory of Music in New York at a salary twenty times what he was earning in Prague. While in America, he was introduced to African American music

(continued)

by his pupil Harry T. Burleigh. He also became acquainted with the music of the Native Americans. Dvořák was the first composer, native or foreign born, to recognize these musical treasures.

After three years in the United States, Dvořák returned to Bohemia, where he became director of the Prague Conservatory. When he died, a national day of mourning was declared in his honor.

Best-Known Works

Chamber music
· String Quartets Nos. 10, 11, and 12

Orchestra
· Concerto for Cello
· Concerto for Violin
· *Slavonic Dances*
· Serenade for String Orchestra
· Symphonies Nos. 8 and 9

Second, Third, and Fourth Movements

The second movement is in a three-part form. The main melody is flowing and sentimental. The middle section of the movement is also melodious, with the first and second violins playing three notes apart.

The third movement has a scherzo-like quality. It contains five brief sections in an A B A B A pattern.

The fourth movement is a rondo, with the pattern of A B A C A B A, which is sometimes termed *sonata rondo*. It has a lively character. It also contains many dotted-note patterns, which Dvořák was fond of using.

TCHAIKOVSKY'S SYMPHONY NO. 4

Much of the music of the Romantic period is luscious and beautiful, but some of it is vibrant and fiery. The fourth movement of Tchaikovsky's Fourth Symphony (see Listening Guide) is such a work. It begins with a flurry of notes, which are then contrasted with a simple Russian folk song melody called "The Birch Tree." The folk melody contains only four lines in an *a a b b* form and has a range of only the first five notes of a minor scale. How different can two themes be?

The movement also cycles back in the development section the stirring introductory music to the first movement. Other characteristics of Tchaikovsky's style can be heard, especially the rapid exchanges of notes among the sections of the orchestra and the gradual buildup to climactic points. It's a real attention-grabbing piece of music.

FIGURE 27.1
THE INTERIOR OF THE NEW MARIINSKY THEATER IN ST. PETERSBURG, RUSSIA. NOTICE THAT SOME OF THE AUDIENCE IS SEATED AT THE SIDES AND BEHIND THE ORCHESTRA, CLOSER TO THE PERFORMERS. IN ADDITION, THE CURVED SURFACES OF THE THEATER CONTRIBUTE TO ITS OUTSTANDING ACOUSTICAL PROPERTIES.

Mimi Hoffer

PIOTR ILICH TCHAIKOVSKY

Symphony No. 4 in F Minor, Op. 36, Fourth Movement (1871)

Genre: Symphony

Form: Sonata

Download 56

9 minutes 26 seconds

Exposition

0:00   First theme with its many fast notes is played forcefully by strings in a major key.

0:16   Second theme (Russian folk melody) introduced by oboe in a minor key.

0:30   Woodwinds and violins exchange two-note figure.

0:50   First theme in major repeated by violins.

1:03   Transition played by brasses and woodwinds.

1:41   Second theme played softly by oboe in minor.

1:58   Woodwinds repeat second theme.

2:12   Second theme played vigorously by French horns.

2:28   Second theme repeated by trombones as violins play swirling notes.

2:42   First half of second theme played quietly by oboe.

2:58   Sections of orchestra rapidly exchange melodic figures.

3:30   First theme played by violins, followed by transition in basses and strings.

Development

4:22   Second theme played by violins in minor.

4:39   Second theme repeated with flute adding contrasting line, then theme repeated in major.

5:12   First part of second theme leads to several rapid exchanges between sections of orchestra.

5:37   Fragments of second theme played by trombones and imitated by trumpets.

6:01   Portion of introduction to first movement played by brasses. French horns and then strings follow as music grows softer.

6:29   Transition begins in French horns as music grows quieter, leading to several slow, silent places.

7:44   Rapid exchanges between woodwinds and violins as music gradually grows louder and higher.

Recapitulation

8:18   First theme returns in violins.

8:29   Transition played energetically by brasses and strings.

(continued)

8:46	Second theme played loudly by brasses.
8:58	Coda with many fast passages and tremolos in violins.
9:19	Movement concludes with timpani and a long, solid chord.

LISTEN TO... this selection streaming online.

WATCH... an Active Listening Guide of this selection online.

WATCH... a performance of this selection online.

DO... an online Listening Practice Activity related to this selection, which your instructor may assign for a grade.

MAIN POINTS OF CHAPTER 27

PRACTICE...
your understanding of this chapter's concepts by working once more with the chapter's Active Listening Guides online.

DO...
online quizzes that your instructor may assign for a grade.

1. Romantic composers, especially in the last half of the nineteenth century, often used the same forms as Classical composers. The musical material they poured into those forms, however, was very different. Often what they included in a form was longer, larger in concept, and much more emotional than what Mozart and Haydn composed.

2. Brahms was especially skilled at working with themes, which gives his music just the right blend of something old and something new.

3. Both diminution and augmentation are found in the first movement of Brahms's Symphony No. 4. In diminution the theme is presented faster (usually twice as fast) as the original. Augmentation is the opposite; the theme appears in much longer note values.

4. Although many fine symphonies and concertos were written in the Romantic period, composers during that time also wrote much chamber music. Dvořák's "American" String Quartet is but one example among many, many possibilities.

5. The fourth movement of Tchaikovsky's Symphony No. 4 contains a good example of the very contrasting nature of themes often found in Romantic music. It also demonstrates the fact that composers during that time brought back in later movements of a work a theme that had appeared in an earlier movement of that work (cyclical form).

Nationalism

28

Learning Objectives

1 Designate the characteristics of nationalistic music.

2 Name some of the "Russian Five" composers, including Mussorgsky.

3 Become familiar with other nationalistic composers from Europe and America, including Smetana.

START...

experiencing this chapter's topics with an online video activity that your instructor may assign.

Romanticism exalted the inherent goodness of humankind in its natural condition. Eighteenth-century intellectuals had considered common folk to be untutored and rough; the Romantics admired them. They thought the life of the simple folk to be good and right because it was largely uncorrupted by society. Furthermore, the life of the common people was a source of subject matter that composers and artists had seldom tapped before.

READ...

the complete chapter text in a rich interactive eBook!

CHARACTERISTICS OF NATIONALISM

When associated with the arts, **nationalism** refers to a deliberate, conscious attempt to develop artworks that are characteristic of a particular country or region. Often, nationalism involves specific subject matter, such as a painting of a national event or an opera about a historical character. Many nationalistic works are also programmatic.

During the nineteenth century, this search for nationalistic expression was mainly an attempt to break away from the prevailing German–Austrian style. Bach, Mozart, Beethoven, Schubert, Liszt, Schumann, Brahms, and Wagner had long ruled the musical world. To men such as Modest Mussorgsky in Russia, Bedřich Smetana in Bohemia, and Edvard Grieg in Norway, it was time for something different. They knew that Russians and Bohemians and Norwegians were as capable of composing music as were the Germans! And they set about proving it.

There was an additional reason for nationalism in the arts during the nineteenth century: It was a time of rising patriotism. Italy and Germany were finally formed as nations. Unfortunately, wars were frequent. In such conflicts a nation's efforts involved the average citizen to a degree unknown in previous centuries. No longer were wars fought largely by professional soldiers for a king. Now the cause was one's country. In short, the times were a good incubator for nationalism in the arts.

In their efforts to assert their independence from foreign influences, some composers indicated the tempo markings and other musical directions in their native language rather than the more internationally accepted Italian. So Debussy wrote *Vif* instead of *Vivace*, Wagner wrote *Schnell*, and some American composers in this century wrote *Lively* or *Fast*, to cite a few examples. The language of the directions does not affect the actual sounds, but it offers an idea of the composers' outlook toward their music.

THE RUSSIAN FIVE

Until well into the nineteenth century, Russia had little musical tradition of its own. The czars imported French and Italian opera as well as French ballet. Michael Glinka (1804–1857) was the first Russian composer to write an opera on a Russian theme. Today he is generally considered to be the father of Russian music.

More important was a group of five Russian composers, known as the Russian Five, who lived in the latter half of the Romantic period. The leader of the informal group was Mily Balakirev (Bal-LA-kee-ref, 1837–1910). He himself was not a talented composer. Instead, he had a different but important role: to persuade other Russian composers that they didn't need to imitate the German style in order to compose good concert music. He urged them to draw on the musical resources in traditional Russian music. Four composers, especially, listened to Balakirev's advice: Modest Mussorgsky, César Cui (1835–1918), Aleksandr Borodin (BOR-o-deen, 1833–1887), and Nikolay Rimsky-Korsakov (1844–1908).

Most of the Russian Five had little formal training in music. Balakirev was self-taught. Cui, an engineer, was not a particularly successful composer. Borodin was a celebrated chemist and an excellent composer. Had he been able to devote more time to composing, his name would probably be far better known in the music world than it is today. His Second Symphony is performed often, as are *In the Steppes of Central Asia* and *String Quartet No. 2*. (*Steppes* are the treeless tracts of land in southeastern Europe and Asia.) His greatest work was an opera, *Prince Igor*, which after his death was completed by Rimsky-Korsakov and Alexander Glazounov (1865–1936).

Rimsky-Korsakov represents a phase of Romanticism called **Exoticism**. Like many other Romantic composers, he felt drawn by the mystery and splendor of Eastern cultures. For example, his best-known work is *Scheherazade*, a tone poem based on the Persian legends in *A Thousand and One Nights*. His "Song of India" from the opera *Sadko* and "Hymn to the Sun" from *Le coq d'or* (*The Golden Cockerel*) are other works that reveal his keen interest in Asia. Rimsky-Korsakov also wrote nationalistic music and worked avidly to advance the cause of Russian music.

MUSSORGSKY'S *BORIS GODUNOV*

Of the Russian Five, the most original was Mussorgsky. He was also perhaps the least skilled technically of the five, but he is the one whose music best represents Russian character and culture. His most significant work, his opera *Boris Godunov* (Figure 28.1), is derived from a play by the great Russian writer Aleksandr Pushkin. It does not follow a sequential plot, as do most operas. Pushkin's play contained twenty-four scenes. Mussorgsky adapted the libretto himself, using only seven scenes and changing them extensively.

The story is about Czar Boris, who ruled from 1598 to 1605. The plot assumes that Boris had the young Prince Dimitri murdered in order to gain the throne, and the murder is presumed to have taken place before the opera begins. Later research has indicated that Boris was innocent of the crime. Boris's feelings of guilt are central to the plot, and they finally lead to his death. There is a scheming Polish princess, who with an ambitious pretender to the throne seeks to capture the Kremlin, the huge Moscow fortress from which the czars ruled.

The scene of Boris's death is one of the most moving in opera. The original final scene has a simpleton beggar alone on the stage, having been tricked out of his most valued coin by a gang of ruffians. He seems to symbolize that the real losers are the Russian people, who suffer from the greed and ambition of those who want to be czar.

The music reveals Mussorgsky's innate musicianship and his flair for the dramatic. The prologue features the Russian people. Afraid for their future after the death of the czar, they pray for a ruler for their land. To encourage a public clamor for himself, Boris sends one of his lieutenants (Prince Shuisky) to tell the crowd that he still refuses to become czar. A chorus of religious pilgrims approaches and sings before the curtain falls.

The coronation scene (see Listening Guide), which follows the prologue, is one of the best-known scenes in the operatic repertoire. It takes place in a courtyard in the Kremlin; the Cathedrals of the Assumption, Annunciation, and the Archangel flank the stage.

Kirill Kudryavtsev/AFP/Getty Images

FIGURE 28.1
CORONATION SCENE FROM *BORIS GODUNOV*

MODEST MUSSORGSKY
Coronation scene from *Boris Godunov* (1870–1872)

Genre: Opera

Form: *A B A*

Download 57

9 minutes 17 seconds

0:00   Gong and tuba sound two long, low notes; brasses play long chords.

0:16   Woodwinds and strings play pizzicato a steady series of notes.

0:50   After a silence, gong and brasses repeat opening music, with church bell added.

1:00   Woodwinds and glockenspiel repeat a steady series of notes.

1:36   Trumpets herald Prince Shuisky, who sings:
       Long live and reign, Czar Boris Feodorovich!

       Chorus: *Long live our great and noble Czar!*

       Shuisky: *Praise him!*

1:56   Chorus sings melody based on Russian folk song.

       As the sun lights all heavens
       So reigns our great and noble Czar Boris!
       Hail to Boris, lord of Russia,
       Hail to our sovereign Boris!
       Long live our Czar!
       Czar, our father, hail.
       We hail thee, our father,
       Our gracious Czar, thou our gracious Czar!
       Great and glorious will thy reign be,
       Father of Russia!

(continued)

| 2:49 | Music changes often between two- and three-beat meter to fit text. |

Sing, rejoice ye, people!
Sing, rejoice ye, Russian people!
Sing, rejoice ye, faithful people!
Sing, rejoice ye, people!
Come, exalt our Czar!

| 3:12 | Trumpet heralds the words of the Boyars. |

BOYARS: *Hail to thee Czar Boris Feodorovich!*
Long life to thee!
As the sun lights all heaven,
So reigns our great Czar, glory!

| 3:36 | Pattern of steady notes from opening of scene is played as chorus continues, with some phrases in whole tone scale |

Czar, our father beloved!
Long life to thee!

| 4:03 | Russian folk song melody returns. |

As the sun lights all heaven,
So reigns our great Czar, glory!
Sing the glory of the Czar of Russia, glory!
Glory! Glory!

| 4:44 | Music becomes quiet as horns hold a long note. Boris sings of his torment: |

My soul is sad!
Against my will strange tremors and evil premonitions oppress my spirit.
O saint long dead,
O thou my royal father!
Thou see'st in heaven the faithful servant's tears!
Look down on me and send a blessing from on high upon my kingdom!
May I be true and merciful, as thou,
And justify my people's praise.

| 6:43 | Boris decides to proceed with his coronation. |

Now let us go and kneel in prayer before the tombs of Russia's kings.
And then the people all shall feast.
Come, ev'ryone from nobleman to serf;
All shall find room, all find an honored welcome!

| 7:21 | After a flurry of sound played by orchestra, sopranos sing. |

Long live and reign our great and noble Czar!

7:31	At this point Mussorgsky specified that church bells should ring freely without any other music.
7:38	Opening music returns.
7:48	Sections of chorus sing "Thou our gracious Czar!" in imitation.

Long life to thee, Czar Boris Feodorovich!
Hail to thee!
As the sun lights all heaven,
So reigns our great Czar of Russia,
Glory and long may he reign!

| 8:32 | Chorus vigorously sings in three-beat meter as low brasses play in two-beat meter. |

Glory! Glory! Glory!

| 9:00 | "Coronation Scene" concludes after chorus sings a final "Glory" and two closing chords played by orchestra. |

 LISTEN TO... this selection streaming online.

 WATCH... an Active Listening Guide of this selection online.

 WATCH... a performance of this selection online.

 DO... an online Listening Practice Activity related to this selection, which your instructor may assign for a grade.

In several ways Mussorgsky was ahead of his time, musically speaking. Twice in the coronation scene a scale containing only whole steps is implied. The scale (called the **whole-tone scale**) would be used quite often twenty-five years later in the music of Impressionistic composers. In addition, there are places in the coronation scene in which two-beat against three-beat meter is implied. Again, such combination of meters (called **polymeters**) would become much more common in the twentieth century. At several places in the orchestral portions of the coronation scene, Mussorgsky has adjacent chords harmonically as far apart as possible. For example, a C major chord is followed by one built on F-sharp. Again, this portends the breaking away from tonal harmony by twentieth-century composers.

The coronation scene from *Boris Godunov* has several notable features:

- The music has a virile, masculine quality. It exudes the rugged, hardy character that one associates with the peasantry of Russia at the beginning of the seventeenth century. Mussorgsky's admiration for the vigor of the Russian people has found its way into his music.

- The words, music, and drama fit together very effectively. Boris's solo is expressive and flexible. It suggests an aria and recitative in which the union of words and music fits perfectly. His prayer sounds somewhat like a chant, which is appropriate because chant is a feature of Russian Orthodox worship.

- The resonant sound of Boris's bass voice gives the impression of a mighty man, the leader of all Russia, a man who can bend steel with his bare hands.

- The scene is filled with color, both visually and musically. A coronation is an impressive event to see.

Mussorgsky's innovations and fresh, nationalistic approach were almost too much for audiences in 1872. Even his friends and admirers had trouble understanding *Boris Godunov*. It was rejected twice for performance by the Imperial Opera. Only after two revisions and a performance of three of its scenes at a benefit concert was all of *Boris Godunov* performed.

Modest Mussorgsky

Sovfoto/Universal Images Group/Getty Images

Modest Mussorgsky (1839–1881) was considered the least accomplished and important of the Russian Five. Today, because of his innovative style and the rugged Russian quality of his music, he is considered the greatest of the five.

He was born into a prosperous landowning family. He showed much talent at the piano at an early age, but he refused to practice and did not seem headed toward a musical career. Instead, he entered a military academy. Soon, he began drinking heavily, but his skill at the piano and good singing voice made him popular at parties. While still in the military, he met Borodin and Balakirev. They sparked his interest in composing, and he soon left the army.

Mussorgsky's musical genius was not recognized at the time, partly because of his own personality. First, there was the heavy drinking and occasional bizarre behavior in public. His drinking led to delirium tremens and his death at the age of forty-two. Second, he was undisciplined about his work and rarely finished anything he started. Much of his music was finished and revised by Rimsky-Korsakov. In the twentieth-century, Russian composer Dmitri Shostakovich (1906–1975) revised his opera *Boris Godunov*.

Best-Known Works

Opera
- *Boris Godunov*
- *Khovanschina*

Orchestra
- *A Night on Bald Mountain*

Piano
- *Pictures at an Exhibition*

BOHEMIA

There is no country of Bohemia today, although at one time it was a distinct area of central Europe with its own language and cultural identity. Today most of it lies in the Czech Republic. This rather small area produced two important composers who promoted its music: Antonín Dvořák and Bedřich Smetana. Throughout most of the nineteenth century, Bohemia was part of the Austrian empire, so the style of Dvořák and Smetana does not differ all that much from the prevailing Romantic style of the time. But its nationalism is expressed in the use of folk melodies and native subject matter.

Smetana's *Moldau*

The *Moldau* (see Listening Guide) is the best known of Smetana's series of tone poems called *Má vlast*. The program that Smetana placed in the score reads:

> Two springs pour forth in the shade of the Bohemian forest, one warm and gushing, the other cold and peaceful. Coursing through Bohemia's valleys, it grows into a mighty stream. Through thick woods it flows as the gay sounds of the hunt and the notes of the hunter's horn are heard ever closer. It flows through grass-grown pastures and low-lands where a wedding feast is being celebrated with song and dance. At night, wood and water nymphs revel in its sparkling waves. Reflected on its surface are fortresses and castles—witnesses of bygone days of knightly splendor and the vanished glory of martial times.

The stream races through the St. John's Rapids, "finally flowing on in majestic peace toward Prague and welcomed by historic Vysehrad," the legendary castle of ancient Bohemian kings. "Then it vanishes far beyond the poet's gaze."

LISTENING GUIDE

BEDŘICH SMETANA
The Moldau from *Má vlast* (1874)

Genre: Tone poem

Download 58

12 minutes 43 seconds

0:00   *Source of river, two springs:* Rippling sounds in flutes, then clarinets.

1:07   *River theme:* Strings play flowing melody.

3:00   *The hunt:* Brasses play fanfare figures.

3:58   *Wedding dance:* Strings and woodwinds play happy dance music.

5:47 *Nightfall and water nymphs in moonlight:* Slow, high notes in violins with rippling sounds in flutes.

8:39 *River theme:* Violins

9:30 *St. John's Rapids:* Brasses and timpani play turbulent music.

10:45 *River theme:* Orchestra plays theme faster and louder.

11:15 *Historic castles:* Brasses play choralelike melody.

12:03 *River fades away:* Long decresendo depicts river fading into distance far beyond poet's gaze.

12:41 *The Moldau* concludes with two forceful chords.

LISTEN TO... this selection streaming online.

WATCH... an Active Listening Guide of this selection online.

WATCH... a performance of this selection online.

DO... an online Listening Practice Activity related to this selection, which your instructor may assign for a grade.

Bedřich Smetana

APIC/Hulton Archive/Getty Images

Bedřich Smetana (1824–1884) was born in a small town in Bohemia, the seventh child of a music-loving brewer. Family activities included playing string quartets at home. Smetana studied for a while in Prague, served as music master for a rich family, and later became pianist for Kaiser Ferdinand, who had abdicated the German throne and was living in Prague. After about ten years, Smetana moved to Gothenburg, Sweden. He earned a good living there, but the climate was bad for his wife's failing health, so he moved back to Prague several years later.

Like Beethoven, Smetana became deaf toward the end of his life. Some of his best compositions were written when he was deaf. Smetana once said that he simply could not write absolute music. Perhaps his feelings of nationalism were too strong to allow him to think of music in absolute terms.

Best-Known Works

Opera
· *The Bartered Bride*

Orchestra
· *Má vlast (My Fatherland)*, which includes *The Moldau*

OTHER NATIONALISTIC COMPOSERS

Norway

Edvard Grieg (1843–1907) was the leading proponent of Scandinavian music. Among his well-known works are the *Peer Gynt Suites*, which were originally composed as incidental music for Henrik Ibsen's play. He also wrote a melodious piano concerto, as well as many shorter piano pieces and chamber works.

Finland

Jean Sibelius (Yon Si-BAY-lee-us, 1865–1957) was Finland's most famous composer. Most of his more nationalistic music was composed early in his career. One of the themes from his tone poem *Finlandia* became the national anthem of Finland. He also used native themes as the basis for program works such as *The Swan of Tuonela* and *Pohjola's Daughter*. The themes in many of his symphonies often have a folklike quality, even if they are not actually folk melodies.

England

The music of Edward Elgar (1857–1934) strikes a consonant note in the hearts of English audiences. Although his music is not very different from that of other Romantic composers, nor is it particularly nationalistic, it possesses a distinctively English quality. Elgar is the composer of *Pomp and Circumstance*, the stately march that is played at so many graduations. His best-known work is *Enigma Variations* for orchestra. Elgar wrote on the score the initials of the friend or family member who is associated with each particular variation. Guessing that person's identity becomes the puzzle or enigma. Fortunately, listeners today can enjoy the beauty of the music without the need to figure out who is being represented.

Several English composers in the early part of the twentieth century are also nationalistic. The most important of these is Ralph Vaughan Williams (1872–1958). His family name is *Vaughan Williams*, not just *Williams*. He helped revive interest in English folk music and also contributed to the improvement in the music of the Church of England. He selected texts for his many vocal works from England's finest poets and used themes from earlier English composers in such works as *Fantasia on a Theme by Tallis*. Other important works of Vaughan Williams include Symphony No. 2 ("The London Symphony") and *Fantasia on "Greensleeves."*

WATCH...
another nationalistic work, from the twentieth century.

Italy

Italian nationalism in the nineteenth century was largely confined to opera. Nationalism in instrumental works did not become evident until the twentieth century in the music of Ottorino Respighi (Res-PEE-gee, 1879–1936). His *Pines of Rome* and *Fountains of Rome* are definitely nationalistic. His style is strongly Romantic, even if the composition dates from the twentieth century.

Spain

Spanish nationalism is found in the music of Isaac Albeniz (1860–1909), Enrique Granados (1867–1916), and Manuel de Falla (FIE-ya, 1876–1946). Each of these composers exploited the rhythms of Spanish dance and the colorful sounds of its music. Although their careers extended into the twentieth century, their music is essentially Romantic in character.

France

As the Romantic era progressed, French composers began to develop a style that was different from the prevailing German style. A truly distinct French style did not appear, however, until the Impressionistic music of Debussy and Ravel, which is presented in Chapter 29.

United States

Nationalistic music was slow to develop in the United States. Very little existed prior to 1900, but from the 1930s through the 1950s such composers as Samuel Barber, Howard Hanson, William Schuman, and especially Aaron Copland had become associated with music's nationalistic movement.

MAIN POINTS OF CHAPTER 28

1. Nationalism refers to the deliberate, conscious attempt by a composer to create a work that is characteristic of a particular country or region. It is achieved by the use of folk songs, dance rhythms, songs about a national hero or event, musical descriptions of a country, and so forth.

2. Part of the impetus for nationalism in the nineteenth century was the desire to break away from the prevailing German-Austrian style that had dominated music for so many years. To indicate their feelings, some composers wrote directions in their native language instead of the traditional Italian.

3. A group of largely self-taught composers emerged in Russia, which was to become known as "The Russian Five." The least technically skilled among them was Mussorgsky, whose opera *Boris Godunov* is still widely performed. He was ahead of his time in his use of whole-tone scales and polymeters.

4. Nationalism did not appear in Spain, Italy, or the United States until the twentieth century.

5. A phase of nationalism known as Exoticism was motivated by an attraction to cultures in India and the Middle East.

 PRACTICE...
your understanding of this chapter's concepts by working once more with the chapter's Active Listening Guides online.

 DO...
online quizzes that your instructor may assign for a grade.

PART 6

Twentieth-Century Music *and* Beyond

	1900	1925
Historical Events	First airplane ● (1903) · Russian Revolution ● (1917) · World War I (1914–1918) · Panama Canal finished (1914)	Great Depression (1929–c. 19
Visual Arts	Munch, *The Scream* (1893) · Kandinsky's work (1896–1944) · Picasso, *Three Musicians* ● (1921) · Rivera's work (1921–1957) · Lipchitz's work (1912–1973)	Mondrian's Cubism (1919–1944) · Braque's work (1891–19
Literature and Theater	Kafka's work (1915–1924) · Joyce's work (1882–1941)	
Philosophy and Science	Freud, key works (1899–1939) · B. Russell's work (1905–1970) · Einstein's theories (1905–1940s)	
Music	Mahler (1860–1911) · Berg's work (1907–1935) · Sibelius's work (1899–1957) · Stravinsky, *Rite of Spring* (top) ▲ (1913) · Rachmaninoff (1873–1943) · Webern's work (1904–1945) · Schoenberg's work (1899–1951) · Bartok's work (1903–1945)	Rodrigo's work (1923–19 · Britten's work (1930–1 · Prokofiev's work (1891–1953) · Villa-Lobos's work (1920–1959) · Shostakovich's work (1926–1975 · Varèse's work (1883–1965) · Hindemith's work (1895–

Yuri Kadobnov/AFP/Getty Images

| 1950 | 1975 | 2000 |

● India becomes nation (1947)

World War II (1939–1945)   ● United Nations founded (1945)   ● Man lands on moon (1969)   ● Gulf War (1990–1991)
                                                                                           ● Soviet Union dissolves (1991)
● Korean War (1950–1953)   Vietnam War (1965–1973)   War in Iraq ● (2003)

Chagall (1887–1985)   Op art (1960s and 1970s)

                              Pop art (1950s and 1960s)

H. Moore's work (1925–1986)

● Orwell, *1984* (1949)   J. K. Rowling, *Harry Potter* (1998)

Solzhenitsyn's work (1962–2008)

Sartre's work (1940–1980)   ● Computers and Internet (1960s–present)

omic energy ● (1945)   Organ transplants (1954)   ● First animal cloned (1996)

Camus's work (1941–1960)

Penderecki's work (1959)

Hovhaness's work (1940–1960)

Cage's work (right) ▶ (1933–1992)

Victor Drees/Hulton Archive/Getty Images

29 Music in the Twentieth Century

START...

experiencing this chapter's topics with an online video activity that your instructor may assign.

Learning Objectives

1 Describe how the twentieth century transformed art and architecture.
2 List the changes in the rhythms, melodies, harmony, timbres, forms, and sources of twentieth-century music.

READ...

the complete chapter text in a rich interactive eBook!

THE TREMENDOUS AND TUMULTUOUS CENTURY

Twentieth-century music may at times be confusing and difficult to understand, but dull it is not. It's as fascinating and challenging as twentieth-century life was. And it definitely was not for the faint of heart, either socially or artistically. It witnessed two world wars and numerous lesser conflicts, a great economic depression and general prosperity, and thousands of discoveries and inventions ranging from organ transplants to computers to exploration in space.

Most of these changes had both benefits and liabilities. For example, as the peoples of the world seemed to be drawing closer together, at the same time they seemed to be becoming more aware of their differences, and in many regions various groups of people worked to assert their particular identities.

Nor did the marvels of technological progress make people any happier. Information is passed along in milliseconds to almost any place in the world, but the quality of what is said often is no better than what hundreds of years ago was written with a quill pen and delivered by hand. Astronauts traveled into space, but they returned to earth and its many problems.

As the twenty-first century unfolds, the pervasive influence of technology grows stronger in many areas of life. It has had a major impact on the amount and type of music people hear, as well as how they think about music. It has also played a very important role in the production and reproduction of music. But, again, it has had both positive and negative results. People today hear much more music than ever before, but they seem to listen to it less and less carefully. As was pointed out in Chapter 1, there is a big difference between just hearing music and really listening to it.

Diverse and complex factors also existed in twentieth-century concert music. It seems to be divided into numerous camps. They include Impressionism, Post-Romanticism, Neoclassicism, Serialism, Primitivism, Expressionism, and Minimalism. Other types are folkloric, experimental, avant garde, and what is considered mainstream. Each of these types represents a view about music and played a role in the development of twentieth-century music.

If twentieth-century music is marked by diversity, dramatic change, and expansion, those same qualities mean that it is also musically very rich. For instance, some twentieth-century music

- Expanded upon the musical elements of earlier music.
- Was influenced by new sources of music, such as Africa and Asia.
- Was the result of sophisticated intellectual efforts.

- Was a revival of musical practices that were once in fashion.
- Was a repudiation of nineteenth-century music.
- Probed new and largely untested ways of creating musical works.

TWENTIETH-CENTURY ART

For much of history, artists played the role that cameras do today. That is, they tried to create an accurate rendition of a person or a scene. But with the invention of photography in the nineteenth century, and especially with its widespread use in the twentieth, the goal of artists changed. Instead of producing images of what was seen, artists became more interested in interpreting what they saw and creating visual objects that are of interest solely for their visual properties. Their use of shape and color became somewhat like composers' use of sounds in music. This change led to a wide variety of types of artworks.

As the twentieth century saw the return to certain techniques used in musical compositions written in earlier centuries, painters also revisited techniques of artists centuries earlier. Pablo Picasso's *Three Musicians* (Figure 29.1) is a type of Cubism called "collage Cubism," in which the impression is given that the portions of the painting are pasted up like pieces of paper (which is what the word *collage* means in French). The separate pieces are fitted together firmly as little architectural blocks. More than pattern concerned Picasso in *Three Musicians*, however. He tried to project the image of musicians as traditional figures of the comedy stage. Their humanness is sensed behind the screen of costumes and masks.

Piet Mondrian developed a completely nonrepresentational, abstract style. He restricted himself to horizontals and verticals and a few simple colors with no shading. In this way it would be virtually impossible to paint a picture of something. In spite of these limitations, Mondrian succeeded in creating lively, attractive paintings. At first glance it may look easy to imitate Mondrian's style successfully, but the limitations actually make it very difficult.

Lee Boltin/Time Life Pictures/Getty Images

FIGURE 29.1

THREE MUSICIANS BY PABLO PICASSO, 1921. THE TWENTIETH CENTURY NO LONGER SAW THE GRANDIOSE WORKS OF ART AND MUSIC THAT MARKED THE ROMANTIC PERIOD. INSTEAD, SMALLER AND MORE PLAYFUL WORKS SUCH AS THOSE OF PICASSO IN ART AND STRAVINSKY IN HIS NEOCLASSICAL COMPOSITIONS REPLACED THEM.

FIGURE 29.2
SNOWING, BY MARC CHAGALL. SOME TWENTIETH-CENTURY ART PROBED THE WORLD OF FANTASY AND PSYCHOLOGY.

An important current in twentieth-century painting was fantasy. Many painters became interested in "the inner eye"—the introspective look at imagination and feeling. Such a view seems to be the artistic counterpart to Freudian psychology and its interest in dreams and the subconscious. Marc Chagall appeared never to lose the memories and dreams of his childhood in a Jewish community in Russia. His painting *Snowing* (Figure 29.2) expresses some of that personal mystery and fantasy. Does it contain shades of the highly successful Broadway musical *Fiddler on the Roof*?

TWENTIETH-CENTURY ARCHITECTURE AND SCULPTURE

Architecture and sculpture varied as much in the twentieth century as painting and music did. New materials such as reinforced concrete, treated glass, and metals that could be shaped and molded became a possibility for architects. No longer did stone need to be piled upon stone to form a wall. A well-known building that illustrates these new possibilities is the Opera House in Sydney, Australia (Figure 29.3), which was designed by JØrn Utzon. It is a fascinating and beautiful structure. It is seen on almost every folder or poster promoting travel to that country.

Even when architects used more traditional materials, they often exhibited bold and imaginative designs. The St. John's Abbey church (Figure 29.4) in Collegeville, Minnesota, was designed by Marcel Breuer. It preserves some of the features of a

FIGURE 29.3
OPERA HOUSE IN SYDNEY,
AUSTRALIA BY JØRN UTZON.

FIGURE 29.4
ST. JOHN'S ABBEY CHURCH,
DESIGNED BY MARCEL BREUER.

traditional church, with a cross and bells in its façade. Yet, the architect created a design that is fresh and modern.

Like painters, sculptors no longer needed to create reproductions of people or objects that needed to look like something recognizable. They become free to fashion stone and metal into shapes that were simply interesting to see. *Aurora* by Mark di Suvero (Figure 29.5) resides outside the National Gallery of Art in Washington, D.C. It possesses imaginative combinations of lines and shapes. Whereas it may seem easy to design

FIGURE 29.5
AURORA BY MARK DI SUVERO.

something like *Aurora*, that is certainly not the case. Everything needs to be blended into a meaningful and interesting pattern.

DESCRIBING TWENTIETH-CENTURY MUSIC

With the Baroque, Classical, and Romantic periods, it is possible to describe their main intellectual and artistic features. That is a much more difficult task with twentieth-century music. Perhaps part of the problem is the lack of perspective; we are simply too close to it. There is an old saying about "not being able to see the forest for the trees."

Part of the reason for the lack of cohesion in twentieth-century music is probably due to the diversity and fragmentation in twentieth-century society itself. Core values and beliefs that prevailed in the Classical and Romantic eras no longer seemed to be in effect.

Equally important is the fact that there is so much music to consider. No longer can an understanding of music be confined to concert music of Europe and America. Music from every part of the globe became available, as well as all types of folk and popular music. Also, more universities and conservatories offered instruction in composition, so more people wrote and made music than ever before. What's more, ever since the Romantic period, composers consciously tried to avoid writing music that sounded too much like any other composer's style. Imitating someone else flew in the face of the idea of creativity as conceived over the past two centuries.

Another reason that it is hard to name one set of standard features for music in the twentieth century is its ever-changing character. For instance, Stravinsky's *Rite of Spring* was modern and novel when it premiered in 1913, but that certainly was not true for long. In fact, it was not even true for Stravinsky a decade later; he had moved on to another style. And Stravinsky was not alone among composers in changing styles.

Some labels are helpful in understanding twentieth-century music, just as period labels such as *Baroque* and *Romantic* are useful in learning about the music of earlier centuries. But such designations should be used with care when discussing twentieth-century music. Composers usually do not like being categorized. They consider their pieces unique works that should be evaluated on their own merits, which is only fair. Still, the use of classifications—the *isms*, for example—can aid in looking at and thinking about the concert music of the twentieth century.

WHAT TO LISTEN FOR IN TWENTIETH-CENTURY MUSIC

Rhythm

Rhythm is a much more important element in twentieth-century music than it was in previous centuries. Some (not all) of the music composed in the twentieth century broke away from the idea of regular metrical patterns. The "tyranny of the bar line" had long since gone. Composers felt free to mix meters, either by actually changing the signature or by displacing the accents. At one point in Stravinsky's *Rite of Spring*, the meter changes with each measure: 3/16, 5/16, 3/16, 4/16, 5/16, 3/16, and so on.

Measures traditionally contained two, three, or four regular beats. New asymmetrical patterns are found in some twentieth-century works. Measures with five or seven beats per measure are used, as well as measures in which the beat pattern is not regular, as in this 8/8 pattern:

$$\text{♩♩♩} \times 3 + 3 + 2$$

Furthermore, musicians felt free to have more than one rhythmic pattern sounding at the same time, what is termed **polyrhythm**, a term introduced in Chapter 2.

Some composers consciously tried to return to rhythmic devices found in folk/ethnic music, such as rhythmic ostinatos—the persistent repetition of short rhythm patterns.

The increased attention given to rhythm had a corresponding increase in the importance of percussion instruments. More percussion instruments were used, and they were featured more prominently. In fact, some works were composed for percussion ensembles; others featured percussion instruments.

Melody

The concept of melody expanded far beyond potentially singable melodies in the traditional major and minor tonalities. Melodies were often no longer warm and flowing as in the preceding century. In fact, melody as such seemed less important in twentieth-century works. Melodies were often conceived nonvocally in their use of wide, awkward leaps and irregular phrases. Sometimes no actual melody can be found in a work. Yet some beautiful melodies exist in the music of the previous century.

Twentieth-century composers broke away from the balanced patterns of phrases found in Baroque and Classical music. No longer were four measures complemented by another four measures. The clearly defined structure of melodies was loosened considerably.

Harmony and Counterpoint

Romantic harmonies are rich and colorful, and chords were built around the traditional pattern of thirds. Twentieth-century composers frequently broke away from that pattern and wrote chords in fourths, fifths, and seconds. More often, however, they added notes to chords just because they wanted that particular sound at that particular place in the music.

Chord progressions in traditional harmony provide a syntax that helps organize the music. Twentieth-century composers did not completely abandon traditional tonal progressions, but they certainly were far less concerned about following them. In fact, not only were they much less interested in tonal centers but some composers also deliberately composed music with no tonal center whatsoever. The principle of dissonance resolving to consonance that prevailed for more than two hundred years was sometimes not followed in twentieth-century music.

Some twentieth-century composers wrote music in two or more keys that sounded at the same time. The term for this technique is **polytonality**. For example, at one point in *Rite of Spring* Stravinsky has an F♭, A♭, C♭ chord in the lower pitches and an E♭, G♭, B♭, D♭, in the upper pitches, a sonority that includes all seven pitches of the C-flat major scale.

Some twentieth-century music was written not in the major/minor keys of the preceding three hundred years but in the modes that prevailed in the Renaissance and earlier periods. This was especially true of music that drew on folk sources.

As the attention given to harmony decreased in the twentieth century, the amount of counterpoint increased. At times, the counterpoint sounds like it was written by a resurrected J. S. Bach. Other twentieth-century counterpoint is very different, because it is filled with dissonance.

Dissonance

The changes in harmony led to one of the things people notice first about twentieth-century music: dissonance. A few composers carried the idea of dissonance to its limit, for example, by asking the pianist to push an elbow down on the keyboard or by specifying a stick that is 14⅜ inches long and pushing it down on the keys. Often dissonance is used to add a certain color to the music, not to create or resolve tension, as it had been

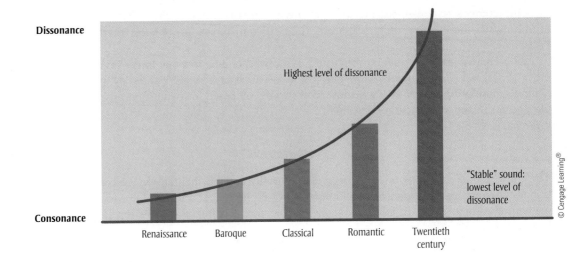

FIGURE 29.6
THE INCREASING USE OF DISSONANCE IN MUSIC THROUGH HISTORY

traditionally employed. In any case, the amount of dissonance in twentieth-century music is much greater than at any other time in history (see Figure 29.6).

Timbre

Twentieth-century composers opened up a new world in terms of timbre with the synthesized sounds and effects available through technology. Even without technology, composers freely milked every possible sound from conventional instruments and the human voice—shrieks, babbling, tongue-clucking, banging, squeaking, buzzing, and sounds made with parts of the instrument removed. Some works for piano call for placing thumbtacks, rubber bands, coins, and other objects on the strings to create different timbres. The technique is called **prepared piano**. A synthesizer can produce almost any sound. It is not limited to the standard timbres of instruments.

The idea of timbre became the central element in some works that consist of an organized series of tone colors rather than themes and melodies.

Form

A few composers wrote works in sonata and other forms. But formal patterns seemed not to be very important to most twentieth-century composers. Some attempted other approaches to organizing their music, and several of these are described in the following chapters.

Sources

Musicians in the twentieth century knew more about music from every historical age and part of the globe than their predecessors did. Ease of communication and improved scholarship into the world's treasure trove of music made this possible. Twentieth-century music is pancultural and panhistorical as no other music has been before. A number of twentieth-century composers drew heavily on elements of music from non-Western cultures, as well as from past times.

The advent of tape and now digital recordings made possible a knowledge of many kinds of music that had not been known before. Also, the field of ethnomusicology has researched many types of music.

MAIN POINTS OF CHAPTER 29

1. The many changes and challenges in the twentieth century had a huge impact on music. They included expanded musical elements, new sources for music, sophisticated intellectual approaches to composing, a revival of some of the musical practices of earlier periods, and new ways of creating musical sounds.

2. The several "isms" in twentieth-century music help to organize its varied styles in one's mind.

3. The element of rhythm became much more important and complex with the use of mixed and asymmetrical meters and polyrhythms.

4. The concept of melody was expanded well beyond the idea of a beautiful theme. Many times melodies are impossible to sing because of their wide range and/or many altered notes.

5. The level of dissonance in harmony and counterpoint increased greatly. Notes were added to chords to achieve a desired sound, and they were sometimes arranged in patterns other than the traditional thirds. Some music was created without any tonal center, whereas other music was polytonal.

6. A wide variety of timbres are heard, both from voices and traditional instruments as well as from electronic instruments.

7. Twentieth-century music was pancultural and panhistorical as no music had ever been before.

 DO...
online quizzes that your instructor may assign for a grade.

30 Impressionism *and* Post-Romanticism

START...

experiencing this chapter's topics with an online video activity that your instructor may assign.

READ...

the complete chapter text in a rich interactive eBook!

Learning Objectives

1 Describe the general characteristics of Impressionism.
2 List the features of Impressionistic music.
3 Describe the characteristics of Post-Romantic music.

The early years of the twentieth century witnessed two types of music that had their roots in the nineteenth century. Impressionism focused on the subtle and fleeting inner impressions of an outer world. It represented a substantial change from the prevailing German/Austrian style. On the other hand, Post-Romanticism was an attempt to pump life into Romanticism by doing more—making works longer and for larger groups. Both Impressionistic and Post-Romantic composers were successful in terms of producing a number of works that are well worth knowing.

CHARACTERISTICS OF IMPRESSIONISM

Impressionism was an artistic viewpoint in which poets, painters, and composers tried to capture something incomplete, of the moment, a sensation. It is based on the belief that experiences in life are largely impressions rather than detailed observations. To achieve this, Impressionists stressed informality and rarely tried to convey a moral or message. They were also fond of nature and commonplace scenes—sunsets, people in casual poses, water lilies in a pond, and the like. Impressionism probably owes its name to painter Claude Monet, who in 1874 exhibited a picture called *Impression—Sunrise*. Critics took up the term to make fun of the new movement.

Several Impressionistic painters, for example, tried to catch the atmosphere of a particular time and place by making rough sketches at two or three different times during the day, because the impression of a scene changed with different lighting. The painting would often be finished in the studio. They also avoided hard outlines and used subtle blending of primary colors.

Some painters used a technique called *pointillism* in which dots of paint are placed close together. Seen up close, the picture looks like a newspaper photo when viewed through a magnifying glass. When viewed from a short distance, however, the dots appear to blend.

In his painting of the Rouen Cathedral (Figure 30.1), Monet was not really trying to represent the cathedral. He did not try to show the entire front of the building or to represent the detail of its stonework. Rather, in a manner characteristic of Impressionistic painters, he used its lines and shapes as objects for the interplay of light, shadow, and color. From his vantage point in a window opposite the church, Monet painted at least thirty nearly identical versions of this scene at different times of day and under varying weather conditions.

Impressionistic poetry and drama were highly symbolic. The writers tried to capture fleeting moments by presenting a sequence of images in words. They intentionally kept their poems in an inconclusive and fragmented condition, which left the meaning up to the reader. Impressionistic writer Maurice Maeterlinck wrote in one

FIGURE 30.1
Monet's Impressionist
Painting of the Rouen
Cathedral

of his essays, "Beneath all human thoughts ... there lies the vast ocean of the Unconscious. All that we know, think, feel, see, and will are but bubbles on the surface of this vast sea."

In one sense, Impressionism represented French nationalism, although it was more of a cultural nationalism than the usual political type. Many works by Impressionistic composers are programmatic. What makes Impressionistic music different from most other program music is that the nonmusical associations are with impressions, not stories or characters.

The Impressionistic movement was unique in the extent to which writers, artists, and musicians knew one another and often worked together. And they held similar points of view about the arts. The painter wanted to capture a fleeting moment on canvas, the author in the printed and spoken word, and the composer in the transitory world of musical sounds. These artists shared a fondness for subtle nuances of light and shadow, vague contours, and veiled thoughts.

Characteristics of Impressionistic Music

- The music has a generally lighter timbre and tone than that of Brahms and Wagner. The size of the orchestra is somewhat smaller. The harp and flute are more prominent, and less use is made of brass instruments.

- The tonal colors are more subtle, including chords with notes added simply because the composer wanted that particular sound. For example, a C E G chord sometimes became a C E G A chord.

- The harmonies have a less functional role in favor of a more tonally colorful role. Sometimes chords move in parallel motion, something that was not allowed in traditional tonal harmony.
- Rhythm is often more subtle and blurred. The metrical pattern is sometimes not easily felt.
- The music has a weaker tonal center, especially when a whole-tone scale is used. All steps in a whole-tone scale are equidistant, so it has no single tonal center.
- There is a limited use of the forms developed in the Classical period and little development of themes. Debussy considered the development of themes to be "musical mathematics."
- Many works are rather short and programmatic.
- The music is sensual and does not attempt to project any messages.

Impressionism partly bridged the change from the Romantic style of the nineteenth century to the music of the twentieth century. It did not leave all its Romantic tendencies behind. Rather, it exemplified the French love of nuance and color and, in so doing, pointed the way toward the future.

DEBUSSY'S "CLAIR DE LUNE"

"Clair de lune" ("Moonlight") is one of Debussy's best-known compositions (see Listening Guide). It is part of his *Suite bergamasque* for piano but is usually heard today as a separate piece. It has also been transcribed for orchestra.

LISTENING GUIDE

CLAUDE DEBUSSY
"Clair de lune" (1890; rev. 1905)

Genre: Character piece

Form: *A B A*

Download 59

5 minutes

0:00   Opening section (A) begins softly with a gradually descending melody.

0:35   A melody repeated

1:25   Music becomes somewhat louder and more animated.

2:02   Contrasting section (B) begins softly.

2:25	*B* melody repeated an octave higher as music grows more intense
2:44	*B* melody repeated quietly
3:13	Opening melody (*A*) returns very softly.
3:50	Phrases of *A* melody repeated several times
4:27	Music gradually fades as chords are played in harplike manner.
4:55	"Clair de lune" concludes very quietly.

 LISTEN TO... this selection streaming online.

 WATCH... an Active Listening Guide of this selection online.

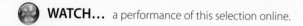 **WATCH...** a performance of this selection online.

 DO... an online Listening Practice Activity related to this selection, which your instructor may assign for a grade.

The opening melody has several places in which the last note of one measure is tied to the first note of the next measure. (In music a **tie** is a curved line connecting two notes of the same pitch indicating that they should sound as one long note.) The effect is to blur the meter of the music at those points. At other points he calls for two equal notes to the beat when the rest of the work uses three. At another place he even specifies *tempo rubato*, indicating rhythmic flexibility.

The skeleton of the melody—its basic notes—is quite simple. It is a descending major scale, to which Debussy merely adds a few alternating notes, almost as decoration. It certainly is not the solid kind of melody that Bach and Beethoven favored! Debussy adds other effects, such as rolling out the notes of some of the chords in a harplike manner instead of having them sounded together, which also tends to obscure the rhythm. At other places he doubles notes of the melody an octave higher, which gives the music a more open, almost haunting effect. The overall effect is luscious and romantic.

RAVEL'S *DAPHNIS AND CHLOE*, SUITE NO. 2

About 1910 Maurice Ravel composed a ballet for the famous impresario of Ballet Russe, Sergei Diaghilev, about whom more will be said in Chapter 32. The story concerns a shepherd, Daphnis, and his love for the beautiful Chloe. Today the ballet's music is most often heard in the form of two suites. Suite No. 2 contains some of Ravel's most Impressionistic music, especially the opening section called "Lever du jour" ("Daybreak"; see Listening Guide). The woodwinds and then the strings provide a rich accompaniment of rippling notes. One can almost sense the glow of the sunrise in the melody. The recording includes a part for chorus in which the singers vocalize on a neutral syllable.

LISTENING GUIDE

MAURICE RAVEL

Daphnis and Chloe, Suite No. 2, "Lever du jour" ("Daybreak") (1910)

Genre: Ballet music

Download 60

5 minutes 31 seconds

0:00   Woodwinds and harps play rippling figures over slow notes in low strings.

0:33   More instruments join in as music begins long crescendo.

0:55   Music reaches climactic point, then begins gradual decrescendo.

1:15   Violas play rich-sounding melody.

pp   *expressively*

1:40   Flute plays brief contrasting figure; then melody resumes in strings.

2:00   Clarinet plays brief contrasting figure; then melody resumes.

2:26   Violins continue melody at higher pitch level as harp and woodwinds again take up rippling figures.

2:50   Chorus sings "Ah" as violins continue melody.

3:07   Trumpets join in as music reaches another climactic point, then begins to grow softer.

3:21   The tempo becomes faster and more dancelike, but—

3:29   soon reaches another climactic point and violins play melody in high notes.

3:54   Strings hold a long, soft note.

4:03   Rippling figure reappears as melody begins again in lower strings, and another gradual crescendo leads to—

4:35   another climactic point by the orchestra and chorus, and then the music grows softer.

5:06   Oboe quietly repeats the same melodic figure several times.

5:30   Clarinet plays some of the figure in augmentation, and piece concludes.

LISTEN TO ... this selection streaming online.

WATCH... an Active Listening Guide of this selection online.

WATCH... a performance of this selection online.

DO... an online Listening Practice Activity related to this selection, which your instructor may assign for a grade.

Debussy, Ravel, and Rachmaninoff

CLAUDE DEBUSSY

Claude Debussy (Deb-yew-SEE, 1862–1918) was born in a small town near Paris. At the age of eleven he entered the Paris Conservatory, where he often revolted against the rules of composition his professors tried to teach him. When he was twenty-two, he won the Prix de Rome, which included study in Italy. Although he did go to Rome, he much preferred the bustle and gaiety of Paris. He also valued the company of painters and writers.

Debussy's early admiration for Wagner faded after a second visit to Bayreuth in 1889, and he developed a dislike for things Germanic. He wrote a number of articles about music, which offered him a chance to vent his feelings. Regarding Wagner, he wrote, "The French forget too easily the qualities of clarity and elegance peculiar to themselves and allow themselves to be influenced by the tedious and ponderous Teuton." He claimed that "beauty must appeal to the senses, must provide us with immediate enjoyment."

Maurice Ravel (1875–1937) followed Debussy both chronologically and stylistically, and this fact has tended to place him in the background despite his many fine compositions. He was born into the family of a mining engineer who had once aspired to be a musician himself. Ravel studied at the Paris Conservatory and, though highly qualified for the award, was four times passed over for the Prix de Rome. The arbitrary nature of these decisions caused a public furor that eventually led to the resignation of the Conservatory's director.

A French patriot, Ravel drove an ambulance along the front lines during World War I. After the war he was recognized as France's greatest composer. He died at the age of sixty while undergoing surgery for a rare brain disease that had seriously affected his speech and motor coordination.

One of his best-known works, and certainly the most unusual, is the hypnotic *Bolero*, in which the same melody and rhythm pattern continue throughout the seventeen minutes of the work.

MAURICE RAVEL

Sergei Rachmaninoff (1873–1943) was born in northwestern Russia. His parents were both amateur pianists, and his mother was his first teacher. Later he studied at the conservatory in St. Petersburg and then Moscow. In his younger days, he revealed much talent, but he tended to be lazy and spent too much time ice skating.

He was equally gifted as a composer and pianist, both of which he emphasized at various times in his life. He first toured the United States in 1909, which led to a contract with Edison Records and then RCA Victor. He immigrated to America after the Communist revolution in 1917, but remained homesick for his native land, and felt a loss of inspiration after that time. Nevertheless, he completed his *Rhapsody on a Theme of Paganini* and Symphony No. 3 while in America. He became ill on a concert tour in 1943, and was diagnosed with lung cancer. He died shortly thereafter.

SERGEI RACHMANINOFF

Best-Known Works of Debussy

Opera
- *Pelléas et Mélisande*

Orchestra
- *La mer*
- *Nocturnes*
- *Prelude to The Afternoon of a Faun*

Piano
- *Images*, Sets 1 and 2
- *Suite bergamasque*

Best-Known Works of Ravel

Orchestra
- *Bolero*
- *Daphnis and Chloe*, Suite No. 2
- *Ma Mère l'Oye (Mother Goose)*

Piano
- *Gaspard de la nuit*
- *Le tombeau de Couperin*

Best-Known Works of Rachmaninoff

Piano
- *Preludes*
- Piano Concertos Nos. 2 and 3

Orchestra
- Symphonies Nos. 2 and 3
- *Vocalise* for Soprano
- *Isle of the Dead*

POST-ROMANTICISM

The Romantic outlook did not go quietly into the night. In fact, elements of it are still found in music being written today—and probably always will be. Some composers who lived at the end of the nineteenth century and into the twentieth continued the Romantic tradition by composing works that were more massive and extensive than those of their predecessors.

Rachmaninoff's *Rhapsody on a Theme of Paganini*

Rhapsody on a Theme of Paganini is one of the best loved of Sergei Rachmaninoff's compositions. It is based on a theme written by the legendary nineteenth-century violin virtuoso Niccolò Paganini. The work opens with a short introduction and one variation before the theme is presented by the violins. It is essentially a simple melody: The same melodic and rhythm pattern is heard in thirteen of the theme's sixteen measures. It is divided into equal halves of an *a b* pattern.

At first, the variations are modest in scope. The piano plays decorative versions of the theme that little by little move farther from it. Variation 7 combines the theme played by the low strings and the Dies irae theme played slowly by the piano. Variation 10 again opens with the Dies irae played by the piano, which is then taken up by the orchestra. The following Listening Guide begins with Variation 18 and goes to the conclusion of the work.

For a number of reasons, this work represents Post-Romanticism well. First, it was composed in 1934, well after the Romantic style had been predominant. Second, the theme is by Paganini, who in some ways was the quintessential Romantic musician. Third, the work includes a quotation of the Dies irae theme, which is associated with death and mystery—favorite topics of Romanticists. Fourth, it is basically a rhapsody containing a free expression of feelings, even though it is in the form of a theme and variations.

Gustav Mahler (1860–1911) and Anton Bruckner (1824–1896) both exhibit one of the traits of Romanticism: a tendency toward musical elephantiasis. Mahler's Third Symphony holds the dubious distinction of being the longest ever written. It takes about one hour and thirty-four minutes, with the first movement alone requiring nearly forty-five minutes to perform. His Eighth Symphony is sometimes called the "Symphony of a Thousand" because it requires so many people to perform it: a huge orchestra, additional brass, and male, female, and children's choirs. Mahler is nevertheless able to handle these musical resources with skill and discretion.

LISTENING GUIDE

SERGEI RACHMANINOFF
Rhapsody on a Theme of Paganini (1934; excerpt)

Genre: Rhapsody

Form: Theme and variations

Download 61

7 minutes 55 seconds

0:00   Theme played by violins

0:16   *Variation 18:* Piano plays sensuous melody based on inversion of theme.

1:01   Orchestra plays theme and then repeats it.

2:31   Piano plays fragments of theme as variation winds down.

2:57   *Variation 19:* Quick tempo, with fast notes in piano that outline theme

3:27   *Variation 20:* Built around two-note figure taken from theme; violins accompany with fast, running notes.

4:00   *Variation 21:* Features piano melody built around notes of chords.

4:25   *Variation 22:* Soft and marchlike

4:52   Music becomes smoother and louder.

5:19   *Variation 23:* Piano and orchestra exchange fragments of theme.

5:41   Short piano cadenza

5:59   *Variation 24:* Piano softly plays fragments of theme. Tempo increases as theme is played by woodwinds and violins.

6:10   Virtuoso passages in piano.

6:45   *Coda:* Piano plays fast notes based on theme.

7:31   Dies irae fragment played by brasses.

7:50   Work concludes somewhat quietly with two short chords.

LISTEN TO ... this selection streaming online.

WATCH ... an Active Listening Guide of this selection online.

WATCH ... a performance of this selection online.

DO ... an online Listening Practice Activity related to this selection, which your instructor may assign

for a grade.

MAIN POINTS OF CHAPTER 30

1. The basic outlook of Impressionism (1890–1920) was that experiences in life are based more on impressions than on detailed observations. Impressionistic artists and composers, who were mostly French, believed that the arts should appeal more to the senses than the intellect.

2. Impressionistic music differed from the prevailing German-Austrian style in several ways:

   - Use of whole-tone scales
   - Smaller orchestra; did not involve the brasses as much
   - Subtle, flexible rhythms
   - Chords that contain added notes
   - Limited development of themes
   - More subtle sound

3. Post-Romanticism expanded on the Romantic outlook of the nineteenth century. Many of its works are larger in scope and longer than those in the Romantic period.

PRACTICE...
your understanding of this chapter's concepts by working once more with the chapter's Active Listening Guides online.

DO...
online quizzes that your instructor may assign for a grade.

The Mainstream

Learning Objectives

1 Provide examples of the characteristics of twentieth-century music in Bartók's Concerto for Orchestra.

2 Identify the folkloric qualities of Villa-Lobos's music.

3 Describe the twentieth-century characteristics of music in a large choral work by Britten.

START...
experiencing this chapter's topics with an online video activity that your instructor may assign.

READ...
the complete chapter text in a rich interactive eBook!

Much twentieth-century music was an expansion and evolution of previous musical styles. It is hard to know what to call this body of "conventional" music. Some writers describe it as **folkloric** because the music was partly derived from folk or ethnic sources, but that was not true of even a majority of this style. *Traditional* is not an accurate word, because most twentieth-century composers broke with nineteenth-century traditions to some extent. *Cosmopolitan* and *eclectic* are not accurate descriptions either, because many composers did not attempt to integrate a variety of musical styles in their compositions. **Mainstream** seems to say it best; it refers to music that is neither experimental nor committed to any one particular approach to writing music.

Three mainstream works are discussed in this chapter: Concerto for Orchestra by Béla Bartók, the Aria from *Bachianas Brasileiras No. 5* by Heitor Villa-Lobos, and the Dies irae from *War Requiem* by Benjamin Britten.

BARTÓK'S CONCERTO FOR ORCHESTRA

Bartók composed his Concerto for Orchestra in the summer of 1943 for a one-thousand-dollar commission from the Boston Symphony Orchestra. "The general mood of the work," he wrote, "represents, apart from the jesting second movement, a gradual transition from the sternness of the first movement and the lugubrious death-song of the third to the life-assertion of the last." The work is called a concerto because single instruments and sections are treated in a concerted way, as in Baroque music. There is also an element of virtuoso performing skill in the concerto. It is one of the masterpieces of twentieth-century music.

First, Second, and Third Movements

Although the movements are independent and no themes are carried over from one movement to another, Bartók considered them as leading from one to another, as was just pointed out. The opening theme of the first movement is based on the interval of a fourth, with appearances of the theme separated by shimmering chords played by the strings. The main theme ascends and descends rapidly and contains a syncopated figure. The second half of this theme is nearly the exact inversion of the first half, with the interval of a fourth again being prominent.

The second movement is entitled "Games of Pairs," because the wind instruments are paired off at specific pitch intervals: the bassoons in sixths, the oboes in thirds, the clarinets in sevenths, the flutes in fifths, and the muted trumpets in seconds. This is the jesting movement that Bartók mentioned in his synopsis. After the five short sections featuring pairs of instruments, the brasses play a chorale accompanied by the snare drum with its snares disengaged. The opening music of the movement follows the chorale, which gives the movement a three-part form.

The third movement is the "lugubrious death-song." The melody is folklike and is played by the oboe. The music is rhapsodic and seems to rise to a peak moment of tragedy.

Fourth Movement

Bartók called the fourth movement "Interrupted Intermezzo" (see Listening Guide). The opening melody has a Hungarian folk quality. The first six complete measures of the theme all begin on the same note—A-sharp—and the five-note pentatonic scale is used. The second melody sounds almost like a waltz, but not quite. Its meter changes often, usually by adding or subtracting half a beat. It gives the music a certain awkward charm. This melody also has a Hungarian folk character and is a reworking of a folk song.

The third theme is different. Bartók adapted a theme from the Seventh Symphony by the Russian composer Dmitri Shostakovitch. That symphony, often referred to as the "Leningrad Symphony," is a somewhat programmatic work that Shostakovitch composed in 1942–1943 during the siege of Leningrad (St. Petersburg today) by the invading German Nazis. Bartók wanted to express his revulsion at Nazi Germany, which had taken over Hungary several years before and caused him to flee his native land. The theme is interrupted by rude noises, which seem to represent the "rough, booted men," as Bartók referred to the Nazi occupiers.

Fifth Movement

The fifth movement is in a large three-part form. It features a theme of nearly continuous running notes and much contrapuntal writing, especially in the B section. The theme of that section is treated fugally, and it appears again at the conclusion of the movement.

Béla Bartók
Concerto for Orchestra, Fourth Movement (1943)

Genre: Concerto

Form: Rondo

Download 62

4 minutes 16 seconds

0:00   Short introduction; then oboe plays A theme.

0:15   Clarinet and flute repeat A theme, then extend it.

0:45   Oboe plays A theme again.

0:59   *B* theme begins in violas.

1:17   Violins play *B* theme as English horn plays contrasting part.

1:41   Oboe again plays *A* theme.

2:05   *C* theme begins in clarinet. Crude noises follow, played by trumpets and woodwinds.

2:21   Trombone plays a glissando.

2:28   Violins play a parody of *C* theme, followed by more blatant noises.

2:40   Inversion of *C* theme, followed by more rude noises.

2:53   Violins and violas play *B* theme.

3:28   English horn plays *A* theme fragment, followed by extended flute solo.

3:49   Flute plays a decorated melody.

4:12   Movement concludes quietly with three quick notes.

LISTEN TO... this selection streaming online.

WATCH... an Active Listening Guide of this selection online.

WATCH... a performance of this selection online.

DO... an online Listening Practice Activity related to this selection, which your instructor may assign for a grade.

Béla Bartók

BÉLA BARTÓK

Béla Bartók (1881–1945) was born in a small city in Hungary. His mother was his first music teacher. After Béla's father died, she became a schoolteacher. They moved quite often, but finally settled in Pressburg (today Bratislava), where Béla studied piano and composition. After finishing his studies at the Royal Conservatory, he concertized throughout Europe.

Bartók and another important Hungarian composer, Zoltán Kodály ("Koh-*die*-ee"), first became recognized outside Hungary as collectors of Hungarian folk music. They lugged their early recording equipment from one village to another, recording the music of the people. In 1907 Bartók became a professor of piano at the Royal Conservatory and spent most of the next thirty years in Budapest. His compositions received little attention outside Hungary until the late 1920s.

After the rise of Hitler and the subsequent collaboration of Hungary with Nazi Germany, Bartók felt impelled to leave his homeland. When he left Hungary, he could take almost nothing with him, so commissions for compositions were an economic necessity. In 1940 he came to the United States to live. He

(continued)

was appointed to a position at Columbia University, primarily to continue his folk music research. He received a few commissions from ASCAP and from jazz clarinetist Benny Goodman.

Bartók's earlier compositions often sounded barbaric, with many thick, dissonant chords. His most recognized works were composed between 1926 and 1937. One of the more interesting is his *Mikrokosmos*, a set of 153 piano pieces in six volumes that are arranged so that the music progresses from simple pieces to works of awesome difficulty.

During the latter part of his life, Bartók appeared to mellow. His music became less dissonant and more accessible. He died of leukemia, with his true stature as a composer still not fully appreciated.

Best-Known Works

Chamber music
· String Quartets Nos. 4, 5, and 6

Orchestra
· Concerto for Orchestra
· Music for Percussion, Strings, and Celesta
· Piano Concerto No. 3

Piano
· *Mikrokosmos*

HEITOR VILLA-LOBOS: *BACHIANAS BRASILEIRAS*

The Brazilian composer Heitor Villa-Lobos was a man of tremendous energy who adopted musical ideas from many sources. His greatest inspiration was the music of the Brazilian people. His *Bachianas Brasileiras* and *Chîros* are filled with rich sounds that alternate between being romantic and boldly dissonant.

Villa-Lobos composed nine *Bachianas Brasileiras*, in which he tried to combine the style of Bach with the indigenous music of Brazil. Villa-Lobos wrote: "This is a special kind of musical composition based on an intimate knowledge of J. S. Bach and also on the composer's affinity with the harmonic, contrapuntal, and melodic atmosphere of the folklore of the northern region of Brazil." The Aria of *Bachianas Brasileiras No. 5* (see Listening Guide) was composed in 1938; in 1945 Villa-Lobos added a second movement to it.

The Aria is for a soprano accompanied by eight cellos—hardly a typical instrumentation. The music is not typical either. During the first third of the work, the singer just vocalizes a luscious melody, first on "Ah" and then for the last third by humming.

The middle section is somewhat like a Brazilian popular song, with its syncopation and frequent changes of tempo. The soloist's melody has an improvised quality.

HEITOR VILLA-LOBOS
Aria from *Bachianas Brasileiras No. 5* (1938)

LISTENING GUIDE

Genre: Aria

Form: *A B A*

Download 63

7 minutes 51 seconds

0:00   Cellos play short introduction.

0:13   Soprano, doubled by a cello, vocalizes melody on "Ah."

1:12   Soprano resumes singing melody.

1:47   Cellos take up melody.

2:01   One cello plays melody.

3:10   Soprano sings middle section.

> *Lo at midnight clouds are slowly passing, rosy and lustrous,*
> *O'er the spacious heav'n with loveliness laden,*
> *From the boundless deep the moon arises wondrous,*
> *Glorifying the evening like a beautiful maiden,*
> *Now she adorns herself in half-unconscious duty,*
> *Eager, anxious that we recognize her beauty,*
> *While sky and earth, yes all nature with applause salute her.*

4:42   *All the birds have ceased their sad and mournful complaining,*

> *Now appears on the sea in a silver reflection*
> *Moonlight softly waking the soul and constraining*
> *Hearts to cruel tears and bitter dejection.*
> *Lo at midnight clouds are slowly passing, rosy and lustrous,*
> *O'er the spacious heavens dreamily wondrous.*

6:32   Soprano hums the melody.

7:24   Music begins to slow down gradually.

7:35   Aria concludes quietly as soprano holds a long note and then moves up one octave.

LISTEN TO... this selection streaming online.

WATCH... an Active Listening Guide of this selection online.

WATCH... a performance of this selection online.

DO... an online Listening Practice Activity related to this selection, which your instructor may assign for a grade.

Heitor Villa-Lobos

Breitenbach/Pix Inc./Time Life Pictures/Getty Images

Heitor Villa-Lobos (1887–1959) was born in Rio de Janeiro, the son of a librarian who was an avid amateur musician and who taught his son cello and strongly encouraged him in music. When Heitor was twelve, his father died, and he composed a piece in his father's memory. Soon Villa-Lobos began playing cello professionally. As a young man, he traveled throughout Brazil and heard the music of its people. Although he never collected folk music in a systematic way, he seemed to absorb it, and it had a major impact on the more than eleven hundred works he composed during his lifetime.

In the 1920s he made two trips to Paris, where he met a number of the composers who were living there at the time. He studied their compositions and absorbed some of their techniques. In the 1930s he was director of music education for Brazil. He drafted a curriculum for its schools and organized several mass concerts, one of which involved forty thousand children! He made several journeys to the United States in the 1940s and founded the Brazilian Academy of Music.

Best-Known Works

Instrumental
- *Bachianas Brasileiras Nos. 1, 5, and 9*
- Concerto for Guitar and Orchestra
- Etudes for Guitar (12)

BRITTEN'S *WAR REQUIEM*

Saint Michael's Cathedral had stood in Coventry, England, since medieval times. During World War II, it was bombed and burned out. Only its walls remained with their mute, empty windows. Rather than rebuild using the former shell of Saint Michael's, it was decided to leave the ruined shell there as a reminder of war's devastation. The entrance to the new cathedral is through the shell of the old one. The new cathedral was dedicated on May 30, 1962, and Benjamin Britten was commissioned to write a work for that occasion (Figure 31.1).

Britten decided to use the traditional Mass for the Dead, or Requiem, as it is more commonly known. But he wanted his *War Requiem* to convey the message of tragedy and despair over the horrors of war. Therefore, he interspersed the words of the Latin Requiem with the antiwar poems in English by Wilfred Owen. Owen was an English soldier who was killed just before the end of World War I. His poems were published posthumously, and they speak to the harshness and futility of war:

> My *subject is War, and the pity of War.*
> *The Poetry is in the Pity . . .*
> *All a poet can do today is mourn.*

Appropriately, Britten dedicated his *War Requiem* to four friends who died in World War II.

War Requiem is a monumental work in six sections, the same ones found in the traditional Requiem Mass. The work requires about eighty-three minutes to perform and calls for orchestra, chorus, boy choir, and three soloists. Its music is neither grand nor glorious, but rather is stark and often quite dissonant. It is highly effective in expressing its message.

FIGURE 31.1
SOLDIERS ATTENDING A SERVICE
IN THE RUINS OF COVENTRY
CATHEDRAL ON MAY 13, 1945,
A FEW DAYS AFTER WORLD WAR II
HAD ENDED IN EUROPE.

The Dies irae is the second section of the *War Requiem*, and only the first portion of it is included in the Listening Guide. Britten used the text of the Dies irae but not the same chant melody that Berlioz and Rachmaninoff used in their works, which were presented in Part V.

Its music is not flowing. Instead, each syllable seems chopped off from its adjacent one. The meter is an asymmetrical seven beats in each measure. The musical effect is one of a limping, twitching march that belies the "wondrous trumpet" phrase in the text and emphasizes "trembling," which is also contained in the text. The rhythmic pattern sounds before each new section for the chorus.

BENJAMIN BRITTEN

Dies irae from *War Requiem*, excerpt from beginning (1962)

Genre: Oratorio, requiem

Form: Strophic with interludes

Download 64

3 minutes 45 seconds

0:00	French horns and trumpet exchange short passages rather quietly.
0:26	Men sing first three lines of the text:

Solvet saeclum in favilla,	The world will dissolve into ashes,
Teste David cum Sibylla	As witness David and the Sibyl.

0:46	Horns and trumpets exchange more passages. Music grows louder.
1:19	Women sing second three lines of the text:

Quantus tremor est futurus,	What trembling there will be
Quando Judex est venturus,	When the Judge shall come;
Cuncta stricte discussurus!	All shall thoroughly be shattered!

1:38	Brasses and percussion play a more extensive passage.
2:12	Chorus, with the brasses continuing to play figures, sings next three lines of the text:

Tuba mirum spargens sonum	The wondrous trumpet, spreading its sound
Per sepulchra regionem	To the tombs of all regions,
Coget omnes ante thronum.	Will gather all before the throne.

2:39	Brasses using mutes continue.
3:13	Chorus sings final three lines of the text somewhat softly:

Mors stupebit et natura,	Death will be stupefied, also nature,
Cum resurget creaturam,	When all creation arises again
Judicanti responsura.	To answer to the Judge.

3:45	After brasses play a few more figures, the section closes quietly.

LISTEN TO... this selection streaming online.

WATCH... an Active Listening Guide of this selection online.

WATCH... a performance of this selection online.

DO... an online Listening Practice Activity related to this selection, which your instructor may assign for a grade.

Benjamin Britten

Erich Auerbach/Hulton Archive/Getty Images

Benjamin Britten (1913–1976) was born in the seacoast town of Lowestoft, England, the son of a dental surgeon and a musical mother. He began putting musical patterns on paper before he was five, and by the time he was six or seven the notes became associated with what he had in mind. By the age of fourteen, he had composed a number of works for piano and voice. He was given a scholarship to the Royal College of Music and by the age of twenty-one was earning his living largely as a composer.

He immigrated to the United States in 1939 but returned to England in 1942. He toured America again several times, usually giving performances with his lifetime companion, tenor Peter Pears.

Britten wrote for every medium and for varied levels of musical difficulty. He was most successful in writing operas, three of which are frequently performed: *Peter Grimes*, *Albert Herring*, and *Billy Budd*. He once said of composing: "It is the easiest thing in the world to write a piece virtually or totally impossible to perform—but ... that is not what I prefer to do; I prefer to study the conditions of performance and shape my music to them."

Best-Known Works

Orchestra and voice
· *War Requiem*
· *Serenade for Tenor, Horn, and Strings*

Choral
· *A Ceremony of Carols*

OTHER MAINSTREAM COMPOSERS

Russia

Dmitri Shostakovitch (1906–1975) was born in St. Petersburg and spent most of his life in Russia when it was under the control of the Communist regime. He entered the Conservatory at St. Petersburg when he was thirteen and composed his First Symphony when he was nineteen. Several times in his career he had problems with the Communist Party because his works were well liked in the West. Public apologies and some politically correct works were required from Shostakovitch to get himself back in good standing. Before he died, he completed his Fifteenth Symphony, making him the first major composer since Beethoven to write more than nine.

England

Ralph Vaughan Williams and Edward Elgar are mentioned in Chapter 28. In addition to these composers, England produced a number of others who contributed to its great tradition of choral music, including William Walton (1902–1983).

France

Following World War I, France went through a strong anti-Romantic reaction. The informal leaders of this movement away from Romanticism were a poet, Jean Cocteau (1889–1963), and an eccentric musician, Erik Satie (Sah-TEE, 1866–1925). Satie reacted to past music in his own inimitable way by writing little compositions entitled, for example, *Three Pieces in the Shape of a Pear*, *Three Flabby Preludes for a Dog*, and *Dried Embryos*. The purpose of such titles was to satirize the seriousness of Romantic composers. On one occasion, Satie composed some music *not* to be listened to. When the audience listened to it, he became irritated and urged them not to.

From this stream of irreverent thought came a group of French composers known as The Six. The most important of these were Darius Milhaud (Mee-YO, 1892–1974), Arthur Honegger (OWN-eh-gair, 1892–1955), and Francis Poulenc (Poo-LAHNK, 1899–1963).

Milhaud lived for a while in Brazil, where he became acquainted with Latin American music. He also visited New York City and heard jazz, which made a lasting impression on him. He was a prolific composer, especially of small works.

Honegger was more conservative than Milhaud. One of his compositions is a tone poem, *Pacific 231*, which depicts a steam engine. By the time he composed it, tone poems had become passé. His most successful works were large in scope, with the oratorio *Le Roi David* (*King David*) being the best known.

Poulenc's music more clearly expresses the Cocteau–Satie outlook. It is charming and pleasant. Most of it was written for small groups, although he also composed two operas.

Latin America

Villa-Lobos is discussed earlier in this chapter. Carlos Chávez (1899–1978) was Mexico's leading composer. His *Symphonia India* is based on Mexican Indian music, and his *Toccata for Percussion Instruments* is an exciting, rhythmic work. It is probably the best-known work for that type of ensemble.

Alberto Ginastera (Hee-nah-STAIR-ah, 1916–1983) was an Argentine composer who achieved fame for his instrumental and vocal works. His music sparkles with Latin American qualities.

MAIN POINTS OF CHAPTER 31

1. Many twentieth-century compositions were not experimental, avant garde, or allied with any particular approach to composing music. They constitute the mainstream of twentieth-century concert music.

2. Some twentieth-century works were influenced by folk music, whereas others were influenced by musical practices that had existed in the Baroque and Classical periods.

3. Bartók's Concerto for Orchestra was titled as a concerto because individual instruments or small groups of instruments are contrasted with one another, somewhat similar to what was done in Baroque music.

4. The music of Villa-Lobos often combines elements of Brazilian folk music with traditional Western concert music. The Aria from his *Bachianas Brasileiras No. 5* is largely a vocalise, which is a song sung on a neutral syllable.

5. Britten's *War Requiem* was commissioned for the dedication of a new cathedral that replaced the one bombed out in World War II. It uses the words and sections of the traditional Requiem Mass, but none of its music.

 PRACTICE... your understanding of this chapter's concepts by working once more with the chapter's Active Listening Guides online.

 DO... online quizzes that your instructor may assign for a grade.

32 Expressionism *and* Primitivism

START...

experiencing this chapter's topics with an online video activity that your instructor may assign.

Learning Objectives

1 List the characteristics of Expressionism in the arts, especially music.
2 Describe Expressionism in Berg's opera *Wozzeck*.
3 Describe the qualities of primitivism in musical works, including Stravinsky's *The Rite of Spring*.
4 Offer some reasons why Stravinsky's *The Rite of Spring* is considered a masterpiece of twentieth-century music.

READ...

the complete chapter text in a rich interactive eBook!

People seem to have known it all along, but in the twentieth century it was exposed and explored as never before: Human behavior is a complex matter that is influenced by competing, contradictory, and sometimes concealed forces. Are humans basically good or fundamentally bad? Is the glass half full or half empty? Is everything folly and meaningless, as the writer of Ecclesiastes says, or does the writer of Psalm 100 have it right with the words "For the Lord is good and his love endures forever"?

Events in Europe in the first twenty years of the twentieth century especially caused people to wonder about the nature of the human race. World War I raged from 1914 to 1918. It was a particularly horrible and senseless war, with the use of poison gas and a million casualties in the trenches of France and elsewhere. And for what purpose? No good seemed to have come from it. No solution resulted that provided political and economic stability. Instead, the ruling houses of Austria, Germany, and Russia were deposed, only to be replaced with confusion and turmoil that soon led to takeovers by repressive totalitarian regimes. It was a great time to be cynical and to see humans as weak and attracted by evil.

It was also a time of questioning the established ways. In Germany, Friedrich Nietzsche's philosophy of "might makes right" was respected and believed. In Vienna, Sigmund Freud was developing his psychoanalytic theories of neuroses, which focused attention on the dark and shrouded aspects of the human mind. Charles Darwin's theories of evolution and the survival of the fittest had challenged the assumptions about the dignity and place of human beings in the scheme of things.

EXPRESSIONISM

Because one role of creative artists is to be commentators on and give expression to the attitudes and feelings of society, it is logical that art and music would reflect European society of that time. The chief artistic style for doing this was **Expressionism**. In a sense, Expressionism was the opposite of Impressionism: Where Impressionism had been essentially happy, bright, and outward looking, Expressionism was morose, dark, and inward looking.

Expressionist painters included Franz Marc, Wassily Kandinsky, Oskar Kokoschka, and Edvard Munch. They tried to shock their viewers with distortions and blatant colors.

Expressionist writers centered on the dark side of people. Elements of Expressionism found their way to the United States in the writings of Franz Kafka. This tradition continued with the American writers William Faulkner and Tennessee Williams and the introspective and profound Irish writer James Joyce.

The poem "The Sick Moon" by the Belgian Albert Giraud is typical of Expressionist poetry. This is its first stanza:

> *You nocturnal deathly sick moon,*
> *Up there in the heavens' dark pillow,*
> *Your look too full with fever*
> *Captivates me like a strange melody.*

The poem attracted the Expressionist composer Arnold Schoenberg, who included it in his set of songs *Pierrot Lunaire (Moonstruck Pierrot)*, which he composed in 1912. The music calls for eight instruments and one singer, who uses a speech–song style called **sprechstimme.** The written pitches in the music for the singer are only approximate, and no sustained pitches are to be produced. Schoenberg's intent was to merge the spoken word and music as much as possible. The effect is eerie and nonvocal in the traditional sense.

Expressionism and Impressionism did have one point in common: Both had a natural affinity among writers, artists, and composers who knew each other. Some were talented in more than one art. The painter Kandinsky wrote plays and poetry, and the composer Schoenberg painted and even exhibited in several shows of Expressionist art.

It would be a mistake to dismiss Expressionism as just a passing fad. Because it touches on and explores a side of human nature, it merits a place in the world of the arts.

Berg's *Wozzeck*

Alban Berg composed *Wozzeck* (VOT-tzek) between 1917 and 1921. He adapted the libretto himself from a play by Georg Büchner, which he saw in 1914. The opera follows a carefully worked-out plan, one that is partly symphonic in nature: These sections differ from the usual exposition/development/recapitulation of sonata form.

Act I	Exposition
Act II	Development
Act III	Catastrophe

Each of the three acts contains five scenes that are organized around a specific musical form or compositional technique. For example, Act III—the one discussed here in the Listening Guide—is organized as a theme and variations.

Scene 1	Variations on a theme
Scene 2	Variations on a single tone
Scene 3	Variations on a rhythm pattern
Scene 4	Variations on a chord
Scene 5	Variations on continuous running notes

A short orchestral interlude is heard between the scenes. Berg did not intend for listeners to be conscious of these forms or techniques. Instead, he wanted the audience to be caught up in the drama and its emotional impact. The techniques used in each case, however, contribute to the dramatic and musical effect.

The story of the opera is about Franz Wozzeck, a poor and rather incompetent soldier. He is persecuted by his sadistic captain and used as a guinea pig by the company's somewhat demented doctor. He is betrayed by his mistress, Marie, who sleeps with another man. Driven to madness, Wozzeck stabs her and later drowns trying to wash the blood off the knife and his hands. In no way does the story resemble one that Mozart might have used for one of his operas!

Prior to Act III, Wozzeck has been driven to desperation by Marie's unfaithfulness, a beating from the man who slept with her, and the actions of the captain and doctor.

The libretto with an English translation of the original German for Act III, Scene 2, appears in the Listening Guide. In it Marie and Wozzeck walk by a pond. She is anxious to get back home, but he wants to sit and talk (Figure 32.1). They comment on the blood-red color of the moon in the sky. After tenderly kissing her, he pulls a knife

FIGURE 32.1
WOZZECK AND MARIE SHORTLY
BEFORE HE STABS HER IN A JEALOUS
RAGE.

Courtesy Indiana University Jacobs School of Music/IU Opera Theater

and plunges it into her throat. Throughout the scene one note is softly but persistently heard. As Marie is stabbed, it is sounded over and over by the timpani. The rhythm pattern of the interlude becomes the musical basis for the next scene.

LISTENING GUIDE

ALBAN BERG

Wozzeck, Act III, Scene 2 (1921)

Genre: Opera

Download 65

Forest path by a pool. Dusk is falling. Marie enters with Wozzeck, from the right.

0:00   MARIE: *Dort links geht's in die Stadt.*
's ist noch weit. Komm schneller!

MARIE: The town lies over there.
It's still far. Let's hurry!

WOZZECK: *Du sollst dableiben, Marie.*
Komm, setz' Dich.

WOZZECK: You must stay awhile, Marie.
Come, sit here.

MARIE: *Aber ich muss fort.*

MARIE: But I must go.

They sit down.

WOZZECK: *Komm. Bist weit gegangen, Marie.*
Sollst Dir die Füsse nicht mehr wund laufen.
's ist still hier! Und so dunkel.—Weisst noch, Marie,
wie lang' es jetzt ist, dass wir uns kennen?

WOZZECK: Come! So far you've wandered, Marie.
You must not make your feet so sore, walking.
It's still, here in the darkness. Tell me, Marie
how long has it been since our first meeting?

MARIE: *Zu Pfingsten drei Jahre.*

MARIE: At Whitsun, three years.

WOZZECK: *Und was meinst, wie lang' es*
noch dauern wird?

WOZZECK: And how long, how long will it still go
on?

She jumps up.

1:22   MARIE: *Ich muss fort.*

MARIE: I must go!

WOZZECK: *Fürchst Dich, Marie?*
Und bist doch fromm! Und gut! Und treu!

WOZZECK: Trembling, Marie? But you are good
(*laughing*) and kind and true!

He pulls her down again on the seat; he bends over her, in deadly earnest.

Was Du für süsse Lippen hast, Marie! | Ah! How your lips are sweet to touch, Marie!

He kisses her.

Den Himmel gäb' ich drum und die Seligkeit, | All heaven I would give, and eternal bliss,
wenn ich Dich noch oft so küssen dürft! | if I still could sometimes kiss you so!
Aber ich darf nicht! Was zitterst? | But yet I dare not! You shiver?

MARIE: *Der Nachttau fällt.* | **MARIE:** The night dew falls.

2:56 | **WOZZECK:** *Wer kalt ist, den friert nicht mehr! Dich wird beim Morgentau nicht frieren.* | **WOZZECK:** (*whispering to himself*): Whoever is cold will shiver no more in the cold morning dew.

MARIE: *Was sagst Du da?* | **MARIE:** What are you saying?

WOZZECK: *Nix.* | **WOZZECK:** Nothing.

A long silence. The moon rises.

MARIE: *Wie der Mond rot aufgeht!* | **MARIE:** How the moon rises red!

WOZZECK: *Wie ein blutig Eisen!* | **WOZZECK:** Like a bloodred iron!

He draws a knife.

MARIE: *Was zitterst?* | **MARIE:** You shiver?

She jumps up.

Was willst? | What now?

3:56 | **WOZZECK:** *Ich nicht, Marie! Und kein Andrer auch nicht!* | **WOZZECK:** No one, Marie! If not me, then no one!

He seizes her and plunges the knife into her throat.

MARIE: *Hilfe!* | **MARIE:** Help!

She sinks down. Wozzeck bends over her. She dies.

WOZZECK: *Tot!* | **WOZZECK:** Dead!

He rises to his feet anxiously and then rushes silently away.

LISTEN TO... this selection streaming online.

WATCH... an Active Listening Guide of this selection online.

WATCH ... a performance of this selection online.

DO... an online Listening Practice Activity related to this selection, which your instructor may assign for a grade.

Scene 3 takes place in a tavern. Wozzeck is almost out of his mind and tries to forget his crime. The music is a dissonant and distorted version of barroom dance music and is played on an out-of-tune piano onstage. Marie's friend Margret sings a weird-sounding folk tune. After a while she notices blood on Wozzeck's hands and sleeve, and she thinks it smells like human blood. He flees in terror as people in the tavern close in on him. The mood of the scene is increased throughout by the twitching, persistent rhythm pattern first heard in the previous interlude. The rhythm pattern has a hypnotic effect and contributes to the sense of horror. Only the tempos at which it is performed are altered to suit the needs of the drama.

In Scene 4 Wozzeck returns to the site of the murder to get rid of the knife. The orchestra adds a macabre, almost surreal tonal backdrop of sounds for his shrieks and shouts. The moon and pond seem to turn to blood as he loses his sanity. He wades into the water to wash the knife and himself.

Alban Berg

Popperfoto/Getty Images

Alban Berg (1885–1935), the son of a factory worker, was born in Vienna. At the age of fourteen he took up composing, an interest that occupied his time when he was confined by asthma and poor health. His father died the next year, leaving the family in difficult financial straits; only the help of a well-to-do aunt allowed Alban to remain in school. After graduation from high school, he took a position as an accountant for the government.

He was largely self-taught until the age of nineteen, when he answered a newspaper ad placed by Schoenberg for composition students. Schoenberg accepted the young man and, because Berg was poor, did not charge him until after more than a year. From then on the lives of the two men seemed woven together. They were mutually supportive of each other when most of their works were received coolly by audiences. Actually, audiences were sometimes extremely hostile to their works.

Berg's place in history is largely the result of his opera *Wozzeck*. Never in good health, Berg died as a result of complications following a bee sting.

Best-Known Works

Chamber music
• Lyric Suite

Opera
• *Lulu*
• *Wozzeck*

Orchestra
• Concerto for Violin

The captain and the doctor—his two tormentors—happen to walk by and hear someone drowning. They offer no help, commenting that the sound of someone drowning "is not good to hear." As Wozzeck drowns, the sounds of the orchestra seem to engulf him. The orchestral interlude that follows is much longer than the other interludes. It presents musical motives associated with Wozzeck's life, and it seems to sob to a close.

Scene 5 is an epilogue that takes place the next morning outside Marie's house. A group of children sing ring-around-the-rosy. The child of Marie and Wozzeck rides a hobby horse. One of the children cruelly taunts the boy: "Hey! Your mother's dead!" At first the child does not understand and continues to ride the horse. The children decide to go see the body. They run off. The child continues to ride for a few more moments, and then he also runs after the other children. The opera does not end with a clear-cut conclusion. The music simply stops.

What is so moving and compelling about *Wozzeck*?

• It is a gripping drama. Its unvarnished realism has a hard-hitting impact that grabs and keeps one's attention.

• The music is excellently crafted to add to the impact of the drama. What the music lacks in traditional beauty is more than made up for in its dramatic power. The audience usually feels emotionally wrung out when *Wozzeck* concludes.

• The music is ingenious in terms of its use of forms and compositional techniques.

PRIMITIVISM

Primitivism was not so much a point of view about art and life as it was a fascination with the art and music of non-Western and nonliterate societies. African sculpture and masks began to interest the artistic world, as did Paul Gauguin's paintings of Polynesian culture

FIGURE 32.2

PAUL GAUGUIN, 1843–1903, *WHERE DO WE COME FROM? WHAT ARE WE? WHERE ARE WE GOING? (D'OU VENONS NOUS ... ?)*, OIL ON CANVAS, 1897. GAUGUIN BELIEVED THAT THE RENEWAL OF WESTERN ART AND CIVILIZATION MUST COME FROM "THE PRIMITIVES" SUCH AS THE POLYNESIAN NATIVES HE PAINTED IN THE SOUTH PACIFIC.

(Figure 32.2). Nineteenth-century writers, artists, and composers had been attracted by the beauty and mystery of the "long ago and far away." In contrast, twentieth-century artists admired the power and vitality of the arts of these societies.

Stravinsky's *The Rite of Spring*

The high point of Primitivism in music was probably reached in 1913 with the premiere of Igor Stravinsky's ballet *La Sacre du Printemps* (*The Rite of Spring*). The music was written for a production by Sergei Diaghilev, impresario of the Ballets Russes. Each year he brought a new and stunning ballet production to Paris. With keen artistic judgment and calculated showmanship, he decided in 1913 to capitalize on the Parisians' interest in primitive art. He chose to produce a ballet about prehistoric ceremonies that culminated in the sacrifice of a human being—a real change from the usual lovely stories found in ballet prior to that time.

The work opens with a bassoon solo in its upper range, giving the music a haunting quality. The pitches of the melody keep returning to the opening note, and the rhythm pattern is irregular, with frequent stops and starts. The introduction contains dissonant, strange sounds with coloristic effects.

In the "Dance of the Adolescents" that follows (see Listening Guide), Stravinsky unleashes the force of rhythm. The effect is like the wild beating of savage drums. Much of the music is quite dissonant, and the rhythm patterns are irregular. A steady series of eighth notes begins with this irregular pattern:

1-2-3-4   1-2-3-4-5   1-2   1-2-3-4-5-6   1-2-3   1-2-3-4   1-2-3-4-5

The "Dance of Abduction" is even wilder. A scampering tune is played by the woodwinds and answered by a French horn call. The meter signatures change often. Polyrhythms are also part of the rhythmic interest of the music.

"Round Dances of Spring" brings some relief from the frenzied music that precedes it. The tempo is slow, and the flutes and other woodwinds play a melody that resembles an American Indian tune.

The music becomes energetic again in "Games of Rival Tribes." The idea of competition is expressed by pitting one section of the orchestra against another, each with its own distinctive music. The music in a number of places is bitonal, which refers to music that is in two different keys at the same time.

The "Entrance of the Sage" brings back the main thematic material with a thick orchestration. The music becomes slower and more majestic at this point. Act I ends with "Dance of the Earth." It also suggests violence and upheaval.

The second and final act of *The Rite of Spring* depicts the sacrifice of a young maiden so that the God of Spring will be satisfied. It is similar in style to the first act but is rarely played apart from the ballet. Just the opposite is true of the music for Act I.

IGOR STRAVINSKY
The Rite of Spring, excerpts from Act I (1913)

LISTENING GUIDE

Genre: Ballet music

Download 66

4 minutes 47 seconds

"Dance of the Adolescents"

0:00	Orchestra plays persistent, driving chords with an irregular pattern of accents.
0:20	Muted trumpet plays short melodic figure that descends by half steps.
0:49	Bassoon plays simple melody derived from previous rhythm pattern.
1:19	Brasses break persistent rhythm with sustained notes; then rhythmic pattern returns.
1:31	Violins play "scooping" notes.
1:43	French horn sounds short melodic figure that is gradually taken up by other instruments.
2:05	Flute repeats French horn melody.
2:21	Trumpets play a third short melody as music grows more active.
2:45	Piccolo plays earlier French horn melody; other instruments follow.

"Dance of Abduction"

3:20	Brasses hold long notes that soon give way to music with a rapid tempo and irregular meter.
3:35	French horns play primitive-sounding motive.
3:58	Woodwinds play melodic figure in dissonant chords.
4:19	Timpani leads, and other instruments respond in irregular metrical patterns.
4:42	Flute plays long, trilled note as "Dance of Abduction" ends.

 LISTEN TO... this selection streaming online.

 WATCH... an Active Listening Guide of this selection online.

 WATCH... a performance of this selection online.

 DO... an online Listening Practice Activity related to this selection, which your instructor may assign for a grade.

Igor Stravinsky

Alvin Langdon Coburn/George Eastman House/Getty Images

Igor Stravinsky (1882–1971) was born in St. Petersburg, Russia, where his father was a singer with the Imperial Opera. Although he studied music, his parents hoped that he would become a lawyer. He studied law at the University of St. Petersburg and composition with Rimsky-Korsakov at the same time.

Stravinsky soon became associated with Sergei Diaghilev, manager of the famous Ballets Russes, who signed the twenty-eight-year-old composer in 1910 after hearing only one of his works. The ballet he composed for the Ballets Russes was *The Firebird*. It was so successful that he was commissioned to write another, *Petrouchka*. Both ballets are based on Russian folk tales. He was then given a third commission for a ballet, *The Rite of Spring*.

Just before World War I, Stravinsky moved to Switzerland. The revolution in Russia cut off his income, and the Ballets Russes disbanded for a while. He lived in Switzerland for eight years while recovering from a serious illness.

After World War I ended, Stravinsky settled in Paris. He became a French citizen and traveled widely as a conductor and pianist. He continued to compose, but he abandoned the style he had used for the three ballets with the Ballets Russes. In 1939 he came to the United States to lecture. World War II prevented his return to Europe, so he settled in Hollywood and became an American citizen. When he was eighty, Stravinsky was the honored guest of President John F. Kennedy at the White House. He was also the subject of a special one-hour program on national television.

Despite superficial changes of style, Stravinsky remained true to his objective concept of music: Because a musical work is something a composer creates, it is essentially an object, not a manifestation of his psyche. Therefore, a composer's works do not need to be consistent personal creations. Skill at composition is what matters; the composer's personality is irrelevant.

Best-Known Works

Ballet
- *The Firebird*
- *Petrouchka*
- *The Rite of Spring*

Chamber music
- Octet
- *L'Histoire du soldat*

Choral
- *Symphony of Psalms*

Opera
- *Oedipus the King*
- *The Rake's Progress*

To listeners hearing it for the first time, *The Rite of Spring* may sound like a jumble of random notes. It may even seem that the players can play anything they want and no one would notice the difference. Such an idea is of course incorrect. Stravinsky carefully planned everything in the score and wrote detailed instructions for playing each part. He tells the timpanist when to change from hard to soft sticks, the French horn players when to tilt the bells of their instruments upward, and the cellists when to retune a string so that a chord can be played on open strings to achieve a more raucous effect.

Musicians generally consider Stravinsky's *The Rite of Spring* to be one of the masterpieces of twentieth-century music. Why?

- Its exploitation of rhythm is exceptional. Stravinsky had an uncanny sense of when to accent notes or change the metrical pattern.

- The themes are used in an imaginative and interesting way. What Stravinsky often did was create a short tune and then repeat it many times, but each time with slight changes. Like every composer whose music has lasted over the centuries, Stravinsky was able to manage the tension between the need for unity and for variety in his music.

- Although a traditional symphony orchestra plays the work, Stravinsky demonstrates great ability to find new timbres and create new sounds.

- Dissonance is also handled in a masterful way. Some chords are very dissonant, but many are not. It's not just that Stravinsky employs dissonant sounds. Rather, it is that he knew *when* to use dissonance—and when not to.

What Is Beautiful? What Is Fascinating?

Stravinsky's *The Rite of Spring* (Figure 32.3) premiered at the Théâtre des Champs Elysées in Paris on May 29, 1913. Stravinsky had written two previous ballets for the great impresario Sergei Diaghilev and the Ballets Russes, and both had been successfully performed in Paris, so both men were already well known there. The premiere was an event of importance among Parisian society, and the theater was filled with dignitaries, royalty, and renowned musicians.

None of them could have anticipated what would happen that May evening. Instead of the expected lovely music, beautiful costumes, and toe dancing, the audience was subjected to some harsh-sounding chords and dancers in not-so-pretty costumes making angular, rough motions. No one knows what set off the audience more, the dancing or the music, but the audience reacted—to an extreme. One writer reported:

> A certain part of the audience, thrilled by what it considered to be a blasphemous attempt to destroy music as an art, and swept away with wrath, began very soon after the rise of the curtain to whistle, to make catcalls, and to offer audible suggestions as to how the performance should proceed.... The orchestra played on unheard.... The figures on the stage danced in time to music they had to imagine they heard.

One critic yelled as loudly as he could, "The music is a colossal fraud!" The ambassador from Austria laughed derisively. One lady reached out into the adjoining box to slap the face of a man who was hissing. Another lady rose majestically in her seat and spat in the face of one of the noisemakers. The eminent French composer Maurice Ravel alone shouted, "Genius!" Backstage, Stravinsky

FIGURE 32.3
A MODERN PERFORMANCE OF IGOR STRAVINSKY'S *THE RITE OF SPRING*

held on to the choreographer, Vaslav Nijinsky, to keep him from going into the audience and fighting with those who disapproved.

Probably no one that evening thought about it in this way, but they were violently disagreeing about the nature of art. Must it always be beautiful? Can't art sometimes stir the emotions and affect people deeply? Can art be *of* life, or must it always be *better than* life?

If nothing else, Expressionism demonstrated that art goes much deeper than beauty in the sense of being pretty. There is nothing pretty about Berg's *Wozzeck* and many sections of Stravinsky's *The Rite of Spring*, but they continue to attract listeners again and again. The poet Keats was right when he wrote, "A thing of beauty is a joy forever." Were he writing that thought today, he would probably revise it to read, "A thing of human emotion is a fascination forever."

Primitivism also appealed to other composers in the years just before World War I. Béla Bartók composed *Allegro Barbaro* for piano in 1911, and several of his other works are wild and rhapsodic. Some of Sergei Prokofiev's early works have driving rhythms and blatant harmonies. Ernest Bloch's Violin Sonata, written in the 1920s, has a hard-driving character.

MAIN POINTS OF CHAPTER 32

PRACTICE...
your understanding of this chapter's concepts by working once more with the chapter's Active Listening Guides online.

1. Expressionism was an artistic point of view that had an inward, dark, and pessimistic outlook on human nature. It was centered in Germany following World War I, and in many ways it was the opposite of French Impressionism.

2. Its music is often dissonant, and it sometimes uses a style of singing called sprechstimme, in which the singer combines singing and speaking.

3. Primitivism refers to works of art, dance, and music that were influenced by non-Western and nonliterate societies. The music often features strong and irregular rhythms and simple short melodies.

4. Stravinsky's music for the ballet *The Rite of Spring* caused a riot to break out at its premiere in Paris in 1913. In addition to its subject matter and unusual costumes, the music is quite dissonant and sometimes bitonal. The rhythm patterns are irregular and contain many polyrhythms.

 DO...
online quizzes that your instructor may assign for a grade.

33 Neoclassicism *and* Tone Row Music

START...
experiencing this chapter's topics with an online video activity that your instructor may assign.

READ...
the complete chapter text in a rich interactive eBook!

Learning Objectives

1 Discuss the chief characteristics of Neoclassical music.
2 Describe the features of music based on a tone row.
3 Differentiate tone row music and serial music.

Styles of music seem to move toward being either products of emotion and feelings or the product of thoughtful intellectual effort. The Baroque style was more emotional than that of the Renaissance. The pendulum then swung back toward intellectual control in the Classical period, but after a few generations it swung back again toward the highly subjective music of the Romantic period.

The twentieth century saw the dichotomy between thought and feeling continue in its music, but with a definite swing toward more intellectually oriented music. One approach was **Neoclassicism**, which seeks to capture the spirit and attitude of the Classical writers, artists, and musicians of the eighteenth century. (The prefix *neo-* actually means "new.") The other approach was tone row music and serial compositions, which are discussed later in this chapter.

NEOCLASSICAL STYLE

The Neoclassical style is evident in Pablo Picasso's painting *The Lovers* (Figure 33.1). If you were to imagine what a picture with such a title would look like, it probably would *not* depict a man and a woman in the cool, detached attitude seen in Picasso's painting. Emotional and passionate it is not. Delicate, sensitive, balanced, and thoughtful it is.

Notice that a minimum of lines and shadings is used, but they achieve the desired effect. Notice also that the figures are dressed not in modern clothing but in garments that seem more like those of the ancient Greeks or Romans. The painting projects an attitude of tender love yet in a restrained way.

Neoclassicism in Music

After *The Rite of Spring*, Stravinsky changed to shorter, more concise music written for a limited number of instruments. Why did he do this? Because of his beliefs about what a composer should do with sound. He wrote: "What is important for the clear ordering of the work, for its crystallization, is that all the ... elements ... should be properly subjugated to the rule of law before they intoxicate us." In Stravinsky's eyes, writing a musical composition is like solving a problem; it is a task to be done by applying the brain. Therefore, music is intended to do nothing except demonstrate the composer's ability to contrive interesting tonal and rhythmic combinations of sounds.

Sometimes Neoclassicism in music has been given the euphonious name "Back to Bach." Several Baroque forms, such as the concerto grosso, were revived during this time, and there was a renewed emphasis on counterpoint. The harpsichord also enjoyed a rebirth of interest, so the allusion to Bach is reasonable.

FIGURE 33.1
THE LOVERS BY PABLO PICASSO
RECALLS THE COOL, QUIET, CLASSIC
QUALITY OF ANCIENT GREEK AND
ROMAN ART. THE FIGURES SEEM AS
DELICATELY POSED AS STATUARY IN
AN ART MUSEUM.

Prokofiev's *Classical Symphony*

The *Classical Symphony* is Op. 25 in Prokofiev's list of works, so it is an early work. To have this symphony follow the style of Mozart and Haydn, he made a number of musical decisions.

- It would not be long. The first movement (see Listening Guide) for example, is just over three and a half minutes—a fraction of the length of most nineteenth-century symphonies.

- It would be for small orchestra. The score does not call for trombones or for percussion other than timpani, and only two instruments are featured on each of the other brasses and the woodwind parts.

- It would contain the types of themes typically found in the Classical style. And, sure enough, the themes are collections of short melodic ideas that are connected. The harmonies are less rich and complex than those found in music of the nineteenth century. One of the themes in the first movement is marked to be played *con Eleganza*—"with elegance."

- It would call for a style of playing that is neat and precise.

- It would follow traditional forms. The first movement is in sonata form, the second movement follows a large three-part form, the third is a stylized dance, and the fourth returns to sonata form.

LISTENING GUIDE

SERGEI PROKOFIEV
Classical Symphony, Op. 25, First Movement (1917)

Genre: Symphony

Form: Sonata

Download 67

3 minutes 46 seconds

Exposition

0:00   Orchestra plays opening chord loudly, followed by violins playing first theme.

0:21   Transition consisting of short melodic fragments begins in woodwinds.

0:48   Second theme played lightly by violins as bassoon plays steady, short notes

1:10   Violins repeat second theme.

1:19   Short codetta

Development

1:32   Silent measure; then violins play part of first theme as music modulates often.

1:42   Melodic fragments are exchanged among the woodwinds.

1:51   Transition played by woodwinds and violins

1:59   Second theme played forcefully by violins followed by other sections of orchestra

Recapitulation

2:33   First theme played by violins

2:42   Transition begins in woodwinds; other sections follow.

3:04   Second theme played very quietly by violins at a high pitch level

3:29   Coda begins as woodwinds and violins outline chords.

3:43   Movement closes in a rush of sound.

LISTEN TO... this selection streaming online.

WATCH... an Active Listening Guide of this selection online.

WATCH... a performance of this selection online.

DO... an online Listening Practice Activity related to this selection, which your instructor may assign for a grade.

SECOND MOVEMENT This movement is quiet and songlike. The main melody seems to be the epitome of delicate, refined beauty.

THIRD MOVEMENT The third movement is a gavotte—sort of. It does have all the features of the **gavotte** of earlier times, but is actually quite twentieth century in its free use of keys. The form is interesting. The movement opens and closes with the same music. Between the two appearances of that music, there are two sections of contrasting music, each repeated. When the second of these sections is repeated, the oboes add a line of counterpoint.

FOURTH MOVEMENT The movement is marked *Allegro vivace* with a metronome marking of 152 beats per minute. In other words, the notes fly by, especially for the violins. Prokofiev reveals his twentieth-century harmonic thinking with a number of interesting key changes. The codetta presents a third theme, which is used prominently in the development section.

It is hard *not* to like Prokofiev's *Classical Symphony*. It has all the attributes of the music of Mozart and his contemporaries—the tuneful themes, the well-thought-out forms, the neatly balanced phrases, and generous amounts of charm and beauty. But Prokofiev has taken those characteristics and added a richer palette of harmonies and treatment of melodies.

Sergei Prokofiev

Roger Viollet/Choumoff/Getty Images

Sergei Prokofiev (1891–1953) was born in a village in southern Russia. His mother taught him to play the piano and encouraged him to compose music. By the time he was nine, he had written a three-act opera. After his family moved to Moscow, Prokofiev studied with outstanding teachers of composition, including Rimsky-Korsakov. Although today we consider those works as almost classical in character, his early compositions were somewhat dissonant, and his teachers thought him something of a musical revolutionary.

After the Communist revolution, he left his homeland and lived in Paris, where he continued to compose and give concerts. In 1933 he decided to return to the Soviet Union, where he was greeted warmly by the public and initially by the government. As he grew older, his music became more mellow.

Following World War II, Prokofiev and Shostakovich were accused of being "formalistic," a vague charge meaning

that their music was considered too sophisticated by government officials. He did not allow governmental pressure to interfere with his work, however.

His style could vary from Neoclassical in the *Classical Symphony* to Neo-Romantic in his ballet *Romeo and Juliet*. He clearly was able, in Stravinsky's words, to subject his compositions "to the rule of law." That fact allowed him to be as Classical or Romantic as he wished at any moment in each musical work. Sergei Prokofiev was one of the giants of twentieth-century music.

Best-Known Works

Ballet
• *Cinderella*
• *The Love of Three Oranges*
• *Romeo and Juliet*

Orchestra
• *Classical Symphony*
• *Lt. Kijé Suite*

• Piano Concertos Nos. 1 and 3
• Violin Concerto No. 2

Piano
• Sonatas (10)

Hindemith's *Kleine Kammermusik*

The full title of Hindemith's work is *Kleine Kammermusik für fünf Bläser*, Op. 24, No. 2, which translated is *Little Chamber Music for Five Winds*. The five instruments are flute, oboe, clarinet, bassoon, and French horn, which constitute the usual woodwind quintet. The work demonstrates Hindemith's Neoclassical tendencies in its sparse use of instruments and in the short, concise format of its movements.

The first movement is cheerful in quality and follows a loose sonata form. The second movement is a subdued and graceful waltz consisting of rather short sections. The third is an elegant slow movement with long melodic lines. The fourth movement is short and fast. It is built around a short, pounding theme that alternates periodically with free-sounding solos for each instrument.

The fifth movement (see Listening Guide) is very fast, with a symmetrical form: A B C B A. The differences among the themes are as much rhythmic as melodic. The first theme has accents falling logically on the beat. In the second theme the accents occur off the beat, while a bass line sounds on the beat. Also, when the pitches of the second theme ascend, the bass line descends in contrary motion, and vice versa. The melodies are not flowing ones. Instead, they are cohesive fragments more in the style of the Classical period. Irregular meter can be seen in the first two themes. In fact, Hindemith changes it so often that he doesn't bother with meter signatures. And he uses chromatic notes so freely that he doesn't bother with a key signature either.

Other Neoclassical Works

Prokofiev was by no means the only composer attracted to Neoclassicism. Stravinsky has already been discussed; the milestone Neoclassical work in classical style was his Octet for Wind Instruments, which he composed in 1923. Other works by Stravinsky that reveal strong Neoclassical tendencies include the ballet *Apollo* (*Apollon Musagète*), *Jeu de cartes* (*Game of Cards*), *Oedipus Rex*, *Pulcinella*, Suites Nos. 1 and 2 for Small Orchestra, and *Symphony of Psalms*.

Although known first for his compositions on Jewish themes, Ernest Bloch (1880–1959) composed two concerti grossi and a number of suites. Several twentieth-century French composers adopted the Neoclassical approach as well. Among them were Jacques Ibert (1890–1962), Francis Poulenc, and Darius Milhaud. A number of American composers also took a Neoclassical approach. They are discussed in Part VII.

LISTENING GUIDE

PAUL HINDEMITH

Kleine Kammermusik für fünf Bläser, Op. 24, No. 2, Fifth Movement (1922)

Genre: Chamber music

Form: Rondo (*A B C B A*)

Download 68

2 minutes 50 seconds

0:00   Lively A theme played by flute, oboe, and clarinet

0:13 B theme has oboe playing off the beat as bassoon plays a line in contrary motion.

0:24 French horn enters with contrasting part.

0:37 All except French horn play figure based on B theme.

0:49 Transition introduced by oboe

1:01 Wide-ranging C theme begins in flute, then repeated with rhythmic accompaniment.

1:39 B theme played quietly by oboe, then repeated with flute as music grows more intense

1:50 Music becomes more dissonant as French horn enters.

1:59 A theme returns in flute, oboe, and clarinet, then French horn.

2:21 Coda begins with clarinet and bassoon playing softly.

2:29 B theme returns forcefully with much dissonance.

2:43 Movement closes with three solid chords.

LISTEN TO... this selection streaming online.

WATCH... an Active Listening Guide of this selection online.

WATCH... a performance of this selection online.

DO... an online Listening Practice Activity related to this selection, which your instructor may assign for a grade.

Paul Hindemith

Paul Hindemith (1895–1963) was born in Hanau, Germany, and his Neoclassical works have a certain Germanic, "academic" quality. As a teenager he played in dance bands and then became a member of the Frankfurt Opera Orchestra. For a while he played viola in the Amar-Hindemith Quartet. He became professor of composition in Berlin, but his modernistic music was banned by Hitler in 1934. He left Germany, lived in Turkey for a few years, and then came to the United States and taught composition at Yale University until 1953. He then returned to Europe and taught at the University of Zürich until his death.

Hindemith composed sonatas for virtually every instrument. He also wrote a large amount of chamber music and a number of motets and choral works. A few of his works were large in scope, including his program symphony *Mathis der Mahler* (*Matthias the Painter*), inspired by three paintings by Mathis Grünewald on the altar at Isenheim, Germany. He also wrote two books on music theory in which he promoted his views about consonance and dissonance.

TONE ROW MUSIC

It had worked for almost three hundred years. From popular songs to symphonies, music had a tonal center around which it functioned. The key of a work may have strayed and for a time become lost, but inevitably it was there and the music returned to it. This principle of a tonal center and the movement of chords in relation to that tonal center seemed as necessary to music as the law of gravity seems to us.

But was it? Arnold Schoenberg did not think so. He and other composers initially wrote works (mostly Expressionistic ones) that centered around no particular key. In short, music that was **atonal**. But Schoenberg was not satisfied. He felt the need to develop a new system for composing. About 1923 he devised a means of "composing with twelve tones," as he termed it.

The heart of Schoenberg's system is its **tone row**. The basic row, which the composer determines before writing the composition, includes the twelve different pitches of the chromatic scale, with no pitch being repeated before the row is complete. In this way no tonal center can be implied, because all the notes in the chromatic scale are treated equally. Although at first glance the idea may seem limited, it has been calculated that there are more than 479,001,600 rows available!

Tone row music is linear, although it does contain some chords. The predetermined row is treated in four ways: (1) the *original*, (2) the **retrograde** (backward, in reverse order), (3) the **inversion** (all intervals reversed from their original direction), and (4) the **retrograde-inversion** (reverse pitch direction and reverse order). Any of the forms of the row can be transposed.

Schoenberg's Variations for Orchestra

As its title implies, the work is a set of variations on a theme. There certainly was nothing new about that. What was new was the use of the tone row theme and the ways in which it is varied.

The overall plan for Variations for Orchestra (see Listening Guide) consists of an introduction, the theme, nine variations, and a finale. The introduction contains a series of sounds including tremolos in the violins and *flutter tonguing* by the flute, which is actually created by a fluttering motion of the tongue.

It also includes a time-honored motive built around the notes B-flat, A, C, and B-natural, which in German spells *B A C H*. Bach himself used this pattern of notes to spell his name as a fugue subject in his last composition, *The Art of the Fugue*. In Germany the musical note *H* is B-natural, and *B* is B-flat. Therefore, the four notes of Bach's name in music are B-flat A C B-natural. Several composers have since written works based on his name as a tribute to him.

The variations are short, sometimes only twenty-three measures long. They often feature small groups of instruments, not the entire orchestra. The finale is longer than any of the variations. The work closes after a final statement of the B A C H motive.

Here is the basic tone row for Variations for Orchestra:

The structure of the music is very carefully planned. For example, the chords are derived from one version of the row, and the number of notes in the melodic phrases corresponds to the number of notes in the chord.

Tone row compositions present problems for listeners not familiar with this type of music. The concept of the row is not hard to understand, but the row itself can seldom be heard in the composition. Furthermore, its chromatic nature makes it difficult to remember. Actually, the row is mainly a compositional technique or approach for composers. Hearing the row as such is not necessary for listeners.

The idea of manipulating timbre also fascinated Schoenberg and other Expressionist composers. He devised a technique for doing that, which he gave the German name **Klangfarbenmelodie**. In German it literally means "manufactured tone color melody." It involves changing the timbre along with the pitch changes. This is accomplished by giving different instruments various notes of the melody so that even though the melody is present, it is not heard in its complete form played on just one instrument.

Schoenberg vigorously denied that his music was cold and intellectual. When the requirements of tone row composition are considered, that denial may seem inaccurate. His music does contain much activity crammed into most of its measures. It seems as if he compressed the dimension of time, causing what happens to the sounds to be much more concentrated than in previous music. Schoenberg obviously did not conceive of music in the rambling dimensions of the Romantic period.

ARNOLD SCHOENBERG
Variations for Orchestra (excerpt; 1928)

Genre: Tone row

Form: Theme and variations

Download 69

1 minute 2 seconds

0:00   Cellos begin with original version of the row.

0:13   Retrograde-inversion of the row begins on a different note from original.

0:31   Retrograde of the row begins on same note as original.

0:42   Inversion of row begins on same note as retrograde-inversion.

0:58   Theme concludes quietly.

(continued)

LISTEN TO... this selection streaming online.

 WATCH... an Active Listening Guide of this selection online.

 DO... an online Listening Practice Activity related to this selection, which your instructor may assign for a grade.

Arnold Schoenberg

Imagno/Hulton Archive/Getty Images

Best-Known Works

Chamber music
- *Pierrot Lunaire*
- Trio for Strings

Orchestra
- Chamber Symphony No. 1
- Variations for Orchestra
- *Verklärte Nacht*

Arnold Schoenberg (SH(R)N-bairg, 1874–1951) was born in Vienna. He began studying violin when he was eight and became an avid participant in amateur chamber music performances. After his father's early death, he went to work as a bank clerk. He had little formal training at an advanced level.

For many years he had shown an interest in composing, and that interest increased until he decided to make it his life's work. He spent two years in Berlin as music director for a cabaret and then returned to Vienna. He served in the Austrian army for two years during World War I. In 1925 he was appointed professor of composition at the Berlin Academy of Arts, where he remained until Hitler came to power. Because of the anti-Semitic actions of the new regime, he decided to leave Germany for the United States, where he taught at the University of California at Los Angeles (UCLA) until his death.

Schoenberg is important in the world of music as much for his leadership and innovative ideas as for his compositions. Prior to 1908 he stood in the tradition of Wagner and composed large Romantic works. About 1908, however, he started turning to music for smaller groups. His music became more contrapuntal and much more chromatic. Over a period of time, he began to write music that had no tonal center. He also moved even further toward Expressionism.

About 1923 he devised the tone row system, which he followed for most of the remainder of his life. This was a system that was to leave its mark on the world of music.

SERIALISM: BEYOND TONE ROWS

Anton Webern (1882–1945) was a student of Schoenberg. Like his teacher, Webern began writing atonal works. Although he composed in the same style as Schoenberg, Webern's music is more austere and economical. Of his thirty-one compositions, the longest is just ten minutes, and all his music can be performed in less than three hours! His dynamic levels are often very soft, and his frail tone row melodies are subtly passed from one instrument to another. If he had written more sparsely, it might seem as if the music disappeared completely (Figure 33.2).

FIGURE 33.2
A STYLE OF PAINTING THAT FEATURES TOTAL INTELLECTUAL CONTROL CAN BE SEEN IN KASIMIR MALEVICH'S *SUPREMATIST COMPOSITION: WHITE ON WHITE.* PAINTED IN 1918, THE WORK IS DEVOID OF ANYTHING EXCEPT WHAT IS ABSOLUTELY NECESSARY.

Digital Image © The Museum of Modern Art/Licensed by SCALA / Art Resource, NY

Webern's Five Pieces for Orchestra

One of Webern's atonal works was his *Five Pieces for Orchestra*, Op. 10 (see Listening Guide). Actually, the use of the word "orchestra" in the title is misleading, because it is not for the usual symphony orchestra. The eighteen instruments include cow bells, guitar, mandolin, and a small reed organ called a harmonium. The fourth piece has the distinction of probably being the shortest work ever written: $6\frac{1}{3}$ measures that take less than thirty seconds to perform. The klangfarbenmelodie technique largely replaces traditional melodies in these pieces.

ANTON WEBERN
Five Pieces for Orchestra, Op. 10, Third Piece

Genre: Atonal work

Download 70

1 minute 28 seconds

0:00   Repeating bell-like sounds played softly. Violin plays an atonal figure.

0:28   Muted horn sounds a few notes.

0:38   Clarinet sounds short figure, followed by muted viola.

0:47   Repeating bell sounds played again.

0:59   Muted trombone plays a short figure.

1:15   Snare drum plays three soft rolls as the Third Piece concludes.

🎧 **LISTEN TO...** this selection streaming online.

🎧 **WATCH...** an Active Listening Guide of this selection online.

🎧 **DO...** an online Listening Practice Activity related to this selection, which your instructor may assign for a grade.

LISTENING GUIDE

Webern expanded the concept of tone row music with the introduction of **Serialism**. In it, the principles of tone row music are carried further with the development of one or more series of pitches within the row. The idea was subsequently extended to rows or series of articulations, dynamic levels, and rhythmic values. The term *articulation* refers to tonguing, slurring, and the style with which notes are played. With these factors established, serialism represented almost complete intellectual control over musical sounds.

Consider the basic row for Webern's Concerto for Nine Instruments:

It can be divided into four subrows. (Brackets have been placed over the four subrows.) In turn, each of these subrows can be divided into three segments, each consisting of two adjacent notes and one that is either a line or a space farther away. The first three notes can be thought of as a miniature row, followed by its transposed retrograde-inversion, retrograde, and inversion.

The Concerto for Nine Instruments begins:

In this example, the groups of three notes are retained, although with **octave displacement**, which is the technique of sounding a pitch in an octave higher or lower from most of the others in the row. The first group is played by the oboe, the second by the flute, the third by the trumpet, and the fourth by the clarinet. In addition, a different rhythm is associated with each three-note group, and different articulations are specified.

Anton Webern

Imagno/Hulton Archive/Getty Images

Anton Webern (1883–1945) grew up and lived most of his life in Austria. He attended Vienna University, eventually earning a doctorate in musicology. In 1904 he became one of Schoenberg's first students, and they became lasting friends and admirers. During most of his career, he held conducting positions, but he changed jobs quite often, sometimes holding a position for less than a year. Following World War I, he helped Schoenberg run the Society for Private Musical Performances. Later he conducted the "Vienna Workers Symphony Orchestra."

World War II was a difficult time for him. He found it hard to make a living and took a job as an editor and proofreader for Universal Edition. Also, one of his sons was killed in the war. Webern himself was accidently shot just after the war ended by an American soldier as he stepped outside his house to enjoy a cigar during a strict curfew, which was in force because of his son-in-law's black market activities.

Although his compositions found limited acceptance from audiences, he had a great influence on other composers, including Stravinsky, who said,

"Doomed to total failure in a deaf world of ignorance and indifference, he inexorably kept on cutting out his diamonds, his dazzling diamonds, of whose mines he had a perfect knowledge."

A number of composers in addition to Stravinsky were attracted to the principles of tone row and serial music and used them in some of their compositions. Other composers made tone row or serial music their dominant style.

MAIN POINTS OF CHAPTER 33

1. Neoclassicism was an attempt by composers and artists to capture the spirit of the Classical period.

2. Neoclassical works feature smaller groups, shorter compositions, classical forms, restrained quality, and melodies consisting of short melodic ideas connected together.

3. Tone row music is based on the twelve pitches of the chromatic scale, which means that the music can have no tonal center; it's atonal. The row is not the actual melody, but rather the framework of pitches around which the composition is built.

4. A tone row can appear in four different versions: the original row, retrograde (backward), inversion (upside down), and retrograde-inversion (backward and upside down).

5. Serialism is the application of the principle of tone row music to other aspects such as dynamic levels, rhythm values, timbres, and articulations.

6. Klangfarbenmelodie is somewhat like pointillism in painting. The various pitches of a melodic line are distributed among several different instruments. Many times the notes are also placed in different octaves.

 PRACTICE...
your understanding of this chapter's concepts by working once more with the chapter's Active Listening Guides online.

 DO...
online quizzes that your instructor may assign for a grade.

34 New Sounds *and* New Techniques

 START...
experiencing this chapter's topics with an online video activity that your instructor may assign.

 READ...
the complete chapter text in a rich interactive eBook!

Learning Objectives

1 Describe the characteristics of chance/aleatory music.
2 Differentiate *musique concrète* and electronic music.
3 Define what is meant by "eclecticism."

With the end of World War II in 1945, the world moved into a new era. In a faltering manner, the nations and peoples of the world started to recover in both a physical and an emotional sense. Most people realized that whatever might happen in the future, things would never be the same again.

Along with the monumental changes that have come about in the nearly seven decades since that time, new generations of composers have been active. New ways of making music have become available through technological advances, and different attitudes about music and music listening have evolved.

From about 1945 to 1960, the competition for leadership in the world of concert music was between those who favored strict control of musical sounds through Serialism and those who favored only a few specifications through chance music and improvisation.

EXTENSIONS OF SERIALISM

Although Schoenberg devised the tone row system in the 1920s, until about 1950 only a few of the major composers were attracted to it. The tone row approach began to find more favor after 1945, partly because of the influence of Webern.

As mentioned previously, Webern extended the idea of a row beyond pitches to include series of articulations, dynamic levels, and rhythmic values. The leading proponents of what is described as **total Serialism** were the French composers Pierre Boulez (b. 1925) and Olivier Messiaen (1908–1992). In one of his works, Messiaen uses one series for the melody, another for the dynamics, and another for the rhythm; each of the series is a different length.

Other composers who favored highly controlled works in the 1950s were Luciano Berio (1925–2003) in Italy, Milton Babbitt (1916–2011) in the United States, and Karlheinz Stockhausen (1928–2007) in Germany. The music they created during those years is very complex, so it is difficult for listeners to perceive and performers to render accurately. Over the years some of these composers changed their approaches to composing.

CHANCE MUSIC

The American John Cage (1912–1992; Figure 34.1) was a major promoter of **chance** or **aleatory music**. The term *aleatory* comes from a Latin word meaning "dice" or "gambler," which in the ancient world signified chance. In such music the sounds are partly the result of chance, so they are unpredictable. A player might be instructed to play anything that comes to mind or just rest. Or the notes can be the result of throwing dice or dropping pages of music on the floor.

FIGURE 34.1
JOHN CAGE

Victor Drees/Hulton Archive/Getty Images

At first glance, such musical practices may seem like a put-on, but they are not. They are the application in music of an existential outlook on life. For centuries Western civilization believed in progress, the idea of moving toward a goal. Through increased knowledge—which in turn led to such practical outcomes as improved medical care, more food, and increased leisure—it was thought that the human race was progressing. However, the idea of progress came under attack in the twentieth century from proponents of existential philosophy and from advocates of Asian religious beliefs. The idea of progress is false, they maintained. There is only change, not progress.

The implications of the only-change, no-goal-toward-which-to-progress philosophy are enormous. It is like removing the goal lines and uprights on a football field and ceasing to keep score or time: The game just happens. About the only assumption that can be made is that the players will eventually tire and stop playing.

This philosophical position rejects the idea that works of art must have meaning. As Cage said, "My purpose is to eliminate purpose." Depicting a can of Campbell's soup or creating a painting that looks as if it came from a comic book (Figure 34.2) is not, as some people believe, a comment on the vulgarity of contemporary civilization. The content of such works is so obvious that it no longer encourages interpretation by the viewer, which is the way the artist wants it. A picture is a picture—and that's all.

John Cage said of his music, "I have nothing to say and I am saying it." In his book *Silence*, Cage urges the composer to "give up the desire to control sound, clear his mind of music [in the usual sense] and set about discovering means to let sounds be themselves rather than vehicles for man-made theories or expressions of human sentiments." Using chance devices to determine sounds is one way in which Cage and others try to get listeners to just consider the sounds and not attempt to read meaning into them.

The epitome of Cage's views was his work *4' 33"*, which premiered in 1955. The pianist simply sits at the piano for four minutes and thirty-three seconds but never plays a sound!

These ideas have been attempted by a number of composers, including Karlheinz Stockhausen. In a complete change from his electronic works of the 1950s, Stockhausen's *Originale* (1961) is based on a series of simultaneous, incoherent "happenings." In one scene the directions are "Pianist and percussionist put on clothes brought in by cloakroom attendant. The pianist takes off his cultic robes and puts on Oriental female costume.... When he is ready, he begins to brew up tea at the piano."

WATCH... a performance of *4'33"* online.

FIGURE 34.2
ROY LICHTENSTEIN'S *WHAAM!* HAS NO MESSAGE. ACCORDING TO LICHTENSTEIN, "STYLISTICALLY, MY WORK IS DEVOID OF EMOTIONAL CONTENT. AND IT'S WHAT I WANT." HE AND HIS MUSICAL COUNTERPART, JOHN CAGE, CREATED WORKS THAT WERE SO OBVIOUS THAT THEY INVITE NO INTERPRETATION. THEY REPRESENT A COMPLETE REJECTION OF THE NINETEENTH-CENTURY BELIEF IN ART AS THE CONVEYOR OF GREAT IDEAS THAT NEED TO BE STUDIED AND PONDERED.

ELECTRONIC MUSIC

As music moved into the 1960s, both serial and chance music faded and electronic music began to receive much more attention. Prior to that time, technologically created and produced music had been confined to a few expensively equipped studios. When the cost of such equipment dropped enough in price, many more composers started to work with computers and synthesizers.

There are two general types of electronic music. One is **musique concrète**. Recordings are made of actual sounds—parts of human speech, the buzzing of an insect, the soothing sound of water running, the shrill sound of a whistle, and so on. Then the recording, which in the 1960s was on magnetic tape, is manipulated by the composer:

- It can be sped up or slowed down.
- It can have other sounds added by splicing.
- Some of the partials of a sound can be filtered out.
- The order in which sounds appear can be arranged and altered.

An American advocate of *musique concrète* was Vladimir Ussachevsky (1911–1990), who was one of the founders of the Columbia–Princeton Electronic Music Laboratory in New York City. *Musique concrète* has been used successfully as background music for movies, plays, and ballets, especially when eerie music is appropriate.

Another type of electronic music consists of sounds produced on electronic equipment such as synthesizers and computers. Such music had its beginning in the Studio for Electronic Music of the West German Radio in the 1950s and today is actively pursued throughout the world.

Technology offers a composer total control over the music, for several reasons:

- There are no performers to alter the music, either intentionally or unintentionally by making mistakes. Once the right button is pushed, the equipment plays exactly what the composer entered into it. Therefore, there is no longer any need for music notation.
- Any pitch is possible, including ones so high that most humans cannot hear them, as well as **microtones**, which are intervals closer than the half steps found on keyboards and many instruments.
- Any combination of pitches is possible.
- Any rhythm is possible, no matter how complex, including multiple rhythms occurring at the same time.
- Any timbre is possible. Electronic devices can filter out or increase partials in a sound to achieve any tone quality the composer wishes.
- Any dynamic level is possible. The sounds can be almost inaudibly soft or so loud that they cause physical damage to the loudspeakers (and listeners' eardrums!). Crescendos and decrescendos can be regulated exactly.
- Any electronically created sound can be combined with any recorded sound in any way the composer desires. Actual sounds of instruments can be *sampled* (recorded) and incorporated into electronic compositions.
- The computer can be programmed in conjunction with other electronic equipment to make some of the decisions in the creation of music. When this happens, the creator of the program becomes to some extent the "composer of the composer."

The world of electronic music has changed rapidly, and it has been around only a few decades in anywhere near the form in which it is found today. No solid repertoire of such music exists. Each new work is to some degree an experiment.

Varèse's *Poème Électronique*

Poème électronique by Edgard Varèse comes as close as any work to being a masterpiece of this type of music (see Listening Guide). It was created in 1958 for the Brussels World Fair and was a part of the pavilion designed by the Swiss architect Le Corbusier (Charles Edouard Jeanneret-Gris, 1887–1965) for the Philips Radio Corporation (Figure 34.3). Not only did Le Corbusier design the exterior, but he also used a planned sequence of colored lights and images to be projected on the interior walls while Varèse's three-track tape was played through 425 loudspeakers.

The interior of the pavilion contained many different shapes and angles. When visitors walked through the building, they were greeted with different colors, images, and musical sounds. Varèse realized that people would not go through the pavilion according to an established path; they were free to move about as they wished, which meant that there was an element of chance in what they encountered. The reactions of the visitors in 1958 to what they saw and heard ranged from anger and fear to curiosity and awe.

Varèse's work certainly represents a break with traditional music. It has no melody, harmony, beat, or meter. Instead, it is a series of organized sounds, mostly of a *musique concrète* nature. They pop in and out of a soundscape that is either interesting or confusing, depending on one's individual inclinations.

The use of electronic music in conjunction with visual images has fascinated both concert and popular composers. The potential of electronic music has hardly been tapped. It offers vast possibilities for working with sounds and images, and many composers today are exploring this new medium.

FIGURE 34.3

THE STRUCTURAL MODEL OF THE PAVILION THAT LE CORBUSIER DESIGNED FOR THE PHILIPS RADIO CORPORATION AT THE WORLD'S FAIR IN BRUSSELS, 1958.

AP Images/Georgios Fefalas/Keystone

LISTENING GUIDE

EDGARD VARÈSE

Poème électronique, beginning (1958)

Genre: Electronic music, Synthesizer

Form: Free

Download 71

2 minutes 50 seconds

0:00	Sounds of a large bell, wiggling sounds, and sirens
0:43	Driplike sounds, followed by something sounding like squawks
0:56	Three-note pattern ascends three times.
1:11	Low sound sustained along with rattling sound, then siren, and more squawks
1:28	Siren sounds are played again and followed by more squawks. Soon more chirping sounds are heard.
2:04	Sound of percussion instruments, as well as siren
2:35	Large bell sound, along with sustained tones

LISTEN TO... this selection streaming online.

WATCH... an Active Listening Guide of this selection online.

WATCH... a performance of this selection online.

DO... an online Listening Practice Activity related to this selection, which your instructor may assign for a grade.

Edgard Varèse

Bernard Gotfryd/Getty Images

Edgard Varèse (1883–1965) lived most of his life in the United States, although he was born in France. Appropriately, his first composition after he moved to his new country was entitled *Amériques*. It called for an orchestra plus an unusual combination of percussion instruments: drums of different types and sizes, siren, rattle, sleigh bells, castanets, glockenspiel, and xylophone. Ten years later he composed a work that is better known today—*Ionization*—which uses thirty-seven different percussion instruments played by thirteen musicians.

Varèse came to music via a different route than most composers. He was trained in engineering and mathematics. His scientific leanings led to his contact in 1927 with engineers at the Bell Telephone Company laboratories to urge them to create machines that would synthesize musical sounds. This request indicates how far ahead of his time Varese was.

When magnetic tape recorders became available in the 1950s, he was the first to explore their potential for music making. Those efforts led to *Poème électronique* in 1958.

Best-Known Works

Electronic
· *Poème électronique*

Flute
· *Density 21.5*

Instrumental
· *Ionization*

ECLECTICISM

Although contemporary music is very pluralistic, with composers writing in widely divergent styles, some composers use what they think is the best of each style. They take various elements from different styles and synthesize music that is uniquely their own, a practice known as **Eclecticism**. They owe allegiance to no musical system or viewpoint, and their compositions are not easily classified. Whether or not Eclecticism is successful depends on the abilities of the particular composer.

Hovhaness's *And God Created Great Whales*

Composed in 1979, *And God Created Great Whales* (see Listening Guide) is a programmatic work that seems like the epitome of twentieth-century eclectic music. The work is integrated into a composition at four different points.

- Portions of the work are aleatory or chance music. Before the appearance of the whales, the orchestra members are instructed to "continue repetition, rapidly and not together in free non-rhythm chaos." Later they are directed to play in a "very wild and powerful" manner.

- A haunting melody in the pattern of the five-note pentatonic scale that sounds as though it came directly from ancient China or Japan. Hovhaness was greatly influenced by the music of Asia.

- Much attention to various tone colors and combinations of sounds. Hovhaness often referred to "points of color" in his music that make it more attractive and interesting. He also explored other sounds from conventional instruments, such as the slide or *glissando* by the trombones and strings.

- An admiration for the whales that inhabit the oceans of the world. In a real sense, it is one of the first of the few "environmental" or "green" compositions in the concert repertoire. Hovhaness composed this work long before "Save the Whales" became a popular cause.

And God Created Great Whales also reveals the mystic, romantic side of Hovhaness. He writes:

> *Free rhythmic passages, each string player independently, suggest waves in a vast ocean sky. Undersea mountains rise and fall in horns, trombones, and tuba. Music of the whales also rises and falls like mountain ranges. Song of the whales emerges like a giant mystical sea bird. Man does not exist, has not yet been born in the solemn oneness of Nature.*

ALAN HOVHANESS
And God Created Great Whales (1970)

Genre: Orchestra with recorded sounds

Download 72

5 minutes 30 seconds

0:00   Strings begin quietly playing many notes at random; music makes a gradual crescendo.

0:20   Brasses play first theme, which is based on pentatonic scale.

Andante maestoso

fff   *ffff*

(continued)

LISTENING GUIDE

0:53   Violins play second theme, which is also based on pentatonic scale with some pizzicato notes.

1:34   Second theme repeated many times as low brasses play long notes and music grows louder.

2:47   More aleatory music.

2:55   Whales enter.

4:03   Aleatory music returns.

4:28   Brasses play the first theme; music grows louder with some "points of color."

5:02   Trombones play glissandos, and then music grows quieter.

5:29   Recording fades just before whales enter again.

LISTEN TO... this selection streaming online.

WATCH... an Active Listening Guide of this selection online.

WATCH... a performance of this selection online.

DO... an online Listening Practice Activity related to this selection, which your instructor may assign for a grade.

Alan Hovhaness

Gordon Parks/Time Life Pictures/Getty Images

Alan Hovhaness Chakmakjian (1911–2000) was born in Somerville, Massachusetts, to Armenian-Scottish parents. Early in his career he dropped his long last name. He seemed destined to bring together the best of two regions of the world, the Occident and the Orient. His musical training in his younger years was largely confined to Boston and the New England Conservatory of Music. In addition, he studied astronomy and Far Eastern music and religions. For a time he taught theory and composition in Boston and was church organist at an Armenian church in Watertown, Massachusetts.

Hovhaness began receiving public attention for his compositions in the late 1940s. He won several awards and grants to study music and compose.

These grants took him to India, Japan, and Korea. He responded with a steady outpouring of compositions.

His musical interests were very cosmopolitan and wide ranging. He once wrote: "I admire the giant melody of the Himalayan Mountains, seventh-century Armenian religious music, classical music of South India, orchestra music of Tang Dynasty China about AD 700, opera-oratorios of Handel." And he admired great whales, too!

Best-Known Works

Orchestra
• *Prayer of St. Gregory*
• *Symphony No. 50* ("*Mt. St. Helens*"):
• *Armenian Rhapsodies*, Nos. 1, 2, and 3

INTO THE TWENTY-FIRST CENTURY

Traditionally if you wanted to listen to a musical work, you either bought a ticket for a performance of it or a good recording of the work. Those types of performances will continue. However, some performances, and perhaps many of them, will be very different as the twenty-first century progresses. Today technology has opened up a vast new world of possibilities. One can only imagine how much more music Mozart might have written if computer music notation programs had existed in the 18th century. Surely innovations such as the iPhone, iPad, and similar devices would have inspired him to explore new worlds of musical creativity.

Consider the recently produced opera *Auksalaq* (Inupiat word for "melting snow/ ice"), created collaboratively by composer Matthew Burtner and media artist Scott Deal. Funded by grants from private foundations and universities, it has been presented several times since 2010. The opera is about the environment and provides an in-depth journey into the vast and remote, yet rapidly changing arctic regions of Alaska and Canada. Created in a new genre termed "telematic," it is quite different from traditional classical opera.

Viewers of this musical work found out about it through traditional ways that people find concerts, as well as through social networking and advertisements. The opera is performed (Figure 34.4) in a space normally associated with music concerts, but the difference here is that for a telematic opera, there is an additional element of audience interactivity. Attendees are asked in the advertisements to bring their own laptop, tablet, or hand-held device in order to participate during the opera's performance with other audience members from disparate locations.

When the performance took place, they were there in person, logged in while listening to the performance so they could also send their own thoughts about the music to a "thought cloud" screen displayed in each performance space. They could do more than just listen. Using an interactive audience-participation software called NOMADS, they became an integral part of the music performance by posting comments and questions, creating elements of the music, and contributing texts for the singers' arias as the performance was in progress. At the world premiere in 2012, audiences attended from locations as far away as Alaska, Indiana, Canada, Norway, and Virginia. The performance was well received and is but one of the many works being created that utilize new ways of enjoying music as a listener.

 WATCH...
a performance of *Auksalaq* online.

Photo by Jill Steinberg 2010

FIGURE 34.4
A Performance of *Auksalaq*

Matthew Burtner and Scott Deal

MATTHEW BURTNER

SCOTT DEAL

Matthew Burtner (b. 1971) is an Alaskan-born composer specializing in noise-based systems, interactive media, and ecoacoustics. He is a professor of music at the University of Virginia and holds a doctorate in composition from Stanford University. He was the first prize winner of the Musica Nova International Electroacoustic Music Competition (Czech Republic). His music has also received honors and awards from organizations in France, Germany, Italy, The Netherlands, and several from associations in the United States.

Scott Deal has performed as a percussionist throughout North America, Asia, and Europe, premiering solo, chamber, and mixed-media works, and can be heard on the Albany, Centaur, Cold Blue, and SCI labels. Deal's recordings have been described as "soaring, shimmering explorations of resplendent mood and incredible scale ... sublimely performed." As a media artist, he was a winner of the prestigious Internet2 IDEA Award. He is a professor of music at Indiana University Purdue University Indianapolis.

CODA

Charles Dickens began *A Tale of Two Cities* with the well-known phrase, "It was the best of times, it was the worst of times ...." This observation seems especially appropriate for the world of concert music today.

It is the best of times in terms of the number of persons composing music, the number of orchestras, public and private financial support, freedom to compose what one wishes, and availability of music of all types at almost all times and in all places. More people are involved with music than at any other time in history. The skill level of performers is far better (with a few exceptions, such as Paganini and Liszt) than in preceding centuries.

But it also seems like the worst of times in terms of the communication and understanding between composers and audiences. As a result, composers sometimes appear to be increasingly elitist and aloof, and the public responds with apathy toward new music.

Nevertheless, musicians in the twenty-first century can build on a rich heritage of music, and technology has made its creation and dissemination far easier and faster than ever before. So, what is the future of music? No one knows, of course. But two predictions seem safe:

- There will always be music. Humanity has found sound and its manipulation too intellectually fascinating and too emotionally satisfying to abandon it. In fact, the indications are that music and the other arts will be valued even more in the years to come. They offer people a counterbalance to a world that often seems impersonal and unfeeling.

- Music in the future will differ from what it was in the past and is today. Creative minds are restless and forever unsatisfied with previous accomplishments. They want to experiment, to try new ways. Truly creative people are simply unable to accept imitations or be content with the efforts of others.

By definition, creativity involves bringing forth something new and unique. And so in the world of music, as with any creative undertaking, there will always be something fresh, new, and different.

MAIN POINTS OF CHAPTER 34

1. Several composers extended Webern's serialism to cover nearly all aspects of a musical work to achieve total serialism.

2. Chance or aleatory music is partly or wholly the product of some chance event, such as rolling dice, dropping pages of music, or allowing performers to play whatever they wish.

3. *Musique concrète* is the recording of sounds and then the manipulation of those sounds by various means.

4. Electronic music is also produced through computers and synthesizers. Over the years this process has progressed from analog recording (continuous but varying power) to recording in digital form (use of digits, usually numbers).

5. Eclecticism is the practice of combining aspects of two or more different styles in the same work.

6. If human experience is a valid guide, it is clear that there will always be music, and that the music of the future will be different from what it is today.

7. New genres such as "telematic" performances connect audiences to the creative process, unbounded by time and space.

 PRACTICE...
your understanding of this chapter's concepts by working once more with the chapter's Active Listening Guides online.

 DO...
online quizzes that your instructor may assign for a grade.

Features of Twentieth- and Twenty-First-Century Music

Melodies	Many nontraditional scales and melodies Often not vocal in character, with an angular contour
Rhythm	Prominent, with much use of irregular meters and complex patterns Polyrhythms Increased role for percussion instruments
Texture	Renewed interest in counterpoint, but homophony still present
Harmony	Often dissonant Some polytonality Some works with *no* tonal center
Dynamic levels	From very soft to extremely loud
Timbre	Conventional instruments and vocal sounds retained, but many new sounds developed from them Wide variety of timbres produced by electronic instruments
Performance media	Much music for small groups, often containing both voices and instruments Synthesizers and electronically amplified instruments Multimedia images and sound, delivered over high-speed Internet connections
Forms	Return to some of the forms used in Baroque and Classical periods
Genres	Opera Ballet music Chamber music Tone row music, serialism Some chance music Electronic music
Other features	Music often intellectually oriented Some techniques adapted from non-Western cultures

PART 7

Music *in the* United States

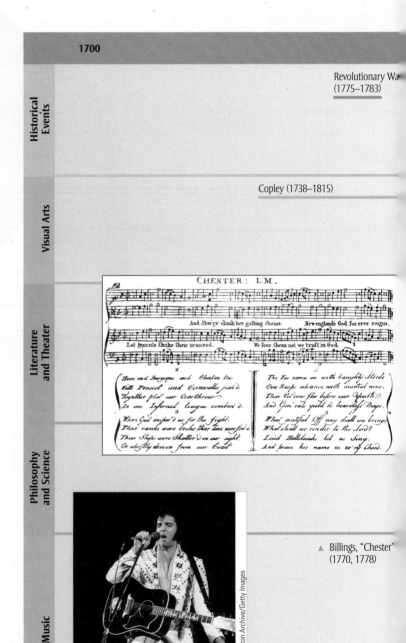

	1700
Historical Events	Revolutionary War (1775–1783)
Visual Arts	Copley (1738–1815)
Literature and Theater	
Philosophy and Science	▲ Billings, "Chester" (1770, 1778)
Music	

Fotos International/Hulton Archive/Getty Images

DEA PICTURE LIBRARY/De Agostini/Getty Images

1900

2000

● Louisiana Purchase (1803)

● War of 1812
(1812–1815)

Westward expansion (1840s–1860s)

Civil War (1861–1865)

● Transcontinental railroad (1869)

World War I (1914–1918)

Great Depression (1929–1940)

World War II (1941–1945)

Korean War ●
(1950–1953)

Terrorist attacks ●
(1993; 2001)

Iraq Wars (1991; 2003)

Vietnam War (1965–1975)

Eakins's work (1870–1916) Wood, *American Gothic* (1930)

...art's work (1777–1828)

● Homer, *Breezing Up* (1876)

Cassatt's work (1888–1926)

F. L. Wright's work (1893–1959)

Saarinen's work (1946–1961)

● Lichtenstein, *Whaam!* (1923–1997)

Pei's work (1917–)

Poe's work (1827–1849)

Cooper's work (1820–1851) Longfellow's work (1839–1882)

● Hawthorne, *The House of Seven Gables* (1851)

Whitman, *Leaves of Grass* ●
(1855)

Twain's work (1869–1910)

Sandburg's work (1919–1967) T. Williams's work (1935–1983)

O'Neill's work (1888–1953) Mailer's work (1948–2007)

M. Graham's work (1894–1991)

Lewis's work (1912–1951)

Frost's work (1913–1963) ● A. Miller, *Death of a Salesman* (1949)

Hemingway's work (1925–1961) Baldwin's work (1924–1987)

● First steamboats (1787)

● Reaper invented (1831)

Lightbulb, phonograph ●
(1879, 1877)

James's work (1863–1916)

Dewey's work (1903–1952) ● TV (1945)

● Automobiles (Early 1900s)

● Airplanes (1903)

● Radio (1906)

● Atomic energy (1945)

● DNA discovered (1953)

Internet (1985) ●

Satellites (1957–present)

Gottschalk's work (1845–1869)

Foster's work (1848–1864)

Sousa's work (1886–1932)

Jazz ●
(Early 1900s to present)

Swing ●
(1930–1945)

Gershwin's work (1898–1937)

● Soul
(1950s & 1960s)

Bernstein's work (1943–1990)

Film music (1939)

Copland's work (1917–1990)

Country ● (1920s–present)
A. C. Beach's work (1883–1944)

W. Schuman's work (1935–1992)

Barber's work (1928–1981)

● Zwilich,
Concerto Grosso
(1985)

J. Williams's work (1932–)

MacDowell's work (1896–1908)

Hanson ● (1896–1981)

Ives (1874–1954) Cage's work (1933–1992) Adams's work (1971)

◄ Rock (bottom left) (1960s–present)

35 American Music before 1920

START...

experiencing this chapter's topics with an online video activity that your instructor may assign.

READ...

the complete chapter text in a rich interactive eBook!

Learning Objectives

1 Describe the evolution of art and music in the United States before 1920.

2 List some of the notable musical activities in America in the nineteenth century.

3 Differentiate the early twentieth-century music of John Philip Sousa and Charles Ives.

The United States of America has a unique history. North America was only thinly populated by Native Americans until the arrival of Europeans in the early part of the seventeenth century. When Europeans did arrive, they came to stay, not just to take the gold and other treasures and head back home, as happened in Central and South America. For the first century and a half after the first settlements, the question was not whether America would be a colony, but whose colony it would be. The English, Dutch, Spanish, and French all laid claims to it at one time or another. New York was once called New Amsterdam; Louisiana was named for King Louis of France; and Florida comes from a Spanish word referring to "the land of flowers."

America represented a fresh start, a chance to develop a new country that was largely unfettered by ties to the past. It was a circumstance that has rarely happened in history. This situation led to the fruition of ideas that today we take for granted—ideas such as all people are created equal and governments should function as democracies. There were no democratic nations in the seventeenth century. The belief in the importance of all people was a revolutionary idea.

Even though the American experience was good for democratic government and the common good of its citizens, it was not so helpful in the development of the arts. They had a slow start in America and did not really flourish until the twentieth century.

Why were the arts slow to develop in America? There are several reasons:

- For much of the first three hundred years of its history, its people were occupied with practical matters related to settling a new land. Except for a tiny number of prosperous families on the eastern seaboard, they had little time for the arts.

- The Puritans, who were among the earliest settlers, thought that art and theater were undesirable. At best, they considered them worthless diversions; at worst, they were products of the devil. The only music permitted in church was the unaccompanied singing of psalms and hymns. Not surprisingly, the first book published in America was the *Bay Psalm Book*.

- America had almost no titled families to patronize the arts. This fact contributed much to the development of a democratic society, but it removed an important source of patrons for composers and artists.

- Initially, Americans brought their language and arts with them from their former lands. They thought that European art and music were superior to whatever might be developed in the colonies or in the young nation. For hundreds of years, the attitude was one of transplanting the superior culture from Europe, not of developing a culture that was distinct and indigenous. In short, Americans suffered from a cultural inferiority complex, a condition that has not entirely disappeared even today. Until well into the twentieth century, it was believed that an aspiring artist, composer, or performer should spend some years studying in Europe.

ART IN AMERICA

American artists were affected by the factors just mentioned. As a result, they developed a simpler, more down-to-earth style than that of European artists. Instead of painting members of the nobility, they painted common people doing common activities. And until the twentieth century their works were not noticeably influenced by intellectual theories about art.

Winslow Homer's *Breezing Up*, painted in 1876 (Figure 35.1), suggests mood, feeling, and atmosphere in a vivid way. The picture of three small boys and a fisherman in a sailboat evokes the pleasure of sailing in a nice breeze. It's a simple, straightforward work of art.

Grant Wood's *American Gothic* (Figure 35.2) is one of the most famous American paintings. It has been parodied, graced doormats and T-shirts, and been seen in cereal commercials. It depicts something very American in its matter-of-fact representation of life. It celebrates the homely, simple virtues of rural life, of America as it once was. The use of the term *Gothic* is intended as an ironic comparison with the massive and complex structures found in the European Gothic tradition. The pointed-arch window of the dwelling in the background is an example of what is sometimes called "carpenter Gothic," which is the American version of a European style carved ornately in stone.

In spite of its slow start, American music is a rich and rewarding type of music to know and understand, especially, of course, for Americans. It is an essential part of a course that covers music listening today.

American music can be divided into three broad categories: folk, popular, and art. American folk music is discussed in Chapter 40. The latter two types are presented in the following chapters.

DEA PICTURE LIBRARY/De Agostini/Getty Images

FIGURE 35.1
Breezing Up (A Fair Wind), 1873–1876, by Winslow Homer (1816–1910), oil on canvas

FIGURE 35.2

AMERICAN GOTHIC BY GRANT WOOD, 1930. THIS PORTRAIT OF AN IOWA FARM COUPLE CONTAINS SOME OF THE SIMPLE BUT STRONG ELEMENTS FOUND IN AMERICAN MUSIC. THE MODEL FOR THE MAN WAS WOOD'S DENTIST.

DEA/M. CARRIERI/DeAgostini/Getty Images

THE EIGHTEENTH CENTURY

The most sophisticated music written in the American colonies before the Revolutionary War was the product of the Moravian communities around Bethlehem, Pennsylvania, and Winston-Salem, North Carolina. These people had come from what is today part of the Czech Republic, bringing with them a rich musical heritage. Besides music for church services, they also wrote chamber works. There were several active composers among the Moravians, but John Frederick Peter (1746–1813) was the most skilled. He immigrated to America in 1770.

Probably the first native-born American composer was a musical amateur, Francis Hopkinson (1737–1791), a friend of George Washington and a signer of the Declaration of Independence. In 1788 he published some songs, for which he also wrote the words. He dedicated the published work to Washington. Washington was humble in his response to Hopkinson:

> I can neither sing one of the songs, nor raise a single note on any instrument to convince the unbelieving, but I have, however, one argument which will prevail with persons of true estate (at least in America)—I can tell them that it is the production of Mr. Hopkinson.

William Billings (1746–1800) was a tanner by trade and later one of a talented number of singing-school masters. He had an insatiable drive to write music and was a firm believer in American music for Americans. He explained in his first collection, *The New England Psalm Singer* (1770), that he would follow his own rules for composition. One of the techniques he used in his hymns was "fuguing," which was an impressive name for simple imitation.

Billings was not modest in making claims about fuguing:

> [Fuguing] is twenty times as powerful as the old slow tunes. Each part striving for mastery and victory. The audience entertained and delighted. Now the solemn bass

demands their attention; next the manly tenor. Now here, now there, now here again!
O ecstatic! Rush on, you sons of harmony.

Whatever Billings lacked in training was offset by his natural musical ability. Despite some rough places, his music possesses a vigor that continues to fascinate many musicians and listeners. A number of Billings's tunes are still performed today. The patriotic tune "Chester" (Figure 35.3) is one of his best known. The melody is in the tenor part, which is the third line from the top. The music has a plain and direct quality.

During the eighteenth century, music in America was not confined to religious situations; a folk music tradition was also developing. Much of this music, as is pointed out in Chapter 40, consisted of adaptations of music from England and much of it was not published.

FIGURE 35.3
A VERSION OF "CHESTER" FROM BILLINGS'S *SINGING MASTER'S ASSISTANT*

America's Patriotic Songs

As is true of a great deal of American culture, much of its patriotic music consists of songs with European roots. The origin of "Yankee Doodle" is unknown, but it was introduced in the colonies by a British doctor named Shackburg about twenty years before the Revolutionary War began. It was first sung by the British to ridicule the New Englanders, who promptly took it over as their own song by adding new verses.

The melody of "The Star-Spangled Banner" was adapted from a popular English drinking song, "To Anacreon in Heaven." This song to an ancient Greek poet was probably composed by John Stafford Smith (1750–1836). The words were written by an American lawyer, Francis Scott Key. During the War of 1812 between the Americans and the British, Key went aboard a British ship in Chesapeake Bay to negotiate the release of a Dr. William Beames, who was being held prisoner by the British. On September 13, 1814, the British fleet sailed up the bay to bombard Fort McHenry, which guarded Baltimore harbor. Before the battle began, Key, Beames, and a companion were transferred to a small boat behind the fleet.

All night Key paced the deck, wondering if the American flag would still be there in the morning. If it were, it would mean that the fort had withstood the challenge and that Baltimore had been saved. "By the dawn's early light" Key could see the Stars and Stripes still flying, and he was moved to begin the poem that is sung today. By that afternoon he had finished it, and a week later it appeared in the *Baltimore American*.

The words were sung for the first time by an actor in Baltimore. It was not officially made the national anthem until 1931.

"My Country 'Tis of Thee" ("America") is sung to the same melody as the British national anthem, "God Save the King (or Queen)," which was written by the English composer Henry Carey (1685–1743). The words sung in this country were written in 1832 by the American Samuel Francis Smith (1808–1895), somewhat by accident. Lowell Mason was searching for music to arrange for children to sing in church. He had been given a collection of songs used in German schools. Not knowing German, Mason had asked Smith, a student at Andover Theological Seminary, to set English words to them in his spare time. It took Smith only half an hour one February day to write his words to the tune, which he did not realize at the time was "God Save the King."

"America, the Beautiful" is sung to a hymn tune, "Materna" ("O Mother, Dear Jerusalem"), by Samuel A. Ward, an obscure organist from Newark, New Jersey. The words were the creation of Katherine Lee Bates (1859–1929), a professor of English at Wellesley College and author of a number of books and poems. She was so impressed by her first visit to the summit of Pike's Peak in Colorado that the opening lines of the poem seemed just to come to her. They were printed in a magazine called *The Congregationalist* on July 4, 1895,

and were subsequently set to several different tunes, but the "Materna" melody is the only one heard with the poem today.

John Philip Sousa's "The Star and Stripes Forever" is discussed later in this chapter. "Hail Columbia!" is another patriotic march. Feeling the need for a song to help unify the young nation, in 1798 Joseph Hopkinson wrote the words and set them to a melody that had been written as an inaugural march for George Washington nine years earlier. The composer of the march is generally believed to be Philip Phile. In those days, America was often referred to as Columbia (the feminine form of Columbus), as can be seen in the designation *District of Columbia* for the national capital area.

"God Bless America" was composed by Irving Berlin (1888–1989), an immmigrant from Siberia who came to America at the age of five. He was a prolific composer of musicals but today is best remembered for his songs. The original version of "God Bless America" was composed for a musical in 1918, but Berlin decided that its solemn quality didn't fit the comedic elements of the show. In 1938 he decided to write a "peace" song, and he recalled his song from twenty years earlier. Singer Kate Smith introduced the slightly revised version in a radio broadcast that December. It was an immediate sensation and has become the unofficial national anthem.

THE NINETEENTH CENTURY

When the nineteenth century began, the former colonies had been the United States of America for little more than a decade. Its population was just over five million people, who lived almost entirely east of the Appalachian Mountains. Most of its goods were still imported from Europe, and there were serious doubts that the young nation would survive. The arts were still in a largely embryonic state. Over the next hundred years, these conditions would change dramatically.

The name *Mason* is an important one in American music. Lowell Mason (1792–1872) wrote many hymns, including "Nearer, My God to Thee," and conducted the Handel and Haydn Society in Boston. Two of his sons founded the piano-manufacturing company of Mason and Hamlin, and a third son became a famous music teacher. Mason led a campaign against some of the religious music of his day, which came into being after the decline of Billings's "fuguing tunes." As part of this effort, Mason published a large number of music collections. Lowell Mason is considered the father of public school music in the United States. He was able to institute music instruction in the Boston elementary schools in 1837.

Not only did America import much of its music, it also imported musicians. European virtuosos found it profitable to tour the United States. The most sensational of these was the singer Jenny Lind, who was advertised by her brilliant promoter, P. T. Barnum, as "the Swedish Nightingale."

An early American piano virtuoso was Louis Moreau Gottschalk (1829–1869). He was a handsome man who cultivated some of the mannerisms of Liszt. He often left his white gloves on the piano for his female admirers to fight over. He wrote sentimental pieces with such tear-jerking titles as "The Last Hope" and "The Dying Poet." "The Banjo," which is based on American rhythms and melodies, became very popular in Europe in the 1850s.

Louis A. Jullian (1812–1860) chose a different approach. He kept his white gloves on as he conducted with his jeweled baton. He played some high-quality music, including some by American composers. But his biggest success was a number titled *Fireman's Quadrille*, during which, as flames burst from the ceiling, the local fire department would rush into the hall to dramatically quench the blaze.

For sheer spectacle no one equaled Patrick Gilmore (1829–1892), a bandmaster who organized supercolossal extravaganzas. One was the Great National Peace Jubilee in Boston in 1869. The performers included a chorus of ten thousand and an orchestra of a thousand, with cannons and a hundred firemen pounding anvils in the "Anvil Chorus" from Verdi's *Il Trovatore*! The only way for Gilmore to top that was to organize a World Peace Jubilee, which he did. For this event he brought Johann Strauss from Vienna to lead his *Blue Danube Waltz*. Although the orchestra was restricted to one thousand players, the chorus was increased to twenty thousand singers. In a letter home, Strauss described his feelings of terror as he stepped before the huge aggregation.

From Jullian's orchestra came a young German violinist named Theodore Thomas (1835–1905), who organized his own orchestra in 1862. Thomas maintained high standards of performance and tried to educate his audiences. In so doing he laid the foundation for the symphony orchestras of today. He traveled widely throughout the United States and for a time was the conductor of the New York Philharmonic. Later, he organized the Chicago Symphony and was its conductor for many years.

The political upheavals in Europe, and especially Germany, in the mid-1800s brought thousands of immigrants to the United States. Some were musicians who soon became affiliated with orchestras and opera companies throughout the country. The European immigrants constituted an audience for the German symphonic music that Thomas's orchestras performed for them.

Late in the nineteenth century, several American composers began to write longer and more sophisticated works. Most of these composers lived around Boston, and almost all of them had studied in Germany at one time or another. For this reason most of their music sounded similar to works of European composers. The "Boston" or "New England" group included George W. Chadwick (1854–1931), Horatio Parker (1863–1919), Arthur Foote (1853–1937), John Knowles Paine (1839–1906), and Amy Cheney Beach (1867–1944), who was the first American woman to write a symphony. She is probably the best known of these composers today. Amy Beach followed the custom of using her husband's first and last names. She signed her works "Mrs. H. H. A. Beach."

Edward MacDowell (1861–1908) had excellent musical training. He studied at the Paris Conservatory when he was eleven years old. After his return to America, he became a professor of music at Columbia University. Most of his works are for piano, including the often played "To a Wild Rose" from *Woodland Sketches*. He also wrote four piano sonatas and two piano concertos. His Suite No. 2 ("Indian Suite") is a landmark because of its early use of Native American music.

THE EARLY TWENTIETH CENTURY

Soon after the turn of the century, the popularity of German Romanticism began to recede in America, only to be replaced by attempts to imitate French Impressionism. The best-known American who wrote in this style was Charles Tomlinson Griffes (1884–1920). He started out composing in the German tradition but later switched to the Impressionistic style of Debussy and Ravel. "The White Peacock" from his

Roman Sketches is frequently performed. Charles Martin Loeffler (1861–1935) also wrote Impressionistic-sounding music.

Sousa and Wind Band Music

Not all music at the turn of the century in America was heard inside concert halls. Some of it was band music that was enjoyed while relaxing on the grass in a park or town square on a warm summer's evening. In the early 1900s, most Americans lived on farms or small towns. Most small towns had a bandstand from which local bands performed, often with more enthusiasm than skill.

The popularity of the band as a concert ensemble—very much an American musical institution—encouraged the development of a number of virtuoso performers, such as Arthur Pryor on trombone and Herbert Clarke on trumpet. It also resulted in a number of composers who wrote marches and overtures for wind bands.

John Philip Sousa thought out "The Stars and Stripes Forever" (Figure 35.4; see Listening Guide) on a ship while returning from Europe. He then wrote it down verbatim when he reached shore. The march follows the traditional march form, except for the addition of a **break**, or **dogfight**, before returning to the main melody of the trio. This march is also famous for the decorative countermelody played by the piccolo when the melody of the trio reappears after the dogfight. By the way, *Dogfight* is a term band directors often use to describe a part of a march in which there is a rapid exchange of musical material among sections of the band.

Although the melody of the trio may seem simple, it is not. It consists of two sections that are each sixteen measures long. These are further divided into four smaller phrases. The rhythm of two notes on the upbeat leading to one longer note pervades the melody. Other than one instance of syncopation, the melody is rhythmically quite straightforward.

Sousa's bands were not large, ranging between forty-eight and fifty-two players. They consisted of about twenty-five clarinet and saxophone players, sixteen brasses, six percussion, and one string bass. Sousa did not perform his marches at as fast a tempo as some directors take them today. He gave them a dignified, not a harried, sound.

FIGURE 35.4

John Philip Sousa on the cover of his most famous work. Sousa wrote more than ninety marches, which are still widely performed today. Much of his music was patriotic.

AP Images

LISTENING GUIDE

John Philip Sousa
"The Stars and Stripes Forever" (1896)

Genre: March

Form: *a a b b c d c d*

Download 73

3 minutes 6 seconds

0:00	March opens with a few introductory measures.

First Strain

0:04	Melody for first strain contains syncopation and features brasses followed by a drum roll.
0:17	First strain repeated.

Second Strain

0:30	Melody for second strain is more energetic.

0:44   Second strain repeated.

Trio

0:58   Music changes key and becomes softer and more songlike.

1:25   "Dogfight" featuring low brasses playing repeated notes in sequence.

1:46   Trio repeated with lively countermelody played by the piccolo.

2:01   Trio with countermelody repeated

2:14   "Dogfight" repeated.

2:36   Trio repeated with brasses playing melody loudly as piccolo plays countermelody.

3:04   "The Star and Stripes Forever" ends with a short, abrupt chord.

LISTEN TO... this selection streaming online.

WATCH... an Active Listening Guide of this selection online.

WATCH... a performance of this selection online.

DO... an online Listening Practice Activity related to this selection, which your instructor may assign for a grade.

John Philip Sousa

John Philip Sousa (1854–1932) is the composer most recognized for contributions to band music. Sousa was born in Washington, DC, of a Portuguese father and a Bavarian mother. The first ten years of his career were spent as a violinist in a theater orchestra. In 1880 he became leader of the US Marine Corps Band. After twelve years he left that position to form his own band. It was very popular (and financially successful) and toured extensively until his death forty years later. He helped develop the sousaphone, a version of the tuba that can be carried over the shoulder while marching. Despite his busy schedule, Sousa found time to compose operettas and marches, as well as write novels and an autobiography. He is remembered today only for his marches and is often referred to as the "March King."

Charles Ives's Symphony No. 2

Ives composed his Second Symphony between 1897 and 1901. It is a rather early work and is somewhat conservative for Ives. Except for having five movements, it is a relatively standard symphony.

FIRST MOVEMENT The movement has a moderate tempo and consists mostly of music for strings. In several respects it is a long introduction, including the fact that it is attached to the second movement without a break.

SECOND MOVEMENT This is a lively movement that features quotations from two old American hymns: "Bringing in the Sheaves" and "When I Survey the Wondrous Cross." The latter of these tunes is played in long note values (augmentation), sometimes with portions of the other themes serving as counterpoint. The hymn tunes are two of the four themes used in the movement.

THIRD MOVEMENT The third movement is slow and melodious.

FOURTH MOVEMENT This movement is slow and majestic.

FIFTH MOVEMENT In this movement (see Listening Guide) Ives quotes from American folk and patriotic songs, in contrast to the second movement and its quotations from hymns. One of the songs is Stephen Foster's "Camptown Races," and another is "Columbia, the Gem of the Ocean." Another melody sounds a bit like Stephen Foster's "Old Black Joe," but it is not. Instead, it is from a work titled *The American Woods* by Brookfield. A fragment of the bugle call "Reveille" is also used. The use of segments of other pieces is often referred to as **quotation music.**

Charles Ives

Labrecht Music & Arts /The Image Works

Best-Known Works

Orchestra
• Symphonies Nos. 2 and 3
• *Three Places in New England*
• *The Unanswered Question*

Organ
• Variations on "America"

Piano
• Sonata No. 2 ("Concord")

Songs
• "The Cage"
• "Lincoln, the Great Commoner"

Charles Ives (1874–1954) was born in Danbury, Connecticut, the son of a bandmaster. His father was no ordinary town bandleader. He encouraged his son to listen carefully and to experiment with different tonal effects. "Stretch your ears" was his advice. So, Charles tried such things as retuning the piano and writing for two bands playing different pieces of music while marching toward each other.

Ives attended Yale University as a music student. After graduation he went to New York City, where he made a fortune in the insurance business. He composed his music alone and had little contact with other musicians. Because he had no need to make money, he did not try to have his compositions published and sold. For this reason, for many years almost no one knew about them. Many of them sat in the barn at his country home in Connecticut. Partly because of health problems, he stopped composing around 1915, almost forty years before his death.

Shortly after the turn of the century, Ives was writing novel harmonies and rhythms that did not appear in Europe for another decade. He experimented with such techniques as polytonality, dissonant counterpoint, atonality, polyrhythms, chords with added notes, unusual melodic intervals, and *sprechstimme*. Ives was also fond of weaving fragments of familiar tunes into his works. He seemed to thrive on the element of surprise and what was novel.

Ives's Symphony No. 3, composed between 1901 and 1904, was awarded the Pulitzer Prize in 1947. The insurance man Ives took the seed of American music planted by the leather tanner Billings a century before and made it flourish. But until the 1940s, no one knew it.

LISTENING GUIDE

CHARLES IVES
Symphony No. 2, Fifth Movement (1897–1901)

Genre: Symphony

Form: *A B A B C*

Download 74

9 minutes 9 seconds

0:00   Opens with violins scurrying through notes rapidly.

0:23   French horns play fragment of Stephen Foster's "Camptown Races."

0:45   Snare drum and piccolo take up short segment of "fife and drum" music.

0:57   Trombone plays fragment of "Camptown Races."

1:14   Strings play opening theme as French horns play fragments of "Camptown Races."

1:47   French horn plays a quiet, tender melody that sounds like a Stephen Foster song.

2:35   French horn repeats songlike melody.

3:04   Woodwinds and violins play a transitional figure that begins somewhat like "Joy to the World." Then trombones play fragments from slow melody.

3:51   Violins play scurrying theme again.

4:09   French horns loudly play fragment of "Camptown Races."

4:31   Snare drum and piccolo play short section of "fife and drum" music.

4:43   Trombones and bassoons play fragment of "Camptown Races."

5:00   Violins play opening scurrying music and are soon followed by woodwinds and low strings playing fragments of "Camptown Races."

5:25   Trombones begin portion of "Columbia, the Gem of the Ocean." Other instruments follow.

5:52   Cello plays songlike melody as flute plays contrasting figures.

6:41   Cello repeats songlike melody.

7:09   Orchestra plays transition.

7:22   French horns forcefully play part of songlike melody.

8:05   Trombones and then trumpets play phrase of "Columbia, the Gem of the Ocean."

8:19   Trumpet plays part of the bugle call "Reveille."

8:22   Trombones play very loudly "Columbia, the Gem of the Ocean" while orchestra provides vigorous accompaniment.

(continued)

8:48 Series of closing chords.

9:05 Movement ends after "Reveille," followed by portion of "Columbia, the Gem of the Ocean" and dissonant chord.

LISTEN TO... this selection streaming online.

WATCH... an Active Listening Guide of this selection online.

WATCH... a performance of this selection online.

DO... an online Listening Practice Activity related to this selection, which your instructor may assign for a grade.

MAIN POINTS OF CHAPTER 35

1. The arts developed slowly in America because:

   • People were occupied with settling the new land
   • The Puritans were suspicious of worldly pleasures, including the arts
   • Almost no wealthy families were available to patronize the arts
   • Americans thought that European music and art were superior

2. The most sophisticated music before the Revolutionary War was the product of the Moravians. Following those years William Billings composed vocal music that is still admired and performed today.

3. The words to most of America's patriotic songs were written and then added to pre-existing melodies.

4. America produced few composers of art music during much of the nineteenth century. The "New England" or "Boston" group emerged toward the end of the century, along with Edward MacDowell, the first composer to use Native American themes in a work.

5. Band concerts were an important part of the American musical scene in the early years of the twentieth century. Known as the "March King," John Philip Sousa was the most successful composer of wind band music.

6. The most innovative American composer in the early years of the twentieth century was Charles Ives. Some of his techniques predated their use by European composers. He often quoted from American songs in his music.

PRACTICE... your understanding of this chapter's concepts by working once more with the chapter's Active Listening Guides online.

DO... online quizzes that your instructor may assign for a grade.

Concert Music
since 1920

Learning Objectives

1 Discover the nationalistic qualities in some American music.
2 Recognize the Neoclassical qualities in some American music.
3 Discuss the minimalistic features found in some musical works.

START...
experiencing this chapter's topics with an online video activity that your instructor may assign.

READ...
the complete chapter text in a rich interactive eBook!

What changes took place in American concert music in the decades following World War I? In a word, *plenty!* To begin with, American composers and American performers came of age. Over the years, they shed their feelings of musical inferiority and gradually assumed a leadership role in the world as performers and as composers.

Part of the reason for the rise of American music was the nation's good fortune in coming out of both world wars with its land virtually unscathed. True, in both wars thousands of American young men died in combat, but their numbers were nowhere near those of Europe and Japan, and the battles took place thousands of miles away from the shores of the then forty-eight states. America did not become exhausted in a struggle for survival or have its cities decimated, as was true of England, Germany, Japan, Russia, and a host of smaller countries.

In addition, a number of outstanding musicians fled to the safety and freedom of the United States prior to and during World War II. Stravinsky, Hindemith, and Schoenberg were but three important composers who came to America. These musicians and composers provided America with an enormous musical infusion.

Over the years, America's training of musicians also became better, until it reached a point where it was no longer necessary to study in Europe to achieve success. Of the three composers featured in this chapter—Aaron Copland, Ellen Taaffe Zwilich, and John Adams—only Copland studied overseas for any length of time, and he was almost two generations ahead of Zwilich and Adams. In fact, today thousands of students from Asia and Central and South America, plus some from Europe, come to the United States to study music at American universities and music schools.

The quality and quantity of concert music in the United States (Figure 36.1) have also been advanced by the National Endowment for the Arts (NEA), which was established in 1965. The NEA represents the first promotion of the arts by the federal government. A sizable portion of the NEA's funds are passed on to state arts councils, which in turn cooperate with and support arts efforts in large and small communities throughout the particular state. A number of major foundations have also continued or increased their support of music.

The United States and Japan have led the world in the development and use of technology for music making and listening. Starting with the phonograph invented by Thomas Edison in 1877 and progressing through radio, television, tape, long-playing records, compact-disc players, CD-ROM and DVDs, and now iPods and mp3 players, with their music and images. The procession of technological advancement has significantly affected, and continues to affect, the music that people hear and how they listen to it.

Although it is impossible for any three works to give the complete picture of the rich and diverse conglomeration of American concert music since 1920, Copland, Zwilich, and Adams each represent an important aspect of its concert musical fabric.

FIGURE 36.1
THE NATIONAL SYMPHONY ORCHESTRA WITH PRINCIPAL CONDUCTOR IVÁN FISCHER IN THE KENNEDY CENTER CONCERT HALL. ALONG WITH THE PUBLIC BROADCASTING SYSTEM (PBS), THE KENNEDY CENTER HAS CONTRIBUTED TO THE GROWTH OF AMERICAN CONCERT MUSIC AT THE NATIONAL LEVEL.

NATIONALISM

Although Nationalism was one of the features of nineteenth-century Romanticism in Europe, it did not appear in American music until well into the twentieth century. Besides, until then only a small amount of concert music was being composed in America, and those few composers were attempting to emulate European models.

The greatest interest in nationalistic music occurred from the 1930s through the 1950s. Composers most associated with this movement were Samuel Barber (1910–1981), Howard Hanson (1896–1981), Roy Harris (1898–1979), William Schuman (1910–1992), and especially Aaron Copland (1900–1990). Barber composed *Knoxville: Summer of 1915* and Adagio for Strings. Hanson wrote an opera, *Merry Mount,* and promoted American music as director of the Eastman School of Music for forty years. Harris composed Symphony No. 4 ("Folksong Symphony"). Schuman wrote *New England Triptych* and an opera, *The Mighty Casey.*

Copland's *Appalachian Spring*

Copland composed *Appalachian Spring* in 1943–1944 for the outstanding choreographer and ballet teacher Martha Graham (Figure 36.2). It is about the courtship and wedding of a couple in rural Pennsylvania in the 1800s. Copland writes some very American-sounding melodies for it, in addition to using the Shaker song "Simple Gifts." The overall spirit of the ballet is calm and its music often hymnlike, which suits the character of the people being portrayed. Today *Appalachian Spring* is heard in an orchestral suite that Copland himself arranged.

Copland provides this synopsis of the score:

1. Very slowly. Introduction of the characters, one by one, in a suffused light. The bride enters, then the groom, a neighbor, and a revivalist and his flock. The music is built around a motive derived from a major chord. Soon a hymnlike melody emerges.

Jerry Cooke/Historical/Corbis

FIGURE 36.2
A Scene From Copland's
ballet *Appalachian Spring*,
with Martha Graham dancing
the bride's role

2. Fast. A sudden burst of unison strings in A major arpeggios starts the action. A sentiment both elated and religious gives the keynote of this scene.

Copland soon combines the high, rapidly moving part with the long notes in the trombones and basses as the flute plays a contrasting line.

3. Duo for bride and her intended—scene of tenderness and passion.

4. Quite fast. The Revivalist and his flock. Folksy feeling—suggestions of square dance and country fiddlers.

5. Still faster. Solo dance of the bride—presentiment of motherhood. Extremes of joy and fear and wonder.

6. Very slowly (as at first). Transition scene to music reminiscent of the introduction.

   Some of the music of this section is derived from the second section.

7. Calm and flowing. Scenes of daily activity for the bride and her farmer husband.

   There are variations on a Shaker tune. This section of *Appalachian Spring* is presented in the Listening Guide.

8. The bride takes her place among her neighbors.

   This section is a quiet coda that balances the introduction. The neighbors depart, and the newlyweds remain "quiet and strong in their new house." The music closes with a serene passage for strings, which sounds, in Copland's words, "like a prayer."

Copland succeeded in writing music that sounds very American. In it he captures the simplicity and strength of a part of American life from its past.

LISTENING GUIDE

AARON COPLAND
Appalachian Spring, Section 7 (1943–1944)

Genre: Ballet music

Form: Theme and variations

Download 75

3 minutes 13 seconds

0:00   "Simple Gifts" melody played by clarinet.

p *simply expressive*

0:34   Variation 1: Oboe and bassoon.

1:04   Variation 2: Violas play melody in augmentation. Strings follow in imitation.

1:52   Variation 3: Trumpets and trombones play melody.

2:17   Variation 4: Woodwinds, slowly and softly.

2:35   Variation 5: Full orchestra in a majestic style.

3:06   Section 7 concludes with a full-sounding chord, followed by sustained note by French horn leading
to next section.

LISTEN TO... this selection streaming online.

WATCH... an Active Listening Guide of this selection online.

WATCH... a performance of this selection online.

DO... an online Listening Practice Activity related to this selection, which your instructor may assign for a grade.

NEOCLASSICISM

In the decades following World War II, a number of composers in America moved toward a more intellectual, Neoclassical style of music. Most of them composed absolute music. The major composers in this group include Roger Sessions (1896–1985), Elliott Carter (1908-2012), and Ellen Taaffe Zwilich (b. 1939).

Zwilich's *Concerto Grosso 1985*

Ellen Taaffe Zwilich's *Concerto Grosso 1985* was commissioned by the Washington Friends of Music to commemorate Handel's three hundredth birthday. Accordingly, she composed a work expressly with Neoclassical elements, including the use of a theme from Handel's Sonata for Violin and Continuo in D Major. Her admiration for the work is clear from what she has said about it:

> I performed [it] many years ago, and I especially love the opening theme of the first movement. ...Throughout [Concerto Grosso 1985] I found myself using compositional techniques typical of the Baroque period, including terraced dynamics, repeated phrases ... techniques I would not normally use, but I felt inspired to do so because of the fact that this piece was based on Handel."

Adhering to Neoclassical practice, Zwilich wrote for a small orchestra and includes a harpsichord. She also gives solo instruments, especially the violin and oboe, prominent roles.

The five movements of *Concerto Grosso 1985* follow a symmetrical pattern, with the last one similar to the first, and the fourth matching the second. The first and fifth use passages from Handel's sonata, with the other movements using shorter quotations.

The first movement (see Listening Guide) contrasts majestic-sounding music in twentieth-century style and its angular melody with Handel's theme. Both the old and new lines have one aspect in common: a repeated rhythmic pattern of short–short–long and a similar melodic outline. Zwilich also adds a long pedal tone in the bass that contrasts with the more dissonant lines above it.

Ellen Taaffe Zwilich

Ellen Taaffe Zwilich was born in 1939 in Miami, Florida, the daughter of an airline pilot. She studied music at Florida State University and the Juilliard School before playing violin for several years in the American Symphony Orchestra under Leopold Stokowski. She also studied composition with Roger Sessions and Elliott Carter. In 1969 she married Joseph Zwilich, who died ten years later.

Since 1975 her career has been a series of commissions, awards, and performances by major symphonies under highly esteemed conductors. In addition to the Pulitzer Prize for Symphony No. 1, she has been awarded the Elizabeth Sprague Coolidge Chamber Music Prize and the Arturo Toscanini Music Critics Award and has received two Grammy Award nominations. She has received a Guggenheim Fellowship as well as grants from the New York State Council on the Arts, the Martha Baird Rockefeller Fund for Music, and the National Endowment for the Arts.

Best-Known Works

Chamber music
• String Quartet

Orchestra
• *Concerto Grosso 1985*
• Concerto for Trombone
• Symphonies Nos. 1 and 2

ELLEN TAAFFE ZWILICH
Concerto Grosso 1985, First Movement (1985)

Genre: Concerto grosso

Form: *A B A B A B*

Download 76

2 minutes 42 seconds

0:00   Orchestra sounds three sustained notes in unison.

0:18   Violins play several angular short–short–long figures as opening note continues.

(continued)

0:35 Violins play Handel's theme while low strings and harpsichord play the continuo part.

0:56 Violins interrupt Handel's theme and play short–short–long figure over a long, low note.

1:15 Oboe continues Handel's melody accompanied by continuo part.

1:32 Short–short–long figure returns in violins and alternates with woodwinds.

1:51 Violins play Handel's melody.

2:03 Short–short–long figure returns in violins over a sustained low note.

2:14 Dissonant chord is held while fragments of short–short–long theme appear.

2:32 Chord grows louder as the movement concludes.

LISTEN TO... this selection streaming online.

WATCH... an Active Listening Guide of this selection online.

WATCH... an interview with this composer online.

DO... an online Listening Practice Activity related to this selection, which your instructor may assign for a grade.

MINIMALISM

At times, twentieth-century composers seemed intent on seeing how *much* they could work into their compositions in terms of techniques and musical ideas. **Minimalism** is a reaction against the technical complexities and highly charged emotional content in much of the concert music of the previous centuries. Minimalist composers are intent on seeing how *little* they can do in their music and yet create something interesting and satisfying to listen to. They take a small amount of musical material and repeat it again and again, usually with small modifications.

Minimalism is sometimes referred to as "trance music," a name that is rejected by Minimalist composers. The effect on listeners of the continual repetition of Minimalist patterns is almost hypnotic. And with good reason. Minimalist music changes very little and does so at a slow rate. These conditions also contribute to the considerable length of most Minimalist music. Minimalist musicians often do not think of their musical works as finished products, but rather as processes. What happens during the music is considered more important than the final result.

Minimalism in music has been largely confined to America. Composers associated with this type of music include Philip Glass (b. 1937), Steve Reich (b. 1936), and John Adams (b. 1947). Glass, who attended the Juilliard School, worked in New York for two years before moving to Paris. While there he was employed copying music for Ravi Shankar, the well-known sitar player. Shankar's Indian music gave Glass an appreciation of the idea of "change within repetition."

Minimalism didn't exactly take off with audiences and critics. Glass had to drive a taxi in the daytime and rehearse his group of six players at night. But success did come over time, including music for the award-winning movie *The Thin Blue Line* (1988) and a song collection, *Songs from Liquid Days* (1986) with Paul Simon and Linda Ronstadt. Rock star David Bowie also made a Minimalist pop album called *Low* in 1977.

Adams's *Short Ride in a Fast Machine*

Short Ride in a Fast Machine (see Listening Guide) exudes energy and fun. It is a short work for orchestra and two synthesizers. The work was composed in 1986 for the Great Woods Festival in Mansfield, Massachusetts. When asked about the title, Adams responded, "You know how it is when someone asks you to ride in a terrific sports car, and then you wish you hadn't." Appropriately, he uses the descriptive term *delirando*, meaning "frenzied," for the work.

Adams shows his Minimalist approach to music by having the brasses play a very rhythmic pattern that evolves as the music flies along:

The repetition of rhythmic motives, which mutate as the music moves along, is the basis for the work. Then there are the insistent sounds of the woodblock. The music tends to propel itself to its frenzied conclusion.

JOHN ADAMS
Short Ride in a Fast Machine (1986)

LISTENING GUIDE

Genre: Program music

Download 77

4 minutes

0:00   Woodblock begins insistent pattern as synthesizers and woodwinds soon join in with faster pattern. Brasses enter with irregular pattern that evolves through several different versions.

0:33   Brasses play even notes; music grows more uneven and dissonant.

1:02   French horns enter with uneven rhythm pattern punctuated by bass drum.

1:43   Brasses play even-note pattern as music gradually grows louder and more dissonant.

Solo trumpet enters. Lower brasses play slow notes in contrast to orchestra.

(continued)

3:22 Brasses continue long notes as music sounds more majestic; horns play persistently repeated notes.

3:50 Portion of earlier music returns.

3:55 Music grows more frenzied until it abruptly concludes.

LISTEN TO... this selection streaming online.

WATCH... an Active Listening Guide of this selection online.

WATCH... John Adams talk about this selection.

DO... an online Listening Practice Activity related to this selection, which your instructor may assign for a grade.

John Adams

Mathew Imaging/WireImage/Getty Images

John Adams was born in 1947 in Worcester, Massachusetts, and grew up in Vermont and New Hampshire. He majored in composition at Harvard, earning both his bachelor's and master's degrees there. In 1971 he accepted a position at the San Francisco Conservatory of Music. From 1978 through 1985, he was composer-in-residence for the San Francisco Symphony. Adams has spoken of himself as "a minimalist who is bored with minimalism." Adams may feel bored with Minimalism, but he gives his music tremendous vitality.

He has written for a wide range of media: orchestra, opera, video, film, and dance. His most widely seen stage events are his two operas, *Nixon in China* (1987, which was telecast on PBS) and *The Death of Klinghoffer* (1991). The former is about President Richard Nixon's historic visit to China after nearly a quarter century of no formal contact between the two nations. In 2002, he wrote *On the Transmigration of Souls* to commemorate the victims of September 11.

Best-Known Works

Opera
· *The Death of Klinghoffer*
· *Nixon in China*

Orchestra
· *Harmonielehre*
· *Harmonium*

Piano
· *China Gates*
· *Phrygian Gates*

MAIN POINTS OF CHAPTER 36

1. A sizable amount of nationalistic American music was composed between 1930 and 1950. Composers Aaron Copland, Samuel Barber, and Howard Hanson promoted American music by using folk songs and writing music about American places and events.

2. Copland was able to retain the interest and respect of trained musicians while writing music that pleased concert-going audiences.

3. As the century progressed, a number of American composers turned to Neoclassicism. Ellen Taafe Zwilich combined elements of Handel's music and its Baroque style with twentieth-century composition techniques in her *Concerto Grosso 1985*.

4. Minimalism is a type of music in which composers make the minimum number of changes, yet still create interesting music. Minimalist composers include Philip Glass, Steve Reich, and John Adams.

PRACTICE...
your understanding of this chapter's concepts by working once more with the chapter's Active Listening Guides online.

DO...
online quizzes that your instructor may assign for a grade.

37 Popular Music *and* Jazz *to* 1950

START...

experiencing this chapter's topics with an online video activity that your instructor may assign.

READ...

the complete chapter text in a rich interactive eBook!

Learning Objectives

1 Describe the roots of popular music in America before 1850.
2 Trace the evolution of popular music through Tin Pan Alley and ragtime.
3 Differentiate the blues from earlier popular music genres.
4 Describe how jazz evolved from earlier musical roots.
5 Differentiate interrelated types of jazz: Dixieland, boogie-woogie, and swing.

Music critic Sigmund Spaeth has asserted that the history of popular music "is an index to the life and history of a nation." All music is an index to some extent, of course, but the popular and folk types seem more closely attuned to experiences of a majority of the people of a nation than music created for the concert hall. In any case, popular music merits investigation.

The term **popular music** implies music that is widely known, usually through commercial enterprises such as sheet music publishers, recording companies, and mass media. In contrast, folk music is passed among the people on an informal basis, with little or no commercial involvement. Furthermore, popular music is much more closely involved with business and economics than is concert music. Although money certainly plays a role in concert music, that role is not nearly as important as it is in popular music.

The popular music discussed here is mostly secular. Large amounts of religious music exists as well, but in white churches the traditional music inherited from Europe prevails. A rich musical tradition also has developed in some black churches, but only recently have scholarly investigations been conducted in this area. A moderate relationship exists between religious and secular music in both black and white churches, which is what one would expect.

POPULAR MUSIC BEFORE 1850

The popular music of colonial America and the early days of the new nation was heavily European in character. Its dances were originally the same ones found in Paris and London. After the Revolutionary War, these dances fell out of favor because of their association with European monarchies, and country dances largely replaced them. For example, a dance imported from France, the cotillion, became the quadrille. It eventually developed into the square dance, which became very popular in nineteenth-century America and is still danced today.

Not much is known about the popular music of the early days of America. Secular songs were not published with words and music together until nearly 1700. Prior to that time, song sheets contained only words. People then must have been guided by an oral tradition regarding which tunes to sing with which set of words, because often the sheets did not indicate a tune. Even if a tune was indicated, that information is of limited usefulness to researchers today, because sometimes the same tune was known by different names.

The **parlor song** was an important type of popular music in early nineteenth-century America. These songs were purchased in sheet music form and sung in the homes of the rapidly expanding middle class. They generally required only modest music-making skill. All of them were in major keys—even the sad songs. The accompaniments, which were usually played on the piano or small pump organ, were rather easy. Many of them were based on Irish folk melodies, which can partly be explained by the large number of Irish immigrants who came to the United States during those years.

The best-known composer of parlor songs was Stephen Foster (1826–1864; Figure 37.1). Although he also wrote lively songs for minstrel shows, he composed "Beautiful Dreamer" and "I Dream of Jeannie with the Light Brown Hair." His parlor songs have a tender, innocent quality that seems quaint to us today.

The texts and moods of parlor songs were usually sentimental and filled with nostalgia, and they often dealt with death. One well-known song of this type was "The Ocean Burial," which began with the words "O! Bury Me Not in the Deep, Deep Sea." Later this song was transformed into "O! Bury Me Not on the Lone Prairie," and it became one of the more popular cowboy songs. It is hard for us today to understand the appeal of sentimental music, just as it would be difficult for people who lived in the nineteenth century to understand why songs today often have so little sentimental quality.

A few popular soloists or groups toured America prior to the Civil War. One was the Englishman Henry Russell (1812–1900). Although he spent only about seven years in the United States, he greatly influenced Stephen Foster and the Hutchinson Family Singers.

The Hutchinson family consisted of three brothers and their sister, and they reached the height of their popularity in the 1840s. Many songs sung by Russell and the Hutchinsons promoted social causes. One song, "The Maniac," drew attention to the terrible conditions in mental asylums at the time. Other songs dealt with women's rights, the abolition of slavery, and the evils of alcohol. Sometimes the music of the Hutchinsons and similar performers was presented in melodramatic scenes that included acting. People today would find such melodramatics comical, but audiences at the time were impressed.

By the time of the Civil War (1861–1865), a popular music–publishing industry was in place. Sheet music was to popular composers at that time what recordings are to popular music today. Without sheet music, it would have been impossible for most people to know the music of Foster or other songwriters.

The Civil War spawned quite a few new songs, or old songs with new words. Some Civil War songs had two sets of words, one for the Union and the other for the Confederacy. Even the melody of "The Star-Spangled Banner" had different words set to it. A few of these Civil War songs, especially Julia Ward Howe's "The Battle Hymn of the Republic" and Dan Emmett's "Dixie," are still sung today.

FIGURE 37.1
Stephen Foster

TOWARD TIN PAN ALLEY AND RAGTIME

Following the Civil War, America witnessed rapid territorial and economic expansion. The transcontinental railroad linking the east and west was completed four years after the end of the Civil War. This was a time of social unrest and of social causes such as the antisaloon movement. During these years, there was much victimization of Native Americans, and the robber barons who built the railroads amassed their fortunes. For the first twenty-five years following the Civil War, popular songs looked to the past more than to the future.

Tin Pan Alley

Beginning about twenty years before the end of the nineteenth century, popular music changed with the emergence of a nationwide music industry for the promotion and publication of songs. The center of this industry was New York City, which dominated both musical theater and popular music. The origin of the term *Tin Pan Alley* has never been clearly determined, and neither has its precise location. It probably started at 28th Street, then moved to 42nd Street, and finally to the Brill Building on 47th Street. Essentially, it referred to the popular music industry, much as the word *Hollywood* refers to the motion picture industry today.

It was (and still is) the nature of the commercial music industry to issue a huge number of songs, most of which had very short lives. Most of the songs barely paid their printing costs. But every so often, a song came along that made its composer and publisher wealthy. The first to reach into the millions in sales was the early 1890s song "After the Ball" by Charles K. Harris. "After the Ball" sold ten million copies at about fifty cents a copy.

To amass large numbers of sales, publishers hired "pluggers" to go into music and department stores to play and sing the publisher's music for the customers. A number of well-known songwriters began as pluggers—Irving Berlin, Jerome Kern, George Gershwin, and others. In addition, publishers made outright payments to performers, who were then mostly in vaudeville, to perform particular songs. The payment to performers for promotional performances was an early version of a now illegal practice known as *payola*.

Tin Pan Alley songs of the 1890s were remarkably similar to one another. They were set in 3/4 waltzlike meter, had a form that consisted of a lead-in verse and a chorus in thirty-two-measure form (*a a b a*, each with eight measures), and simple harmony. Some of these Gay Nineties songs include "Meet Me in St. Louis" (a song promoting the World's Fair there in 1904), "In My Merry Oldsmobile," and "The Bowery." There were some songs about women betrayed ("Only a Bird in a Gilded Cage") and some Irish American songs ("My Wild Irish Rose" and "Who Threw the Overalls in Mistress Murphy's Chowder?"). By the way, the decade of the 1890s was termed the *Gay Nineties* because it was relatively prosperous and trouble-free.

Scott Joplin

Michael Ochs Archives/Getty Images

Scott Joplin (1868–1917) was born near Texarkana, Texas. He showed much musical talent, learning to play the banjo, and to some extent the piano, on his own. He then studied with a local classically trained teacher and began a career as an itinerant pianist. He settled for a number of years in Sedalia, Missouri, where he played at the Maple Leaf Club, which provided the name for his most successful ragtime piece. In 1899 "Maple Leaf Rag" sold one million copies.

In 1900 Joplin moved to St. Louis to work more closely with his publisher, John Stark. Two years later, his first major composition was a ballet suite that included ragtime music. An opera, *Guest of Honor*, followed, but

the music for it has since been lost. In 1907 Joplin moved to New York and wrote an instruction book on ragtime music, which over time earned him the informal title "King of Ragtime." After his contract with Stark ran out in 1909, he made many piano rolls. Joplin also devoted much of his attention to an opera, *Treemonisha*, for which he wrote both the libretto and the music and planned the choreography. It was not successful and was performed only once during his lifetime in 1915. The opera's failure contributed to his failing health. By 1916 he had to be institutionalized, and he lived less than two more years. *Treemonisha* was published and staged in 1972 and awarded the Pulitzer Prize in 1976.

Ragtime

Ragtime existed in two related forms. One form consisted of popular songs; it was popular between 1890 and 1920. The other form was for piano and was a forerunner of jazz. Ragtime songs were usually peppy tunes. They have balanced phrasing and key centers, two beats to the measure, and catchy melodies with lots of syncopation accompanied by steady, even chords in the bass. They are sectional in form. Some of the better-known titles include "Hot Time in the Old Town," Irving Berlin's "Alexander's Ragtime Band," which is basically a march instead of a rag, and "Way Down Yonder in New Orleans."

Although many ragtime songs were written, today rags are known almost exclusively as solo piano music. The most recognized composers of piano rags were Ben Harney (1871–1938), Tom Turpin (1873–1922), and, most notable of all, Scott Joplin. Piano rags, as many a pianist has discovered, are not easy to play well. Both Harney and Joplin wrote instruction books for playing them.

The rise of piano rags paralleled the rapid increase in the sales of pianos in America between 1890 and 1920, after which a decline began. Piano rags also benefited from the development of the mechanical player piano, which worked via small holes punched in rolls of paper that were pulled across pneumatic tubes connected to the keys. In fact, some rags existed only on piano rolls and not on sheet music. The performance of "Maple Leaf Rag" (see Listening Guide) was originally a piano roll made by Joplin himself.

Ragtime did not follow the path through Tin Pan Alley to the public, as did most popular music. Instead, its home was the large and small cities of the Midwest—St. Louis, Sedalia, and Kansas City in Missouri; Moline, Illinois; New Albany, Indiana; and Oskaloosa, Iowa; as well as Memphis and Indianapolis.

LISTENING GUIDE

SCOTT JOPLIN
"Maple Leaf Rag" (1899)

Genre: Ragtime music

Form: *a a b b a c c d d*

Download 78

2 minutes 98 seconds

0:00   The *a* section (or *strain*) begins in major with steady chords and syncopated melody.

0:19   The strain repeated.

0:37   The *b* strain begins higher and descends.

0:54   The *b* strain repeated.

1:12   The *a* strain returns.

1:30   The *c* strain begins in a new major key.

1:47   The *c* strain repeated.

2:04   The strain returns in original major key.

2:21   The strain repeated.

2:36   "Maple Leaf Rag" ends with two solid chords.

LISTEN TO... this selection streaming online.

WATCH... an Active Listening Guide of this selection online.

WATCH... a video of this selection online.

DO... an online Listening Practice Activity related to this selection, which your instructor may assign for a grade.

Three major developments in the 1920s brought an end to ragtime and major changes in the popular music industry:

1. The rapid demise of sheet music and piano roll sales and a corresponding rise in the sale of recordings.
2. The advent and development of commercial broadcasting. In January 1922 there were twenty-eight broadcasting stations; by December of that year, there were 570.
3. The introduction of sound motion pictures in 1927. Within two years of that date, 320 songwriters and composers were working in Hollywood.

BLUES

The **blues** began as folk music. Their musical characteristics are discussed in Chapter 41, but a few words listing musical features can't provide the true flavor of the blues. Beyond their lowered notes in the scale and *a a b* pattern of lines covering twelve measures, there is something about a singer's tone quality, small shadings of intonation, and basic melancholy feeling that makes the blues sound "blue." The vocalist always sings alone of his or her personal and usually unhappy feelings. Blues songs are not for a vocal ensemble.

The first publication of blues dates back to 1912, but the high point of their popularity came in the 1920s and early 1930s with performances by vaudeville singers. The best-known blues singers were Ma Rainey (Gertrude Pridgett, 1886–1939) and Bessie Smith.

Bessie Smith

Gilles Petard/Redferns/Getty Images

Bessie Smith (1894–1937) was born in Tennessee but was "discovered" singing in Selma, Alabama, when she was contracted by Columbia Records in New York. Between 1924 and 1927 her recordings of the blues sold more than two million disks, making her the highest-paid black performer of the time. She died as the result of an automobile accident in 1937.

In popular music, and certainly in the blues, the performer is far more important than the writer of the music; often the writer is hardly mentioned. Smith was successful because she projected a magnetism that comes through, even though the recordings of the 1920s lack the fidelity of recordings today. But her success can be attributed even more to her expressive singing voice and style. She adjusted her tone quality and added subtle nuances in pitches to make her singing memorable.

Smith's "Lost Your Head Blues"

Bessie Smith recorded "Lost Your Head Blues" (see Listening Guide) in 1926. She is joined on the recording by two other jazz greats: Fletcher Henderson on piano and Joe Smith on trumpet. Although each *a* line is repeated, Smith varies it slightly.

BESSIE SMITH
"Lost Your Head Blues" (1926)

Genre: Blues

Form: Strophic, *a a b*

Download 79

2 minutes 52 seconds

0:00   Short introduction.

0:11   The *a* line is based entirely on tonic, or I, chord. Short trumpet break follows Bessie's singing.

> *I was with you baby…*

0:22   Repeat of *a* line is mostly based on subdominant, or IV, chord, but returns to tonic at the end. Another trumpet break follows.

> *I was with you baby …*

0:32   The *b* line is mostly based on dominant, or V, chord, but concludes on tonic, followed by a trumpet break.

> *Now since you got plenty …*

The rest of the verses follow the same pattern, except for the final verse, when the breaks also occur in the middle of lines.

0:43   *Once ain't for always … (Repeat)*
        When you get a good gal …

1:16   *When you were lonesome … (Repeat)*
        But since you've got money …

1:48   *I'm gonna leave … (Repeat)*
        But I'll write you …

2:19   *Days are lonesome … (Repeat)*
        I'm a good old gal …

2:50   Song concludes quietly.

LISTEN TO… this selection streaming online.

WATCH… an Active Listening Guide of this selection online.

WATCH… a video of this selection online

DO… an online Listening Practice Activity related to this selection, which your instructor may assign for a grade.

JAZZ

The roots of **jazz** are complex, but certainly some of them reach back to the African heritage of African Americans. Other influences include minstrel show music, work songs, blues, French-Creole and Latin American music, and especially ragtime.

The traditional beginning of jazz lies with the brass bands that played for funerals in New Orleans. As a part of the procession to the grave site, the band played solemn versions of hymns like "Nearer My God to Thee." After the burial, the band would assemble a couple of blocks away from the cemetery and break into a ragtime version of a hymn or tune like "Didn't He Ramble." The bands were competitive in their ability in *cutting* or *bucking*, the terms for such playing. The style eventually moved to the red-light district and the bordellos of New Orleans.

Like folk music, jazz was created by generally untrained musicians who could not have written down what they played or sang, even had they wanted to. Actually, some of the early jazz musicians didn't want to learn to read music because they claimed it might hinder their creative abilities. But jazz differs in two ways: (1) It sprang up in the cities, so its roots are urban; and (2) only a few people perform jazz, while many listen.

Elements of Jazz

MELODY The most notable feature of jazz melodies is the **blue notes**. These notes are created by altering the major scale by lowering the third, fifth, or seventh steps. The chords that accompany these notes are not altered, however, so there is a dissonance between the lowered melody note and the note in the chord. The result, however, is not so much dissonance as it is a particular tonal effect.

HARMONY Traditional jazz harmony is as conservative as a church hymn. Most chords consist of the three primary triads used for harmonizing most simple songs: tonic (I), dominant (V), and subdominant (IV). As jazz matured, however, its harmonic palette became much richer and more sophisticated.

RHYTHM Jazz assumed many of the rhythmic characteristics of ragtime—a meter of two beats per measure combined with a countless variety of syncopated melodic figures. Jazz rhythms cannot be written precisely in traditional notation. Jazz musicians make small deviations in timing and emphasis, which most trained musicians cannot execute without guidance and practice.

TIMBRE Jazz has its own tonal colors. Certain instruments and certain styles of playing have become associated with jazz. The saxophone was intended to be a concert instrument, but jazz players took it up and produced a different timbre. Brass instruments in jazz often use mutes. Some of these mutes have distinctive names, such as *cup*, *wah-wah*, and *plunger*, which originally was a rubber sink plunger.

The style of singing jazz is quite different from that used for singing an art song or a folk song. Jazz singers employ more colors and "bend" the pitch for expressive effect.

The idea of "note bending" was a vocal technique derived from field hollers. It was picked up by instrumentalists and used in jazz.

FORM Jazz has no overall form that applies to all its styles. The form generally consists of a series of variations on a simple harmonic pattern. As mentioned previously, the blues have a traditional pattern of three lines set in an *a a b* pattern. Sometimes the singer does not sing all the way through a section, and an instrumentalist fills in with a short solo called a *break*.

IMPROVISATION Making up music on the spot is fundamental to jazz. Traditionally, jazz was not written down, but, as it developed, it was often arranged with at least some of the music notated. The extemporaneous creation of music gives jazz an ever-fresh quality. Improvising in jazz is based on the chords of the tune. Players are not confined to just the notes of the chords, especially as jazz has evolved, but they are aware of them and make up their music accordingly.

Typically, the players in a jazz performance agree that they will play a certain piece in a particular key. They also agree on an order in which each player is featured, although it can be changed during the performance by a nod of the head. Each player in turn improvises a chorus while keeping in mind the harmony of the song. Often for the final time through the piece, everyone joins in simultaneous improvised counterpoint. Only the musical instincts and good ears of the players, as well as the basic chord patterns of the piece, keep the music together.

Often during jazz improvisation, the melody can no longer be detected in the mosaic of sound. This happens because players sound many notes in addition to the former melody, and the tune becomes pretty well obscured.

Types of Jazz

Until the end of World War I, jazz had been mostly confined to the South, especially New Orleans. A number of factors led to the movement "up the river" to St. Louis, Chicago, and other cities in the North. One was the closing of Storyville, the red-light district in New Orleans. The US Navy had Storyville shut down because it was concerned about its impact on the physical and moral health of the servicemen. Many jazz musicians who worked in the bordellos lost their jobs and had to seek work elsewhere.

In addition, during World War I many young men, who had previously never thought they would see much more than the area where they grew up, were assigned to military camps and bases all over the United States. Furthermore, travel between cities by train was easy and not too expensive, if one was willing to ride coach class. If a jazz piano player lost his job in New Orleans, he could buy a ticket and head for St. Louis or Chicago. One of the best-known bands to make such a move was Joe "King" Oliver's Creole Jazz Band (Figure 37.2).

DIXIELAND The predominant type of jazz in the 1920s was **Dixieland**. It consisted of music in two beats to the measure with a strong upbeat and a "busy" quality when several players were improvising at the same time. The bands were small, usually four to seven players. Originally, they did not include drums; keeping the beat was the piano player's job. Drums were added in later years. Dixieland bands loved to describe their music as being "hot," which meant that it was somewhat faster and louder than people were accustomed to at the time.

The song "Come Back, Sweet Papa" (see Listening Guide) is a good example of Dixieland style. The tune was written by Paul Barbarin and Bob Russell, but in jazz what

FIGURE 37.2
JOE "KING" OLIVER'S CREOLE
JAZZ BAND

the players do with a tune is much more important than the original tune. If a recording had been made of "Come Back, Sweet Papa" a day or even a few minutes after the version that can be downloaded, it would be similar but not exactly the same, because the players make up some of what they play as they go along.

"Come Back, Sweet Papa" was recorded by Louis Armstrong and his Hot Five in Chicago on February 22, 1926. On the recording Armstrong plays cornet. Other instruments heard on the recording are trombone, sax/clarinet (the same player doubling), piano, and banjo. Notice that there are no drums in the Hot Five.

The recording has a twangy quality, due largely to the inadequacies of recording equipment in 1926. It could be remastered today to sound "warmer," but why? Part of its charm lies in its original timbre.

Scat singing was an instrumental style of singing introduced by Armstrong in a recording of a song called "Heebie Jeebie." It sets syllable sounds without meaning to an improvised vocal line. The sounds are usually sung quite quickly. The best known scat singer was Ella Fitzgerald.

LISTENING GUIDE

LOUIS ARMSTRONG
"Come Back, Sweet Papa" (1926)

Genre: Dixieland jazz

Form: Variations on tune

Download 80

2 minutes 32 seconds

0:00	Short introduction played by trumpet and saxophone.
0:08	Sax plays chorus.
0:28	Sax repeats chorus.
0:48	Trumpet takes up chorus as trombone adds melodic figures.
1:08	Trumpet repeats chorus.
1:27	Trombone plays sliding notes (glissando), and trumpet continues as clarinet improvises contrasting part.
1:49	Piano plays chorus.
2:08	Clarinet, trumpet, and trombone play chorus together.
2:26	Piece concludes with characteristic rhythm figure.

LISTEN TO... this selection streaming online.

WATCH... an Active Listening Guide of this selection online.

DO... an online Listening Practice Activity related to this selection, which your instructor may assign for a grade.

BOOGIE-WOOGIE After the Great Depression hit in 1929, for economic reasons people often hired only a piano player rather than a six- or seven-piece band. This situation encouraged the development of a type of jazz piano playing called **boogie-woogie**. It features a persistently repeated bass figure over which the player improvises trills, octave tremolos, and other melodic figures. Boogie-woogie was often called "eight to the bar," because the repeated bass part has eight notes per measure.

Louis Armstrong & Duke Ellington

LOUIS ARMSTRONG

DUKE ELLINGTON

Louis Armstrong (1900–1971) was born on the Fourth of July into a poor and unstable New Orleans family. As a boy he became involved with street life and at the age of twelve was sentenced by the juvenile court to the Colored Waifs' Home. It was there that he learned to play the cornet. After two years in the home, he was released; he did odd jobs and played whenever the opportunity presented itself.

Good fortune struck when Joe "King" Oliver took an interest in Armstrong, including sending him jobs that he couldn't accept himself. In 1919 Oliver moved to Chicago, and Armstrong was recognized as the best trumpet player in New Orleans. Two years later Oliver telegraphed Armstrong to join him in Chicago. Two years after that, Fletcher Henderson offered him a job with his outstanding band in New York.

After leaving Henderson's band some years later, Armstrong led several groups of his own, including the Hot Five. By the 1940s he was featured on many radio shows and appeared in a number of films. His last movie was *Hello, Dolly!* In his later years, he sang as much as he played. He served as a goodwill emissary for the US State Department on a number of worldwide tours.

Armstrong is considered the first great improvising soloist. He established a high standard of performance that has lasted for generations. In so many ways, he caught the elusive quality and joy of jazz.

Edward Kennedy "Duke" Ellington (1899–1975) lived a very different life from that of Louis Armstrong. Ellington was born in Washington, D.C., into the middle-class family of a butler. He studied both art and music when he was young, and his piano lessons included instruction in the popular ragtime style of the day. Although he was successful in his art studies, he decided on music and formed a band that played at social events in the Washington, D.C., area.

In 1923 he joined a five-piece combo called The Washingtonians and went to New York. Success didn't come easily, but three years later he was playing at the Cotton Club, which at that time was the most expensive nightclub in Harlem. It catered to white audiences who wanted to hear good jazz.

Over the years, Ellington's band was responsible for many musical innovations, including the use of echo chambers in recordings to increase reverberation (which became standard practice later), the flatted fifth, the amplified bass, and the baritone saxophone. By the 1950s his group's popularity seemed to be declining, but a stunning performance at the Newport Jazz Festival in 1956 revived it. He composed a number of sacred works in his later years and made goodwill tours for the US State Department. Jazz bands were noted for a high turnover rate. Not so with Ellington. For example, Harry Carney, his baritone sax player, was with him for forty-seven years!

Ellington's compositions were partially group efforts. He would begin playing a musical idea on the piano, and other members of the band would join in and add ideas. He would then massage these ideas into a final composition. Duke Ellington and his band left a legacy of elegant jazz.

SWING By 1935 jazz had progressed from small groups improvising in Dixieland style to intricate arrangements for bands of twelve to nineteen players. Much of their music was written down. Many pieces were played in four rather fast beats per measure, and the chords were far more complex than they had been in earlier jazz. The term **swing** may well have come from the bouncy quality of the music.

The Swing Era or Big Band Era was a time when audiences danced. Its concert halls were such places as the Roseland Ballroom in New York and the Palladium in Hollywood. It was also a time when the more successful bands had regular broadcasts over national radio networks.

Improvisation was still an important part of swing. Arrangers marked places for a soloist to *ad lib*—to improvise at liberty or at will. And there were many outstanding soloists: Gene Krupa on drums, Harry James on trumpet, Coleman Hawkins on saxophone, Artie Shaw and Benny Goodman on clarinet, and others. It was also the era of outstanding bands: Glenn Miller, Paul Whiteman, Les Brown, Count Basie, Woody Herman, and especially Duke Ellington. These bands had outstanding arrangers who had as much to do with the musical results as the composers of the tunes. Ellington's "Take the 'A' Train" (see Listening Guide) is typical of swing music.

DUKE ELLINGTON
"Take the 'A' Train" (1941)

LISTENING GUIDE

Genre: Big band jazz

Form: *a a b a*

Download 81

2 minutes 55 seconds

0:00　　Short introduction, then saxes play first part (*a*) of the tune.

0:17　　Saxes repeat first part of the tune.

0:29　　Saxes play a contrasting section (*b*).

0:40　　Saxes play *a* theme again.

0:51　　Saxes play *a* variant of the tune as a muted trumpet improvises contrasting part.

1:02　　Variant of *a* section is repeated.

1:15　　Muted trumpet continues with *b*.

1:28　　Trumpet and saxes repeat variant of *a*.

1:37　　Modulation to new key.

1:43　　Saxes embellish variant of *a* as trumpet improvises. Then variant is repeated.

2:07　　Trumpet and saxes play variant of *b*, concluding with a cascading chord sounded by trumpets and trombones.

2:17　　Saxes play original *a* tune against lively rhythmic pattern in trumpets.

2:28　　Saxes quietly repeat part of *a* several times as music slowly fades.

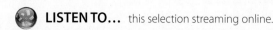
MAIN POINTS OF CHAPTER 37

1. The parlor song was a common type of popular music in the nineteenth century. It was intended for amateur performers in the home.

2. Tin Pan Alley became the name for the popular music industry around 1880. At that time, popular songs existed in sheet music form and were promoted by song pluggers in stores.

3. Two important forerunners of jazz were blues and ragtime. Blues included blue notes (lowered thirds, fifths, and sevenths in the melody) and followed a twelve-bar form. Ragtime was primarily for piano and contained much syncopation in a lively two-beat meter.

4. America's greatest contribution to the world of music, jazz, developed early in the twentieth century in New Orleans. It has a variety of roots, but its African American heritage is clearly the most important one.

5. Jazz consists largely of improvisations on popular songs. It contains much syncopation, lively rhythms, blue notes, and distinctive tone colors, and features such instruments as the saxophone and trumpet played with a jazz quality.

6. Dixieland has a lively, "busy" quality when the small group of players improvise at the same time.

7. Boogie-woogie, composed for piano, featured an ostinato bass figure played by the pianist's left hand while the right hand played many decorative notes and melodic figures.

8. The swing era (1935–1950) featured bands of fifteen or more players playing music for dancing. Arrangements consisted of popular tunes that had a bouncy quality.

38 Popular Music since 1950

START...

experiencing this chapter's topics with an online video activity that your instructor may assign.

Learning Objectives

1 Describe the nature of the popular music industry.
2 Discuss the different types of blues and soul music.
3 List the characteristics of country music.
4 Describe the features of rock music.
5 Name some of the less well known types of popular music.
6 List the features of modern jazz.

READ...

the complete chapter text in a rich interactive eBook!

The United States today still has some of the features of the 1950s. Its governmental structure and economic system are largely unchanged, and most of its core beliefs and values are still somewhat intact. But in other ways, America has moved far from what it was in 1950. That is certainly true of its popular music.

POPULAR MUSIC TODAY

Three conditions have affected American popular music in major ways. One is the huge progress in music recording and playback technology. In the past seventy-five-year period, popular music recording technology has progressed from long-play 33-rpm discs to CDs and then to downloadable MP3s. Playback technology has moved from sizable speakers connected to a record-playing unit to hand-held devices that also serve as telephones and cameras and can easily access the Internet. This makes YouTube and similar programs available, which opens up huge sources of music at no cost.

A second factor significantly affecting music is the increased audience for music, in terms of both numbers and diversity. The population of the United States is nearly two and a half times larger than it was in 1950, which means that the market for music is correspondingly that much larger. Equally important is the fact that the market for music has also become much more diverse. For example, in 1950 three networks dominated television. Those networks are still around, but the number of channels, especially on cable, and choices of television programs, have increased exponentially, while the percentage of viewers of network shows has decreased significantly. No longer is music marketed by just a few large companies.

Music is now marketed to sizable segments of the population. Several of these are ethnic groups, while others are related to age levels. There are radio programs that feature the music of nearly every decade from 1970 forward and stations that broadcast in languages other than English and promote products for particular segments of the population.

The third condition is the combination of sizable segments of American society and the increased diversity of popular music, especially hip hop, has led to a powerful musical-economic combination. It consists of three industries: clothing, entertainment, and snack foods. Products in these three areas are often so intertwined that economically it's impossible to separate one from another. Sometimes a fad begins in entertainment, including music, while at other times it is instigated by fashions. In one sense,

FIGURE 38.1
RED HOT CHILI PEPPERS AND BRUNO MARS PERFORMING DURING THE PEPSI SUPER BOWL XLVIII HALFTIME SHOW IN 2014.

it doesn't matter. The combination is a powerful one, involving hundreds of millions of dollars in profits for various individuals and companies (Figure 38.1). Just recall the slogan from the early-1970s Coca-Cola commercial "I'd like to teach the world to sing" to realize the size and impact of this combination.

For these reasons, it is impossible in one chapter, or even an entire book devoted to the topic of popular music, to offer adequate coverage of even the most prominent types. For example, one source lists these types: African, avant-garde, blues, Caribbean and Latin American, Brazilian, other Latin, comedy, country, Asian, East Asian, South and Southeast Asian, easy listening, electronic, folk, hip hop, jazz, pop, rhythm and blues, rock, and reggae. For this reason, this chapter must be limited to an overview of the main types of popular music.

Types of Popular Music

Generalizations about the types and styles of popular music are difficult for more reasons than the ones just mentioned. For one, it is difficult to classify the various types of rock and other forms of popular music. One can easily come up with five different types of rock and at least three different types of country music. Each is slightly different from the other, but all of them share certain general, overall characteristics.

This situation isn't helped by the fact that performers sometimes move from one category to a different one. Justin Timberlake, for example, is both an actor, appearing in films such as *The Social Network* (2010) and *Inside Llewyn Davis* (2013), and a pop singer (Figure 38.2). Even groups aren't stable. After being highly successful as a group, some have split up and gone their individual ways. Others are successful for only a few years (for only a few months, in some cases) and then are hardly heard from again.

David Wolff - Patrick/Redferns/Getty Images

FIGURE 38.2
JUSTIN TIMBERLAKE

David Wolff - Patrick/Redferns/Getty Images

FIGURE 38.3
POP SENSATION LORDE

WATCH...
an example of mainstream popular music online.

Mainstream Popular Music

Although popular music is as much a sociological and economic phenomenon as it is musical, a number of popular performers and musicians have created some truly imaginative pieces of music. Sometimes these works represent crossovers between popular and concert music. In other cases, popular performers have demonstrated much creativity and originality. Whatever the case, popular music is a fascinating mix of many kinds of music that have been influenced by a number of factors.

Rising Stars

A sensible question to ask is: How do popular singers rise to the national and international spotlight? How are they "discovered"? How does talent emerge from relative obscurity to such high levels of visibility? This phenomenon is not entirely new, but in the mainstream of the music of Western civilization it is a product of modern society.

Think of The Beatles' meteoric rise to fame in the 1960s. Their appearance on the Ed Sullivan television show spawned both a cultural and a musical revolution—fueled by mass media. In the twenty-first century, the phenomenon has been further magnified by programs such as *America's Got Talent*, as well as by internationally broadcast talent shows. Audiences are asked to "vote" for their favorite acts, and competitors advance through several rounds of competition.

While not U.S. born, one example of such recent talent is the New Zealand singer-songwriter Lorde, whose full name is Ella Yelich-O'Connor (Figure 38.3). She began recording in 2011 at the age of fifteen and the next year self-released her five-song album

The Love Club EP on the Internet's SoundCloud. In 2013 the work was commercially released by Virgin Records, and a year later her song "Royals" won top rock song at the Billboard Music Awards. By 2014 her music had sold more than 1 million copies worldwide.

Clearly, the Internet, YouTube, daily talk shows, and the whole of the entertainment industry have contributed to her fame. It will be important to observe how the passing of time judges the enduring quality of her work—and thus the reason for including this young singer in this chapter.

Popular music is enduring, but in a very dynamic way. We are not sufficiently removed in time to truly know how this singer and others will be regarded generations from now. Perhaps this is instructive in appreciating the enduring legacy of the composers and artists who have been studied in previous chapters.

BLUES AND SOUL

Two important types of American popular music were born in the rural South. And just as the South was segregated on the basis of race until about forty-five years ago, its popular music also had strong racial associations. The *blues* was the music of the blacks, and *country* was the music of the whites.

Blues began as a type of folk music that is described in Chapter 41. As many African Americans migrated over the years from the South to the cities of the North, the blues moved with them. It spoke of the harsh life that they encountered in the northern cities. The acoustic guitar was replaced by the electric guitar, and piano, drums, and other instruments were added to accompany the singers. The music became louder than before, and blues singers often adopted a shouting style, even though they usually used a microphone. The style of piano playing was similar to what was used in boogie-woogie, with its heavy left-hand repeated patterns. Drums were eventually added as well.

Rhythm and Blues

By the 1950s saxophones and backup vocal ensembles had completed the migration of the blues from the country to the city. And it had acquired a new commercial name: **rhythm and blues**. Entertainers such as Chuck Berry (b. 1926; Figure 38.4) and Bo Diddley (1928–2008) created a music that became the basis of rock and roll, which began to appear in the mid-1950s.

Motown Records was a major force in promoting rhythm and blues. It was founded in Detroit in 1958 by then–auto worker and part-time songwriter Barry Gordy, with seven hundred dollars he borrowed from his credit union. The name *Motown* is a contraction of "Motor Town," a nickname sometimes given to Detroit.

Motown Records carefully developed its stars and their recordings, including choreography and arrangements slicked up for white audiences. In addition to the Supremes (Figure 38.5), its major stars were Smokey Robinson, The Temptations, Stevie Wonder (Figure 38.6), and Michael Jackson (Figure 38.7). In 1988 Motown Record Corporation was sold to MCA, Inc. for $61 million.

Michael Jackson (1958–2009) was a giant in the world of popular music. Born the seventh child in a musical family, he began his musical career performing with his brothers in the Jackson 5. Soon he began creating his own music and dances. His 1982

FIGURE 38.4
Chuck Berry

FIGURE 38.5
The Supremes

FIGURE 38.6
Stevie Wonder

FIGURE 38.7
Michael Jackson

album *Thriller* easily holds the world's sales record at 200 million. During his career he is estimated to have sold 750 million albums worldwide! He also won thirteen Grammy awards and twenty-six American Music Awards. He was instrumental in establishing MTV as a viable artistic outlet. Although plagued by personal problems later in his life, he maintained his many musical and benevolent activities. His death was declared a homicide due to an overdose of drugs administered by his doctor.

WATCH...
a video of Michael Jackson online.

Soul

Rhythm and blues gradually gave way to a more general concept of African American music: **soul**. This term is somewhat nebulous, but it is strongly associated with the racial and cultural identity of African Americans. Musically, it is a synthesis of blues, jazz, and gospel. On the surface its prominent musical characteristics are not all that different from those of rock. But underneath there lies a wealth of subtle tonal and rhythmic nuances that make soul distinctive and highly expressive.

RAP

Rap became a popular music phenomenon in the 1990s and is still popular today. It is half spoken, not sung in the usual sense of the word, with strong, persistent rhythm. The most notable feature of rap is its messages, which contain simple rhymes. Song topics originally included violence, resentment of authority, and aggression in harsh and unvarnished terms.

In its rather short history, rap has tended to divide into two categories. One is "gangsta rap" with its angry, violent messages, and heavy rhythm. The other, sometimes called "pop rap," speaks to unity and has more melodic interest. Queen Latifah's "Unity," for example, addresses issues of mutual respect and community values.

COUNTRY MUSIC

Country music was (and still is) the "people's music" among the whites in the South. It began as folk music but evolved into a national phenomenon and a huge commercial enterprise.

Characteristics of Country Music

SINGING STYLE The style of singing is a direct carryover from the style used for folk songs. It has a lonesome quality and is sung with a clear tone and no vibrato. It tends to be nasal and slightly tense or strained. Often singers let their voice "break" to add emotion to a moment in a song. Above all, the singing projects sincerity, or it is just not country music.

INSTRUMENTS Country music is traditionally played on stringed instruments—the fiddle, dulcimer, guitar, banjo, and mandolin. The *mandolin* is associated with Italy but became widely used in some types of country music. The *fiddle* is a violin played in a distinctive way with a straight, penetrating tone, short and rapid bow strokes, and much sliding from one note to another. Some country music festivals have fiddling contests in which fiddlers perform antics, such as playing the instrument behind their backs or holding the bow between their legs while moving the fiddle with their hands and arms.

MELODY AND HARMONY Country music is simple and direct. As it became more popular, major and minor scales replaced the extensive use of the older modal scales. Its songs are mostly harmonized with the three primary chords found in so much music in the Western world: tonic, dominant, and subdominant.

WATCH...
two country music videos online.

RHYTHM The rhythm is simple, with only a little syncopation. Most of the songs are two beats to the measure.

TEXTS The texts of country songs are an interesting blend of realism and sentimentality. Topics include death, drinking, nostalgia, loneliness, and, the perennial favorite, heartbreak.

Michael Ochs Archives/Getty Images

FIGURE 38.8
COUNTRY GREAT HANK WILLIAMS

Development of Country Music

The move of country music away from its folk status to the world of popular music coincides with the widespread use of recordings and radio in the 1920s. Record companies realized the commercial potential of what was then called *hillbilly* music. They recorded singers such as Uncle Dave Macon from Tennessee, the Carter Family from Virginia, Gid Tanner and his Skillet Lickers from Georgia, and especially Jimmie Rodgers from Mississippi.

Radio broadcasts were vital to the growth of country music because a large part of its audience lived in remote, rural, mountainous areas. The radio show that eventually became the Grand Ole Opry started in 1925 on WSM in Nashville with two unpaid performers and no commercial sponsor!

The first major country music star was Jimmie Rodgers (1897–1933) from Meridian, Mississippi, who was known as the "Singing Brakeman" because he had worked on the railroad earlier in his life. His music career was short—only six years. But during those years, he recorded 111 songs and sold twenty million records, an amazing feat for that time.

Hank Williams died at the age of twenty-nine from a combination of alcoholism and barbiturates prescribed by a con-man doctor.

Country music had a close cousin in country-western music. Part of the commercial success of this music was due to the popularity of movies about cowboys and the music performed in them.

Country music grew rapidly after World War II. The most important name in country music from the early 1950s was Hank Williams (1923–1953; Figure 38.8), who had a short career. He and his band, the Drifting Cowboys, recorded such perennial favorites as "Your Cheatin' Heart," "I'm So Lonesome I Could Cry," and "Hey, Good Lookin'." Other important names include Johnny Cash, Tennessee Ernie Ford, Merle Haggard, Patsy Cline, and Loretta Lynn, whose life story was made well known in her autobiography and subsequent movie, *Coal Miner's Daughter*.

Types of Country Music

The success of country music led to several variants in its style. **Rockabilly**, as its name suggests, was strongly influenced by rock. It was mostly the product of Sun Records and was represented by Carl Perkins (1932–1998), Elvis Presley (1935–1977), and Jerry Lee Lewis (b. 1935).

A third variant, **bluegrass**, attempted to return country music to its traditional roots. It has no songs about truck drivers or urban situations. Only acoustic (nonelectric) instruments are used, and its song topics return to the less commercial ones of early years. Bluegrass music can largely be credited to one man, Bill Monroe (1911–1996; Figure 38.9), who grew up in Kentucky.

Country music's growth (Figures 38.10 and 38.11) has made Nashville "Music City, USA," complete with a new Grand Ole Opry House in 1975, television and recording studios, publishing houses, agents, and amusement parks.

ROCK

It would be easy to say that **rock** is the musical progeny of a union between blues and country music, because it contains important elements of both. But it is much more than that.

Rock often vents strong feelings of revolt. As one writer has said, rock "expressed a visceral impatience with sociopolitical norms."

Michael Ochs Archives/Getty Images

FIGURE 38.9
BILL MONROE

FIGURE 38.10
DOLLY PARTON

FIGURE 38.11
TAYLOR SWIFT

Although rock first appeared in the mid-1950s, it did not begin to dominate the popular music scene until the mid-1960s. The fact that these years also witnessed the emergence of the baby-boomer generation as college-age young people at the same time as the turmoil over the Vietnam War can hardly be a coincidence.

Rock had its start with a Cleveland disc jockey named Alan Freed, who played rhythm and blues. He probably coined the term **rock and roll**, as it is used today, as he called his radio program "Moondog's Rock and Roll Party." Later Freed moved to New York City as a disc jockey for WINS, which soon became that city's leading popular music station.

At about the same time, white groups began recording their own versions of rhythm and blues. The first such hit was Bill Haley's (1925–1981) "Rock around the Clock." It was the theme song for the 1955 motion picture *Blackboard Jungle*, in which rebellious students smashed a teacher's valuable collection of jazz records. Later it was the theme for the popular television show *Happy Days*.

Elvis Presley (Figure 38.12) was soon to follow with songs such as "Heartbreak Hotel," which in 1956 succeeded in both the black and white segments of the market—something that rarely happens. Presley is easily the most remembered country-rock star. His singing and personal magnetism greatly enlarged the audiences for both country and rock music. His recordings sold an astounding one *billion* worldwide, with 111 albums or singles going gold, platinum, or multiplatinum. In addition, he appeared in thirty-three films and sang hundreds of concerts. The public's fascination with Presley continues. His home, Graceland, in Memphis is the second most visited home in the United States; only the White House exceeds it.

WATCH...
Elvis online.

Fotos International/Archive Photos/Getty Images

FIGURE 38.12
ELVIS PRESLEY, THE KING IN THE YEARS SINCE HIS DEATH, HE
IS REPORTED TO HAVE BEEN SEEN IN HUNDREDS OF DIFFERENT
PLACES.

Characteristics of Rock

RHYTHM The heart of rock is its strong beat. Often the beat is incorporated in a simple melodic figure played in the bass parts. Another feature of rock rhythm is its prominent *backbeat*. The backbeat is what audiences clap along with: 1-2-3-4, 1-2-3-4. In some types of rock, this backbeat is incorporated with other rhythm patterns to create a complex combination of rhythms.

MELODY AND HARMONY The melodies and harmonies of rock are strongly influenced by folk music. It has an elemental simplicity. Rock has more songs written in the modes than other types of music, which again reveals some of its folk heritage.

TIMBRE The tonal qualities of rock depend on the particular style. "Hard" rock is very loud with distorted sounds, which is not true of "soft" or "pop" rock. Rock's sounds are almost always amplified electronically, which affects the timbre of the music. The style of singing can vary from raucous, almost shouted sounds of undetermined pitch to energetic but tuneful. Singers work hard at developing individual styles that listeners can easily identify.

LYRICS The form of a rock song is usually built around its lyrics. Songs are often strophic and have more verses than traditional Tin Pan Alley songs. Often lines of text are freer in phrase lengths than the usual thirty-two measures in *a a b a* form. Some rock music uses sophisticated lyrics in terms of rhyme schemes and frame of reference, and sometimes the lyrics do not follow metrical patterns.

PERFORMANCES Most rock musicians are very conscious of visual effects. Some have experimented with subjective mental states in concerts and on videos, or what has often been termed "psychedelic" rock. Some of these images have been fantasy, some subliminal, and some probably influenced by drugs. Because of the enormous amount of money that top rock stars earn, they can afford the best in terms of lighting and other visual and sound effects. Rock concerts usually involve much more than just music. They include stunning lighting and dramatic effects to captivate their audiences.

Developments in Rock since 1965

BRITISH INFLUENCE The close relationship between British and American popular music has a long history. Therefore, it was not surprising when two British groups, The Beatles (Figure 38.13) and the Rolling Stones, became very influential in the American rock music scene. In fact, after the mid-1960s the rock music styles of the two countries became almost indistinguishable from each other.

FOLK ROCK Rock had its urban folk form in the music of Bob Dylan (b. 1941), who was associated with Greenwich Village in New York City. He infused his music with both folk qualities and social protest lyrics. Other singers of folk rock included Judy Collins and Joni Mitchell.

FUSION The combination of two or more different musical styles is called **fusion**. The fusion of rock with other styles was inevitable, given its enormous popularity. One fusion

FIGURE 38.13
THE BEATLES: RINGO, JOHN, PAUL, AND GEORGE

FIGURE 38.14
CHICAGO

FIGURE 38.15
BRUCE SPRINGSTEEN

occurred between rock and jazz. Several groups successfully blended these two types of music. Blood, Sweat and Tears, and Chicago (Figure 38.14) perform a variety of types of rock music. The combination of styles is heard particularly in the treatment of rhythm. Some of these works were considerably longer than the usual rock song, as are the working-men's anthems of Asbury Park, NJ, singer-songwriter Bruce Springsteen (Figure 38.15).

Another fusion involved the influence of classical music in rock. Three British musicians or groups achieved recognition for this type of music: Keith Emerson, the Bee Gees, and Deep Purple. Emerson, with Greg Lake and Carl Palmer, also produced popular versions of music by such composers as Copland and Mussorgsky.

George Harrison and The Beatles were among the first, if not *the* first, to include elements of Asian music in their rock works. Indian music especially attracted Harrison.

SATIRE AND PUNK One piece of evidence regarding the maturing of rock was its increasing use of satire. Frank Zappa (b. 1940) and the Mothers of Invention engaged in theatrics and put-ons that caused audiences to wonder about the seriousness of it all. Zappa himself kept interviewers guessing about the nature of his artistic intentions with his rambling and unclear statements.

While Zappa may have been having fun with audiences, *punk* rock was deliberately being rebellious. The feelings of rebellion were directed at both the norms of society and the rock establishment, which these performers thought had sold out to commercial interests. The musical impact of these groups was probably less than their social impact, as they sometimes engaged in repulsive behavior in their performances. Punk rock groups did not lack for interesting names, including Weirdos, Sex Pistols, the Lewd, the Mutants, the Ghouls, Flesheaters, Slash, Search and Destroy, Circle Jerks, Crime, Damage, and Destroy All Music.

Music Videos

The present generation of young people is sometimes described as "the Video Generation." It has grown up with visual images provided by television and other technology. And these images are not just pictures or designs, but frequent, often rapid-fire moving images that flash across a screen. Even on network television, one shot is almost never maintained for more than a second or two. The time span can be much shorter in music videos.

It was only a matter of time before popular music began to combine music and visual images. This effort led to the establishment of MTV (Music Television) in the early 1980s. Initially, the purpose of the videos was the promotion of recordings. One of the early and most widely recognized music videos was Michael Jackson's "Thriller," which was taken from his 1983 album of the same name.

Music videos can be divided into four main types:

- Videos that present a performer in a concert format
- Videos that present music in a dance format
- Videos that present a story, which may or may not relate directly to the lyrics of the song
- Videos that present fantasy images, often on the premise of a dream

WATCH...
a music video by Mariah Carey.

Music videos rely heavily on the manipulation of images, using computers and other technological equipment.

Any survey of a musical style is limited in the amount of information it can provide and in the conclusions it can draw. This seems especially true of rock, because it changes so rapidly and because it is a complex economic-social-psychological-musical phenomenon. Whatever else may be said of rock, it is truly a fascinating topic and a creative type of music.

OTHER TYPES OF POPULAR MUSIC

Although soul, country, and rock cover much of the popular music scene since 1950, they certainly do not account for all of it. Several other types of popular music were influential as well.

Latin American

Latin American music has influenced the popular music of the United States since at least the 1920s, when the husband-and-wife team of Vernon and Irene Castle popularized the tango. By the 1930s the *rumba* had become a popular dance. Cuban music soared in popularity as "The Peanut Vendor" recorded by Don Azpiazú became the first Cuban hit record.

Interest in Latin American music reached a high point in the 1950s and 1960s with the popularization of the *mambo*. The person most responsible for the interest in this dance music was Tito Puente (1923–2000; Figure 38.16), who was born in New York City of Puerto Rican parents. His most successful recording from this period was "Dance Mania."

The 1970s saw the advent of a "hot" style of Latin American music called *salsa*. It originated in the Cuban nightclubs in the 1940s, from where it spread to the rest of the Caribbean and then on to the United States. Three cities became known as the "salsa triangle": San Juan in Puerto Rico, Miami, and New York.

Another type of Latin American music is associated with the American West. Austin, Texas, became the center for an amalgamation of Mexican and country music called *Tex-Mex*. The best-known singer of Latin American music in the 1970s was Linda Ronstadt. She grew up in Tucson, Arizona, the daughter of a part-Chicano father.

Although *reggae* originated in Jamaica in the 1960s, it did not become widely known in the United States until fifteen or so years later. Reggae features accents on the backbeat with simple melodies and few chord changes. Bob Marley (1945–1981) and the Wailers presented colorful sounds that became popular with the 1976 song "Roots, Rock, Reggae."

The interest in Latin American music is strong. In 1992 Puente recorded "Numero 100," his one hundredth recording. The Miami Sound Machine with Gloria Estefan (Figure 38.17) is another example of Latin American music that appeals to a wide audience.

FIGURE 38.16
DIZZY GILLESPIE AND TITO PUENTE

WATCH…
Gloria Estefan online.

MODERN JAZZ

Jazz reached a turning point in the 1950s: It became more sophisticated—gone was the strong beat that people could dance to. In its place was a music that began for the first time to be considered seriously as concert music by its audiences and many of its performers. No longer was it music for the players; instead it became music for listeners. In the process, jazz lost its appeal to the young people, who moved to rock and rhythm and blues. The share of the radio and record market occupied by jazz slipped to about 2 percent.

The change began with a style of jazz called bebop or, more common, bop. It was the product mainly of Charlie "Bird" Parker (1920–1955) and Dizzy Gillespie (John Birks, 1917–1993; Figure 38.19). Bop contains nearly continuous syncopation, dissonant chords, and freely developed melodies. Dizzy Gillespie defined bop by saying that in bop you go *Ba-oo Ba-oo Ba-oo* instead of *Oo-ba Oo-ba Oo-ba*.

Bop groups were usually small combos, not the big bands of the 1940s. The string bass was often responsible for maintaining the beat. Some of its musical passages were

FIGURE 38.17
GLORIA ESTEFAN AND THE MIAMI SOUND MACHINE

WATCH...
Miles Davis and his band in a jam session in which each player has a chance to improvise.

played in unison, often with lots of notes. Miles Davis (1926–1991), Dave Brubeck (1920–2013; Figure 38.18), and the Modern Jazz Quartet turned toward a "cool" style of jazz. Their music was more intellectual and well ordered, and it was also performed by small groups.

Brubeck's "Blue Rondo a la Turk"

Dave Brubeck's "Blue Rondo a la Turk" (see Listening Guide) reveals its more sophisticated nature in its title. First, it alludes to rondo form in which the same music returns several times with other music interspersed between its appearances. Second, it refers to Turkish music and its frequent use of asymmetrical rhythm patterns. Appropriately, the first section of the piece opens with nine rapid beats per measure arranged in a 1 2, 1 2, 1 2, 1 2 3 pattern. "Blue Rondo a la Turk" also has a "cool," intellectual quality, especially in its long sax and piano solos.

A less well-understood type of jazz is called **free jazz**. It was first developed by Ornette Coleman (1926–1967) about 1960. Other practitioners of this style include John Coltrane (1926–1967) and Cecil Taylor (b. 1929). Free jazz usually involves collective improvising, no predetermined chord progressions or tonality, playing deliberately out of tune, and expanded forms that are longer than those usually encountered in jazz.

Gai Terrell/Redferns/Getty Images

FIGURE 38.18
DAVE BRUBECK

LISTENING GUIDE

DAVE BRUBECK
"Blue Rondo a la Turk" (1959)

Genre: Modern jazz

Form: Rondo

Download 82

3 minutes 52 seconds

0:00	"Turkish" part of the work begins, with fast and unusual rhythm pattern. Piano, bass, and drums play nine fast notes in a 2 + 2 + 2 + 3 pattern, with every fourth measure in a 3 + 3 + 3 pattern.
0:11	Saxophone joins in.
0:22	Piano, bass, and drums continue without saxophone.
0:45	Saxophone enters as piano drops out.
1:07	Saxophone plays main thematic idea again.
1:18	Piano begins transition based on main theme.
1:53	Music suddenly changes to four-beat meter with a more leisurely character. This is briefly interrupted three times by the opening music.
2:14	Saxophone begins lengthy improvised "blues" solo accompanied by bass and drums.
3:52	Recording fades.

 LISTEN TO... this selection streaming online.

 WATCH... an Active Listening Guide of this selection online.

 WATCH... a video of this selection online.

 DO... an online Listening Practice Activity related to this selection, which your instructor may assign for a grade.

Some jazz composers, notably Miles Davis, moved to electronic sounds and changes that made the jazz-based compositions. Davis's "Bitches Brew," created in 1969, uses a number of electric instruments and an almost rocklike rhythm pattern that is ornamented with Latin American figures. In 1995 Wynton Marsalis (b. 1961; Figure 38.19) and his Septet followed in Davis's footsteps with "Citi Movement," a thirty-seven-minute-long ballet. These compositions represent high artistic aspirations. Jazz has indeed moved far from what its founding fathers back in New Orleans started early in the twentieth century.

FIGURE 38.19
Wynton Marsalis

MAIN POINTS OF CHAPTER 38

1. Blues, rhythm and blues, and soul were developed by African Americans. Their most important offspring is jazz.

2. Country music and variants of it were developed by whites in the south. Nashville is the home of country music and has become very successful commercially.

3. Country music features simple melodies and harmonies, often a "lonesome" slightly nasal singing style, and realistic and sometimes sentimental lyrics.

4. Variants of country music include bluegrass (no electric instruments or commercial lyrics), rockabilly (a combination of country and rock), and country-western (cowboy songs on western topics).

5. Rock music developed in the 1960s and became very popular. Its characteristics include a strong beat and especially a strong backbeat, many melodies that reveal the influence of folk music, sometimes very loud singing and playing, forms that follow the lyrics instead of a traditional pattern, and generally today stunning visual and dramatic effects at its concerts.

6. Originally rock was known as rock 'n' roll. Later variants include soft rock, acid rock, punk rock, fusion, and satirical rock.

7. Jazz became much more sophisticated as it made the transition from a type of performers' music to a style intended for listeners. Several of its variants include bop with its small group playing music containing much syncopation, cool jazz with its much more intellectual qualities, and free-form jazz that has no predetermined chords.

8. Additional types of popular music include Latin American with its salsa, reggae from the Caribbean, and rap.

 PRACTICE...
your understanding of this chapter's concepts by working once more with the chapter's Active Listening Guide online.

 DO...
online quizzes that your instructor may assign for a grade.

39 Music *for* Stage *and* Film

START...

experiencing this chapter's topics with an online video activity that your instructor may assign.

READ...

the complete chapter text in a rich interactive eBook!

Learning Objectives

1 Discuss some of the types of popular music that preceded the Civil War.

2 Describe the features of Broadway musicals.

3 Explain the nature and condition of opera in America.

4 Explain the role of music in films.

5 Describe the development of music in films.

Music for stage performance and film is somewhat different from concert music. Such music does not stand alone. It always involves a visual element and usually drama. Composers therefore face somewhat different requirements when writing for stage or film. They need to create music that is effective in tandem with the action and story with which they are working. In spite of this apparent limitation, this requirement has produced a body of beautiful and interesting music.

EARLY CONCERTS

Public performances of music in the 1700s were mostly confined to four cities: Philadelphia, New York, Boston, and Charleston. These performances were hardly concerts in the current sense of the word. They included songs, dances, recitations, card tricks, and even balancing acts. Audiences were noisy, and performers often had to request them to be quiet. In fact, for many years some of the audience was allowed to sit onstage. On bad nights the audience threw nuts, fruit, and even bottles at the performers!

No clear division existed between popular and concert music in stage productions, a situation that lasted until about 1830. Songs were almost always included in early public performances, but few of those songs have survived. A few types of musicals existed. Most of these had skeletal plots around which composers created some songs, but most of the music for these stage productions has been lost.

MINSTREL SHOWS

An indigenous American type of stage show is the **minstrel show**, which developed in the decades before the Civil War. These shows enjoyed enormous popularity and existed well into the twentieth century. They featured exaggerated portrayals of black people by white performers wearing blackface. After the Civil War, blacks became the main performers in minstrel shows. The shows consisted of songs, dances, jokes, skits, and satirical speeches.

Originally, there were only four performers seated in a semicircle. They didn't sit still for long, however; they were almost constantly in motion, even when sitting. Banjo and fiddle players occupied the middle two seats. The other two performers were logically called "end men." They played the bones and tambourine and engaged in entertaining

384

horseplay. The *bones* were two small clappers played with the fingers. They were originally animal bones but were later made of hardwood.

The music for minstrel shows was generally in a major key, had a lively tempo, and contained much repetition of short motives. The well-known song "Dixie" has each of these characteristics. Two names are especially associated with the music for minstrel shows: Stephen Foster (1826–1864) and Dan Emmett (1815–1904). Emmett composed "Dixie" while working with a minstrel show company.

VAUDEVILLE

Late in the 1800s, a new and important form of stage entertainment appeared: **vaudeville**. It descended from minstrel shows, the English music hall, and the "burlesque" type of entertainment offered in saloons. Vaudeville usually consisted of a succession of individual acts—singers, dancers, jugglers, magicians, and animal acts. They were typically headed by a well-known comedian or singer.

By the turn of the century, vaudeville was playing in thousands of theaters across the United States. It thrived into the days of silent movies, with which it often shared the stage. Many performers who later became famous through the movies, radio, or television got their start in vaudeville: Sophie Tucker, George M. Cohan, Jimmy Durante, Jack Benny, and Ed Wynn, to name a few. Interestingly, vaudeville left no discernible body of music.

MUSICAL COMEDY AND BROADWAY MUSICALS

The Black Crook, first produced in 1866, is often credited with being the first American musical. Actually, it was quite European in character; the more-American musical comedies were at least a generation or more in the future. Along the way, three European-born and trained composers contributed to the development of this genre of music: Victor Herbert (1859–1924), Rudolf Friml (1879–1972), and Sigmund Romberg (1887–1951). Their stage works, called *operettas*, were filled with beautiful melodies, and their stories were pure escapism. Many of them were placed in exotic locations and times.

Probably the richest time period for **musical comedy** was the thirty years between Jerome Kern's *Show Boat* (1927) and Leonard Bernstein's *West Side Story* (1957). Other notable composers of musical comedies during this time include Richard Rodgers and Oscar Hammerstein II, Frederick Lowe and Alan Jay Lerner, Cole Porter, and Irving Berlin. The stories became more real, and the music was integrated more logically into the story line. No longer were songs just strung together around a flimsy plot. Actually, some of the musical comedies during these years had quite serious stories, along with some comedy—*South Pacific*, *Show Boat*, *Lady in the Dark*, *Carousel*, *The King and I*, and others. These musicals consisted of one good tune after another. Some of the songs were not only quite expressive but also rather sophisticated. Artistic dance scenes were often incorporated as well.

Bernstein's *West Side Story*

West Side Story (music by Leonard Bernstein and lyrics by Stephen Sondheim) is an updated version of Shakespeare's *Romeo and Juliet*. Instead of rival families, however, there are rival gangs; one is Puerto Rican (Sharks) and the other native New Yorkers (Jets). Maria is Puerto Rican, and Tony is of Polish descent. They meet and fall in love at a dance, but the obstacles to their happiness cannot be overcome. Tony unintentionally kills Maria's brother in a gang fight. Then Tony is told falsely that Maria has turned against him, so he allows himself to be stabbed. He dies in Maria's arms. The movie version of *West Side Story* won the Academy Award for Best Picture in 1961.

The song "Tonight" (Quintet; see Listening Guide) appears before the gang fight (rumble). The two gangs, the Jets and the Sharks, each claim that the other started the feud and that they will whip the other. Anita (girlfriend of Maria's brother) looks forward to a time of lovemaking after the fight. Maria and Tony are consumed with thoughts about their newfound love. Each of the two gangs and three individuals is positioned apart, both in staged versions and in the film. The music provides wonderful counterpoint of the different moods and music expressing those moods.

Since *West Side Story*, musical comedies have moved away from the emphasis on the composer and the songs. The librettist, director, and choreographer have assumed new importance. Some musicals are built around a concept rather than a story. *A Chorus Line* and *Cats* are two such "concept" musicals.

LISTENING GUIDE

LEONARD BERNSTEIN
"Tonight" (Quintet) from *West Side Story* (1957)

Genre: Musical comedy

Download 83

3 minutes 37 seconds

0:00   Orchestra plays fast, rhythmic music as steady notes are sounded by the low instruments.

0:07   The two gangs, the Jets and the Sharks, alternate in claiming how they are going to beat the other gang in the upcoming fight. They also exchange charges about who will start it.

1:07   Anita eagerly anticipates making love with Bernardo after the "rumble."

1:26   Tony sings the song "Tonight" that he and Maria sang together earlier in the musical.

2:18   The orchestra takes up the "rumble" music again.

2:23   The Jets urge Tony to be present for the upcoming gang fight.

2:40   Maria sings "Tonight" as the Jets continue to urge Tony.

3:06   Tony joins Maria in singing "Tonight" while the Jets and the Sharks sing in anticipation of the events to come and accuse each other of starting the fight.

3:30   The "Quintet" concludes with both gangs, Tony, Maria, and Anita singing the word "Tonight" as the orchestra sounds a long, brilliant chord.

LISTEN TO... this selection streaming online.

WATCH... an Active Listening Guide of this selection online.

WATCH... a performance of this selection online.

DO... an online Listening Practice Activity related to this selection, which your instructor may assign for a grade.

Leonard Bernstein

Leonard Bernstein (1918–1990) was born in Lawrence, Massachusetts, of Russian-Jewish parents. His businessman father moved the family to Boston shortly after Leonard's birth. Leonard graduated from the Boston Latin School and Harvard University. Later, he studied at the Curtis Institute in Philadelphia.

During his career he developed a number of successful television programs on musical topics, appeared as a piano soloist, and composed a variety of types of music. For a decade he was conductor of the New York Philharmonic Orchestra.

Best-Known Works

Ballet
• *Fancy Free*
• *On the Town*

Musical
• *West Side Story*

Orchestra
• *Candide: Overture*

Operatic Musicals

A noteworthy trend in music for the stage in recent years is a growing number of successful musicals that are virtually operas—every word in them is sung. Three examples of this trend are *The Phantom of the Opera* by Andrew Lloyd Webber (Figure 39.1) and *Les Misérables* and *Miss Saigon* by Claude-Michel Schonberg. There are, however, several differences between them and the operas of Mozart, Verdi, and other composers as performed by the major opera houses of Europe and the Americas.

- The style of singing is more like what is heard in musicals.
- The singing is amplified, although no microphones are visible and the sound levels are not particularly loud.
- The vocal parts are technically less demanding; no outstanding singing ability is required.
- The accompanying orchestra is small.
- They are sung in English in English-speaking countries.
- They contain one or more humorous sections and characters.
- The action onstage moves at a faster pace. The performances of *Les Misérables* in New York used a rotating stage that made sixty-three turns in each performance.

These major musicals have international roots; they are no longer just Broadway musicals. Lloyd Webber is British and Schonberg is French. Furthermore, these musicals opened in London and Paris, respectively, and came to New York after having enjoyed success overseas.

The Phantom of the Opera is based on a story about a phantom (who is actually a man with a terribly scarred face) who haunts the Paris Opera House. It has been made into at least two movies and a stage play. The plot revolves around the love of the phantom for a beautiful young soprano. He sabotages the efforts of the opera managers to promote her place in the company. He also tries to win her affection and keep her from her fiancé. His efforts fail.

FIGURE 39.1
THE PHANTOM OF THE OPERA ACTORS EMMY ROSSUM AS CHRISTINE DAAE AND GERARD BUTLER AS ERIK IN *THE PHANTOM OF THE OPERA*

Schonberg's *Les Misérables* and *Miss Saigon* were both originally written in French with the text by Alain Boubil. English translations were carefully prepared later. *Les Misérables* is probably the world's most popular musical. It was also made into a highly successful film in 2012.

Les Misérables is based on the novel by the French writer Victor Hugo. It tells of a man, Jean Valjean, who while young committed a petty crime for which he spent several years in jail. Although initially bitter after his release, his feelings change after being befriended by a kindly priest. He eventually adopts a new name and becomes a factory owner and mayor of his town, but is still pursued by an unrelenting police inspector. One of his good deeds is to raise as his own an illegitimate girl, Cosette. Her mother had worked for a while in Valjean's factory, but she had fallen on hard times and died while Cosette was quite young.

Times are hard in France in the 1830s, and Valjean joins a band of students who hope to bring about another revolution to better the lives of the poor. The revolution fails because the people do not rise up as they did in 1789. Valjean saves Cosette's fiancé, who was one of the revolutionaries, by carrying him unconscious through the sewers of Paris to safety. The young man recovers, and the couple marry. Finally, they learn the truth about all that Valjean has done for them. *Les Misérables* closes with Valjean being escorted into heaven by Cosette's mother and the stirring marching song of the revolutionaries.

Miss Saigon is a much more contemporary story about Chris, a U.S. Marine in the Vietnam War, who falls in love with a Vietnamese girl named Kim. Despite his best efforts, he is forced to leave her behind when the Americans withdraw. Two years later, now married to an American woman, Chris learns that Kim is alive and that he has a young son in Vietnam. He returns to see her and the child. Kim, realizing that the best hope for her son's future is with his father in America, decides to give him up to Chris. In her grief-stricken state, she commits suicide, dying as Chris bends over her in anguish as the curtain falls.

WATCH...
a performance of this selection online.

AMERICAN OPERA

Opera has never been as popular in America as it has in many European countries. Some of the reasons for this are mentioned in Chapter 12, but certainly the lack of operas in English is significant. Another probable reason is the lack of an American aristocracy to fund and support opera.

It is not that American composers have failed to write several first-rate operas. Rather, it is that only a few of them seem to have achieved a permanent place in operatic repertoire. One candidate for this permanent status is Howard Hanson's *Merry Mount*, which is based on a story by Nathaniel Hawthorne set in New England.

Another candidate is *The Medium* by Gian-Carlo Menotti, who was born in Italy but immigrated to the United States when he was seventeen. *The Medium* is based on a grisly story of a devious old lady who claims to communicate with the dead in fake séances. Eventually, her conscience begins to bother her, and she imagines that something clutched her throat during a séance. Disaster follows. *The Medium* uses only five singers and an actor who plays the role of a person who is deaf and cannot speak. Its orchestra is very small; there is no chorus, and it lasts for less than an hour.

Menotti's *Amahl and the Night Visitors* was one of the first operas composed for television. After its premiere on the *Hallmark Hall of Fame* in 1951, it became an annual Christmas telecast for nearly two decades.

Gershwin's *Porgy and Bess*

The opera that has secured for itself a solid place in American operatic repertoire is not a true opera but rather, in the composer's words, a "folk opera." *Porgy and Bess* by George Gershwin is based on a story by Dubose Heyward set in Charleston, South Carolina. It is about a beggar named Porgy, who cannot walk and must get around in a goat cart. Gershwin could see the dramatic possibilities in the story and decided to compose an opera based on it.

To make the story as real as possible, Gershwin has the characters speak many of their lines instead of singing recitatives. He also incorporates the music of the black people of Charleston—the blues and features of jazz—into the opera. Although he does not include actual folk songs, the music has a folklike quality. Its jazz elements are written down rather than made up on the spot.

The story of *Porgy and Bess* (Figure 39.2) is filled with tragedy. Porgy leads a lonely life; Bess, a loose-living woman, comes to town with her lover, Crown. Neither Bess nor Crown is accepted by the people of Catfish Row. Crown kills a local man in a fight, and Bess takes refuge from the police in Porgy's shanty. Their relationship grows into genuine love.

When Crown learns of Bess's love for Porgy, he sets out to kill him. In the fight between the two men, Crown is stabbed and dies. Porgy is taken off to jail on suspicion of murder.

Now is the moment the character Sportin' Life has been waiting for. He represents the easy, evil life that Bess left behind when she moved in with Porgy. Because Porgy may never be freed from jail, Sportin' Life is able to persuade Bess to go back to New York with him.

But Porgy is released, and when he returns home, he finds Bess gone. "Where is she?" he asks. "New York," answer his neighbors. *Porgy and Bess* closes with the pathetic scene of Porgy climbing into his goat cart to go to New York to find Bess.

The song "Summertime" (see Listening Guide) appears near the beginning of the opera and helps establish the opera's setting. The mood is lazy and relaxed as the mother sings her baby to sleep. The accompaniment suggests a gentle rocking motion. The song includes some vocal devices such as a slide, or glissando, and a little catch on the word *cry.*

Sahm Doherty/Time Life Pictures/Getty Images

FIGURE 39.2
Opera Singers in Performance Opera singers Donnie Ray Albert and Clamma Dale in a Kennedy Center production of *Porgy and Bess.*

George Gershwin
"Summertime" from *Porgy and Bess* (1934–1935)

Genre: Opera

Download 84

2 minutes 28 seconds

0:00 Introduction soon falls into a gentle rocking sound between two notes.

0:25 Soprano begins:

Moderato

p Sum - mer - time _____ an' the liv - in' is eas - y, _____

(continued)

1:21   Song continues with much the same melody as singers join in accompanying part.

One of these mornin's…

2:12   After a long note on the word *by*, during which the accompaniment plays some chromatic harmony, the song ends quietly.

LISTEN TO… this selection streaming online.

WATCH… an Active Listening Guide of this selection online.

WATCH… a performance of this selection online.

DO… an online Listening Practice Activity related to this selection, which your instructor may assign for a grade.

George Gershwin

Fine Art Images/Heritage Images/ Getty Images

George Gershwin (1898–1937) was born and educated in Brooklyn, New York. His family was poor but was able to afford piano lessons for him. At the age of sixteen, he was employed as a song-plugger by a Tin Pan Alley publisher, and his career in music began. He often collaborated with his brother, Ira, who wrote the lyrics for many of George's songs.

Although successful and eventually financially well off, Gershwin was ambitious about composing concert music. His first big success came with *Rhapsody in Blue* in 1924. He originally composed it for piano and jazz orchestra; later he asked Ferde Grofé to arrange the orchestral parts. Whatever he lacked in developing musical ideas he more than made up for in his sparkling tunes and moving melodies.

George Gershwin died in Hollywood of a brain tumor after unsuccessful surgery to save his life.

Best-Known Works

Orchestra
· *An American in Paris*

Orchestra and piano
· Concerto in F
· *Rhapsody in Blue*

Opera
· *Porgy and Bess*

Musicals
· *Of Thee I Sing*
· *Girl Crazy*
· *Strike Up the Band*

MUSIC FOR FILMS

In a sense, commercial movies have almost never been silent. In the small, low-priced theaters a pianist pounded out music at appropriate places as the film flickered by on the screen. In upscale theaters small- to medium-sized orchestras played music especially composed for the film. This body of theater music has now been largely forgotten.

The Role of Music in Films

Today, of course, music is an integral part of almost every commercial film, even showings of old silent movies. Watch a familiar movie. Now, turn off the sound, and watch two or three minutes without the music. Is the experience the same? Does the momentum of the story line move ahead? Is the dramatic impact of the movie the same? What is missing?

The musical score of course—because music contributes to a film in a number of ways. And these ways are not new to composers. Remember from Chapter 25 that Berlioz used the *idée fixe* (fixed idea) in his *Symphonie fantastique* to associate particular scenes, images, and a character (Harriet Smithson) with a melody. In his opera *Götterdämmerung*, Wagner used the "leitmotiv" to represent law, fire, maidens, the castle, and redemption by love. Even earlier, in "Spring" from the *Four Seasons*, Vivaldi used individual musical melodies to represent outdoor sounds of nature.

Most of today's film composers have studied this music and know it well. Their approach is much the same. Remember the movie *Jaws*, with music by John Williams? The two-note theme appears with increasing intensity each time the shark is anticipated or appears. So, music is truly an integral part of movie music because:

- It creates a more convincing atmosphere of a particular time and place. A scene with a ship sailing through the seas calls for one kind of music, and a scene in a crowded bar requires another.

- It gives viewers cues about the unspoken thoughts of the characters or the yet-unseen implications of a situation. If a man is looking at a woman and he is filled with feelings of love and desire, the music can project his feelings. In many ways, music can express such feelings better than words.

- It provides neutral filler or background sound. Although such music is of little interest in itself, it does fill the empty places in a film.

- It helps build a sense of continuity in a motion picture. This is done by associating certain music with a particular character or situation.

- It supports and contributes to the buildup of a scene, including giving the film a solid ending. Almost no movie ends in silence, even if it lacked much of a musical score.

Development of Music for Films

It wasn't much of a beginning back on October 6, 1927, with *The Jazz Singer*, the first motion picture with music. The sound portion consisted of just five songs, including Irving Berlin's "Blue Skies." Its sound quality was vastly inferior to what we are used to today. To help the picture succeed, Warner Brothers picked a well-known vaudeville performer, Al Jolson. Impressive by today's standards or not, *The Jazz Singer* opened the door, and soon "all-talking, all-singing, all-dancing" films would follow.

It was as though a great divide had been reached that separated silent movies from films with sound. Within a few years of *The Jazz Singer*, Hollywood was attracting top musical talent for its productions. Many of the best Broadway composers and arrangers worked there—George Gershwin, Jerome Kern, Irving Berlin, Cole Porter, and Harold Arlen.

At first glance, composing some music to serve the five purposes described earlier would seem to stifle creative quality. After all, the music must match the film to the second, so little development of musical ideas is possible. Either because of or in spite of these limitations, a number of excellent composers established their professional reputations through their film music—Miklos Rozsa, Erich Korngold, Henry Mancini, Alfred Newman, Dimitri Tiomkin, James Horner, Max Steiner, Jerry Goldsmith, Maurice Jarre, Bernard Herrmann, and John Williams, among others. Some of their music has found a life apart from the movie for which it was made in terms of commercial recordings. Some of it has almost assumed a folklore status, such as the shrieking sounds from the violins that Herrmann wrote for the soundtrack for Alfred Hitchcock's *Psycho* and Williams's ominous throbbing sounds for the shark in *Jaws*.

Bernard Hermann

Bernard Hermann (1911–1975) grew up in New York City, the son of Russian-Jewish parents. He studied music at New York University and the Juilliard School of Music. The 1930s were a decade when network radio was very important. He joined the Columbia Broadcasting System in 1934 as conductor and several years later become its main conductor. It was during this time that he met and then worked with Orson Welles on his Mercury Theater broadcasts. When Welles moved to Hollywood to make motion pictures, Hermann went with him. Between 1941 and 1976 he composed music for sixty films, the final being *Taxi Driver* for Martin Scorsese. However, he is best known for the many films he scored for Alfred Hitchcock.

Hermann was especially sensitive to the need for the music to contribute to the film. He usually demanded to see the script before he would agree to compose its music. On several occasions he rejected a script while using some not-so-nice language to describe it. They finally had a falling out in 1966, when Hitchcock demanded a jazzier, more modern score for *Torn Curtain*.

Best-Known Works

Film scores
- *Citizen Kane*
- *Anna and the King of Siam*
- *The Day the Earth Stood Still*
- *Vertigo*
- *North by Northwest*
- *The Birds*
- *Taxi Driver*

FIGURE 39.3
PSYCHO III STAR AND DIRECTOR ANTHONY PERKINS, IN FRONT OF THE "PSYCHO HOUSE" ON THE UNIVERSAL BACK LOT, 1986.

Hermann's Music for *Psycho*

Music in a film should, when necessary, contribute to the drama and mood of the film. One film score that achieved this goal in an exemplary way is Bernard Hermann's score for Alfred Hitchcock's 1960 film *Psycho* (Figure 39.3). Because Hitchcock filmed the movie in black and white to better fit the grim mood of the story, Hermann decided to have its score be monochromatic in that the music is played only by string instruments. In doing so, he created some very memorable film music.

The excerpt from the score, often called "Prelude" (see Listening Guide), is played after the young woman (Janet Leigh in the film) has stolen a large amount of money from her employer and is nervously driving out of town with it. She keeps looking back to see if someone is following her. The music has a nervous, agitated quality about it that enhances the feeling of tension. The music could easily be a twentieth-century concerto grosso for strings with its accented notes, dissonant chords, and persistent, driving rhythm.

"The Murder" (see Listening Guide) is the minute-long segment of the film score that everyone seems to know and remember. (It seems *much* longer than one minute when you view the film.)

The young woman grows tired and decides to stop for the night. The only place she can find is the seedy Bates Motel. It is run by a psychopathic young man (Tony Perkins in the film; Figure 39.3) who is keeping his dead mother's body in

BERNARD HERMANN
"Prelude" from *Psycho* (1960)

Genre: Film music

Download 85

2 minutes 3 seconds

0:00	Upper strings play an energetic, driving music with many repeated notes.
0:03	Short melodic figure is repeated several times.
0:32	Brief lyrical melody enters and is repeated.
0:43	Energetic, driving music returns.
1:06	Brief lyrical melody returns.
1:17	Energetic music returns.
1:35	Brief lyrical melody returns.
1:44	Short melodic figure is repeated in different octaves.
2:00	Music concludes quietly.

 LISTEN TO... this selection streaming online.

WATCH... an Active Listening Guide of this selection online.

DO... an online Listening Practice Activity related to this selection, which your instructor may assign for a grade.

BERNARD HERMANN
"The Murder" from *Psycho* (1960)

Genre: Film music

Download 86

59 seconds

0:00	Violins play short, high glissando notes that sound like shrieks. Lower strings soon enter also playing shrieking notes.
0:14	Shrieking notes are repeated starting with the violins.
0:25	Shriek sounds end as the lower strings play pairs of long, low notes.
0:57	Murder scene music concludes on a long, low note.

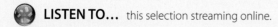 **LISTEN TO...** this selection streaming online.

WATCH... an Active Listening Guide of this selection online.

 WATCH... a performance of this selection online.

 DO... an online Listening Practice Activity related to this selection, which your instructor may assign for a grade.

AF Archive/Alamy

FIGURE 39.4
JANET LEIGH, SCREAMING AS SHE IS ABOUT TO BE STABBED.

WATCH...
a YouTube gallery of the work of recent outstanding movie composers.

PRACTICE...
your understanding of this chapter's concepts by working once more with the chapter's Active Listening Guides online.

DO...
online quizzes that your instructor may assign for a grade.

an upstairs room in their old Victorian house up the hill from the motel. He imagines that his mother is commanding him to do evil things, among them murdering the young woman (Figure 39.4). This he does while she takes a shower. The final part of the segment shows her blood flowing slowly down the drain. Originally Hitchcock did not intend to have any music during this scene, as hard as that is to imagine today. The music has a tremendous impact on the scene, and it's the main reason why those shrieking sounds are so famous.

MAIN POINTS OF CHAPTER 39

1. Music for stage and film is created to contribute to a dramatic situation. Some of it is of a quality that is beautiful and interesting to listen to, apart from what is seen in the film or on stage.

2. Minstrel shows were an early form of stage entertainment. They consisted of songs, dances, jokes, and skits by whites portraying blacks. Vaudeville was another type of variety show with music. It was supplanted by sound motion pictures.

3. Operetta and many of the earlier musical comedies consisted of fanciful stories with pretty songs. Later, some musicals were quite serious. A few recently popular musicals are virtually operas in that every word in them is sung.

4. Opera has not achieved the popularity in America that it enjoys in Europe, although several excellent operas have been composed by Americans.

5. Music contributes to the impact of a film in several ways. It provides an atmosphere, gives clues about unspoken thoughts, provides continuity, and creates a background

PART 8

Music *around the* World

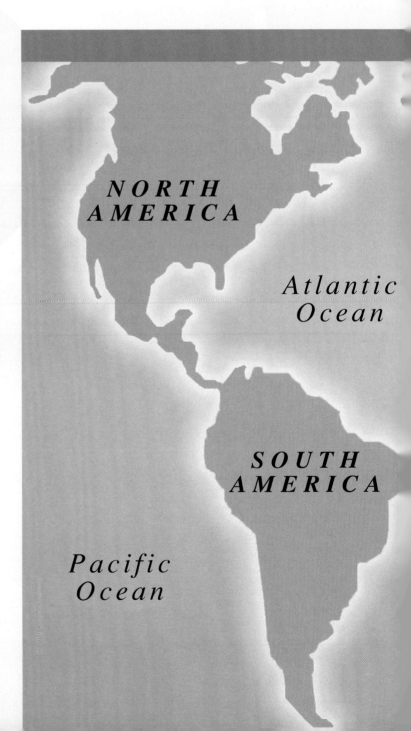

NORTH AMERICA

Atlantic Ocean

SOUTH AMERICA

Pacific Ocean

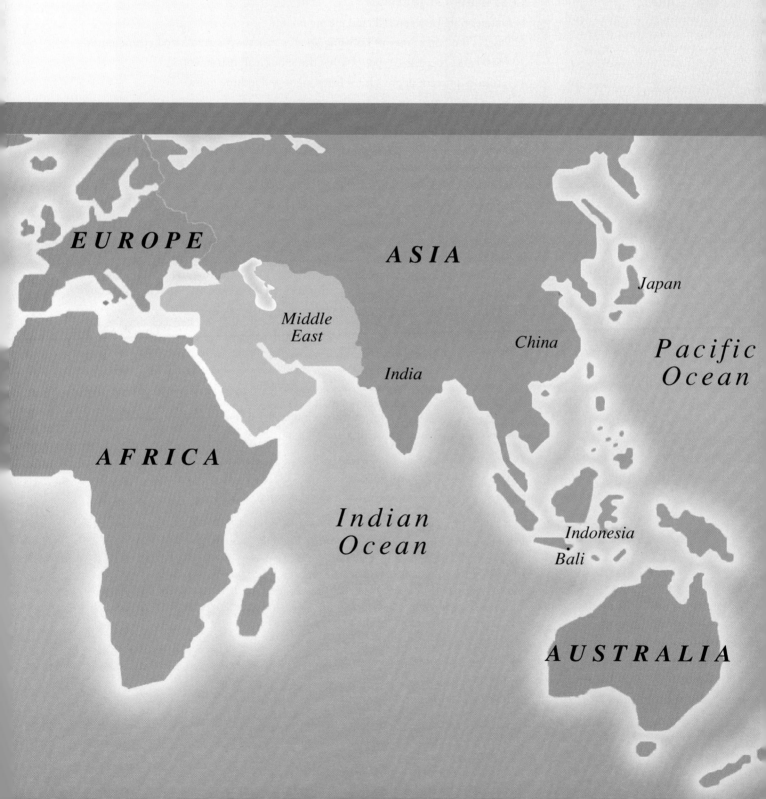

40 Folk *and* Ethnic Music

START...
experiencing this chapter's topics with an online activity that your instructor may assign.

Learning Objectives
1 Differentiate between folk and ethnic music.
2 Discuss the importance of knowing about various types of folk and ethnic music.
3 Classify the four basic types of folk/ethnic musical instruments.
4 Utilize a different approach for listening to folk/ethnic music.

READ...
the complete chapter text in a rich interactive eBook!

What's different about a song of the Huron in America, the music of the Bantu in Africa, the traditional chantey of English sailors, and Hindu religious music in India? It's a good question and a topic that merits attention.

WHAT ARE FOLK AND ETHNIC MUSIC?

Folk music is different from concert music because it is the music of the common people of a particular nation or ethnic group. And because it is the music of a sizable group of people, it has qualities that cause the people of a particular culture to like and remember it. It is music that has been tested by a large segment of people or a nation. If it had not met with their approval, it would have been forgotten and passed into oblivion. Western concert music is a type of ethnic music because it is a product of a particular civilization. As used in this book, however, *ethnic* refers to non-Western music.

Music also exists that can be identified with a particular group of people but is not the product of those people. Such music is often referred to as **ethnic**. It is also representative of its particular culture but not of the music of the common people of that culture.

All folk music is ethnic music because it is the product of a particular culture. But the opposite is not true: Not all ethnic music is folk music, because usually ethnic represents the efforts of a small, somewhat elite group of musicians.

KNOWING FOLK AND ETHNIC MUSIC

Why learn about folk and ethnic music? Such music does not appear on programs in the concert halls of Europe and America, nor is it played on radio stations other than educational ones, and even there only rarely. Recordings of most such music are limited, and they are sold only in a few specialized music stores.

In spite of this situation, there are at least three good reasons for learning about folk and ethnic music: (1) Elements of such music often find their way into concert music. (2) Folk and ethnic music reflect the attitudes and values of a culture. (3) Today we encounter other cultures and their music more frequently.

INFLUENCE OF FOLK AND ETHNIC MUSIC

Composers and musicians have often been influenced by folk and ethnic music, sometimes more than they like to admit. Occasionally over the past two hundred years, actual folk tunes have been used in symphonies and other concert music. In other cases, even if no actual folk melodies are used, composers have written folklike tunes. Melodies from concert music have also appeared occasionally in popular music.

Popular music has also been very much influenced by folk music, both in America and around the world. Often the popular music in an African or Asian country is a blend of its traditional folk/ethnic music idioms and Western popular music. The balance between indigenous folk music and popular music can vary considerably. Some contains a lot of folk or ethnic qualities, whereas other popular music has only a little.

But more than melodies are involved here. Composers sometimes appropriate and adapt ideas they hear in folk and ethnic music. They take a rhythmic or melodic pattern and alter it for use in a composition. For example, Aaron Copland drew heavily on elements of square dance music in his "Hoe-Down" from *Rodeo*, which was presented in Chapter 1.

Reflecting Culture

Music and the other arts are windows to the culture in which they exist (Figure 40.1). They represent the attitudes and values of a people. The sensitivity and subtlety of Japanese *koto* music, for example, says more about Japanese character and beliefs than can a thousand words.

Knowing the politics, history, and economy of a nation is certainly worthwhile. It is also valuable to have a sense of its character, its cultural "soul." The former provides basic factual information; the latter provides insight into a society's character.

FIGURE 40.1
A Cultural Heritage is kept alive by this North American Indian taking part in a drum circle during a powwow in Los Angeles.

The Global Village

Two hundred years ago, most people were born, lived, and died in the same small geographic area. The customs and way of life of that area were all they ever experienced or knew about. How different it is today! The journey across the Atlantic from England to America used to require month or more on a sailing ship, but today it is covered in about six hours on a jet. Mail and news, once transported by ship, are now instantaneous via satellite and other technology. A famine or war in some far-off place such as Somalia used to be scarcely noticed, if it was known at all. Today such tragedies are seen live on television in vivid color.

It's a fact: People have contact with and are affected by other peoples around the world to a degree that no one could have imagined a hundred years ago. Each year since 1900, the people of the world have been drawn closer and closer together. Today we do live in a "global village."

Not only have travel and communication been made vastly quicker and easier but also peoples from many diverse cultures are becoming U.S. citizens in ever-increasing numbers. Even small towns in the heartland of America have recent emigrants from Southeast Asia and Latin America; no longer are immigrants confined to large cities such as Los Angeles, Miami, or New York. Ethnic radio stations and newspapers in languages other than English are commonplace. The yellow pages of telephone books list a wide array of restaurants featuring ethnic foods, and mosques and temples now stand beside Christian churches and Jewish synagogues.

THE IMPORTANCE OF FOLK AND ETHNIC MUSIC

When a nation wishes to demonstrate its best qualities and character, it usually turns to its arts. For decades the U.S. Department of State has been sending musicians and other performers on tours of other countries. *Porgy and Bess* was one of the first works to be selected for such a tour, for instance. In turn, many other nations take pride in sending their orchestras, choral groups, and dancers to tour America.

These efforts have become increasingly important as nations grow closer together through increased commerce and governmental contacts. For example, the Washington National Opera has recently expanded contacts with various embassies, including holding its major social and fund-raising events at the new embassies of both Russia and China. Not only have these occasions led to greater financial and governmental cooperation, they also presented promising young performers and the music of the host country. In short, music has a value that reaches well beyond itself. America would certainly be poorer artistically, financially, and in its international relations without music and the other arts.

It is important, therefore, to know about and understand the other residents of our global village, including their cultures and their arts. Learning about the music of other peoples is no longer an academic exercise. It has become an essential aspect of being an educated person. Not only is it useful to know something about folk/ethnic music, it is also important to respect and honor the music of other cultures. Their music and way of life are as logical and right for them as ours are for us.

HOW ARE FOLK AND ETHNIC MUSIC DIFFERENT?

What is different about most folk and ethnic music? What features do most such music have in common?

Lack of Uniformity

A symphony by Mozart is published in notation. Therefore, when it is performed by competent musicians, it sounds similar from one performance to another. As for musical instruments, a modern B-flat clarinet is very much like thousands of other B-flat clarinets.

It's different with most folk music. A song may be performed in a particular way by an individual, and another person in the same culture living only a few miles away may perform it quite differently. A homemade musical instrument is truly one of a kind, although it may be similar to other instruments. The lack of uniformity makes it difficult to determine which version of a song is the most authentic one. That fact makes study of various kinds of music even more interesting and challenging.

Creation

Folk and ethnic music are usually created by an individual, which is also true of concert music. But there the similarity ends. In concert music, the composer is closely identified with his or her composition—Beethoven's Fifth Symphony, Prokofiev's Third Piano Concerto, and so on. On the other hand, the originator of a folk melody is rarely known. In fact, he or she might not even admit to such an accomplishment, because in some cultures songs are supposed to be gifts from the gods. Besides, in folk music no one seems to know or care who created a song.

Individual Changes

There is another reason that the creator of a folk song is seldom recognized. Once the song is created, a process of modification begins. Performers usually feel free to make changes, generally small ones. Over the years a song can evolve to become quite different from how it started out. A folk song is a living organism; it is ever changing. That is one of the virtues of folk music.

Importance of the Performers

Because folk music is seldom set in notation, and because modifications are accepted and even encouraged, performers of folk and ethnic music have a much more important role than they do in Western concert music. No longer are they confined to the role of being a re-creator of a work from notation. They can become at least co-creators of the music.

Improvisation

One of the reasons that performers have such an important role is that often they are expected to *improvise*—to make up music on the spot. However, they do not usually improvise out of thin air—that is, without any guidelines at all. Each type of music (African, Hindu religious, jazz, and so on) has performance traditions and practices that musicians are expected to follow. It's a bit like a basketball team: The players have some plays or plans for scoring and defense, but usually they have to adjust them on the spot, depending on what the other team does. They operate within a system, but yet they have the freedom to try their own ideas when it seems desirable.

Audience

Today we are used to having music performed for an audience, either in person or by listening to a recording. In the case of folk and ethnic music, the audience, if there is one at all, is much less important. In many parts of the world, music is performed at events in which everyone participates; there are few listeners as such. Some of the time, the music is performed as part of a ceremony to appease to or to thank gods, which makes a human audience irrelevant.

When an audience becomes unimportant, performers no longer need to worry about people *liking* their music. It also removes any commercial considerations, because no tickets or royalties are possible. Therefore, folk and most ethnic music is created for reasons other than to make money.

Subtleties, Shadings, and Sophistication

Each type of music contains a number of small things that contribute much to its character and are an integral part of the music. For example, in some styles of music the performers "bend" or "shade" certain tones in a melody to make the music more expressive. Shading is an integral part of traditional Japanese music. In its traditional culture it is believed that a melody sung without such inflections lacks expression. Such sophisticated subtleties are easily overlooked by listeners not familiar with the particular musical style, because the music already sounds so different to them.

In general, when a musical style is strong in one element, it is relatively undeveloped in some others. African music, for example, is noted for its rhythms, but its other aspects are less notable. Balinese music contains a kaleidoscope of timbres, but it does not have the harmonic or melodic interest of many other types.

Most folk and ethnic music consists of short works, often songs. True, some African rituals last for hours, but the same music tends to be repeated over and over with only slight variations. Without a system of notation, works of music are usually rather short-winded. This short length doesn't allow much time for the development of themes, something that is important in Western concert music.

Oral Tradition

Much of the world's music is never rendered in notation. Yet some of the music that has existed for hundreds of years has not, as far as can be determined, been forgotten or changed in a noticeable way. How is this possible? By passing it from one person or generation to another by word of mouth, what is known as **oral tradition**. It is difficult for those of us who are used to preserving thoughts in writing or through recordings to understand the ability that people can acquire to remember what they hear. When they want or need to, people can recall quite accurately, especially if the song or story is not too long.

Some of the music described in the following chapters is ethnic music, not folk music. This is especially true of the music of Bali, India, Japan, and China. American and European popular music has, and continues to have, a major impact on popular music throughout the world. A popular song in Japan or Brazil or India, for instance, often contains elements of Western popular music, as well as the musical traditions of that particular country. These songs are hybrids. Technology and ease of travel by airplane have indeed brought the human race closer together, especially in the area of popular music.

Preservation

Until about a hundred years ago, almost no one seemed to care about preserving folk or ethnic music. Western intellectuals did not seem to consider it worth saving, and the musicians who created and performed it seemed happy with what oral tradition had given them. Over the years, interest in preserving and studying folk and ethnic music increased. Today a number of ethnomusicologists with recorders and notepads are working and living in many parts of the globe in an attempt to preserve this vast musical treasure.

FOLK/ETHNIC INSTRUMENTS

A vast number of musical instruments have been created throughout the world. Although each has unique characteristics, folk/ethnic instruments have been classified by scholars into four broad groups according to the way they produce sounds.

Aerophones

This category comprises instruments that are played by blowing. The most common of these are flutes. Some are played sideways, as we are accustomed to seeing today, but many are played straight in front of the player's mouth. One type of flute found among the natives of Oceania and Hawaii is blown through the nose.

Some reed **aerophones** are also found. Some of these use a double reed like that of an oboe; others have a single reed and mouthpiece like that of a clarinet. The *pungi* played by snake charmers in India is an example of a reed instrument (Figure 40.2). Actually, the music is wasted on the snakes, which have no hearing. The snakes respond to the swaying body of the charmer. In case you were wondering, the snake's fangs have been removed.

FIGURE 40.2
AEROPHONE A SNAKE CHARMER PLAYS FOR A PAIR OF COBRAS IN VARANASI, INDIA.

© Luisa Puccini/Shutterstock.com

Animal horns are simple instruments that approach the buzzing of the lip membranes on brass instruments. They are hollowed out and blown from the small end. The Jewish *shofar* is one such instrument.

WATCH...
a performance of an unusual ideophone online.

Ideophones

These are the percussion instruments other than drums. Bells, chimes, xylophones, and rattles are all examples of **ideophones** (Figure 40.3).

FIGURE 40.3
IDEOPHONES IN BALI, GAMELAN MUSICIANS PLAY TRADITIONAL IDEOPHONES.

Membranophones

Membranophones are all the types of drums encountered throughout the world. Drums are constructed from wood, metal, coconut shells, and clay. Some are struck with sticks, others are hit with the hand or fingers, and friction drums are rubbed with a piece of animal hide. Some have straight sides, others taper in, and a few have the shape of an hourglass.

WATCH...
a demonstration of a talking drum online.

Chordophones

This fourth group includes all string instruments (Figure 40.4). Most of these are plucked—harps, lyres, and zithers. The strings on some **chordophones** are struck with mallets, and a few are bowed as on a violin or cello.

Unlike orchestral instruments, which are quite standardized, folk instruments lack uniformity. They may be similar to one another, but no two are alike. And they are traditionally taught individually, usually by rote. Because there are few instruction books for learning to play them, and the way they are played varies widely.

WATCH...
a performance of a group playing zithers online.

MUSIC AND CULTURE

All the many types of music in the world are products of particular societies and cultures. Although all societies have some type of music, many do not even have a word for music. In some instances, it's the same as the word for "work." In one Native American tribe the word means "song," and it includes dancing and ritual.

As has been pointed out, music and the other arts provide much insight into the character and customs of a people. The cultural difference between a piano concerto by Prokofiev,

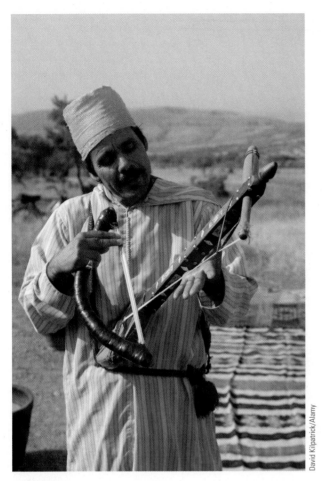

David Kilpatrick/Alamy

FIGURE 40.4

A CHORDOPHONE, IN THIS CASE A FOLK FIDDLE, PLAYED BY A TRADITIONAL MOROCCAN PLAYER AND SINGER NEAR MARRAKESH, MOROCCO.

for example, and a song of the Aleuts in Alaska lies in the relative importance of the cultural elements. In the case of the Aleut music (and almost all other folk and ethnic music), a knowledge of language, customs, thought forms, and other aspects of culture is necessary for a good understanding of the music. The Prokofiev piano concerto is much more able to stand alone. It is not as embedded in everyday culture, at least to most of us in Western civilization it isn't.

It is, of course, possible to analyze a folk or ethnic work apart from its cultural setting, but the music can lose much of its meaning when this is done. In fact, some Indian scholars object to putting Hindu ragas in notation and to discussing only the features of the music. They are correct in their concern for the cultural relevance of the music, but the amount of time one can devote to learning about any given type of music is limited. Therefore, we have no choice but to consider mainly the musical aspects in college-level music courses.

LISTENING TO FOLK AND ETHNIC MUSIC

Listening to folk or most ethnic music requires a somewhat different approach from what is needed for listening to concert music (Figure 40.5). Listening to what happens in a melody and the rhythm of a work is still necessary, but the listener must also consider the cultural factors.

Here is but one example of this fact. An ethnomusicologist studying Mexican music wanted to hear a certain song that was sung for a particular festival. He located the performer, who didn't want to sing it. "We're not having the festival now," he explained. Finally, the man was coaxed into singing it, but he broke into laughter before finishing it. Why? Because singing the song apart from the festival seemed ridiculous to him.

One way to think about and listen to folk and ethnic music is to imagine two columns. One column is under the heading *Musical* and the other is under the heading

FIGURE 40.5

IN *FOLK* AND *ETHNIC* MUSIC, SOCIOCULTURAL CONSIDERATIONS OUTWEIGH MUSICAL FACTORS, WHEREAS IN ART/CONCERT MUSIC, THE OPPOSITE IS TRUE.

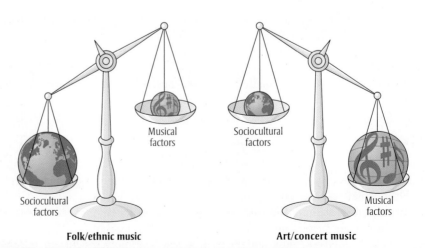

Musical factors

Sociocultural factors

Sociocultural factors

Musical factors

Folk/ethnic music

Art/concert music

© Cengage Learning®

Sociocultural. Here is an example that could easily be true of much of the music from Africa.

Musical	Sociocultural
Drums in several sizes	From Africa
Polyrhythms	Highly trained drummers
Very steady tempo	Everyone participates
Call-and-response	Male drummers and soloist
Some improvisation	Aspects of a tonal language
Simple melody	Simple dances to music
Phrases often repeated	Performed "by ear"—no notation
African singing style	Instruments of skins and gourds

As with most types of music, several hearings of the same piece are recommended so that you become somewhat accustomed to the style. Keep in mind, too, that the folk music was not created as concert music, but it is very effective in relating its message and in representing a culture.

MAIN POINTS OF CHAPTER 40

1. Folk music is the music of the common people of a particular nation or ethnic group. Ethnic music is identified with a particular culture and is usually performed by trained musicians.

2. It is important to know something about folk/ethnic music because elements of it are sometimes found in concert music; it reveals the attitudes and values of a culture; and the peoples of the world today are interconnected as never before.

3. Performers of ethnic music are often expected to improvise. Each type of music, however, has performance traditions and practices that the musicians are expected to follow.

4. Folk/ethnic music differs from concert music in several ways:

   - Creators of such music are usually unknown.
   - Performers usually feel free to make small changes in it.
   - Some of it is largely improvised within the guidelines of the type of music.
   - The response of an audience, if there is one, is not important.
   - It contains subtleties that are easily missed by persons who are unfamiliar with that type of music.
   - Much of it does not exist in notation, but is preserved by oral tradition.

5. Folk/ethnic instruments can be divided into four groups according to how they produce sounds.

   - Aerophones produce sound when air is blown into them.
   - Ideophones are percussion instruments other than drums such as rattles and xylophones.
   - Membranophones include the wide variety of drums with heads made from animal skin.
   - Chordophones include all types of string instruments.

6. Cultural elements are more important in folk/ethnic music than they are in concert music.

 DO...
online quizzes that your instructor may assign for a grade.

41 Folk Music *of* Europe *and the* Americas

START...
experiencing this chapter's topics with an online video activity that your instructor may assign.

READ...
the complete chapter text in a rich interactive eBook!

Learning Objectives

1 Describe the nature of folk music in western and eastern Europe.
2 Identify types and features of American folk music.
3 Outline the development of African American folk music.
4 List the features of folk music in Central and South America.

Europe stretches from the Ural Mountains in Russia several thousand miles west to England and Ireland. With the settling of North and South America by the various nations of Europe, the culture of western European civilization was transported across the Atlantic Ocean and later halfway around the world to Australia and New Zealand. The emigrants from Europe came upon lands already occupied by Native Americans in the north and Incas, Aztecs, and other peoples to the south. Later, slaves were brought to the Western Hemisphere from Africa.

The resulting combination of music from multiple countries and sources is a wealth of music styles, with each influencing and enriching the others.

WESTERN EUROPEAN FOLK MUSIC

European folk music is built around the features presented in Part I. These include melody, harmony, timbre, accompaniment, form, subject matter, and rhythm.

Melody

Melodies are built on the seven-note major and minor scales. In addition, many folk melodies use seven-note scales other than major or minor, or what are termed *modes*. A few pentatonic scales are encountered, particularly in Eastern Europe. A **pentatonic scale** has five notes in the pattern of the black keys on a piano. Generally, the range of the melodies is about one octave, and they do not contain many repeated notes.

Harmony

Accompanying chords are built in thirds, with the three primary chords predominating. The presence of harmony is an important difference between Western music and much of the music of other parts of the world.

Timbre

The style of singing found in Western folk music is natural and relaxed, at least to Western ears. Many folk singers use little vibrato, and no attempt is made to impress listeners with the singer's vocal prowess. The instruments used in folk music are equally unpretentious. The guitar, accordion, harmonica (mouth organ), dulcimer, and other easily transported instruments are generally used. The dulcimer looks like a long, flat violin with three strings. It is placed on the player's lap and plucked with a quill. Two of its strings produce a drone.

Although most Western folk music consists of songs, there is a body of instrumental music associated with dances. The fiddle tunes found in western Europe and America are part of this tradition.

Accompaniment

Originally, folk music was often performed without any accompaniment. Most of it is now accompanied by an instrument, however, which is often played by the singer.

Form

A characteristic of Western folk music is the singing of different sets of words to the same melody. As mentioned in Chapter 23, the musical term for the repeating of a song with different verses, or *stanzas*, is **strophic**. Although some European folk songs have twenty or more stanzas, four or five is typical.

Subject Matter

European folk songs include a larger percentage of epic tales and love sentiments than is found in other cultures. One important type of song is the **ballad**. Its words tell a story, often a sad one, in five or more stanzas. Traditionally, ballads are sung by one singer. In English ballads the singer usually relates a tale about someone else, which gives the song a sense of detachment. In American ballads the singer often sings about himself or herself, but an attitude of detachment is nevertheless retained.

Rhythm

The rhythm of Western folk music is regular and metrical. Traditionally, ballads have a common iambic meter and stanzas of four lines in which a four-foot line alternates with a three-foot line.

Although European folk music is not noted for its complicated rhythms, it certainly is enough so the group performing *Riverdance* can develop some stunning dance routines.

 WATCH...
a performance from *Riverdance* online.

Ballads

"Barbara Allen" (see Listening Guide) is a good example of a ballad as well as of many characteristics of Western folk music. It is the most popular ballad of the Western world and hundreds of versions exist. Samuel Pepys wrote of singing "Barbara Allen" on January 2, 1666, in London. Both the English and the Scots claim the song, and some ninety-eight versions of it were found in Virginia alone!

ENGLISH BALLAD
"Barbara Allen" (late 1600s)

Genre: Ethnic music

Form: Strophic, ballad

Download 87

4 minutes 28 seconds

0:00	The first verse begins after a short guitar introduction.	
0:08	1. In Scarlet town where I was born, there was a fair maid dwellin', made many a youth cry well a-day, and her name was Barb'ry Allen.	

0:32   2. Twas in the merry month of May, when green buds they were swellin', Sweet William came from the west country, and he courted Barb'ry Allen.

(continued)

LISTENING GUIDE

0:55	3.	He sent his servant unto her,
		to the place where she was dwellin',
		"My master's sick, bids me call for you,
		if your name be Barb'ry Allen."

1:20	4.	Well, slowly, slowly she got up,
		and slowly went she nigh him,
		but all she said as she passed his bed,
		"Young man, I think you're dying."

1:42	5.	He turned his pale face to the wall,
		and busted out a cryin',
		"Adieu, adieu, my dear friends all,
		Be kind to Barb'ry Allen."

2:05	6.	Well, lightly tripped she down the stairs.
		she heard those church bells tollin',
		and each bell seemd to say as it tolled,
		"Hard-hearted Barb'ry Allen."

2:27	7.	And she looked east, and she looked west.
		She seen his pale corpse a-comin',
		"Lay down, lay down that corpse of clay,
		that I may look upon him."

2:55	8.	"Oh, mother, mother go make my bed,
		go make it long and narrow.
		Sweet William died for me today.
		I'll die for him tomorrow."

3:20	9.	They buried Sweet William in the old
		churchyard.
		They buried Barbara beside him.
		Out of his grave grew a red, red rose,
		and out of hers a briar.

3:48	10.	They grew and grew up the old church wall,
		'till they could grow no higher.
		And at the top, twined in a lovers' knot,
		the red rose and the briar.

LISTEN TO... this selection streaming online.

WATCH... a performance of this selection online.

WATCH... an Active Listening Guide of this selection online.

DO... an online Listening Practice Activity related to this selection, which your instructor may assign for a grade.

In addition to its metrical rhythm, "Barbara Allen" has a simple melody that is largely built out of the notes of its main chord. The singer on the recording, Pete Seeger, uses a plain, unemotional style as he accompanies his singing on a guitar. Notice also that even though the text is sad, the melody doesn't reflect that fact. Maybe it's because the song is telling about what happened to someone else. A balled is not a "woe's me" song.

EASTERN EUROPEAN FOLK MUSIC

Americans tend to think that Europe ends with Germany or Poland, which is not really accurate. Another thousand miles east of Berlin lies Moscow, the capital of the huge Russian Federation with its rich culture. In many ways, its folk music is not greatly different from that of Eastern Europe, but it does reveal influences of the music from contacts with Asian cultures.

The video in this chapter's online engagement activity shows a concert at which a wide variety of Russian folk music was presented. The athletic style of dancing is a feature of the Cossacks from southern Russia.

Another country in Eastern Europe is Hungary. It's one of the smaller nations that has maintained its identity through several invasions and occupations by larger European and Middle Eastern powers including German, Russia, and Turkey. As is true of several other European counties, it has a sizable ethnic minority that has contributed to its culture.

WATCH... a video of a native Hungarian instrument online.

The cimbalom is a native instrument from Hungary that is often played by gypsies. It is a chordophone that produces sounds when its strings are struck with a mallet. It is also similar to a piano, in that its sounds may be damped by the use of a foot pedal.

NORTH AMERICAN FOLK MUSIC

Just as English is the predominant language in the United States, the British Isles are the main source of its folk music (Figure 41.1). Many songs were imported from England, and many others are patterned after British types. Folk music scholars in the early twentieth century found Elizabethan English folk songs better preserved in remote Appalachian hamlets than in England itself. The style of performance is also closely related to its English heritage.

Non-British music came to America in the nineteenth century in various immigrant groups. In a few cases, their music was incorporated into the culture. For example, "Du, du liegst mir im Herzen" is a German song that has been adopted into the culture; "Alouette" is a French-Canadian example; "Chiapanecas" ("Mexican Clapping Song") is a Latin American contribution that is clapped and stomped at many major-league ballparks.

Some non-British songs have had new words set to their melodies. The Pennsylvania Dutch song "Marjets wann ich uffschteh" became "Go Tell Aunt Rhody." (The word *Dutch* as used in *Pennsylvania Dutch* is a distortion of *Deutsch*, which is the German word for "German.") Unfortunately, much non-British music was lost in America. Still, there are various types of American folk music.

Gary Miller/Getty Images

FIGURE 41.1
FOLK ARTIST SHAWN COLVIN

Work Songs

Songs that accompany labor are not characteristic of American folk music, except for sea chanteys and African American music. **Chantey** is pronounced "shantey." "Blow the Man Down" is an example of a sea chantey. Its words hardly convey a deep message:

> Come all ye young fellows that follow the sea,
>   to the way haye, blow the man down,
> And pray, pay attention and listen to me,
>   give me some time to blow the man down.

Occupational Songs

Although few songs accompanied work, many of them were about work. Cowboy ballads, which were modeled after the English ballad, often had a melancholy tone. In "The Cowboy's Lament," the dying young man says:

> Get sixteen gamblers to carry my coffin
> Six purty maidens to sing me a song,
> Take me to the valley and lay the sod o'er me,
> For I'm a young cowboy an' know I done wrong.

The development of the railroads provided another source for occupational songs. Some of them are about men who built the railroads ("Drill, Ye Tarriers, Drill"), some describe famous personalities ("John Henry" and "Casey Jones"), and others tell about particular trains ("Wabash Cannonball").

"The Ox-Driving Song" tells about the troubles of the teamsters who drove their wagons over muddy roads and washouts:

> When I got there, the hills were steep,
> 'twould make any tenderhearted person weep
> to hear me cuss and pop my whip
> and see my oxen pull and slip.

Dance Music

The most important type of folk dancing was square dancing. If no instruments were available, the dancers sang the music as they danced. Usually, the words had little significance; sometimes words were added simply to complete a line of music. A good example of dance music is "Skip to My Lou":

Flies in the buttermilk, two by two,
flies in the buttermilk, two by two,
flies in the buttermilk, two by two,
skip to my Lou, my darling!

CHORUS:
She's gone again, skip to my Lou,
she's gone again, skip to my Lou,
she's gone again, skip to my Lou,
skip to my Lou, my darling.
My girl wears a number nine shoe,
my girl wears a number nine shoe,
my girl wears a number nine shoe,
skip to my Lou, my darling.

CHORUS

WATCH...
Lindsey Stirling's contemporary fiddle playing and a traditional bluegrass celebration online.

Dance music was often played on fiddles. Most of the tunes, called **hoedowns** or **breakdowns**, were in a fast tempo with two beats to the measure. Their heritage is the reels and hornpipes from the British Isles. Jigs were also popular fiddle music for dancing. Fiddle tunes had some imaginative titles: "Devil's Dream," "Lost Indian," "Orange Blossom Special," "Leather Britches," and others.

The fiddle and the violin are the same—sort of. The difference comes in the way they are played. Fiddlers handle the bow somewhat differently and hold the instrument lower in front of the chest (Figure 41.2). No vibrato is used. One old catalog lists a "Special Stradivarius Model" for $9.95, including bow, case, extra strings, instruction book, and fingering chart!

Self-Expression

Many songs, in both folk and concert music, serve to express deep feelings. The white spiritual "The Wayfaring Stranger" is one example:

I'm just a poor, wayfaring stranger,
A-trav'ling through this world of woe,
Yet there's no sickness, no toil, no danger,
In that fair land to which I go.
I'm goin' there to see my mother,
I'm goin' there no more to roam,
I'm just a-goin' over Jordan,
I'm just a-goin' over home.

"A-goin' over Jordan" refers to dying.

Arrangements

Sometimes composers find songs that they consider worth arranging for concert or recital hall performance. They leave the original melody largely intact and devise an

FIGURE 41.2
PERFORMANCE ARTIST LINDSEY STIRLING, QUARTER-FINALIST IN *AMERICA'S GOT TALENT* 2010, COMBINES CLASSICALLY INSPIRED FIDDLE-STYLE PLAYING WITH DANCE MOVES FROM TODAY.

Taylor Hill/FilmMagic/Getty Image

accompaniment for piano or orchestra. Aaron Copland did this with the Shaker song "Simple Gifts."

The accompaniment for "Simple Gifts" is in keeping with the text and melody by being open and uncluttered. There are only very brief introductory measures based on the melody for each section of the song. Sometimes the chords are sounded off the beat in a subtle way, but generally everything is plain and understated.

Native American Music

Native Americans came to the Americas during the Ice Age thousands of years ago, when an ice bridge existed across the Bering Strait between Siberia and Alaska. Their music differs very much from that of the English tradition.

The functional nature of Native American music is apparent in the names given to the rituals. A sun dance or a rabbit dance (Figure 41.3) was created for a specific purpose. Sometimes that purpose was to appease or influence spirits, and at other times it was to sing about events in life.

Native American instruments traditionally consisted of a variety of drums, usually played with sticks. Many types of rattles were also developed. Several kinds of flutes were played, especially by the men, who performed love music on them to impress their chosen young women.

The Native American population was never large by modern standards, and it was spread over a vast land area. It was no more than one to two million in all of the United States and Canada. Its music differs according to the particular tribe and geographic location.

Among many examples of Native American music is that created by the Siberian Yupik peoples in Alaska. One community is on St. Lawrence Island in the Bering Sea just a short distance from the eastern coast of Russia. In the village of Savoonga, population about 700, the subsistence diet consists of largely whale meat, fish, and seal, because almost nothing grows in that climate. Their island environment is a habitat shared with walrus, seals, whales, and other marine mammals. The main musical instrument of the Yupiks is a frame drum about two feet in diameter covered by a marine mammal membrane—usually made from walrus stomach. It is played using a drumstick crafted from driftwood. They make much use of these drums (Figure 41.4) as they dance and chant, often in formal and informal social settings.

The Yupik culture incorporates dance as a means of storytelling. The combination of chant and dance varies stylistically depending on the specific region where the tribes live. The Yupiks in central Alaska tend to use longer and more sustained phrases than do the villages to the north. These days, most performances take place in gatherings in school gyms or community halls.

- The Eskimos and the tribes of the Pacific Northwest developed music characterized by nonstrophic forms, complex rhythms, and small melodic intervals.
- The tribes of California and the extreme Southwest sing with a harsh vocal sound. Their songs consist of two or more separate sections that are repeated, alternated, and interwoven.

FIGURE 41.3
A NATIVE AMERICAN DANCER

FIGURE 41.4
ALASKAN NATIVE DRUM

- A third broad area includes Utah, Nevada, and the interior of northern California. In this region the singing is more relaxed in style, and the songs are made up of paired phrases, with each phrase repeated.
- A fourth type of Native American culture is distinguished more by language than geography. It consists of the Navajo, Apache, and some western Canadian tribes. Their melodies have a wide range, and male singers freely perform in high, falsetto voices.
- The Pueblo and Plains tribes display more tension in singing and favor a two-part song form.
- Native American songs in the eastern and southern parts of the United States feature singing responsively, with shouts tossed back and forth between leader and group.

Music of Native America has not had much effect on the other types of American music for two reasons. First, most Native Americans did not live close to non–Native Americans. They have often lived apart on reservations, and their music has tended to be confined to the tribe. No Native American music was found in concerts before about 1890, and even today there are very few works that show the influence of this music.

Second, Native American music is quite different from Western music. In some respects, it is more Asian than Western. When one culture incorporates music from another, the two styles are likely to be similar. Some change—but not too much—is accepted in a musical style. In the few instances in which Native American music has been incorporated into compositions, it has been changed quite a bit.

AFRICAN AMERICAN MUSIC

In a complex and pluralistic society such as the United States, the sources of the cultural mixture are hard to determine, so it is difficult to know which aspects of African American music were transplanted from Africa and which were developed in America. In any case, some of the African rhythmic ideas, call-and-response patterns, love of instruments, and improvisation are now part of American music. Africans brought something perhaps more important than any technical features: a strong interest in music and a desire to involve listeners in the music.

Calls and Hollers

One early and important feature of African American folk music was the spontaneous individual calls and hollers heard in the fields and other workplaces. Their purpose was to relieve loneliness and stress, as well as to express feelings. Sometimes hollers were used to warn other slaves of impending danger.

Musically, they were short melodic fragments that were highly decorated. They were mostly improvised. Few calls and hollers were recorded before they largely disappeared, but they played a role in the development of the blues, which led directly to jazz.

Spirituals

An important form of African American religious folk music was the **spiritual**. Until after the Civil War, these songs existed by oral tradition among blacks. The first book of spirituals containing both words and music was not published until 1867.

During Reconstruction, several colleges for the recently freed slaves were established in the South by various church groups. To help raise money by giving concerts, singing groups were formed at these colleges, most notably the Fisk Jubilee Singers at Fisk University in Nashville (Figure 41.5). Initially, the group sang a variety of songs, but no spirituals. They soon found, however, that spirituals were enthusiastically received by

WATCH...
a modern spiritual performance online.

Michael Ochs Archives/Getty Images

FIGURE 41.5
THE FISK JUBILEE SINGERS IN
SEVEN YEARS, THEY RAISED
$150,000, A LARGE AMOUNT OF
MONEY AT THAT TIME.

audiences. The Fisk Jubilee Singers were both a musical and a financial success as they toured New York City; Washington, D.C.; and Europe.

Spirituals drew heavily on biblical texts. Some of these texts use Bible stories as thinly veiled parallels to the plight of the African Americans as slaves. The spiritual "Go Down, Moses" is a good example:

> When Israel was in Egypt's land,
>   Let my people go.
> Oppressed so hard they could not stand,
>   Let my people go.

Spirituals were sung with much inflection and subtlety. What is seen in the notation of a spiritual is only the skeletal outline for what was actually sung. In fact, quite a bit of improvising took place during the singing. Spirituals were originally sung by a group, not a solo singer.

Folk Blues

Blues songs were the most important type of secular folk music among African Americans. In contrast to spirituals, blues songs were for individual singers to cry out against life's problems. The topics of the blues ranged from problems with work (too much or not enough), crime, infidelity, loneliness, and rejection. These sentiments were generally sung in a three-line form (*a a b*).

> My mama told me before I left home,
> My mama told me before I left home,
> You better let them Jacksonville women alone.

Furthermore, lines of the blues are harmonized in a rudimentary way. The musical interest was in the way the melody was sung. Blues singers tend to slide between pitches to put more emotion in the music. Many embellishments are also added. Usually, singing blues is accompanied by the guitar. Sometimes it is played in "bottleneck" style by running a knife blade on the strings, which creates a timbre something like that of a Hawaiian guitar.

Work Songs

Songs created to accompany work are definitely a contribution of African Americans. The song text is not always related to the job at hand; often the words are only to supply a pleasant accompaniment to labor.

Instruments

Particular instruments are prominent in African American folk music, just as they are in Africa. Some instruments are conventional; others are intended to provide sound effects. Included in the latter category are washboards, pans, cowbells, bottles, various clappers, and the gutbucket. It is an inverted washtub with a rope pulled through it, which is connected to a stick. The pitch is varied according to the tension the player exerts on the stick and thereby the rope.

LATIN AMERICAN MUSIC

Latin American music includes a wide variety of types, partly because the music of Spain, the parent culture of Central and South America, is so varied. Spanish music includes the music of the gypsies and the Basque people of northern Spain, Arabian influences resulting from six hundred years of occupation by the Moors, and French influence from Provence. With the Spanish conquests in the New World, elements of its music were transported to the Americas.

In addition to the influences of Spanish and Portuguese colonialism, the music of Central and South America was heavily influenced by African music brought by black slaves. This influence is especially strong in Haiti and the other Caribbean nations of Cuba, Jamaica, and Trinidad, the Guianas on the northern coast of South America, and northern Brazil. Central and South America also have large Indian populations, which in some areas have retained their native languages. Recent emigrations from Asia have also played a role in the music of Latin America.

What has resulted from the contacts among these four groups is a varied and wonderfully mixed heritage. Many countries have terms for these mixed cultures, such as *mestizo* (Native American and Spanish), *mulato* (African and Spanish), and *zambo* (African and Native American).

Since the Spanish came to the New World, the various types of music have been adapted so much that it is often impossible to tell the origins of a particular style of music. For example, the *bolero* was originally Spanish, but in Cuba its rhythm became more complex. Among other features that carried over from Spanish music are the frequent use of rhythms having three notes to the beat, the presence of a line of harmony moving parallel to the melody but three notes below, and melodies with a narrow range.

Mexican music is largely Spanish in character, more so than most Latin American music. Although some Mexican Indians have retained their musical heritage, Indian influence is not significant in Mexican music. The Mexicans have a narrative type of song called a **corrido**. Like the English ballad, it relates a happening or tells a story.

Instruments play an important role in Mexican music and are sometimes featured in interludes of songs. The often-heard *mariachi band* consists of from three to twelve performers playing violins, guitars, trumpets, and other instruments (Figure 41.6).

Another type of Latin American music is the **son**, which appeared during the early part of the twentieth century and became a popular urban type of music played by groups consisting of strings and percussion. In the recording of "Sones de Hausteca" associated with this book (see Listening Guide), the violin player shows the influence of the virtuoso style of concert violinists in the United States. Two of the male singers sing in parallel thirds, which is typical of Mexican music. At times, the harmony and melody don't fit together all that well.

WATCH...
a mariachi band perform online.

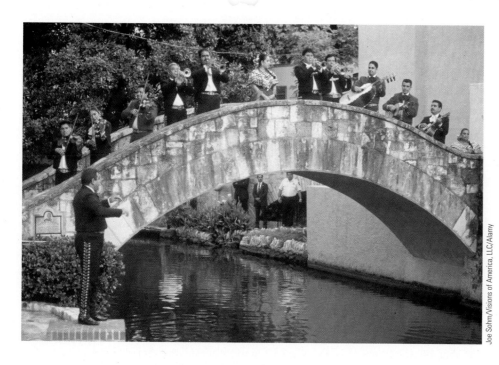

FIGURE 41.6
**MARIACHI BAND ON RIVER
WALK.** A MARIACHI BAND
PERFORMS ON A FOOTBRIDGE IN
SAN ANTONIO, TEXAS.

Joe Sohm/Visions of America, LLC/Alamy

MEXICAN FOLK SONG
"Sones de Hausteca"

Genre: Ethnic music

Form: *Son*

Download 88

1 minute 48 seconds

0:00	Violinist begins and is soon accompanied by guitar.
0:30	Male singer enters, sometimes sliding his voice up into falsetto (false high voice).
0:40	Two other men join in, singing in thirds.
0:49	Soloist sings the melody.
0:57	Violinist solos with many fast notes.
1:38	Rhythmic pattern with short repeated notes is heard in violin and guitar.
1:48	Recording fades.

LISTEN TO... this selection streaming online.

WATCH... an Active Listening Guide of this selection online.

DO... an online Listening Practice Activity related to this selection, which your instructor may assign for a grade.

LISTENING GUIDE

SOUTH AMERICAN MUSIC

WATCH...
Peruvian flute music online.

The nations of South America have rich musical culture. It is similar in many ways to that of Latin American nations like Mexico, but South America has a number of different instruments as well as nations in which Portuguese is spoken instead of Spanish. And the populations of some of its countries, especially Argentina, contains large subgroups of immigrants from Europe. An instrument that is heard often in Peru is a flute consisting of a row of bamboo pipes that the player blows across as he or she maneuvers the instrument to sound different pitches.

MAIN POINTS OF CHAPTER 41

1. European folk music is similar to American folk music in most respects. Melodies in the five-note pentatonic scale are encountered more often, especially in the music of Eastern Europe.

2. Many European folk songs are strophic, with different verses sung to the same melody. Ballads are songs in which the singer relates a story, often a sad one, in five or more verses.

3. American folk music is a mixture of music from many different sources, especially the British Isles.

4. Several types of American folk music can be identified. They include work and occupational songs, dance music, and songs in which singers express their feelings.

5. Dance music was often played on violins (fiddles). Square dancing with its quick tempo and duple meter was the most prevalent type of dance music.

6. Music of native Americans varied a great deal according to tribe and region. Most of it is functional music. It is quite different from most Western music and therefore not easily assimilated into it.

7. Music instruments of native American cultures are frequently made from materials found in the natural environment, including animal skins that are the product of subsistence living.

8. Many features of African American music have been incorporated into American music. These include spontaneous calls and hollers, spirituals, work songs, and folk melodies in which individual singers cry out against life's problems.

9. Latin American music is a mixture from a variety of sources, especially Spanish, Indian, and African. Mexican music includes a ballad-like *corrido* and small instrumental groups called *mariachi*.

PRACTICE...
your understanding of this chapter's concepts by working once more with the chapter's Active Listening Guides online.

DO...
online quizzes that your instructor may assign for a grade.

Music *of* Africa *and* the Middle East

42

Learning Objectives

1 Discuss features of African music and its performance.
2 Describe the main characteristics of Middle Eastern music.
3 Identify the features of Jewish folk music.

 START...
experiencing this chapter's topics with an online video activity that your instructor may assign.

 READ...
the complete chapter text in a rich interactive eBook!

The continent of Africa (Figure 42.1) is a huge landmass about a fourth larger than all of North America. The Sahara extends for thousands of miles across its upper half. To the south of the Sahara are the black peoples whom we usually associate with that continent. For the remainder of this book, the word *African* refers to the music from the southern two-thirds of the continent.

To the north of the Sahara, and especially to the east extending from Egypt in the northeastern corner to Iran and Pakistan north of India, lies what is often referred to as the Middle East. These peoples are largely Muslim, with Turks and Arabs being the largest ethnic groups. Sitting in the middle among these countries is Israel, with its unique heritage.

The musics of sub-Saharan Africa and the Middle East contain many differences within them, and this discussion can offer only a small sample of each overall type of music.

AFRICAN MUSIC

What are the main characteristics of the music of the peoples who live south of the Sahara? Many of the features of folk music mentioned in Chapter 41 are found in African music, but several are particularly important.

FIGURE 42.1
AFRICA AND THE WORLD

Relationship with Language

African languages are tonal in character. In such languages the meaning of sound varies depending on the pitch and manner in which it is spoken. Because they are tonal, African languages have a musical quality about them. There is a strong similarity between the songlike quality of a language and the music of the people who speak it. At best, rendering non-Western music in notation can only approximate the actual sounds.

Even the drums used in some African music attempt to imitate the pitches and inflections of the language. These "talking drums" are capable of sending messages that are clearly understood by the people who speak that particular language. Actually, the drums do not "talk" so much as they signal. The process is similar to how bugle calls functioned at one time in an army. You saw a video on how drums work in Chapter 40.

Here is an example of how the pitches of a language influence the rhythm and pitches found in the music:

Text	"Wo ho te sen?" ("How do you do?")
Tone levels	Low high, low high
Rhythm	Short long, short long
Melody	

FIGURE 42.2
MEN PERFORMING AT KOPEYIA DRUMMING VILLAGE IN GHANA

Association with Dance

Just as language is closely related to African music, so is dance. Dance is used in rituals, worship, celebrations, and for recreation. It is also considered a natural accompaniment to the music. Some dances are for just the men, while women participate in others. Much of the time, anyone can join in the dancing, often to be observed and rewarded with coins if the dancer was judged to be good by the onlookers. Few people are passive when African music is being performed.

Rhythm

The music played by groups of percussion instruments best illustrates the complexity of rhythm in African music (Figure 42.2). The music starts out simply with a basic rhythm, or "time line," which might be compared with the role of the bass drum in a marching band in keeping the group together. Soon other percussion instruments are added over the time line part until as many as five distinct rhythm patterns are sounding at the same time—polyrhythm. Then enters the master drummer, who plays the rhythm of a particular piece of music. After a while he gives a rhythmic signal to change to another piece. This process continues until the performance is completed.

Several other points should be mentioned about African instrumental ensembles, especially as found in Ghana and other West African countries.

- Rarely do African drummers tap their feet; they do not think of following a beat as do Western musicians.
- Not only do the rhythm patterns of the various instruments differ but also they do not begin at exactly the

same moment, as is usually true in Western music. In fact, they would lose some of their rhythmic flavor if they did.

- Often it is unclear whether the meter is in two or three beats. At one moment the pattern seems to be clearly two beats to the measure, but a little while later a three-beat pattern may be perceived. This metric ambiguity makes the music more fascinating.

Improvisation

There is less improvising in African percussion ensembles than is generally supposed. The musicians are often playing preexisting music that has been passed on by oral tradition. Performers, especially master drummers, are allowed to make small changes and alterations in the music, partly to relieve tedium. African musicians do not, however, play whatever they happen to feel like playing. They perform within certain clearly understood guidelines.

Functional Music

Music is very much a part of the daily lives of Africans. For example, it is called on to cure illnesses, appease gods, and celebrate the births of babies. There are songs for praising cattle, telling about animal hunts, and paddling a canoe. There is also some music that is simply for entertainment, and a small amount that is played for ceremonies involving a king or chief.

A few African men earn their livelihood from their music making, especially drummers. These musicians learn their trade from infancy. They are carefully taught, often by their fathers, and they do not perform publicly until they become truly competent as young adults.

Because most African music is functional, it does not take place in a performer/audience situation. Musical performances are truly participatory events in which there is little distinction between performer and audience. Because African music is functional, its musicians want their work to have an impact. They do not care whether it is considered "beautiful" in the sense that Western musicians often think about music.

Lack of Uniformity

It has been estimated that sub-Saharan Africa contains between five hundred and seven hundred languages or dialects. Four major languages exist just in the small nation of Zambia. These languages are so different that commerce and government are conducted in English, which was used when Zambia was Northern Rhodesia and under British control. In Kenya, it is not unusual for people to speak as many as three languages— examples are English, Swahili, and one or more tribal dialects such as Maa (spoken by the Maasai tribe) as well as others in regions reflecting the colonization period.

Such diversity of languages is significant in that continent's music because its music and languages are virtually inseparable. Therefore, the music of one tribe may differ a lot from that of another only a few miles away. And the music that is so vital to one tribe often makes little sense to other tribes, even though they both sound like African music to people in Europe and America.

Form

African music features what is termed *call-and-response* form. In this form a leader sings or plays a phrase, and then the group responds with its rendition of the phrase. The pattern is something like a game of musical tennis. Sometimes the response is not identical because members of the group will make small alterations in what they have heard. At other times, the response begins before the original phrase is completed, and the result is a brief period of simple counterpoint.

Some African songs follow a pattern in which the original melody returns or is set in a two-part form.

WATCH...
a video of a native African choir online.

Melodic Characteristics

African melodies are often altered and ornamented with slight changes of pitch, trills, slides, and other decorative notes. Some of the scales on which the music is based are not very different from those found in Western music, but the style in which they are used is quite different.

The tone quality of singing is very open and forceful. Changes of dynamic level are limited.

Beliefs about Music and Instruments

Africans have strong beliefs about the spirit of an instrument. For example, a drum is not just a drum; instead, it has an almost human quality. The maker of a drum wants to make sure the drum "speaks" as it should. So he may unobtrusively pick up pebbles from the yard of a woman known to be a gossip to put in the drum. In addition, he may add a piece of lion skin so that the drum will roar, a piece of frog skin to help the drum remain supple, and pieces of metal so that it will rattle. Other musical instruments are similarly "doctored" to achieve a more interesting sound.

Instruments

 WATCH...
a video of an African talking drum online.

Drums hold the dominant position among African musical instruments. They are constructed of various materials and are made in a variety of sizes. Some are played with the hands; others are played with sticks. An especially interesting drum has an hourglass shape with strings connecting its two heads.

The *mbira*, or thumb piano, is a feature of African music (Figure 42.3). It usually has about eighteen short strips of metal or cane that sound against a resonating box. Simple flutes are also found in African music, as is a single-string instrument called a *gonje*, which is played with a bow.

Other African instruments include a gourd with beads strung around it. It is shaken in performance, often by a woman. A double bell that looks like a cowbell is also heard, as are various rattles, hand claps, and whistles.

P. Kayukwa/lebrecht/The Image Works

FIGURE 42.3
Mbira

 WATCH...
a video of a mbira online.

MIDDLE EASTERN MUSIC

As mentioned earlier, the term *Middle East* usually refers to the Arab world that extends thousands of miles from the northwest coast of Africa from Casablanca on the Atlantic Ocean to the eastern borders of Pakistan north of India (see Figure 42.4). The people who inhabit this vast stretch of land are more united in their religious faith—Islam—than by their culture or language. The people of Iran, for example, consider themselves Persian and speak Farsi, not Arabic. The Turks constitute another major segment of the Middle East, whereas another large segment is centered in Egypt and yet another stretches across North Africa.

Although the land encompassed by the Middle East is large, the population is not, at least in comparison with that of Africa, Europe, or the Far East. The people tend to be spread along the shores of the Mediterranean Sea and the Indian Ocean. They are no more homogeneous than are the peoples of sub-Saharan Africa.

Music of the Middle East is in a difficult situation because most musicians, especially those who perform popular music, are considered low class. Also, in Islam only restrained chanting is allowed of verses from the Koran. The situation is not helped by the fact that in the Middle East music is based on complex and confusing theories that vary from one area to another. Some of these theories maintain that the best music encourages a trancelike higher level of life.

Most Middle Eastern music is monophonic. Singers, who are usually men, produce a tense, nasal tone quality. They also improvise many ornaments to the basic melodic line. Rhythm is treated very freely, which permits singers and instrumentalists to add

FIGURE 42.4
THE MIDDLE EAST

© 2016 Cengage Learning®

David Taylor Photography/Alamy

FIGURE 42.5
EGYPTIAN MUSICIAN PLAYING A REBAB

their own decorative notes to the music. The ornamental figures are very prominent in "Segah," which is from Iran (see Listening Guide).

A number of instruments are associated with music from the Middle East. One is the *ud*, which is a plucked string instrument with a pear-shaped body. Another string instrument is the *rebab* (Figure 42.5), which is generally considered the direct ancestor of the violin. The *tombak* is a drum in the shape of an hourglass that is played with the fingers.

There are few concerts in the Middle East. Most performances are informal, many times in cafés. In that setting one may sip a drink while listening. Also, at family festivities, music and dance play a celebratory role for special occasions or just for social gatherings.

IRAN
"Segah"

Genre: Ethnic music

Download 89

2 minutes 2 seconds

0:00	Violin plays an ornamented melody.
0:31	Singer begins a free-sounding melody with many vocal trills.
0:55	Violin plays a more elaborate melody.
1:10	Singer adds many vocal trills to the melody.

(continued)

LISTENING GUIDE

1:47   Violin again plays highly decorated melody.

2:02   Recording fades.

LISTEN TO... this selection streaming online.

WATCH... an Active Listening Guide of this selection online.

WATCH... a video of a Segah online.

DO... an online Listening Practice Activity related to this selection, which your instructor may assign for a grade.

Jewish Music

Israel is situated in the middle of the Arab world, which over the centuries has created many political tensions and wars. Modern Israel is very different from its neighbors. Not only is it the only well-established democracy in the region; it is also much more Western and up-to-date. It is a nation with a fascinating history.

Over the centuries Jewish religious music has remained rather well unified, in spite of the Diaspora in the middle ages and subsequent centuries, which was the scattering of the Jewish people from Palestine to many different parts of the world. Judaism was much less evangelistic than Christianity. It tended to keep its faith within the group, and it seldom incorporated regional music into its worship.

The traditional religious music of Judaism consisted of prayers and invocations, not anthems and other ensemble music. Today its religious music varies according to the degree of orthodoxy. The more orthodox congregations permit only unaccompanied chanting by cantors; the more liberal congregations (at least in the United States) often employ Gentile instrumentalists and singers and allow them to perform adaptations of music written for Christian worship (with some words changed). The orthodox chants are similar to some of the chants adopted by the early Christian Church (see Chapter 7). A few Jewish melodies have been adapted for use as hymn tunes in Christian churches.

The modern nation of Israel was founded in 1948, and most of its population emigrated there from other countries—Poland, Ethiopia, and many other nations, and in recent years, especially Russia. These immigrants have retained some of the musical influences of their former lands, so it is not unusual, for example, for German Jews to sing German or Yiddish songs or for Armenian Russian Jews to sing songs of their former homeland. In addition, the influence of the Middle East and its Arab culture has also been felt. When Israelis sing Arab songs, however, they sing them in a Jewish style.

Because the common bond among the people of Israel is religious, not ethnic, attempts have been made to create a new and unifying folk music tradition. New popular songs have been composed with texts on economic and political topics. Folk songs in Israel today are accompanied by tambourines, accordions, and guitars—instruments that represent Israel's diverse musical heritage.

The best candidate for a type of popular Jewish music is its ensembles that play klezmer music. Its small bands are made up of a variety of instruments, but they feature the clarinet, which wails out Jewish melodies. The songs are mainly in minor keys, often with a slow beginning and a rapid concluding tempo.

WATCH... a video of a klezmer song performed online.

MAIN POINTS OF CHAPTER 42

1. African music features complex rhythms, some improvisation according to traditional guidelines, and call-and-response form. It varies a great deal from tribe to tribe and is usually associated with dancing.

2. African instruments include a wide variety of drums, rattles, and the thumb piano. Africans ascribe almost human qualities to their instruments. "Talking drums" imitate the pitches of a particular language and are used for signaling purposes.

3. Middle Eastern music is largely monophonic, with its melodic line highly ornamented in a rhythmically free manner. It is inhibited somewhat by the fact that most musicians have a low social status and complex theories about music.

4. Several instruments are used in Middle Eastern music, including the plucked string *ud* and a drum with an hourglass shape.

5. The music of Israel is very cosmopolitan, except for its religious music, which varies according to the degree of orthodoxy of the particular congregation.

 PRACTICE...
your understanding of this chapter's concepts by working once more with the chapter's Active Listening Guides online.

 DO...
online quizzes that your instructor may assign for a grade.

43

Music *of* Asia

START...
experiencing this chapter's topics with an online video activity that your instructor may assign.

Learning Objectives

1 Explain the characteristics of the music of India.
2 Describe the features of Chinese music.
3 List the characteristics of Japanese music.
4 Discuss the features of Balinese music.
5 Describe the features of Australian music.

READ...
the complete chapter text in a rich interactive eBook!

What do the three-note songs of the Aborigines of Australia, the ragas of India, and the gamelan music of Bali have in common? In many ways they are different, but each comes from that vast portion of the world called Asia and its related countries along the Indian and Pacific oceans.

MUSIC OF INDIA

India is overwhelming. About 13 percent of the world's people live there. Somewhat protected from outside influences by the giant Himalayan Mountains to the north and the vast Indian Ocean to the south, India developed a unique and fascinating civilization (Figure 43.1). Where else does one encounter snake charmers, wandering holy men (some of whom wear no clothes), the ritual bathing in the Ganges River, opulent wealth alongside unbelievable poverty, and the superb Taj Mahal?

And where else does one find music like Indian classical music? Its roots reach back at least two thousand years, and it has existed largely unchanged since then. Today Indian classical music still thrives, but along with it is heard popular music from movies, some rock music from England and America, traditional hymns as well as other Christian music, and even some wind band music that is a carryover from the more than 250 years of English rule.

In a country as large as India, it is not surprising to find sizable differences and diversity. So, its classical music tends to divide into two major types: the *karnataka* music of southern India and the *Hindustani* music of northern India. The music of the north was influenced by Persia and the culture of the Middle East as the result of invasions from those countries over the centuries. It contains more improvisation and showy music. The music of the south is more traditional and is based on composed songs. It also sounds busy and contains more ornamented melodic lines.

What makes Indian music, from both the south and the north, special?

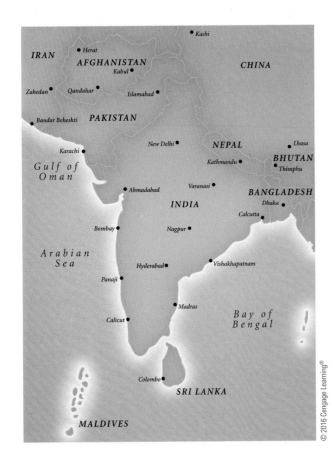

FIGURE 43.1
INDIA AND ITS NEIGHBORS

© 2016 Cengage Learning®

424

Ragas

It would be easy to describe a raga as a scale or melodic formula, but that would neglect its important affective and philosophical overtones. **Ragas** are intended to express and generate feelings—"colors of the mind." Each raga is thought to have a personality of its own with its own rules. Usually, ragas are associated with particular human emotions, Hindu deities, seasons of the year, and so on.

Theoretically, thousands of ragas exist, but only about fifty are performed today. They vary in length, but the average is about twenty to twenty-five notes. Two tones tend to stand out in each raga, one being four or five notes higher than the other. The basic raga is treated to many alterations, including slides, pitch bending, and other figures.

The following is a raga from northern India. The small noteheads indicate slides or zigzag figures, and the brackets mark off the phrases.

Instead of using the metrical rhythms found in Western music, both concert and popular, Indian musicians use rhythmic cycles of anywhere from 5 to 128 beats, called **talas**. Most talas are 5 to 8 beats long. Below is an example of a 14-beat tala. The slash marks in this example indicate how the beats are organized into subgroups.

/ • • • • • / • • / • • • / • • • • /   (5 + 2 + 3 + 4)

Musical Instruments

Indian scholars have grouped musical instruments into three classes, based on how the sound is produced.

STRING INSTRUMENTS The first category includes instruments that produce sound by plucked or bowed strings. The instrument that is most associated with Indian classical music is the *sitar*. It is a large, complicated instrument with five strings for playing the melody and thirteen more strings that ring in sympathy with the melodic strings. It has a bowl-shaped body made from wood and a row of pegs along the neck. A similar instrument found in southern India is the *veena*, which has fewer strings and a gourd or papier-mâché jug-shaped resonator attached to the neck.

WIND INSTRUMENTS These include bamboo flutes and the clarinet-like *pungi*, which is the instrument of choice among snake charmers.

PERCUSSION INSTRUMENTS These are instruments on which the sound is produced by striking. These consist mostly of a wide variety of drums. The most important of these is the double-headed *tabla*, which consists of two small drums played with the hands and fingers. There are also percussion instruments that produce sound by striking a solid object such as a gong.

Performances

Concerts of Indian music are informal (Figure 43.2). Although people in the audience sometimes sit on chairs, traditionally the performers sit on mats. They may count time with their hands, converse with one another, or offer comments and encouragement to the players. There is no printed program because the entire performance is not planned out. In fact, Indian musicians do not rehearse together before a concert. A concert consists partly of existing songs and partly of improvised music. Performances may last as long as three to four hours without an intermission. They are often held at cultural clubs that offer a series of programs that include music, dance, drama, and movies.

The performers sit on the floor and do not play from notation. The group is usually small, consisting of one singer and several instrumentalists. There is little or no applause

WATCH...
a video of a sitar performance online.

WATCH...
a video of a tala in a raga online.

John Henry Claude Wilson/Robert Harding World Imagery/Getty Images

FIGURE 43.2
MAN PLAYING A SITAR NEXT TO A
MAN PLAYING A TABLA

at the conclusion of the concert. (Western musicians would find the lack of applause very unnerving, to say the least.) The audience simply leaves, except for a few persons who hang around to chat with the performers.

Texture

Indian music has a layered texture. The top layer consists of the singer or solo instrument. The second layer is the drone that is a part of most Indian classical music. It is played by one or more tambouras, which is a large string instrument that sounds a few pitches almost continuously throughout the music. The lowest layer consists of percussion. This layer is performed by the tabla player and sometimes other instruments like the tambourine. Ten musicians constitute a large ensemble by Indian standards; the number is usually fewer than that.

The three layers—the flute, the drone, and the tablas—can easily be heard in "Raga Hansa-Dhwani" (see Listening Guide), which is included in the recordings for this book. The flute player improvises on a type of five-note pentatonic scale over the drone part. The rhythmic structure consists of a cycle of sixteen beats sounded by the tabla player. The "Hansa-Dhwani" is an evening raga that conveys the joyful mood of a bird flying.

LISTENING GUIDE

INDIA
"Raga: Hansa–Dhwani"

Genre: Ethnic music Drone, flute, tablas

Form: Raga

Download 90

2 minutes 13 seconds

0:00	Drone begins
0:02	Flute enters playing a melody with many decorative notes.
0:14	Tabla starts its rhythmic cycle.
0:25	Three instruments continue. Flute improvises short phrases based on a pentatonic scale.
1:13	Tempo quickens slightly.

| 1:39 | Flute "bends" the pitch of several notes. |
| 2:13 | The recording fades. |

 LISTEN TO... this selection streaming online.

WATCH... an Active Listening Guide of this selection online

DO... an online Listening Practice Activity related to this selection, which your instructor may assign for a grade.

Form

Indian music is balanced between composed music and music that is improvised by the performers. Performances normally contain four types of improvisation.

- The performance begins with an opening—a free-sounding improvised section based on the raga. It is performed without the tala.
- The next portion is quite rhythmic and works through variations and combinations of groups of notes.
- A third section consists of improvisation on one melodic line. The music of this section gradually becomes more elaborate and showy.
- The fourth section fits both the raga and the tala of the composition. If it is sung, no words are used. Instead, the performer sings the Indian note names—*sa, ri, ga,* and so on. The section grows more complex as it moves along.

Today in India a prospective musician studies either Western or Indian music. Few musicians know both types well. Indian music is usually learned from a religious teacher, a *guru,* who traditionally receives no pay for his lessons. The guru's purpose is to guide his disciple spiritually and musically.

Cultural Outlook

All music is interwoven with its cultural setting. In the case of India, that setting is highly otherworldly and laced with religious belief. Indian musicians see music as the mystical transfer of human emotion into sound. They even have a special word for it— *bhava.* They believe that without *bhava* the music lacks feeling and "soul."

Traditions and beliefs seem unchangeable in India. One of these beliefs involves the obligation of a musician to preserve the music and pass on to the next generation what the guru taught. There is also the belief, at least among some musicians, that performing a raga apart from its nonmusical association violates cosmic laws and may cause some calamity. One Indian musician told a European musicologist, "You in the West play love music when there is no love and winter music in the summer. No wonder you had several large wars in the twentieth century."

CHINESE MUSIC

China and India have a number of things in common (Figure 43.3). Both possess very large populations; one out of every five human beings is Chinese. Both also have music traditions that reach back thousands of years. And in both countries, music is very much interwoven with philosophy. In fact, one early Chinese emperor ordered

FIGURE 43.3
SOUTHEAST ASIA

WATCH...
a video of an erhu online.

WATCH...
a video of a Chinese opera
online.

musicians and astrologers to work together in calculating the length of pipe to be the standard pitch for music during his reign, because he wanted it to be in harmony with the universe.

Much Chinese music is built on the five-note pentatonic scale. It consists mostly of melody; harmony is largely absent. The most distinctive features of Chinese music are the instruments used to play it and the resulting timbres. String instruments are especially important. One such instrument is the *pipa*, which is like a four-string lute with its pear-shaped body. Another is the *erhu*, which is a two-string fiddle with strings made of silk. An instrument that is strummed like an autoharp is also used. In addition, several types of flutes are played, as are double-reed instruments. The percussion section includes cymbals and, of course, a gong. No brasses are found in traditional Chinese music. A few large orchestras existed in China, which was rare outside the West.

The Chinese developed a unique type of opera. Heroic roles are sung with a rasping sound; heroines sing with a high, thin, sound. The lines of opera consist of short phrases separated by instrumental interludes. The percussion instruments maintain a steady rhythm, and the sections of the music are concluded with a cymbal crash. It requires years of training to perform Chinese opera correctly.

Chinese music has a spotty history. At times it thrived; at other times it barely survived. After the fall of the last dynasty in 1911, China was declared a republic and the old music of the court went out of fashion. Since 1949 the Communist Party has ruled the mainland, and the traditional, sophisticated music was definitely discouraged. The Chinese government has become much more flexible in recent years. Some of the Chinese musical tradition is being preserved on Taiwan, but that country has rushed to adopt Western culture, including its music.

JAPANESE MUSIC

Much of the classical music of Japan was transported there by Chinese and Korean musicians around the eighth century. For many years it was performed mainly by court musicians, Buddhist priests, and scholars. It reached its peak in the seventeenth and eighteenth centuries, when by orders of its emperors Japan isolated itself from contact with foreign nations. Today Western-style music, both concert and popular, dominate the musical scene in Japan.

One of the features of Japanese music is the *koto*, which is a large instrument with thirteen strings. The performer sits with the instrument laid horizontally in order to pluck its strings. Its strings are stretched over a soundboard about six feet long and are plucked and manipulated by the player. The bridges that hold the strings up off the body can be moved for different tunings.

Much music has been composed for the koto, both solo and in combination with voices or other instruments, such as the *shakuhachi* (a simple bamboo flute) and the *shamisen* (a three-string instrument); see Figure 43.4. Even though a small group of musicians may perform koto music, they play the same basic melody but with different ornamentation and little or no harmony. Generally, Japanese music uses the five-note pentatonic scale. It is subtle and refined, and much attention is devoted to the tone color, pitch, ornamentation, and nuance of the sounds.

Japanese girls playing the flute, "koto" and samisen, c.1880 (hand coloured albumen print on card), Japanese Photographer. (19th century)/Private Collection/The Stapleton Collection/Bridgeman Images

FIGURE 43.4
SHAMISEN, KOTO, AND
SHAKUHACHI

Japanese girls playing the flute, "koto," and samisen, c. 1880 (hand-colored albumen print on card), Japanese Photographer (19th century)/Private Collection, The Stapleton Collection/Bridgeman Art Library

"Hakusen no" ("A White Fan") contains many features of traditional Japanese music (see Listening Guide). It consists of a single line without an accompaniment consisting of chords or contrasting line, as is found in almost all Western music. The singer's tone is more nasal than Westerners are accustomed to. In addition, both the singer and bamboo flute (*shakuhachi*) shade tones so that the sounds sometimes slide from one to another. The percussion instruments offer only a minimum of rhythmic pattern.

WATCH...
a video of a koto being
played online.

JAPAN
"Hakusen no"

Genre: Ethnic music

Download 91

1 minute 18 seconds

0:00   Guitarlike instrument plays introductory notes.

0:18   Singer begins; song contains some sliding notes.

0:34   Simple percussion sounds begin.

0:48   Flute plays long sliding notes.

1:38   Singer sings low notes as guitarlike instrument continues.

LISTEN TO... this selection streaming online.

WATCH... an Active Listening Guide of this selection online.

DO... an online Listening Practice Activity related to this selection, which your instructor may assign for a grade.

LISTENING GUIDE

BALINESE MUSIC

Bali is one of the islands in the large series that make up the country of Indonesia. The cultural level of this island of less than three million people, who live in an area about the size of Delaware, has rightfully earned it a special place in the world of music and dance. Each village on Bali—and there are about fifteen hundred of them—has at least one instrumental group called a **gamelan** (Figure 43.5). Its music is strictly ensemble music, with little attention to individual parts or players. Traditionally, gamelan was played in courts, but more recently many are heard in concerts and in conjunction with shadow plays, in which shadows of puppets are projected on a screen. These performances present musical dramas on life and death, good and evil, justice and injustice, and other philosophical topics.

Gamelans can range from four to thirty players, with instruments in pairs, one using the pentatonic scale and the other a version of a seven-note scale. The tuning of these scales is not precisely the same. These small pitch differences between them and the other instruments give the music a more shimmering quality.

The main instrument in many gamelans is the xylophone with metal keys. Other instruments include bamboo flutes, which are played in front of the player, not sideways. Drums, gongs, and cymbals of various sizes are also used. The larger drum is considered the male; the smaller one the female. Drummers direct the ensemble by setting the tempo and signaling changes in dynamic levels and transitions between sections. There are also gamelans consisting of other instruments, especially the *angklung*. It is made of hollow bamboo pieces of different lengths that are rattled back and forth to produce sound.

Gamelan music consists of large rhythmic cycles that are subdivided into smaller cycles. The melodies take place within this rhythmic framework. There are distinct melodic modes within the division of the scale. The main melodic line is often available in a type of notation, which uses the numbers 1 2 3 5 6 in recognition of the pentatonic scale. The parts for most of the other players are memorized.

To people unaccustomed to Balinese music, it may sound like a rain of pretty sounds. Those sounds, however, are sophisticated and subtle, and the result of careful planning. "Gender Wajang" (see Listening Guide) is typical of gamelan music with its pentatonic scale and shimmering timbres. Only a small amount of "Gender Wajang" is included on the recording. It is part of a much longer performance.

FIGURE 43.5
AN INDONESIAN GAMELAN

BALI (INDONESIA)
"Gender Wajang"

Genre: Ethnic music

Download 92

1 minute 45 seconds

0:00	Melody figure alternates between two pitches that gradually grow softer and lower.
0:35	Music becomes louder.
0:42	New melody appears built on a five-note pentatonic scale.
0:48	Music seems to pause several times after repeated notes.
1:09	The tempo speeds up and then slows down.
1:37	Another pause and repeated notes.
1:44	Recording fades.

LISTEN TO... this selection streaming online.

WATCH... an Active Listening Guide of this selection online.

WATCH... a video of a gamelan online.

DO... an online Listening Practice Activity related to this selection, which your instructor may assign for a grade.

MUSIC OF AUSTRALIA

Adjacent to Asia, Australia is one of the world's continents, including the country as well as neighboring islands. One example of the music of this land mass is that of the Aborigines in Australia. Almost all of Australia's population came from Europe, especially England. However, the Aborigines were there long before the arrival of Europeans in the eighteenth century. These people had developed a culture of their own, which included language and music.

A novel feature of their music is the didgeridoo. This term, invented by English-speaking people, is actually a word representing how the instrument sounds. More accurate is the aboriginal term for the instrument. It's a large instrument made from a log that termites have hollowed out. It is then cleaned and shaped to create a wind instrument that has no keys or mouthpiece as such, even though it is a wind instrument. And it does require a lot of wind to play it successfully. There is nothing else like it in the world.

WATCH...
a video on playing a didgeridoo online.

MAIN POINTS OF CHAPTER 43

1. Melodies in Indian classical music are developed around ragas, which are melodic patterns that express "colors of the mind." Rhythm in Indian music is based on talas, which are rhythmic cycles usually consisting of five to eight beats.

PRACTICE...
your understanding of this chapter's concepts by working once more with the chapter's Active Listening Guides online.

DO...
online quizzes that your instructor may assign for a grade.

2. Instruments associated with Indian music include the sitar (a string instrument), pungi (a wind instrument), and tabla (small drums that are played with the fingers).

3. Indian music is very intertwined with religious beliefs. Indian musicians believe music is the mystical transfer of human emotion into sound.

4. Chinese music is based on the five-note pentatonic scale. It features instruments such as the pipa, erhu, flutes, and percussion.

5. Japanese music features the koto, which is a large plucked string instrument. The music uses the five-note pentatonic scale and is refined and subtle in character.

6. The island of Bali in Indonesia is famous for its gamelans, which are instrumental ensembles. The main instruments are xylophones with metal bars, flutes, and percussion. The gamelan uses both the five-note pentatonic scale and a version of a seven-note scale.

7. The didgeridoo is a unique Australian Aboriginal instrument.

Glossary

absolute music Music that is free of extramusical associations.

a cappella Unaccompanied choral music.

accent The emphasis placed on a note, usually by playing it louder.

accidental A sharp, flat, or natural sign that alters a pitch by one half step.

aerophone Any instrument that generates sound by vibrating a column of air.

aleatory music Music in which the sounds are partly or entirely the result of chance.

alto (contralto) The lower, heavier female voice.

aria An accompanied solo song, usually of some length and complexity, in an opera, oratorio, or cantata.

art music Music intended for careful attention to its sounds and expressive qualities.

art song A musical setting of a text by a composer for solo singer and piano.

atonal Music that is not in any key or tonality.

augmentation A compositional technique in which the note values of a theme are all lengthened proportionally.

backbeat The second beat in a measure.

ballad An English narrative song told in simple verses.

ballade A short, melodic piano piece.

ballet Music and bodily movements combined for artistic purposes.

bar See *measure*.

baroque The style of music the prevailed from 1600 to 1750.

bass The lower, heavier male voice.

basso continuo See *continuo*.

basso ostinato A phrase in the bass line that is played again and again.

beat The pulse or throb that recurs regularly in music.

bebop See *bop*.

bel canto Literally, "beautiful singing" in Italian. Often it refers to a style of opera in the first part of the nineteenth century that featured much vocal technique and beautiful singing.

berceuse Instrumental pieces in a moderate tempo and accompaniment reminiscent of rocking a cradle.

binary form A balanced two-part form, *ab*.

bluegrass A type of country music in which acoustic instruments are used in an attempt to better capture the original qualities of country music.

blue note A note in major scale—usually the third, fifth, or seventh—that in jazz is lowered one half step while the harmony remains in major.

blues A type of song associated with African Americans in which a solo singer sings about some hardship; the usual form of the blues is *a a b*.

bolero A Spanish dance adapted by the Cubans, who made its rhythm more complex.

boogie-woogie A jazz piano style featuring a repeated figure in the bass part and a highly decorated melody line.

bop (bebop) An advanced jazz style for a small group, involving nearly continuous syncopation and a flowing melodic line.

break Contrasting section in the trio of a march; sometimes called "dogfight."

broadside A ballad printed on one sheet of paper, with a text often discussing political matters.

broken chord The notes of a chord sounded one after another rather than simultaneously.

broken style Notes of a chord played sequentially, not simultaneously.

cadence A melodic or harmonic formula that gives a sense of phrase ending. In poetic usage it sometimes refers to beat or tempo.

cadenza A section in which a soloist plays a free paraphrase on the themes of the work.

call-and-response The form found in African music in which phrases of music are exchanged between soloist and group.

calls Melodic phrases sung by the African American slaves while working in the fields.

canon Music in which one or more lines imitate one another for almost the entire work.

cantata A vocal composition in several movements for solo voices, instruments, and usually a chorus; it is usually based on a religious text.

cantus firmus A preexisting melody that is used as the basis for a polyphonic vocal work.

chaconne A work featuring variations on a pattern of chords repeated throughout the work.

chamber music Instrumental music in which each part is performed by only one player.

chance music Music in which some or all events are the product of chance.

chanson A French polyphonic song of the seventeenth century.

chantey An English or American sailors' song.

character piece A short keyboard work expressing a mood or idea, composed during the Romantic period.

chorale A stately hymn tune used in the German Lutheran Church.

chord The simultaneous sounding of three or more pitches.

chordophone Any instrument that produces sound by vibrating strings.

choreographer The person who designs the movement of dancers.

chorus (1) A sizable group of singers that sings choral music. (2) A section of an opera, oratorio, or cantata sung by a chorus.

chromatic Melodic or harmonic movement by half steps.

classical music The popular term for concert music.

Classical period The prevailing style of music from 1750 to 1820.

coda (codetta) The concluding portion of a section or movement, usually giving the impression of an ending.

concert music Music created for the intellectual and psychological satisfaction it provides.

concert overture An overture not associated with an opera or drama.

concerted style Music in which one section of a performing group contrasts with another section or a soloist.

concerto A multimovement work consisting of music that contrasts a soloist with an orchestra or band.

concerto grosso A multimovement work contrasting a small instrumental group with a large group.

consonance A group of simultaneous sounds that seems agreeable or restful.

continuo (basso continuo) A bass line for keyboard and other instruments in which the player is given only a succession of single notes and other symbols from which to fill out the remainder of the harmony. Also, the instruments that play the continuo part.

corrido A Mexican narrative song.

counterpoint Two or more independent lines with melodic character occurring at the same time.

countersubject The secondary theme in a fugue.

country music A type of music containing folklike qualities that is especially popular with the white culture of the American South.

crescendo (cresc.) The music should gradually become louder.

cyclical form The appearance of a theme from one movement in another movement of a multimovement work.

decrescendo (decresc.) The music should gradually become softer.

development (1) The manipulation of themes in a musical work. (2) The section in sonata form devoted to the development of themes.

Dies irae The traditional Gregorian chant sung at funerals.

diminution The proportional reduction of all note values in a theme.

dissonance A group of simultaneous sounds that seems disagreeable or harsh.

divertimento A pleasant but not very complex instrumental work, usually consisting of stylized dances.

Dixieland A jazz style for a small group of players, consisting of two beats per measure and a rather lively tempo.

doctrine of affections (doctrine of affects) The Baroque practice of attempting to project states of feeling and ideas in music.

dodecaphonic music See *tone row music.*

double exposition The use of two expositions in a concerto, one for the orchestra and the other featuring the soloist.

downbeat The first beat of a measure, which usually receives the greater emphasis.

drone A low, continuous sound that lasts throughout a piece of music.

dynamics The amount of loudness in music.

Eclecticism The practice of combining what the composer believes to be the best features of several different styles.

electronic music Music produced through synthesizers and electroacoustic instruments.

encore A short work played at the end of a concert in response to an audience's applause.

ensemble e An instrumental or vocal performing group.

episode Sections of a fugue in which the subject is not present.

equal temperament A system of tuning, in which the intervals are adjusted to divide the octave into twelve equal parts.

estampie An instrumental dance during the Middle Ages.

ethnic music Music that is characteristic of a particular culture or group of people.

etude A short instrumental work stressing some technical aspect of playing the instrument.

Exoticism A phase of Romanticism that draws on scenes from Asia and the Middle East.

exposition (1) The opening section of a fugue. (2) The opening section in sonata form.

Expressionism An early twentieth-century style that emphasized subjective and often disturbing emotions.

falsetto voice The "false" high voice that can be produced by males.

fanfare Short, brilliant-sounding music, usually featuring brass instruments.

fantasia A free-sounding instrumental work.

fantasie A short, free-sounding instrumental work.

figured bass A shorthand system of numbers and accidentals used by keyboard players in Baroque music for indicating chords.

finale The final movement of a multimovement work.

fine arts Type of art in which objects are created only for the psychological satisfaction that people find in them.

folk music The music of the common people of a society or geographic area.

folkloric A type of twentieth-century music that contains folklike qualities.

form The pattern or plan of a musical work.

free jazz A sophisticated type of jazz containing few stylistic guidelines.

frets Metal strips on the fingerboard of a guitar and similar instruments that help the player in finger placement.

fugato A short section of a work containing phrases of music in imitation.

fugue A composition in which the main theme (subject) is presented in imitation in several parts.

fusion The combination of two or more musical styles.

galant style The light, decorative style generally associated with the eighteenth-century French court.

gamelan A Balinese instrumental ensemble.

genre The term referring to a type or classification of music.

glissando A very rapid sliding of notes up or down a scale.

grace note A short decorative note that has no assigned rhythmic value.

Gregorian chant The monophonic chant originally sung unaccompanied in Latin by monks and priests in the Roman Catholic Church.

harmonic series (overtone series) The order in which overtones of a pitch occur.

harmony The simultaneous sounds of several pitches, usually in accompanying a melody.

hoedown A portion of a square dance.

homophony The texture consisting of a line of melody with accompaniment.

idée fixe **(fixed idea)** A theme that is transformed at various places in a composition.

ideophone A percussion instrument other than drums.

imitation The repetition of a theme in another part or line or a few beats later.

impressionism An artistic viewpoint that emphasizes overall impressions rather than detailed or intellectual observations.

impromptu A short piano composition in a style that sounds improvised.

improvisation Music that is made up on the spot, usually according to stylistic guidelines.

incidental music Music composed to be performed in conjunction with a drama.

interval The distance between two pitches.

inversion (1) Turning a melody upside down so that an ascending interval descends, and vice versa. (2) Rearranging the notes in a chord so that its basic note is no longer the lowest one.

jazz An African American style of music developed in twentieth-century America that is characterized by improvised playing and syncopated rhythms.

key center See *tonic*.

key signature The pattern of sharps or flats at the beginning of a line of music that indicates which notes are to be altered by one half step.

Klangfarbenmelodie "Manufactured tone color melody"; melodies made up of different timbres.

leitmotiv A motive or theme that is associated with a particular character or idea in the music dramas of Richard Wagner.

libretto The text of an opera or oratorio.

Lied The German word for "art song." The plural of *Lied* is *Lieder.*

liturgy A ritual for public worship.

madrigal A free, secular, imitative work for voices.

mainstream Twentieth-century music that is neither experimental nor committed to a particular compositional viewpoint.

major scale A series of seven different pitches within an octave, with half steps between the third and fourth steps and the seventh and eighth steps.

Mass (1) The celebration of Holy Communion (Eucharist) in the Roman Catholic Church. (2) The musical setting of the Ordinary of the Mass.

measure A group of beats marked as a separate unit in music notation.

medieval motet An unaccompanied work composed during the medieval period for voices, using a cantus firmus from Gregorian chant, with other parts in vernacular languages added, and often containing complex rhythmic and melodic relationships.

medieval period The style of music that prevailed from approximately 1100 to 1450.

melody A series of consecutive pitches that form a cohesive musical entity.

membranophone Any instrument that produces sounds from a skin or other membrane.

meter The regular pattern of stressed and unstressed beats.

meter signature The two numbers, one above the other, at the beginning of a piece or section of a longer work that indicate the metrical pattern and how it is notated.

microtone An interval of less than a half step.

minimalism Music in which the composer makes as few changes as possible but still seeks to create an interesting work.

minor scale A series of seven pitches within an octave, with a half step between the second and third steps.

minstrel show A popular form of entertainment in the latter part of the nineteenth century and early twentieth century consisting of a variety of lighthearted acts performed by actors in black face.

minuet and trio A three-part form in three-beat meter and the style of a minuet.

modes As used today, scale patterns containing seven pitches other than major or minor.

modulation Changing the tonal center as the music progresses, usually without a break.

monody A texture used in the early Baroque consisting of one melody with simple accompaniment.

monophony One melodic line without any accompaniment.

motet A sacred composition for voices.

motive A short musical idea that is a unifying element in a musical work.

movement A large independent section of an instrumental composition.

musical (musical comedy) A type of theater that features music as well as actions, scenery, and costumes.

music drama The term Richard Wagner used for his operas in which he tried to strike a balance between the music and the dramatic action.

musique concrète Natural sounds that are recorded and then modified and organized by a composer into a musical composition.

mute A device for muffling or dampening the sound of an instrument.

nationalism A deliberate, conscious attempt to develop artworks that are characteristic of a particular country or region.

Neoclassicism "New classicism"; music created according to the rational outlook of the Classical period.

nocturne A type of nineteenth-century character piece for piano; originally, the word meant "night music."

octave A pitch that has twice or half the frequency of vibrations of another; usually the two pitches have the same letter designation.

octave displacement Using a note with the same letter name as a previous note but in another octave.

Op. (opus) Meaning "work" in Latin, it usually appears with a number to indicate the order in which the composer's works were written.

opera A drama set to music in which the lines of text are sung with orchestral accompaniment.

opera buffa Comic opera of the eighteenth and nineteenth centuries.

opera seria Dramatic opera, usually dealing with serious subject matter.

opus Latin for "work;" used to identify a composer's compositions.

oral tradition The process in which music is preserved by people through hearing the music, remembering it, and then performing it.

oratorio A sizable work for chorus, soloists, and orchestra, usually on a religious topic, that is performed without scenery, costumes, or acting.

Ordinary The parts of the Mass that are ordinarily included, regardless of church season: Kyrie, Gloria, Credo, Sanctus, and Agnus Dei.

organum The name for the early polyphonic music of medieval times.

ostinato A short, persistently repeated melodic, rhythmic, or harmonic pattern.

overture An instrumental introduction to a vocal work or an orchestral suite.

parlor song A sentimental type of song popular in the nineteenth century.

passacaglia A repeated set of variations based on a melodic ostinato in the lowest-pitched part.

passion An oratorio based on the suffering of Jesus on Good Friday, according to one of the four Gospels.

pedal (pedal point) A long note or notes that persist over an extended period of time while harmonies change.

pentatonic scale A five-note scale, usually with the pattern of whole steps and half steps encountered on the black keys of the piano.

phrase A rather short, logical segment of music; it is comparable to a clause or phrase in language.

pitch The perceived highness or lowness of a musical sound.

pizzicato Notes on a string instrument that are played by the player's fingers plucking the string instead of using the bow.

polymeter The presence of two or more meters at the same time.

polyphony Music in which two or more melodic lines of approximately equal importance are sounded at the same time.

polyrhythm Two or more rhythm patterns occurring simultaneously.

polytonality Two or more tonal centers sounding at the same time.

popular music Music created primarily for commercial purposes.

post-Romanticism Works in the Romantic style composed after it was the prevailing style.

prelude (1) A short instrumental work. (2) A piece to be played as an introduction.

prepared piano A practice sometimes used in twentieth-century music in which tacks, chewing gum, paper, and other objects are placed in the mechanism of the piano so that it sounds different timbres.

Primitivism Music that seeks to contain rhythmic power and blatant expression.

program music Instrumental works associated by the composer with an extramusical idea or object.

program symphony A multimovement programmatic work for orchestra.

Proper The portion of the Mass that is "proper" for a designated day in the church year.

quotation music Music that makes extensive use of quotations from other music.

raga A melodic formula used in the music of India.

ragtime A forerunner of jazz, usually for piano in a marchlike style.

rap A type of African American music that consists of rapid delivery of words in a singsong style.

realization A keyboard player performing the music indicated by the figured bass.

recapitulation The section of sonata form in which the themes from the exposition are repeated.

recitative A style of singing that covers its text expressively, usually in an economical and direct way.

relative major (or minor) Major and minor scales that have the same key signature.

Renaissance motet A sacred vocal composition developed during the Renaissance.

Requiem The funeral Mass of the Roman Catholic Church.

retrograde The reverse version of a melody or tone row, in which the first note becomes the last, and so on.

retrograde-inversion The upside-down and backward version of the tone row.

rhythm The flow of music in terms of time.

rhythm and blues A term for African American popular music.

rhythmic modes The constant repetition of certain rhythm patterns, much like poetic meters.

ritornello form The orchestral form in which themes at the beginning of a concerto grosso return later in the movement.

rock (rock and roll) A popular style of music that contains features of both rhythm and blues and country music.

Rococo The decorative, light style prevalent in the eighteenth-century courts, especially France.

Romantic period The style of music that was prevalent from about 1820 to 1910.

rondo A form in which the theme appears three or more times with contrasting sections between its appearances.

rubato A performer's slight deviations from a strict tempo.

run A series of rapidly moving, scalewise notes.

saltarello A lively type of folk dance.

sampling The recording of a short segment of an instrument for inclusion in electronic music.

scale A series of pitches that proceeds upward or downward according to a prescribed pattern.

scherzo (1) The third movement of some symphonies and other works, usually in a playful style. (2) An independent work for piano composed during the Romantic period.

secular music Music that is worldly or nonsacred.

sequence The immediate repeating of a phrase or figure at a different pitch level from the original.

Serialism The application of the principles of tone row music to elements such as dynamic levels and articulations.

sforzando A loud, accented note or chord; it is indicated by the letters *Sfz*.

son A Mexican balladlike song.

sonata (1) A Baroque multimovement work for solo instrument. (2) A multimovement work for piano and another instrument, or for piano alone.

sonata form A form consisting of an exposition section, followed by a development section, and then a recapitulation of the themes from the exposition.

soprano The higher, lighter female voice.

soul A general term for several types of African American music.

spiritual A religious song unaccompanied by a choir, usually associated with African American churches.

Sprechstimme A vocal style that is a combination of speaking and singing.

strophic form A song in which several verses of words are sung to the same melody.

subject The main theme of a fugue.

suite (1) A collection or group of stylized pieces of dance music. (2) A collection of parts of a larger work such as a ballet or opera.

swing A type of popular music containing many jazz influences that was arranged for big bands.

symphonic poem See *tone poem*.

symphony A large multimovement work for orchestra.

syncopation The displacement of an accent so that it occurs where it is not normally expected or does not occur where it is expected.

tala A rhythmic cycle of beats found in the music of India.

tempo The speed of the beats in a piece of music.

tenor (1) The higher, lighter male voice. (2) The line in a medieval motet that contains the phrases from Gregorian chant.

ternary form A three-part form, *aba*, in which the opening music returns.

terraced dynamics Abrupt changes in levels of loudness.

text painting (word painting) The compositional technique of having the musical sounds reinforce the words being sung.

texture The basic setting of the music: monophonic, homophonic, or polyphonic.

theme A central melody in a musical work.

theme and variations A work consisting of a theme and altered versions of that theme.

theme transformation The alteration of a theme that retains its characteristic intervals of melody or rhythm pattern.

through-composed song A song that contains no repetition of lines of music.

timbre Tone quality or tone color in music.

time signature See *meter signature*.

Tin Pan Alley The name associated with the popular music industry.

toccata A showy work, usually for a keyboard instrument.

tone poem A sizable orchestral work of program music.

tone row (twelve-tone or dodecaphonic music) A composition based on a row of pitches that uses each of the twelve tones in an octave.

tonic (tonal center) The specific pitch around which a piece of music is centered.

tonic chord A chord built on the first degree of a major or minor scale.

transcription An adaptation of a musical work for an instrument or voice for another instrument or voice, or for a group of either.

tremolo The very rapid alternation between or repeating of pitches.

trill The rapid alternation between a pitch and the adjacent higher pitch.

trio sonata A Baroque sonata written for three players on melody accompanied by the continuo line.

troubadour French noblemen who created love poems and songs in the thirteenth century.

twelve-tone music See *tone row music*.

variation A section of music in which the melody, harmony, or rhythm of a theme is repeated with some changes.

vaudeville A popular type of stage entertainment in the early twentieth century consisting of music and other variety acts.

vibrato Slight, rapid fluctuations of pitch.

virtuoso A very technically skilled performer.

vocalise A song sung without words, usually sung on a single vowel sound.

voice (1) The human voice. (2) A part in an instrumental composition, especially a fugue.

Western music Music of Europe and the Americas.

whole-tone scale A scale in which the octave is divided into six whole steps.

wind band (wind ensemble) An ensemble comprising wind and percussion instruments.

Listening Guides INDEXED BY COMPOSER

Index of Composer Biographies

Index